D1731990

CULTURAL HERITAGE LAW AND POLICY

Series Editors

PROFESSOR FRANCESCO FRANCIONI

*Professor of International Law and Human Rights and Co-Director of the
Academy of Academic Law at the European University Institute, Florence*

PROFESSOR ANA FILIPA VRDOLJAK

*Associate Dean (Research) and Professor of Law at the University
of Technology, Sydney*

Confronting Colonial Objects

CULTURAL HERITAGE LAW AND POLICY

The aim of this series is to publish significant and original research on and scholarly analysis of all aspects of cultural heritage law through the lens of international law, private international law, and comparative law. The series is wide in scope, traversing disciplines, regions, and viewpoints. Topics given particular prominence are those which, while of interest to academic lawyers, have significant bearing on policy-making and current public discourse on the interaction between art, heritage, and the law.

Confronting Colonial Objects

Histories, Legalities, and Access to Culture

CARSTEN STAHN

OXFORD
UNIVERSITY PRESS

OXFORD
UNIVERSITY PRESS

Great Clarendon Street, Oxford, OX2 6DP,
United Kingdom

Oxford University Press is a department of the University of Oxford.
It furthers the University's objective of excellence in research, scholarship,
and education by publishing worldwide. Oxford is a registered trade mark of
Oxford University Press in the UK and in certain other countries

© Carsten Stahn 2023

The moral rights of the author have been asserted

First Edition published in 2023

Published in the United States of America by Oxford University Press
198 Madison Avenue, New York, NY 10016, United States of America

British Library Cataloguing in Publication Data

Data available

Library of Congress Control Number: 2023943279

ISBN 978–0–19–286812–1

DOI: 10.1093/oso/9780192868121.001.0001

Printed and bound by
CPI Group (UK) Ltd, Croydon, CR0 4YY

Links to third party websites are provided by Oxford in good faith and
for information only. Oxford disclaims any responsibility for the materials
contained in any third party website referenced in this work.

Preface and Acknowledgements

The taking and return of cultural artefacts is one of the most discussed topics in the art world and international relations. It is present wherever we go, often on our own doorsteps. Many Western museums are major tourist attractions. They host many objects or human remains, whose colonial histories or 'ghostly presences' pose intriguing questions in relation to the past and present or raise painful memories in the eyes of those affected. How should we confront these challenges? These questions are not only at the heart of expert discussions or curatorial policies but go to the core of societal identities. The ethics, institutional practices, and public perceptions surrounding contested objects are shifting. The significance of the moment is captured by the striking words of Bénédicte Savoy on the occasion of the historic French return of twenty-six objects from Dahomey to modern-day Benin: 'Just as there was a before and after the fall of the Berlin Wall, there will be a before and after the return to Benin of the works looted by the French army in 1892.'[1] These returns are the tip of the iceberg of a movement which has gained new traction after many decades of struggle, silence, or delay.

Coloniality was mediated through material things. The life story and transformation of objects provide ample evidence that cultural objects were not only sites of colonial violence, domination, or commodification but also symbols of resistance or agents in their own right, which transformed attitudes in Western societies. Human remains became the incarnation of the body politics of colonialism. Although the debate on restitution and return of stolen or looted cultural objects is as old as humanity, cultural takings in the colonial era have received limited structural attention. Colonial violence has remained in the shadow of the holocaust. Amadou-Mahtar M'Bow, former Director-General of UNESCO, recalled in 1978 that the return of cultural assets to communities of origin 'cannot be solved simply by negotiated agreements and spontaneous acts'.[2] However, in the process of UN decolonization, the link between history, identity, and access to culture was marginalized, despite calls for restitution. For a long time, return was treated as an issue of cultural diplomacy. Change was mainly driven by developments of indigenous rights and the gradual humanization of cultural heritage law.

Over the past decade, the restitution movement has reached a tipping point. We witness a growing consciousness of the ongoing remnants of colonial injustice,

[1] Farah Nayeri and Norimitsu Onishi, 'Looted Treasures Begin a Long Journey Home from France' *New York Times* (28 October 2021).
[2] Amadou-Mahtar M'Bow, 'A Plea for the Return of an Irreplaceable Cultural Heritage to Those Who Created It' (Paris: UNESCO, 1978).

changing museum ethics, and professional practices, as well as new ways to confront issues of ownership or access to culture. Sustainable Development Goal 16 lists 'recovery and return of stolen assets' as an express target. Change is driven by civil society pressure, return claims, professional networks, curators or individual institutions, greater transparency, the establishment of new art institutions in the Global South—often more modern than their Western counterparts, new forms of collaboration between museums and communities in provenance research, governance or display, and new prospects of sharing objects. They provide the building blocks for a new era of engagement.

This book seeks to take stock of these developments and to contribute to the emerging strand of literature on cultural colonial takings and their contemporary significance. One challenge is positionality. Should this be done by a Western author if there is already a diversity gap in contemporary academic publishing? On the one hand, this is an ethical dilemma which must be openly acknowledged. There is a pressing need to diversify scholarship, foreground local knowledge systems, and/or strengthen the voices of those who have advocated for change, but have received less attention in discourse. On the other hand, it is important to stimulate critical inquiry and memory in Western societies who struggle to re-engage with their own past. As Chimamanda Adichie said at the opening of the Humboldt Forum in Berlin: 'We cannot change the past but we can change our blindness to the past'.[3] The study seeks to heed the call by Open Restitution Africa to ensure more inclusive referencing and engagement with non-Western voices and perspectives.[4]

The work addresses colonial objects in the broad sense, i.e. colonized cultural objects and bodies. It starts from the premise that the underlying challenges can only be addressed through the interplay of different lenses: justice, ethics, and human rights. It illustrates how colonial agents reinvented social and scientific narratives to justify takings throughout different periods of colonial history and shows synergies with contemporary arguments advanced in the discourse on restitution and return, including the re-construction of identities through restitution processes. It explains the dual role of law, as imperial tool and language, and as instrument of resistance and transformation. It points out blind spots in cultural heritage law and new ways to deal with colonial heritage, drawing on collaborative practices, experiences with successful returns, and synergies with transitional justice concepts. It proposes a relational cultural justice approach to overcome impasses, which have created stalemate and impeded dialectical engagement. It does not portray restitution or return as golden standard for all objects. It rather places

---

[3] Humboldt Forum, Keynote speech by Chimamanda Adichie (22 September 2021) https://www.humboldtforum.org/en/programm/digitales-angebot/digital-en/keynote-spreech-by-chimamanda-adichie-32892/.

[4] Molemo Moiloa, *Reclaiming Restitution: Centering and Contextualizing the African Narrative* (Open Restitution Africa, 2022) https://openrestitution.africa/wp-content/uploads/2022/09/ANF-Report-Main-Report.pdf.

the emphasis on the need to search forms of consent in relation to ownership, presentation, or conservation, based on the nature of objects, structural injustice, and contemporary relations. The core idea of the relational model is to foster new collaborative relationships between holding institutions, countries, or communities of origin and local stakeholders. It argues at the same time that contemporary engagement should not be reduced to issues of return, but identifies strategies and remedies beyond restitution.

A key part of the manuscript is devoted to micro-histories, biographies, or 'necrographies' of objects. They often speak for themselves. They illustrate the narratives of takings, unexpected twists and turns in the lives of objects, different ontologies, and forms of encounter. These stories do not only offer fascinating insights about colonial politics, world history, or the branding of art forms, but also offer new ways to understand the ways in which racial science and market forces influenced the shaping of international law.

The study challenges the argument that all takings of cultural objects qualify as looted art or theft. But it also questions the premise that colonial acquisitions were lawful, simply because they involved some type of consent, exchange, or compensation. It relies on the concept of entanglement to recognize these complexities. It argues that legality should be regarded as a spectrum, with different degrees of legality or illegality ('entangled legalities'), and develops principles of relational justice to disentangle these dichotomies. It illustrates some of the risks and blind spots of current return practices, such as the dominant focus on spectacular objects or continuing double standards in relation to natural history objects.

Major parts of the text were written during the Covid-19 pandemic. They are not only inspired by interdisciplinary scholarly perspectives, but by many virtual seminars, podcasts (e.g. 'Stuff the British Stole'), and news platforms, such as the invaluable 'Restitution Matters' project, open access sources (e.g. Kwame Opoku's entries on Modern Ghana), and actual and virtual conversations with friends and colleagues. It takes into account developments until March 2023.

I wish to thank Ingrid Samset from Leiden University College for her careful reading and invaluable comments and Charlotte Perez for her critical editorial reading. I also wish to express my gratitude to colleagues from the Leiden Cultural Heritage Centre (Pieter ter Keurs, Evelien Campfens), the Grotius Centre for International Legal Studies, and Queen's University Belfast, and our students for inspiring discussions and exchange of ideas. Particular thanks are also owed to Francesco Francioni and Ana Filipa Vrdoljak for including this work in the Series on Cultural Heritage Law and Policy, to Nicola Prior for her careful copy-editing, and to colleagues at OUP (Merel Alstein, Robert Cavooris, and Lane Berger) for making this book a reality.

The work is made available open access in order to enable broad engagement by readers and audiences in all parts of the globe. It is not only geared towards experts, but is meant to encourage discussion on the responsibilities and moral choices we face in our daily actions when we encounter contested objects. I hope it will not be the end or the beginning of the end, but rather the end of the beginning of a more open, equal, and transparent discourse on ways to confront entangled objects, and a means to translate new visions into action. It is dedicated to my mother, who explored the fascination of different heritage traditions in her travels and exposed me to new worlds.

The Hague, March 2023

Preface to Carsten Stahn's book

Confronting Colonial Objects: Histories, Legalities, and Access to Culture

This book is a timely and important contribution to the current debate on the impact of colonialism and of de-colonization on the legal status of cultural property and on the difficult issue of reparation and restitution of objects obtained by war, colonialism, and coercion from colonized peoples. In the past twenty years this theme has attracted vast and increasing attention on the part of scholars, museums, media, collectors, and experts in provenance research. Important museums of the world have been facing increasing scrutiny from media, academics, and law enforcement officials over the extent to which their collection may include cultural objects looted during the colonial period. This has produced unprecedented reactions at the political level—such as the commitment undertaken in 2017 in a public speech by the French President Macron to inaugurate a policy of gradual return to African countries of cultural objects removed during the colonial period and now part of the collections of national museums. As we know, this political pronouncement has been followed by the influential *Rapport Savoy/Sar sur la restitution du patrimoine africaine*. This move has been followed by the adoption by important museums in Europe and the United States of plans intended to root out looted artefacts in their collections.

In this climate of changing cultural mores, this book addresses the topic through the lens of three interrelated legal-theoretical contexts: justice, ethics, and human rights. In this multidisciplinary perspective, the author raises the important question of whether the Western legal and social construct that defines the concept of cultural property and its relation to society may be shared, or may even be compatible, with the cultural understandings and legal traditions of the colonized people. The answer is, obviously, a negative one. Hence also a negative evaluation of the role played by international law in legitimizing the mass appropriation of cultural objects by the colonizing powers. But the most important question that remains to be answered concerns the role that international law can play today in remedying past injustices and ensuring the return of cultural objects wrongly removed from colonial territories. Today, international law provides a framework of multilateral instruments designed to facilitate the restitution or return of cultural objects illegally removed from their country of origin. However, as we well know, these instruments—such as the 1970 UNESCO Convention and the 1995 UNIDROIT Convention—are not technically capable of addressing the restitution of colonial loot because they have no retroactive effect. However, this formal legal obstacle to the application of the above instruments to colonial loot does not relieve us from the duty to remedy past cultural injustices that continue to display their harmful effects in present time. This is what the author of this book successfully attempts to do through the lens of justice, ethics, and human rights.

Francesco Francioni and Ana Filipa Vrdoljak

Contents

Table of Contents

Table of Cases

NATIONAL CASES

INTERNATIONAL CASES

Table of Instruments

NATIONAL INSTRUMENTS

Australia

List of Abbreviations

AFFORD	African Foundation for Development
AJIL	American Journal of International Law
Art.	Article
AU	African Union
BC	Before Christ
CARICOM	Caribbean Community
CETS	Council of Europe Treaty Series
CLR	Commonwealth Law Reports
CO	Commonwealth Office
Co.	Company
DLR	Dominion Law Reports
ECOWAS	Economic Community of West African States
EEF	British Egypt Exploration Fund
EJIL	European Journal of International Law
EMOWAA	Edo Museum of West African Arts
EU	European Union
FAO	Food and Agriculture Organization
GA	General Assembly
GAOR	General Assembly Official Records
HCA	High Court of Australia
HMS	His (or Her) Majesty's Ship
IBA	International Bar Association
ICCPR	International Covenant on Civil and Political Rights
ICESCR	International Covenant on Economic, Social and Cultural Rights
ICLQ	International & Comparative Law Quarterly
ICOM	International Council of Museums
ICPRCP	International Committee for Promoting the Return of Cultural Property
IFAN	Institut Français d'Afrique Noire
ILA	International Law Association
ILC	International Law Commission
ILO	International Labour Organization
IMO	International Museums Office
JICJ	Journal of International Criminal Justice
LJIL	Leiden Journal of International Law
LRT	Legacy Restoration Trust
MBRA	Mutually Beneficial Return Agreement
NADA	Native Affairs Department Annual
NAGPRA	Native American Graves Protection and Repatriation Act
NATLA	Nama Traditional Leaders Association

NCMM	National Commission for Museums and Monuments of Nigeria
NFT	Non-fungible token
NMVW	National Museum of World Cultures
NZPCC	New Zealand Privy Council Cases
OIOC	Oriental and India Office Collection
PhD	Doctor of Philosophy
RIAA	Reports of International Arbitral Awards
SCC	Supreme Court of Canada
SCR	Supreme Court Reports
TGV	Train à Grande Vitesse
TWAIL	Third World Approaches Towards International Law
UK	United Kingdom
UN	United Nations
UNDRIP	United Nations Declaration on the Rights of Indigenous People
UNESCO	United Nations Educational, Scientific and Cultural Organization
UNIDROIT	International Institute for the Unification of Private Law
UNTS	United Nations Treaty Series
US	United States
V&A	Victoria and Albert Museum
VOC	Vereenigde Oostindische Compagnie
WIC	West India Company
ZaöRV	Zeitschrift für ausländisches öffentliches Recht und Völkerrecht

1

Confronting Colonial Heritage

Introducing Entanglements, Continuities, and Transformations

It is in the heart of London, in one of its museums
An object which often occupies my thoughts
It is a wooden tiger, whose claws tear at
The red mannequin of an English Soldier …*

> Henri-August Barbier, 'The Sultan's Joujou',
> *Iambes et poèmes* (1837)

1 Setting the scene

It is an intriguing view, which has inspired poets, writers, or painters. A uniformed man, wearing a red coat and a low crowned black hat, lies on his back. His eyes are almost closed. He is attacked by a life-size wooden tiger, who crawls on top of him. The tiger fleshes his teeth into the man's neck. You can virtually hear the animal roar. The body of the tiger contains a built-in ivory keyboard. It pushes air through a pipe inside the man's throat. The playing makes the man's left arm rise and fall. It produces grunting and wailing sounds, which convey the distress of the victim. The tiger is called Tipu's tiger (also Tippoo's tiger), named after the 'Tiger of Mysore', an Indian sultan (1750–1799), who ruled the Kingdom of Mysore during British colonial expansion in Southern India in the late eighteenth century. Today, the object is behind glass doors. It is one of the most illustrious artefacts in the Victoria and Albert Museum in London.

The story of this iconic object[1] represents the tensions of colonial history like hardly any other cultural object.[2] Its making, acquisition, and diverging perception

All urls provided in the book were accessed on 1 March 2023

* English translation from French original 'Le Joujou du Sultan' ('Il est au cœur de Londres, en l'un de ses musées, Un objet qui souvent occupe mes pensées: C'est un tigre de bois, dans ses ongles serrant, Le rouge mannequin d'un Anglais expirant').

[1] See Mildred Archer, *Tippoo's Tiger* (London: Her Majesty's Stationery Office, 1959); Susan Stronge, *Tipu's Tigers* (London: V&A Publishing, 2009); Arthur W. J. G. Ord-Hume, 'Tipu's Tiger: Its History and Description' (1987) 3 *Music and Automata* 21–31, 64–80. On Tipu Sultan, see G. A. Henty, *The Tiger of Mysore: A Story of the War with Tippoo Saib* (London: Blackie & Son, 2001, 1896).

[2] Cultural objects are typically defined by their significance to states, individuals, non-state entities, or groups. See Christa Roodt, 'Restitution of Art and Cultural Objects and Its Limits' (2013)

Confronting Colonial Objects. Carsten Stahn, Oxford University Press. © Carsten Stahn 2023.
DOI: 10.1093/oso/9780192868121.003.0001

pose intriguing questions about the self-understanding of modern society, its relation towards the past and contemporary identity and the role of international law itself in colonial encounters. The depiction of the object tells a more complex story about the dynamics of local and colonial rule in South-east Asia, the diverse nature of colonial violence, rivalry among colonial powers, and the transformation of the meaning of cultural objects over time.

1.1 Tipu's story

The artefact blurs boundaries between subject and object. It was originally commissioned in the 1790s by the Tipu Sultan, a Mysore ruler known for his attachment to tigers.[3] The object stood as a symbol of his own rule.[4] The sultan allied with France in order to counter expansion of the East India Company in the Anglo-Mysore wars between 1769 and 1799.[5] The tiger became a metaphor of the Sultan's

---

46 *Comparative and International Law Journal of Southern Africa* 286–307, 287. See also Art. 2 of the UNIDROIT Convention of 24 June 1995 on Stolen or Illegally Exported Cultural Objects (1995) 34 ILM 1332, which refers to objects 'which, on religious or secular grounds, are of importance for archaeology, prehistory, history, literature, art or science and belong to one of the categories listed in the Annex' to the Convention. On cultural colonial objects, see John Henry Merryman (ed.), *Imperialism, Art and Restitution* (Cambridge: Cambridge University Press, 2006) Jeannette Greenfield, *The Return of Cultural Treasures* (3rd edn, New York: Cambridge University Press, 2007); Ana Vrdoljak, *International Law, Museums and the Return of Cultural Objects* (Cambridge: Cambridge University Press, 2006); James A. R. Nafziger and Ann M. Nicgorski, *Cultural Heritage Issues: The Legacy of Conquest, Colonization and Commerce* (Leiden: Brill, 2009); Dan Hicks, *The Brutish Museums: The Benin Bronzes, Colonial Violence and Cultural Restitution* (London: Pluto Press, 2020); Bénédicte Savoy, *Africa's Struggle for Its Art: History of a Postcolonial Defeat* (Princeton: Princeton University Press, 2022); Alexander Herman, *Restitution: The Return of Cultural Artefacts* (London: Lund Humphries, 2022); Pierre Losson, *The Return of Cultural Heritage to Latin America* (London: Routledge, 2022); Angelika Epple, Thomas Sandkühler, and Jürgen Zimmerer (eds.), *Geschichtskultur durch Restitution? Ein Kunst-Historikerstreit* (Köln: Böhlau Verlag, 2021); Jos van Beurden, *Treasures in Trusted Hands* (Leiden: Sidestone Press, 2017); Jos van Beurden, *Inconvenient Heritage* (Amsterdam: Amsterdam University Press, 2022); Wazi Apoh and Andreas Mehler, 'Mainstreaming the Discourse on Restitution and Repatriation within African History, Heritage Studies and Political Science' (2020) 7 *Contemporary Journal of African Studies* 1–16; Teresa McGuire, 'African Antiquities Removed during Colonialism: Restoring a Stolen Cultural Legacy' (1990) 1990 *Detroit College of Law Review* 31–70; Evelien Campfens, 'The Bangwa Queen: Artifact or Heritage?' (2019) 26 *International Journal of Cultural Property* 75–110; Sebastian M. Spitra, 'Civilisation, Protection, Restitution: A Critical History of International Cultural Heritage Law in the 19th and 20th Century' (2020) 22 *Journal of the History of International Law* 329–354. See also generally Francesco Francioni and Ana Vrdoljak, *The Oxford Handbook of International Cultural Heritage Law* (Oxford: Oxford University Press, 2020).

 [3] The scene has synergies with the death of the son of Sir Hector Munro, a British General who had defeated Tipu's father in the second Anglo-Mysore war (1780–1784). Munro's son, himself a cadet of the East India Company, was mauled by a Bengal tiger on Saugor Island near Calcutta in 1792. Colin Munro, 'Thus Were the British Defeated' (2018) 40 *London Review of Books* 20–21.
 [4] Tipu allegedly claimed that he preferred to live 'two days like a tiger' than 'two hundred years like a sheep'. See Alexander Beatson, *A View of the Origin and Conduct of the War with Tippoo Sultaun* (London: G. and W. Nicol, 1800) 153–154.
 [5] He even invited Napoleon Bonaparte to join the struggle against British rule.

kingship. It illustrated his resistance to British invasion. It contrasted the emblem of the East India Company, which depicted a lion.[6]

Tipu's tiger is not only an artefact, but also an instrument, a musical 'automaton'. Its making reflects emerging patterns of globalization through colonial relations. The object represents the highest state-of-the art of technical craftsmanship at the time. The tiger was produced by local artists in collaboration with French organ-makers. It was located in the music room of Tipu's palace at Seringapatam, the capital of Mysore (now called Srirangapatna) in Southern India.

The role and reception of Tipu has changed considerably throughout history. The tiger was seized during the Siege of Seringapatam in 1799, when British forces looted and pillaged Tipu's palace and the city. Its taking formed part of an emerging culture of imperial collecting.[7] The official historical note of the Victoria and Albert Museum describes the acquisition as follows:

> The invading army stormed through a breach in the ramparts and, in the ensuing chaos, Tipu and a great many of his soldiers, generals and the citizens of the town were killed. The victorious troops then rampaged through the city, looting valuables from the palace and from private houses, until Colonel Arthur Wellesley (later the Duke of Wellington) gave an order for hanging and flogging which quickly restored order. The contents of the royal treasury were then valued and divided between the men of the East India Company Army by the Prize Agents over the next weeks, in accordance with the conventional practice of the period. Some time later, the tiger was discovered in the music room of the palace and was shipped to London, where it arrived in 1800. It was sent to East India House, the headquarters of the East India Company which housed a library and new museum, and soon became one of the most popular exhibits.[8]

When Tipu's tiger arrived in London, it sparked considerable attention. The tiger quickly became a sensational object. Placed on British soil and displayed in the East India House, it became a symbol of British victory over India and the vanquishing of Britain's rival France. The object was viewed as an illustration of the brutality of Tipu's own rule, rather than as symbol of resistance against colonial violence. This reading of the image coincided with orientalist conceptions of Indian leaders as cruel tyrants and a broader fascination in European society with exotic cultures, warfare, and differences between East and West.

---

[6] Jean-Marie Fournier, 'Tippoo's Tiger' European Romanticisms in Association (9 August 2019) http://www.euromanticism.org/tippoos-tiger/. See also Kate Brittlebank, 'Sakti and Barakat: The Power of Tipu's Tiger. An Examination of the Tiger Emblem of Tipu Sultan of Mysore' (1995) 29 *Modern Asian Studies* 257–269.

[7] See generally Maya Jasanoff, 'Collectors of Empire: Objects, Conquests and Imperial Self-fashioning' (2004) 184 *Past and Present* 109–135.

[8] See Victoria and Albert Museum, Search the Collection, 'Mechanical Organ: Tippoo's Tiger' http://collections.vam.ac.uk/item/O61949/tippoos-tiger-mechanical-organ-unknown/.

The British Press presented the 'musical tiger' as an illustration of the 'deep hatred of Tippoo Saib towards the English nation', who amused 'himself with a sight of this miserable emblematical triumph'.[9] An entry of the Penny Magazine of the Society for the Diffusion of Useful Knowledge from 1835 reflects the colonial propaganda and orientalization of foreign rule, which served as justification for colonial expansion:

> Whether made for Tippoo himself or for some other Indian potentate a century and a half earlier, it is difficult to convey a more lively impression of the mingled ferocity and childish want of taste so characteristic of the majority of Asian princes than will be communicated at once by this truly barbarous piece of music.[10]

The displacement, public display, and reception changed the status of the object. Under Tipu's rule, the tiger was a private possession of the sultan. The act of looting converted it into a war trophy and public object. It developed into a cultural reference with historical and cultural significance to multiple audiences. For British audiences, it marked a symbol of colonial power and victory, which became part of national identity through reproduction in literary works[11] or political cartoons.[12] For Indians, it symbolized resistance towards colonial policies.

Nowadays, Tipu's Tiger represents a cultural icon in its own right. It is a global object, which is the subject of multiple poems,[13] books,[14] video clips, podcasts,[15] and replica. It carries multiple, and partially, conflicting meanings. In post-colonial Britain, it is no longer merely a symbol of the victory of colonial rule, but also a reminder of the violence of imperial expansion. In India, public opinion remains divided. For some, Tipu is a powerful illustration of the struggle for independence from British rule, for others, a reminder of a dark period in history which involved

---

[9] St James's Chronicle or the British Evening Post, 'Musical Tyger' Issue 6605 (17–19 April 1800)   https://www.khanacademy.org/humanities/art-asia/south-asia/x97ec695a:1500-1850-deccan-south/a/tipus-tiger .

[10] See Penny Magazine of the Society for the Diffusion of Useful Knowledge (15 August 1835) (London: Charles Knight, 1835) 319–320. See also Amal Chatterjee, *Representations of India, 1740–1840: The Creation of India in the Colonial Imagination* (London: Macmillan, 1998) 174.

[11] English Romantic poet John Keats included a reference to Tipu's Tiger in his satirical poem 'The Cap and Bells', after visiting the London offices of the East India Company ('That little buzzing noise … comes from a plaything of the Emperor's choice, from a Man-Tiger-Organ, prettiest of his toys').

[12] *Punch*, a British weekly magazine, ran a cartoon on 'The British Lion's Vengeance on the Bengal Tiger' in 1857, which shows a lion attacking a tiger killing a European. It symbolized the defeat of the Indian Rebellion of 1857 by the East India Company. See *Punch*, Vol. 33, (22 August 1857) 76–77 http://www.victorianweb.org/periodicals/punch/53.html.

[13] See e.g. Marianne Moore, 'Tippoo's Tiger (New York: Phoenix Book Shop, 1967).

[14] See *supra* note 1; Kate Brittlebank, *Tiger: The Life of Tipu Sultan* (New Delhi: Juggernaut, 2016).

[15] See Marc Fennell, Stuff the British Stole, Episode 1, 'A Tiger and a Scream' (22 November 2020)   https://www.abc.net.au/radionational/programs/stuff-the-british-stole/a-tiger-and-a-scream/12867626.

repressive local rule, including destruction of temples and churches and killings during Tipu's reign as sultan.[16]

This story highlights the complex problems raised by the treatment of cultural colonial objects which are treated in this book, i.e. material objects with a cultural expression[17] collected in colonial contexts, namely in externally[18] or internally[19] colonized societies from the early sixteenth to the twentieth centuries.[20] As the story of Tipu shows, cultures speak to us through their objects. Many cultural colonial objects have a dual nature. They are part of material culture ('cultural property') and become part of heritage, in the sense that they carry a historical and symbolic meaning that transcends their origins and evolves over time. Their history is often connected to violence, domination, or conquest between civilizations, nations, or communities.[21] Cultural objects have been treated in similar narratives as colonial subjects, such as the 'exotic' or the 'other'. Colonial ideology was mediated through material things, including cultural takings. Collection became a means to classify them. Cultural appropriation persists not only through ownership in the physical sense, but also through control over the contemporary representation, meaning or display of objects, or their commercial exploitation. They are sometimes qualified as 'orphans' by curators since their provenance, authors, or original meanings remain unknown.

1.2 Premise, positionality, and methodology

These cultural dimensions of colonialism have been marginalized in practice and discourse. Colonialism was also a 'cultural project of control', driven by the scramble for curiosities, prestige, the appropriation of material culture, and the production of imperial hierarchies, which 'enabled conquest, and was produced by it'.[22] This

---

[16] NDTV, 'Tipu Sultan Jayanti: Life of "Tiger of Mysore" and Controversy around Him (10 November 2018) https://www.ndtv.com/india-news/tipu-sultan-jayanti-life-of-tiger-of-mysore-and-controversy-around-him-1945322.

[17] Vrdoljak, *International Law, Museums and the Return of Cultural Objects*, 7, who refers to the 'movable physical manifestations of the culture of an occupied people'.

[18] This is the classic form of colonialism. See Robert Blauner, 'Internal Colonialism and Ghetto Revolt' (1969) 16 *Social Problems* 393–408, 395.

[19] Internal colonialism refers to a condition of oppression or subordination of one group over another inside the boundaries of the state which colonized it. It involves intra-state economic and social domination or exploitation. See generally Robert J. Hind, 'The Internal Colonial Concept' (1984) 26 *Comparative Studies in Society and History* 553.

[20] Jos van Beurden uses a narrower definition. He defines them as objects of 'cultural or historical importance' that were 'acquired without just compensation or was involuntarily lost during the European colonial era' in order to distinguish them from objects that were regularly purchased or goods which were specifically produced for European visitors. See Van Beurden, *Treasures in Trusted Hands*, 39.

[21] Margaret M. Miles, *Art as Plunder: The Ancient Origins of Debate about Cultural Property* (New York: Cambridge University Press, 2008).

[22] Nicholas B. Dirks, *Castes of Mind: Colonialism and the Making of Modern India* (Princeton: Princeton University Press, 2001) 9.

entanglement is not only reflected in colonial violence, but also in science (pale-ontology, anthropology, archaeology), circulation and trade of cultural objects or human remains, missionary activity, curatorial policies, knowledge production and everyday practices (photography,[23] imagery).[24] The scramble for cultural objects and human remains complemented the exploitation of primary resources. It was driven by transnational networks and extended to countries that were not colonial powers or colonized in the geographical sense.[25] Cultural appropriation or exploitation was not limited to extractive colonial contexts in the Global South, but also occurred in the Global North (e.g. *inuit* culture in Greenland, Sámi culture, British–Irish rela-tions[26]), albeit on a lesser scale.[27] It covered multiple types of objects with cultural significance: artefacts, human remains, or fossils.[28] Many objects were hidden in mu-seum storage throughout the twentieth century. These shadows of colonial history affect not only ethnological museums, but all genres of museums and collections.

This book builds on the idea that humans and things constitute each other[29] and that materiality matters for identity. It is in line with the 'material turn' in law and history,[30] which seeks to understand human behaviour through the story of objects

---

[23] Daniel Foliard, *The Violence of Colonial Photography* (Manchester: Manchester University Press, 2022).

[24] Luis Eslava, *Local Space, Global Life: The Everyday Operation of International Law and Development* (Cambridge: Cambridge University Press, 2015).

[25] On Scandinavian colonialism, see Magdalena Naum and others (eds.), *Scandinavian Colonialism and the Rise of Modernity: Small Time Agents in a Global Arena* (New York: Springer, 2013); Raita Merivirta, Leila Koivunen, and Timo Särkkä, 'Finns in the Colonial World' in Magdalena Naum and others (eds.), *Finnish Colonial Encounters: From Anti-Imperialism to Cultural Colonialism and Complicity* (New York: Springer, 2021) 1–38.

[26] The debate on the repatriation of the remains of Irish giant Charles Byrne reflects the ongoing rem-nants of colonial sensitivities in British-Irish relations. See Thomas L. Muinzer, 'A Grave Situation: An Examination of the Legal Issues Raised by the Life and Death of Charles Byrne, the "Irish Giant"' (2013) *International Journal of Cultural Property* 23–48, 37, who argues that 'Northern Irish identity within the context of the United Kingdom' is 'robust enough' to support claims for return based on a 'community of origin' identification. See Chapter 5.

[27] See Magdalena Naum and Jonas M. Nordin, 'Situating Scandinavian Colonialism' in Magdalena Naum and Jonas M. Nordin (eds.), *Scandinavian Colonialism and the Rise of Modernity* (New York: Springer, 2013) 3–16, 4–5.

[28] Paul P. Stewens, Nussaïbah B. Raja, and Emma M. Dunne, 'The Return of Fossils Removed under Colonial Rule' (2022) 8 *Santander Art and Culture Law Review* 69–94.

[29] As Martin Skydstrup has argued, the idea that an 'intrinsic identity' is vested in an object, 'being forever attached to a social entity - be that a group, community, region or nation - is compromised by the simple fact that the status of an object is constantly subject to ongoing processes of cultural redefinition'. See Martin Skrydstrup, 'Righting Wrongs? Three Rationales of Repatriation and What Anthropology Might Have to Say About Them' in Gabriel Mille and Jens Dahl (eds.), *Utimut. Past Heritage: Future Partnership. Discussions on Repatriation in the 21st Century* (Copenhagen: Greenland National Museum and Archives & International Work Group for Indigenous Affairs, 2008) 56–63, 58. On the agency of objects, see Chris Gosden, 'What Do Objects Want?' (2005) 12 *Journal of Archaeological Method and Theory* 193–211.

[30] See e.g., Neil MacGregor, *A History of the World in 100 Objects* (New York: Penguin, 2013); Jessie Hohmann and Daniel Joyce, *International Law's Objects* (New York: Oxford University Press, 2018); Daniel Ricardo Quiroga-Villamarín, 'Beyond Texts? Towards a Material Turn in the Theory and History of International Law' (2021) 23 *Journal of the History of International Law* 466–500, Carl Landauer, 'The Stuff of International Law' (2021) 31 *EJIL* 1049–1078. On the material turn in cultural heritage, see Daniel Miller, *Stuff* (New York: Wiley, 2009.

and the relations between persons and things. The stories of objects, and their treatment in legal and institutional frames, serve as a site to understand broader questions of justice, inequality, and power under international law. Cultural colonial takings involved takings of histories, knowledge, ideas and beliefs through the removal or conversion of physical things. The role of objects, and their changing identities shaped not only Western colonial markets, artistic classifications, or the transformation of institutions, but also the frames and gaps of cultural heritage law or discourses around the justification of the colonial project itself. Many of the takings reveal open scars and ongoing effects in contemporary relations.

The term cultural colonial object itself is reductionist. It often reflects a meaning attached to things as a result of their dislocation or transformation in Western culture. It is understood in a broad way here, capturing colonized objects and bodies and the fluidity between personhood and things.[31] It includes 'subject-objects',[32] i.e. objects of religious, cultural, spiritual, historical, or artistic significance which are associated with subject qualities or human attributes by a nation, society, or identifiable group. It takes into account that things which appear to be 'mere' objects from the perspective of the Western viewer may be associated with qualities of personhood[33] or spiritual power[34] in societies or communities of origin, or be regarded as subjects (e.g. ancestors or 'citizens in exile').[35] The notion is at the same time more flexible than the notion of cultural property',[36] which theorizes items through the lens of property, possession or ownership relations, or the term 'cultural heritage',[37] which defines artefacts through their bond to history and identity

---

[31] It is broader than the notion of objects mentioned in Article 1(a)–(k) of the 1970 UNESCO Convention on the Means of Prohibiting and Preventing the Illicit Import, Export and Transfer of Ownership of Cultural Property, 14 November 1970, 823 UNTS 231.

[32] On the evolution of subject–object relationship in material culture, see also Friedemann Yi-Neumann and others (eds.), *Material Culture and (Forced) Migration: Materialising the Transient* (London: UCL Press, 2022) 8–11.

[33] Many civilizations regard material objects not only as physical objects, but as an embodiment of the spirit of ancestors and a means to connect to them, which needs to be protected for the benefit of future generations. Objects may turn into animated subjects through rituals or engagement with the spiritual power or energy that they embody. See Tular Sudarmadi, *Between colonial legacies and grassroots movements: exploring cultural heritage practice in the Ngadha and Manggarai Region of Flores* (PhD Dissertation, Amsterdam: 2014) 30 https://research.vu.nl/ws/portalfiles/portal/42127428/compl ete+dissertation.pdf.

[34] Souleymane Bachir Diagne has argued that objects do not only present art, but constitute a language for African philosophy and cosmology.

[35] See Ciraj Rassool, 'Restoring the Skeletons of Empire: Return, Reburial and Rehumanisation in Southern Africa' (2015) 41 *Journal of Southern African Studies* 653–670, 653, 669.

[36] Article 1 of the 1954 Hague Convention for the Protection of Cultural Property in the Event of Armed Conflict defines cultural property within the meaning of the Convention as 'movable or immovable property of great importance to the cultural heritage of every people'. It includes objects with 'artistic, ethnographic, archaeological, or historical value'. See John Henry Merryman, 'Two Ways of Thinking about Cultural Property' (1986) 80 *AJIL* 831–853, 831. On the diverse understandings, see Lyndel Prott and Patrick J. O'Keefe, ' "Cultural heritage" or "cultural property"?' (1992) 1 *International Journal of Cultural Property* 307–320; Roger O'Keefe, 'The Meaning of "Cultural Property" under the 1954 Hague Convention' (1999) 46 *Netherlands International Law Review* 26–56.

[37] The notion of cultural heritage is broader than culture property. Its preservation is linked to the identity of communities or groups, and their link with the present and future, which is continuously

of people. It covers man-made material objects, such as archaeological objects, ethnographic artefacts, historical monuments, or artistic objects, including masks, sculptures, ritual objects, or jewellery. It may also include certain natural objects, such as human remains[38] or funeral objects, whose human and spiritual dimension may transcend their physical features.[39]

This work presents both the different facets of colonial violence and their enduring effects, and possible avenues to renew relations. It pleads for a new age of engagement with objects and their histories in order to address some of the stereotypes, false dichotomies, or impasses, which have characterized discourse on collecting practices, provenance, object identities, or impediments to return for centuries. It argues that cultural objects have a dual function. They do not only reflect cultural identity or value, but serve at the same time as carriers of different forms of violence and memory, and as agents of transformation which may facilitate new relations through their affective qualities, locality, or modes of representation or display. It suggests that ideas of cultural relational justice and object mobility may serve to transcend the traditional divide between cultural nationalism and cultural internationalism, challenge post-colonial continuities and promote new object possibilities and just relations.

One challenge, which needs to be addressed up-front, is the issue of positionality.[40] Presenting object histories may involve semantic traps, inherent biases, risks of misrepresentation or 'othering'.[41] The question who speaks, and

---

(re)created. The concept includes non-material cultural elements. It has been extended through different international conventions, such as the Convention Concerning the Protection of the World Cultural and Natural Heritage, 16 November 1972, 1037 UNTS 151, the Convention on the Protection of the Underwater Cultural Heritage, 2 November 2001, 2562 UNTS 3 or the Convention for the Safeguarding of the Intangible Cultural Heritage (17 October 2003) 2368 UNTS 1. See generally Janet Blake, 'On Defining the Cultural Heritage' (2000) 49 *International and Comparative Law Quarterly* 61–85; Manlio Frigo, 'Cultural Property v. Cultural Heritage: A "Battle of Concepts" in International Law?' (2004) 86 *International Review of the Red Cross* 367–378; Francesco Francioni, 'Beyond State Sovereignty: the Protection of Cultural Heritage as a Shared Interest of Humanity' (2004) 25 *Michigan Journal of International Law* 1209–1228; Craig Forrest, *International Law and the Protection of Cultural Heritage* (London & New York: Routledge, 2010).

[38] Ruth Redmond-Cooper (ed.), *Heritage, Ancestry and Law: Principles, Policies and Practices in Dealing with Historical Human Remains* (Builth Wells: Institute of Art and Law, 2015). On legal protection, see Ryan M. Seidemann, 'Bones of Contention: A Comparative Examination of Law Governing Human Remains from Archaeological Contexts in Formerly Colonial Countries' (2004) 64 *Louisiana Law Review* 545–588; Jie Huang, 'Protecting Non-Indigenous Human Remains under Cultural Heritage Law' (2015) 14 *Chinese Journal of International Law* 709–734. For a discussion of return, see Steven Gallagher, 'Museums and the Return of Human Remains: An Equitable Solution' (2010) 17 *International Journal of Cultural Property* 65–86.

[39] Article 12 of UN Declaration on the Rights of Indigenous Peoples, GA Resolution 61/295 (13 September 2007) UN Doc A/RES/61/295 (UNDRIP) makes express mention of human remains and distinguishes them from other cultural property. Under the 1970 UNESCO, human remains may be covered under different notions: 'property relating to history', 'products of archaeological excavations or discoveries', or 'objects of ethnological interest'.

[40] Ingrid Samset, 'Towards Decolonial Justice' (2020) 14 *International Journal of Transitional Justice* 596–607, 607.

[41] Carol Ann Dixon, *The 'Othering' of Africa and Its Diasporas in Western Museum Practices* (PhD, Sheffield: 2016).

who is listened to, or silenced, is central to narratives of cultural takings, return, or restitution. One might ask whether it is appropriate at all for a white Western scholar to trace object histories and engage with the heritage of Empire,[42] even though colonial narratives, scientific discourses, and epistemic violence have been central to cultural dispossession, identity-taking, and colonial injustice. As Open Restitution Africa has shown, despite the cardinal role of voices from the Global South in the restitution movement as of the 1960s (e.g. Ekpo Eyo, Folarin Shyllon, Kwame Opoku, Zahi Hawass, Monica Hanna) and the growing knowledge production on the topic of restitution and return over the past years, academic writing and discourse remains heavily dominated by Western voices and centred on certain iconic objects.[43] This makes it necessary to diversify discourse and foreground non-Western positions in order to counter a replication of past inequalities and silencing in contemporary knowledge frames and practices. A critical interrogation of colonial practices by Western voices is a double-edged sword. It may contribute to a rethinking of past and contemporary approaches by the Global North and Europe. But it also carries inherent limits and ambiguities. As Olúfémi Táíwò has cautioned in his critique of decolonial approaches, defining the colonized merely through the colonial experience is ambivalent, since it may reduce moral or political agency.[44] Any Western perspective may easily become entangled in its own contradictions or perpetuate inequalities. It may render other voices less visible or present dilemmas of inequality, structural injustice, or oppression through the voice of 'a dominant group', rather than those who have been marginalized ('whitesplaining').[45] These dilemmas cannot be fully solved, but must be openly addressed and confronted. They require particular care in the use of voice, the framing of concepts, and the choice of methods.

This study seeks to mitigate these tensions through a critical methodology, acknowledgement of epistemic dilemmas, and polyphonic perspectives on events, narratives, or object meanings. It operates on the premise that critical inquiry into colonial takings and approaches to restitution or return may serve to reveal contradictions and injustices of the past, question racial science and commodification of objects, identify false universalities, bring out the diversity and pluri-vocality of law in the past, take distance from discriminatory semantics, point out colonial continuities, and show respect for diversity and other epistemologies. It uses several methods in order to address risks of bias and positionality.

---

[42] The entry of the Africa collection of the Humboldt forum in Berlin alludes to this positionality with a quote from Robin DiAngelo's 'White Fragility' at the entrance: 'I have a white frame of reference and a white worldview'.

[43] Molemo Moiloa, *Reclaiming Restitution: Centering and contextualizing the African Narrative* (Johannesburg: Open Restitution Africa, 2022), at https://openrestitution.africa/wp-content/uploads/2022/09/ANF-Report-Main-Report.pdf.

[44] Olúfémi Táíwò, *Against Decolonisation: Taking African Agency Seriously* (London: Hurst, 2022).

[45] Matiangai Sirleaf, 'Do You Have to Say that You Are Black?' in *Third World Approaches to International Law Review*, TWAILR: Reflections #43/2022 (15 June 2022).

A first technique is the idea of 'contrapuntal reading', developed by Edward Said.[46] It relies on the principle that colonial relations can only be meaningfully understood through the perspective of imperialism and the resistance to it and require simultaneous engagement with 'the metropolitan history' and counter histories.[47] As Priyamvada Gopal has shown in her work on Insurgent Empire, colonialism and racism have triggered multiple forms of resistance by people whose contributions have been hidden or erased from memory.[48] The counter-narratives brought out in object studies and legal analysis here challenge the position that takings were fine according to the relevant standards of the time. The often-repeated claim that takings were legal according to colonial law or the absence of legal prohibitions has a 'counter-factual character'.[49] The picture is far more complex. Many Western agents knew that certain practices, such as grave robbing or the takings of human remains, conflicted with professional ethics, instructions for ethnographic collecting, or minimum standards of humanity.[50] They were aware that cultural takings were not necessarily based on free and informed consent of indigenous populations, and sometimes expressed regret in hindsight. This is reflected in certain communications between museums and agents.[51] Some remains were exported from Australia or New Zealand in violation of laws banning trade or export.

[46] Said relied on this technique to read texts through the perspective of both the colonizer and the colonized and bring out what is excluded in speech. He wrote: 'We must therefore read the great canonical texts with an effort to draw out, extend, give emphasis and voice to what is silent or marginally present or ideologically represented in such works. The contrapuntal reading must take account of both processes—that of imperialism and that of resistance to it, which can be done by extending our reading of the texts to include what was once forcibly excluded' Edward W. Said, *Culture and Imperialism* (New York: Knopf, 1993) 78–79. It is applied here to analysis of discourses and practices.

[47] Ibid, 51. On challenges to Eurocentric world views of collections, see Germaine Warkentin and Carolyn Podruchny (eds.), *Decentring the Renaissance: Canada and Europe in Multidisciplinary Perspective, 1500-1700* (Toronto: University of Toronto Press, 2001); Amy Lonetree, *Decolonizing Museums: Representing Native America in National and Tribal Museums* (Chapel Hill: University of North Carolina Press, 2012), Vanessa Watts, 'Indigenous Place-Thought and Agency Amongst Humans and Non Humans' (2013) 2 *Decolonization: Indigeneity, Education & Society* 20–34.

[48] Priyamvada Gopal, *Insurgent Empire Anticolonial Resistance and British Dissent* (London: Verso, 2020). See also Nuno Domingos, Miguel Bandeira Jerónimo, and Ricardo Roque, *Resistance and Colonialism: Insurgent Peoples in World History* (Cham: Springer, 2020); Balakrishnan Rajagopal, *International Law from Below: Development, Social Movements, and Third World Resistance* (Cambridge: Cambridge University Press, 2003).

[49] Yann LeGall and Gwinyai Machona, 'Possessions, Spoils of War, Belongings' *VerfBlog* (2 December 2022) https://verfassungsblog.de/possessions-spoils-of-war-belongings/.

[50] Paul Turnbull, 'The ethics of repatriation: reflections on the Australian experience' in Cressida Fforde, C. Timothy McKeown, and Honor Keeler (eds.), *The Routledge Companion to Indigenous Repatriation* (London: Routledge, 2020) 927–949.

[51] LeGall and Machona refer to communications between physician Hermann Kersting (1863–1937) and Felix von Luschan from 27 June 1900, in which Kersting admitted that certain objects were 'looted from the big village Napári during a small war' in Dagbon, or a letter dated 27 March 1899 from Lieutenant Valentin von Massow (1864–1899), a colonial officer in German Togoland, to van Luschan, in which he argued that he had largely collected 'war booty' (*Kriegsbeute*) during military campaigns and expeditions, which carries low ethnographic value because of its non-professional means of collection. LeGall and Machona 'Possessions, Spoils of War, Belongings'.

The analysis of Western sources shows that colonial narratives, archives, or semantics have often concealed the violence of takings, the protest or resistance concerning exploitation or dispossession, or attempts to reclaim objects taken by explorers, traders, colonial officers, missionaries, or soldiers. Contemporary forms of resistance are not limited to vocal protest or activism, such as Emery Mwazulu Diyabanza's actions to reclaim 'stolen property' from Africa',[52] but also through implicit rejection or disinterest in elitist or distant museum structures, or the decision not to engage. Archiving and storage of objects may be perceived as a 'burial'. These perspectives must be brought out.

At the same time, it is misleading to romanticize local agency or present local chiefs or leaders merely as passive victims of colonial violence. This work seeks to present both the stories unpinning the taking, commodification or social transformation of cultural objects, and the gaps, biases, or complicity of legal frameworks, as well as counter-narratives and forms of resistance to colonialism or racism, which have received lesser attention. 'Contrapuntal readings' are incorporated through integration of multiple standpoints, narratives and voices from the Global South and alternatives reading of the law, which have been sidelined in positivist accounts.

A second feature, which informs this study, is the recognition of the structural nature of colonial violence. The colonial encounter was marked by 'unequal power relationships and a self-image of the cultural superiority of those in power'.[53] This condition affected not only the exercise of power or the construction of law, but also the ideologies, discourses, knowledge frames or aesthetics governing objects. As Franz Fanon stated in 'The Wretched of the Earth', for 'the native, objectivity is always directed against him'.[54] Colonial values and biases were embedded in both museum histories and legal frameworks. This has repercussions for the approach towards law and history. They are not neutral, but products of their time which need to be put into context. Tracing histories of dispossession, knowledge frames or law in the colonial period requires a normative repositioning, including critical reading, the integration of counter-perspectives or other World views, or imagination beyond the colonial model. In many instances, it is impossible to gain one true or authentic story. Colonial narratives carry risks of bias. Alternative accounts were often transmitted through oral histories.

Accepting histories and laws of the time as authentic or neutral frames consolidates structural inequality. A contemporary account requires contextualization and 'critical redescription',[55] as Anne Orford has put it, what matters are not only

---

[52] He has been branded as the 'Robin Hood of Restitution'. See Kate Brown, 'Mwazulu Diyabanza, the Robin Hood of Restitution Activism' *Art News* (12 January 2021).

[53] German Museums Association, *Guidelines for German Museums: Care of Collections from Colonial Contexts* (Berlin: German Museum Association, 2021) 23.

[54] Frantz Fanon, *The Wretched of the Earth* (New York: Grove Press, 1963) 77.

[55] Anne Orford, 'In Praise of Description' (2012) 25 *LJIL* 609–625.

the stories themselves but the way in which they are told. Past and contemporary narratives and methods of scientific classification contain discriminatory elements or vocabulary which conceals the violence of the past. The political economy of takings affected semantics. For instance, terms like 'collecting', 'gifting', or 'war booty' present takings as innocent or neutral acts, which hide the brutal or concerted methods of dispossession or imply that objects were free to be taken, like finds. Legal institutions, such as the application of 'prize law' procedures,[56] provided a means to acquire title over looted objects. The rising international 'market' for objects in the twentieth century was not predominantly driven by local interests in trade, exchange, or gift-giving, but largely a result of the 'unequal networks of power and capital established by colonialism'.[57]

These contradictions need to be set into context. Narratives of colonial agents regarding the taking of objects cannot be taken for granted as true or authentic accounts of collection or taking. Rather, they are presented here, sometimes in their original form, to reveal the inherent contradictions, gaps or biases of colonial practices and the ever-changing justifications for colonial takings. The overall purpose is to tell a 'history of histories'.[58]

A third key element of the methodology is the use of a micro-historical approach, focused on stories that emerge through objects. This approach provides a perspective on the past which reflects the nature of colonial networks and their operation. It is used to examine the dislocation and pathways of objects, the semantics and justifications of takings, their diverse meanings, as well as continuities and change in attitude regarding return or restitution. Object stories provide important insights about colonial history, as well as gaps, biases or strategic uses of the law in the colonial period, and its aftermath. They illustrate methods of collecting, colonial exploitation and knowledge production, the nexus between racial science and the birth of modern museums, the transformation and protection of cultural heritage, as well as the contestations and reclamations of cultural objects.

A central concept is the idea of 'object biography'.[59] It draws on the interrelation between things and people. It takes into account that the 'life story' of objects is constantly built and transformed through the relationship between the location, context, and meanings of an object.

[56] James L. Hevia, *English Lessons: The Pedagogy of Imperialism in Nineteenth-Century China* (Durham: Duke University Press, 2003) 83–84.

[57] Independent Group of Experts, 'Ethical Principles for the Management and Restitution of Colonial Collections in Belgium' (June 2021) 1.2.1.

[58] On complicity between historians and empire, see Priya Satia, *Time's Monster: History, Conscience and Britain's Empire* (London: Allen Lane, 2020).

[59] Janet Hoskins, 'Agency, Biography and Objects' in Chris Tilley and others (eds.), *Handbook of Material Culture* (London: Sage, 2006) 75–84; Kate Hill (ed.), *Museums and Biographies: Stories, Objects, Identities* (London: Boydell and Brewer, 2012).

This concept is helpful to understand how things may 'tell the stories of people' and to accommodate the multiple identities or subject-like attributes of objects.[60] It has been used to tell expanded histories of objects, challenge colonial narratives from a bottom up-perspective or tell stories of resistance and resilience.[61] It may be traced back to anthropologists Arjun Appadurai[62] and Igor Kopytoff,[63] who introduced the idea of a life-story approach towards objects. It was developed by Alfred Gell who argued that 'art objects are the equivalent of persons, or more precisely, social agents'[64] which can have an agency of their own[65] in relation to those who created them, look at them, or use them.[66] The idea of agency is shared by network theorists (e.g. Bruno Latour)[67] who accept that things may take on subject-like qualities, since they generate actions, define contexts or create meanings in relations between humans and things.[68] Jane Bennett has defended the idea that objects create trajectory by their 'vibrant materiality'.[69]

Such approaches challenge the predominant view in Western property law, according to which human beings own material objects. They have been applied in colonial contexts to understand the taking and transformation of objects. For instance, William Mitchell used the idea of 'bad objecthood' in order to explain the destruction, confiscation or conversion of sacred objects by missionaries.[70] Bénédicte Savoy has spoken of 'translocations'.[71] Jos van Beurden has referred

---

[60] Janet Hoskins, *Biographical Objects: How Things Tell the Stories of People's Lives* (London: Routledge, 1998).

[61] Haidy Geismar, 'In Defence of the Object Biography' (2021) 19 *British Art Studies* 1 https://doi.org/10.17658/issn.2058-5462/issue-19/conversation/003.

[62] Arjun Appadurai (ed.), *The Social Life of Things: Commodities in Cultural Perspective* (Cambridge: Cambridge University Press, 1986).

[63] Igor Kopytoff, 'The cultural biography of things: commoditization as process' in Appadurai, *The Social Life of Things*, 64–91.

[64] Alfred Gell, *Art and Agency: An Anthropological Theory* (Oxford: Oxford University Press, 1998) 7.

[65] Gell refers inter alia to 'idols' which are 'not depictions, not portraits, but (artefactual) bodies' creating religious agency. Gell, *Art and Agency*, 98–99.

[66] Liana Chua and Mark Elliott note that Gell's observation that 'objects have agency' is 'almost axiomatic' nowadays. See Liana Chua and Mark Elliott, 'Introduction: Adventures in the Art Nexus' in Mark Elliott and Liana Chua (eds.), *Distributed Objects: Meaning and Mattering after Alfred Gell* (New York: Berghahn Books, 2013) 1–24, 1. For a critique, see Howard Morphy, 'Art as a Mode of Action: Some Problems with Gell's Art and Agency' (2009) 14 *Journal of Material Culture* 5–27.

[67] Bruno Latour has extended network theory to relations between things and persons or between things. See Bruno Latour, *Reassembling the Social: An Introduction to Actor-Network-Theory* (Oxford: Oxford University Press, 2005).

[68] Letizia Caronia and Luigina Mortari, 'The Agency of Things: How Spaces and Artefacts Organize the Moral Order of an Intensive Care Unit' (2015) 25 *Social Semiotics* 401–422. Claire Wintle has argued that objects forge 'social relationships, individual and collective identities across time and space'. See Claire Wintle, *Colonial Collecting and Display: Encounters with Material Culture from the Andaman and Nicobar Islands* (Oxford: Berghahn Books, 2013) 2–3.

[69] Jane Bennett, *Vibrant Matter: A political ecology of things* (Durham, NC: Duke University Press, 2010).

[70] William John Thomas Mitchell, *What Do Pictures Want? The Lives and Loves of Images* (Chicago: Chicago University Press, 2005) 166.

[71] Bénédicte Savoy, Felicity Bodenstein, and Merten Lagatz (eds.), *Translocations: Histories of Dislocated Cultural Assets* (New York: Colombia University Press, 2022).

to the 'amputated biography' of objects in order to capture the knowledge gaps in provenance histories.[72] Dan Hicks has introduced the alternative concept of 'necrography', i.e. story of the death of objects in order to challenge the idea of linear transformation and take into account that object identities may disappear, for instance through their 'burial' in museum storages.[73]

The life-story approach is used here in order to trace the changing meanings of cultural colonial objects through processes of dislocation, and the ways in which museums shape the interpretation or demise of objects.[74] Colonial takings show certain recurring patterns. For instance, objects were often initially taken as curiosities, war trophies or 'fetishes'. Their removal affected their meaning. They became a symbol of the enlightened quest for knowledge or colonial victory in the imperial mind. Some objects were placed in public collections or gradually became objects of national prestige. Others were used as 'scientific' objects to showcase racial superiority or colonial difference. Throughout the twentieth century, many objects were requalified as a form of art, sometimes under degrading terms, such as 'primitive art'[75] or as universal objects, e.g. patrimony of humanity. In today's world, they take on 'decolonial' features. They are not only artefacts or works of art, but also reminders of colonial injustice and its histories, and the need to confront this past in former colonial powers and colonized societies.

Methodologically, this approach is a useful way to critically examine object trajectories and new ways to engage with them. It serves to trace the intellectual history and cultural significance of cultural takings, including their nature as identity or dignity takings. It helps to understand the diverse meanings of objects, including their transformation from trophies, idols or ethnological objects to affective objects or works of art, and the epistemic dimensions of colonial violence. It also provides a space to interrogate the ontologies of objects and investigate alternative object conceptions, such as the qualification of objects as 'witnesses to history',[76] subjects ('ancestors'), the comparison of human remains to 'missing persons'[77] or their transitional nature from an ontological perspective, i.e. their in-between state pending restitution.[78] Such perspectives open new avenues to explore whether

---

[72] Van Beurden, *Inconvenient Heritage*, 52.

[73] Hicks, *The Brutish Museums*, 236–239.

[74] On object transformation through conflict, see Leora Auslander and Tara Zahra (eds.), *Objects of War: The Material Culture of Conflict and Displacement* (Ithaca, NY: Cornell University Press, 2018).

[75] Colon Rhodes, *Primitivism and Modern Art* (London: Thames & Hudson, 1994); Marianna Torgovnick, *Gone Primitive: Savage Intellects, Modern Lives* (Chicago: The University of Chicago Press, 1990).

[76] Lyndel Prott, *Witnesses to history: a compendium of documents and writings on the return of cultural objects* (Paris: UNESCO, 2009).

[77] Ciraj Rassool, 'Human Remains, the Disciplines of the Dead, and the South African Memorial Complex' in Derek R. Peterson, Kodzo Gavua, and Ciraj Rassool (eds.), *The Politics of Heritage in Africa: Economies, Histories, and Infrastructures* (Cambridge: Cambridge University Press, 2015) 133–156.

[78] Noémie Etienne, 'Who Cares? Museum Conservation between Colonial Violence and Symbolic Repair' (2022) 5 *Museums & Social Issues* 1 DOI: 10.1080/15596893.2022.2057413.

transitional justice concepts, such as access to truth or access to justice can be applied to cultural colonial objects, and to what extent museums are not only guardians of heritage, but sites of transformative justice.

Some of the analysis is grounded in post-colonial theory (*Said*, *Fanon*, *Spivak*) or TWAIL approaches.[79] They are used to bring out the violence of colonial takings, to highlight the biases, gaps, and complicities of legal frameworks and to motivate the plea for alternative frames. However, it is also important to acknowledge their weaknesses. Post-colonial theorizations may blur the complexity of colonial histories, through a focus on domination, inequality, hierarchies or divides between colonizers and colonized. They underpin a case for return or restitution, and transformation of heritage approaches, but often remain sceptical in relation to the prospects of promoting change through law. They may also have disempowering effects. For instance, portraying indigenous or African cultural heritage merely through the perspective of 'looted art' places the emphasis almost exclusively on the past and may marginalize the contribution of contemporary artists to local and global culture.[80]

Care in the choice of semantics is an integral element of a critical methodology. Revisiting vocabulary and pluralizing discourse is in itself an important means of countering epistemological violence. Some legal terms of art are at odds with the relational dimensions of culture. For instance, notions such as 'cultural property' or 'ownership' may convey material understandings of objects, which marginalize the complexity of subject-object relations. The term 'collecting' is an umbrella notion, which may conceal the lack of consent or the entangled forms of consent in military, missionary, or other forms of takings in colonial power structures. The notion of 'gift' or exchange may silence the structural inequality of the political economy of colonial transactions. The term 'taking' better reflects the extractive logic behind takings, which is not limited to objects procured through force or coercion, but also extends to 'scientific' or other missions undertaken in colonial contexts. The notion of 'return', used throughout this work, goes beyond legal restitution in the narrow sense. It covers returns, including cross-border relocations of cultural and

---

[79] See Bhupinder S. Chimni, 'Past, Present and Future of International Law: A Critical Third World Approach' (2007) 8 *Melbourne Journal of International Law* 499–515; Antony Anghie, 'Finding the Peripheries: Sovereignty and Colonialism in Nineteenth-Century International Law' (1999) 40 *Harvard International Law Journal* 1–71, Luis Eslava and Sundhya Pahuja, 'Beyond the (Post)Colonial: TWAIL and the Everyday Life of International Law' (2012) 45 *Verfassung und Recht in Übersee* 195–221. On 'dark sides' of international cultural heritage law, see Lucas Lixinski, *International Heritage Law for Communities: Exclusion and Re-Imagination* (Oxford: Oxford University Press, 2019) 240–251. TWAIL literature on cultural heritage is rare, see e.g., Bharatt Goel, ' "All Asiatic Vague Immensities": International Law, Colonialism and the Return of Cultural Artefacts' TWAILR: Reflections, No. 41/2022.

[80] For instance, the finding in the report by Felwine Sarr and Bénédicte Savoy, *The Restitution of African Cultural Heritage: Toward a New Relational Ethics*, November 2018 http://restitutionreport2018.com/sarr_savoy_en.pdf

(Sarr and Savoy Report) that 90 per cent of African heritage is located the out of the continent sends ambivalent messages about the richness of contemporary cultures.

heritage objects, based on legal, ethical, and moral grounds.[81] It is not meant to express the absence of legal obligations, as suggested in UNESCO practice.

2   Tensions between empire, cultural dispossession, and protection of cultural objects

Historically, the removal of cultural colonial objects is closely related to dilemmas of cultural imperialism,[82] and discourses of humanity and civilization,[83] which go back to ancient civilizations.[84]

2.1   Ancient roots of the civilizatory paradox

The taking of cultural objects has been prominent means of expanding empire since Ancient Greek and Roman times.[85] They have been claimed as spoils of war ('To the victor belong the spoils') and were shown in public processions. Cultural takings served multiple purposes. They were used to signal victory, facilitate subjugation, or fund public treasures and warfare.[86] However, they were early on constrained by ideas of moderation, reputation, or honour. In some cases, culturally significant objects were returned several decades, or even centuries later. For instance, in 480 BC Persian King Xerxes plundered the statues of Harmodios and

---

[81] See Piotr Bienkowski, 'A Critique of Museum Restitution and Repatriation Practices' in Conal McCarthy (ed.), *The International Handbooks of Museum Studies: Museum Practice* (London: John Wiley & Sons, 2015) 431–453, 443.

[82] 'Cultural imperialism' involves cultural domination or oppression of less powerful societies by force or through removal of cultural commodities. The notion emerged in the second half of the twentieth century in the context of post-colonial, historical, and media studies. See Edward Said, *Culture and Imperialism* (New York: Vintage Books, 1993); Herbert Schiller, *Communication and Cultural Domination* (New York: International Arts and Sciences Press, 1976); Bernd Hamm and Russell Smandych (eds.), *Cultural Imperialism: Essays on the Political Economy of Cultural Domination* (Toronto: University of Toronto Press, 2005); John Tomlinson, *Cultural Imperialism: A Critical Introduction* (Baltimore: Johns Hopkins University Press, 2001); Ryan Dunch, 'Beyond Cultural Imperialism: Cultural Theory, Christian Missions, and Global Modernity' (2002) 41 *History and Theory* 301–325.

[83] See Brett Bowden, ' The Colonial Origins of International Law: European Expansion and the Classical Standard of Civilization' (2005) 7 *Journal of the History of International Law* 1–24, Antony Anghie, *Imperialism, Sovereignty and the Making of International Law* (Cambridge: Cambridge University Press, 2005), Ntina Tzouvala, *Capitalism as Civilization* (Cambridge: Cambridge University Press, 2020).

[84] Wilhelm Treue, *Art Plunder: The Fate of Works of Art in War and Unrest* (Basil Creighton tr, New York: The John Day Company, 1961); Ivan A. Lindsay, *The History of Loot and Stolen Art from Antiquity until the Present Day* (2nd ed., Austin: Unicorn, 2014); Colin Renfrew, *Loot, Legitimacy and Ownership: The Ethical Crisis in Archaeology* (London: Duckworth, 2000).

[85] Chris Godsen, *Archaeology and Colonialism: Cultural Contact from 5000 BC to the Present* (Cambridge: Cambridge University Press, 2004) 154.

[86] Patty Gerstenblith, 'Protecting Cultural Heritage in Armed Conflict: Looking Back, Looking Forward' (2009) 7 *Cardozo Public Law Policy & Ethics Journal* 677, 678.

Aristogeitos (known as the Tyrannicides) from the Acropolis during the occupation of Athens. The two marble statues, depicting the men who assassinated the tyrant Hipparchus symbolized the birth of Athenian democracy.[87] They were later returned by Alexander the Great, who sought to appease Athenians for the wrongs of the Persian wars.[88]

In ancient Greece, plunder of religious sites, such as temples, was condemned on religious or moral grounds. The Greek historian Polybius (210–128 BC)[89] advocated 'magnanimity' and restraint in warfare. In 218 BC, Macedonian King Philip V and his troops destroyed religious property in Thermos, the religious and political centre of Aetolia, during the first Macedonian war. Polybius criticized the destruction of religious shrines by Philip as a violation of principles of just and reasonable conduct within ancient warfare in a famous passage of his work *The Histories*.[90] He argued that the unrestrained destruction of cultural objects taints the reputation of victorious powers and compromises prospects of peace.[91] He condemned Roman looting practices, such as the plunder of Greek sanctuaries on Sicily (211 BC),[92] arguing that it makes it harder to govern defeated populations since it causes feelings of loss and resentment[93]—an argument which returned later in the context of 'savage warfare'.[94]

Roman practices navigated between conflicting rationales: the desire to defeat and crush enemies, in particular barbarians, on the one hand, and incentives to show restraint in order mitigate the risks of revenge by the enemy, on the other. They illustrate a 'civilizational paradox'[95] which runs through the history of the

---

[87] Margaret M. Miles, 'War and Passion: Who Keeps the Art?' (2017) 49 *Case Western Reserve Journal of International Law* 5–21, 8.

[88] Jennifer Finn, Alexander's Return of the Tyrannicide Statues to Athens (2014) 63 *Historia: Zeitschrift für Alte Geschichte* 385–403.

[89] Polybius often viewed as an early defender of the protection of art and cultural property in warfare. See John Thornton, 'Polybius in Context: The Political Dimension of the Histories' in Bruce Gibson and Thomas Harrison (eds.), *Polybius and His World: Essays in Memory of F. W. Walbank* (Oxford: Oxford University Press, 2013) 213–230; Miles, 'War and Passion', 10. For a critique, see Jonathan Williams, 'From Polybius to the Parthenon: Religion, Art, and Plunder' in Christopher Smith and Liv Mariah Yarrow (eds.), *Imperialism, Cultural Politics, and Polybius* (Oxford: Oxford University Press, 2012) 278–297, 283, arguing that Polybius took a pragmatic stance.

[90] See generally Adriaan Lanni, 'The Laws of War in Ancient Greece' (2008) 26 *Law and History Review* 469–489.

[91] He stated: 'To do wanton damage to temples, statues and all such works with absolutely no prospect of any advantage in the war to our own cause or detriment to that of the enemy must be characterized as the work of a frenzied mind at the height of its fury. For good men should not make war on wrong-doers with the object of destroying and exterminating them, but with that of correcting and reforming their errors, nor should they involve the guiltless in the fate of the guilty, but rather extend to those whom they think guilty the mercy and deliverance they offer to the innocent'. See Polybius, *The Histories of Polybius*, Book 5 (W. R. Paton tr, G. P. Putnam's Sons, Loeb Classical Library, 1922) 31 http://penelope.uchicago.edu/Thayer/E/Roman/Texts/Polybius/5*.html. Emma Nicholson, 'Polybios, the Laws of War, and Philip V of Macedon' (2018) 67 *Historia: Zeitschrift für Alte Geschichte* 434–453, 435.

[92] See Polybius, *Histories*, 9.10 (Spoils of Syracuse).

[93] Ibid.

[94] See Chapter 6.

[95] Daniel R. Brunstetter, 'A Tale of Two Cities: The Just War Tradition and Cultural Heritage in Times of War' (2018) 4 *Global Intellectual History* 1–20, 6.

seizure of objects from antiquity to the twentieth century: Objects of civilized enemies, such as equals to Rome, benefited from rudimentary protection, through
civic attitudes or limits to retribution and to punishment, based on principles of
magnanimity, humility, or honour. Non-civilized entities, i.e. 'savage' and 'barbarian' enemies, were not seen worthy of protection and subject to plunder or
spoliation.[96]

The idea to protect cultural property is reflected in Cicero's famous Verrine
Orations.[97] Cicero (106–43 BC) built on Polybius' critiques in order to condemn
the appropriation of sacred images or objects in peacetime, including objects
which depict gods or belong to a sanctuary, temple, or shrine. He stressed that
Verres unduly turned public and religious artefacts into private property through
their forced removal, contrary to Roman customs and social conventions. He accused Verres of 'un-Roman' behaviour, including acquisition of objects at derisory
purchase prizes, equating his conduct to illegitimate private theft.[98] His orations
served as an important precedent for the protection of antiquities and material
heritage. They allowed to differentiate the legitimacy of looting based on a set of
different criteria, including the sacred or secular context of objects, their taking in
times of war or peace and their removal for private or public purposes.[99] Cicero's
ideas were later taken up by scholars, such as Hugo Grotius (1583–1645), Emer de
Vattel, or Quatremère de Quincy, but not applied consistently.

Roman imperial expansion was marked by a 'dichotomy between civilization
and barbarism'.[100] Romans distinguished the 'civilized "us"—the populus' from
the 'barbarian "Other"—the gentes'.[101] Cultural heritage of 'barbarians', who wor-
shiped other gods or were deemed to be cruel and unpredictable, enjoyed lesser
protection than civilized nation or city states.[102] This distinction facilitated the
forced acculturation of culturally diverse populations into the Roman empire.
Surrender to Rome meant surrendering 'people, the city, fields, water, boundaries,
shrines, utensils, all things divine and human into the dominion of ... the Roman
people'.[103] Romans relied on the concept of the law of prize and booty (*jus praedae*)

---

[96] On perceptions of 'civilization and community in the ancient mind', see David J. Bederman,
International Law in Antiquity (Cambridge: Cambridge University Press, 2009) 267–280.

[97] They concerned the prosecution of Gaius Verres, the Roman governor of Sicily, in 70 BCE.
Margaret M. Miles, 'Cicero's Prosecution of Gaius Verres: A Roman View of the Ethics of Acquisition of
Art' (2002) 11 *International Journal of Cultural Property* 28–49.

[98] Thomas D. Frazel, '"Furtum" and the Description of Stolen Objects in Cicero "In Verrem" 2.4'
(2005) 26 *The American Journal of Philology* 363–376, 367.

[99] Gerstenblith, 'Protecting Cultural Heritage in Armed Conflict', 679.

[100] It may be traced back to Greek thinking. See W. R. Jones, 'The Image of the Barbarian in Medieval
Europe' (1971) 13 *Comparative Studies in Society and History* 376–407, 379–380

[101] Michel Bouchard and Gheorghe Bogdan, 'From Barbarian Other to Chosen People: The
Etymology, Ideology and Evolution of "Nation" at the Shifting Edge of Medieval Western Christendom'
(2015) 17 *National Identities* 1–23, 7.

[102] See with respect to the Carthage, Brunstetter, 'A Tale of Two Cities', 6.

[103] Alexander Gillespie, *A History of the Laws of War: The Customs and the Laws of War with Regards
to Civilians in Times of Conflict*, Vol. 2 (Oxford: Hart Publishing, 2011) 220.

to justify takings. Over time, Rome became 'a museum of pillaged masterpieces from Greece, Egypt, and Asia Minor'.[104]

2.2 Reincarnations in just war doctrine and scholastic scholarship

These distinctions re-emerged in different form in just war doctrine, where ideas of civilization were closely connected with Christianity. For instance, the Crusades were partly justified to defend and recuperate Christian property. Medieval just war doctrine allowed Christians to protect or reclaim their own cultural heritage from unjust occupiers.[105] During the sack of Constantinople, the capital of the Byzantine Empire, in 1203, crusader armies looted many ancient and medieval cultural treasures from palaces, churches, monasteries, and libraries—including the famous bronze horses of St. Mark.

In the sixteenth century, Spanish scholastic scholars advocated limits to conquest and destruction of cultural property. They criticized unrestrained looting, pillage, or exploitation in the new territories discovered by Spain and argued that all humans, including 'barbarians' are protected by certain secular natural law principles. In his famous lecture 'On the Indians', Francisco de Vitoria (1486–1546) recognized that non-Christian populations in the New World enjoy property protection, irrespective of their faith: 'Unbelief does not destroy either natural law or human law; but ownership and dominion are based either on natural law or human law; therefore they are not destroyed by want of faith.'[106]

However, the 'civilizational paradox' persisted despite the recognition of the equality of humans under natural law. Vitoria defended the view that natives are 'unfit to found or administer a lawful State up to the standard required by human and civil claims'.[107] This finding foreshadows the 'standard of civilization' promoted in colonial expansion.[108] In *De Indis*, Vitoria specified several 'just titles by which the barbarians of the New World passed under the rule of the Spaniards', including the freedom to spread 'the Christian religion' (Second just title) and the authority to use of force and coercion 'in defence of the innocent against tyranny' (Fifth just title). He argued that the refusal of the natives to allow the new rulers to 'preach and announce the Gospel' constitutes 'a wrong committed by the barbarians against the

---

[104] See Bruce Montgomery, 'Reconciling the Inalienability Doctrine with the Conventions of War' (2015) 78 *The American Archivist* 288–316, 294.

[105] Brunstetter, 'A Tale of Two Cities', 8–9.

[106] See Francisco de Vitoria, *De Indis et de Ivre Belli Relectiones* (ed. Ernest Nys, trans. John Pawley Bate, Washington, DC: Carnegie Institution of Washington, 1917) 123.

[107] ibid 160–161.

[108] Brett Bowden, 'In the Name of Progress and Peace: The "Standard of Civilization" and the Universalizing Project' (2004) 29 *Alternatives: Global, Local, Political* 43–68; Gerrit W. Gong, *The Standard of Civilization in International Society* (Oxford: Clarendon Press, 1984).

Spaniards', which enables the latter to take control, and 'if necessary take up arms and declare war on them'.[109] He also acknowledged that 'the Spaniards may prohibit the barbarians from practising any nefarious custom or rite', such as human sacrifice or cannibalism, and overthrow them in order to 'defend' natives from 'tyranny and oppression'. He wrote:

> [The Spaniards] may also force the barbarians to give up such rites altogether. If they refuse to do so, war may be declared upon them, and the laws of war enforced upon them; and if there is no other means of putting an end to these sacrilegious rites, their masters may be changed and new princes set up.[110]

This argument gave Spanish conquerors leeway to impose colonial authority if native populations failed to allow the expansion of Christian faith or to adjust their own customs to the new standards of civilization.[111] This logic was applied inter alia by Spanish Conquistador Hernán Cortés (1485–1547) in order to justify the conquest of the Aztec Empire and the destruction of the temples of Tenochtitlan, including the Great Temple (Temple Mayor) in 1521.[112] The protection of cultural property remained thus unequal.[113]

2.3 Renaissance and Enlightenment

The Renaissance period in the fifteenth and sixteenth centuries sparked a renewed interest in appreciation of cultural objects across Europe, including a rediscovery of Roman and Greek culture. Art was regarded as an universal expression of beauty. The interest in art and antiquities triggered an urge for both collection and preservation. In elite circles, plunder was perceived as a barbaric act, which manifested a lack of culture. In practice, however, it remained a part of warfare. It endured throughout the seventeenth century, and was common during the Thirty Years'

---

[109] Vitoria, *De Indis*, Second possible title, for the spreading of the Christian religion, para. 12.

[110] Vitoria, *De Indis*, Fifth just title, in defence of the innocent against tyranny, para. 15.

[111] Gillespie, *A History of the Laws of War*, 237.

[112] Cortés explained his rationale in his Third Letter to Emperor Charles V: 'Seeing that they were so rebellious and showed such determination to defend themselves to the death, I inferred two things: first that we should recover little or none of the treasures they had taken from us, and the other, that they gave occasion and forced us to totally destroy them. This last reason caused me the greater grief, for it weighed on my soul and made me reflect on what means I might employ to frighten them, so that they should realise their error and the injury they would sustain from us; and I kept on burning and destroying the towers of their idols and their houses.' Letters of Cortes to Emperor Charles V, Vol 2, (Francis Augustus MacNutt, 1908) Third letter (15 May 1522) 81 https://en.wikisource.org/wiki/Letters_of_Cortes_to_Emperor_Charles_V_-_Vol_2/Third_letter,_May_15,_1522.

[113] Scholastic doctrine left leeway to destroy sacred places, such as Aztec temples of Tenochtitlan, and replace them by novel monuments, if they hindered the spread of Christian civilization. See Brunstetter, 'A Tale of Two Cities', 11.

War (1618–1648) and in civil war.[114] These experiences led to calls for restraints on looting and plunder, based on considerations of humanity and community. For instance, Hugo Grotius argued in his Laws of War and Peace (1625) that looting of sacred objects may contravene natural law ideas of a humane society. He recalled Polybius' plea for moderation in relation to the plunder of cultural ornaments and stated the destruction of religious objects for reasons other than military necessity shows total disregard of the 'laws and ties of our common humanity'.[115] This argument grounded protection of cultural property in universal ideas. Plundering religious or cultural artefacts conflicted with an emerging cosmopolitan identity. A number of seventeenth-century treaties, such as the Dutch-Spanish Treaty of Münster (1648) included provisions on the restitution of cultural property[116] and reaffirmed the protection of private property from seizure in warfare.[117] They provided a legal framework for voluntary return of displaced cultural property to the estates of the Holy Roman Empire, in the absence of a customary rule in relation to restitution of cultural objects.[118]

In the era of the Enlightenment, new rationalist conceptions of warfare strengthened calls for the protection of cultural property. Seventeenth and eighteenth-century doctrine differentiated no longer formally between Christian and non-Christian enemies, but rather between cultural taking in just and unjust war. In his Social Contract (1762), Jean-Jacques Rousseau (1712–1778) famously compared war to a duel between governments, directed against sovereigns and their armies, rather than civilians or subjects.[119] The laws of war increasingly distinguished between combatants and civilians. In the eighteenth century, 'works of art and the contents of collections were spared, as royal places were spared, on the ground of the personal courtesy supposed to be due from one prince to another'.[120] The legitimacy of plunder of cultural objects was more openly constrained by rationales

---

[114] For instance, during the sack of Heidelberg during the Thirty Years' War, manuscripts of the famous Palatine Library were looted by Maximilian, Duke of Bavaria, and offered to Pope Gregory XV. See Tullio Scovazzi, 'The "First Time Instance" as Regards Restitution of Removed Cultural Properties' (2012) 19 Agenda Internacional 9–19.

[115] Hugo Grotius made this point in Chapter 12 of Book III of Laws and War of Peace in which argued that objects containing artistic or historic value ought to be spared by virtue of the principle of moderation. See Ch. 12, Sections V–VII, in particular VII. See Hugo Grotius, Rights of War and Peace (A. Campbell tr, New York & London: Walter Dunne, 1901) 367.

[116] Article 24 required restitution of all goods that had been seized or confiscated because of the war, and also applied to plunder and loot.

[117] On the seventeenth century, see Hugh Trevor-Roper, The Plunder of the Arts in the Seventeenth Century (London: Thames & Hudson, 1970).

[118] Montgomery, 'Reconciling the Inalienability Doctrine', 295.

[119] Rousseau stated: 'War then is a relation, not between man and man, but between State and State, and individuals are enemies only accidentally, not as men, nor even as citizens, but as soldiers; not as members of their country, but as its defenders. Finally, each State can have for enemies only other States, and not men.' See Jean Jacques Rousseau, The Social Contract (1762) Book 1, 7–8 (G. D. H. Cole tr) https://socialpolicy.ucc.ie/Rousseau_contrat-social.pdf.

[120] See William Edward Hall, A Treatise on International Law (A. Pearce Higgins (ed.), 8th edn, Oxford: Clarendon Press, 1924) 505.

of military necessity. For example, in the mid-eighteenth century, Emer de Vattel (1714–1767) developed Grotius' ideas in his *The Law of Nations or the Principles of Natural Law* (1758). He argued that warfare should focus on the destruction of the armed forces of the enemy and promoted the protection of sanctuaries, tombs, and other buildings of cultural significance in warfare. He stated:

> For whatever cause a country is ravaged, we ought to spare those edifices which do honour to human society, and do not contribute to increase the enemy's strength—such as temples, tombs, public buildings, and all works of remarkable beauty. It is declaring one's self an enemy to mankind, thus wantonly to deprive them of these monuments of art.[121]

Cultural property was thus protected by proportionality considerations, which postulated moderation in the treatment of adversaries. These protections coincided with a recognition of the transgenerational value of cultural objects, and their quality as property of humanity. Art itself became a form of 'secularized religion' in the Europe, with museums turning into modern equivalent of former temples.[122] Vattel's brief reference to the aesthetics of objects ('works of remarkable beauty') has been celebrated as the 'earliest expression of true cultural property internationalism',[123] although it was heavily qualified by military necessity.[124]

The emerging restraints regarding the appropriation of cultural property in the eighteenth century were challenged by the Napoleonic Wars. The late eighteenth and the turn of nineteenth centuries saw a rise in cultural nationalism, i.e. importance of cultural property to national history and identity. Factors such as the rise of democracy, the undermining of hereditary sovereigns, and the space role of 'people in wars and national politics' prompted both a rediscovery of the importance of national cultural property[125] and cynic uses of rationales of 'civilization' in order to justify the appropriation and removal cultural objects. The French Revolution and the Napoleonic period spurred a sentiment that only enlightened and civilized nations could appreciate the full value of cultural objects.[126] A nostalgic, and

---

[121] Emmerich De Vattel, *The Law of Nations*, Book III, § 168.

[122] Bénédicte Savoy, '"You Were Sending Out, This Way and That, Paintings" Restitutions and Emotions: A Few Reflections for a Long-Term Approach' *Arts & Sociétés* https://www.sciencespo.fr/art setsocietes/en/archives/1214.

[123] See John Henry Merryman, 'Cultural Property Internationalism' (2005) 12 *International Journal of Cultural Property* 11–39, 14.

[124] Vattel added: 'Nevertheless, if we find it necessary to destroy edifices of that nature in order to carry on the operations of war, or to advance the works in a siege, we have an undoubted right to take such a step.' See Vattel, *The Law of Nations*, Book III, § 168.

[125] See Elazar Barkan, 'Amending Historical Injustices: The Restitution of Cultural Property: An Overview' in Ealazar Barkan and Ronald Bush, *Claiming the Stones/Naming the Bones: Cultural Property and the Negotiation of National and Ethnic Identity* (Los Angeles: Getty Research Institute, Getty Publications, 2002) 16, 18.

[126] See Dorothy Mackay Quynn, 'The Art Confiscations of the Napoleonic Wars' (1945) 50 *American History Review* 437–460.

deeply nationalist and patriarchal reading of liberalism was used as justification to 'repatriate objects' and build new collections. Post-revolutionary France regarded itself as the centre of the free and enlightened world. Cultural objects became an important symbol of political power and triggered rivalry among Western powers:

> Because it was universally accepted that the cultural lineage of Europe flowed from Egypt to Greece to Rome, whatever nation was in possession of the major antiquities of these ancient civilizations became symbolically the torch-bearer of Western culture.[127]

Napoleon sought to recreate Paris as a 'new Rome' and instructed his armies not only to conquer land in Europe and Egypt, but to collect art and cultural artefacts.[128] He charged scientists and artists with a mandate to retrieve, choose and relocate objects from Belgium or Italy to the Louvre.

France considered itself as the natural home for cultural treasures of conquered states. Nationalist discourse at the time relied not only on the doctrine of the spoils of war, but rather on idea of 'liberating' cultural artefacts.[129] For instance, a famous petition supported by French artists stated:

> The Romans once an uncultivated people, became civilized by transplanting to Rome the works of conquered Greece. Thus ... the French people . . naturally endowed with exquisite sensitivity, will ... by seeing the models from antiquity, train its feeling and its critical sense ... The French Republic, by its strength and superiority of its enlightenment and its artists, is the only country in the world which can give a safe home to these masterpieces. All other Nations must come to borrow from our art, as they once imitated our frivolity.[130]

The displacement of cultural objects was justified by multiple rationales: the claim that objects were under threat of destruction in host countries (Italy), that French museums were the safest place for conservation, that 'repatriation' to France was necessary to protect civilization or restore it (Egypt), or that seizure was a legitimate trophy of war (e.g. Brandenburg gate Quadriga).[131] Napoleon used a legal loophole to justify transfer of works of art. Many removals from churches, galleries, or public art collections were legitimized through treaties or peace settlements, in

---

[127] Patricia Mainardi, 'Assuring the Empire of the Future: The 1798 Fete de la Liberte' (1989) 48 *Art Journal* 155–163, 160.

[128] Montgomery, 'Reconciling the Inalienability Doctrine', 297.

[129] See John Alan Cohan, 'An Examination of Archaeological Ethics and the Repatriation Movement Respecting Cultural Property (Part Two)' (2004) 28 *Environs: Environmental Law and Policy Journal* 4–115, 17.

[130] Quynn, 'The Art Confiscations of the Napoleonic Wars', 438–439.

[131] David Gilks, 'Attitudes to the Displacement of Cultural Property in the Wars of the French Revolution and Napoleon (2013) 56 *The Historical Journal* 113–143, 119–131.

which defeated powers were forced to give up objects. Formally, the looting was thus justified as a consensual acquisition, rather than as a booty of war.[132] Consent was used as a disguise to justify the legality of confiscation. For instance, many objects seized by Napoleon in Italy at the end of the eighteenth century were justified as compensation payments or transferred through peace agreements, including the famous of horses of St Mark, which were removed from Venice to the Louvre on the basis of the treaties of Milan and Campo Formio.[133] The works to be seized and removed were specified in treaty instruments or identified by a specialized Commission, set up by France.

This rise of cultural nationalism, under the guise of 'civilization' conflicted with cosmopolitan views of cultural property, developed by certain intellectuals in the latter half of the eighteenth century. For instance, French archaeologist Antoine Chrysotome Quatremère de Quincy (1755–1849) had claimed in his Letters to Miranda on the plan to abduct the monuments of Italy (1796) that the seizure and displacement of cultural objects conflicts with the integrity of objects and their value to humanity.[134] He argued that objects ought to be protected against removal, since they form part of a common European cultural heritage.[135] He understood himself as member of a 'universal republic of arts and sciences', which serves the 'improvement of the human race' and 'belongs to all peoples'[136], and argued that 'stripping the galleries of Rome and Italy is not spreading, but dispersing the Enlightenment'.[137]

His critique of the removal of art was shared by some members of the National Institute of Arts and Sciences.[138] Napoleon's strategies, and his justification of cultural nationalism in the name of 'civilization', stood in direct contradiction with this universalist vision of cultural objects, defended by some thinkers at the end of the eighteenth century.[139]

---

[132] See Stephan Wilske, 'International Law and the Spolis of War: To the Victor the Right of Spoils?' (1998) 3 UCLA Journal of International Law & Foreign Affairs 223–282, 245.

[133] The Treaty of Peace and Friendship between France and Venice, signed at Milan on 16 May 1797, and the Treaty of Campo Formio of 17 October 1797 between the French Republic and the Austrian Empire were used to justify the removal of cultural objects by Napoleon.

[134] Antoine Chrysotome Quatremère de Quincy, 'Letters on the plan to abduct the monuments of Italy' in Antoine Chrysotome Quatremère de Quincy, Letters to Miranda and Canava on the Abduction of Antiquities from Rome and Athens (Chris Miller and David Gilks trs, Los Angeles: Getty Research Institute, 2012) 9.

[135] He stated: 'The arts and sciences have long formed in Europe a republic whose members, bound together by the love of and the search for beauty and truth, which from their social contract are much less likely to isolate themselves in their respective countries than to bring the interests of these countries into closer relation, from the cherished point of view of universal fraternity'. Antoine Chrysotome Quatremère de Quincy, 'Extracts from Letters to General Miranda 1796' in Lyndel V. Prott (ed.), A Compendium of Documents and Writings on the Return of Cultural Objects (Paris: UNESCO, 2009) 19, 23.

[136] Ibid, 20.

[137] Ibid, 25.

[138] Mainardi, 'Assuring the Empire of the Future', 156.

[139] See also Merryman, 'Cultural Property Internationalism', 16.

Following the defeat of Napoleon, European Allies took active steps to reverse the excesses of the Napoleonic wars and 'repatriate' cultural property. France sought to retain cultural property acquired during the wars and to negotiate a corresponding clause in the peace settlements at the Congress of Vienna.[140] But the Allies insisted that cultural objects taken by force or acquired by treaty should be returned to the country of origin. Lord Viscount Castlereagh, the English plenipotentiary, played a leading role in the negotiation of the post-war settlements. He pleaded in favour of return, based on the inseparability of cultural objects from the country to which they belonged, i.e. the link between cultural objects, people, and land. He claimed in a note to the ministers of the other Allied Powers was that Napoleon's spoils were 'contrary to every principle of justice and the usages of modern warfare'[141] and refused to accept armistice agreements or treaty provisions as a valid title to acquisition of ownership. He argued that 'spoliations, under cover of treaties ... were more flagrant, if possible', than overt acts of pillage[142] and insisted that Allied powers had the 'duty' to 'facilitate' the 'return these objects to the places from whence they were torn'.[143]

European powers followed this argument and negotiated returns, based on Castlereagh's reasoning and the presumed protection of cultural property under eighteenth century principles. The Congress of Vienna settlements marked an important shift in the justification of return of cultural property. As Charles De Visscher has noted:

[t]he restitution ordered by the Allied Powers was based on the very general principle of the integrity of the artistic heritage of conquered nations; once recognized, this principle tends to condemn as having an unlawful purpose, any cession, even conventional, of an art object, which is imposed under moral duress.[144]

This practice openly refuted Napoleon's postulate that France's alleged role as representative of civilization or heir to Western culture legitimizes cultural acquisition by force or through treaty settlements or reparation claims procured through duress. About half the cultural property seized by Napoleon since 1793 was returned to the countries of origin.

The settlements were far less determinate in relation to return of objects taken from non-European contexts.[145] Many of the arguments that Napoleon used to

---

[140] Louis XVIII argued in 1814 that 'the masterpieces of the arts belong to us forevermore, by rights more stable and sacred than those of conquest'. Mainardi, 'Assuring the Empire of the Future', 156.

[141] Note Delivered by Viscount Castlereagh to the Allied Ministers, and Placed upon their Protocol, Respecting the Restitution of the Works of Art, Paris (11 September 1815), in 'Parliamentary Debates from the Year 1803 to the Present Time' (1816) 32 *Hansard* 297, 298.

[142] Note Viscount Castlereagh, 301. See also Charles de Visscher, *International Protection of Works of Art and Historic Monuments* (Washington, D.C.: U.S. Department of State, 1948) 823, 826.

[143] Note Viscount Castlereagh, 299.

[144] De Visscher, *International Protection of Works of Art and Historic Monuments*, 826.

[145] See Barkan, 'Amending Historical Injustices', 19.

legitimize the taking of objects, such as paternalistic accounts of civilization, the victory of liberty and science over tyranny,[146] or reliance on the inability of local societies to 'rescue' their cultural treasures, share striking parallels with justifications for the removal of objects from colonies and protectorates. The principles of inseparability and protection of cultural objects, which were forcefully advocated by powers (e.g. Great Britain, Belgium, Netherlands, Prussia, Spain, Italy) at the Congress of Vienna in inter-European relations, were not equally applied to non-European entities, such as Egypt. None of the objects taken from non-Europeans were returned. In 1816, only one year after the Congress of Vienna, the same Great Britain, which relied so vigorously on ideas of cultural integrity and national identity to seek the return of Napoleon's plundered art, validated the purchase of the famous marbles, removed from the Greek Parthenon in 1800 by Lord Elgin, and thereby legitimized his questionable acquisition.[147] Even progressive voices, such as Quatremère de Quincy, shared a narrow Eurocentric understanding of the protection of cultural heritage and defended Elgin's removal of the marbles from the 'oriental' Ottoman Empire by a 'seemingly contradictory argument', namely the value of display in the British museum.[148] Legal writers remained divided whether the arrangements at the Congress of Vienna 'had violated international rules or established new ones'.[149] The Western-centric understanding of arts and sciences in the Enlightenment left glaring gaps in relation to colonial takings. It marginalized other civilizations and ways of engaging with the world.

2.4   Conflicting tensions in the nineteenth century

The nineteenth century was marked by the rise of the modern nation-state, the building of national identity through culture, and a changing world order. The idea of a nation's right to cultural heritage gained broader acceptance among European states. Material culture, monuments and museums were important means to demonstrate political power, build the identity of nation states or preserve and develop the cultural identity of communities. This transformation strengthened the move for the preservation and protection of cultural property. In a famous ruling concerning the seizure of art from a US vessel (*The Marquis de Someruelos*) in the War of 1812 between the United States and England of 1812, the British Court of Vice-Admiralty in Halifax, had found that:

---

[146] Quynn, 'The Art Confiscations of the Napoleonic Wars', 439.
[147] John H. Merryman, 'Thinking about the Elgin Marbles' (1985) 83 *Michigan Law Review* 1880–1923, 1881.
[148] Debbie Challis, 'The Letters of A. De Quincy' (2013) 63 *Classical Review* 599–601, 600.
[149] Wayne Sandholtz, 'Plunder, Restitution, and International Law' (2010) 17 *International Journal of Cultural Property* 147–176, 153.

[t]he arts and sciences are admitted amongst all civilized nations, as forming an exception to the severe rights of warfare, and as entitled to favour and protection. They are considered not as the peculium of this or that nation, but as the property of mankind at large, and as belonging to the common interests of the whole species.[150]

The aftermath of the post-1815 restitutions, converging interests in the protection of cultural objects and identity, emerging ideas on the universal nature of cultural objects, and experiences in nineteenth century warfare prompted a transnational network of scholars, diplomats, and professionals to push for the 'civilization' of the laws of war. For instance, in 1836, UK international lawyer Henry Wheaton recognized in his influential treatise on international law that cultural property is protected by customary international law. He argued that:

By the ancient law of nations, even what were called *res sacrae* were not exempt from capture and confiscation ... But by the modern usage of nations which has now acquired the force of law, temples of religion, public edifices devoted to civil purposes only, monuments of art, and repositories of science, are exempted from the general operations of war ... This extension extends even to the case of an absolute and unqualified conquest of the enemy's country.[151]

As of the mid-nineteenth century, the protection of cultural and artistic property found its way into the codifications of the laws of war. The Lieber Code (1863), which was commissioned by US President Abraham Lincoln during the Civil War and inspired subsequent codifications, expressly required parties to a conflict to protect 'classical works of art, libraries, scientific collections or precious instruments' from damage and destruction[152] and penalized 'all destruction of property not commanded by the authorized officer', as well as 'all pillage or sacking, even after taking a place by main force'.[153] The Code allowed parties to a conflict to remove 'works of art, libraries, collections, or instruments belonging to a hostile nation or government' for 'the benefit of the said nation' but specified that 'ultimate ownership' was to 'be settled by the ensuing treaty of peace'.[154]

Cultural property protection was addressed in all major subsequent codifications in the nineteenth and early twentieth centuries, including the 1874 Project

---

[150] Court of Vice-Admiralty at Halifax, 'The Marquis de Someruelos' (21 April 1813) in James Stewart, *Reports of Cases, Argued and Determined in the Court of Vice-Admiralty at Halifax in Nova-Scotia* (London: Butterworth and Son, 1814) 482–486, 483.

[151] Henry Wheaton, *Elements of International Law with Sketch of the History of Science, Vol. 2* (Philadelphia: Carey, Lea and Blanchard, 1836) 252, para. 5.

[152] Instructions for the Government of Armies of the United States in the Field (Lieber Code) (24 April 1863) Art. 35.

[153] Lieber Code, Art. 44.

[154] Ibid, Art. 36.

of an International Declaration Concerning the Laws and Customs of War,[155] the 1880 Oxford Manual on the Laws of Land Warfare, drafted by the Institute of International Law,[156] and the 1899 and 1907 Hague Conventions on Laws and Customs of War on Land.[157] However, despite some opposition,[158] the justifications for protection of cultural property, and in particular claims for protection grounded in the link between people and objects, remained inherently linked to the identity of Western nation-states. The 'civilizatory paradox' that has governed cultural property protection since antiquity, never went fully away.

Enlightenment principles, such as reason, progress, or humanism, were treated as the predominant domain of white Europeans. Codifications relating to the laws of war and corresponding protections in the nineteenth century were focused on the ideal of regulating constraints on warfare between 'civilized nations'. The concept of civilization, which was originally related to Christianity,[159] became more strongly associated with theories of evolution, racial science and categories or classes of civilization.[160] It was determined based on alignment of others with European social and cultural practices, systems of political organization or government.[161] The 'governed and enlightened nations of "civilized" Europe' formed 'the norm to which the "barbarous" might aspire'.[162]

---

[155] Project of an International Declaration Concerning the Laws and Customs of War, Brussels, 27 August 1874 (Brussels Declaration) Art. 8.

[156] International Law Institute, Manual, *The Laws of War on Land,* 9 September 1880, Art. 34.

[157] Hague Convention (II) with Certain Powers, with Respect to the Laws and Customs of War on Land, 29 July 1899; Hague Convention (IV) with Other Powers Respecting the Laws and Customs of War on Land (18 October 1907).

[158] Swiss international lawyer Johann Caspar Bluntschli argued in his manual on the modern international law of civilized nations (1878) that the looting of cultural monuments and treasures, which used to be common in the revolutionary wars at beginning of the century, now ran counter to public conscience and legal norms, since such objects have no direct connection with the State or the war, but serve the peaceful culture of the nation. Johann Caspar Bluntschli, *Das moderne Völkerrecht der civilisierten Staaten als Rechtsbuch dargestellt* (Nördlingen: C. H. Beck, 1878) 41–42. He qualified the intentional destruction of cultural monuments and works of art by occupying powers as an act of barbarism which cannot be justified by military necessity. Ibid, 363.

[159] Henry Wheaton still wrote in 1864 that 'public [international] law, with slight exceptions, has always been, and still is, limited to the civilized and Christian people of Europe or to those of European origin', excluding 'barbarians of Africa' or the 'savage tribes of North America. Henry Wheaton, *Elements of International Law* (3rd edn, London: Sampson Low, Son and Company, 1863) 16–17.

[160] Brett Bowden, 'The Ideal of Civilisation: Its Origins and Socio-Political Character' (2007) 7 *Critical Review of International Social and Political Philosophy* 25–50.

[161] Authors such as James Lorimer drew on Montesquieu to distinguish civilized, barbarous, and savage societies, which are incapable of 'municipal organization'. James Lorimer, *The Institutes of the Law of Nations* (Edinburgh and London: William Blackwood & Sons, 1883) Vol. I, 101, Vol. II, 191. The question of whether an entity was deemed to be civilized depended inter alia on the form of political organization, 'whether its government was sufficiently stable to undertake binding commitments under international law', and to what extent it 'was able and willing to protect adequately the life, liberty and property of foreigners'. Georg Schwarzenberger, 'The Standard of Civilisation in International Law' in George W. Keeton and Georg Schwarzenberger (eds.), *Current Legal Problems* (London: Stevens & Sons Ltd., 1955), 212–234, 220.

[162] Brett Bowden, 'The Colonial Origins of International Law: European Expansion and the Classical Standard of Civilization' (2005) 7 *Journal of the History of International Law* 1–24, 15; Edward Keene, 'The Standard of 'Civilisation', the Expansion Thesis and the 19th-century International Social Space' (2014) 42 *Millennium Journal of International Studies* 651–673.

Nineteenth-century international law distinguished wars fought in Europe from colonial warfare. Instruments, such as the Lieber Code, were replete with civilization narratives and distinctions between 'civilized' and 'barbarous armies'.[163] Protection of cultural property was governed by double standards.[164] The universalist arguments that Quatremère de Quincy or the *Marquis de Someruelos* case invoked in relation to cultural objects were not transposed to other cultures. The interests of humanity that were advocated came in variations and gradations: civilized humanity continued to be differentiated from the humanity of barbarians or savages.[165] Hierarchies of race coincided with hierarchies of culture. While artefacts from Persia, China or Japan were recognized as art, objects from Africa, Oceania or Native Americans continued to be treated as fetishes or curiosities.

At the end of the nineteenth century, some authors relied on utilitarian considerations, and arguments of cultural internationalism in order in order to defend the taking of cultural property in warfare. For instance, James Lorimer questioned in 1884 whether 'the careful removal and appropriation' of 'works of art', such as Napoleon's removal of Italian or Spanish works to the Louvre, conflicts with the 'interests of humanity or of civilisation', if they are 'retained uninjured, and made equally accessible for learned and artistic purposes, and for general culture and enjoyment'.[166] Henry Maine adopted a similar reasoning. He recognized the broad accessibility of objects as an important criterion to assess the legality of capture. He relied on an assessment of progress in infrastructure and technological advancement in order to determine the most appropriate place of retention.[167] Arguments like these validated the forcible removal of cultural objects from their place of origin, based on technological progress.

Such narratives captured the schizophrenic justification of cultural takings in the colonial period. European powers claimed that they had a 'civilising responsibility', namely a 'responsibility to promote civilization and institute good government in the countries under their imperial authority'.[168] They used this argument to legitimize the taking and removal of objects, which led to cultural dispossession or destruction in societies of origin.[169]

---

[163] Lieber Code, Art. 24.

[164] In the negotiation of the Hague Conventions of 1899 and 1907, it was heavily debated to what extent the laws of war should apply in relation to non-civilized entities. See Chapter 6. See also Spitra, 'Civilisation, Protection, Restitution', 332–338.

[165] James Lorimer, *The Institutes of the Law of Nations. A Treatise of the Jural Relations of Separate Political Communities*, Vol. 1 (Edinburgh and London: Blackwood and Sons, 1883) 101.

[166] Ibid, Vol. 2 (Edinburgh/London: William Blackwood & Sons, 1884) 78.

[167] Maine invoked this argument in relation to the return of sculptures and paintings to the Italian cities after the Congress of Vienna. He wrote: 'As I say, the one tenable argument against their restoration was the greater convenience to the civilised world of their being left in Paris; but in an age of railways their distance in Italy is no appreciable inconvenience.' See Henry S. Maine, *International Law* (London: John Murray, 1890) 198.

[168] Edward Keene, *Beyond the Anarchical Society: Grotius, Colonialism and Order in World Politics* (Cambridge: Cambridge University Press, 2002) 78.

[169] On this central contradiction, see also Ana Vrdoljak, 'International Law, Museums and the Return of Cultural Objects' in Lyndel V. Prott, *Witnesses to History* (Paris: UNESCO, 2009) 193, 194.

3 Current manifestations

In our contemporary age, many of these contradictions have continuing relevance. As scholars, such as Edward Said have shown, traces of imperialism and coloniality, i.e. the ideas underpinning the rationalization of colonial world views, remain ever-present in the representation of cultural objects, control over discourses, or processes of cultural reproduction.[170] Civilizatory divides, double standards, or risks of cultural appropriation have persisted or re-emerged in novel forms.

The colonial period has been marked by a 'massive unidirectional flow' of cultural and historical objects and human remains from Asia, the Americas, the Pacific region or Africa to Europe'.[171] Most of the objects taken were placed in Western museums or collections, sometimes with limited knowledge of their origins.[172] Many objects were collected from a position of superiority.[173] They were acquired in contexts of structural injustice (e.g. settler colonialism, extractive colonialism), taken in the name of science or religious conversion, used to showcase difference, study 'primitive' cultures, or save 'declining civilizations' or validate the colonial project. As both Aimé Césaire and Albert Memmi[174] have argued, such practices 'decivilized' not only the colonized, but also the colonizer.

The physical removal of cultural objects causes enduring harm and alienation. It involved not only economic or cultural loss, but identity-taking and disempowerment.[175] It commodified objects, transformed epistemologies, or destroyed systems of knowing in societies of origin.[176] As Achilles Mbembe has shown in his *Critique of Black Reason*, these forms of cultural 'expropriation' have created sentiments of inferiority and 'humiliation' in formerly colonized societies.[177]

---

[170] Said, *Culture and Imperialism*. On museums and colonial collecting, see Sally Price, *Primitive Art in Civilized Places* (Chicago: University of Chicago Press, 1989); Tim Barringer and Tom Flynn, *Colonialism and the Object: Empire, Material Culture and the Museum* (London: Routledge, 1997); Tony Bennett, *Pasts Beyond Memory: Evolution, Museums, Colonialism* (London: Routledge, 2004); Sarah Longair and John Macleer (eds.), *Curating Empire: Museums and the British Imperial Experience* (Manchester: Manchester University Press, 2012); John Mackenzie, *Museums and Empire: Natural History, Human Cultures and Colonial Identities* (Manchester: Manchester University Press, 2009).

[171] Jos van Beurden, 'Decolonisation and Colonial Collections: An Unresolved Conflict' (2018) 133 *BMGN: Low-Countries Historical Review* 66–78, 73. See also Folarin Shyllon, 'Unravelling History: Return of African Cultural Objects Repatriated and Looted in Colonial Times' in James Nafziger and Ann Nicgorski (eds.), *Cultural Heritage Issues: The Legacy of Conquest, Colonization and Commerce* (Leiden: Brill Publishers & Martinus Nijhoff, 2010) 159–168.

[172] Sarr and Savoy Report, 3.

[173] Said speaks of 'positional superiority'; see Edward Said, *Orientalism* (New York: Vintage Books, 1978) 7.

[174] Albert Memmi, *The Colonizer and the Colonized* (Boston: Beacon Press, 1965).

[175] Catherine Lu, 'Colonialism as Structural Injustice: Historical Responsibility and Contemporary Redress' (2011) 19 *Journal of Political Philosophy* 264; Catherine Lu, *Justice and Reconciliation in World Politics* (Cambridge: Cambridge University Press, 2017).

[176] Linda Tuhiwai Smith, *Decolonizing Methodologies. Research and Indigenous Peoples* (London and New York: Zed Books; Dunedin: University of Otago Press, 1999) 58–59.

[177] Achille Mbembe, *Critique of Black Reason* (Durham and London: Duke University Press, 2017).

Seretse Khama, former President of Botswana, has described the ongoing effects in striking terms:

> We should write our own history books to prove that we did have a past, and that it was a past that was just as worth writing and learning about as any other. We must do this for the simple reason that a nation without a past is a lost nation, and a people without a past are a people without a soul.[178]

The separation of objects from societies of origin, and their retention in museum spaces raises not only issues of justice or access to culture, but also questions relating to the ontology of objects. Objects were seen as cultural property, evidence of history, or cultural trends or through aesthetic lenses, rather than as living objects. Display practices focus on aesthetics, beauty, and preservation, rather than ritual or spiritual functions of objects. This transforms material culture.[179] As Ghanaian art historian and writer Oforiatta Ayim has noted, '[I]f you look at our knowledge systems and you look at how objects are seen and animated—they are not these graveyards of a mausoleum, there is a spirit and an aliveness to them.'[180] Although claims of protest or return have been filed throughout the colonial period,[181] these issues were marginalized in the decolonization process in the 1950s and 1960s. The Pan-African Cultural Manifesto, adopted by the Organization of African Unity on the occasion of the First Pan-African Cultural Festival held in Algiers from 21 July to 1 August 1969, made an important connection between colonial resistance and survival through culture. It stated:

> The preservation of our culture saved us from the attempts made to turn us into peoples with no soul nor history. Our culture protected us … [T]he colonized peoples have never given up their inner identity … African culture, impeded in its development, found a refuge in its language, in its customs, songs, dances, beliefs and so on … and in spite of its diminution, it proved to be an essential bulwark of resistance to colonial intrusion.[182]

---

[178] Seretse Khama, Speech of Chancellor at University of Botswana, Lesotho, and Swaziland graduation ceremony (15 May 1970) *Botswana Daily News* (19 May 1970) http://www.thuto.org/ubh/bw/skquote1.htm.

[179] Anthropologist George W. Stocking has vividly described this process of re-contextualization: '[O]bjects of "material culture"—which in traditional contexts often had spiritual value—are re-spiritualized (in Western terms) as aesthetic objects, at the same time that they are subjected to the processes of the world art market'. George W. Stocking (ed.), *Objects and Others: Essays on Museums and Material Culture* (Madison: University of Wisconsin Press, 1998) 6.

[180] Nosmot Gbadamosi, 'Stealing Africa: How Britain Looted the Continent's Art' *Aljazeera* (12 October 2021) https://www.aljazeera.com/features/2021/10/12/stealing-africa-how-britain-looted-the-continents-art.

[181] At the UN, official requests for return have been discussed since the 1970s.

[182] Organization of African Unity, Pan-African Cultural Manifesto, Algiers, July 1969 (1970) 17 *Africa Today* 25–28, 25–26. It added '[C]ulture has been and will remain a weapon. In all cases, armed struggle for liberation was and is a pre-eminently cultural act'. Ibid, 27.

Some states, like Zaire (now the Democratic Republic of the Congo) took a fierce stance against colonial cultural interference and called for return of cultural heritage removed during colonialism. President Mobuto Sese Seko (1930–1997), made this point expressly in the General Assembly in 1973:

> During the colonial period we suffered not only from colonialism, slavery, economic exploitation, but also and above all from the barbarous systematic pillaging of all our works of art. In this way the rich countries appropriated our best, our unique works of art, and we are therefore poor not only economically but also culturally.
>
> What I am telling you is fundamental, because every rich country, even if it does not possess all the masterpieces of its best artists, has at least the bulk of them. Thus, Italy has those of Michelangelo; France, Renoir ... That is why I would also ask this General Assembly to adopt a resolution requesting the rich Powers which possess works of art of the poor countries to restore some of them so that we can teach our children and our grandchildren the history of their countries.[183]

In 1978, former UNESCO Secretary General Amadou-Mahtar M'Bow issued a 'Plea for the Return of an Irreplaceable Cultural Heritage to those who Created It' in 1978. He called for the sharing or return of important cultural property with states of origin and recognized that the return cannot 'be solved simply by negotiated agreements and spontaneous acts'.[184] He stressed that return is about more than giving back physical objects. He justified this approach by the close interrelation between cultural objects, the histories, stories, and meanings surrounding them, and the relational aspects of returns:

> The return of a work of art or record to the country which created it enables a people to recover part of its memory and identity, and proves that the long dialogue between civilizations which shapes the history of the world is still continuing in an atmosphere of mutual respect between nations.[185]

However, these urgent call for actions fell largely on deaf ears. Cultural heritage instruments contain 'double standards' in relation to the protection of cultural colonial objects. While attacks on cultural heritage in times of armed conflict have increasingly been banned under international law,[186] the issue of the treatment

---

[183] UN Doc A/PV 2140 and Corr 1 (1973) 28 UN GAOR (2140th plen mtg) paras 176–178.
[184] Amadou-Mahtar M'Bow, 'A Plea for the Return of an Irreplaceable Cultural Heritage to those who Created It' (7 June 1978) http://www.unesco.org/culture/laws/pdf/PealforReturn_DG_1978.pdf.
[185] Ibid.
[186] See Convention for the Protection of Cultural Property in the Event of Armed Conflict with Regulations for the Execution of the Convention (14 May 1954) 249 UNTS 240, Art. 4. Article 8 of the Rome Statute of the International Criminal Court contains war crimes prohibitions relating cultural property in international and non-international armed conflict ('[i]ntentionally directing attacks against buildings dedicated to ... art [or] science ... [and] historic monuments ... provided they are

of colonial objects has received very limited attention.[187] Former colonial powers have largely succeeded to silence debates on restitution or return in legal instruments. Treaty instruments and cultural heritage law perpetuated the *status quo*. Specific language was introduced to distinguish colonial takings from contemporary forms of looting or illicit trafficking of cultural objects. Settler societies, like Canada, Australia, New Zealand, or the United States[188] have created legal frameworks for return claims of indigenous communities.[189] However, objects taken in extractive colonial contexts have mostly been returned as an act of comity, rather than out of a sense of legal obligation[190] in order not to set precedents and avoid the formation of a customary rule.[191] This practice wrongly implies that international law has nothing to say about the legality or conditions of takings in the colonial period or contemporary practices of return.

The status and treatment of objects continues to reflect 'civilizatory paradoxes' of the past. For instance, contemporary knowledge systems theorize objects through dichotomies, such as art versus anthropology, cultural versus natural objects, contemporary versus traditional art, etc. Such categorizations may introduce artificial hierarchies or suppress alternative frames of reference, such as understandings by indigenous communities.[192]

Government and public institutions have relied on the ambiguity of the law, the global significance of objects and the value of international guardianship, the need for provenance research, or the alleged risks of return to countries of origin in order to question or reject claims of return.[193] Concepts such as 'common heritage', which

---

not military objectives'). See generally Patrick O'Keefe, *The Protection of Cultural Property in Armed Conflict* (Cambridge: Cambridge University Press, 2006). On norm change, see Wayne Sandholtz, *Prohibiting Plunder: How Norms Change* (Oxford: Oxford University Press, 2007).

[187] The Hague Conventions of 1899 and 1907 on Laws and customs of War on Land increased protections for cultural objects, but did not create any express obligations of return in case of violation.

[188] The US Native American Graves Protection and Repatriation Act, 25 USC Ch 32 (16 November 1990) (NAGPRA) is an influential example of domestic legislation on indigenous rights that promoted successful returns and serves partially as an example for other colonial contexts as well. On NAGPRA, see Chapter 6. See also Sangita Chari and Jaime M. N. Lavallee (eds.), *Accomplishing NAGPRA. Perspectives on the Intent, Impact, and Future of the Native. American Graves Protection and Repatriation Act* (Corvallis: Oregon State University, 2013).

[189] See Elizabeth M. Koehler, 'Repatriation of Cultural Objects to Indigenous Peoples: A Comparative Analysis of U.S. and Canadian Law' (2007) 41 *The International Lawyer* 103–126; Marina Hadjioannou, 'The International Human Right to Culture: Reclamation of the Cultural Identities of Indigenous Peoples under International Law' (2005) 8 *Chapman Law Review* 193–221, 201.

[190] In the UNESCO Intergovernmental Committee for Promoting the Return of Cultural Property, return of colonial artefacts was approached on moral, rather than legal grounds. See also Campfens, 'The Bangwa Queen', 93.

[191] See Hui Zhong, *China, Cultural Heritage, and International Law* (New York: Routledge, 2018).

[192] Elizabeth Cook-Lynn, 'Who Stole Native American Studies?' (1997) 12 *Wicazo Sa Review* 9–28, 14.

[193] See James Cuno, 'Culture War: The Case against Repatriating Museum Artifacts' (2014) 93 *Foreign Affairs* 119–129. For example, Julien Volper, ethnographic curator at Royal Museum for Central Africa in Tervuren argued that returns would transform Western collections into 'a graveyard'. See Julien Volper, 'Défendons nos musées!' *Le Figaro* (14 September 2017). See also Merryman, 'Thinking About the Elgin Marbles', 1895 ('If the principle were established that works of foreign origin should

emphasize the 'universal' value of colonial cultural objects, have been used to justify the desirability of international custodianship or to encourage actors in the Global South to frame their own laws and practices after the social conventions of Western collections. Such a logic is reflected in the 2002 Declaration on the Importance and Value of Universal Museums, signed by eighteen prominent museums,[194] and has been defended by authors, such as Neil McGregor, the former director of the British Museum, James Cuno,[195] or Tiffany Jenkins, who has argued that universal museums situate objects in a 'wider, richer framework of relationships' where they 'provoke questions, illustrate relationships, and take on an elevated meaning'.[196]

Museum displays have continued to reproduce epistemic forms of violence. Objects have not only been dispossessed, but also been reappropriated through colonial collecting. Some museums have integrated indigenous curatorial models. However, in many cases, curatorial practices have centralized the history of object collectors, rather than their provenance, the histories of their creators or acts of resistance against takings. Digitization and novel means of reproduction have created new possibilities to share objects, but also opened new sites of struggle over ownership rights, access, or circulation. The return of digital surrogates, instead of original objects, provides a comfortable way to protect the integrity of Western collections, without critical inquiry into provenance or conditions of access in source communities.[197]

Recent decades have witnessed a turn towards more critical engagement with colonial legacies.[198] The image of the universal museum as public space has come under challenge.[199] The 1980s marked a turning point in relation to repatriation of

---

be returned to their sources, as Third World nations increasingly demand in UNESCO and other international fora, the holdings of the major Western museums would be drastically depleted'). For a discussion of cases, see Michael J. Reppas, 'Empty "International Museums" Trophy Cases of Their Looted Treasures and Return Stolen Property to the Countries of Origin and the Rightful Heirs of Those Wrongfully Dispossessed' (2007) 36 *Denver Journal of International Law and Policy* 93–123.

[194] See Declaration on the Importance and Value of Universal Museums (December 2002) https://www.hermitagemuseum.org/wps/portal/hermitage/news/news-item/news/1999_2013/hm11_1_93/?lng. For a discussion, see Neil G. W. Curtis, 'Universal Museums, Museum Objects and Repatriation: The Tangled Stories of Things' (2006) 21 *Museum Management and Curatorship* 117–127.

[195] James Cuno (ed.), *Who Owns Antiquity? Museums and the Battle over Our Ancient Heritage* (Princeton: Princeton University Press, 2008); James Cuno (ed.), *Whose Culture? The Promise of Museums and the Debate over Antiquities* (Princeton: Princeton University Press, 2009).

[196] Tiffany Jenkins, *Keeping Their Marbles. How the Treasures of the Past Ended up in Museums—And Why They Should Stay There* (Oxford: Oxford University Press, 2016) 123.

[197] It detracts from structural questions, such as reforms of inalienability laws in Western jurisdictions. For a critique, see Kimberly Christen, 'Opening Archives: Respectful Repatriation' (2011) 74 *The American Archivist* 185–210, 187.

[198] See Wolfgang Kaleck, 'On Double Standards and Emerging European Custom on Accountability for Colonial Crimes' in Morten Bergsmo, Wolfgang Kaleck, and Kyaw Yin Hlaing (eds.), *Colonial Wrongs and Access to International Law* (Brussels: Torkel Opsahl Academic EPublisher, 2020) 1–41.

[199] Museums are spaces with legal or moral decision-making power over provenance or restitution. Dan Hicks has qualified them as a 'weapon, a method and a device … to legitimize, extend and naturalize new extremes of violence within corporate colonialism'. See Hicks, *The Brutish Museums*, 15.

indigenous objects. Indigenous campaigns for the return of human remains and increased attention to the social conditions of indigenous groups and the destruction of indigenous heritage prompted legislative change and changes in cultural policy in settler contexts, such as Australia, New Zealand, or the US. They paved the way for increased transnational repatriations of human remains.[200] In recent years, several collections in Europe, North America, or the Asia-Pacific region have started to critically re-examine collecting histories and pay greater attention to the violent contexts in which objects have been acquired. In 2018, French President Emmanuel Macron commissioned a ground-breaking study, the Sarr and Savoy report, to investigate the modalities of return of objects from France, including potential changes of French law. The report advocated a radical rethinking of past acquisitions of colonial art and their treatment.[201] It stressed that 'destruction and collection are the two sides of the same coin' and encouraged a reconception of the role of museums.[202] It suggested a new relational ethics, arguing that the very objects, which have 'become diasporas', are 'the mediators of a relation that needs to be reinvented' through a process of return.[203]

New legal instruments and museums have been created to facilitate returns. For instance, the African Charter for Cultural Renaissance mandates African States to 'take steps to put an end to the pillage and illicit traffic of African cultural property and ensure that such cultural property is returned to their countries of origin'.[204] The African Union initiated steps for a new Model Law on the Protection of Cultural Property and a framework for negotiations on return.[205] The request for return of the Parthenon Marbles by Greece kept the issue alive in inter-European debates.

The return movement is at a tipping point.[206] Requests for return (e.g. Benin, Egypt, Nigeria), grass-root civil society initiatives, or protests have triggered greater reflexivity beyond classical settler colonial contexts. The display of human remains or the auctioning of objects are increasingly causing public outrage or indignation (*colère publique*),[207] signalling changes in morality and public consciousness.[208] Spectacular events, such as the Dahomey returns by France and the

---

[200] Timothy McKeown, 'Indigenous repatriation: The rise of the global legal movement' in Cressida Fforde, C. Timothy McKeown, and Honor Keeler (eds.), *The Routledge Companion to Indigenous Repatriation* (London: Routledge, 2020) 23–43.

[201] Sarr and Savoy Report, 19–20.

[202] Ibid, 15.

[203] Ibid, 39.

[204] Charter for African Cultural Renaissance, 6th Ordinary Session of the Assembly of the African Union in Khartoum, Sudan (24 January 2006) Art. 26.

[205] African Union, Draft Concept Note for the Continental Consultations on the Restitution of Cultural Property and Heritage (29 November 2021).

[206] Jean d'Aspremont and John Haskell, *Tipping Points in International Law* (Cambridge: Cambridge University Press, 2021).

[207] Emile Durkheim, *The Division of Labour in Society* (W. D. Halls tr, Basingstoke: Palgrave, 2013) 79.

[208] For instance, in 2022 the Vanderkindere auction house in Brussels was forced to cancel the sale of three skulls of Africans killed during the colonial period. See also Chapter 8.

increasing global commitment to the return of the Benin bronzes looted in the 1897 punitive expedition challenge the retention of objects taken by force.[209] Some cultural objects have been returned by private museums or universities. 'Specially affected' countries, such as the Netherlands,[210] Germany,[211] or Belgium,[212] the Arts Council in England[213] and particular museums (e.g. the Smithsonian institution[214]) have issued new ethical policies or guidelines to deal with colonial collections. They point towards a shift in ethics from retention towards targeted returns, a change in ethical approaches by 'specially affected' countries. In some cases, such as the return of the Ngonnso figure to Cameroon,[215] museums have committed themselves to return objects donated under unequal power relations.[216] Some countries—like Belgium—have adopted a new legislative framework to facilitate return of cultural colonial objects.[217] Following his apology to indigenous groups in Canada, Pope Francis expressed a commitment towards restitution of colonial objects, where possible, based on the seventh commandment ('You shall not steal'). However, there is still limited formal recognition of a legal obligation to return.

Legislative barriers to return continue to exist under domestic heritage legislation (e.g. UK, France).[218] Return openly challenges past stereotypes about 'Africa and the Orient' and causes fears regarding the admission of 'illegal possession'.[219] Certain guidelines, such as the 2022 Arts Council guidance, seek to change practices in a pragmatic way, by presenting return as a technical and neutral procedure. Such a framing carries the risk of replicating the silencing of structural injustices

[209] See Carsten Stahn, 'Beyond "To Return or Not to Return": The Benin Bronzes as a Game Changer?' (2022) 8 *Santander Art and Culture Law Review* 29–68.

[210] National Museum of World Cultures, 'Return of Cultural Objects: Principles and Process', 2019; Council for Culture, Report, Advisory Committee on the National Policy Framework for Colonial Collections, Guidance on the way forward for colonial collections (22 January 2021).

[211] German Museums Association, *Guidelines for German Museums: Care of Collections from Colonial Contexts* (3rd edn, Berlin: German Museums Association, 2021).

[212] Independent Group of Experts, 'Ethical Principles for the Management and Restitution of Colonial Collections in Belgium' (June 2021).

[213] Arts Council, 'Restitution and Repatriation: A Practical Guide for Museums in England' (Manchester: Arts Council England, 2022).

[214] Smithsonian Ethical Returns Working Group, 'Values and Principles Statement' (Washington: Smithsonian Institution, 2022).

[215] The figure symbolizes the foundation of the Nso dynasty. It was reclaimed by a civil society initiative 'BringBackNgonnso'.

[216] See Chapter 4. Hermann Parzinger, the President of the Prussian Cultural Heritage Foundation, argued in this context that the 'special—especially spiritual—significance of an object for the society of origin can also justify a return.

[217] On the Belgian framework law of 3 July 2022 on restitution and return, see Marie-Sophie de Clippele and Bert Demarsin, 'Pioneering Belgium: Parliamentary Legislation on the Restitution of Colonial Collections' (2022) 8 *Santander Art and Culture Law Review* 277–294. The law does not include human remains or archives.

[218] For instance, the British Museum Act of 1963 poses strict barriers for deaccessioning of objects held by the museum. See Chapter 9. On the divide between a case-by-case approach or a general framework for restitution in France, see Xavier Perrot, 'Colonial Booty and Its Restitution: Current Developments and New Perspectives for French Legislation in This Field'(2022) 8 *Santander Art and Culture Law Review* 295–310.

[219] Jonathan Harris, *The New Art History: A Critical Introduction* (London: Routledge, 2001) 275.

and epistemic violence, which have driven colonial takings. Meaningful engagement with the past requires a broader reckoning with ongoing heritage of empire, including acknowledgement of ethical and legal wrongdoing, fresh relational strategies to build a new future, and new thinking about the role of the museum.[220]

Overall, relatively few objects have been returned. There is a risk that the 'scramble for return' may remain confined to very specific object categories and continue to sideline acknowledgement of wrong or a structural commitment to repair. Actual returns may fuel cultural nationalist narratives in societies of origin or create divides between state authorities, local communities, or families.

4 New horizons

This book examines both the past histories and transformation of objects over time, and the prospects and critiques of the new age of engagement.

The opening part investigates the rationalization and modes of taking of cultural colonial objects between the sixteenth and the twentieth centuries. The first chapters (Chapters 2–5) identify recurring historical patterns in cultural takings. They distinguish roughly three periods: (i) early takings (c. sixteenth to eighteenth centuries); (ii) the systematization of collection between the eighteenth and the mid-nineteenth centuries, with the emergence of modern nation state, scientific organization of knowledge and the birth of modern museums;[221] and (iii) the scramble for cultural objects and human remains as of the mid/late nineteenth century. They show that cultural property played a central role in liberal theories of progress and civilization. Cultural exploitation was justified by some of the same rationales and rhetoric of civilization or protection as economic exploitation or territorial expansion. It was not only driven by curiosity, quest for knowledge, trade, or material profit, but by a means of enhancing national prestige or demonstrating power.[222] In the nineteenth century, many takings were inherently linked to racial science. They became a means to showcase cultural superiority or destroy local cultures, sometimes as a by-product of a collecting mania, through confiscation, removal, commodification, and 'othering'. With the increasing recognition of the artistic value of objects throughout the twentieth century, objects were used to

---

[220] See Dan Hicks, 'UK Welcomes Restitution, Just not Anti-Colonialism' *Hyperallergic* (26 August 2022).

[221] Janet Owen, 'Collecting Artefacts, Acquiring Empire: Exploring the Relationship between Enlightenment and Darwinist Collecting and Late Nineteenth-century British Imperialism' (2006) 18 *Journal of the History of Collections* 9–25.

[222] On the gradual transformation of colonialism from an externalized, and company-driven undertaking into a 'national project', see Gurminder K. Bhambra, 'Colonial Global Economy: Towards a Theoretical Reorientation of Political Economy' (2021) 28 *Review of International Political Economy* 307–322.

highlight the value of colonies to home audiences or competing colonial powers or to expand national collections.

The subsequent chapters (Chapters 6–9) analyse how the colonial condition and the commodification of objects shaped the framing and silences of legal frameworks in the twentieth century and contemporary approaches towards return. They show the dual face of law and legal practices in relation to takings and returns, namely their complicity in the creation and maintenance of colonial injustices, and their ability to serve as instrument of resistance, challenge historical conceptions, and open possibilities for transformation. The book develops a theory of legal entanglement, which takes into account the legal complexities of cultural takings in contexts of systemic injustice. It challenges the classical argument, repeated in discourse, that cultural colonial takings were in line with ideas of justice at the time, or the assumption that they can only be assessed merely from a moral perspective, in light of the Eurocentric nature of the international legal order. It makes a case that past takings need to be assessed by reference to plural legal orders and that contemporary legalities are shaped by a web of norms governing relations to objects, including human rights guarantees, such as dignity or access to culture.

Ultimately, the study argues in favour of a relational understanding of cultural heritage, which encourages greater transparency of colonial collections, novel forms of consent or ownership for objects taken in a context of structural inequality, broader structures of participation and representation in discourses over return, contextualization of provenance research, and more inclusive cultures of memory. It develops principles of relational cultural justice.

The work as a whole brings out certain macro points, which highlight the close interconnection between colonial violence, cultural takings, and civilizatory discourses, the historical and legal entanglements of objects, and fresh ways to engage with the heritage of empire.

4.1 Agents of resistance, agents of Empire

A first point is the close link between the extractive logic of colonialism and the removal or destruction of culture. The extractive nature of colonial relations applied not only to raw materials, natural resources, labour, or human capital, but also to cultural objects. It encompassed diverse types of objects: Royal regalia or sovereign objects, sacred and religious objects, historical/archaeological objects, as well as human remains and natural history specimen.

Certain regalia, sacred objects or body parts were taken since they were viewed as symbols of protest or resistance against colonial subjugation or Christianity. However, colonial conditions affected not forcible takings, such as trophy hunting, taking of war booty, or punitive raids, but also more 'innocent' forms of transactions by explorers or private individuals, such as commercial or scientific acquisitions. As the Belgian Ethical Principles for the Management and Restitution of Colonial Collections note, markets were 'formed not only by local need but also responded directly' to the demands created by the colonial condition.[223] Both capitalist market economy and the advancement of European 'science' provided an umbrella to extract cultural artefacts, human remains, fossils or natural objects, such as plants or animals. Scientists and travellers collected bio-cultural objects in foreign cultures, based on the alleged premise that they were under threat of extinction or extermination.[224] Even 'scientific' or 'linguistic' missions could take on violent and coercive features, due to their close entanglement with colonial power structures or networks. In many contexts, objects were not freely circulated or exchanged, but confiscated, appropriated, or acquired by traders, military officers, missionaries, or colonial authorities based on colonial power relations.

The violence went beyond physical removal. It involved identity loss, cultural appropriation, and different forms of exploitation.[225] Collectors used cultural heritage as war trophy, object of racial science, market commodity or symbol of prestige, sometimes based on their association with past cultures. In some cases, post-colonial governments later invoked object identities in order to seek and justify their retention as national patrimony, while sidelining the interests of affected communities. Archaeology was used to secure privileged access to antiquities, control over export regimes and support the prestige or power of Western elites.

Through their taking or commodification, many objects acquired partly new identities. Collectors, museums, collectors, art professionals and markets asserted ownership and property rights, ascribed new meanings to objects, without regard to their original meaning in societies of origin, or converted objects, by inventing new frames of reference ('curios', 'fetishes', ethnological objects, 'primitive art'). Objects gained market value, as artistic objects, were auctioned or stored in collections or became a source of attraction for visitors in colonial expeditions or museums, generating revenue or symbolic capital for the colonial project. Several objects, such as Nefertiti, the Pergamon Altar, or the Aksum obelisk became icons of fascist ideology. In many cases, the meaning of objects changed. Processes of archiving and classification neutralized the violence and cruelty.[226] They perpetuated 'extractivism' and 'control'.[227] Objects are thus not only symbols of past colonial violence, but carriers of its epistemologies and enduring effects. On some

---

[223] Independent Group of Experts, 'Ethical Principles for the Management and Restitution of Colonial Collections', 1.2.1.

[224] On the coloniality of natural history collecting, see Caroline Drieënhuizen and Marieke Borren, 'Editorial' (2023) *Locus-Tijdschrift voor Cultuurwetenschappen* https://locus.ou.nl/locus-dossier-doorwerkingen-van-natuurhistorische-kolonialiteit/redactioneel.

[225] Timothy Clack and Mark Dunkley (eds.), *Cultural Heritage in Modern Conflict: Past, Propaganda, Parade* (London: Routledge, 2022).

[226] Achille Mbembe, 'The Power of the Archive and Its Limits' in Carolyn Hamilton and others, *Refiguring the Archive* (Dordrecht: Kluwer, 2002) 19–26, 22.

[227] Anna Brus and Martin Zillinger, 'Introduction: Transforming the Post/Colonial Museum' in Anna Brus and others (eds.), The Post/Colonial Museum, *Zeitschrift für Kulturwissenschaften*, 11–29, 19.

occasions, their taking was a form of 'epistemicide'[228] which deprived colonial subjects of their knowledge systems, introduced new frames of classification and establishment new types of control over culture, knowledge, and history. Today, many objects carry counter-hegemonic features. They are both symbols of empire and of the role that colonial objects may take in producing a new modernity.

4.2   Perpetual reinvention of coloniality and racial capitalism

A second element is the link between object histories and the transformation of justificatory discourses for takings. Cultural takings drove the reinvention of justifications of colonialism, and different ways of engaging with objects. Takings were carried out by colonial networks. They were shaped by competition among colonial powers. Objects were removed for political, military, economic or religious reasons. However, they also carried agency. They influenced the colonial project. They challenged colonial stereotypes or forced colonial powers to constantly adapt or reinvent narratives of justifications in order to legitimize acquisition or destruction. In that sense, the engagement with material culture transformed the colonial encounter.

Early takings were not only justified by military defeat, triumph, or rationales of compensation, but also driven by curiosity, the quest for knowledge, and an urge to collect unknown or spectacular objects. The emergence of the encyclopedic museum at the end of the eighteenth century[229] had an impact on takings and removals. It stimulated traders, explorers, or colonial officials to collect objects. They were not only taken because of their material value, but also due to the prestige associated with their acquisition or their association with past glory (e.g. ancient civilizations).

Cultural takings were influenced by theories of racial difference and ideas of racial hierarchy 'with the European at the top, followed by Asians, Africans and aboriginals'.[230] They influenced the conquest of Americas and were used to rationalize colonial relations between Europeans and non-Europeans. With the birth of social Darwinism in the nineteenth century, scientific motives gained broader importance. Objects were collected to classify people and races, study colonial subjects, or 'preserve' dying cultures. At the peak of colonial era, pseudo-scientific narratives were actively used to conceal the brutality of takings. Racial science

---

[228] Fazil Moradi, 'Catastrophic Art' (2022) 34 *Public Culture* 243–264.

[229] James Cuno, *Museums Matter: In Praise of the Encyclopedic Museum* (Chicago: University of Chicago Press, 2011); Donatien Grau (ed.), *Under Discussion: The Encyclopedic Museum* (Los Angeles: Getty Research Institute 2021).

[230] Tayyab Mahmud, 'Colonialism and Modern Constructions of Race: A Preliminary Inquiry' (1999) 53 *University of Miami Law Review* 1219–1246, 1223; Subhadra Das and Miranda Lowe, 'Nature Read in Black and White: Decolonial Approaches to Interpreting Natural History Collections' (2018) 6 *Journal of Natural Science Collections* 4–14.

made violence more acceptable and less visible, according to the conditions of the time. It gave collectors and colonial agents a rational and utilitarian pretext for the removal of cultural objects or human remains. Explorers, soldiers, or museum officials relied on the 'scientific' importance of objects in order to justify transgressions of traditional moral or professional codes. Collecting itself was infused by colonial ideology, othering, and 'white projection', i.e. stereotypes and imaginations about foreign cultures.[231]

This is reflected in object biographies. Several collectors mistakenly associated objects from Africa with different civilizations, based on the misguided belief that they were too sophisticated to originate from the continent. For instance, Cecil Rhodes shared great admiration for the famous Zimbabwe birds (now a national symbol), taken from the Great Zimbabwe. Excavators believed that were made by Phoenicians or Arabs.[232] A similar misconception arose in the context of the taking of the Benin bronzes. They were initially perceived as artefacts of 'savages'.[233] Experts questioned whether they originated from the Edo culture. When Commissioner and Consul-General of the Niger Coast protectorate, Ralph Moor (1860–1909) described some of the items collected, he characterized them as 'hideously-constructed brass heads'.[234] German archaeologist Leo Frobenius was persuaded that they were 'of Greek origin'.[235] When it became clear that they were indeed from Africa, and not from any other culture, they reinvigorated the intense promotion of colonial collecting. It was thus the discovery of the value of the objects which drove its renewed scramble, and made it necessary to revisit justifications for takings. The discoveries challenged the idea of cultural superiority. Takings were justified by additional considerations, such as the need to gain knowledge and better understanding about administered populations for purposes of colonial governance, the idea demonstrating the value of colonies to home audiences, or the building of museum collections.

Human rights discourse had imperial features. As Mahmood Mamdani has argued, for centuries of colonial history 'major interventions' have been justified as 'humanitarian' under the umbrella of the 'civilising mission'.[236] For example, France invoked ideals drawn from the French Revolution, namely the republican virtues of liberty, equality, and fraternity, to justify the 'liberation' of populations in Asia and Africa from their 'despotic' rulers.[237] Britain actively used oriental tropes,

---

[231] Hicks, *The Brutish Museums*, 37 ff.

[232] See Chapter 4.

[233] Elazar Barkan, 'Aesthetics and Evolution: Benin Art in Europe' (1997) 30 *African Arts* 36–41.

[234] Despatch from Consul-General Moor to the Marquess of Salisbury, Benin City (24 February 1897).

[235] Leo Frobenius, *Voice of Africa* (London: Hutchinson & Co., 1913) 98.

[236] Mahmood Mamdani, *When Victims Become Killers: Colonialism, Nativism, and the Genocide in Rwanda* (Princeton, NJ: Princeton University Press, 2001) 78.

[237] Alice L. Conklin, 'Colonialism and Human Rights: A Contradiction in Terms? The Case of France and West Africa, 1895–1914' (1998) 103 *The American Historical Review* 419–442. The operations were sometimes expressly qualified as 'humanitarian interventions'. See Antoine Rougier, *La Théorie de L'Intervention D'Humanité* (Paris: Pedone, 1910) 43.

such as the idea of the native 'pirate' or the 'piratical headhunter', to justify forcible expansion in Asia.[238] It relied on causes, such as the suppression of slavery or human sacrifice, to justify colonial subjugation in West Africa.[239] This argument conflated patterns of victimization. As Samson Ukpabi has noted, claiming 'that all the expeditions were undertaken purely from the humanitarian point of view' is 'to beg the issue':

> In all the wars, there were both major and contributory causes, and the [colonial] governors ... often tended to give undue emphasis to points that only deserved passing remarks ... [S]ince most of the evidence comes from the despatches of these same governors, and little from the other side, the difficulties placed in the path of an historian who wishes to get at the roots of the matter are enormous.[240]

The most prominent justification for taking of cultural objects is the 'salvage' and 'rescue' narrative. It has roots in cultural anthropology, extends to natural history collection '(salvage ecology')[241] and runs like a consistent pattern through collecting history, ranging from the taking of Parthenon marbles by Lord Elgin[242] or the removal of the Pergamon Altar by Carl Humann[243] to the collection of ethnological or spiritual objects from populations which were deemed to face extinction, such as the famous Luf boat, removed by the German merchant company Hernsheim & Co. from Papua New Guinea.[244] This narrative is grounded in an ambivalent mixture of alleged heroism and nostalgia. It sought to legitimize cultural takings as an altruistic or benevolent act, while ignoring that the removal itself contributed to the demise of the culture, which was deemed to be 'rescued'. It paved the way for some of the contradictory protectionist practices of museums, which invoked cultural internationalist narratives in order to avoid or delay return of objects or to justify retention of objects, based on better conditions of preservation or broader access.[245] This practice shifted justifications from ideas of cultural superiority to discourses of technological advancement.

Cynically, some of the same narratives served as a basis for the commodification and marketing of objects on the art market. Many of the objects taken were not meant to be marketed and commodified, but gained monetary value through their

---

[238] Farish A. Noor and Peter Carey (eds.), *Racial Difference and the Colonial Wars of 19th Century Southeast Asia* (Amsterdam: Amsterdam University Press, 2021) 73–150.

[239] Inge Van Hulle, *Britain and International Law in West Africa: The Practice of Empire* (Oxford: Oxford University Press, 2020).

[240] Samson C. Ukpabi, 'British colonial wars in West Africa: Image and reality' (1970) 20 *Civilisations* 379–404, 388.

[241] Danielle L. Gilbert, 'Possessing Natural Worlds: Life and Death in Biocultural Collections' (2022) 25 *Locus: Tijdschrift- voor Cultuurwetenschappen* https://edu.nl/d476x.

[242] See Chapter 2.

[243] See Chapter 6.

[244] See Chapter 4.

[245] See Chapter 8.

removal and the dynamics of the art market. As Donna Yates has shown, auction houses and dealers have replicated popular stereotypes and colonial images, such as native savagery (head-hunting, cannibalism), sexism, exotic and romanticized depictions of travels and methods collection, and tales of white saviour in order the emphasize the rare, exotic, or authentic nature of objects.[246] Some of the same violence that was used to justify takings became thus a means to increase the value of objects on the newly emerging markets. Categories, such as 'native' or 'primitive' were both mechanisms of control and domination, and an expression of the 'discontent of the civilized with civilization', i.e. the longing or imagination of the virtues of a simpler life in Western minds.[247]

These practices show that cultural extraction and appropriation was closely associated with a logic of 'racial capitalism'[248] which permeated colonialism, namely the exploitation of the social and economic value of the art and culture of marginalized people. As Anna Arabindan-Kesson has shown in relation to textiles, this method forms part of the 'aesthetic, institutional, and material pasts of art history itself'.[249] At the peak of colonialism, the removal of cultural objects or human remains occurred in the context of a 'system of racialized extraction' which operated through 'capitalist processes of profit-making and race-making'.[250] The taking of objects contributed to racial stratification,[251] by dividing humanity into a hierarchy of 'races', and was used for processes of profit-making to increase the wealth and power of collectors, auction houses, museums, or colonial collections. It contributes to ongoing colonialities in the treatment of objects.

4.3 Complicity of collectors, museums, and racial science

The complicity of collectors, museums, and racial science was an essential factor in the massive removal of objects and human remains as of the late nineteenth century. The General Act of the Berlin Conference gave the green light for a scramble for objects. It awarded special protection to 'Christian missionaries, scientists and explorers, with their followers, property and collections'.[252] Collecting became a

---

[246] Donna Yates, 'Violence as a Value Enhancer in the Art Market' *Items* (1 March 2022).

[247] Arthur Lovejoy and George Boas, *Primitivism and Related Ideas in Antiquity* (Baltimore: Johns Hopkins Press, 1997 [1935]) 7.

[248] Cedric Robinson, *Black Marxism: The Making of the Black Radical Tradition* (Chapel Hill & London: University of North Carolina Press, 1983); Nancy Leong, 'Racial Capitalism' (2013) 126 *Harvard Law Review* 2151–2226.

[249] Anna Arabindan-Kesson, *Black Bodies, White Gold: Art, Cotton, and Commerce in the Atlantic World* (Durham, NC and London: Duke University Press, 2021) 114.

[250] Carmen G. Gonzalez and Athena D. Mutua, 'Mapping Racial Capitalism: Implications for Law' (2022) 2 *Journal of Law and Political Economy* 127–201, 174.

[251] William Edward Burghardt Du Bois, *Black Reconstruction in America, 1860-1880* (New York: Harcourt Brace & Company, 1935).

[252] General Act of the Berlin Conference on West Africa (26 February 1885) Art. 6(2).

national enterprise. Emerging ethnological museums started to issue guidelines and instructions for takings. They were eager to obtain authentic objects from previously unexplored communities or exotic objects which 'deviated from the Western aesthetic canon'. They prepared wish lists of objects. Experts joined colonial missions to facilitate acquisition and/or document provenance. In prominent military campaigns, such as the Maqdala or Benin 'expeditions', the taking of cultural objects was premeditated and supported by non-military personnel.[253] Both cultural objects and human remains became highly sought after commodities on the emerging markets.[254] Not only did they contribute to the scientific prestige of collections; they were also used to market the colonial project and study colonial subjects.

The veil of objectivity associated with 'science' overshadowed ethical or moral constraints. Individual explorers or collectors did not necessarily support colonial expansion and exploitation, but became part of 'collecting' networks and profited from the underlying structures. For instance, ethnologists such Felix von Luschan (1854–1924) questioned theories of biological racial difference[255] and openly challenged the stereotype that African societies lacked civilization or artistry, but contributed to their cultural exploitation. Some collectors were aware of the contradictions and injustices of takings, or realized them in hindsight (e.g. Michel Leiris), but rationalized them through their alleged benefit for 'science' and knowledge of colonized people.

The bio-politics of colonialism became visible. Human body parts were more openly treated as commodities or trade items.[256] Human skulls marked the 'holy grail' of evolutionary science in nineteenth century 'race theory'. Skull-digging became a recurrent phenomenon in colonial contexts. Skulls were taken as war trophies, extracted from graves, or collected from detention sites and shipped to the metropolis for skull measuring and racial science.[257]

Evolutionary theory and racial distinctions shaped not only the collection of human remains, but also the search for human origins and specimen. Human fossils were treated as 'natural history objects'. They were collected to rationalize theories of human difference. They were of equal or sometimes even greater importance to nations and communities than cultural objects.[258] Museum display

---

[253] See Chapter 3 and Lucia Patrizio Gunning and Debbie Challis, 'Planned Plunder, the British Museum, and the 1868 Maqdala Expedition' (2023) 66 *The Historical Journal* 1–23.

[254] Independent Group of Experts, 'Ethical Principles for the Management and Restitution of Colonial Collections', 1.2.1.

[255] John David Smith, 'W.E.B. Du Bois, Felix von Luschan, and Racial Reform at the Fin de Siècle' (2002) 47 *American Studies* 23–38, 36.

[256] See Chapter 5.

[257] For instance in East Timor, Portuguese officials and collectors profited from indigenous trophy-taking in order to acquire skulls and human remains for 'scientific' purposes. See Chapter 4.

[258] Some fossils may qualify as cultural objects and might thus be 'covered by the right of access to culture'. See Stewens, Raja, and Dunne, 'The Return of Fossils Removed under Colonial Rule', 79.

did not only give prominence to objects, but also alienated societies of origin from their material culture.

4.4 A cycle of distancing, discursive silencing, and erasure

Distancing, discursive silencing and erasure are common features in both the histories of takings and approaches towards restitution and return. They have actively contributed to colonial amnesia in institutional and legal practices. As anthropologist and historian Michel-Rolph Trouillot (1949–2012) has shown in relation to the Haitian Revolution, silences are not just part of 'any historical narrative',[259] but are inherently connected to power, inter alia produced in the tracing of facts and events, the creation of historical sources, the production of archives, or the development of historical narratives.[260] The histories of cultural colonial objects illustrate this close interconnection. Many of the individual object stories show how deeply discourses on 'punitive expeditions' or other takings have been affected by colonial ideology, othering, narratives of cultural superiority, or pseudo-scientific pretexts. These factors have contributed to dis-narration of facts, e.g. selective and positional story-telling, disregard of alternative accounts, or erasure of counterfactuals. Only a few collectors, such as professional collectors, certain missionaries, or experts[261] made systematic efforts to explore and document object meanings. This has resulted in knowledge gaps or silences. They are reproduced in archives, provenance research, or display practices. They dehistoricize or depersonalize object stories and have facilitated processes of object conversion, which gradually erase the past. This culture of silencing or disremembering is part of the process of appropriation itself.

This pattern is replicated in legal and institutional practices regarding restitution and return. In major international legal frameworks until the 1990s, states used discursive silencing or created temporal and spatial distances to takings in order to frame discourse in moral, rather than in legal terms, maintain power relations, and facilitate market dynamics.[262] As Bénédicte Savoy has shown, national actors, such as governments or public institutions in European circles, often failed to build critical memory, made limited efforts to engage with object histories proactively, or even concealed uncomfortable truths. For instance, in Germany, the issue was approached from scratch, again, since the 1970s, and treated as if nothing had happened, each time it came back to the surface.[263] Alternative strategies, such

---

[259] Michel-Rolph Trouillot, *Silencing the Past: Power and the Production of History* (Boston: Beacon Press, 1995) 27.

[260] Ibid, 26.

[261] See Chapter 4.

[262] See Chapter 7.

[263] See Savoy, *Africa's Struggle for Its Art*.

as loans, joint exhibitions, or voluntary returns were used as means to evade the debate on restitution. In contemporary discussions, these dilemmas come back in different forms in the drafting of guidelines or policies, namely through implicit reproduction of colonial knowledge structures, distracted accounts of past and contemporary legal responsibilities, the framing of return as a national issue, or the failure to confront past biases and take responsibility.[264]

4.5   Entangled objects

A recurring contradiction is the complex entanglement of cultural colonial objects. The conditions of taking are difficult to qualify in hindsight. Some objects were expressly produced on local markets to respond to the growing demand for 'authentic' objects. However, it is misleading to assume that colonial acquisitions were lawful simply because they involved some type of consent, exchange, or compensation, or to claim that they were accepted in the past but are considered unethical today.

Australian anthropologist Nicholas Thomas has drawn attention to the 'conflicted transcultural history of colonialism'.[265] He has qualified material artefacts as 'entangled objects', in order to express the complex entanglement of material culture in colonial encounters and challenges to classical conceptions of reciprocity in commerce and transactions.[266] The concept of entanglement is also useful to understand the legal conditions of acquisitions. Cultural colonial objects have a hybrid nature with different shades of legality, ranging from takings under force[267] or without consent to 'objects whose acquisition was in breach of the colonial legal concepts and morality of the period'.[268]

The idea of 'legal entanglement' provides a new way to accommodate existing problems, by setting legalities into context. It challenges the premise that 'there are no rules under international law which prohibited the acquisition of cultural goods during colonial rule'.[269] It encourages a multi-normative perspective on takings.[270] It suggests that conditions of taking cannot be evaluated only based on codified rules

---

[264] See Chapter 8. Hicks criticizes the 2022 Art Council guidance for 'active erasure' of the 'guiding principles, rationale, and ethos of what cultural restitution has become in the 2020s'. See Hicks, 'UK Welcomes Restitution, Just not Anti-Colonialism'.

[265] Nicholas Thomas, *Entangled Objects: Exchange, Material Culture, and Colonialism in the Pacific* (Cambridge: Harvard University Press, 1991) 26.

[266] Ibid.

[267] Jos van Beurden notes that in 1900 'almost 40 percent' of the objects contained in the Tervuren Museum in Belgium were 'war-related'. See Van Beurden, 19, 71.

[268] German Museums Association, *Care of Collections from Colonial Contexts*, 2021, 58.

[269] See Carola Thielecke and Michael Geißdorf, 'Collections from Colonial Contexts: Legal Aspects' in German Museums Association, *Care of Collections from Colonial Contexts*, 153–164, 160.

[270] See Carsten Stahn, 'Confronting Colonial Amnesia: Towards New Relational Engagement with Colonial Injustice and Cultural Colonial Objects' (2020) 18 *JICJ* 793–824.

and principles of international law,[271] but must take into more fluid principles and the legal order of colonized entities.[272] This approach flows from a contrapuntal reading of the law. It is based on the premise that the international legal order was more pluralist than portrayed in normative codifications or colonial practices.[273] It encompassed both legal norms and more fluid 'principles of humanity' and 'dictates of public conscience', grounded in natural law. This was inter alia recognized in treaty practices with First Nations (e.g. the US, New Zealand), jurisprudence in settler colonial contexts or imperial courts,[274] which recognized that colonized entities were not lawless spaces. They often had their own unwritten laws or customs, protecting treatment, access, and custody of sacred, ceremonial, or communal objects or human remains. For instance, the idea of inalienable cultural property, and its intergenerational character, which has been invoked as a bar to takings in Western contexts, also applies in other societies. It calls into question the taking of objects, which are 'not subject to individual ownership by anyone', and 'cannot justly be transferred by any individual', including persons who belong 'to the relevant culture'.[275]

Cultural takings did not occur in a legal void, but involved legal wrongdoing or 'unconscionable takings', conflicting with 'principles of equity'.[276] They conflicted with expected standards of behaviour under minimum principles of humanity or dignity,[277] principles of cultural protection and integrity asserted among 'civilized' nations, professional codes, or domestic customs and practices. There are at least three common forms of 'entanglement', which have affected takings: coercion, entangled consent, and entangled authority, i.e. lack of authority to alienate objects (e.g. sacred, spiritual, or communal objects). They continue to produce effects in the present. Certain objects have been taken in legal grey zones or under uncertain conditions, but carry cultural importance for societies of origin in the present as symbols of colonization or resistance thereto (e.g. the Gweagal shield).[278]

---

[271] International law itself is understood in a broad and relational sense, namely as set of practices, discourses and interpretations which shape social interaction, and are simultaneously shaped by them. See Gidon A. G. Gottlieb, 'Relationism: Legal Theory for a Relational Society' (1983) 50 *University of Chicago Law Review* 567, 569.

[272] On local customary law in nineteenth century Benin, see Oluwatoyin Sogbesan and Tokie Laotan-Brown, 'Reflections on the Customary Laws of Benin Kingdom and Its Living Cultural Objects in the Discourse of Ownership and Restitution' (2022) 8 *Santander Art and Culture Law Review* 9–28.

[273] See Chapter 6. Lauren Benton has used the notion of 'interpolity law' to characterize the normative pluralism.

[274] See Chapter 6.

[275] Erich Hatala Matthes, 'Repatriation and the Radical Redistribution of Art' (2017) 32 *Ergo* 931–953, 936.

[276] Geoffrey Robertson, *Who Owns history?* (London: Biteback, 2019) 170.

[277] Bernadette Atuahene has argued that property dispossessions qualify as 'dignity takings' in cases where 'the state takes property from a class of people that it considers sub persons'. See Bernadette Atuahene, 'Takings as a Sociological Concept: An Interdisciplinary Examination of Involuntary Property Loss' (2016) 12 *Annual Review of Law and Social Science* 171–197, 178. See Chapter 7.

[278] See Agnieszka Plata, 'The Aboriginal Shield from the Collection of the British Museum: A Case Study from the Perspective of Recent Developments' (2022) 8 *Santander Art and Culture Law Review* 139–160.

4.6 Dual role of law

This discussion is interrelated with a broader inquiry into the role of law in colonial contexts. As other studies have shown[279], law has a complex relationship with colonial power. It had a dual face. It served as handmaiden to the colonial enterprise or constituted the colonial condition, but also stimulated resistance or transformation.[280] This is also reflected in relation to cultural takings and restitution or return of objects.

International law had an ambivalent role. It simultaneously tolerated cultural takings (e.g. through legal grey zones) and imposed constraints on the conduct of colonial powers or provided space for contestation or resistance. The 1899 and 1907 Hague Conventions distinguished colonial expansion from situations of occupation and left grey zones in relation to colonial warfare. Colonial powers did not necessarily deny the applicability of the laws of war in colonial contexts, but claimed greater flexibility and discretion in their application. Catherine Elkins has referred to a 'legalized lawlessness'.[281] The rule of 'colonial difference' served to adjust the degree of permissible violence to the methods and degree of 'civilization' of the enemy.[282]

Later, cultural heritage instruments upheld double standards through distancing and silencing. International treaty instruments, such as the 1954 Hague Convention, the 1970 UNESCO Convention, or the UNIDROIT Convention were limited in their temporal scope of application or contained colonial clauses, which left the application to dependent territories within the discretion of former colonial powers.[283] The legal regime was geared at contemporary forms of looting or illicit trafficking of cultural objects, rather than historical colonial takings. Based on this logic, colonial provenance almost became an reassurance for purchasers on global markets.

However, there is also a less discouraging side to the story. Law was not monolithic.[284] It was also used to challenge or transform colonial rule.[285] Colonial subjects filed petitions and challenged property takings in order to protect their

---

[279] Sally Engle Merry, 'Law and Colonialism' (1991) 25 *Law & Society Review* 889–922; Jonathan Saha, 'A Mockery of Justice? Colonial Law, the Everyday State and Village Politics on the Burma Delta, c.1890—1910' (2012) 217 *Past & Present* 187–212; Martti Koskenniemi, 'Colonial Laws: Sources, Strategies and Lessons' (2016) 18 *Journal of the history of International Law* 248–277.

[280] See also Carsten Stahn, 'Reckoning with Colonial Injustice: International Law as Culprit and as Remedy? (2020) 33 *LJIL* 823–835.

[281] Caroline Elkins, 'The "Moral Effect" of Legalized Lawlessness' (2018) 44 *Historical Reflections* 78–90, 84.

[282] Colonel C. E. Callwell, *Small Wars: Their Principles and Practices* (Lincoln: University of Nebraska Press, 1996).

[283] See Chapter 7.

[284] John L. Comaroff, 'Colonialism, Culture, and the Law: A Foreword' (2001) 26 *Law & Social Inquiry* 305–314.

[285] Laura Benton, 'Evil Empires? The Long Shadow of British Colonialism' *Foreign Affairs* (July/August 2022)

rights through legal procedures. Some scholars, leaders or courts contested colonial justifications or struggled to reconcile imperial violence with their conceptions of law or liberal government. For instance, Bartolomé de las Casas (1484–1566) defended a right of natives to resist conquest and tyranny by the conquistadors, and argued that the Spanish Crown should restore Inca sovereignty and return treasures back to natives, since Peru had not consented to conquest.[286] Edmund Burke justified a right of resistance against abuse by East India Company in the Impeachment Trial of Warren Hastings.[287] Domestic courts recognized constraints emanating from respect of non-Western forms of sovereignty ('native sovereignty') in the nineteenth century.[288] Contemporary human rights and cultural heritage instruments have challenged state-centred and protectionist vision of cultural colonial objects, and the assimilation of indigenous peoples and their culture into settler societies.[289]

The treatment of restitution and return is marked by a similar duality. Law has been used to both support and constrain the case for return of colonial objects. This dichotomy is reflected in international treaty and institutional practice. States have tended to shy away from recognizing formal legal responsibility for historical takings. They have preferred to frame returns as moral acts or voluntary commitments, undertaken on a case-by-case basis in the context of international cooperation and development assistance. The interests of colonized entities were sidelined.[290] Return became thus a matter of inter-colonial relations.[291]

In the context of UNESCO, states distinguished colonials returns formally from restitutions in order to avoid recognition of wrongdoing.[292] UNESCO created the Committee for Promoting the Return of Cultural Property to its Countries of Origin[293] in the late 1970s to fill gaps of the 1970 Convention. This mechanism addressed the problem primarily through diplomacy and negotiated solutions, namely dialogue, meditation, or conciliation, rather than a formal legal obligation of return.

In the 1990s, the 'emperor' returned in new clothes. Market rationales prevailed over return claims in the negotiation of the UNIDROIT Convention.[294] The rise of

---

[286] Bartolomé de las Casas took this position in his work on the Treasures of Peru. See Chapter 5.

[287] See Chapter 6.

[288] Ibid.

[289] Instruments such as UNDRIP or NAGPRA accommodate different conceptions of ownership and repatriations, based on the communal or spiritual value of objects. See Chapter 6.

[290] Article 24 of the Treaty of Versailles framed the return of the skull of a Tanzanian resistance leader (the 'Mkwawa head') as inter-state obligation between Germany and the UK, the new colonial power, without any reference to colonial subjects, i.e. the rights of descendants.

[291] See Chapter 5.

[292] The differentiation between the notions of 'return' and 'restitution' is reflected in the 1995 UNIDROIT Convention, which distinguishes 'restitution of stolen cultural objects' from 'return of illegally exported cultural objects' (Chapter 3).

[293] On the Committee, see Vrdoljak, *International Law, Museums and the Return of Cultural Objects*, 211 ff; Folarin Shyllon, 'The Recovery of Cultural Objects by African States through the UNESCO and UNIDROIT Conventions and the Role of Arbitration' (2000) 5 *Uniform Law Review* 219–240, 222 ff.

[294] See Chapter 7.

cultural internationalism, and the casting of objects from former colonies as 'world heritage', impeded new solutions. Return was perceived as a threat to the integrity of global collections, market dynamics or national prestige in holder countries. Some of these narratives still persist in contemporary guidelines or policies on colonial collections which reduce duties to moral or ethical obligations.[295]

However, it is not all doom and gloom. Law has also been used to challenge or reverse colonial biases and double standards. Return claims, challenging the taking of objects, have a long-standing history. They were used in different colonial contexts.[296] For instance, in 1867, Māori leaders filed a petition for the return of an ancestral meeting house (Te Hau ki Turanga), which had taken with government approval in the New Zealand wars.[297] In 1872, Emperor Yohannes of Ethiopia requested the return of a manuscript, the *Kivera Negust* ('Glory of the Kings') from Queen Victoria. It contained the laws of Ethiopia, as well important historical documentation.[298] It had been taken in the Magdala loot by Lord Napier.[299] The king justified the case for return by the argument he was unable to govern his country without the manuscript, since his people would 'not obey' his orders 'without it.'[300] It was returned by the Trustees of the British Museum in the same year. Requests for return of iconic objects, such as Nefertiti[301] or objects taken in the 1897 raid of Benin[302] have been made since the interwar period.

Later, pressure from human rights movements and indigenous groups led to the adoption of specific frameworks to address objects and human remains taken from indigenous populations. As of the 1970s, many settler colonial societies have created specific laws and procedures to facilitate the repatriation of cultural objects and human remains.[303] UNDRIP expressly recognized the right of indigenous

---

[295] The report of the Dutch Advisory Committee on the National Policy Framework for Colonial collections states expressly that 'the handling of requests to return cultural objects is not so much a legal as an ethical question', due to the application of statute of limitations, the non-retroactivity of international conventions and the imprecision of 'standards and principles of international humanitarian law', see Summary of report Advisory Committee, 2. See Chapter 8.

[296] See Lars Müller, 'Returns of Cultural Artefacts and Human Remains in a (Post)colonial Context' Working Paper 1/2021 (Magdeburg: Deutsches Zentrum Kulturgutverluste, 2021).

[297] See Chapter 4.

[298] Edward Ullendorff and Abraham Demoz, 'Two Letters from the Emperor Yohannes of Ethiopia to Queen Victoria and Lord Granville' (1969) 32 Bulletin of the School of Oriental and African Studies, University of London 135–142. It marked one of first official restitution request made by an 'African ruler'. See Richard Pankhurst, 'Ethiopia, the Aksum Obelisk, and the Return of Africa's Cultural Heritage' (1999) 98 *African Affairs* 229–239, 233.

[299] See Chapter 3.

[300] Ullendorff and Demoz, 'Two Letters from the Emperor Yohannes of Ethiopia', 135.

[301] Pierre Lacau, the Director of the Egyptian Antiquities Department, started a campaign for the return of Nefertiti in 1923. In 1930, the Museum in Cairo sought the return of the bust in exchange for other objects, and a lifting of the ban of excavations. See Chapter 3.

[302] In 1935, Oba Akenzua II requested the return of two throne stools taken in the 1897 'punitive expedition' in order to preserve the history of the Kingdom of Benin. Germany was only willing to return replicas of the stools. See Audrey Peraldi, 'Oba Akenzua II's Restitution Requests' (2017) 1 *Kunst & Kontext* 23–33.

[303] See Chapter 7.

peoples to 'use and control' their 'ceremonial objects' and their 'right to the repatriation of their human remains'.[304] Domestic courts in Italy[305] or Colombia[306] have relied on international legal norms, such as the right to self-determination, indigenous rights or cultural heritage principles, to justify a duty to return colonial objects under international law. The recognition of the right to access of culture under international human rights law provided new options to groups or communities to claim access or return. These developments challenge the idea that return is merely a moral, rather than a legal issue.

4.7 Interplay of justice, ethics, and human rights

How should takings and return be approached from a contemporary point of view? The micro-histories and practices traced here suggest that existing legal entanglements can only be 'disentangled' through an intersectional perspective, namely the interplay of justice, ethics, and human rights.

A main argument developed in this book is that the treatment of cultural colonial objects is neither a purely moral, nor a purely legal question,[307] but rather situated at the intersection of three different angles: justice,[308] ethics,[309] and human rights.[310] It requires consideration of all three perspectives, i.e. 'justice, morality, and human rights'.[311] This intersectionality is needed to take into account the complexities of colonial injustice. Each of the three perspectives has its own added value.

Ethical perspectives provide an important role since they offer flexibility to determine fair and just solutions, i.e. to do 'the right thing'.[312] The formalism of legal frames may silence or legitimize past injustice, or produce outcomes that are

---

[304] UNDRIP, Art. 12 (1).

[305] Alessandro Chechi, 'The Return of Cultural Objects Removed in Times of Colonial Domination and International Law: The Case of the Venus of Cyrene' (2008) 18 *Italian Yearbook of International Law* 159–181.

[306] In the Quimbaya Treasure case, the Constitutional Court of Colombia justified the duty to return inter alia on the basis of UNDRIP. See Diego Mejía-Lemos, 'The "Quimbaya Treasure," Judgment SU-649/17' (2019) 113 *AJIL* 122–130.

[307] See Sophie Schönberger, 'Restitution of Ethnological Objects: Legal Obligation or Moral Dilemma?' (2016) 81 *Museumskunde* 45–48; Thérèse O'Donnell, The Restitution of Holocaust Looted Art and Transitional Justice: The Perfect Storm or the Raft of the Medusa? (2011) 22 *EJIL* 49–80.

[308] Charlotte Joy, *Heritage Justice* (Cambridge: Cambridge University Press, 2020).

[309] See also Kamil Zeidler, *The Restitution of Cultural Property* (Gdansk: Gdansk University Press, 2016), Roodt, 'Restitution of Art and Cultural Objects and Its Limits', 286.

[310] Tullio Scovazzi, 'Diviser c'est détruire: Ethical Principles and Legal Rules in the Field of Return of Cultural Property'(2011) 94 *Rivista di Diritto Internazionale* 341, 392.

[311] Robert Peters, *Complementary and Alternative Mechanisms beyond Restitution: An Interest-oriented Approach to Resolving International Cultural Heritage Disputes* (EUI PhD, Florence: 2011) 157; Elazar Barkan, 'Introduction: Reparation: A Moral and Political Dilemma' in Jon Miller and Rahul Kumar (eds.), *Reparations: Interdisciplinary Inquiries* (Oxford: Oxford University Press, 2007) 2.

[312] Arts Council, 'Restitution and Repatriation: A Practical Guide for Museums in England', 14.

perceived as unfair or unjust. It is often impossible to remedy past wrong. As Lea Ypi has rightly noted, in certain cases 'the best way to make amends for our past wrongful behaviour is to grant people what they want, regardless of why they want it and even if what they want is not something they may have been entitled to in the first place'.[313] These limits explain why ethical categories have been at the forefront of approaches to facilitate return of Nazi-looted art[314] or human remains.

However, ethical categories cannot be read in isolation of the law. A pure reliance on ethical principles may deny the complexity of legal relations and concepts in the past. Nineteenth-century international law itself was based on a complex blend of positivist and natural law principles. Reducing justice to ethics may marginalize the legal nature of wrong or present return as a benevolent gesture, rather than as something that is owed.

The human rights lens has added value because of its transformative potential. It provides a prospective rather than a retrospective vision of colonial injustice. It focused on contemporary relations towards objects. It is not dependent on demonstration of past wrongdoing, but provides a means to address ongoing violation of cultural rights in contemporary relations. It challenges historical blind spots, such as the state-centric vision of international law. It offers a basis for non-state entities, such as groups or communities, to make claims or enjoy participatory rights in decision-making processes, even though they may have lacked standing or legal personality in the colonial era. It recognizes that protection of cultural heritage is not tied to fixed conception of the past (e.g. an 'authentic' or 'frozen' culture), but dynamic and intertemporal.[315] This openness is essential to address problems of continuing cultural affiliation, which may arise in return claims, partly as a result of colonial practices.

At present, the debate in ethics is ahead of the law. This creates discrepancies between holocaust restitutions and colonial injustice. One way to mitigate these divides is the development of legal principles on restitution and return of cultural colonial objects, which enable a balancing of competing norms and case-by-case solutions.[316] Some concrete guidance may be drawn from newly emerging guidelines or policies in relation to colonial collections. They differ in content, but reflect a common set of criteria, which can serve as inspiration. They use, in principle, two sets of criteria, to assess cultural returns: justice-related criteria, which justify return by wrongdoing or unjust enrichment, and arguments of cultural

---

[313] Lea Ypi, 'What's Wrong with Colonialism' (2013) 41 *Philosophy & Public Affairs* 158–191, 187.

[314] The turn to ethics is reflected in post-Second World War instruments and the Washington Conference Principles on Nazi-Confiscated Art (3 December 1998). See Chapter 8.

[315] This has been recognized by the Human Rights Committee in its interpretation of Art. 27 ICCPR. See Human Rights Committee, *Apirana Mahuika et al. v. New Zealand*, Communication No. 547/1993, UN Doc. CCPR/C/70/D/547/1993 (2000), para. 9.4; *Ilmari Lansman et al. v. Finland*, Communication No 511/1992, UN Doc CCPR/C/52/D/511/1992 (1994) para. 9.3.

[316] See Chapter 9.

significance,[317] which are more closely embedded in cultural rights.[318] This dual focus extends the case for restitution or return of objects beyond 'looted art' or coercively acquired objects. It justifies the case for redistribution of cultural objects, based on both conditions of takings, and their relational significance in and throughout the world.

Both sets of criteria have a basis in law. They may be grounded in cultural heritage principles. The application of justice-related criteria, such as wrongdoing or unjust enrichment, is supported by the prohibition of cultural takings without free and informed consent[319] or the duty not to benefit from exploitation of peoples subjected to colonial or foreign occupation for cultural gain.[320] They may justify return *ex officio*, i.e. irrespective of demonstration of cultural significance. The cultural significance criterion allows return even in the absence of past wrong. It finds legal support in the right of people and communities to maintain and develop cultural identity and enjoy access to their culture,[321] the principle of 'cultural integrity'[322] or the protection of 'intangible cultural heritage'.[323]

4.8 Museums as transitional justice spaces

Both the complicity of museums in colonial violence and their current role in the debate over return pose novel challenges for the identity and understanding of museums, including their role as guardians of the 'tangible and intangible heritage of humanity'.[324] The ideas of universality, which have been associated with models of the encyclopedic or the universal museum, have come under serious critique.[325] Many museums are in search of a new museology in light of their colonial heritage. A critical question is whether and how they can address their own past, develop their own identity beyond conservation or containment, and have a transformative

---

[317] In 2022, Hermann Parzinger, President of the Prussian Cultural Heritage Foundation noted in the context of the decision to return the statue of Ngonso that return is not limited to looted objects: 'The special—especially spiritual—significance of an object for the society of origin can also justify a return'. See Deutsche Welle, 'Germany to Return Looted Artifacts to Africa' (29 June 2022).

[318] See Chapter 8.

[319] See UNDRIP.

[320] Tullio Scovazzi, 'The "First Time Instance" as Regards Restitution of Removed Cultural Properties' (2012) 30 *Agenda Internacional* 9–19, 18.

[321] Vrdoljak, *International Law, Museums and the Return of Cultural Objects*, 301–302.

[322] Tullio Scovazzi and Laura Westra, 'The Safeguarding of the Intangible Cultural Heritage According to the 2003 UNESCO Convention: The Case of First Nations of Canada' (2017) 1 *Inter Gentes* 24–44, 39. It also protects economic aspects central to a communities' culture. See Jeremie Gilbert, 'Indigenous Peoples, Human Rights, and Cultural Heritage: Towards a Right to Cultural Integrity' in Alexandra Xanthanki and others (eds.), *Indigenous People and Cultural Heritage: Rights, Debates, Challenges* (Leiden: Brill, 2017) 20–38, 34–36.

[323] See Chapter 7.

[324] See ICOM Definition, adopted by the 22nd General Assembly in Vienna, Austria, on 24 August 2007.

[325] See Chapter 8.

role in relation to colonial injustice.[326] For instance, Priya Basil has suggested to consider the museum as 'a kind of cultural Truth and Reconciliation Commission', which invites 'people and artists in communities from which belongings were taken, as well as other artists and even museum visitors, to share—through exchanges, workshops, displays—in shaping other kinds of landscapes for belonging', and a 'space of reparation' where 'stories' serve 'as a form of compensation or even as reparations'.[327] Others plead that the form of the museum itself should be rethought, since the '[m]aster's tools will never dismantle the master's house'.[328]

Traditionally, core ideas and concepts of transitional justice (truth, reparation, memorialization) applied by states in such contexts have been linked to physical violence against persons. However, museums need to confront some of the same issues (e.g. accountability, engagement with victims or survivors, repair) that public institutions face in the aftermath of conflict or processes of political transitions.[329] The social biography of objects shows that the boundaries between violence against objects and violence against persons become blurred in relation to cultural colonial takings, which are linked to identity loss or loss of history. This makes it pertinent to draw analogies or borrow from the methods and lessons learned in this field. Institutions inevitably become involved in discourses of historical injustice and measures to come to terms with the past. Emerging practices in curatorial ethics or museology suggest that many of them apply transitional justice methods and concepts, knowingly or unknowingly, in attempts to confront the remnants of colonial violence in their collections.[330]

Under modern museum ethics, documentation of object histories is no longer an act of convenience, but inherently linked to transparency requirements, knowledge-sharing and cooperation with countries and communities of origin.[331] In colonial contexts, it becomes a form of truth-seeking into object histories. It should not only be conducted reactively, but also a proactive basis, even in the absence of return claims.[332] It requires broad epistemic frames and collaborative

---

[326] Some associate the role of museums with 'social repair'. See Etienne, 'Who Cares?' 5. On narratives and memorialization, see also Alice Procter, *The Whole Picture: The Colonial Story of the Art in Our Museums and Why We Need to Talk about It* (London: Cassell, 2020).

[327] Priya Basil, 'Writing to Life' (2021) 19 *British Art Studies* 1 https://doi.org/10.17658/issn.2058-5462/issue-19/conversation/p17.

[328] Audre Lorde, 'The master's tools will never dismantle the master's house' in Audre Lorde, *Sister Outsider: Essays and Speeches* (Berkeley: Crossing Press, 2007) 110–114.

[329] Padraig McAuliffe, 'Complicity or Decolonization? Restitution of Heritage from 'Global' Ethnographic Museums' (2021) 15 *International Journal of Transitional Justice* 678–689, Alessandro Chechi, 'The return of cultural objects displaced during colonialism. What role for restorative justice, transitional justice and alternative dispute resolution?' (2023) 6 *International Journal of Restorative Justice* 95-118, 103.

[330] The synergies between transitional justice methods and the search for a new museology in relation to colonial collections are reflected in the turn to relational ethics. See Chapter 7.

[331] See Art. 6 (1) ICOM Code of Ethics.

[332] Independent Expert Group, 'Ethical Principles for the Management and Restitution of Colonial Collections', 3.2.

structures. According to a relational account, provenance research needs to involve new forms of inquiry into colonial histories, which go beyond property or owner-ship relations. They cannot be based solely on archives or Western narratives, but require engagement with oral histories in societies of origin, knowledge-sharing, and joint research, or reconnection of objects with their intangible meanings. The role of the curator is to trace and develop different object narratives, rather than to produce an authoritative expert account on art historic significance.[333] Integrating local sources may challenge images of passivity and diversify perspectives on vic-timization. The more objects are equated to subjects (e.g. ancestors, human re-mains), the more provenance research becomes a cultural equivalent of the right to truth in transitional justice, namely a right to truth in relation to the provenance of objects.

The increasing need to establish object histories or engage with returns claims equates museums to spaces of transformative justice. Even though museums are not necessarily able to restore the *status quo*, they can contribute to object trans-formation, in the sense of facilitating a transition from unjust towards just rela-tions.[334] In this way, they take on a transitional justice role. For instance, if an object taking involved desacralization or dehumanization, return may become a means to renew relations towards objects. It is not only a means for the institution to come to terms with its own past, but contributes to transformation of relations towards ob-jects. In addition, return processes can have restorative justice features.[335]

In museum practice, memorialization[336] is part of the educational function of museums and the ethics of labelling and display. Cultural takings are often a form of 'memory-cide'. Museums holding cultural colonial objects are carriers of know-ledge and memory. They must exhibit objects in a conscientious and inclusive manner.[337] Memory processes are related to the pursuit of 'a dialogic truth' and the need to confront 'marginalization, exclusion, negative stereotyping, dehumaniza-tion and denialism'.[338] They need to go beyond a 'Never again' logic in holocaust

---

[333] Nancy Proctor, 'Digital: Museum as Platform, Curator as Champion, in the Age of Social Media' (2010) 53 *Curator* 35–43, 38.

[334] Jennifer Balint, Julie Evans, Nesam McMillan, and Mark McMillan, *Keeping Hold of Justice: Encounters between Law and Colonialism* (Ann Arbour: University of Michigan Press, 2020) 100.

[335] The process itself may carry transformative value, by strengthening the agency of claimants or the dignity of objects.

[336] Memorialization is geared at 'understanding the mechanisms of oppression and dehumanization' preceding 'large-scale violence', opening up 'debate on the causes and consequences of past violence' and 'the need to build a different future'. See Report of the Special Rapporteur on the promotion of truth, justice, reparation and guarantees of non-recurrence, 'Memorialization processes in the context of serious violations of human rights and international humanitarian law: the fifth pillar of transitional justice' UN Doc. A/HRC/45/45, 9 July 2020, para. 59.

[337] The turn to relational ethics places emphasis on contextualization of objects, engagement with the narratives and experiences of people behind objects, consultation with communities, or sharing of knowledge. See Ethical Principles for the Management and Restitution of Colonial Collections in Belgium, 5.2, 5.5.

[338] Report, 'Memorialization processes', para. 33.

or atrocity crime discourse[339] and address structural features behind colonial violence, such as epistemic violence and the 'broader ethics and historical legacies of the scientific racism' that shaped collections.[340] Returns require strategies to resocialize objects and revive cultural memory in order to reconnect objects to societies of origin, and disconnection strategies in order to preserve critical memory.

4.9   Relational cultural justice as a bridge to break impasses in restitution discourse

A macro argument of this book is that relational approaches form part of a broader cultural relational justice model, which is needed to address some of the traditional limitations and impasses in relation to restitution and return. Cultural nationalism and cultural internationalism have played a central role in both the justification of takings, and impediments in relation to return. The debate has turned in circles for many decades, based on false binaries, which have framed return as an either/or question. Recurring bottlenecks are: (i) object-centric versus people centric readings of cultural objects; (ii) the global artistic and scientific value of objects versus their role in national or local identity politics; (iii) the need for preservation, guardianship, and care in international collections versus their use as symbols of living cultures; (iv) the importance of global access and visibility versus their invisibility in the Global South; or (v) the encyclopedic value of museums versus the spectre of the 'empty museum'.

Some voices stress that contemporary semantics of restitution may continue to disguise colonial violence or mark a 'new spectacle', through governments or museums conceal historical responsibilities and maintain control over narratives and the history of the past.[341] It is thus essential to go beyond restitution, namely treat restitution and return as a process which goes beyond the mere transfer or circulation of objects. The idea of relational justice provides a conceptual frame to address some of these structural divides and to go beyond classical approaches. It provides a method to determine where objects rightfully belong and to enable new relations towards objects. It relies on three elements: (i) the need to find a new contemporary basis of consent for entangled objects; (ii) the development of more inclusive procedures, in line with rights of access to cultures; and (iii) strategies to enable new object possibilities and engagement, including in the post-return stage.[342] It makes

---

[339]   For a critique of the ability of transitional justice to address colonial wrong, see Mohamed Sesay, 'Decolonization of Postcolonial Africa: A Structural Justice Project More Radical than Transitional Justice' (2022) 16 *International Journal of Transitional Justice* 254–271.

[340]   Independent Expert Group, 'Ethical Principles for the Management and Restitution of Colonial Collections', 5.7.

[341]   Fazil Moradi, 'Restitution of Looted African Art Just Continues Colonial Policies: Much More Is at Stake' *The Conversation* (13 October 2022).

[342]   See Chapter 9.

it necessary to view cultural takings as more than a 'tragic event',[343] namely to confront colonial histories and re-engage with responsibilities for past takings, epistemic violence, and ongoing forms of discrimination or dispossession.

The need to establish new forms of consent may be grounded in both past violations[344] and contemporary rights of access of culture. It opens prospects for various intermediate solutions, which go beyond the classical return or not to return divide. It takes into account that return is not always the 'golden rule'[345] or the most appropriate solution.[346] The main point of the relational model is to find new ways of agreement towards contemporary forms of owning or display of objects, even if they may have been acquired lawfully according to the standards of the time. This model finds support in the justice-related criteria (wrongdoing or unjust enrichment) and arguments of cultural significance, supported by principles in cultural heritage law. It is inter alia reflected in the separation of recognition of ownership and the decision on physical location, which has been adopted in Germany's strategy regarding the return of Benin or objects or Belgium's policies on colonial objects.[347] It restores equality and may enable a more open discourse on location, display or sharing.

Museums have something to gain from this process. A transfer of property rights may entail restriction in use, new forms of curatorship or changes in benefits from intellectual property rights, but it does not necessarily entail cultural loss. As the 2022 Arts Council Guidance on Restitution and Repatriation states, it provides an 'opportunity for museums to develop their collections knowledge and research, to build relationships with originating communities, to open up dialogue around contested items and to create opportunities for discourse and discussion around cultural heritage'.[348] It may allow 'emotions and memories to set in', relinquish control and enable new ontological encounters, changing the way in which 'objects, persons, and epistemic things' are known.[349] It leaves room for mutually beneficial return agreements and recognizes the wide spectrum of options to enable access to culture, such as sharing arrangements, new stewardship models, exchanges, loan-agreements, including loans from the Global South to Western collections, object circulation or digitalization. A redistribution responds not only to justice

---

[343] Moradi, 'Catastrophic Art', 255.

[344] Andreas von Arnauld has argued that violation of ethical principles may create a contemporary obligation to negotiate with the victims of historical injustice or their descendants, i.e. 'meaningful negotiations in order to come to an agreed solution'. See Andreas von Arnauld, 'How to Illegalize Past Injustice: Reinterpreting the Rules of Intertemporality' (2021) 32 *EJIL* 401–432, 426, 432.

[345] See Liv Nilsson Stutz, 'Claims to the Past. A Critical View of the Arguments Driving Repatriation of Cultural Heritage and Their Role in Contemporary Identity Politics' (2013) 7 *Journal of Intervention and Statebuilding* 170–195, 185.

[346] It may 'whitewash' responsibility towards the past, in the absence of a proper process, shift postcolonial continuities to the national realm, or create secondary conflicts in societies of origin.

[347] See Chapter 9.

[348] Art Council, 'Restitution and Repatriation: A Practical Guide for Museums in England', 2.

[349] Brus and Zillinger, 'Introduction: Transforming the Post/Colonial Museum', 19.

concerns, but also reflects the inter-civilizational significance of objects better than their retention in a few selected 'universal museums'.[350] This is in particular evident in relation to objects, which are currently hidden in storage in Western collections.

A second element is the initiation of an open and inclusive process on the past and future of objects, which goes beyond inter-state negotiation[351] and offers possibility for participation of affected groups, communities, or stakeholders (e.g. descendants of former rulers).[352] This process is important to identify the plural meanings, cultural values and ontologies of objects, to accommodate different positions and identify strategies on a case-by-case basis, in line with justice criteria and the cultural, social, and economic value of objects.

Finally, it is important to recognize that restitution or return of objects itself is only one aspect of engaging with the remnants of colonial injustice. It is essential to complement such processes with restitution of knowledge or information or additional cooperation or assistance to returns (e.g. support for local infrastructure and institutions), which facilitate access to objects after return and enable new engagement.

4.10   Temple versus agora: Changing museum structures, interconnectivity, and object mobility

The issue of restitution and return is inherently connected to the debate about the future role of the museums, connectivity, and object mobility.

Museums are ever-changing. The dilemmas of colonial injustice pose essential questions about the institution of the museum as such. A classical social critique of museums is that they are spaces of social distinction. The debates surrounding taking and distribution of cultural colonial objects force Western collections to rethink their structures and transform from temples of knowledge, science, or education into more open spaces of civic encounter and mutual engagement (*agorae*). They push museums to increase transparency regarding contentious histories, to combine exhibition with ongoing research and inquiry, to recentre perspectives,

---

[350] Matthes, 'Repatriation and the Radical Redistribution of Art', 943–946.

[351] Jochen von Bernstorff and Jakob Schuler, 'Wer spricht für die Kolonisierten? Eine völkerrechtliche Analyse der Passivlegitimation in Restitutionsverhandlungen' (2019) 79 *ZaöRV* 553–577, 576.

[352] They derive participatory rights from protection of cultural rights under international human rights law, such as Art. 15(1)(a) of the Covenant on International Economic, Social and Cultural Rights, Art. 27 of the International Covenant on Civil and Political Rights. They are supplemented by specific cultural heritage protections. See the preamble of the UNESCO Convention on Intangible Cultural Heritage, Arts. 2(3) and 7(1) of the UNESCO Convention on the Protection and Promotion of the Diversity of Cultural Expression (20 October 2005) 2440 UNTS, or Art. 3(8) of the UNIDROIT Convention. Art. 18 UNDRIP states that 'indigenous peoples have the right to participate in decision-making in matters which would affect their rights, through representatives chosen by themselves in accordance with their own procedures, as well as to maintain and develop their own indigenous decision-making institutions'.

i.e. to question dominant knowledge frames and provide space for alternative per-spectives, to enhance marginalized voices, enable storytelling and emotional forms engagement with objects, set objects in context with contemporary works[353] or provide opportunities for social healing or repair.[354] They also encourage a more diverse museum landscape and the development of new or alternative forms of museums.

This process of diversification challenges the classical argument that returns are not feasible due to lack of capacity. Many institutions in the Global South are putting in place structures to receive objects. Part of their value lies in fact that they do not necessarily imitate classical approaches, but open new ways of seeing and engaging with the histories of objects.[355] For instance, museums such as the Museum of Black Civilizations in Dakar, challenge dominant Western narra-tives.[356] In many settler colonial contexts, indigenous people have pushed to 'indi-genize' the institution of the 'museum' and created cultural community centres that relate histories of objects closer to intangible heritage. The museum itself may not be the most appropriate space for certain objects, such as ceremonial or sacred ob-jects, or objects that are not meant to be preserved, but are to be renewed in society.

The debate on returns further opens new questions relating to interconnectivity and object mobility. Opponents to return have invoked issues of conservation and preservation and global access in order to justify retention. These arguments are losing force with the changing knowledge infrastructure, digitization, and evolving visions regarding the identity of museums. Technically, the sharing of objects is not necessarily confined to one space. Multi-media technologies and digital and vir-tual formats offer new ways to present and engage with objects. This development opens new prospects for object mobility in the large sense, i.e. circulation of know-ledge and ideas, interconnectivity, and sharing of objects.

Digitalization reopens the fundamental question to what extent museums define their identity in material terms, i.e. through preservation, or physical ownership of objects, or through provision of knowledge, content, or contextualization. Should they understand themselves more as 'temples', i.e. as guardians of civilizatory

---

[353] One critique is that the prominent space given to 'looted art' may sideline the contributions or value of contemporary artists or objects.

[354] Csilla E. Ariese and Magdalena Wróblewska, *Practicing Decoloniality in Museums: A Guide with Global Examples* (Amsterdam: Amsterdam University Press, 2022).

[355] The District Six Museum in Cape Town, one the 'Sites of Conscience' in South Africa, goes new ways, by promoting a 'critical non-racialism' as a method to engage with the past. The ANO Institute of Arts and Knowledge in Ghana Novel has developed the idea of the mobile museum in order to chal-lenge the monolithic or static form of museums. See ANO Institute of Arts and Knowledge, Mobile Museums https://www.anoghana.org/mobilemuseums. This model bring objects to communities, in-corporates their input, and thereby stimulates new thinking about the ways in which the value and meaning of objects is created.

[356] The museum tells colonial histories from an African perspective. See Sabrina Moura, 'The Museum of Black Civilisations, between History and Utopia' (2021) *Zeitschrift für Kulturwissenschaften*, 107–122.

treasures and knowledge, or as *agorae*, i.e. an open market place for dialogue and the circulation of ideas and knowledge? Many Western museums have digitalized collections or receive visitors online. Such museums can function more easily without holding large quantities of authentic objects. This makes it easier to justify de-accessioning of objects, in particular those which are not publicly shown.[357] Digital restitution can be a useful first step to come to an agreement, where objects should be placed or whether and how they might be shared or circulated. It cannot replace the authenticity of material objects and their aura,[358] and may create access or ownership dilemmas in communities of origin. But it provides greater prospects for the sharing of knowledge, the visibility of objects across spaces, and potential agreements on the distribution of objects.

The concept of object mobility also provides a means to address the long-standing critique that return will simply create novel intra-state conflicts between different stakeholders in countries or societies of origin, or replicate patterns of cultural nationalism, to the detriment of cultural communities. Experiences in Mali or New Zealand have shown that that such conflicts may be mitigated through joint stewardship models, or the sharing and circulation of objects between museums and stakeholders.[359] Curatorial practice offers innovative methods to display the absence of objects in Western collections. This may contribute to preservation of critical memory in the Global North.

The dynamic developments in this field over the past decade mark not only a brick in the wall in the century-long dispute over return, but a seismic shift offering new prospects and lenses. They challenge some of the old dichotomies of the restitution debate and highlight at the same time the limits of the concept of restitution. A targeted focus on restitution of objects alone may conceal greater structural challenges. Cultural justice requires more comprehensive socio-economic measures to address the broader epistemic and economic consequences of cultural colonial takings, including reconsideration of artistic or legal frames, education, reanimation of traditions, knowledge and know-how, building of infrastructure and connections to contemporary works of art, or rethinking of modes of commercial exploitation, intellectual property frames, or access to objects.[360] Ultimately, cultural colonial objects are essential in framing a new modernity and reimagining the idea of the museum itself.

---

[357] For example, a museum may still reach a global audience, based on images, documentation, or replica, even if it reduces its collection of material objects.

[358] Walter Benjamin argued in 1936 that in 'even the most perfect reproduction', one thing is lacking: 'the here and now of the work of art—its unique existence at the place at which it is to be found. The history to which the work of art has been subjected as it persists over time'. See Walter Benjamin, 'The Work of Art in the Age of Its Technological Reproducibility' (Michael W. Jenning tr) (2010) 39 *Grey Room* 11–37, 13.

[359] See Chapter 9.

[360] Howard W. French, *Born in Blackness: Africa, Africans, and the Making of the Modern World, 1471 to the Second World War* (New York: Liveright, 2022).

2

Expanding Empire: Curiosity, Power, and Prestige

1 Introduction

> I reckon … that in fact eloquence can be uttered from no human being … as out of the inspection and study of images and things, which we put in order and are able to compare.[1]

These are the words of Samuel Quiccheberg, one of the founders of museology in sixteenth century Europe. He encouraged knowledge production and categorization in his treatise on 'Inscriptions or Titles of the Most Complete Theatre' (1565) in order to inspire princes and noblemen to collect objects for purposes of knowledge production. His idea reflects the ideal of collecting in the Renaissance, which was driven by the urge for discovery, humanism, and science:

> [A] wave of new products, new knowledge, and new words swept over Europe, stimulating openness, wonder excitement, and imagination…. Curiosity, both cause and consequence of the discoveries and previously considered dangerous to the soul, was increasingly seen as a virtue.[2]

This spirit guided some of the takings in the colonial period. They were marked by a striking contradiction. They were guided by a quest for knowledge and exploration of the cultures of colonial subjects, but also as a means of exploiting or destroying their cultures.

Early takings, ranging from the sixteenth to the eighteenth centuries, lacked systematicity. Objects were taken for different reasons: as war trophies, for power, prestige or personal gain, upon request, or out of fascination with the foreign cultures or the natural world. The discovery voyages were driven by curiosity and the search for rare and exotic objects in European societies. Colonial companies,

---

[1] Samuel Quiccheberg, *Inscriptiones Vel Titvli Theatri Amplissimi* (Antonio Leonardis tr, Munich: Monachii, 1565) 26–27 in Stephanie Jane Bowry, *Re-thinking the Curiosity Cabinet: A Study of Visual Representation in Early and Post Modernity* (PhD, University of Leicester, 2015) 349–350.
[2] Genese Grill, 'Portals: Cabinets of Curiosity, Reliquaries and Colonialism' (2016) 39 *The Missouri Review* 38–62, 45–46.

Confronting Colonial Objects. Carsten Stahn, Oxford University Press. © Carsten Stahn 2023.
DOI: 10.1093/oso/9780192868121.003.0002

such as the British or Dutch East India company established extensive collections of natural specimens and man-made objects, including weapons, jewelry, sculptures, or artefacts.[3] Some objects found their way initially into curiosity cabinets. They were established in the sixteenth and seventeenth centuries to understand the 'the universal nature of things'.[4] These collections constituted predecessors to the naissance of museums[5] and contributed to the emergence of different fields of science, such as geology, anthropology, botany, and medicine. They encompassed weapons, libraries, antiquities, and natural objects such as plants, clothes, or other items reflecting human craftsmanship or technological advancement at the time. These cabinets were a 'microcosm'. Each object represented an entire region or population, a 'summary of the universe'.[6]

With scientific progression and the diversification of sciences, methods of collecting became more systematic and organized. Scientific disciplines such as archeology, natural history, ethnography or anthropology, developed in the course of the nineteenth century. Knowledge was organized along such distinctions. Scholars and curators started to organize objects in art collections or curiosity cabinets, based on origins, forms, materials, or meaning. Collection of cultural artefacts was no longer focused on rare or curious objects. It became more common to search for objects that are representative of world knowledge and cultures.[7] Ethnographic collections emerged and expanded, based on anthropological rationales, such as the desire 'to know and understand the history of man'.[8]

Collection and removal of objects became an inherent part of colonial strategies,[9] and not only one of its consequences. Colonial power structures created a new system of ordering the world, industry of knowledge production, and a race and a market for cultural objects.[10] Acquisition was promoted through a global network structure[11], including geographies of power, transnational

---

[3] Arthur MacGregor, *Company Curiosities: Nature, Culture and the East India Company, 1600–1874* (London: Reaktion Books, 2018). Practices, such as the display of Tipu's Tiger in the house of the East India Company, show this close relationship between imperial power and fascination with the 'other'.

[4] Oliver Impey and Arthur MacGregor (eds.), *The Origins of Museums: The Cabinet of Curiosities in Sixteenth and Seventeenth Century Europe* (Looe, UK: House of Stratus Press, 2001) xvii.

[5] Some collections set the foundations for establishment of museums, such as the comprehensive collection by British physician Sir Hans Sloane, which included African and Native American ethnographic objects and facilitated the creation of the British Museum in 1753.

[6] See James Clifford, *The Predicament of Culture: Twentieth-Century Ethnography, Literature and Art* (Harvard: Harvard University Press, 1988) 227.

[7] Alexandra Sauvage, 'To Be or not to Be Colonial: Museums Facing their Exhibitions' (2010) 6 *Culturales* 97–116, 106.

[8] On the alleged 'humanitarian' foundations, see Ribi Forclaz, *Humanitarian Imperialism: The Politics of Anti-Slavery Activism, 1880-1940* (Oxford: Oxford University Press, 2015).

[9] Frederick Cooper and Ann Laura Stoler, 'Between Metropole and Colony: Rethinking a Research Agenda' in Ann Laurer Stoler and Federick Cooper (eds.), *Tensions of Empire: Colonial Cultures in a Bourgeois World* (Berkeley: University of California Press, 1997) 1–58.

[10] See Chris Gosden and Chantal Knowles, *Collecting Colonialism: Material Culture and Colonial Change* (Oxford: Berg, 2001).

[11] Alan Lester, *Imperial Networks: Creating Identities in Nineteenth-Century South Africa and Britain* (London: Routledge, 2001).

movements, discursive networks, and local actors. It involved not only colonial agents, private companies, collectors, or scientists, but also institutions, such as museums, which participated in the taking or circulation of objects and their display.[12]

Legal instruments, such as protectorate agreements, colonial laws, or the Final Act of the Berlin Conference[13] served as formal sources to legitimate transactions or changes in ownership, but were at the same complicit in dispossession, commodification, or perpetuating inequalities.[14] Catherine Lu has used the term 'structural injustice' to capture the disempowering or alienating features of colonial encounters. This logic applies to cultural colonial objects. Many of them may be qualified as 'legally entangled objects', i.e. as objects of cultural or historical importance shaped by a context of indirect violence or structural inequality.[15] This context casts doubt on the voluntary nature of dispossession or change of title, even in the absence of direct physical violence.

This chapter explores the genealogy and different modes of extractive colonial collecting. It develops a typology of takings and forms of violence. It then illustrates practices through selected micro-histories of objects taken from the sixteenth to the mid-nineteenth centuries. These histories demonstrate how objects influenced 'colonial identities, imperial networks, and cross-cultural exchange'[16] and the actions of individuals in colonial settings. The object stories show that the objectification and taking of things was not only driven by curiosity, commercial interests, or an urge for preservation of cultural heritage ('rescue' ideology, nostalgia), but an inherent part of inter-colonial rivalry, performative features, and the method of colonization,[17] bolstering the colonizers' claim to superiority, and involving a taking of ownership and cultural identity.[18]

---

[12] On museums and empire, see Tim Barringer and Tom Flynn, *Colonialism and the Object: Empire, Material Culture and the Museum* (London: Routledge, 1997); Tony Bennett, *Pasts Beyond Memory: Evolution, Museums, Colonialism* (London: Routledge, 2004); Sarah Longair and John Macleer (eds.), *Curating Empire: Museums and the British Imperial Experience* (Manchester: Manchester University Press, 2012).

[13] Matthew Craven, 'Between Law and History: The Berlin Conference of 1884-1885 and the Logic of Free Trade' (2015) 3 *London Review of International Law* 31–59.

[14] See Antony Anghie, *Imperialism, Sovereignty and the Making of International Law* (Cambridge: Cambridge University Press, 2005) 3; Mahmood Mamdani, *Citizen and Subject: Contemporary Africa and the Legacy of Late Colonialism* (Princeton: Princeton University Press, 1996) 124.

[15] On socio-cultural dimensions of imperialism, see Cooper and Stoler, *Tensions of Empire: Colonial Cultures in a Bourgeois World*.

[16] Claire Wintle, *Colonial Collecting and Display: Encounters with Material Culture from the Andaman and Nicobar Islands* (Oxford: Berghahn Books, 2013) 2.

[17] On settler colonialism, see e.g. Patrick Wolfe, 'Settler Colonialism and the Elimination of the Native' (2006) 8 *Journal of Genocide Research* 387–409; Lorenzo Veracini, *Settler Colonialism: A Theoretical Overview* (New York: Palgrave Macmillan, 2010).

[18] Sarah Longair, 'The "Colonial Moment" in the Lives of Objects from the Swahili Coast' in Prita Meier and Allyson Purpura (eds.), *Worlds on the Horizon: Swahili Arts across the Indian Ocean* (Illinois: Krannert Art Museum, 2018) 130–145, 132.

1.1 The violence of takings

Colonial takings are a particular category of cultural appropriation. As cultural anthropologist Pieter ter Keurs has noted: 'Collecting is never a neutral activity. All collecting, certainly in the context of colonialism, is political.'[19] The very act of taking can be seen as a structural form of violence. It involved an erasure of the history and identity of colonized societies or served as a means to assert cultural superiority. It was part of extractive policies, cultural exploitation, or competition with other colonial powers. In some contexts, cultural dispossession became a mode of governance, or better governmentality,[20] namely a means to 'control through collection, description, and classification.'[21] By removing items, commodifying them, and inscribing other meanings onto them, colonizers sought to undermine the ability of the colonized to maintain their own life-world. Collectors often ignored the immediate political context since colonialism was considered to be a 'normal state of affairs'.

Boris Wastiau has provided a vivid account of the violence of colonial collecting in the Belgian Congo. He has described the system of cultural appropriation as follows:

> Most acquisitions for the museum were made according to the colonizer's rules, which implied a payment, but seldom according to the Congolese's ethical standards, especially with regard to human remains. Not all acquisitions were made in this way and many were not made for museums in the first place. If immediate violence in the process of collecting was not the norm, albeit common, acquisitions took place within an extremely violent system that damaged African traditional cultures through 'pacification campaigns', the establishment of closely monitored 'chefferies indigenes', and missionary work principally. The outcome was a country that irremediably lost a massive part of its cultural heritage in the span of a few decades.[22]

---

[19] Pieter ter Keurs, 'Collecting in the Colony: Hybridity, Power and Prestige in the Netherlands East Indies' (2009) 37 *Indonesia and the Malay World* 147–161, 147.

[20] Michel Foucault's concept of governmentality refers to the process of governing and the mentality of government, including the 'modes by which, in our culture, human beings are made subjects'. See Michel Foucault, 'The Subject and Power' (1982) 8 *Critical Inquiry* 777–795, 777. On the role in colonial collecting, see Tony Bennett, 'Anthropology, Collecting and Colonial Governmentalities' (2014) 25 *History and Anthropology* 137–149.

[21] Sarah van Beurden, *Authentically African: Arts and the Transnational Politics of Congolese Culture* (Athens, OH: Ohio University Press, 2015) 5.

[22] Boris Wastiau, 'The Legacy of Collecting: Colonial Collecting in the Belgian Congo and the Duty of Unveiling Provenance' in Paula Hamilton and James B. Gardner (eds.), *The Oxford Handbook of Public History* (Oxford: Oxford University Press, 2017) 460–478, 472.

Structurally, the violence of collecting goes beyond conquest, coercion, robbery, or theft. It includes epistemic forms of violence.[23] Knowledge production and scientific expeditions in the Enlightenment era were closely connected with the European colonial project. Modern individualism and secular scientific worldviews were regarded as superior to 'indigenous knowledge systems'. Collecting practices introduced a new classificatory system for collections, museums, or knowledge systems. They defined new ways of seeing, displaying, or engaging with objects, and organized knowledge according to certain clusters and categories, including distinctions between natural and cultural objects[24] or artefacts and art. At the peak of colonial expansion in the nineteenth century, colonized societies were used as laboratories to study racial differences.[25] Museums, scientists, and private agents were complicit in this enterprise. They issued detailed instructions for the collection of artefacts, sacred objects, ornaments, or human remains. As Ciraj Rassool has noted:

> The museum is not only an institution of modernity and ordered citizenship, but is the primary institutional form of empire. It was made and is being remade and adapted through both sides of empire's history: by a rapacious and violent empire of plunder and pacification, and by empire as 'benevolent colonisation', humanitarianism and trusteeship over people and things.[26]

1.2 Justificatory discourses

Colonial authorities, agents, or individuals invoked a mix of different narratives and rationales to justify acquisition. They sought to ground removal in legal justifications, such as legitimate reprisals or reparation, alleged 'humanitarian' motives, the 'rescue' or preservation of objects, and different forms of consent in order to legitimize their taking in the eyes of competing powers or public audiences at home. They used ambiguities in the law or created legal structures to give acquisitions an appearance of consent or legality.

Rights of conquest were rarely invoked in isolation. The taking of objects as spoils of war was often accompanied by other justificatory narratives, which were deemed to provide additional legitimation for ownership. The need to suppress slavery or human sacrifice was often invoked as the rationale to legitimize 'the

---

[23] Gayati Chakravarty Spivak, 'Can the Subaltern Speak?' in Cary Nelson and Lawrence Grossberg (eds.), *Marxism and the Interpretation of Culture* (Basingstoke: Macmillan Education, 1988) 271–313.

[24] Samuel J. M. M. Alberti, *Nature and Culture: Objects, Disciplines and the Manchester Museum* (Manchester: Manchester University Press, 2009).

[25] Helen Tilley, *Africa as a Living Laboratory: Empire, Development, and the Problem of Scientific Knowledge, 1870-1950* (Chicago: University of Chicago Press, 2011).

[26] Ciraj Rassool, 'Restoring the Skeletons of Empire: Return, Reburial and Rehumanisation in Southern Africa' (2015) 41 *Journal of Southern African Studies* 653–670, 658.

European conquest of Africa' to home audiences.[27] Colonial powers relied on the concept of 'punitive expeditions' in order to justify forcible responses to violations of treaty arrangements, restrictions on trade, or resistance to colonial agents. Some takings were designated as forms of reparation or compensation, following the examples of the Napoleonic wars. This was a convenient technique to recuperate expenses incurred by the colonial enterprise and signal submission. In many cases, the captured artefacts were later displayed in public collections in Europe in order to highlight the presumed triumph of civilization and law and order over less 'civilized' subjects and legitimize colonial policies in the eyes of domestic audiences.[28]

In other cases, the collection of objects was defended as a service to colonial subjects, namely as a means to secure their advancement or protection or the preservation of artistic mastery, memory, and culture. This 'saviour' logic is a recurring rhetorical figure in colonial politics. For instance, the seizure and sale of cultural objects was sometimes justified as a means to secure assets for the 'future development of the protectorate'.[29] In this way, colonial powers made 'the subjugated pay the cost for their own subjugation'.[30] In other situations, removal was justified as a benevolent act, carried out in the interests of foreign cultures or for the care and preservation of the objects themselves.[31]

In again other cases, objects were acquired as part of culture of collecting, for instance to complete existing collections or to compete with other colonial powers.[32] Orientalization, i.e. the 'othering' of cultures, was an integral part of justifying cultural dispossession. The display of cultural colonial objects was often a means to showcase Western superiority and support racially motivated justifications of colonial rule and the 'civilizing mission'. It triggered a fascination with exotic and mysterious cultures in Western society. Ethnological museums became 'part of the colonial infrastructure' and 'places where colonial knowledge was produced and presented'.[33] Later, the rebranding of some of 'these objects as art' in the twentieth

---

[27] See Robin Law, 'Human Sacrifice in Pre-Colonial West Africa' (1985) 84 *African Affairs* 53–87, 54. For example, the punitive expedition to Benin in 1897 was justified as a response to human sacrifice and an alleged violation of the duty of the Oba of Benin to open the territory to trade. See Chapter 3.

[28] For instance, Britain formally justified its seizure of the famous Koh-i-noor diamond after the end of the Second Anglo-Sikh War of 1848–1849 as an act of reparation, formalized through of a treaty of surrender. See 3.2.3

[29] Mary Lou Ratté, *Imperial Looting and the Case of Benin* (Master's Thesis, University of Massachusetts, 1972) 80 https://scholarworks.umass.edu/cgi/viewcontent.cgi?article=3034&context=theses.

[30] Staffan Lundén, *Displaying Loot: The Benin Objects and the British Museum* (PhD Dissertation, University of Gothenburg, 2016) 148.

[31] Lord Elgin argued that the purchase and transfer of the Parthenon Marble to the British Museum was an 'act of rescue', justified by the lack of care for classical Greek heritage under the reign of the Ottoman Empire. See 3.3.3. The removal of the famous Rosetta stone at the beginning of the nineteenth century was in part legitimized through Egypt's inability to secure the safety of its own heritage. See 3.2.1.

[32] Wastiau, 'The Legacy of Collecting', 460–478.

[33] On the history of ethnographic collecting, see Helen Tilley and R. J. Gordon (eds.), *Ordering Africa: Anthropology, European Imperialism and the Politics of Knowledge* (Manchester: Manchester University Press, 2007); Tony Bennett, 'Anthropology, Collecting and Colonial Governmentalities'

century allowed colonial powers to shift 'civilising narratives',[34] present themselves as 'custodians' of the cultural heritage of colonies and justify their own rule.[35] This argument relies on the problematic assumption that Western societies are better equipped than societies of origin to appreciate and interpret their cultural heritage.

Many colonial agents developed a certain 'nostalgia'[36] for the culture of colonized people. Renato Rosaldo has called this 'imperialist nostalgia'.[37] It is based on a paradox. The taking and display of objects involved the longing for an often 'self-interpreted', idealized, or 'romanticized' past[38] and an urge to preserve or restore past traditions.[39] However, it was at the same time a means to undermine the culture of the colonized or contribute to their peril. It 'negated all prior existence of indigenous ideas about heritage, and existing preservation policies, as well as their appropriation and transformation by imperial powers.'[40]

From the late-eighteenth century to the twentieth century, feelings of loss or care for an imagined past and the will to preserve or reconstruct these identities drove many agents to collect objects. For instance, military agents, colonial administrators, explorers, or private collectors acquired or looted Egyptian, Greek, or Javanese artefacts, based on fascination with great ancient civilizations. With the rise of social Darwinism, this urge was extended to indigenous or 'primitive' objects. As Caroline Drieënhuizen has argued, this form of colonial nostalgia became part of a 'social and political strategy':

> Nostalgic feelings helped the colonial elite … to constitute and fashion their identity through the transference of memories. In so doing, they were able to cope with challenges in the present, to ease both spatial and political transitions, and to feel grounded in diverse social and cultural contexts … [Colonial nostalgia] influenced not only personal, but also collective identities, as people donated their

---

(2014) 25 *History and Anthropology* 137–149; Zachary Kingdon, *Ethnographic Collecting and African Agency in Early Colonial West Africa: A Study of Trans-Imperial Cultural Flows* (New York, London: Bloomsbury Visual Arts, 2019).

[34] As Sarah van Beurden has shown in her study of the Congo, 'objects' themselves have undergone transformation in this process. They constituted 'artefacts of science, players in the construction of narratives about the "civilizing mission"', and eventually art'. See Sarah Van Beurden, 'The Value of Culture: Congolese Art and the Promotion of Belgian Colonialism (1945–1959)' (2013) 24 *History and Anthropology* 472–492, 473.

[35] Ibid, 474.

[36] See Fred Davis, *Yearning for Yesterday: A Sociology of Nostalgia* (New York: Free Press, 1979) 1–30; William Cunningham Bissell, 'Engaging Colonial Nostalgia' (2005) 20 *Cultural Anthropology* 215–248.

[37] Renato Rosaldo, 'Imperialist Nostalgia' (1989) 26 *Representations* 107–122.

[38] Caroline Drieënhuizen, 'Objects, Nostalgia and the Dutch Colonial Elite in Times of Transition, ca. 1900-1970' (2014) 170 *Bijdragen tot de Taal-, Land- en- Volkenkunde* 504–529, 507.

[39] This tension is reflected in the notion itself, which derives from two Greek notions: 'nostos, i.e. 'to return home' and 'algia', 'a painful condition'. Rosaldo, 'Imperialist Nostalgia', 108.

[40] Astrid Swenson, 'The Heritage of Empire' in Astrid Swenson and Peter Mandler (eds.), *From Plunder to Preservation: Britain and the Heritage of Empire, c.1800–1940* (Oxford: Oxford University Press, 2013) 3–28, 16.

objects to national museums which defined and represented through display collective memories. As a result, dominant versions of colonial nostalgia determined ... perceptions of the national colonial history.[41]

In connection with saviour ideologies, this sense of nostalgia served to create moral comfort or uplift, but concealed at the same time historical complicity in cultural dispossession[42] and engagement with colonial wrong.[43]

Cultural takings were not merely justified by reasons of personal enrichment or institutional glory, but rationalized through different utilitarian considerations, including civilizing rationales, care-taking, and preservation of material culture in the name of other cultures or humanity. These narratives concealed the violent nature of colonial collecting. Colonial powers acted as judges and juries of their own actions. They used heroic images and narratives ('saviour', altruism) and pseudo-scientific justifications and reinventions of culture to validate cultural dispossession.

1.3 Forms of acquisition

The nature of objects taken and the modalities of acquisition differ among types of agents (e.g. military, missionaries, traders) and contexts. Some artefacts were obtained through purchase or gift exchange, while others were looted or acquired through force, or removed by missionaries or scientists.[44] Many objects were collected during scientific or commercial expeditions. Colonial companies[45] and administrators played a key role in the acquisition of ethnographic and other objects.

1.3.1 Punitive expeditions

Certain objects were acquired by force, namely through so-called 'punitive expeditions'.[46] These operations involved 'measures short of war' carried out in response

---

[41] Drieënhuizen, 'Objects, Nostalgia and the Dutch Colonial Elite in Times of Transition', 525.

[42] On silences in historical narratives, see Michel-Rolph Trouillot, *Silencing the Past: Power and the Production of History* (Boston: Beacon Press, 1995).

[43] Rosaldo, 'Imperialist Nostalgia', 120.

[44] See Jos van Beurden, *Inconvenient Heritage* (Amsterdam: Amsterdam University Press, 2022) 28–40.

[45] On corporate colonialism, see Grietje Baars, *The Corporation, Law, and Capitalism: A Radical Perspective on the Role of Law in the Global Political Economy* (Chicago: Haymark Books, 2020); Elizabeth Comack, 'Corporate Colonialism and the "Crimes of the Powerful" Committed Against the Indigenous Peoples of Canada' (2018) 26 *Critical Criminology* 455–471.

[46] See David Pizzo, 'Punitive Expeditions' in Gordon Martel (ed.), *The Encyclopedia of War* (Hoboken, New Jersey: Wiley-Blackwell, 2012) https://doi.org/10.1002/9781444338232.wbeow507. On the Togo-Hinterland Expedition in 1894/1895 in which German colonial officials plundered ethnographic objects in order to repress local uprising, see Jan Hüsgen, 'Colonial Expeditions and Collecting: The Context of the "Togo-Hinterland Expedition" of 1894/1895' (2020) 4 *Journal for Art Market Studies* 1–12. On looting, see Colin Renfrew, *Loot, Legitimacy and Ownership: The Ethical Crisis in Archaeology* (London: Duckworth, 2000).

to alleged wrongdoing. They involved use of force, extortion, spoliation, or theft.[47] The term 'expedition' illustrates the contradictions of colonial discourse. Such operations were carried out to justify plunder and forcible acquisition of cultural objects in colonial contexts, at a time when cultural property was increasingly protected in Europe through peace treaties, natural principles, or emerging codifications of customs of war.[48] They were carried out to crush resistance against colonial expansion or avenge violations of obligations by local rulers. They were formally justified as responses to treaty violations by local leaders or for 'civilizing' purposes.[49] Punitive measures were justified as retaliatory measures, sanctioning violations of such treaty obligations.[50] The corresponding violence, theft, and exploitation was often concealed from the public[51] or rationalized through 'humanitarian' rhetoric. Punitive expeditions were common across colonial powers. They led to the acquisition of many objects that were otherwise difficult to obtain, such as royal treasures, religious or ritual artefacts, or objects of historical importance.[52]

1.3.2 Commerce and colonial collection

Other objects were acquired through commerce or private expeditions. Throughout the nineteenth century, colonial expansion promoted a new scientific organization of world and increased interest in disciplines, such as ethnography, anthropology, and natural history. Collection became popular to respond to an increasing fascination in Europe with objects from 'primitive expansion cultures'. It had performative features. Colonial artefacts were collected and publicly displayed and served partly demonstrate the power of the colonial rulers.[53] Collecting was geared at originals, i.e. authentic objects that were created before encounters with the colonizers. Many colonial powers relied on scientists or companies to collect antiquities and ethnographic objects. Scientific and racial motives were often mixed. Collection was driven by a dual ambition: to 'control the "other" human being by collecting his or her objects' and the urge to satisfy 'the collector's own ... needs'.[54]

---

[47] On forcible collection, see Tim Barringer, *The South Kensington Museum and the Imperial Project* (London: Routledge, 1997); Margot Finn, 'Material Turns in British History: I: Loot' (2018) 28 *Transactions of the Royal Historical Society* 5–32.

[48] See Chapters 1 and 6.

[49] For instance, treaties with West African rulers included clauses requiring them to prohibit human sacrifice or slavery.

[50] Inge van Hulle, 'British Humanitarianism, International Law and Human Sacrifice in West Africa' in Inge van Hulle and Randall C. H. Lesaffer, *International Law in the Long Nineteenth Century (1776-1914)* (Leiden: Brill, 2019) 105–125.

[51] Bernard Porter, '"Empire, What Empire?" Or, Why 80% of Early- and Mid-Victorians Were Deliberately Kept in Ignorance of It' (2004) 46 *Victorian Studies* 256–263, 260–262.

[52] For instance, a large number of objects in the Belgian Tervuren Museum were procured through forcible operations. See Maarten Couttenier, *Congo tentoongesteld*, (Leiven: Acco, 2005) 198.

[53] On the interplay between metropole and colony, see Cooper and Stoler, 'Between Metropole and Colony'.

[54] Ter Keurs, 'Collecting in the Colony', 160.

Article 6 of the General Act of the Berlin Conference protected these types of acquisition, by mandating colonial powers to 'protect and favour all religious, scientific or charitable institutions and undertakings created' to support colonial rule, instruct 'the natives', and bring them 'the blessings of civilization'.[55] This contributed to a stark rise in cultural colonial objects in European collections at the beginning of the twentieth century.[56] The presence of large ethnographic collections, presenting 'primitive cultures', became a part of the self-identity of museums[57] and a means to educate and demonstrate prestige through colonial exhibitions.[58]

The colonial encounter and presence of collectors created new opportunities for exchange and markets for the commodification of objects.[59] Both the influx of traders, missionaries, and colonial administrators and the local population's desire for fashionable European goods led to a trade in objects, through broader regional and transnational networks of circulation and involved informal systems of exchange.[60] Certain objects were specifically produced locally for this market or for export.[61] Local elites contributed to the collection or commodification of objects or culture of collecting.[62] Some local actors became agents for colonial powers or foreign traders, located and acquired objects, and thus became complicit in the loss of cultural heritage. However, in many instances, the circumstances of acquisition are doubtful,[63] because the trade relationship was based on economic and political pressure or initiated through coercion or threat, challenging the fair or voluntary nature of commercial transactions.[64]

---

[55]   See Art. 6 of the General Act of the Berlin Conference on West Africa (26 February 1885).

[56]   2019 German Museum Guidelines, 48.

[57]   See generally Tony Bennett, *Pasts Beyond Memory. Evolution, Museums, Colonialism* (London: Routledge, 2004).

[58]   Sauvage, 'To Be or not to Be Colonial', 107.

[59]   See Kingdon, *Ethnographic Collecting and African Agency in Early Colonial West Africa*, 48.

[60]   In some regions, European goods became local status symbols. Some native rulers relied on Western traders or missionaries as advisers. See generally Raymond Corbey, *Tribal Art Traffic: A Chronicle of Taste, Trade and Desire in Colonial and Post-Colonial Times* (Amsterdam: Royal Tropical Institute, 2000).

[61]   Andrew Zimmerman, *Anthropology and Antihumanism in Imperial Germany* (Chicago: University of Chicago Press, 2001).

[62]   Röschenthaler describes this in relation to Douala sculptures from Cameroon: '[P]eople sold their sculptures, at first secretly. Soon individual owners began doing so publicly, as did the secret societies as a whole. A trader would then sell the works at Douala. From there, they found their way to Europe ... Although some sculptures could be ritually removed and later renewed, the influence of the missionaries was not without detrimental impact on the artistic production of the local population'. See Ute M. Röschenthaler, 'Max Esser's 'Bakundu Fetishes?' (1999) 32 *African Arts* 76–96, 80. The diary entries of German businessman Max Esser suggest that he acquired four Douala sculptures ('fetishes') in Bakundu villages on an exploratory trip to Cameroon in 1896 'in exchange for an accordion' and 'some goods' after 'lengthy negotiations' with the chief and the local 'sorcerer'. Ibid, 78.

[63]   Larissa Förster, 'Der Umgang mit der Kolonialzeit: Provenienz und Rückgabe' in Iris Edenheiser and Larissa Förster (eds.), *Museumsethnologie: Eine Einführung* (Berlin: Dietrich Reimer, 2019) 78–103, 85.

[64]   This is inter alia recognized in the German Guidelines on Collections from Colonial Contexts, which note that 'colonial officials' had often 'extensive knowledge of local law', as a result of which 'it can generally be assumed that Europeans were aware when they "illegally" acquired sacred objects from locals, for example, which should not have been for sale'. German Museums Association, *Guidelines*

Both colonial officials and private actors from European contexts were aware from their own traditions that public property or certain protected objects cannot be acquired or appropriated by private individuals. But they did not necessarily apply such restrictions to cultural colonial objects. For instance, Richard Kandt (1867–1918), a German colonial administrator in German East Africa (Rwanda), famously wrote in 1897 to Felix van Luschan (1854–1924), the Deputy Director of the Ethnological Museum in Berlin: 'In general, it is difficult to obtain an object without using at least some force. I believe that half of your museum is stolen'.[65] It is documented through diaries or correspondences that certain 'collectors' were aware of the problematic origin of their holdings[66] or went beyond instructions to acquire objects.

1.3.3 Missionary collecting

Missionaries contributed actively to cultural dispossession or destruction in Africa, Asia, or the Pacific.[67] They were often closely connected to colonial authorities and an important part of the 'triangle of government, business and Church'.[68] Some missionaries developed expert knowledge on objects and established large collections, based on their interest in 'salvaging, studying and seeking to understand' objects.[69] Local communities sometimes gave up objects voluntarily as a result of missionary activities. However, such transactions cannot be viewed in isolation of the structural context of 'giving' and 'taking'.[70] The veneration of powerful non-Christian objects triggered an 'iconoclash'.[71] Catholic imperial theology left no space for indigenous African religions, based on the idea of a Judeo-Christian covenant with god, which justified the *extra ecclesiam nulla salus* (no salvation outside the church) doctrine.[72] Removal or destruction of objects was considered as a gateway towards conversion.

---

on Dealing with Collections from Colonial Contexts (Berlin: German Museums Association, 1st edn, 2018) 67.

[65] Correspondence Richard Kandt to Felix von Luschan, SM-PK, EM, 712, 1897/1544, Bl. 230. See also Regina Sarreiter, 'Ich glaube, dass die Hälfte Ihres Museums gestohlen ist' in Anette Hoffmann, Britta Lange, and Regina Sarreiter, *Was Wir Sehen. Bilder, Stimmen, Rauschen. Zur Kritik anthropometrischen Sammelns* (Basel: Basler Afrika Bibliographien) 43–58.

[66] On correspondences from Hermann Kersting and Lieutenant Valentin von Massow in German Togoland, see Yann LeGall and Gwinyai Machona, 'Possessions, Spoils of War, Belongings' *Verfassungsblog* (2 December 2022) https://verfassungsblog.de/possessions-spoils-of-war-belongings/.

[67] Barbara Lawson, "Missionization, Material Culture Collecting, and Nineteenth-Century Representations in the New Hebrides (Vanuatu) (1994) 18 *Museum Anthropology* 21–38, 34 ('vital aspect of missionization')

[68] Van Beurden, *Inconvenient Heritage*, 189.

[69] Alison Bennett, *Material Cultures of Imperialism in Eastern Africa c. 1870-1920: A Study of Ethnographic Collecting and Display* (PhD, University College London: 2019) 116.

[70] Van Beurden, *Inconvenient Heritage*, 189.

[71] Bruno Latour, 'What Is Iconoclash? Or Is there a World beyond the Image Wars?' in Peter Weibel and Bruno Latour (eds.), *Beyond the Image-Wars in Science, Religion and Art* (Cambridge, Mass.: MIT Press, 2002) 14–37.

[72] Leyten, *From idol to art*, 148.

Some objects were acquired for personal reasons, or based on in interest in indigenous cultures. Others were collected, confiscated, or destroyed because they were associated with witchcraft, sorcery, or magic or deemed to have 'negative' psychological influence on locals, impeding conversion to Christianity. They constituted 'bad objects of imperialism', in terms of William Mitchell's theory of objecthood.[73] For instance, in the South Pacific, Africa, or Asia, missionaries from different congregations called on locals to abandon or destroy 'fetishes', i.e. objects associated with a heathen, pagan culture. They collected, confiscated, or burned ritual objects or religious artefacts, sometimes under fierce resistance[74] and/or based on the mistaken impression that they constituted idols and objects of worship. Collection and acts of conversion became the indicators of the success of the mission. In some cases, objects were collected as trophies or booty and shown in missionary exhibitions to showcase the need and impact of missionary work in relation to primitive cultures.[75] Other objects were 'gifted' to museums.

The Vatican even established its own Ethnology Museum. It results from a large-scale missionary exhibition (the 1925 Vatican Exhibition), organized by Pope Pius XI (1857–1939) in 1925. The exhibition hosted 100,000 items sent from all parts of the world. 40,000 objects were retained by the Vatican. Pius XI decided to create the Vatican Ethnology Museum so that 'dawn of faith among the infidel of today can be compared to the dawn of faith which ... illuminated pagan Rome'.[76] The museum reflects the colonial entanglement of missionary work, which was guided by beliefs in European superiority. It came to serve as 'a didactic and scientific museum at the service of missions'.[77] It hosts more than 60,000 objects, including 'approximately 10,000 from Africa', '10,000 from the Americas', '20,000 from Asia, and '6,000 from Oceania'.[78] The objects were displayed for 'exotic otherness'. The collection was officially justified by the idea that artefacts were donated by missions, state representatives or even indigenous groups. However, the structural conditions, under which donations were made in colonial contexts, such as the imbalances in

---

[73] William John Thomas Mitchell, *What Do Pictures Want? The Lives and Loves of Images* (Chicago: Chicago University Press, 2005) 166.

[74] For examples of resistance, see Van Beurden, *Inconvenient Heritage*, 184–185.

[75] One example is the collection of *korwar* figures by Dutch missionary Frans van Hasselt for the Utrecht Missionary Society in Northwest New Guinea. See Raymond Corbey and Frans Karel Weener, 'Collecting While Converting: Missionaries and Ethnographics' (2015) 12 *Journal of Art Historiography* 1–14. Methodist missionary George Brown collected a vast amount of artefacts in the South Pacific at the end of the nineteenth century in the name of salvation of souls. See Richard Eves, 'Commentary: Missionary or Collector? The Case of George Brown' (1998) 22 *Museum Anthropology* 49–60. Some missionaries supported punitive expeditions, including Brown. On the collection of the London Missionary Society, see Chris Wingfield, 'Scarcely More than a Christian Trophy Case? The Global Collections of the London Missionary Society Museum (1814–1910)' (2017) 29 *Journal of the History of Collections* 109–128.

[76] This is stated in an official publication authorized by the Vatican Museums: Metropolitan Museum of Art, *The Vatican Collections: The Papacy and Art* (New York: Harry Abrams, 1982) 226.

[77] Ibid, 226.

[78] Ibid, 227.

Catholic missions or the suppression of indigenous traditions by settler colonial governments, are only beginning to be more critically investigated.[79] It took centuries until the Holy See finally admitted that the 'doctrine of discovery', which was invoked to legitimize colonial conquest, is 'not part of the teaching of the Catholic Church' since it did 'did not adequately reflect the equal dignity and rights of indigenous peoples'.[80]

1.3.4 *Gifts*

The argument of the 'gift' is a recurring justification in relation to the acquisition of colonial objects.[81] As French anthropologist Marcel Mauss has shown, gifts have played an important role in 'inter-societal' relations to foster solidarity and establish social bonds.[82] Gift exchange was a common practice in the colonial era. It was used to show hospitality or part of treaty-making ceremonies. For instance, both the British and the Dutch East India Company often exchanged gifts with local rulers in order to legitimize their presence.[83] Some exchanges were grounded in diplomacy and reciprocity, while others are more closely related to unequal power relations between colonial officials and local chiefs. The conditions are difficult to assess in hindsight, since the process of 'gifting' carried risks of misinterpretation, in light of differing social conventions. As Alison Bennett has noted:

> Gifts served as political envoys, and were part of the navigation of new political and social spaces. They paved the way for new relations and the exercise of elite local agency. However, gifting was a complex act that often involved intense negotiation, and the possibility of rapid alterations in the balance of power for either party in the exchange. It served to create a relationship or association between

---

[79] Kwame Opoku, 'Could the Catholic Church's Ethnology Museum be holding artefacts with doubtful histories?' *Pambazuka News* (26 February 2015). For instance, the museum contains objects confiscated by the Canadian government in the 1885 Nicole Winfield, 'Vatican Says They're Gifts; Indigenous Groups Want Them Back' *AP News* (21 July 2022).

[80] Holy See Press Office, 'Joint Statement of the Dicasteries for Culture and Education and for Promoting Integral Human Development on the "Doctrine of Discovery"' (30 March 2023) https://press.vatican.va/content/salastampa/en/bollettino/pubblico/2023/03/30/230330b.html. In April 2023, Pope Francis made a pledge for an openness towards restitution ('To the extent that one can make restitution, which is a necessary gesture, it is better to do it. There are times when one cannot... But to the extent that one can make restitution, let it be done, please, this is good for all. So as not to get used to putting one's hands in other people's pockets'. See Holy See, 'Apostolic Journey of His Holiness Pope Francis to Hungary, 28–30 APRIL 2023' (30 April 2023), https://www.vatican.va/content/francesco/en/speeches/2023/april/documents/20230430-ungheria-voloritorno.pdf.

[81] Grégoire Mallard, 'The Gift as Colonial Ideology' in Grégoire Mallard, *Gift Exchange: The Transnational History of a Political Idea* (Cambridge: Cambridge University Press, 2019) 85–120.

[82] See generally Marcel Mauss, *The Gift: The Form and Reason for Exchange in Archaic Societies* (Abingdon: Routledge, 2002). Mauss argued that gift exchange creates a social expectation that the 'debt' needs to be repaid.

[83] Frank Birkenholz, 'Merchant-kings and lords of the world: Diplomatic gift-exchange between the Dutch East India Company and the Safavid and Mughal empires in the seventeenth century' in Tracey A. Sowerby and Jan Hennings (eds.), *Practices of Diplomacy in the Early Modern World c. 1410–1800* (London: Routledge, 2017) 219–236.

individuals and groups, but also signified different things for those on either side of the exchange.[84]

In certain contexts, the term 'gift' may cover up the violent history of acquisition. For instance, it became means to show allegiance to colonial rulers[85] or part of customary tribute schemes.[86] In the eyes of the colonized, even ordinary civilians, such as commercial agents or explorers, were easily seen as representatives of the colonial state, or associated with its power. Even voluntary interactions can therefore not be fully detached from the colonial context.[87]

1.4 Changing contexts

One of the most striking features of cultural colonial objects is their changing meaning. Many objects are unique historical testimonies that have undergone social metamorphosis and transformation through their taking and commodification. The colonial encounter has ruptured predestined pathways or created new social meanings. Objects have acquired multiple, and sometimes conflicting, identities. They may constitute trophies of war, symbols of anti-imperial resistance, sacred objects, cultural property, art, administrative items (e.g. documented archival material), or legally disputed artefacts at the same time.

In some cases, object histories reflected in Western collections or the display of things as 'objects' marks a form of epistemic violence. For instance, many of the classifications or names, which collectors used when they collected cultural material, sometimes based on guidance notes by museums, were replicated in the documentation and 'cataloguing' practices of museums.[88] They often contained limited input from source communities. In this way, colonialities persisted in the knowledge infrastructure of collections.

Roughly speaking, cultural takings in the colonial era can be divided into different phases: (i) a period of early collection, from the sixteenth to the eighteenth centuries; (ii) the systematization of collection between the eighteenth and the mid-nineteenth centuries, with the rise of the modern nation state, increasing scientific organization of world knowledge and the birth of modern museums; and

---

[84] Bennett, *Material Cultures of Imperialism in Eastern Africa c. 1870-1920*, 159.

[85] For instance, in 1908 King Ibrahim Njoya offered the throne of King Nsangu, as a 'gift' to the German Emperor Wilhelm II. See Chapter 4.

[86] On the Quimbaya Treasure, see 3.4.2.

[87] As cultural anthropologist Larissa Förster has noted, it is convenient to look 'only at one's own historically grown legal system' and ignore the condition and 'historical legal system of the "others"'. Larissa Förster, 'Whoever's Right' *Blog: How to move on with Humboldt's legacy* (2018) https://blog.uni-koeln.de/gssc-humboldt/en/whoevers-right/.

[88] On North American practices, see Hannah Turner, *Cataloguing Culture: Legacies of Colonialism in Museum Documentation* (Vancouver: University of British Columbia Press, 2020).

(iii) the 'scramble' for cultural objects during colonial expansion as of the mid/late nineteenth century, based on theories of social Darwinism, cultural exploitation, and competition among colonial powers, and increased interest in the public display of 'primitive' objects.[89] All three periods show recurring modes of acquisition and certain overlapping justificatory discourses.

2   Methods of collection from the sixteenth to the mid-eighteenth centuries

Collection of cultural artefacts and treasures was an integral part of colonial expansion as of the sixteenth century, the discovery of the 'New World' and trade relations with Africa, the Far East, and South-east Asia.[90] Conquistadores, missionaries, military, or government agents and colonial companies played an important role in this process. Depending on the circumstances, objects were either destroyed or acquired through different means: force and coercion, purchase, or missionary collecting and gift exchange. Objects in the 'New World' were seized on ideological or religious grounds, to finance expeditions and conquest or to enrich the metropolis.[91] Some items found their way into curiosity cabinets. The objects in these collections were not yet systematically ordered according to scientific or artistic categories. Their content and focus often depended on the tastes and individual interests of the collectors and their networks. More systematized collection started in the eighteenth century. In some cases, the collection of objects shaped the image of empire 'at home'.[92] As Maya Jasanoff has argued, by 'exploring, collecting and classifying foreign cultures', collectors 'both bridged and defined boundaries between Europeans and non-Europeans'.[93]

2.1   Spanish conquest of Central and South America

An early example is the Spanish conquest of Central and South America.[94] It was marked by cultural destruction or plunder of ancient civilizations. Spanish

---

[89] See also Jos van Beurden, *Treasures in Trusted Hands* (Leiden: Sidestone Press, 2017) 53–79, who distinguishes 'early migration of objects' and 'peak in migration of objects'.

[90] Arthur MacGregor, *Curiosity and Enlightenment: Collectors and Collections from the Sixteenth to Nineteenth Century* (New Haven: Yale University Press, 2007); Maya Jasanoff, *Edge of Empire: Lives, Culture, and Conquest in the East, 1750–1850* (New York: Alfred A. Knopf, 2005).

[91] Roger Atwood, *Stealing History: Tomb Raiders, Smugglers, and the Looting of the Ancient World* (New York: St. Martin's Griffin, 2006).

[92] Maya Jasanoff, 'Collectors of Empire: Objects, Conquests and Imperial Self-Fashioning' (2004) 184 *Past & Present* 109–135, 112.

[93] Ibid, 113.

[94] On returns, see Pierre Losson, *The Return of Cultural Heritage to Latin America* (London: Routledge, 2022)

conquest imposed a new culture, language, or religion on the local inhabitants. Sites of pre-Columbian cultures, such as temples or shrines were systematically destroyed on religious or economic grounds. In 1511, Spanish King Ferdinand II (1452–1516) explicitly instructed *conquistadores* to collect gold in the new colonies, and claimed a fifth of all captures ('the royal fifth'). This led to a systematic search for gold and silver treasures and looting or destruction of Aztec temples, Maya treasures and religious objects or codices. Many gold and silver objects were taken as war booty and melted down in order to facilitate transport. In light of the violent context, it is difficult to determine which objects were acquired in a consensual way.

The fine line between consent and coercion is illustrated by the defeat of the ninth Aztec emperor of Mexico, Montezuma II (1466–1520). In 1518, conquistador Hernán Cortés (1495–1547) declared war on the Aztec empire. Montezuma sought to appease Cortés through extravagant 'gifts', such as silver and golden armbands, earrings, necklaces, gold ornaments, shields, and helmets covered in turquoise mosaic or feather fans. Cortés sent the 'gifts' to Spain, but decided to attack Tenochtitlan in 1520, where he imprisoned the emperor and looted his palace. The acquisition of Aztec treasures thus resulted from a combination of force and exchange. The grey zones between coercion and gift are illustrated by the ongoing controversy between Mexico and the Museum of Ethnology in Vienna (Austria) over the return of the famous headdress of Montezuma ('Kopilli Ketzalli'), which belonged to Montezuma.[95] The headdress is made out of more than 400 precious quetzal plumes, mounted in gold. It stands as a symbol of the wisdom and power of the Aztec empire and sovereignty of native cultures. Its acquisition remains contested among historians. According to one reading, Cortés looted it from Montezuma. According to another theory, it formed part of the welcoming presents offered to Cortés in 1519, as evidenced by a letter of Cortés which mentions a 'feather headdress' as part of the gifts to the Spanish king. Based on this ambiguous context, it has been rightly branded as a mix between the two, namely a 'stolen gift'.[96]

The treasures of the Inca empire (now Peru) were acquired by Spain in a similar way, namely through coercion, looting, and consent. The Inca empire was the largest and richest kingdom in the Americas at the time. The Inca used gold and silver as ornaments and decoration for their temples and palaces. In 1532, Spanish conquistador Francisco Pizarro (1478–1541) ambushed the last Inca ruler, Atahualpa

---

[95] Khadija von Zinnenburg Carroll, 'The inbetweenness of the vitrine: Three parerga of a feather headdress' in Paul Basu (ed.), *The Inbetweenness of Things: Materializing Mediation and Movement between Worlds* (London: Bloomsbury, 2017) 23–36.

[96] Magda Michalska, 'The International Dispute over Montezuma's Tiara' *Daily Art Magazine* (25 November 2020) https://www.dailyartmagazine.com/dispute-montezumas-tiara/. See also Pierre Losson, *Claiming the Remains of the Past: The Return of Cultural Heritage Objects to Colombia, Mexico, and Peru* (PhD, City University of New York, 2019) 44, arguing that it may have been a 'gift' by Montezuma to Charles V or as 'part of the spoils of the ransack of Montezuma's palace'.

(1502-1533) and held him for ransom. The emperor sought to regain his freedom through an enormous ransom, namely one large room filled with gold, and two rooms with silver objects, amounting to over 13,000 pounds of 22 karat gold and twice the amount of silver. Atahualpa's subjects compiled these treasures in a period of eight months and handed them over to the Spanish forces in exchange for his return. They were divided among Pizarro and his conquistadors, and the Spanish crown. After receipt of the ransom, Pizarro did not release Atahualpa, but killed him in 1533 and confiscated the treasures of the Temple of the Sun in the Inca capital of Cuzco. The temple was plated with 700 gold sheets, each of which depicted a divine Inca god. Many gold and silver objects were melted down. Some artistic treasures were preserved and later exhibited in Spain. Atahualpa's death marked the beginning of the end of the Inca Empire.

These examples illustrate that law was used as an inherent strategy in justifying conquest. Spanish agents relied on surrender instruments, truces, and alliances to justify submission. As Lauren Benton has noted: 'Spanish chronicles, correspondence, and contracts reporting the interactions with Indians narrated raids and sometimes brutal violence against Indians as logical responses to threats and as reactions to betrayal in the form of breaking the terms of truces, alliances, and agreements to surrender.'[97] These narratives of conquest must be read with caution, since they constructed legitimizations for cultural takings and negated the will of local subjects to maintain their own polities.[98]

2.2 Corporate colonialism

Britain and the Netherlands relied heavily on state sponsored or controlled trade companies to expand their spheres of influence. They outsourced overseas expansion to merchant corporations, such as the British and Dutch East India companies.[99] Both companies were created in the first decade of the seventeenth century. They were vested with chartered powers, enabling them to carry out trade and diplomacy or seize territorial possessions. This unique status turned them into *sui generis* entities. They were more akin to state companies than 'purely commercial' organizations.[100] Their hybrid nature allowed them to operate simultaneously as associations of private merchants and quasi-sovereigns.

---

[97] Laura Benton, 'The Legal Logic of Conquest: Truces and Betrayal in the Early Modern World' (2018) 28 *Duke Journal of Comparative & International Law* 425–448, 439.

[98] Ibid, 439 ('Declarations by Indians that they were vassals of the king implied incorporation but not the dissolution of their political communities').

[99] Charles Henry Alexandrowicz, *An Introduction to the History of the Law of Nations in the East Indies* (Oxford: Clarendon Press, 1967).

[100] Philip J. Stern, *The Company-State: Corporate Sovereignty and the Early Modern Foundations of the British Empire in India* (Oxford: Oxford University Press, 2011) 6.

2.2.1   British East India Company

The British East India Company was created in 1600 through a royal charter from Queen Elizabeth I, with a monopoly of trade with Asia. Its initial mandate was to procure, exchange, or obtain valuable commodities from India. This commercial interest was closely related to empire-building.[101] The company competed for market access with other European powers, such as Portugal, the Netherlands, or France. It created outposts and 'factories' abroad. Territorial expansion created needs of security of protection. The company soon required reinforcements in order to secure its activities. It was vested with the power to recruit its own soldiers, use emergency powers, or declare war on other entities. It signed treaties or treaty-like agreements with Indian states and local rulers in order to build alliances, collect tributes, or establish indirect rule. It made industrial production in India subservient to the industries of Great Britain.

The exercise of political power in independent or autonomous states required company representatives to act like sovereigns, rather than merchants. They formally relied on agreements in order to establish structures of empire.[102] They were necessary to legitimize power vis-à-vis local entities. However, coercion and treaty-making were closely intertwined. As Martine van Ittersum has argued, treaty-making was not necessarily 'an alternative to conquest and war, but was, in fact, integral to the process of European possession and indigenous dispossession': 'Europeans who ventured overseas in the early modern era did not aim to enter into equal treaties with indigenous rulers or peoples, but to conclude agreements that advanced their own claims to trade and/or territory.'[103]

The growing influence of the East India Company in India was facilitated by the decline of the Mughal empire. Territorial conquests started in Bengal, the richest of the Mughal provinces, in 1756. The victory by East India Company forces, led by Robert Clive (1725–1774)[104] over Bengal at the Battle of Plassey in 1757 secured British influence over the Indian sub-continent and consolidated the position of the company. It started to function more like an imperial government rather than a company.[105] It ruled India from the 1770s until 1858 with a private army. Over

---

[101] See William Dalrymple, *The Anarchy: The Relentless Rise of the East India Company* (London: Bloomsbury, 2019).

[102] Saliha Belmessous (ed.), *Empire by Treaty: Negotiating European Expansion, 1600-1900* (Oxford: Oxford University Press, 2015); Saliha Belmessous (ed.), *Native Claims: Indigenous Law against Empire, 1500-1920* (Oxford: Oxford University Press, 2012).

[103] Martine van Ittersum, 'Empire by Treaty? The role of written documents in European overseas expansion, 1500-1800' in Adam Clulow and Tristan Mostert (eds.), *The Dutch and English East India Companies: Diplomacy, Trade and Violence in Early Modern Asia* (Amsterdam: Amsterdam University Press, 2018) 153, 155.

[104] Clive built his own collection of artefacts and memorabilia. See Mildred Archer, Christopher Rowell, and Robert Skelton, *Treasures from India: The Clive Collection at Powis Castle* (London: Herbert Press in association with The National Trust, 1987).

[105] See Huw V. Bowen, *The Business of Empire: The East India Company and Imperial Britain, 1756–1833* (Cambridge: Cambridge University Press, 2009) 182–218.

time, its commercial form created conflicts with its governance mandate. It used its large amount of autonomy in colonial territories in order to please shareholders and put profits before the welfare of persons. It relied on martial law, collected taxes, and developed into an army of 260,000 men at the beginning of the nineteenth century. It exploited its subjects through colonial trade policies and treated military booty as a fast and lucrative way to ensure shareholder returns.

Seizing objects as military booty was both a proof of victory and form of tax collection, which glued national and locally recruited troops together. Britain developed military prize procedures in order to prevent uncontrolled looting, provide an inventory of prize collection, and ensure a fair distribution of war booty and proceeds of sales. However, in practice, these procedures were not always fully complied with since they were burdensome, required documentation of provenance of items, and delayed gratification. Looting continued to be more attractive.[106] In fact, the very term 'loot' emerged in connection with the violence of the East India Company in British India. The 'plundering' was referred to as 'lūṭ' in Hindi, and came to be understood as pillage or theft in English dictionaries in the eighteenth century.[107]

(i) Colonial looting: The story of Tipu's tiger

Company agents and soldiers became complicit in the looting of cultural artefacts in the context of submission and conquest of local rulers.[108] A famous example is the looting in the British–Mysore wars, which led to extensive cultural takings. The company captured the treasury of the Tipu sultan, who was viewed as one of the main British foes in eighteenth century India, after the battle of Seringapatam in 1799. Lord Richard Wellesley (1760–1842), the governor-general of India between 1797 and 1805, allegedly sought to prevent the looting of artefacts and royal objects, such as Tipu's throne,[109] but could not stop the army from capturing and distributing precious objects and artefacts as spoils of war to soldiers.

The conquest of Seringapatam was a punitive expedition designed to overcome the sultan's resistance to the extension of trading routes and expansion of the East India Company. The siege of the city was driven by economic rationales, but officially justified by Tipu's tyrannic rule.[110] Tipu was presented as a despot who tortured British soldiers and forced his subordinates to convert to Islam.

---

[106] Margot Finn, 'Material Turns in British History: I: Loot' (2018) 28 *Transactions of the Royal Historical Society* 5–32.

[107] The notion became common after the Indian Mutiny (1857–1858). See James Hevia, *English Lessons: The Pedagogy of Imperialism in Nineteenth-Century China* (Durham and London: Duke University Press, 2003).

[108] Arthur MacGregor, *Company Curiosities: Nature, Culture and the East India Company, 1600–1874* (London: Reaktion Books, 2018).

[109] The throne was looted and dismantled. Individual parts were sold or distributed as prized trophies.

[110] Krishna Manavalli, 'Collins, Colonial Crime, and the Brahmin Sublime: The Orientalist Vision of a Hindu-Brahmin India in The Moonstone' (2007) 4 *Comparative Critical Studies* 67–86, 74. Lord Cornwallis had already expressed concerns in 1792 during the negotiation of the Treaty of

The victory over Tipu on 4 May 1799 was celebrated as an historical triumph. Lachlan Macquarie (1962–1824), a British officer, described the moment as follows in his journal:

> The final result of this glorious and memorable Day, was, that our Troops were in Complete Possession of Tippoo Sultaun's Fortress and Capital in less than an hour from the commencement of the assault; the Sultaun himself, and a great many of his principal officers, killed in the Storm; his sons and all his Family our Prisoners; and all his immense Riches and Treasures in our Possession.[111]

Cultural looting became an inherent part of the history of Seringapatam.[112] The looting was chaotic, with indiscriminate plunder, leading to a dispersal of objects. Arthur Wellesley (1769–1852), who fought as a colonel in the battle, wrote to Richard Wellesley:

> Nothing therefore can exceed what was done on the night of the 4th. Scarcely a home in the town was left unplundered … jewels of the greatest value, bars of gold … have been offered for sale in the bazaars of the army by our soldiers, sepoys, and followers.[113]

Major General David Baird, the leader of the British troops, reported that Tipu's palace was 'filled with soldiers and (to their shame be it said) officers, loading themselves with gold and jewels'.[114] Tipu's library, his clothes and even his slippers were 'were taken as a trophy of his defeat'.[115] An eye-witness account of the discovery of Tipu's tiger in his music room illustrates the 'orientalization' of Tipu:

> In a room appropriated for musical instruments was found an article which merits particular notice, as another proof of the deep hate, and extreme loathing of Tippoo Saib towards the English. This piece of mechanism represents a royal Tyger in the act of devouring a prostrate European. There are some barrels in

---

Seringapatam: '[F]aithless and violent as Tippoo's character was known to be, I judged it incumbent upon me to be prepared to support by force if it should prove necessary the rights that we had acquired.' Cornwallis to Directors, Conclusion of Treaty with Tipu Sultan, (5 April 1792) IOR/H/251, 91–107, 94,

[111] Lachlan Macquarie, 'Original Account of Siege of Seringapatam' OIOC, Home Misc. 814.

[112] Jasanoff, 'Collectors of Empire' 126 ('the scale of looting at Seringapatam was unprecedented, so was the degree to which the spoils reached civilians').

[113] Arthur Wellesley Wellington and Arthur Richard Wellesley Wellington, *Supplementary Despatches and Memoranda of Field Marshal Arthur, Duke of Wellington, K.G., 15 vols* (London: Murray, 1858) I, 212.

[114] Theodore Edward Hook, *The Life of General the Right Honourable Sir David Baird, 2 vols* (London: Richard Bentley, 1832) I, 221.

[115] See Martin Moran, 'Tipu Sultan's Slippers and Colonel Mordaunt's Cock Match: Footwear, identity and violence in eighteenth-century India' Oxford University Open Educational Resources (Oxford: 2019) 272–281, 277 open.conted.ox.ac.uk.

imitation of an Organ, within the body of the Tyger. The sounds produced by the Organ are intended to resemble the cries of a person in distress intermixed with the roar of a Tyger. The machinery is so contrived that while the Organ is playing, the hand of the European is often lifted up, to express his helpless and deplorable condition. The whole of this design was executed by Order of Tippoo Sultaun. It is imagined that this memorial of the arrogance and barbarous cruelty of Tippoo Sultan may be thought deserving of a place in the Tower of London.[116]

The narrative of Tipu as a tyrannic or savage ruler contrasted with his recorded 'affection of literary pursuits' and his large library, which was deemed to become 'the most curious and valuable collection of oriental learning and history that has yet been introduced into Europe'.[117] Tipu's portrayal as a cruel and 'barbarous', rather cultivated leader, allowed the East India Company to rationalize the violence and present the operation towards the public as an act of liberation, protecting the local population from savage rule.[118] Through this justification, the company restored its own image in the eyes of the British public.[119] The taking of objects was justified as a legitimate collection of war booty after victory.[120] The success of the expedition marked 'a watershed in the East India Company's portrayal of itself as a ruler'.[121] The company, a commercial body 'assumed the manners of a conquering state',[122] while side-lining a colonial rival: France.[123]

The Treaty of Srirangapatna, concluded after the fall of Tipu between the company and the new Maharajah of Mysore on 1 September 1799 required Tipu's successor to pay an annual tribute and not to conduct foreign relations. The company retained a military presence and claimed the authority to order reforms and control the governance of the state. It 'derived an undoubted' right of conquest from the 'justice, and success, of the late war' with the Tipu sultan.[124]

---

[116] Narratives Sketches of the Conquest of the Mysore, Effected by the British Troops and Their Allies, in the Capture of Seringapatam, and the Death of Tippoo Sultaun; May 4, 1799 (London: West and Hughes, 1800) 98–99. See Estefania Wenger, *Tipu Sultan: A Biography* (New Delhi: VIJ Books (India) PVT Ltd, 2017).

[117] Narratives Sketches of the Conquest of the Mysore, 100–101.

[118] Peter Marshall, 'Cornwallis Triumphant: War in India and the British Public in the Late Eighteenth Century' in Lawrence Freeman, Paul Hayes, and Robert O'Neill (eds.), *War, Strategy, and International Politics* (Oxford: Clarendon Press, 1992) 71–72.

[119] See Michael Soracoe, *Tyrant! Tipu Sultan and the Reconception of British Imperial Identity, 1780-1800* (Dissertation, University of Maryland, 2013) https://drum.lib.umd.edu/handle/1903/14889.

[120] Disordered plunder and predatory activities by individuals were regarded as violations of accepted military practices according to the standards of the time. See Richard Davis, *Lives of Indian Images* (Princeton: Princeton University Press, 1997) 154.

[121] Jasanoff, 'Collectors of Empire', 128.

[122] Ibid, 128.

[123] Ibid, 125.

[124] Alexander Beatson, *A View of the Origin and Conduct of the War with Tippoo Sultaun* (London: G. and W. Nicol, 1800) 206–207.

The Tipu sultan died during the attack. However, the story of the conquest of Seringapatam lived on through Tipu's tiger. The object itself was reinvented through its capture. Tipu had originally commissioned the artefact as a means of self-fashioning, i.e. to demonstrate his power and authority.[125] The taking as a war trophy reversed the symbolism. The East India Company produced a 'Seringapatam medal'[126] in order to reward soldiers who had participated in the siege and capture of Seringapatam. The coin presented a British lion overpowering Tipu's emblem, the tiger. In Britain, the object came to be seen as a symbol justifying the establishment of colonial authority over India and the domination of uncivilized cultures. This transformation shows that 'taking possession of another culture's objects can be a way to assert mastery over that culture.'[127] With the victory at Seringapatam, the company experienced the virtue of collecting and displaying objects in 'order to promote a new self-image', and later established its own museum as a showcase for the trophies of imperial war.'[128]

(ii) Tightened scrutiny

In the 1830s, the East India Company allegedly pursued plans to dismantle the Taj Mahal and ship the marble to collectors in London in order to stabilize the finances of the company after the first Anglo-Burmese War (1824–1826). The Governor-General of British India, Lord William Bentinck, auctioned marbles from the Agra fort in 1830 in order to raise funds. This sale outraged the public.[129] A large amount of Indian antiquities and sculptures, displayed in the British Museum, were collected in the eighteenth century by Major General Charles Stuart, a commander of the East India Company army.[130] He counts as one of the first collectors of Indian sculptures at the time, but faced accusations of disfiguring temples and stealing idols.[131]

The autonomy and governance of the company was criticized by prominent public figures in Britain. It was accused of fraud and abuse after the pillaging of

---

[125] See Chapter 1.

[126] See Thomas Carter and William Henry Long, *War Medals of the British Army, and How They Were Won* (London: Norie and Wilson, 1893) 15.

[127] Barrett Kalter, 'Shopping, Collecting, and Feeling at Home' (2008) 20 *Eighteenth Century Fiction* 469–477, 473.

[128] Jasanoff, 'Collectors of Empire', 122.

[129] Sraman Sircar, Demolishing the Taj: Ending the Saga of the Taj Committee (14 June 2020) https://www.heritagewalkcalcutta.com/post/tajcommittee3.

[130] British Museum, Tantra at the British Museum: Collecting histories: Collecting and the East India Company https://www.britishmuseum.org/exhibitions/tantra-enlightenment-revolution/tantra-collecting-histories. The British Museum states: 'We do not know how Stuart acquired these sculptures. He may have bought some of them, but it's also possible others were removed from sites without permission.'

[131] See Jörg Fisch, 'A Solitary Vindicator of the Hindus: The Life and Writings of General Charles Stuart (1757/58-1828)' (1985) 1 *The Journal of the Royal Asiatic Society of Great Britain and Ireland* 35–57, 51–52. Allegations of theft were not proven. Fisch notes: 'His whole attitude towards Hinduism and the Indians indicates rather a benevolent and paternalistic relationship than that of a thief. With constant complaints he would more over have risked difficulties with his superiors, and there are no indications of this.' Ibid, 52.

Bengal. Economist Adam Smith criticized the company's monopoly over trade and argued that it was neither good as merchant, nor as sovereign.[132] In 1783, Edmund Burke and Charles James Fox proposed a Bill (the India Bill) in the British Parliament to replace the company leadership by a panel of parliamentary commissioners. In his famous speech in the Impeachment Trial of Warren Hastings,[133] the company's Governor-General, Burke, noted that 'the Company never ... made a treaty which they have not broken'[134] and that the company's aims of commerce, geared at economic profit, are irreconcilable with its responsibilities as quasi-governmental organization, requiring it to act for the welfare of the population.[135] Yet, at that time, the company was already 'too big to fail'. It received financial support and continued to function until 1874, under stricter scrutiny of a governmental board of control which was entitled to give orders.

2.2.2 Dutch East India Company
The Dutch rivals of the British East and West India, namely the Dutch East (Vereenigde Oostindische Compagnie, VOC) and West India (WIC) Companies, were established in 1602 and 1621. The constituted the international arm of the Dutch Republic. Their corporate form was closely linked to executive and quasi-governmental powers. For instance, the VOC was entitled to negotiate treaties, explore and govern new territories as part of trade expansion, develop currency, punish, and imprison perpetrators or wage war. It had 70,000 employees and signed over 500 treaties with Asian rulers. Jan Pietersz Coen (1587–1629), the chief executive of the VOC in the East Indies, already recognized the close nexus between trade and the use of force in 1614. He noted that the company cannot carry on 'trade without war' nor wage 'war without trade'.[136] It used both legal tools and pragmatism, as well as war and diplomacy to achieve its goals.

The VOC relied extensively on treaty practices to establish new alliances, trade relations, and acquire key commodities in Asian trade. Based on its commercial mandate, it sought to secure the most profitable treaty regimes. Monopoly-driven trade agreements were heavily debated inside the company, but became the 'axiom of commercial policy'.[137] The company negotiated agreements, requiring parties to

---

[132] Gregory M. Collins, 'The Limits of Mercantile Administration: Adam Smith and Edmund Burke on Britain's East India Company' (2019) 41 *Journal of the History of Economic Thought* 369–392.

[133] See Chapter 6. See also Mithi Mukherjee, 'Justice, War, and the Imperium: India and Britain in Edmund Burke's Prosecutorial Speeches in the Impeachment Trial of Warren Hastings' (2005) 23 *Law and History Review* 589–630.

[134] See Edmund Burke, Speech Fox's East India Bill (1 December 1783) 20 https://quod.lib.umich.edu/e/ecco/004807298.0001.000/1:2?rgn=div1;view=fulltext.

[135] Burke invoked notion of trust, in order to plead for greater accountability. Ibid, 8–9.

[136] Letter from Jan Pietersz Coen to the executive of the Company (27 December 1614); Justus M. van der Kroef, 'The Decline and Fall of the Dutch East India Company' (1948) 10 *The Historian* 118–134, 119.

[137] Sinappah Arasaratnam, 'Monopoly and Free Trade in Dutch-Asian Commercial Policy: Debate and Controversy within the VOC' (1973) 4 *Journal of Southeast Asian Studies* 1–15, 1.

sell their goods to the VOC in perpetuity, in return for the company's protection. These trade monopolies were combined early on with plans to create colonies of merchants and farmers, through settlers and VOC employees in order to restrict indigenous trade and the influence of competing powers, such as Great Britain or Portugal.[138] These agreements placed large areas under the exclusive control of the company and dominated trade relations in Asia, including long-distance trade between India and the Indonesian Archipelago. Many of them were 'framed in the Western European tradition of treaty making, with little or no attempt to accommodate local practices.'[139] This triggered misunderstandings, conflicting expectations, mutual recriminations, or even war in some cases.[140]

Monopolistic treaty arrangements became a key instrument to justify territorial extension. The VOC claimed the right to use force to sanction breaches of the agreements. Although some company officials remained critical of the use of violence, use of force was ultimately viewed as a necessary means to secure respect of the company and protect agreements[141] and led to expansion in the 1640s and 1650s.

The policies of the company were supported by Hugo Grotius' legal theories, who defended use of force as the *ultima ratio* method of retaliation in case of breach of contractual obligations (*pacta sunt servanda*).[142] This logic justified continued domination and colonial expansion under the banner of consent, in the Indonesian archipelago and other places:

> [T]the Company's tactics and mode of operation were to lure or pressure local rulers into treaties that were beneficial to the Company. When the former came to realise that the treaties ran contrary to their own interests, the Company could defend them on Grotian principles by claiming that they were entered into without coercion by autonomous subjects of law, and thus were legally binding and had to be observed.[143]

Territories were treated as extensions of the company's interests. The company took ownership of cultural objects in the context of military operations or retaliations. For instance, in 1691 the VOC captured sixteen Hindu temple statues as

---

[138] Ibid, 4.

[139] Leonard Andaya, 'Treaty Conceptions and Misconceptions' (1978) 134 *Bijdragen tot de Taal-, Land- en Volkenkunde* 275–295, 287–288.

[140] Ibid, 291.

[141] Arasaratnam, 'Monopoly and Free Trade in Dutch-Asian Commercial Policy', 2–3.

[142] Martine van Ittersum has argued that Grotius' arguments contributed significantly to the legitimization of Western imperialism and colonization. See Martine J. van Ittersum, *Profit and Principle: Hugo Grotius, Natural Rights Theories and the Rise of Dutch Power in the East Indies 1595-1615* (Leiden: Brill, 2006).

[143] Carl Fredrik Feddersen, *Principled Pragmatism VOC Interaction with Makassar 1637-68, and the Nature of Company Diplomacy* (Oslo: Cappelen Damm Akademisk, 2017) 75.

spoils of war in a military contest against a local ruler in Malabar on the East coast of India. These 'statues from Kerala' come into the possession of VOC governor Nicolaes Witsen (1641–1717), who had an extensive collection of 'curiosities' and auctioned them in 1728.[144]

In the war on Kandy (1761–1765) in Ceylon (Sri Lanka), the VOC pillaged the city and the temple of the king of Kandy in order to break a rebellion against the VOC, tacitly supported by the king.[145] Kandy was of key strategic importance for the company in order to retain the monopoly over trade with cinnamon. In 1765, VOC forces took jewels, textiles, and arms from the king's palace as war booty, including a blue and gold ceremonial cannon (the 'Cannon of Kandy'), bearing the symbols of the king.[146] It was later displayed in the cabinet of curiosities of the Prince of Orange and the Rijksmuseum in Amsterdam.[147] One year later, VOC forces looted objects from local rulers in Sulawesi (Indonesia).[148]

The VOC came gradually into conflict with local rules through its growing military and governmental power and its insistence in trade monopolies, and captured cultural objects in some operations as part of the effort to break local resistance. However, territorial expansion created at the same time an interest in foreign societies, which coincided with the ideas of the Enlightenment.

In 1778, VOC official Jacob Cornelis Matthieu Radermacher (1741–1783) created the Batavian Society of Arts and Sciences in Jakarta,[149] the administrative and cultural headquarters of the company in South-east Asia. The society was created as a private institution, involving VOC members. It was the first European institution of learned societies in Asia, designed to analyse the cultural and scientific aspects of the East Indies, including its society and natural environment. After the VOC was replaced by a Dutch colonial administration, the society turned into a museum. It came to play an important role in relation to cultural appropriations under Dutch colonial policy. It decided which objects should stay in the colony and which objects should be moved to the metropolis.[150] It thereby established an additional level of decision-making, which ensured that certain artefacts remained in Indonesia.

---

[144] See Van Beurden, *Treasures in Trusted Hands*, 58.

[145] See J. C. Nierstrasz, *In the Shadow of the Company: The VOC (Dutch East India Company) and Its Servants in the Period of Its Decline (1740-1796)* (PhD, Leiden, 2008) 71–77.

[146] Van Beurden argues that it was already established in the 1970s that the cannon constitutes 'a fairly clear-cut case of war booty'; see Van Beurden, *Inconvenient Heritage*, 61.

[147] Van Beurden, *Treasures in Trusted Hands*, 58. Sri Lanka has requested the return of the cannon since 1980. In July 2023, the Rijksmuseum agreed to return it as part of its first colonial returns to the country, along with five other objects taken by the VOC in the plunder of Kandy.

[148] Ibid.

[149] Peter Boomgaard, 'The Making and Unmaking of Tropical Science: Dutch Research on Indonesia, 1600-2000' (2006) 162 *Bijdragen tot de Taal-, Land- en Volkenkunde* 191–217.

[150] Van Beurden, *Inconvenient Heritage*, 61. Van Beurden, *Treasures in Trusted Hands*, 65, 78.

2.3 Missionary 'collecting' and traders and explorers

The acquisition of cultural objects by soldiers and trade companies was complemented by the increase of missionaries and priests, which followed and supported
trade and territorial expansion. The attitude towards cultural objects differed. In
some cases, missionaries shared an interest in the welfare of the indigenous people
and their culture. In other cases, they treated them as 'heathen' objects. For example, missionaries played a key role in the destruction of Maya culture. They destroyed manuscripts and religious symbols. The ambivalent attitudes are reflected
in the practices of Spanish bishop Diego de Landa Calderón (1524–1579). He me-
ticulously studied Mayan scripts and culture, but qualified Maya codices as proof
of diabolical practices and burnt many of them in order to combat idolatry. He
wrote in his *Relacíon de las Cosas de Yucatan* (*Relation on the Incidents of Yucatan*):

> We found a large number of books in these characters and, as they contained
> nothing in which were not to be seen as superstition and lies of the devil, we
> burned them all, which they (the Maya) regretted to an amazing degree, and
> which caused them much affliction.[151]

Only four of them were spared, and ultimately found their way to different places
in Europe: the Dresden Codex, the Madrid Codex, the Paris Codex, and the
Grolier Codex.

A similar tension is reflected in the collecting of missionaries in Africa. The
Catholic Church sent missionaries to the Congo from the seventeenth century.
They collected indigenous objects in order to understand native cultures and explore how they could be converted to Christianity. Some indigenous objects were
destroyed as a 'sort of rite of passage'.[152] Others were preserved and taken in order
to study and lecture on cultures in Africa. In this way, some of 'the earliest African
art collections in America' emerged as a byproduct of missionary collecting.[153]

Similarly, traders and explorers collected souvenirs and curiosities wherever
they went. They acquired objects through purchase, exchange, or mere taking. This
type of collection was not systematic, i.e. geared at acquiring 'either representative samples of a totality or artifacts of particular kind'.[154] The collection of ethnographic objects was mostly driven by curiosity, fascination with newly encountered
people, or the social prestige associated with objects from distant land and cultures
in European elites. As Alexandra Sauvage has noted:

---

[151] See Inga Clendinnen, *Ambivalent Conquests: Maya and Spaniard in Yucatan, 1517-1570*
(Cambridge: Cambridge University Press, 2nd edn, 2003) 70.
[152] Raymond Corbey, *Tribal Art Traffic: A Chronicle of Taste, Trade and Desire in Colonial and Post-
Colonial Times* (Amsterdam: Royal Tropical Institute, 2000) 65.
[153] Mary Rhoads Martin, *Legal Issues in African Art* (PhD, University of Iowa, 2010) 43.
[154] Thomas, *Entangled Objects*, 138. They qualified artefacts as 'curios'.

[T]he European aristocracy developed a taste for the art of collecting objects that would glorify their military career and give them social prestige. Collected objects were 'curiosities' because they came from geographically distant territories ... cabinets of curiosities mixed hundreds, or thousands of objects, that came to be classified in three sections: naturalia (with animal, vegetal and mineral elements), artificialia (creations of Western man, such as paintings, weapons, astrolabes and telescopes) and exoticas (anything that came from faraway lands, either natural or manufactured, and that was perceived as uncanny or bizarre by the European eye).[155]

This is well illustrated by some of the objects collected by the VOC, which found their way initially into such 'cabinets of curiosities'.

2.4   Gifts

Other objects were acquired as gifts. Gift exchange was common in South-east Asia. VOC officials often offered gifts to local rulers as an investment into future relations, and received gifts in return. For example, Dutch forces received indigenous arms from Indonesian rulers, in exchange for presents from Dutch royalty.[156] Missionaries sometimes claimed to receive objects 'in exchange for presents'.[157] In other cases, gifts were offered to avoid conquest or retaliation. As highlighted earlier, Atzec and Inca rulers offered treasures to Spanish *conquistadores* in order to avoid occupation or pay ransom. For instance, Montezuma offered his welcome treasures to Cortés as a form of bribe, namely as a means to drive him away. Gift exchange was thus not always based on free and voluntary conduct.

3 The systematization of collection between the eighteenth and the mid-nineteenth centuries

Between the late-eighteenth century and the mid-nineteenth century, collection of artefacts gained a new dimension through the birth and identity politics of the modern nation state in Europe, explorations of Asia, Pacific, and North America,

---

[155] Alexandra Sauvage, 'To Be or not to Be Colonial: Museums Facing their Exhibitions' (2010) 6 *Culturales* 97–116, 102–103.

[156] Van Beurden, *Treasures in Trusted Hands*, 56.

[157] See Wastiau, 'The Legacy of Collecting', 468, citing a missionary statement from the record of the Tervuren Museum: 'Here is a little information about the conditions of acquisition of the masks. I never raid and comb out villages and I do not buy them either while travelling, because I do not want to be burdened by these cumbersome and generally dirty objects, but they are brought to me in exchange for presents ... The carving I recently acquired was only given up to me after long palavers.'

the establishment of large museum collections,[158] and the scientific organization of world knowledge. Treatment of cultural objects was marked by divides between rising cultural nationalism in European societies, on the one hand, and the othering of non-Western cultures, on the other. Practices of collecting during eighteenth century explorations focused on economically valuable objects and cultural 'curiosities'. They became more systematically organized in the nineteenth century. Indeed, nineteenth century nationalism was related to imagined communities and identities.[159] Collecting and displaying objects were part of social imagination.[160] They were partly driven by the urge of societies to portray themselves in the legacy of great ancient traditions.

3.1 Imperial collecting between cultural nationalism and cultural elevation

In Europe, material culture came to be seen as an important element of national identity. European nations celebrated cultural heritage as a national legacy. The need to collect, preserve, and conserve heritage, including ancient and own histories, was regarded as an important role of the state, and a means to demonstrate civilization and national progress. Access was extended beyond upper levels of society. States presented material remains of their ancestors in national museums. Museums gained a broader public role. They were seen as sites to promote public education and good citizenship.[161] For instance, the British Museum became publicly accessible in 1759.[162] The Louvre opened its doors to the public in 1793.

This development influenced collection of artefacts at the beginning of the nineteenth century. It was marked by 'tensions between Enlightenment and Romanticism, between universalism and particularities, between classifications and feelings, and European nationalism paired with a strong political and military involvement in non-European regions'.[163] Imperial collecting had a double foundation. It was associated with political rationales and national glory, and at the same time inspired by ideas that rational and scientific study of objects would bring

---

[158] Tony Bennett, *The Birth of the Museum: History, Theory, Politics* (London: Routledge, 1995); Tony Bennett, *Pasts Beyond Memory: Evolution, Museums, Colonialism* (London: Routledge, 2004).

[159] Benedict Anderson, *Imagined Communities: Reflections on the Origin and Spread of Nationalism* (London, New York: Verso, 2006).

[160] Marieke Bloembergen and Martijn Eickhoff, 'A Wind of Change on Java's Ruined Temples' (2013) 128 *BMGN: Low Countries Historical Review* 81–104, 83.

[161] Sauvage, 'To Be or not to Be Colonial', 107.

[162] The museum was established in 1753. On the broader trend across Europe, see Staffan Lundén, *Displaying Loot: The Benin Objects and the British Museum* (Gothenburg: Gothenburg Archaeological Theses, 2016) 57.

[163] Pieter ter Keurs, 'Agency, Prestige and Politics: Dutch Collecting Abroad and Local Responses' in Sarah Byrne and others (eds.), *Unpacking the Collection: One World Archaeology* (New York: Springer, 2011) 165–182, 169.

human progress. European powers competed for influence and prestige, based on ideas of progress and romantic nostalgia. This competition enhanced the incentive to justify the acquisition abroad through political or military means and coincided with national interests in justifying colonial expansion. Early nineteenth-century nationalism stimulated the collection of objects and trophies from outside Europe, based on strife for power and prestige, economic benefit, and ownership over the origins of European culture.[164] The museum became a 'social tool' to promote the cultural identity of the 'modern West'.[165]

The dual focus, i.e. the pride and glory associated with cultural collection, and the interest in other cultures, also for purposes of colonial administration, transformed approaches to collection of colonial artefacts and justification of their taking. While war-related and coercive justifications persisted, they were complemented by additional rationales, such as 'rescue' or preservation of objects or 'scientific' objectives. Archeological and anthropological methods were used to study human remains and cultural objects in colonial societies, including indigenous populations.

Collecting was part of or closely associated with the colonial structures that suppressed domestic societies through violence.[166] Colonized peoples were defined in binary opposition to advanced Western cultures, namely as exotic and inferior societies, which reflect 'primitive' stages of European cultural development in need of protection and development.[167] Such narratives provided the gateway for 'salvage' narratives, i.e. the idea to protect objects from decline or neglect by natives,[168] or pseudo-scientific justifications of takings by colonial agents, explorers, or professionals.

In settler colonial contexts, states started to pay attention to indigenous cultures. For example, US authorities collected and exhibited Native American artefacts at the beginning of the nineteenth century. Australian museums began to collect artefacts of indigenous peoples as of 1830.[169] European colonial powers started to establish museums in Asia and Africa throughout the eighteenth and nineteenth centuries. For instance, in 1784, the British East India Company created the Asiatic Society in Kolkata. It opened a museum in 1814, carrying manuscripts, sculptures, or paintings. In some contexts, colonial powers introduced specific legislation to protect native heritage against collection by soldiers, scientists, or competing

---

[164] Ibid, 181.
[165] Sauvage, 'To Be or not to Be Colonial', 99.
[166] See Pieter ter Keurs (ed.), *Colonial Collections Revisited* (Leiden: CNWS Publications 2007).
[167] Tulaar Sudarmardi, *Between Colonial Legacies and Grassroots Movements: Exploring Cultural Heritage Practice in the Ngadha and Manggarai Region of Flores* (PhD, University of Amsterdam, 2014) 35.
[168] See also Marieke Bloembergen and Martijn Eickhoff, *The Politics of Heritage in Indonesia* (Cambridge: Cambridge University Press, 2020) 34.
[169] Sudarmardi, *Between Colonial Legacies and Grassroots Movements*, 34.

powers. Some items were sent to specialized museums in the metropolis, rather than cabinets of rarities.

These developments are well reflected by the transformation of the Batavian Society for Arts and Sciences. It became a symbol of the self-legitimation of colonial rule through preservation of Hindu or Buddhist antiquities It turned into a space for the search, collection, and preservation of artefacts in the Dutch East Indies. In 1822, Dutch Governor-General Godert van der Capellen (1778–1848) established a commission which was designed to search, collect, and store cultural artefacts and prevent plunder by Chinese or local agents.[170] Experts and government officials were specifically instructed by decree actively to search for important cultural objects, such as Javanese artefacts.[171] They were first examined and then either retained by the Museum of the Batavian Society or shipped to the Netherlands for inclusion in the Dutch national collection.[172] Removal was justified by the interest in the preservation of objects or better conditions of guardianship in the metropolis. In 1840, the Dutch governor declared indigenous temples and artefacts as public property of the colonial power and made removals of antiquities subject to government approval.[173] This decree prevented private collectors or soldiers from exporting antiquities.[174] As Marieke Bloembergen and Martijn Eickhoff have argued, this branding of cultural artefacts as 'national property' marked a key moment for the legitimation of colonial identity through preservation of Java's cultural treasures: 'Care for archaeological sites ... was officially transformed from a state-regulated civil responsibility to an obligation of the –internally expanding – colonial state itself that aimed to prevent interference from other colonial powers.'[175]

In this way, Dutch colonial authorities gained monopoly power of cultural heritage in the East Indies, and expanded the practices of VOC that had protected the Dutch monopoly over trade. Later, the Batavian Society sent agents to accompany military expeditions throughout the archipelago against indigenous kingdoms and polities in order to search and treasures in Aceh, Lombok (1894),[176] and Bali (1906–1908).[177] The museum thus became both an object and agent of colonial collecting.

---

[170] Bloembergen and Eickhoff, *The Politics of Heritage in Indonesia*, 38–39.

[171] Lunsingh Scheurleer, 'Collecting Javanese Antiquities. The Appropriation of a Newly Discovered Hindu-Buddhist Civilization' in Ter Keurs, *Colonial Collections Revisited* 71–114.

[172] A famous example of these are the three Singasari statues, which were sent to the Netherlands in 1819 or the statue of the Buddhist goddess Prajnaparamita, which was sent in 1823.

[173] Van Beurden, *Treasures in Trusted Hands*, 78.

[174] Ter Keurs, 'Collecting in the Colony', 154. External agents had already started to collect Hindu-Buddhist statues before the decree.

[175] Bloembergen and Eickhoff, *The Politics of Heritage in Indonesia*, 42.

[176] See Chapter 3.

[177] Jos van Beurden, *The Return of Cultural and Historical Treasures: The Case of the Netherlands* (Tropenmuseum: KIT Publishers, 2011) 31.

3.2 The quest for prestige and trophy: Objects acquired through military operations and occupation

From the end of the eighteenth century to the mid-nineteenth century, military power or colonial occupation played an important role in the acquisition of artefacts. Many objects were collected through or as a result of coercive power. European nationalism led to an increased interest in cultural artefacts. Domination of other kingdoms or non-Western societies was seen as a form of power and glory, or associated with benefits and progress. Cultural objects were not only 'grabbed' or taken as war booty as a byproduct or consequence of conquest or colonial expansion, but sometimes actively targeted and pursued in the national interest, because of their prestige and economic or symbolic value.

3.2.1 French/British acquisition of the Rosetta stone in Egypt (1799–1801)

The close interplay between nationalism, conquest, and taking cultural artefacts in order to civilize 'others' is reflected in the story of the famous Rosetta stone.[178] The stone is an Egyptian relic. It contains a bilateral decree by Egyptian priests, written in Egyptian and Greek, in honour of the succession of Ptolemy V. Its dual inscription was essential to decipher Egyptian hieroglyphics. The stone was initially public property of Egypt, which was a province of the Ottoman Empire at the time. It was discovered and taken by Napoleon during the French occupation of Egypt in 1798.[179]

Napoleon's conquest of Egypt had strong synergies with colonial missions of the nineteenth century. It was driven by a mix of imperial rationales and civilizing motives, i.e. the idea to rewrite the history of Ancient Egypt through Western civilization. Napoleon defended the military expedition inter alia as an attempt 'to free Egypt from oppressive Ottoman rule'.[180] He brought 165 scholars and scientists with him in order to document cultural history and introduce modern Western science in Egypt. Egyptian antiquities were desired objects. French forces retrieved the Rosetta stone on 15 July 1799 at a fort near the Egyptian port of el-Rashid (ancient Rosetta), where it was built into an old wall. The French commander, Lieutenant Pierre-Francois Bouchard (1772–1832), recognized the historical significance and confiscated the stone. It was brought to the Institut d'Egypte in Cairo, which was established by Napoleon to study ancient Egyptian arts and sciences and select artefacts for transport from Egypt to France. The discovery was reported in the *Courier of Egypt*, the military journal of the French expedition, in 1799. It

---

[178] Jonathan Downs, *Discovery at Rosetta: The Stone that Unlocked the Mysteries of Ancient Egypt* (London: Constable, 2008) 210–215; Josh Shuart, 'Is All Pharoah in Love and War: The British Museum's Title to the Rosetta Stone and the Sphinx's Beard' (2004) 52 *University of Kansas Law Review* 667–720.

[179] Dalia N. Osman, 'Occupier's Title to Cultural Property: Nineteenth-Century Removal of Egyptian Artifacts' (1999) 37 *Columbia Journal of Transnational Law* 969–1002.

[180] John Alan Cohan, 'An Examination of Archaeological Ethics and the Repatriation Movement Respecting Cultural Property (Part Two) (2004) 28 *Environs* 4–112, 15.

stated that 'the stone offers great interest for the study of hieroglyphic characters' and may even provide 'the key' to their understanding.[181] The removal highlights the selective application of cultural protections to non-European peoples. The taking marked an illegitimate taking of cultural property,[182] disguised by rationales of military authority and purposes of study and conservation.

After the defeat of French troops in 1801 by British and Ottoman forces, the British Empire claimed the Rosetta stone and other Egyptian artefacts as war booty in a treaty of surrender. British agents were expressly instructed to seize the Egyptian antiquities captured by Napoleon. French General Abdallah Jacques de Menou (1750–1810) argued that France should be entitled to retain monuments and works of art acquired by the Commission of Sciences and Arts. However, the Capitulation Treaty of Alexandria required France to forfeit to England 'all the curiosities, natural and artificial, collected [in Egypt] by the French Institute'.[183] It stated that all antiquities collected by France constitute public property and shall be 'subject to the disposal of the generals of the combined army'.[184] Menou and French officers were initially reluctant to transfer the stone. There are conflicting accounts of how it was taken. In a letter to the Society of Antiquaries from 1910, Colonel Tomkyns Hilgrove Turner (1766–1843) claimed that he seized it from Menou and carried it away with a gun-carriage ('devil-cart').[185] Edward Daniel Clarke (1769–1822) presented a less militaristic account, arguing that the stone was secretly surrendered by a French officer and a member of the Institute to a British delegation, including Richard William Hamilton, Lord Elgin's private secretary, in a warehouse in Alexandria, which hosted Menou's belongings.[186] This account portrayed the handover almost as an act of salvage from violence.

The stone turned from a French into a British trophy. It was transported to England by boat. Turner qualified it as a 'proud trophy of the war', almost a *spolia optima*, not 'plundered from defenseless inhabitants, but honourably acquired by the fortune of war'.[187] In 1802, King George III donated the stone to the British Museum. Egypt was not given any say in this process. French scholars remained opposed to the transfer of objects to their colonial rival. They were allowed to retain smaller objects, such as papyri.

---

[181] *Courier de l'Egypte*, No. 37 (15 September 1799) 3–4.

[182] Cohan, 'An Examination of Archaeological Ethics and the Repatriation Movement Respecting Cultural Property', 18–19. See also Van Beurden, *Treasures in Trusted Hands*, 70 ('It can be defined as war booty because of the involvement of the French army and because the British captured many treasures from the French, thus definitely turning them into war booty').

[183] Articles of Capitulation of Alexandria, Article XVI (1801) in Robert Wilson, *History of the British Expedition to Egypt* (London: Egerton, 1803) 346–353.

[184] Ibid.

[185] Letter dated 30 May 1810 from Colonel Tomkyns Hilgrove Turner to Nicholas Carlisle, Secretary to the Society of Antiquaries, 'An Account of the Rosetta Stone in Society of Antiquaries' (1812) 27 *Archaeologia* 212–214.

[186] Jonathan Downs, 'Romancing the Stone' (2006) 56 *History Today* 48–54.

[187] Letter dated 30 May 1810, from Turner to Nicholas Carlisle, 213–214.

The legal evaluation of the taking remains contested. Some argue that the seizure was at best morally wrong.[188] Others question whether the persons who represented Egypt at the time of the Capitulation Treaty, namely Osman Bey, the Ottoman provincial governor, and Hassan Kapudan Pasha, the commander of forces in Alexandria, had the right to surrender Egyptian antiquities or whether they did so compelled by force.[189] Egyptologist Monica Hanna has challenged British ownership on the basis that 'the Ottoman empire', which formed part of the 'combined army', never 'gave up' its 'share of the claim' under Article 16 of the Treaty of Alexandria.[190]

Napoleon's crusade of Egypt triggered a race for Egyptian culture in the early nineteenth century and promoted the emergence of Egyptology as a scientific discipline.[191] Through the colonial encounter and its scientific decoding, the stone has become part of overlapping cultural identities.[192] Egyptian voices, such as Zahi Hawass, former Secretary General of the Supreme Council of Antiquities in Egypt, have requested its return.

3.2.2 Looting of the palace of the Sultan of Yogyakarta (1812) and Raffles' Java collection

The British interregnum of the Dutch East Indies between 1811 and 1816 under the leadership of British Lieutenant-Governor Thomas Stamford Raffles, the founder of modern-day Singapore,[193] illustrates the interrelation between coercion, appreciation of past cultures, and colonial politics at the beginning of the nineteenth century.

Raffles sought to consolidate British power in Java after the victory of British–Indian forces over Dutch rulers in 1811. In June 1812, he conquered the palace of Sultan Hamengkubuwono II in Yogyakarta (the *kraton* of Yogyakarta) in order to expand the rule of the East India Company in Java.[194] The sultan counted among the most influential rulers in Indonesia. Raffles received word of a potential plot, by which the ruler of Surakarta sought to persuade Sultan Hamengkubuwono II to rise against British rule. He used this argument to promote 'regime change'. He argued that the sultan had 'shown himself unworthy of the confidence of the British Government and unfit to be further entrusted with the administration delegated to

---

[188] See Robertson, *Who Owns History?*, 180.

[189] Jonathan Downs, 'Questioning Britain's Legal Title to the Rosetta Stone' (4 April 2010) https://jdownsrosetta.wordpress.com/2010/04/04/questioning-britains-legal-title-to-the-rosetta-stone/.

[190] Monica Hanna, 'The Rosetta Stone Betrayal and the West's Obsession with Ancient Egypt' *The National News* (2 September 2022).

[191] Richard Carrott, *The Egyptian Revival: Its Sources, Monuments, and Meaning 1808–1858* (Berkeley: University of California Press, 1978); Melanie Byrd, *The Napoleonic Institute of Egypt* (PhD, Florida State University, 1992) 262.

[192] Downs, *Discovery at Rosetta*, 215 ('erected by the priests of the pharaoh, discovered by French savants, and preserved by British scholars, the Rosetta Stone unites two of the elder states of Europe with the most ancient of western civilizations').

[193] On Raffle's policies on Java, see John Bastin, 'Raffles and British Policy in the Indian Archipelago, 1811-1816' (1954) 27 *Journal of the Malayan Branch of the Royal Asiatic Society* 84–119.

[194] Tim Hannigan, *Raffles and the British Invasion of Java* (Singapore: Monsoon Books, 2012).

him'.[195] He defeated the sultan in the conquest of Yogyakarta in 1812. British and Indian soldiers plundered royal treasuries and manuscripts, including court archives and literary works. They forced the sultan and his followers to hand over their personal jewel encrusted daggers (*kris*) and gold ornaments.

Raffles justified the seizure and distribution of war booty in a communication to Lord Minton, the Governor-General of India, based on a similar practices in India. He stated:

> The universal opinion [has been] that in places carried by assault, the army was entitled to make an immediate distribution of treasure and jewels.[196]
>
> The Craton [kraton] having fallen by assault, it was impracticable to make any provision for Government to [re]cover the expences [sic] of the undertaking; consequently, the whole plunder became Prize to the Army. It is considerable, but it could not have fallen into better hands. They richly deserved what they got.[197]

Some of the treasures and the dagger of the sultan were sent to Calcutta in order to demonstrate the submission of Java to British rule. The dethroned sultan was sent into exile in Penang and the newly designed Sultan, Hamengkubuwono III, was required to acknowledge the 'supremacy of the British Government over the whole Island of Java' in a treaty.[198] Indonesian resistance continued after the British return of Java to Dutch rule in the Java wars of the 1820s under the leadership of Prince Diponegoro, who had been present during the looting.

The looting of the palace of the sultan contrasted with Raffles' general commitment to make preservation of cultural artefacts part of British governance policy. He was both a product of the Enlightenment and a cultural imperialist. His approach to collection went beyond the collection of curiosities. He shared an appreciation for the history and culture of Java, wrote a book on the history of Java in 1817, drawing on earlier works by a naturalist, and started to collect artefacts, long before he establishment of ethnographic museums in the 1830s.[199] He instructed British and Dutch experts to study archeological sites and objects and reanimated the Batavian Society. He believed that Java was once a great civilization which could prosper again under British rule.[200]

---

[195] Peter Carey, *The British in Java, 1811–1816: A Javanese Account* (Oxford: Oxford University Press, 1992) 416, note 92.

[196] Peter Carey, *The Power of Prophecy: Prince Dipanagara and the End of an Old Order in Java, 1785–1855* (Leiden: Brill, 2007) 347.

[197] Ibid, 348.

[198] Tim Hannigan, 'The Red-Coat Conquest of Yogyakarta' *Jakarta Globe* (21 June 2012) http://tahannigan.blogspot.com/2013/05/the-british-assault-on-yogyakarta-in.html.

[199] Thomas Stamford Raffles, *The History of Java* (London: Black, Parbury and Allen, 1817).

[200] See Alexandra Green, 'Raffles' Collections from Java: European Evidence of Civilization' (2 February 2019) https://www.nhb.gov.sg/acm/whats-on/lectures/2feb2019_green ('the British could help recover Java's lost past and thereby improve its future').

Under his governance, preservation and protection of cultural objects gained an important political dimension. Raffles actively called for the conservation and collection of Javanese antiquities in order to legitimize British rule over the previous misrule by the VOC and the governance by local rulers which contributed to the decay of Java's cultural treasures.[201] His collection was thus driven by civilizatory ideas, influenced by theories of the Enlightenment,[202] and colonial logics of emancipation. He thought that British control over Java would add to the prestige and glory of the Empire. He started collecting artefacts in order to convince politicians in the metropole that it was worth it to maintain British rule and administer the island as a British protectorate.[203] He collected a large amount artefacts, including 130 masks, sculptures, and puppets, some of which go back to court cultures from the seventh century. They were later transferred to the Indian museum in Calcutta and the British Museum. A ship with his manuscripts and notes on the collection sank in 1824. It is thus not entirely clear how many of his artefacts were looted and how many were 'collected'.[204]

3.2.3 The acquisition of the Koh-i-Noor (1849): symbol of power and colonial superiority

The acquisition of the famous Koh-i-Noor diamond is a paradigm example of the close nexus between military submission, cultural takings, and the strife for power and prestige.[205] It was transferred from the Maharaja of Lahore to the Queen by a treaty-forced cession.[206] It turned from an object of violence into an object representing the glory of the Empire.[207]

The diamond has a long cultural history as an emblem of power, passing between dynasties of rulers in South-east Asia.[208] Its name may be traced back to

---

[201] Bloembergen and Eickhoff, *The Politics of Heritage in Indonesia*, 36

[202] See British Museum, 'Sir Thomas Stamford Raffles' https://www.britishmuseum.org/about-us/british-museum-story/people-behind-collection/sir-thomas-stamford-raffles ('The objects instead show that Raffles chose items that were exotic, but which could be considered indicative of a high level of civilisation according to European standards').

[203] See British Museum press release, 'Sir Stamford Raffles: Collecting in Southeast Asia 1811-1824' (2019) https://www.britishmuseum.org/sites/default/files/2019-11/Raffles-press-release.pdf ('He acquired objects to show his European audience that Javanese society was worth colonising').

[204] British Museum, Sir Thomas Stamford Raffles' ('There has been a popular perception that Raffles' theatrical collections were taken from the central Javanese court of Yogyakarta which was attacked by the British on Raffles' orders in 1812. Stylistic analyses show that most of the puppets and musical instruments were produced elsewhere, particularly the north coast of Java where Raffles was particularly friendly with the courts').

[205] See Vivek K. Hatti, 'India's Right to Reclaim Cultural and Art Treasures from Britain under International Law' (2000) 32 *George Washington Journal of International Law and Economics* 465–496; Saby Ghoshray, 'Repatriation of the Kohinoor Diamond: Expanding the Legal Paradigm for Cultural Heritage' (2007) *31 Fordham International Law Journal* 741–780.

[206] Ghoshray, 'Repatriation of the Kohinoor Diamond', 751 ('History, therefore, leaves no doubt that the Kohinoor was not a generous gift, but rather a spoil of war handed over by a boy king to his conqueror, Queen Victoria').

[207] Danielle C. Kinsey, 'Empire, Diamonds, and the Performance of British Material Culture' (2009) 48 *Journal of British Studies* 391–419, 419.

[208] Jeanette Greenfield, *The Return of Cultural Treasures* (New York: Cambridge University Press, 1989) 148.

Nader Shah Afshar (1688–1747), Shah of Persia from 1736 to 1747, who conquered Delhi in 1739 and looted the stone from the Mughal Empire where it formed part of a 'Peacock Throne' of the Mughals. The shah reportedly said 'Koh-i-Noor!' ('Mountain of Light') when he saw the stone. It returned to India in 1813, when Afghan Sultan Shuja Shah Abdali Durrani (1785–1842), ruler of the Durrani Empire, handed it over to Maharaja Ranjit Singh (1780–1839), the leader of the Sikh empire, in return for sanctuary. Singh wore the diamond as jewelry and used it in official meetings, including encounters with European rulers. It was disputed whether it constituted private or public property.

The gemstone was acquired by Britain after the end of the Second Anglo-Sikh War (1848–1849), when British and Bengal forces of the East India Company annexed Punjab and defeated the Sikh army at the battle of Battle of Gujrat (1849), which opposed company rule. Following the victory, the company signed the Treaty of Lahore on 29 March 1849 with Maharaja Duleep Singh (1838–1893), the ten-year-old grandson of Maharaja Ranjit Singh, who was in line for the throne. The treaty was meant to legitimize the annexation. The young Maharaja resigned 'for himself, his heirs, and his successors all right, title, and claim to the sovereignty of the Punjab, or to any sovereign power whatever'.[209] The diamond was claimed as 'reparation' for the expenses occurred by the company in the Anglo-Sikh War. The treaty stated that '[a]ll the property of the State, of whatever description and Chapter wheresoever found, shall be confiscated to the Honourable East India Company, in part payment of the debt due by the State of Lahore to the British Government and of the expenses of the war'.[210] Article 3 added that '[t]he gem called the Koh-i-Noor, which was taken from Shah Sooja-ool-moolk by Maharajah Runjeet Singh, shall be surrendered by the Maharajah of Lahore to the Queen of England'.[211]

It is clear from this text that the diamond was not merely a 'gift' by Maharaja Duleep Singh. The young Maharajah was compelled to give up the diamond as a result of military defeat. He later claimed that it was unjustly taken from him without compensation. The circumstances show that the British Governor-General in India, James Andrew Broun-Ramsay, the future Lord Dalhousie (1812–1860), had a specific interest in acquiring the diamond for the crown, and pushed for its handover.

Dalhousie took special measures to preserve the diamond from war booty by the East India Company. According to traditional prize procedures, the company would have taken the stone in order to sell it or share the profits with soldiers. Much to the regret of the directors of the East India Company,[212] Dalhousie initiated the

---

[209] Treaty of Lahore, Art. 1.
[210] Ibid, Art. 2.
[211] Ibid, Art. 3.
[212] This is illustrated by his letters. He wrote later: 'The Court [of the East India Company] you say, are ruffled by my having caused the Maharajah to cede to the Queen the Koh-i-noor; while the "Daily

treaty clause with Maharaja Duleep Singh in order to offer the diamond to Queen Victoria.[213]

Historically, the surrender of the diamond was more than a gesture of submission after conquest. The stone was deliberately picked by Dalhousie in light of its history and symbolism. Dalhousie did not seek to capture the diamond for economic benefit, but rather because of its prestige and glory for the British Empire,[214] namely to place 'the historical jewel of the Mogul Emperors in the Crown of his own Sovereign', as he wrote in letters.[215]

He revealed his motivation in his diaries. He stated:

> The Koh-i-Nur [sic] has ever been the symbol of conquest. The Emperor of Delhi had it in his Peacock Throne. Nadir Shah seized it by right of conquest from the Emperor. Thence it passed into the hands of the King of Kabul. While Shah Shuja ul-Mulk was king, Ranjit Singh exorted [sic] the diamond by gross violence and cruelty. And now when, as the result of unprovoked war, the British Government has conquered the kingdom of the Punjab, and has resolved to add it to the territories of the British Empire in India, I have a right to compel the Maharaja of Lahore, in token of his submission, to surrender the jewel to the Queen, that it may find its final and fitting resting-place in the crown of Britain. And there it shall shine, and shine, too, with purest ray serene. For there is not one of those who have held it since its original possessor, who can boast so just a tide to its possession as the Queen of England can claim after two bloody and unprovoked wars.[216]

The acquisition occurred at a time when the British monarchy was in search for an illustrious diamond to portray its grandeur and keep up with other monarchs in Europe (France, Russia, Portugal).[217] It may thus have been inspired by rivalry and competition among European powers.

News" and my Lord Ellenborough [Governor-General of India, 1841–44] are indignant because I did not confiscate everything to her Majesty, and censure me for leaving a Roman Pearl in the Court ... I was fully prepared to hear that the Court chafed at my not sending the diamond to them, and letting them present it to Her Majesty, They ought not to do so-they ought to enter into and cordially approve the sentiment on which I acted thus. The motive was simply this: that it was more for the honour of the Queen that the Koh-i-noor should be surrendered directly from the hand of the conquered prince into the hands of the sovereign who was his conqueror, than it should be presented to her as a gift—which is always a favour—by any joint-stock company among her subjects. So the Court ought to feel. As for their fretting and censuring, that I do not mind—so long as they do not disallow the article. I know I have acted best for the Sovereign, and for their honour, too.' See Ghoshray, 'Repatriation of the Kohinoor Diamond', 750.

[213] Kinsey, 'Empire, Diamonds, and the Performance of British Material Culture', 393.
[214] Kinsey, 'Empire, Diamonds, and the Performance of British Material Culture', 395 ('It is thus clear that what compelled to reserve the Koh-i-particular, was not its physical makeup but, rather, the stone's biography way that British conquest in India could be written').
[215] Ibid, 395.
[216] Ibid, 396.
[217] Ibid, 397.

The Koh-i-Noor was presented to the British public at the 1851 Great Exposition in London, together jewels from the Lahore treasure. The conditions of how it was obtained were concealed. It was presented as a 'gift' from Maharaja Duleep Sing to Queen Victoria.[218] The display triggered a mixed reaction by the public. It was appreciated for its historical value, rather than its ornamental beauty. Prince Albert decided to cut and restyle the stone in order to enhance its brilliancy and make it fit for representational purposes of the British monarchy. Through this transformation, Britain reappropriated the diamond. It became a contested part of the crown jewels of the British monarchy. India has requested the return of the diamond after its Independence in 1947. However, the ownership relations are complex, with claims by descendants of Maharaja Ranjit Singh and other nations. In 2023, Queen Consort Camilla decided not to wear the controversial Koh-i-Noor diamond during the coronation of King Charles III, but to be crowned with Queen Mary's crown.[219]

3.2.4 *The 'Benjarmasin Diamond' (1859): From sovereignty object to colonial burden*

The collection of the Benjarmasin diamond,[220] a 70-carat gem stone captured by the Dutch in the context of the 'wars of succession' in the Sultanate of Benjarmarsin in Borneo, shares striking parallels with the story the Koh-i-Noor. It is the Dutch equivalent of the capture of a symbol of sovereignty in a military expedition. The Dutch intervention destabilized the sultanate and consolidated Dutch rule, following the end of the reign of Sultan Adam Alwasih Billah (1786–1857) between 1825–1857.[221] The diamond was initially offered to King Willem III (1849–1890) as an ornament for the crown. It was ultimately placed in the cabinet of curiosities, polished, and cut for sale and later stored in museums. It has been officially designated as 'war booty' in the Rijksmuseum.[222]

The story of acquisition reflects the close entanglement between commercial interests and violence in the Dutch East Indies.[223] The Sultanate of Banjarmasin, located in the southern region of Borneo (Kalimantan) enjoyed strategic importance

---

[218] Ibid, 403–404.

[219] Sean Coughlan, 'Controversial Diamond Won't Be Used in Coronation' *BBC News* (14 February 2023).

[220] Caroline Drieënhuizen, 'Een "lelijk vuil ding": een diamant in het Rijksmuseum en de doorwerking van koloniaal denken' (26 September 2017) https://carolinedrieenhuizen.wordpress.com/2017/09/26/een-lelijk-vuil-ding-een-diamant-in-het-rijksmuseum-en-de-doorwerking-van-koloniaal-denken/.

[221] See Ita Syamtasiyah Ahyat, 'Politics and Economy of Banjarmasin Sultanate in the Period of Expansion of the Netherlands East Indies Government in Indonesia, 1826-1860' (2012) 3 *Tawarikh: International Journal for Historical Studies* 155–176.

[222] See Rijksmuseum, 'The Banjarmasin Diamond, anonymous, c. 1875' https://www.rijksmuseum.nl/en/collection/NG-C-2000-3.

[223] See M. Idwar Saleh, 'Agrarian Radicalism and Movements of Native Insurrection in South Kalimantan (1858-1865)' (1975) 9 *Archipel* 135–153.

for maritime commerce, the pepper trade, and mining since the seventeenth century. On 4 May 1826, Sultan Adam signed an agreement with the Dutch colonial government in Batavia. It granted the Dutch suzerainty in return for the protection of the sultanate against foreign aggression or native insurgency and annual compensation payments. The agreement also gave the government influence on decisions of royal succession. It specified that the determination of royal family successions and the designation of the local governor (the *Mangkubumi*), who acted as liaison between the sultanate and Dutch government require the approval of the Netherlands Indies.[224] The treaty thereby gave the Dutch considerable influence over the governance of the sultanate.

Dutch scientists discovered the large diamond collection of Sultan Adam during a scientific expedition in 1835. The sultan wore precious jewels and gemstones as ornaments. The treaty prerogatives gained significant importance after Sultan Adam's death on 1 November 1857. It led to a succession dispute. The sultan had originally proposed Sultan Hidayatullah II of Banjar (1822–1904), the legitimate son of Crown Prince Sultan Muda Abdurrachman, as his successor. However, in 1856, the Dutch forced Sultan Adam to recognize Sultan Tamdjid, an illegitimate son of Muda Abdurrachman, as crown prince and successor, based on military threats.[225] They favoured Sultan Tamdjid, because he was favourable to Dutch interests[226] and more likely to grant them full control over the mining regions of the sultanate.[227] Sultan Adam nominated Tamjid as successor and Hidayat as governor (*Mangkubumi*).

This designation sparked local resistance. Hidayat was backed by the aristocracy. Tamdjid lacked the support of the royal family or nobility.[228] His proposed rule was viewed with suspicion:

> The century-old belief that after the death of the 12th king of Ban jar the country would be falling into alien hands raised fear and tension among people in the rural areas. It was believed that the reigning Sultan, as illegitimate son, would bring evil and bad luck to the people and the country. All the irrational fear, rising tension and acute frustration made the situation more critical, since the enemies were the white infidels, who violated the adat, endangered religion, humiliated the beloved old king and insulted the right of the adat-chosen candidate for the throne who was only given the occupation of a Mangkubumi.[229]

---

[224] Ahyat, 'Politics and Economy of Banjarmasin Sultanate', 158.
[225] The message was conveyed through the sending of a Dutch war ship, the Admiral van Kinsbergen, to Banjamarsin. See Ahyat, 'Politics and Economy of Banjarmasin Sultanate', 167.
[226] Ibid, 164.
[227] Saleh, 'Agrarian Radicalism and Movements of Native Insurrection in South Kalimantan', 143 ('The Dutch secret aim was that in the near future, the coal area could be wholly transferred to them, as government land').
[228] Ahyat, 'Politics and Economy of Banjarmasin Sultanate', 168.
[229] Saleh, 'Agrarian Radicalism and Movements of Native Insurrection in South Kalimantan', 144.

The determination of Tamjid as successor by the Dutch authorities triggered a period of violent insurrection and power struggles between Tamjid and Hidayat, which led to a takeover of Dutch rule. Dutch forces, led by Colonel Augustus Johannes Andresen (1808–1872), entered Borneo in April 1859 and pushed Tamjid to resign in order to restore order. When Hidayat declined the offer to take over as new sultan, the Dutch abolished the Sultanate and placed the territory under control of the Dutch government in Batavia, through a decree issued on 17 December 1859 and a proclamation of 11 June 1860. They also confiscated the sultan's wealth and treasures, including the 70-carat gemstone.[230] It was called the 'Banjarmasin' diamond. The stones were declared to be part of Dutch state property. These confiscations had important symbolic meaning. Not only did they remove personal regalia, but they also deprived local rulers of their sovereign power, identity, or legitimacy.

The Batavia society decided which pieces of the treasure should be retained in Indonesia or sent to the Netherlands. The diamond was perceived as a symbol of sovereignty and sent to the Netherlands in 1862. Like the Koh-i-Noor, it was meant to became a royal object in its new context, namely a gift for King William III. However, the stone turned out to be far less popular than assumed. The king refused to accept it, probably in light of the high costs associated with its cutting and polishing. The Dutch parliamentarian Fransen van de Putte described the diamond as an 'ugly dirty thing' that needs to be 'cleaned up'.[231] The Dutch museum of natural history refused to exhibit it. The Minister of Colonies decided to have it cut in order to sell it as a commercial object. The stone was transformed into a shaped 36-carat diamond. But it did not attract sufficient interest from buyers. The resized diamond was then offered to the Rijksmuseum as a symbol of the subjugation of the Banjarmasin empire. The museum remained initially reluctant to accept the diamond, because it had lost some of its historical significance through the process of transformation. In 1902, the stone entered the collection of the museum, as a permanent loan from the Minister of the Colonies, without official registration in the inventory. It was exhibited in 1937, together with the Lombok treasures, as a national trophy, i.e. as a reminder of the glory of Dutch military history and colonial power relations.[232] In 2021, the Dutch Advisory Committee on the National Policy Framework for Colonial Collections named the diamond as a primary example of involuntarily lost cultural heritage, which should be returned unconditionally.[233]

---

[230] Willem Adriaan Rees, *De Bandjermasinsche Krijg van 1859–1863: Nader toegelicht* (Arnheim: D. A. Thieme, 1867) 35; Drieënhuizen, 'Een "lelijk vuil ding"'.

[231] Drieënhuizen, 'Een "lelijk vuil ding"'.

[232] Ibid.

[233] Advisory Committee on the National Policy Framework for Colonial Collections, *Guidance on the Way Forward for Colonial Collections* (The Hague: Council for Culture, 2021) 2, 55.

3.3 Imperial collecting to care and preserve: Semi-public, semi-private acquisition in the service of exploration and civilization

The context of the Enlightenment and the birth of modern sciences also influenced other modes of collecting. Colonial officials, private collectors, and experts joined forces or built networks to search for antiquities and ethnographic objects. Some of them started as 'private' activities before they received formal backing by ruling authorities. Colonial administrations began to organize and support semi-private, semi-public expeditions in order to explore domestic cultures and legitimate their own presence beyond commercial or war-related rationales. Missionaries increased their presence in colonial territories in the process of colonial extension.

Collecting was driven by a mix of considerations: quest for knowledge and understanding of foreign cultures, curiosity regarding ancient civilizations, the desire to collect, preserve, or own objects and civilizing motives, legitimating colonial authority, or demonstrating superiority of rule or faith. Heroic and paternalistic justifications for the collection of objects were invoked more openly. It became popular to argue that colonial agents are better equipped than local authorities to care for or preserve ancient cultural heritage. This 'rescue narrative' was grounded in distrust of local rulers or other colonial powers, and the need for legitimation of the colonial enterprise at home and abroad.

3.3.1 *Cook's voyages/Gweagal shield*

In the eighteenth century, collection of cultural objects expanded through maritime and land exploration. The voyages of James Cook are an early example of semi-private, semi-public collection during the 'formative' stage in history. Cook himself represents the archetype of the European fascination with discovery, exploration, and exoticism. His voyages were officially carried out to map and explore the world, but laid the basis for the colonization of Australia and the Pacific.[234] Cook was charged to observe the transit of the planet Venus at Tahiti in his first voyage (1768–1771), to search for the 'southern continent in the second (1772–1775), and to look for the Northwest Passage in the third (1776–1780). During his travels, he collected more than 2,000 ethnographic and natural objects and documented many of the traditions and ancestral ways of life of indigenous peoples. Some were acquired through gift exchange and genuine transactions; others involved unilateral appropriation or even violence. The objects collected during the voyages preceded the birth of anthropology. Many of them were later incorporated into ethnographic museums. Important collections gathered by members of Cook's

---

[234] Nicholas Thomas and others, *Artefacts of Encounter: Cook's Voyages, Colonial Collecting and Museum Histories* (Dunedin: Ottago University Press, 2016); Wilfred Shawcross, 'The Cambridge University Collection of Maori Artefacts, Made on Cook's First Voyage' (1970) 79 *Journal of the Polynesian Society* 305–348.

explorations, such as those by botanist Joseph Banks (1743–1820)[235] or naturalist Johann Reinhold Forster (1729–1798) and his son Georg Forster (1754–1794) laid the foundations for the emergence of new scientific disciplines. The British Museum started to display ethnographic objects representing material cultures of the Pacific in a systematic fashion after Cook's third voyage.

In Europe, Cook was celebrated as an explorer, who mapped the world in cartographic terms and gathered evidence and knowledge of previously unknown cultures. However, his travels and encounters also laid the foundations for the extension of empire and new forms of settler colonialism. Encounters with indigenous cultures ranged from peaceful reception, active local interest in exchange, or even extended relationships with local communities, leading to acquisition of Tahitian and Māori artefacts,[236] to clashes and opposition, such as the violent encounter with the Gweagal people in Australia. During his 1770 expedition to Australia, Cook collected a number of aboriginal artefacts and cultural heritage. Afterwards, many of the objects collected became symbols of national history and identity and showcased Britain's role on the world stage. The stories or romanticized portrayals of Cook's encounters with indigenous people opened the path for dispossession or colonization.

This tension is represented by the dispute over the 'shield of the Gweagal people',[237] currently held in the British Museum. It has become a symbol of indigenous resistance to encounters with Cook, namely as a witness to acts of violence in the first contacts between Cook and aboriginal Australians. The shield is made out of wood from a red mangrove tree, found in Australia at the time, and it carries a hole. The shield's provenance and its violent acquisition remain contested.[238] It is undoubtedly a 'rare, early example and undoubtedly a highly significant expression of the heritage of the particular Aboriginal groups concerned'.[239] One theory is that it was taken by Cook and his crew in his encounter with Aboriginal Gweagal people in Botany Bay on the south-east coast of Australia in 1770. Entries in the journals of Cook and his botanist James Banks describe an incident in which Cook opened fire on two Gweagal men, who sought to prevent his landing in Botany Bay. One of the men grabbed a shield in his defence.[240] The museum

---

[235] Neil Chambers, 'Joseph Banks, the British Museum and Collections in the Age of Empire' in R. G. W. Anderson and others (eds), *Enlightening the British: Knowledge, Discovery and the Museum in the Eighteenth Century* (London: British Museum Press, 2003) 99–112.

[236] Nicholas Thomas, 'A Case of Identity: The Artefacts of the 1770 Kamay (Botany Bay) Encounter (2018) 49 *Australian Historical Studies* 4–27, 13.

[237] Katrina Schlunke, 'One Strange Colonial Thing: Material Remembering and the Bark Shield of Botany Bay' (2013) 27 *Continuum: Journal of Media and Cultural Studies* 18–29; Maria Nugent and Gaye Sculthorpe, 'A Shield Loaded with History: Encounters, Objects and Exhibitions' (2018) 49 *Australian Historical Studies* 28–43.

[238] Thomas, 'A Case of Identity', 10.

[239] Ibid, 10.

[240] Schlunke, 'One Strange Colonial Thing', 19–20. J. C. Beaglehole (ed.), *The Journals of Captain James Cook* (Cambridge: Cambridge University Press for the Hakluyt Society, 1955–67) vol. I,

has presented it for a long time as the shield that Cook fired at in 1770. However, it is questionable whether the shield in the British Museum is indeed the one from Botany Bay. The shield has been examined by firearms specialists, who confirmed that the hole is not from a gunshot. The wood, red mangrove, does not stem from Botany Bay.[241]

These uncertainties regarding the object biography do not affect its cultural and educational importance. The shield has been reclaimed by Australian Gweagal descendants as an early and rare example of aboriginal culture.[242] It has relevance to the colonial encounter because it reflects the idea of resistance or defence against power. It 'offers material evidence of a pre-colonial Aboriginal sovereign power',[243] which has later been derecognized through colonization, and reflects ongoing struggles over space and belonging.[244] An important change in direction is the decision by Cambridge University in 2023 to return four spears taken by James Cook from Botany Bay in 1770 to descendants of their former owners, i.e. the La Perouse Aboriginal community in Australia. It justified the return by the exceptional cultural significance of the spears as 'the beginnings of a history of misunderstanding and conflict' and their importance to aboriginal communities and all Australians.[245]

The 'trade' of preserved Māori heads may also be traced back to Cook's first voyage.[246] In New Zealand, Joseph Banks managed to exchange used clothes, namely a pair of white linen underpants, for the preserved head of a Māori boy that was offered to him. Banks acknowledged in his journal that the transaction was not entirely free from coercion. He noted that he threatened the Māori with his 'musquet' in order to complete the exchange.[247] The incident was typical of later

---

304–306; J. C. Beaglehole (ed.), *The Endeavour Journal of Joseph Banks, 1768–1771* (Sydney: Angus and Robertson, 1963) vol. II, 54–55, 133.

[241] Marc Fennell and Nick Wiggins, 'A Shield, Some Spears, and the Symbolism People Find in the Stuff the British Stole' *ABC News* (25 January 2021).

[242] Rodney Kelly, a descendant of a Gweagal man shot in Botany Bay, led a campaign for return of the shield after it was displayed in Canberra in March 2016.

[243] Sarah Keenan, 'The Gweagal Shield' (2017) 68 *Northern Ireland Legal Quarterly* 283–290, 290; Robertson, *Who Owns History?*, 191–194.

[244] As Sarah Keenan has argued: 'The dispute over this shield goes well beyond questions of individual ownership and genealogy ... Whatever conclusions about the shield's provenance are reached by the British Museum and its invited experts, the fact remains that this shield is an Aboriginal object in the possession of an institution whose entitlement to it remains grounded in the racist notions of cultural and intellectual superiority which saw it displayed in its cabinets in the first place'. See Sarah Keenan, 'How the British Museum Changed Its Story about the Gweagal Shield' Australian Critical Race and Whiteness Studies Association, *Kardla (Fire) News* (18 May 2018).

[245] Trinity College Cambridge press release, 'Aboriginal Spears to Be Returned to Traditional Owners' (2 March 2023).

[246] See Chapter 5.

[247] John Cawte Beaglehole (ed.), *The Endeavour Journal of Joseph Banks, 1768–1771, Vol. 2* (Sydney: Public Library of New South Wales, 2nd edn, 1963) 31.

exchanges and contributed to the creation of an international market for Māori relics in the nineteenth century.[248]

3.3.2 Semi-public, semi-private acquisition by colonial officials in Java

The trend towards targeted search and collection of antiquities is reflected in the semi-public, semi-private practices of acquisition by Dutch and British agents at beginning of the nineteenth century in Java. Collection of objects was driven by a 'combination of personal, civic and state-related emotions'[249] under unequal power relations. It created close links between Dutch and British officials. Both of them viewed Javanese antiquities as surviving objects of a far advanced civilization, i.e. the South-east Asian equivalent of Greek–Roman culture, but shared scepticism against the ability of Javanese rulers to take care of their own heritage. They collected objects for private and public reasons, and defended their actions as acts of liberation for the benefit of material culture.

The Dutch governor of East Java, Nicolaus Engelhard (1761–1831), was one of the first Europeans who studied Javanese temples on his trips and interactions with Javanese leaders in Surakarta and Yogyakarta. Like Raffles, he was not a profit-driven, 'ignorant and destructive temple-looter',[250] but an admirer of Javanese artefacts, who relied on colonial logics to justify their appropriation. Engelhard visited temple ruins. He ordered the clearance of objects in order to enable proper appreciation. In 1803, he discovered the decaying Singhasari temple in the forests of Malang. He removed the statues of the thirteenth-century Hindu period in East Java, and arguing that natives did not 'honour' their temple ruins and 'had little value or respect for them'.[251] He argued that local inhabitants did not show sufficient care for the objects and that their taking protected them against acts of vandalism.[252] This narrative contrasted with views according to which locals wanted to hide objects from native rulers and Europeans.[253] Reports confirm that he regarded himself as the legitimate owner, arguing that the 'statues had been ceded to him as private property by the previous government'.[254] This turned the statues

---

[248] D. Wayne Orchiston, 'Preserved Maori Heads and Captain Cook's Three Voyages to the South Seas: A Study in Ethnohistory' (1978) 73 *Anthropos* 798; Robert Paterson, 'Maori Preserved Heads: A Legal History' in Peter Mosimann and Beat Schönenberger (eds.), *Kunst & Recht 2017/Art & Law 2017* (Bern: Stämpfli Verlag, 2017) 71–85.

[249] Marieke Bloembergen and Martijn Eickhoff, 'A Wind of Change on Java's Ruined Temples: Archaeological Activities, Imperial Circuits and Heritage Awareness in Java and the Netherlands (1800–1850) (2013) 28 *BMGN - Low Countries Historical Review* 81–104, 102.

[250] Roy Jordaan, 'Nicolaus Engelhard and Thomas Stamford Raffles: Brethren in Javanese Antiquities' (2016) 101 *Indonesia* 39–66, 40.

[251] Sarah Tiffin, 'Raffles and the Barometer of Civilisation: Images and Descriptions of Ruined Candis in "The History of Java"' (2008) 18 *Journal of the Royal Asiatic Society* 341–360, 357.

[252] Jordaan, 'Nicolaus Engelhard and Thomas Stamford Raffles', 43.

[253] Tiffin, 'Raffles and the Barometer of Civilisation', 357, referring to a report according to which 'the Inhabitants had concealed the figure just described, and many others not only from all Europeans ... but from their own native Chiefs').

[254] Jordaan, 'Nicolaus Engelhard and Thomas Stamford Raffles', 43.

in fact 'a gift to himself', since he was the commanding authority at the time.[255] They were later shipped to the Netherlands, together with another iconic object, the Prajñaparamita of Java, which was collected in 1819 by a VOC official near the Singhasari temple and offered to the Dutch king.[256]

British collectors used similar arguments of neglect and cultural deterioration to justify removal of objects during the British rule over Java. They claimed that they 'discovered' the artefacts and sent some of them to the Museum of the East India Company in Calcutta. For instance, Colonel Colin Mackenzie (1754–1821), the main military engineer of the British-Indian forces in Java, was mandated by Raffles to search for antiquities. He collected the 'Pucangan stone', an eleventh-century artefact with important inscriptions in Sanskrit and Old Javanese (Charter of Pucangan) during the period of Raffles' administration in 1812 and sent it to Calcutta. It became known as the 'Calcutta stone'.[257]

Raffles himself removed a tenth-century stone, with ancient Javanese inscriptions, the Sangguran stone, from the region of Malang and shipped it to Calcutta in 1813. He offered the stone as a token of appreciation, i.e. a 'gift', to his superior, Lord Minto, the Governor-General of India. It is known as the 'Minto stone'. It was moved to Scotland, but later returned to Indonesia.[258] The way in which it was presented suggests that Raffles considered himself entitled to give away Javanese heritage. These examples highlight the double standards governing appropriation of ancient cultural artefacts. Removal by locals was perceived as an act of 'destruction', whereas removal by colonial agents was qualified as an act of rescue or 'preservation'.[259]

3.3.3 'Rescue' of the Parthenon Marbles (1801–1805)

The most famous illustration of the 'rescue' ideology at the beginning of the nineteenth century is the removal of the Parthenon Marbles by the British Ambassador to the Ottoman Empire, Thomas Bruce, the seventh Earl of Elgin (Lord Elgin, 1766–1841), and their subsequent purchase by the 'British nation' in 1816, following an extensive debate in Parliament. It has become a global symbol of the struggle over cultural return.[260]

---

[255] Ibid.

[256] Bloembergen and Eickhoff, *The Politics of Heritage in Indonesia*, 40.

[257] Nigel Bullough and Peter Carey, 'The Kolkata (Calcutta) Stone and the Bicentennial of the British Interregnum in Java, 1811–1816' International Institute for Asian Studies, Newsletter Vol. 74 (Summer 2016)   https://www.iias.asia/the-newsletter/article/kolkata-calcutta-stone-bicentennial-british-interregnum-java-1811-1816.

[258] Ibid.

[259] Tiffin, 'Raffles and the Barometer of Civilisation', 357.

[260] On a defence of retention, see Noel Malcolm, *The Elgin Marbles, Keep, Lend or Return? An Analysis* (London: Policy Exchange, 2023). On the legal dimensions, see Catharine Titi, *The Parthenon Marbles and International Law* (Berlin: Springer, 2023), Alexander Herman, *The Parthenon Marbles Dispute* (London: Bloomsbury, 2023).

The 'rescue' idea was one of the main justifications for the acquisition of the marbles by the British state. It is expressly reflected in the report of the House of Commons Select Committee on the Earl of Elgin's Collection of Sculptured Marbles from 1816, which recommended the purchase of the collection from Elgin. It compared the marbles to neglected objects that were open to abuse and in need of protection. It stated that:

> [n]o country can be better adapted than our own to afford an honourable asylum to these monuments of the school of Phidias, and of the administration of Pericles; where secure from further injury and degradation, they may receive that admiration and homage to which they are entitled, and serve in return as models and examples to those, who by knowing how to revere and appreciate them, may learn first to imitate, and ultimately to rival them.[261]

This argument fits with cultural nationalist narratives of the nineteenth century, which viewed culture as a part of nationhood and national prestige. It has strong parallels to the justifications used by Napoleon. It is an expression of the strife for national glory and competition between European powers. The purchase transformed the marbles from a piece of ancient civilization into a national icon of the British nation.[262] It allowed Britain to present itself as the modern equivalent of the 'cradle of democracy' in classical Athens and as a saviour of Western civilization.[263] For instance, Elgin himself saw the removal as a 'service to the arts in England' and took pride in the fact that even Napoleon had not acquired 'such as thing from all his thefts in Italy'.[264] It reflected at the same time biases towards the ability of the Ottoman Empire to appreciate and take care of Greece's cultural heritage. The acquisition stood in marked contrast to the British position on Napoleon's lootings, emerging ideas on protection of cultural property based on the bond between objects and nations (*Quatremère de Quincy*), or their value to humankind (*Marquis de Someruelos* case), and the treaty-based protections of cultural heritage under the Congress of Vienna settlements.[265] For instance, Quatremère de Quincy famously

---

[261] See House of Commons, Report of the Select Committee on the Earl of Elgin's Collection of Sculptured Marbles (25 March 1816) 15.

[262] Fiona Rose-Greenland, 'The Parthenon Marbles as Icons of Nationalism in Nineteenth-century Britain' (2019) 13 *Nations and Nationalism* 654–673.

[263] See Timothy Webb, 'Appropriating the Stones: The "Elgin Marbles" and English National taste' in Barkan, *Saving the Stones*, 51–96.

[264] William St Clair, *Lord Elgin and the Marbles: The Controversial History of the Parthenon Sculptures* (Oxford and New York: Oxford University Press [1967], 1998) 100.

[265] Derek Fincham, 'The Parthenon Sculptures and Cultural Justice' (2013) 23 *Fordham Intellectual Property, Media and Entertainment Law Journal* 943–1016, 973–974. William Richard Hamilton, Elgin's former private secretary, argued in the Congress of Vienna negotiations in 1815 that 'works are considered so sacred a property, that no direct or indirect means are to be allowed for their being conveyed elsewhere than where they came from'. See Letter from Hamilton to Elgin about 15 October 1815, quoted in Philip Hunt and A. H. Smith, 'Lord Elgin and His Collection' (1916) 36 *Journal of Hellenic Studies* 163–372, 332.

argued in the context of Napoleon's looting of Italy that the integrity of works of art can be destroyed through their decomposition ('to divide is to destroy').[266] The removal of dismembered pieces is particularly damaging from a perspective of material culture since it affected the integrity of the Parthenon as a whole.

Greece was under the occupation of the Ottoman Empire when Lord Elgin started his works on the Parthenon. At the time, the Parthenon was a sacred temple and a national shrine, which was controlled by a Turkish governor (the Voivide) and a warden (the Disdar). They protected the marbles and ruins from spoliation by visitors and tourists. Elgin shared admiration for the classical works and their values and meanings. Originally, he did not intend to remove sculptures and artefacts, but sought to make drawings and produce plaster replicas for his future country house (Broomhall)[267] and 'improve artistic appreciation and taste among his countrymen'.[268] He composed a team, under the leadership of Italian artist Giovanni Battista Lusieri (1755–1821), and instructed them with the works.

When progress proceeded more slowly than anticipated, Philip Hunt (1772–1838), the Chaplain to Lord Elgin, advised him in a memorandum to seek permission from Ottoman authorities 'to erect scaffolding and to dig where they may wish to discover the ancient foundations' and to gain the 'liberty to take away any sculptures or descriptions *which do not interfere with the works or walls of the Citadel*'.[269] The idea was to allow excavations to discover buried marble sculptures, but not necessarily to obtain permission to remove marbles from the 'works or walls' of the Parthenon itself, as the last sentence indicates.[270] Hunt suggested Elgin apply for a 'firman', i.e. a formal decree from the sultan, granting him permission to expand the works.

Elgin benefited from the circumstance of the time. He had a good standing with Ottoman authorities, since Britain had assisted Turkey in defeating Napoleon's forces in Egypt. He claimed that he obtained such an official decree from the Sublime Porte, the central government of the Ottoman Empire. But there is no record of negotiations with Sultan Selim III (1761–1808), the supreme head of the Ottoman Empire. The only document existing is the Italian translation of an official letter, signed by the Acting Grand Vizier Kaimakam Pasha in July 1801, which

---

[266] Quatremère de Quincy, *Letters to Miranda and Canova on the Abduction of Antiquities from Rome and Athens* (Chris Miller and David Gilks trs, Los Angeles: Getty Research Institute, 2012) 100.

[267] Elgin wrote in a letter of 10 July 1801: ' I should wish to collect as much marble as possible. I have other places in my house which need it, and besides, one can easily multiply ornaments of beautiful marble without overdoing it; and nothing, truly, is so beautiful and also independent of changes of fashion.' See Letter from Elgin to Lusieri (10 July 1801), quoted in Hunt and Smith, 'Lord Elgin and His Collection', 192.

[268] See British Committee for the Reunification of the Parthenon Marbles, 'The History of the Marbles' https://www.parthenonuk.com/about-bcrpm/history-of-the-marbles.

[269] Emphasis added. Letter from Philip Hunt to Lord Elgin (31 July 1801), quoted in Hunt and Smith, 'Lord Elgin and His Collection', 190. See also St Clair, *Lord Elgin and the Marbles*, 87.

[270] Robertson, *Who Owns History?*, 64.

was kept by Hunt.[271] It has been questioned whether the original of the document constituted a 'firman' in the formal sense, since it was not issued by Sultan Selim III and did not contain an order.[272] It may have been a 'friendly letter' rather than a formal authorization.

The document did not necessarily provide a title to remove the marbles. The English translation of the Italian document stated that Elgin's five painters should not be 'disturbed, nor in any way impeded by the Commandant of the Castle, nor any other person, and that no one meddle with their scaffolding, and implements, which they may have made there; and should they wish to *take away any pieces of stone* with old inscriptions, and figures, that no opposition be made'.[273]

The key passage of this translation, referring to 'any pieces of stone', is misleading. The Italian original uses the terms *qualche pezzi di pietra*, which means *some* or *a few* pieces of stone. The wording can therefore not be legitimately interpreted to justify the large-scale removal of objects, later carried out by Elgin,[274] which reportedly comprised 'seventeen figures from the Parthenon pediments; fifteen metopes; fifty-six slabs of the temple friezes; one caryatid column; four pieces of the temple of victory; thirteen marble heads; a large assortment of carved fragments, painted vases, sepulchral pillars and inscribed albas'.[275] Moreover, the context of the passage suggests that it applies to objects found through excavations, rather than removal of existing sculptures of the Parthenon.[276] As William St Clair has noted:

> The firman confers no authority to remove sculptures from the buildings or to damage them in any way. On the contrary it seems certain that the Ottoman government, if they considered the point at all, only intended to grant permission to dig and take away, which is all they had been asked for in Hunt's memorandum. Nor is there is any indication that at the time either Elgin or any of his entourage believed that the firman gave permission to make removals from the buildings.[277]

Elgin exploited the ambiguity of the document to excavate fallen pieces of sculpture and remove them from the Acropolis. His team removed the first metope, the frieze of the Parthenon, and other structural marbles. The removals clearly exceed

[271] William St Clair, 'Imperial Appropriations of the Parthenon' in John H. Merryman (ed.), *Imperialism, Art and Restitution* (Cambridge: Cambridge University Press, 2006) 65–97, 78.
[272] Vassilis Demetriades, Was the Removal of the Parthenon Marbles by Elgin Legal? https://publicati ons.parliament.uk/pa/cm199900/cmselect/cmcumeds/371/371ap15.htm. Dyfri Williams, 'Lord Elgin's Firman' (2009) *Journal of the History of Collections* 1–28, 11.
[273] Emhasis added. See Williams, 'Lord Elgin's Firman', 7.
[274] Christopher Hitchens, 'The Elgin Marbles' in Christopher Hitchens, Robert Browning, and Graham Binns, *The Elgin Marbles: Should They be Returned to Greece?* (London: Verso, 1997) 16, 61 ('Even a most free and lavish translation of the Italian tongue cannot twist these words into meaning a whole shipload of sculptures, columns and caryatids').
[275] Fincham, 'The Parthenon Sculptures and Cultural Justice', 976.
[276] John Merryman, 'Thinking about the Elgin Marbles' (1985) 83 *Michigan Law Review*, 1880–1923, 1899.
[277] St Clair, *Lord Elgin and the Marbles*, 89.

the scope of the alleged 'firman'.[278] Hunt was visibly uncomfortable with the turn of events. He recognized this in a letter of 21 August 1801 in which he stated that 'there are envious people who will not fail to represent what has been done here as a violence to the fine remains of Grecian sculpture'.[279] Thomas Lacey, an engineer, who was asked by Elgin to assist him was even more direct. He wrote to Hunt on 8 October 1801 that he would 'embark for Athens to plunder temples and commit sacrilege'.[280] Elgin's team offered illustrious gifts to the Voivode and Disdar in order to encourage them to turn a blind eye to the removals. In October 1802, Elgin received additional documents from the Sublime Porte, which were deemed to reassure the Voivode and Disdar of the legality of his actions.[281]

John Merryman has argued that Elgin obtained title to displace the Parthenon marbles through ex post acquiescence of Ottoman authorities after 1801. He noted that:

[t]here is evidence that the Ottomans twice ratified what Elgin had done. For one thing, it appears that Elgin caused the Sultan to issue additional firmans addressed to the Voivode and Disdar of Athens, in which the Sultan generally sanctioned what these local officials had done for Elgin and his party. For another, a large shipment of Marbles was held up in Piraeus (the port of Athens) because the Voivode, under pressure from the French, refused to give his permission for their embarkation. Eventually the Ottoman government gave written orders to the Athenian authorities to permit the shipment, and the Marbles were allowed to leave for England.[282]

According to his view, the removal was immoral, but not illegal under these circumstances.[283] However, this argument has remained contested.[284] Although it is

---

[278] Elgin evaded this in the hearing before the Parliamentary Committee. When asked whether 'the Turkish Government' knew that he 'was removing statues under the permission' he 'obtained from them' he simply replied: 'No doubt was ever expressed to me.' Hunt was more ambiguous. When he was asked whether 'the firman gave direct permission to remove figures and pieces of sculptures from the walls of the temple' he said: 'That was the interpretation that the Governor was induced to believe.' See Memorandum submitted by Mr Jules Dassin (May 2000) https://publications.parliament.uk/pa/cm199 900/cmselect/cmcumeds/371/0060504.htm.

[279] Hunt to Elgin (21 August 1801) in St Clair, *Lord Elgin and the Marbles*, 95, fn. 32.

[280] Memorandum submitted by Mr Jules Dassin (May 2000) https://publications.parliament.uk/pa/ cm199900/cmselect/cmcumeds/371/0060504.htm.

[281] Lusieri to Elgin (28 October 1802) in Hunt and Smith, 'Lord Elgin and His Collection', 235.

[282] Merryman, 'Thinking about the Elgin Marbles', 1899.

[283] See also Izidor Janzekovic, 'A Series of (Un)Fortunate Events: The Elgin Marbles' (2016) 16 *Journal of Art Crime* 55–76, 63 ('Even though with the first firman [Elgin], arguably, crossed the line, they now legalized these actions post factum') 69 ('Turks have later approved of Elgin's actions at least two more times. The first time in 1802, Elgin has requested a new firman in Constantinople for the worrisome Disdar and Voivode. And then again in 1810, when the new firman was guaranteed by Elgin's successors, ambassador Adair, and it allowed them to load the last major part of the collection on the ships and ship it to England').

[284] David Rudenstine has argued that 'the widely held assumption that the Ottomans gave Lord Elgin permission—whether prior or subsequent—to remove the marbles is no more than a grand illusion'. See David Rudenstine, 'Lord Elgin and the Ottomans: The Question of Permission' (2002) 23 *Cardozo*

clear that Elgin's men did not simply walk 'off undetected with tons of antiquities in the middle of the night' and that Ottoman officials were 'fully cognizant of the scale of the undertaking',[285] consent remained ambiguous.[286]

Representatives of the Ottoman Empire continued to contest Elgin's title to remove the marbles from Greece. The content of a letter issued by the Grand Vizier to the Voivide in 1802 suggests that Lusieri was only given permission to draw monuments, but not to remove antiquities.[287] In 1809, the British ambassador Robert Adair was told by Ottoman officials that 'Lord Elgin had never had permission to remove any marbles in the first place'.[288] On 31 July 1811, Alidair shared the doubts in a letter to Lord Elgin. He noted that, in the view of Bartolomeo Pisani, the chief interpreter of the British embassy, Elgin had not acquired any sort of rights of ownership in the marbles:

> Mr Pisani more than once assured me that the Porte absolutely denied your having any property in those marbles. By this expression I understood the Porte to mean that the persons who had sold the marbles to your Lordship had no right so to dispose of them.[289]

Any possible ex post acquiescence was heavily influenced by bribes. Elgin used his influence as representative of the British Crown to acquire and remove the objects in his personal capacity. He gave handsome gifts and an important sum of money to Turkish governors, which are recorded in his account books.[290] For instance,

Law Review 449–547, 453. See also David Rudenstine, 'The Legality of Elgin's Taking: A Review Essay of Four Books on the Parthenon Marbles' (1999) 8 *International Journal of Cultural Property* 356–376, 371 (the 'major premise underlying this enduring controversy - that the Ottomans gave Elgin legal title to the marbles which he then transferred to the British government - is certainly not established and may well be false').

[285] Rudenstine, 'Lord Elgin and the Ottomans', 465, fn. 75.

[286] The website of the British Museum continues to rely on the consent theory. It states: 'He was granted a permit (firman), and between 1801 and 1805 acting under the oversight of the relevant authorities, Elgin removed about half of the remaining sculptures from the ruins of the Parthenon. He also obtained permission to have removed sculptural and architectural elements from other buildings on the Acropolis, namely the Erechtheion, the Temple of Athena Nike and the Propylaia ... His actions were thoroughly investigated by a Parliamentary Select Committee in 1816 and found to be entirely legal, prior to the sculptures entering the collection of the British Museum by Act of Parliament.' See British Museum, 'The Parthenon Sculptures' https://www.britishmuseum.org/about-us/british-museum-story/objects-news/parthenon-sculptures.

[287] See Robertson, *Who Owns History?*, 71; Eleni Korka, 'New Archical Evidence' in Fani Mallouchou-Tufano and Anna Malikourti (eds.), *200 Years of the Parthenon Marbles in the British Museum: New Contributions to the Issue* (Athens: Society of Friends of the Acropolis, 2016) 52–61, 56.

[288] St Clair, *Lord Elgin and the Marbles*, 155.

[289] Theodore Theodorou, Robert Adair's letter to Lord Elgin http://www.adairtoelgin.com/#_ftn9.

[290] William St Clair writes: 'The financial accounts reveal that the bribery in Athens amounted to about one-quarter of the total costs of removing the antiquities. The figures include presents in kind, mainly telescopes, guns, horses, and jewellery that were presented to high officials in Athens on particular occasions, but exclude the payments made to high officials of the central government in Constantinople. Almost everyone connected with the operations in Athens, high and low officials, secretaries, couriers, soldiers, and the paid workmen, and sometimes their families, enjoyed gifts and

there is evidence that the shipment of goods was bought by bribes. William St Clair has noted that the 'scale of these payments went beyond any ritual exchange of gifts and courtesies, normal and lavish though such rituals were in the Ottoman empire'.[291] He stated:

> The military governor received payments in the first year alone equivalent to thirty-five times his annual salary. The governor was given more, and even larger amounts that do not appear in the accounts were paid to officials in Constantinople ... The paradigm point is this. No administrative or judicial system can be expected to withstand such a weight of political influence and money. This is imperialism in action, destroying not only monuments but the local administrative and legal infrastructure.[292]

Such bribes affect the legitimacy of consent. Elgin did not 'purchase' the marbles, or acquire them in good faith. He simply removed them through illegitimately obtained consent and his influence as ambassador, in an attempt to 'rescue' some of them from ruin. This conduct was suspect even by British standards. As David Rudenstine has argued: '[t]he idea that British law turned a blind eye towards a British ambassador tendering a bribe to a foreign official so that that official would exercise discretionary authority in favor of the ambassadors private gain is an important and seemingly specious claim'.[293] In addition, one may doubt whether local authorities had the power to take decisions regarding the alienation of national property, which formed part of a public and religious monument.

Elgin's justification for the acquisitions remained weak. When he was pushed by the House of Commons Select Committee to explain why he did not keep a record of the terms any permissions, he stated:

> No, I never did; and it never occurred to me that the question would arise; the thing was done publicly before the whole world. I employed three or four hundred people a day; and all the local authorities were concerned in it, as well as the Turkish Government.[294]

Elgin completed the last shipment from Athens to Britain in 1812. The arrival of the marbles in London caused both enthusiasm and critique. British poet George

---

distributions of money, sugar, coffee, wine, rum, and other benefits. By far the largest amounts went as financial payments to the two key Ottoman officials, the voivode and the disdar.' See William St Clair, 'The Elgin Marbles: Questions of Stewardship and Accountability' (1999) 8 *International Journal of Cultural Property* 391–521, 402.

[291] Ibid, 402.
[292] St Clair, 'Imperial Appropriations of the Parthenon', 79.
[293] Rudenstine, 'Lord Elgin and the Ottomans', 468.
[294] Hunt and Smith, 'Lord Elgin and His Collection', 336.

Gordon Byron (1788–1824) openly criticized Elgin and his acts as vandalism or looting, which damaged the unity of the Parthenon and violated national patrimony. In a poem entitled 'Childe Harold's Pilgrimage', published in 1812, Byron stated:

> Dull is the eye that will not weep to see
> Thy walls defaced, thy mouldering shrines removed
> By British hands, which it had best behoved
> To guard those relics ne'er to be restored.[295]

It is thus no surprise that the term 'elginism' became a synonym for cultural plunder in nineteenth century France.

Elgin developed a multi-faceted salvage narrative in order to justify his actions. He argued that the removal did not only save the sculptures from decay or destruction or promote arts and culture in Britain, but also prevented their capture by France. He thereby used Britain's rivalry with France to defend his actions to the public.

In 1815, Elgin filed a request with the House of Commons in order to determine whether Britain would seek to purchase the marbles on behalf of the public. The House of Commons Select Committee examined the legality of Elgin's acquisition. It questioned Elgin inter alia on the 'salvage' theory, asking Elgin why he 'did not do anything to rescue them, in any other way than to bring' the marbles 'away' in the way he 'found' them.[296] Elgin replied: 'No; it was impossible for me to do more than that; the Turkish government attached no importance to them in the world.'[297]

The Committee ultimately endorsed the acquiescence theory, based on the hearings, justifying acquisition by the alleged lack of protest by Ottoman officials or the Greek population.[298] The report, dated 25 March 1816, confirmed that, according to the evidence, 'no displeasure was shown by the Turkish Government, or the local population, and that no attempt was made to conserve the remains which were exposed to frequent injury'.[299] It recommended the purchase in order to offer 'honourable asylum' to the treasures. In the subsequent parliamentary debate, the House of Commons decided to approve the purchase and pay £35,000 to the Trustees of the British Museum in order to enable it to buy the marbles. The motion was approved by a majority of eighty-two votes, with thirty votes against it.

---

[295] See George Gordon Byron, *The Complete Works of Lord Byron, Vol. 2* (Paris: Galignani and Co., 1835) 85

[296] Hunt and Smith, 'Lord Elgin and His Collection', 337.

[297] Ibid, 337.

[298] Parliamentarian John Morritt had argued before the Committee that '[i]n his opinion the Greeks were decidedly and strongly desirous that the marbles should not be removed from Athens'. Ibid, 339.

[299] Ibid, 340.

The debates showed conflicting positions. Mr Henry Bankes, the Chairman of the Select Committee and trustee of the British Museum, supported the purchase. He distinguished Elgin's acquisition expressly from Napoleon's methods. He stated: '[t]here was nothing like spoliation in the case, and that it bore no resemblance to those undue and tyrannical means by which the French had obtained possession of so many treasures of art, which he rejoiced to see again in the possession of their rightful owners'.[300] Bankes also supported the 'salvage' justification. He argued that the treasures were

[m]aking rapid strides towards decay, and the natives displayed such wanton indifference as to fire at them as marks. They had also been continually suffering, from the parts carried off by enlightened travellers. The greatest desire, too, had been evinced by the government of France to become possessed of them.[301]

Other speakers were more reserved. Some opposed the purchase on economic grounds. Others formulated more fundamental critiques. Mr Hugh Hammersley opposed the acquisition on 'justice' grounds. He argued that the marbles had been 'improperly taken' and that Great Britain holds them only 'in trust till they are demanded by the present, or any future, possessors of the city of Athens'.[302] Mr Sergeant Best argued that he could not agree to the purchase since the 'marbles had been brought to this country in breach of good faith'.[303]

In following decades, arguments reflecting the 'justificatory' discourse of the British empire were used to defend the retention of the marbles in the British Museum.[304] Public narratives downplayed the way in which Elgin used his ambassadorial role to remove the sculptures and relied on saviour rhetoric and the museum's ability to present the marbles to the world in order to maintain the status quo.

The acquisition remained contested in legal doctrine. For instance, Jeanette Greenfield has argued that 'Elgin's men did in peacetime what would no longer have been acceptable even in time of war'.[305] Charles de Visscher has openly criticized the 'rescue thesis', based on the fact that the Marbles were an integral part of the Parthenon Temple itself. He stated:

It is very doubtful, however, whether the arguments put forth can actually justify the irreparable damage resulting from his action. The fact is that the principle of

---

[300] Ibid, 343.
[301] Ibid, 343.
[302] Ibid, 344.
[303] House of Commons, Debate Elgin Marbles (7 June 1816) in *The Parliamentary Debates from the Year 1803 to the Present Time*, Vol. 34 (London: Hansard, 1816) 1038.
[304] St Clair, 'Imperial Appropriations of the Parthenon', 82.
[305] Greenfield, *Return of Cultural Treasures*, 88.

the unity and integrity of a monument of such extraordinary artistic and historic value clearly outweighs any other consideration here. Neither the possibility of spoliation at the hands of foreigners, nor the likelihood of defacement or destruction of the monuments on the Acropolis— these were motives later cited by Lord Elgin—had the dual character of certainty and imminence that might have justified so serious a step.[306]

The questionable methods of taking certainly turned the Parthenon marbles into a legally entangled object.[307] The removal stood in stark contrast to European principles on the protection of the integrity of art works. It also marked a clear abuse of rights by Elgin. As Hersch Lauterpacht has argued, 'there is no legal right, however well established, which could not, in some circumstances, be refused recognition on the ground that it has been abused'.[308] The taking, influenced by official capacity and bribes, and exceeding the possible authorization under the firman, crossed the 'imperceptible line between impropriety and illegality, between discretion and arbitrariness, between the exercise of the legal right … and the abuse of that right'.[309]

The presence of the marbles in Britain had an impact on social attitudes and aesthetics in Britain. In Britain, 'Greek superseded Roman art as the ideal, both in high and in popular culture'.[310] The British Museum claimed that the marbles became part of its own identity. The Greek government regards them as an integral part of its national identity, namely as a symbol of the 'freedom of the people and a resistance to tyranny in all its forms'.[311]

The decade-long discussions on return reflect many of the 'red herrings' used in the restitution debate. The British Museum defended its own claim based on a mixture of arguments, drawing on the alleged legality of acquisition, the importance of the marbles to British identity, the capacity of the museum to display them in connection with other universal heritage objects, and the inalienability provisions under the 1963 British Museum Act. Greece in turn has continued to contest the British Museum's ownership, based on their improper removal[312] and their

---

[306] Visscher, *International Protection of Works of Art and Historic Monuments*, 828.

[307] On the legal case for return, see Geoffrey Robertson, Norman Palmer, and Amal Clooney, *The Case for the Return of the Parthenon Sculptures* Report (31 July 2015).

[308] Hersch Lauterpacht, *The Development of International Law by the International Court* (London: Stevens & Sons, 1958) 164.

[309] On abuse of rights in the context of the trusteeship obligations of administering powers, see ICJ, *Voting Procedure on Questions relating to Reports and Petitions concerning the Territory of South West Africa*, Advisory Opinion of 7 June 1955, Separate Opinion Judge Lauterpacht [1955] ICJ Rep. 67, 90, 120.

[310] Merryman, 'Thinking about the Elgin Marbles', 1908.

[311] Alexander Herman, *Restitution: The Return of Cultural Artefacts* (London: Lund Humphries, 2021) 25

[312] Harrison Jacobs and Tessa Solomon, 'Greece Rejects Possibility of Parthenon Marbles "Loan" in New Statement' *Art News* (6 January 2023) ('We repeat, once again, our country's firm position that it does not recognize the British Museum's jurisdiction, possession and ownership of the Sculptures, as they are the product of theft').

cultural importance to Greek identity. In 2021, the UNESCO Intergovernmental Committee for Promoting the Return of Cultural Property urged the UK to negotiate return of the Parthenon sculptures to Greece. Secret negotiations led to proposals to facilitate return based on a partnership agreement, involving reciprocal exchange of objects or a long-term 'loan' to Greece in order to bridge the conflicting positions of both sides.[313] According to contemporary polls carried out by the Parthenon Project, a majority of the British public (54 per cent) supports return of the sculptures.[314]

3.4 Gifts

The practice of gifts exchange was influenced by colonial power relations between the late-eighteenth century and the mid-nineteenth century.[315] For instance, the presence and control of the East India Company changed the culture of gift-exchange in India. Indian rulers were controlled through treaties. This context converted what was originally 'a form of present-giving and prestation' under Mughal rule into 'a kind of "economic exchange"'.[316] In the eighteenth century, company officials based their authority on contractual obligations and good governance. They started to collect taxes and exercise executive, judicial, or legislative powers. Gifts became a ritual expressing loyalty and subordination,[317] and took on more contractual features.[318]

3.4.1 The dagger of Prince Diponegoro

The close link between gifts and colonial violence is illustrated by the acquisition of the dagger of Prince Diponegoro (1785–1855), a hero of anti-colonial resistance in Java. Diponegoro's resistance caused financial damage to the VOC. Dutch General Hendrik Merkus de Kock sought to end his resistance to colonial rule through peace negotiations. He charged Colonel Jean-Baptiste Cleeren, field commander in eastern Bagelen, with the mandate to negotiate with Diponegoro and lure him

---

[313] Tom Seymour, 'British Museum's hopes of a "loan arrangement" for the return of the Parthenon Marbles imperilled ahead of Greek elections' *The Art Newspaper* (13 January 2023); Alex Marshall, 'After 220 Years, the Fate of the Parthenon Marbles Rests in Secret Talks' *NY Times* (17 January 2023). See also Chapter 8.

[314] Tessa Solomon, 'New UK Advisory Board Chaired by Former Culture Minister Calls for Return of Parthenon Marbles' *Art News* (14 October 2022) https://www.artnews.com/art-news/news/parthenon-marbles-news-uk-advisory-board-return-1234643159/.

[315] Margot C. Finn, 'Colonial Gifts: Family Politics and Exchange of Goods in British India, c. 1780–1820' (2006) 40 *Modern Asian Studies* 203–231.

[316] Bernard S. Cohn, 'Representing Authority in Victorian India' in Eric Hobsbawm and Terence Ranger (eds.), *The Invention of Tradition* (Cambridge: Cambridge University Press, 1983) 165–210, 172.

[317] Ibid, 172.

[318] The reception of gifts was viewed more critically by Parliament and company directors, who sought to limit practices of corruption and bribes. Ibid, 171.

to 'good faith' discussions in De Kock's headquarters at Magĕlang in Central Java. Cleeren gave Diponegoro the 'mistaken impression' that would be able to walk away from the negotiations if the terms were unacceptable to him.[319] Diponegoro appeared to trust Colonel Cleeren.[320] When it became clear to General De Kock that Diponegoro would not surrender unconditionally, he forced him to accept his demands and arrested him on 28 March 1830.[321] Cleerens obtained Diponegoro's dagger, a costly weapon with golden decoration, and presented it as a 'gift' to King Willem I on 11 January 1831. Although it is not fully clear how Cleeren gained possession of the dagger, it is 'highly likely' that he received it at his initial peace negotiations with Diponegoro in order 'to seal the gentleman's agreement given by Cleerens that the Dutch would negotiate in good faith'.[322] The context of the acquisition suggests that it is a 'gift' acquired under irregular circumstances. It was returned by the Netherlands in March 2020.

3.4.2 The Quimbaya treasure
In certain cases, gifts were made after independence from colonial powers. A notorious example is the Quimbaya treasure,[323] a collection of pre-Columbian objects donated by Colombian President Carlos Holguín to Spain in 1893. It shows how the strife for prestige and power by ruling elites may lead to cultural loss to the detriment of people and indigenous groups under the influence of past colonial relations. The artefacts were removed from two tombs in the Cauca river valley in Colombia by gravediggers in 1890. President Holguín purchased a large part of the collection.

The treasures were first shown in a public exhibition in Bogota. In 1893, the President decided to 'gift' 122 objects to the Spanish government, without seeking authorization from the Colombian Congress.[324] The objects were offered to Spain in the context of an exhibition commemorating the 'discovery of America', held in Madrid in 1892, and the World Exhibition in Chicago in 1893. The President had developed a close relationship to the Spanish monarchy. The donation was made to enhance national prestige, namely to present the degree of civilization of

---

[319] Peter B. R. Carey, 'Raden Saleh, Dipanagara and the Painting of the Capture of Dipanagara at Magĕlang (28 March 1830)' (1982) 55 *Journal of the Malaysian Branch of the Royal Asiatic Society* 1–25, 7.

[320] Peter Carey, *The Power of Prophecy; Prince Dipanagara and the End of an Old Order in Java, 1785–1855* (Leiden: KITLV Press, 2007) 669, fn. 55.

[321] Justus M. van der Kroef, 'Prince Diponegoro: Progenitor of Indonesian Nationalism' (1949) 8 *The Far Eastern Quarterly* 424–450, 448.

[322] Peter Carey, 'Reflections on the Return of the Diponegoro's Dragger Kiai Nogo Siluman' https://langgar.co/reflections-on-the-return-of-the-diponegoros-dragger-kiai-nogo-siluman/.

[323] See Alicia Perea Caveda and others, 'Pre-hispanic Goldwork Technology: The Quimbaya Treasure, Colombia' (2013) 40 *Journal of Archaeological Science* 2326–2334; Diego Mejía-Lemos, 'The "Quimbaya Treasure," Judgment SU-649/17' (2019) 113 *AJIL* 122–130; Losson, *Claiming the Remains of the Past*, 58–69.

[324] Mejía-Lemos, 'The "Quimbaya Treasure', 123.

pre-Columbian culture before Spanish conquest and to express gratitude to the Regent Queen of Spain, Doña María Cristina de Absburgo Lorena, who had served as arbitrator in a border dispute with Venezuela. Holguín viewed the collection as a remnant of past pre-Hispanic civilization.[325] The gift caused some protest in civil society. However, ultimately the strife for global recognition and prestige prevailed over the interests of the local population.[326] The objects were first placed in the National Archaeological Museum in Madrid, and later transferred to the Museum of the Americas, where it became one of the most important items in the collection.

Colombia has sought to recover the treasures since the 1970s. In 2006, domestic lawyers filed complaints with domestic courts in Colombia, seeking to compel the Colombian government to demand their return from Spain through UNESCO's Intergovernmental Committee for Promoting the Return of Cultural Property to its Countries of Origin or its Restitution in case of Illicit Appropriation. They argued that Holguín had alienated national Colombian patrimony in violation of cultural property protections under Colombian law at the time.[327] In 2017, the Colombian Constitutional Court[328] found that President Holguín lacked the power to gift objects purchased with public funds without approval of Congress and the conclusion of a treaty transferring ownership.[329] It even held, based on a contested reasoning, that this manifest breach affected the validity of Colombia's consent internationally[330] and conflicted with the *jus cogens* nature of the right of self-determination and rights of indigenous peoples.[331] Spain has refused to return them, arguing that the treasures were validly acquired and have become part of national patrimony. The dispute shows both the close entanglements of gifts with the strife for recognition and prestige in post-colonial relations, and difficulties arising from the appropriation of the past through national discourses.

4 Conclusions

Ultimately, these diverse object histories offer several general insights about colonial takings, which are also replicated in later practices. The first one is the close connection between empire and control over culture. Taking was an expression of colonial power. Not all colonial officials or corporate agents who acquired objects were driven by the desire to further the imperial project. However, they became complicit in it. Cultural takings were a means to facilitate colonial expansion,

---

[325] Losson, *Claiming the Remains of the Past*, 61.
[326] Ibid, 59, 62.
[327] Ibid, 66.
[328] Constitutional Court of Colombia, Judgment SU-649/17 (19 October 2017).
[329] Mejía-Lemos, 'The "Quimbaya Treasure", 124.
[330] Ibid, 127–128.
[331] Ibid, 128.

legitimize the colonial project, its violence, or costs to audiences 'at home', or to cover the expenses of expeditions or military operations. Objects were often treated as 'the objects of "others"', i.e. as objects of cultures which were 'experienced' as alien.[332] Some of them were collected out of sheer curiosity,[333] for their rarity or exotic nature, or their ability to tell stories and provide proof of contact with foreign cultures. The fact that they are referred to as 'curios' reflects the power asymmetry and process of subjection of the colonized. Others were taken as trophies (e.g. regalia). The forcible acquisition of objects (e.g. as trophies of war) stood in contradiction to the proclaimed narratives or justifications of coercion. Many acquisitions or collections illustrated the sophistication, rather than the lack of civilization of the conquered subjects, and/or caused admiration.[334]

Power and culture intersected in complex ways. Cultural takings signalled national prestige, domination or submission or marked strategic responses to rivalry powers. As Jessica Ratcliff has noted, '[i]nter-imperial rivalry may have driven [East India] Company collecting as much, if not more, than perceptions of any immediate use of the collections for the administration of Company territories and trade'.[335] Collecting had performative features, i.e. 'seeing', 'showing', 'representing', or 'staging'.[336] Such theatric features increased towards the end of the nineteenth century, when colonial exhibitions and the bio-politics of colonialism turned 'othering' into spectacle. The very act of displaying objects became a form of epistemic violence.

The birth of modern museums enhanced the strife for national prestige and the accumulation of encyclopedic knowledge. The example of the Parthenon marbles shows the exploitation of the structures of empire and the abuse of rights to gain ownership over culture within Europe. In other parts of the world, cultural extractions became a means of enhancing power and prestige of colonial empire under the premise of discovery, commerce, or scientific classification. Objects gained a different social meaning or were reinvented in their novel context.[337] The diversification and professionalization of museums increased the power to 'show and tell' stories about empire through objects.[338] In some cases, objects were used to construct social 'differences' or demonstrate moral superiority. In other cases, they

---

[332] George W. Stocking (ed.), *Objects and Others: Essays on Museums and Material Culture* (Wisconsin: University of Wisconsin Press, 1998), 4.

[333] Jasanoff, *Edge of Empire: Lives, Culture, and Conquest in the East, 1750–1850*, 64.

[334] Bennett, *Material Cultures of Imperialism in Eastern Africa*, 229.

[335] Jessica Ratcliff, 'Hand-in-Hand With the Survey: Surveying and the Accumulation of Knowledge Capital at India House During the Napoleonic Wars' (2019) 73 *Notes and Records* 149–166, 160.

[336] Sylviane Leprun, *Le théâtre des colonies: scénographie, acteurs et discours de l'imaginaire dans les expositions, 1855–1937* (Paris: L'Harmattan, 1986).

[337] Jasanoff, 'Collectors of Empire', 128 ('collecting is about reinvention').

[338] Tony Bennett speaks of an 'exhibitionary complex'. See Tony Bennett, 'The Exhibitionary Complex' in Reesa Greenberg, Sandy Nairne, and Bruce W. Ferguson (eds.), *Thinking about Exhibitions* (London: Routledge, 1996) 82

became symbols of prestige and self-identification in their environment. For instance, in Britain, many items collected in India 'appeared in the exhibitions as tokens of loyalty to the heir to Queen Victoria, newly created Empress of India, rather than examples of Indian manufacturers'.[339] The acquisition of objects transformed not only colonized societies, but also the identity of the 'imperial homeland'. Certain iconic objects, such as Tipu's tiger, the Gweagal shield, or the kris of Dipenegoro remained symbols of resistance and struggle against colonial power in the eyes of affected societies and mobilized continuing requests for return.

Many of these contradictions re-emerged in cultural takings at the peak of the colonial era, such as the looting of the 'Chinese Summer Palace', the Maqdala pillage, or the hunt for the Benin bronzes. A recurring feature is the absence of the story of scientific racism in collections, and the friction between the initial branding of some objects as legitimate military trophy or symbol of colonial superiority, and their subsequent recognition as protected objects of art.

[339] Tim Barringer, 'The South Kensington Museum and the colonial project' in Tim Barringer and Tom Flynn (eds.), *Colonialism and the Object: Empire, Material Culture and the Museum* (London and New York: Routledge, 1998) 11–27, 22.

3

Collecting Mania, Racial Science, and Cultural Conversion through Forcible Expeditions

1 Introduction

At the German Colonial Congress in 1902, Felix von Luschan noted:

> What we cannot secure and save for posterity in the next few years is facing complete extinction and can never be procured again. Conditions and institutions that have developed peculiarly over the course of millennia are changing almost from one day to the next under the influence of the white man; it is time to snatch quickly before it becomes forever too late.[1]

This statement describes, like no other, the scramble for cultural colonial objects in the heyday of colonial collection, and its cynical justification by rationales of salvage, science, and conservation.

The collection of cultural objects increased significantly, both in quantity and diversity, between the mid-nineteenth and the mid-twentieth centuries.[2] At the time, the industrial revolution was well on its way. This prompted 'a new sense of superiority' among European powers: 'Europe had made a leap into an exciting world of economic prosperity and unprecedented technical mastery of nature; new hopes were connected to individualism, liberalism and democracy.'[3] Collecting became an integral part of colonial policies and practice.[4] The expansion of territorial control, commerce and colonial governance, and competition among European powers triggered an increasing need to 'justify' the colonial project in

---

[1] Felix von Luschan, 'Ziele und Wege der Völkerkunde in den deutschen Schutzgebieten' in *Verhandlungen des Deutschen Kolonialkongresses 1902* (Berlin: Dietrich Reimer, 1902) 163–174, 165.

[2] Annie E. Coombes, *Reinventing Africa; Museums, Material Culture and Popular Imagination in Late Victorian and Edwardian England* (New Haven: Yale University Press, 1997); Claire Wintle, *Colonial Collecting and Display* (Oxford: Berghahn Books, 2013); Chris Gosden and Chantal Knowles, *Collecting Colonialism: Material Culture and Colonial Change* (Oxford: Berg 2001).

[3] Erik Ringmar, 'Liberal Barbarism and the Oriental Sublime: The European Destruction of the Emperor's Summer Palace' (2006) 34 *Millenium* 917–933, 930.

[4] Chris Gosden and Chantal Knowles, *Collecting Colonialism Material Culture and Colonial Change* (London: Routledge, 2020).

Confronting Colonial Objects. Carsten Stahn, Oxford University Press. © Carsten Stahn 2023.
DOI: 10.1093/oso/9780192868121.003.0003

different contexts: in external affairs, in the metropolis, and in relations regarding the colonized. The Berlin Conference of 1884–1885 facilitated a 'collection boom'.[5] It became a tipping point for the systematic search for objects, including not only iconic artefacts, but also objects of everyday life. The gathering of collections on 'primitive peoples' was framed as a 'scientific' enterprise, through which European nations sought to present themselves as the apex of human civilization. With the growing trade and commodification of objects, ownership and display was used to justify the often costly and demanding maintenance of colonial power towards home audiences. Cultural takings were thus both a means of colonization and a technique to justify colonial domination. They were justified by a complex mix of realist, ideological, and strategic rationales, which go beyond war booty, prestige, and exploration: (i) Colonial subordination and submission, sanction against resistance, or exploitation; (ii) self-definition and display of superiority through othering, racial theories, and display of primitive objects; and (iii) justification of the 'civilizing mission'.

The massive transfer of objects was driven by the rise of racial science, capital flows between colonies and Europe, the expansion of public museums and colonial exhibitions, and broader consumerist cultures, including the commodification of 'oriental' or 'primitive' cultural artefacts. Objects were obtained through public and private channels: military and scientific expeditions, excavations, individual and missionary collecting, trade, or institutionalized collection in the name of museums. Through the acquisition of cultural objects, colonizing countries took ownership of colonized entities, not only in a physical or territorial sense, but also socially, culturally, historically, and economically. Territorial agents and administrators became central in the collection of objects. Museum curators relied on private agents and missionaries in order to extend their collections.

This chapter traces the link between evolutionary and racial science and the scramble for objects since the mid-nineteenth century, based on micro-histories of multiple forcible expeditions, carried out by different colonial powers (France, the UK, Belgium, Germany). It argues that 'scientific' discourse contributed to the advancement of two central premises of the colonial project: the idea of racial superiority and the image of the 'vanishing' of other cultures. It uses micro-histories of forcible takings in order to illustrate different forms of colonial violence, recurring patterns, and semantics, and the networked nature of takings, including the role of individuals agents and museums. It shows that colonial takings were driven by conflicting narratives which centralized colonizers and erased counter-narratives of colonized communities. It demonstrates that cultural takings challenged at the time some of the premises of colonial ideology. The artistic value of objects increased not only the scramble for objects, but forced colonial agents, collectors,

---

[5] Jos van Beurden, *Inconvenient Heritage* (Amsterdam: Amsterdam University Press, 2022) 33, 34, referring to an 'explosion in the taking of objects without consent or compensation'.

and museums to rethink some their world views. The violence behind the takings has prompted calls for return long after the facts. In modern times, objects taken in punitive expeditions have become the forerunners of new engagement with the colonial past.

2 The ambivalent use of science

As of the mid-nineteenth century, human sciences, and in particular theories of cultural evolutionism and scientific progress, drawing on perceived differences between colonizers and natives, gained a key role in colonial ideologies and power relations.[6] Colonial discovery and expansion facilitated scientific advancement in certain fields of science, such as biology, medicine, ecology, geography, or anthropology.[7] Colonial powers in return relied on racial science and anthropological knowledge to justify or facilitate colonial rule.[8] They treated colonial extensions as laboratories for science.[9] Colonial entities became spaces of observation and experimentation for medical, anthropological, or other purposes.[10]

Social Darwinism[11] and racial theories[12] contributed to the expansion of colonial rule over non-European peoples and the development of the 'civilizing mission'.[13] They mixed evolutionary theories with sociology, psychology, and philosophy. They relied on the idea that some people were more 'fit or socially

---

[6] See Joseph M. Hodge, 'Science and Empire: An Overview of the Historical Scholarship' in Brett M. Bennett and Joseph M. Hodge (eds.), *Science and Empire: Knowledge and Networks of Science across the British Empire, 1800-1970* (London: Palgrave Macmillan, 2011) 3–29; Lewis Pyenson, *Civilizing Mission: Exact Sciences and French Overseas Expansion, 1830-1940* (Baltimore: Johns Hopkins University Press, 1993); Lewis Pyenson, *Cultural Imperialism and Exact Sciences: German Expansion Overseas, 1900-1930* (New York: Peter Lang, 1985); Lewis Pyenson, *Empire of Reason: Exact Sciences in Indonesia, 1840-1940* (Leiden: Brill, 1989).

[7] See Talal Asad (ed.), *Anthropology and the Colonial Encounter* (New Jersey: Humanities Press, 1973).

[8] Andrew Zimmerman, 'Adventures in the Skin Trade: German Anthropology and Colonial Corporeality' in Glenn Penny and Matti Bunzl, *Worldly Provincialism: German Anthropology in the Age of Empire* (Ann Arbor: University of Michigan Press, 2003) 156–178, 171–172.

[9] Helen Tilley, *Africa as a Living Laboratory Empire, Development, and the Problem of Scientific Knowledge, 1870–1950* (Chicago: University of Chicago Press, 2011).

[10] On human remains, see Chapter 5.

[11] Charles Darwin's developed his theory of natural selection in his work *On the Origin of Species* in 1859. Darwin coined the term 'struggle for survival', but did not advocate an extension of his theories to human life or racial differences. His theories were used in the second part of the nineteenth century by philosophers and scientists like Herbert Spencer (1820–1903) or Karl Pearson (1857–1936) to develop what has become known as 'social Darwinism'. Spencer developed the concept of 'survival of the fittest' and applied it to human societies and nations. See generally Gregory Claeys, 'The Survival of the Fittest and the Origins of Social Darwinism' (2000) 61 *Journal of the History of Ideas* 223–240; James Alen Rogers, 'Darwinism and Social Darwinism' (1972) 33 *Journal of the History of Ideas* 265–280; Richard Weikart, 'The Origins of Social Darwinism in Germany, 1859–1895' (1993) 54 *Journal of the History of Ideas* 469–488.

[12] See Nancy Stepan, *The Idea of Race in Science* (London: Macmillan, 1982).

[13] Like Darwin himself, social Darwinists were not necessarily pro-imperial. They relied on Darwin to explain the struggle between individuals and included struggles among 'white' European nations.

advanced' than others to survive on the globe ('survival of the fittest') or that cultural evolution emerges in stages, working 'their way up from savagery to civilization through the slow accumulations of experimental knowledge'.[14] Such theories provided a 'veneer' and breeding ground for imperialistic expansion in line with the spirit of the time. European powers promoted their colonial expansion and justified 'salvage' of other 'civilizations', based on belief in natural selection, racial differences, and advancement of European nations, as reflected by their self-proclaimed technological and social progress.

Social Darwinism had a double impact. It provided colonial powers with a theory to justify superiority, based on the law of nature, and enhanced the competition and the 'race' between Western powers to build empires, based on theories of survival. For instance, British sociologist Benjamin Kidd (1858–1916) argued that the main quality which gives superiority to a society or race in the social struggle is the willingness of its members to subordinate personal interests to the interest of society.[15] He claimed that tropical races were unable to administer themselves and that imperialism was necessary to foster social evolution in colonies,[16] based on 'qualities such as humanity, strength, righteousness, and devotion'.[17] This reasoning rebranded colonial exploitation as an act of altruism in the interest of the survival of others.

Social Darwinism also provided, at least, an implicit basis for a hierarchization of civilizations and emerging patterns of racial discrimination. At the end of nineteenth century, scientists disagreed over what race meant, and how it was constituted. Social Darwinism reinforced the idea that differences between races are determined and inherited biologically. It turned racial difference into a constituent element of colonial justification. Francis Galton (1822–1911), one of the founders of eugenics, even went so far to argue in his 'Inquiries into Human Faculty and Its Development' (1883) that '[t]here exists a sentiment, for the most part quite unreasonable, against the gradual extinction of an inferior race'.[18]

The turn to social and racial science provided a backbone of the 'civilizing mission' which played a key role in the psychology of colonialism.[19] Racial theorists

---

[14] American anthropologist Lewis Henry Morgan (1818–1881) made this argument in 1877 in his work on ancient society. See Lewis Henry Morgan, *Ancient Society, or Researches in the Lines of Human Progress from Savagery through Barbarism to Civilization* (New York: Henry Holt and Company, 1877) 3.

[15] Benjamin Kidd, *Social Evolution* (London: Macmillan and Co., 1894).

[16] Benjamin Kidd, *The Control of the Tropics* (London, 1898) 53–57.

[17] Ray Hall Byrd, *Social Darwinism and British Imperialism, 1870-1900* (PhD, Texas Tech University, 1971) 86 https://ttu-ir.tdl.org/bitstream/handle/2346/13602/31295008643008.pdf;sequence=1.

[18] Francis Galton, *Inquiries Into Human Faculty and Its Development* (London: Macmillan, 1883, 2nd edn, 1907) 200.

[19] Douglas Lorimer, 'Theoretical Racism in Late-Victorian Anthropology, 1870-1900' (1988) 31 *Victorian Studies* 405–430; Patrick Bratlinger, 'Victorians and Africans: The Genealogy of the Myth of the Dark Continent' (1985) 12 *Critical Inquiry* 106–203, Tayyab Mahmud, 'Colonialism and Modern Constructions of Race: A Preliminary Inquiry' (1999) 53 *University of Miami Law Review* 1219.

argued that the 'black' and the 'white' races are not entirely different, but sufficiently similar to form part of the same species (monogenism) and enable assimilation and progressive development of 'backward' peoples.[20] This conception of the racial 'other' provided a seemingly objective reason to mould colonies after the ideal of European standards. As Ana Popović has argued:

> [b]y producing 'proof' of racial differences scientists could easily explain the occupation of African territories and then justify the exploitation of their land. First, they were able to use the evolutionary theory to explain the 'backwardness' of African peoples and the 'superiority' of the white race. Then, they could advocate for the 'civilization mission', in which the 'superior' race was supposed to educate the 'inferior race' … According to the logic of the late-19th century scientific discourse, although the black race could never become completely 'white', they could be 'civilized' to a certain degree, their 'savage' customs could be changed and brought closer to the Western ideals.[21]

This reasoning is present in many of the justifications that were advanced to justify colonial violence, resulting in the looting of cultural objects. It also spurred the interest in anthropological collection and the taking of cultural objects for the purposes of securing the survival of cultures under threat of demise. This mix of racism and 'humanitarianism' culminated in the evolutionary model of Frederick Lugard (1858–1945), who argued for the 'advancement of the subject races' and 'the development of material resources for the benefit of mankind' in territories 'unsuited for white settlement' in his defence of Britain's Dual Mandate in tropical dependencies in 1922.[22]

Colonialism itself became more 'scientific'. Colonial collecting 'supported, appropriated and formulated anthropological, geographical and medical knowledge'.[23] Scientists developed a more articulate interest in the documentation and study of foreign cultures, including human anatomies, anthropological classification and racial differences. These classifications were highly complex, encompassing different degrees of 'whiteness' and/or race in each colony. This led to a more systematic collection of everyday objects and their classification, supported by governmental and colonial administrations and in line with emerging methods of field research at the time. British archaeologist Augustus Pitt Rivers

---

[20] Patrick Petitjean, 'Science and the Civilizing Mission: France and the Colonial Enterprise' in Benedikt Stuchtey (ed.), *Science across the European Empires, 1800-1950* (Oxford: Oxford University Press, 2005) 107–128, 115.

[21] Ana Popović, 'Late Victorian Scientific Racism and British Civilizing Mission in Pears' Soap Ads' (2015) 3 *Pulse: the Journal of Science and Culture* 99–112, 106.

[22] Frederick Lugard, *The Dual Mandate in British Tropical Africa* (Edinburgh: Blackwood and Sons, 1922) 606.

[23] Elizabeth Edwards, 'Photographic Uncertainties: Between Evidence and Assurance' (2014) 25 *History of Anthropology* 171–188, 172.

(1827–1900) developed guidelines for the collection of anthropological objects, based on 'evolutionary sequences' ('typologies') and racial classifications.[24] Collection was facilitated by new media, such as photography and film.

Evolutionary theories and fears of the extinction of civilizations or races started to affect practices and justifications of collections. They drove two key assumptions of colonial ideology. They promoted the stereotype that other communities beyond the metropole/Europe were less advanced and contributed to idea that other communities were destined to perish. The expansion of Western civilization and culture in the colonial era was increasingly perceived as a factor contributing to the decline of indigenous cultures in scientific circles. The fear of the 'vanishing savage' with the advance of civilization became a 'constant theme'.[25] Physician and ethnologist James Cowles Prichard, the founder of British anthropology, highlighted this risk as early as 1839. He noted:

> Wherever Europeans have settled, their arrival has been the harbinger of extermination to the native tribes. Whenever the simple pastoral tribes come into relations with the more civilised agricultural nations, the allotted time of their destruction is at hand; and this seems to have been the case from the time when the first shepherd fell by the hand of the first tiller of soil. Now, as the progress of colonization is so much extended of late years, and the obstacle of distance and physical difficulties are so much overcome, it may be calculated that these calamities, impending over the greater part of mankind, if we reckon by families and races, are to be accelerated in their progress; and it may happen that, in the course of another century, the aboriginal nations of most parts of the world, will have ceased entirely to exist.[26]

This concern over loss and extinction reinvigorated cultural collection and anthropological throughout the nineteenth century. It stimulated a 'salvage' ethos in scientific circles, which justified the need for accurate and systematic collection in order to recover and preserve foreign peoples and cultures in the race against extinction through colonial expansion and expanding settler communities.[27]

This 'salvage' logic was allegedly meant to protect 'civilization' and to support the preservation of traditional structures in administered territories for purposes of imperial administration, but contributed at the same time to their destruction, by removing emblems of living culture and identity, prioritizing certain forms of

---

[24] See David K. van Keuren, 'Museums and Ideology: Augustus Pitt-Rivers, Anthropological Museums, and Social Change in Later Victorian Britain' (1984) 28 *Victorian Studies* 171–189.

[25] Jacob Gruber, 'Ethnographic Salvage and the Shaping of American Anthropology' (1970) 72 *American Anthropologist* 1289–1299, 1294.

[26] James Cowles Prichard, 'On the extinction of human races', *Monthly Chronicle of the Aboriginal Protection Society* (London, 1839).

[27] Gruber, 'Ethnographic Salvage and the Shaping of American Anthropology', 1296.

agricultural production for purposes of extraction, and assuming social control or creating denigrating distinctions among people through labels, such as tribes, Indians etc. Annie Coombes has highlighted this paradox:

> By speeding the inevitability of such destruction, anthropologists encouraged the expansion of the market in ethnographia and boosted the already multiple values assigned to the discipline's objects of study thus enhancing the status of anthropological 'knowledge', while simultaneously ensuring that those societies who produced such material culture maintained their position at the lower end of the evolutionary scale, since they were destined not to survive.[28]

Hosted in collections in the metropolis, cultural objects became 'signifiers' of the sovereignty and cultivation of imperial powers.[29] They were often displayed or presented based on cultural hierarchies or racial stereotypes articulated in evolutionary theories.[30]

3 The new age of ethnological museums and collections

Late nineteenth-century colonialism triggered a new age of anthropological museums and collections, driven by cultural competition of European nations.[31] Things were collected because they were 'culturally or humanly "interesting"'.[32] As James Clifford has noted: '[A] story of human development was told. The object ... ceased to be primarily an exotic 'curiosity' and was now a source of information entirely integrated in the universe of Western Man.'[33] Many colonial powers created special museums to house ethnographic artefacts and antiquities from Africa, Asia, or South America between 1880 and 1920.[34] Colonial museums reflected scientific debates, colonial understandings of objects, and approaches

---

[28] See Annie Coombes, 'Museums and the Formation of National and Cultural Identities' (1988) 11 *Oxford Art Journal* 57–68, 62.

[29] Ibid, 61.

[30] On 'primitivity' as a temporal concept, see Johannes Fabian, *Time and the Other: How Anthropology Makes Its Objects* (New York: Columbia University Press, 1983) 17–18.

[31] Adam Kuper, *The Museum of Other People: From Colonial Acquisitions to Cosmopolitan Exhibitions* (London: Profile Books, 2023).

[32] Clifford, *The Predicament of Culture*, 227.

[33] Ibid, 227–228.

[34] See Annie E. Coombes, *Reinventing Africa: Museums, Material Culture, and Popular Imagination in Late Victorian and Edwardian England* (New Haven, CT: Yale University Press, 1994); Tim Barringer and Tom Flynn (eds.), *Colonialism and the Object: Empire, Material Culture, and the Museum* (London: Routledge, 1998); H. Glenn Penny, *Objects of Culture: Ethnology and Ethnographic Museums in Imperial Germany* (Chapel Hill, NC: University of North Carolina Press, 2002); Alice Conklin, 'Civil Society, Science, and Empire in Late Republican France: The Foundation of Paris's Museum of Man' (2002) 17 *Osiris* 255–290.

towards the relationship between colonial powers and colonial subjects.[35] They became repositories of colonial collecting, classified objects, or mandated the collection of artefacts.

At the same, anthropological and ethnological studies became complicit in the colonial endeavour:

[A]nthropology was not only to be used to understand and help control people, but it was also to be used as a measure of imperialistic competition. The colonial policies of the British, Germans and French were fiercely contrasted, political and economic motives for the collection of ethnographic materials were becoming as important as the scientific.[36]

Museums and collections benefited from colonial structures and shared their knowledge with colonial agents.[37] They supported scientific expeditions or actively incentivized military personnel, colonial officials, private collectors or missionaries to acquire artefacts. Through their display of objects, they contributed to popular stereotypes, similar to colonial exhibitions. In this way, they were 'part of the colonial infrastructure and networks as well as places where colonial knowledge was produced and presented'.[38] They provided a space for evolutionist theories in international exhibitions that recreated 'African and other "primitive" villages for the education and entertainment of their national working classes'.[39]

Some museums have a clear colonial origin. For instance, the Royal Museum for Central Africa in Tervuren was built on the initiative of King Leopold II in order to publicize the newly acquired Congo Free State in the International Exposition of 1897.[40] It was initially set up as a tool to educate the Belgian public and attract potential national or international investors to the economic opportunities in the Free State. The colonial exhibition encompassed ethnographic objects (e.g. spears, arrows, masks),[41] stuffed wild animals, products from the Congo, and a replication of an indigenous village, in which Congolese men, women, and children from different ethnic groups were asked to imitate tribal life in the colony. The exhibition

---

[35] See John MacKenzie, *Museums and Empire: Natural History, Human Cultures and Colonial Identities* (Manchester: Manchester University Press, 2009).

[36] James Urry, 'Notes and Queries on Anthropology and the Development of Field Methods in British Anthropology, 1870-1920' (1972) *Proceedings of the Royal Anthropological Institute of Great Britain and Ireland* 45–57, 49.

[37] On the British experience, see Sarah Longair and John Macleer (eds.), *Curating Empire: Museums and the British Imperial Experience* (Manchester: Manchester University Press, 2012).

[38] German Guidelines 2019, 49. See MacKenzie, *Museums and Empire*, 7 ('tools of empire').

[39] Jean Muteba Rahier, 'The Ghost of Leopold II: The Belgian Royal Museum of Central Africa and Its Dusty Colonialist Exhibition' (2003) 34 *Research in African Literatures* 58–84, 63.

[40] For a survey, see Debora L. Silverman, 'Diasporas of Art: History, the Tervuren Royal Museum for Central Africa, and the Politics of Memory in Belgium, 1885–2014' (2015) 87 *Journal of Modern History* 615–667.

[41] Ibid, 619.

portrayed the Congo 'as a land of chaos, savagery' or slavery, and the Belgian colonizers as liberators who 'put an end to slavery and to expose[d] Central African
peoples to "civilization"'.[42]

Afterwards, the colonial exhibition was turned into a permanent collection. The
Congo Museum itself opened its doors in 1898. A large number of objects were
collected in a violent context, i.e. by military force.[43] In 1908, the Free State, which
was initially run as a fictive state in the possession of King Leopold II, formally became a Belgian colony.[44] The museum became the central point for the collection
of objects. It had the authority to determine whether objects should be retained in
Tervuren, or whether they should be placed in other museums or be returned for
preservation in the Congo. It encouraged military personnel, civil servants, missionaries, traders, or scientists to collect objects in order to document cultures that
were bound to disappear. Until the 1920s, the presentation of objects reproduced
narratives of the 'civilizing mission', Western superiority and race-dominated evolutionist anthropology, in line with Belgian colonial discourse at the time. Official
collectors and museum curators recorded the provenance of objects. The documentation often concealed the precise way of acquisition, including collection
through force, coercion, or under unfair conditions. Provenance labelling was kept
ambiguous in records. As Boris Wastiau reports:

> the most frequent terminology used in correspondence with curators described
> objects as 'collected' or 'taken in', 'sheltered', or 'gathered' by the collectors. They
> were 'made to reach' the museum, 'sent', 'expedited', or they just 'arrived at the
> museum'. Others were 'found' or 'brought forth' by the Congolese to the col-
> lectors ...The notion of 'find' must be understood broadly. It could cover any type
> of acquisition, fair or unfair, commercial or not.[45]

After the First World War, and in particularly in the 1930s, discourse changed with
the growing recognition of ethnological objects as art, as reflected by Franz Boas'
work *Primitive Art*.[46] The very notion of 'primitive art' continued to reflect cultural
narratives of colonial superiority,[47] but expressed greater artistic appreciation for
the works. Artefacts were seen more broadly as objects that reflected the value of

---

[42]   See Rahier, 'The Ghost of Leopold II', 66.

[43]   In 1897, 3,008 out of 7,598 objects were war-related. See Von Beurden, 'Decolonisation and
Colonial Collections', 71.

[44]   Joseph Conrad, *Heart of Darkness* (4th ed., New York: Norton, 2006) 99–113; Neal Ascherson, *The
King Incorporated: Leopold the Second and the Congo* (London: Allen & Unwin, 1963).

[45]   Boris Wastiau, 'The Legacy of Collecting: Colonial Collecting in the Belgian Congo and the Duty
of Unveiling Provenance' in Paula Hamilton and James B. Gardner (eds.), *The Oxford Handbook of
Public History* (Oxford: Oxford University Press, 2017) 460–478.

[46]   Franz Boas, *Primitive Art* (Cambridge, Mass.: Harvard University Press, 1927).

[47]   In the 1970s, the notion was replaced by other terms, such as 'nonwestern' or 'tribal art'. See Fred
Myers, 'Primitivism, Anthropology, and the Category of "Primitive Art"' in Christopher Tilley and
others, *Handbook of Material Culture* (London: Sage, 2006) 267–283, 267.

the colony to Belgium. They became 'a positive motivating factor instead of a negative affirmation of the need for colonial rule'.[48]

In Denmark, the National Museum in Copenhagen, founded in 1819, played a similar role as the Tervuren Museum in Belgium in relation to Danish colonial objects.[49] It was both a site of study and a central repository for objects, including ancient Inuit remains, colonial works from Greenland, and ethnographic materials from the nineteenth century, which had been taken in order to protect presumably vanishing cultures from disappearance.[50]

In France, the *Musée d'Ethnographie du Trocadéro* constituted the first anthropological museum.[51] It was created for the World Fair in Paris in 1878. It became a host of colonial objects with the expansion of the 'civilizing mission' in French colonial policy, which was designed to extend the 'benefits' of Western civilization to backward and oppressed people in Africa, Asia, and the Pacific region.[52] The museum provided the public and colonial agents with information on the colonized populations and societies. It was meant to preserve objects and reflect the history and customs of cultures facing extinction, either through colonization or societal change. It received objects inter alia from military expeditions. For instance, twenty-seven objects from the plundering of the palace of Dahomey were handed over to the museum between 1893 and 1895.[53] As of the late 1920s, the museum developed a more ethnological orientation under the leadership of anthropologist Paul Rivet (1876–1958). It integrated anthropological objects from the French Natural History Museum. Rivet sought to 'humanize colonial policy' and promote greater respect of cultural diversity in colonial administration and the French policy of colonial association, at a time when nationalism and fascism were on the rise.[54] He stressed the interconnection between human cultures and presented artefacts from Africa or Asia thematically on a par with European objects. The museum was closed in 1935 and transformed into the 'Museum of Man' (*Musée de l'Homme*).[55]

The 1931 Colonial Exposition in Paris, which was deemed to educate the French public about the virtues of the colonies and to 'demonstrate the generosity,

---

[48] See Sarah Van Beurden, 'The Value of Culture: Congolese Art and the Promotion of Belgian Colonialism (1945–1959)' (2013) 24 *History and Anthropology* 472–492, 474.

[49] Van Beurden, *Treasures in Trusted Hands*, 163.

[50] Mille Gabriel, *Objects on the Move: The Role of Repatriation in Postcolonial Imaginaries* (PhD: University of Copenhagen, 2010) 108.

[51] See Nélia Dias, *Le Musée d'Ethnographie du Trocadéro 1878-1908. Anthropologie et Muséologie en France* (Paris: CNRS, 1991); André Delpuech, Christine Laurière, and Carine Peltier-Caroff (eds.), *Les Années folles de l'ethnographie: Trocadéro 28–37* (Paris: Muséum national d'histoire naturelle, 2017).

[52] See Alice Conklin, *A Mission to Civilize: The Republican Idea of Empire in France and West Africa, 1895-1930* (Stanford: Stanford University Press, 1997).

[53] Sarr and Savoy Report, 52.

[54] Nélia Dias, 'Le musée d'ethnographie du Trocadéro: un musée colonial?', *Encyclopédie pour une histoire numérique de l'Europe*, ISSN 2677–6588 https://ehne.fr/fr/node/21471.

[55] Alice L. Conklin, *In the Museum of Man: Race, Anthropology, and Empire in France, 1850-1950* (Ithaca: Cornell University Press, 2013).

humanitarianism, and suitability of France for colonial rule'[56] led to the creation of the Musée permanent des Colonies (Colonial Museum).[57] The museum was originally modelled after the Tervuren Museum. Like its Belgian counterpart, it gradually reoriented policies of collecting and presenting objects after the 1930s. Indigenous artefacts were transformed into 'exotic primitive art'.[58] This transformation is reflected in changing title. It was first renamed the *Musée de la France d'Outre-mer* (Museum of French Overseas Territories) in 1935 and then the *Musée National des Arts Africains et Oceaniens* (Museum of African and Oceanic Arts) in 1960.

In Germany, the aftermath of the 1885 Berlin Conference and the rising preoccupation with 'salvage' anthropology led to a stark increase in acquisition of colonial objects. It was reinforced by a network of collectors. Ethnological museums emerged in the second half of the nineteenth century in cities like Leipzig (1862), Berlin (1869), or Hamburg (1879), and later in Cologne (1901), Frankfurt (1904), or Stuttgart (1911). The acquisition of German colonies and the interest in objects triggered a wave of collection. A decision by the German Bundesrat in 1891 specified that the Ethnological Museum in Berlin should be the primary site to host objects acquired by public funds or by officials or soldiers of the German Empire. It was extended to military and colonial officers in 1896, and marked the incentive actively to search and collect objects through colonial networks. As a result of this, the collection of the museum grew from around 7,000 objects in 1884/85 to around 50,000 objects during the colonial era. A similar trend is visible in other museums. For example, more than 90 per cent of the 25,000 objects of the Linden Museum in Stuttgart were acquired before the end of the German colonialism in 1920.[59] The ethnological museum in Munich acquired 27,000 objects between 1907 and 1916.[60] At the turn of the twentieth century, museums faced capacity limits:

> Boxes brimming with artifacts that had been packed away for decades were stacked to the ceilings of basement rooms, storage sheds, and offices ... [T]he overwhelming disorder of things forced German ethnologists to cancel public tours ... and engage in heated debates about the very nature und purpose of such collecting and display.[61]

---

[56] Thomas August, 'The Colonial Exposition in France: Education or Reinforcement?' (1982) 6/7 *Proceedings of the Meeting of the French Colonial Historical Society* 147–154, 148.

[57] Patricia A. Morton, 'National and Colonial: The Musée des Colonies at the Colonial Exposition, Paris, 1931' (1998) 80 *The Art Bulletin* 357–377.

[58] See Anne Monjaret and Mélanie Roustan, 'A palace as legacy: The former French colonial museum: perspectives from the inside' (2017) 22 *Journal of Material Culture* 216–236, 221.

[59] Gesa Grimme, *Provenienzforschung im Projekt Schwieriges Erbe: Zum Umgang mit kolonialzeitlichen Objekten in ethnologischen Museen* (Stuttgart: Linden-Museum, 2018) 59.

[60] Sigrid Gareis, *Exotik in München: museumsethnologische Konzeptionen im historischen Wandel am Beispiel des Staatlichen Museums für Völkerkunde München* (München: Anacon, 1990) 100.

[61] Glenn Penny, *Objects of Culture: Ethnology and Ethnographic Museums in Imperial Germany* (Chapel Hill: University of North Carolina Press, 2002) 1. The anthropological museum in Leiden was flooded with objects in 1895. See Van Beurden, *Inconvenient Heritage*, 34.

The relationship between ethnology and colonialism was complex. Colonial struc-tures provided the backbone of ethnographic fieldwork. Many German ethnol-ogists and anthropologists were initially liberals, who opposed racial hierarchies, but became complicit in colonial collecting. For instance, Adolf Bastian (1826–1905), the founder and curator of the Royal Museum of Ethnology in Berlin, stood in a liberal humanist tradition, which is typical of nineteenth-century German ethnology.[62] He was sceptical of Darwin's evolutionary theories and believed in a common humanity, but upheld the distinction between 'peoples of nature' (*Naturvölker*) and 'peoples of culture' (*Kulturvölker*), coined by Johann Gottfried Herder.[63] This was in line with voices who related the beginnings of art to peo-ples of nature in the 1890s.[64] Bastian was a passionate defender of 'salvage anthro-pology'. His goal was to 'collect everything'[65] in order to prevent the disappearance of native material culture. He used the colonial context for collection and analysis of cultural artefacts,[66] until he was replaced in 1909 by his successor Felix von Luschan (1854–1924). Of course, through such takings, collectors themselves con-tributed to the disappearance of cultures.

Von Luschan became one of most influential ethnologists in Imperial Germany. He was a 'liberal' who had worked under Bastian. He used the structures and net-work of colonial empire as a 'natural laboratory for science'. He was marked by contradictions. He challenged racial theories that advocated hierarchies among 'superior' and 'inferior' peoples and defended the unity of mankind. Contrary to other contemporaries, such as Max Buchner (1866–1934), the director of the ethnological museum in Munich, he was one of the first to recognize that the famous Benin bronzes are 'great and monumental native African art' that is 'not second to contemporary European art'.[67] He fought to 'save them for science' and saw them as evidence against racism. He acquired Benin bronzes from auction houses after the punitive expedition in 1897 before systematic collection started in Britain. Through his network, he managed to collect 580 Benin objects by 1919,

---

[62] Penny, *Objects of Culture*, 14–15. On different strands in anthropology, see also Fredrik Barth and others, *One Discipline, Four Ways: British, German, French, and American Anthropology* (Chicago: University of Chicago Press, 2005).

[63] Peter Monteath, 'German anthropology, nationalism and imperialism: Georg von Neumayer's Anleitung zu wissenschaftlichen Beobachtungen auf Reisen' (2020) 31 *History and Anthropology* 440–461. 450. See also Alfred Vierkandt, *Naturvölker und Kulturvölker. Ein Beitrag zur Socialpsychologie* (Leipzig: Duncker und Humboldt, 1896).

[64] Ernst Grosse, *Die Anfänge der Kunst* (Freiburg and Leipzig: Mohr, 1894).

[65] Penny, *Objects of Culture*, 51.

[66] Bastian noted in a letter: 'That military campaigns can bear fruit for scientific fields of research and can be exploited for this purpose, is evidenced by multiple examples—recently again through the results of the conquest of Benin—and already proven most sensationally during the earlier French ex-pedition to Egypt, which (through concomitance of a staff of 120 academics, artists, technicians and engineers) laid the groundwork for the magnificent blossoming of Egyptology following the discovery of the Rosetta stone, the key to decoding hieroglyphics, which threw a flood of light onto the grayness of prehistoric times.' See Penny, *Objects of Culture*, 110.

[67] Stefan Eisenhofer, 'Felix von Luschan and Early German-Language Benin Studies' (1997) 30 *African Arts* 62–94, 63.

which is more than twice the amount of bronzes that remained in London (280). However, in practice, he also employed collection in the service of imperialism.

Von Luschan was aware of the 'violent' apprehension of objects in the course of colonial expansion.[68] He knew that the Benin bronzes were acquired by force. He called the ethnological museum 'the greatest monument to our colonial troops'.[69] Between 1899 and 1901, he used the context of the anti-imperial Boxer rebellion in China to secure the collection of Chinese artefacts for the Berlin museum.[70] In 1906, he acknowledged that 'the governors of the individual protectorates and a large number of doctors, public servants and officers are fully conscious of the scientific and practical importance of anthropology and support our efforts purposefully and emphatically'.[71] He thus both challenged and upheld scientific racism.[72] The 1914 instructions on collection of objects, edited by von Luschan and ethnologist Bernhard Ankermann (1859–1943), encouraged collectors actively to search the homes of 'natives' in order to seize objects that may not be available for purchase.[73] The amount of ethnographic objects acquired under his leadership caused storage and display problems. Objects were collected during a short period of time. Inventories were drawn up hastily. Many acquisitions were insufficiently documented.[74]

The collection of Karl von Linden (1838–1910), which led to the creation of the Linden Museum in Stuttgart, emerged in a similar way. Von Linden acquired objects over two decades for the public association preceding the museum.[75] He relied on an extensive network of correspondence. Objects were collected by colonial officials, military units in German colonies, executives or employees of colonial companies, and missionaries and diplomats.[76] During his twenty-year tenure, the collection increased from approximately 300 objects in 1886 to around 63,000 objects.[77] Acquisitions grew rapidly in the second half of the 1890s. Many objects were formally presented by donors as a gift to the King of Württemberg. In this way,

---

[68] Kristin Weber, 'Objekte als Spiegel kolonialer Beziehungen: Das Sammeln von Ethnographica zur Zeit der deutschen kolonialen Expansion in Ostafrika (1884–1914)' in Marc Seifert et al. (eds.), *Beiträge zur 1. Kölner Afrikawissenschaftlichen Nachwuchstagung (KANT I)* (Cologne: University of Cologne, 2007) 1–24, 12.

[69] Monteath, 'German anthropology, nationalism and imperialism', 457.

[70] Penny, *Objects of Culture*, 107–108.

[71] Monteath, 'German anthropology, nationalism and imperialism', 452–453.

[72] John David Smith, 'W.E.B. Du Bois, Felix von Luschan, and Racial Reform at the Fin de Siècle' (2002) 47 *American Studies* 23–38.

[73] Felix von Luschan and Bernhard Ankermann, *Anleitung zum ethnologischen Beobachten und Sammeln* (Berlin: Georg Reimer, 1914) 9 ('[Y]ou have to rummage through the huts of the natives, because the people rarely bring everything for sale themselves, and there are things that you never get to see, even during longer stays in the country, if you don't go looking for them yourself').

[74] This continues to complicate provenance research. See Chapter 8.

[75] Württemberg Association for Commercial Geography and Promoting of German Interests Abroad (Württembergischer Verein für Handelsgeographie und Förderung deutscher Interessen im Ausland).

[76] Grimme, *Provenienzforschung im Projekt Schwieriges Erbe*, 20.

[77] Ibid, 20.

von Linden was able to bypass the primary role of the Berlin museum, much to the regret of Luschan.[78] Statistics demonstrate that collection emerged essentially through colonial structures. As much as 35 per cent of the objects were acquired by military personnel in the colonies; 21 per cent were collected by employees, owners, or shareholders of companies involved in colonial transactions. In addition, 18 per cent were gathered by members of the colonial administration.[79] The museum was essentially built through colonial expansion and colonial structures.

Even though the acquisition of objects by scientists or museums was not always guided by racial prejudices,[80] their collection and presentation fed into dominant narratives of cultural superiority inherent in colonial discourse. General Pitt Rivers even specified in a deed of gift to the University of Oxford that materials in the Pitt Rivers collection should be displayed according to his 'general principle' and 'mode of arrangement', which reflects classifications and evolutionist thinking of nineteenth-century collecting practice.[81]

4 Sociological transformation

The massive and systematic taking of objects and their classification and commodification changed both object meanings and colonial policies. With the rise of anthropology and ethnology, many objects were initially regarded as 'objects of science'. However, the display, representation, and reception led to a gradual aesthetization of objects in many collections.[82] Art historian Svetlana Alpers has referred to the 'museum effect' through which the museum turns 'all objects into works of art'.[83] This also applies to cultural colonial objects. Objects were more commonly regarded as artistic or cultural goods, forming part of a human cultural heritage, rather than as 'objects of science' or natural history objects.[84] They came to be valued for their craftsmanship or aesthetic qualities.

Throughout the twentieth century, Central and West African or Asian sculptural objects were increasingly collected and displayed as art objects, reflecting the 'beauty' of non-Western cultures. The Benin bronzes are an early example of this

---

[78] Ibid, 22.

[79] Ibid, 18–19.

[80] Elazar Barkan, *The Retreat of Scientific Racism: Changing Concepts of Race in Britain and the United States between the World Wars* (Cambridge: Cambridge University Press, 2011).

[81] Deed of Gift and Declaration of Trust on behalf of the University of Oxford in respect of the Anthropological Collection offered to the University by Major-General Augustus Henry Lane Fox Pitt Rivers, accepted by the University on 7 March 1883, *University Gazette* (13 May 1884).

[82] Van Beurden, 'The Value of Culture', 482.

[83] Svetlana Alpers, 'The Museum as a Way of Seeing' in Ivan Karp and Steven D. Lavine (eds.), *Exhibiting Cultures: The Poetics and Politics of Museum Display* (Washington, DC: Smithsonian Institution Press, 1991) 25–32, 26.

[84] For instance, the Javanese Prajñaparamita statue was originally collected in 1823 as a curiosity and to portray primitive indigenous culture. It was returned to Indonesia in 1978 as an artistic masterpiece.

process. Their discovery challenged the assumption that African sculpture lacked tradition or artistic sophistication. They called into question the 'primitiveness' of Benin society and thus deviated from stereotypes about the inferiority of non-Western cultures prevailing at the time. The reception of objects by the 'primitive art' movement and sculptures of artists, like Pablo Picasso or Henri Matisse, led to a 'westernization' of artefacts and cultural practices.[85] Objects were considered as art, irrespective of their original social use or function, e.g. as ritual or religious objects or items of daily life.

This trend and the influence of modernism became visible in museum practice in the 1930s. For instance, objects in the Tervuren Museum or French collections were gradually branded as 'modern art'.[86] Their 'recognition as masterpieces' made them suitable for 'Western collectors and museums' and increased their value as cultural commodities.[87]

Objects developed an agency of their own. They changed the narratives surrounding the justification of the colonial project. As Sarah van Beurden has argued, 'the older narrative of the "civilizing mission", in which the objects were proof of the need for the transformation of "primitive" African cultures, shifted towards a rhetoric of cultural guardianship'.[88] Colonization was no longer justified solely by primitive or backward nature of communities outside the metropole, but by other narratives which centred the positionality of the colonizer, such as the value of colonies to the metropole, or the 'heroism' of colonial powers who brought these treasures to light. Objects were used to showcase the value of colonies and the welfare of the colonial state. Collectors, administrators, or museums took credit for 'saving' or 'protecting' cultural objects and increasing their value beyond the moment of taking. Cynically, the violence behind the taking itself became a factor of attraction, which increased the market value of objects.

A similar conversion is visible in relation to intangible heritage. Colonial shows and exhibitions transformed indigenous cultural heritage into social 'capital'. They relied on exotic traditional customs in order to attract audiences and promote colonialism. For instance, the 1931 Paris exhibition attracted 30 million visitors over a period of six months. Many exhibitions contained 'living villages', which involved hundreds of people brought from colonies in Africa or Asia.[89] These practices commodified traditional cultures. Native rituals and practices were performed as spectacles for public entertainment. The shows played with the interest in primitive artefacts and erotic performances in order to 'sell' the colonial project to the

---

[85] Reproductions of 'primitive' statues came to be associated with Western modernist traditions, such as works by 20th century artists, rather than their original cultures.

[86] Frans Ohlbrechts, *Quelques chefs-d'oeuvre de l'art africain des collections du Musée royal du Congo belge, Tervuren* (Tervuren: Musée Royal du Congo belge, 1952).

[87] Van Beurden, 'The Value of Culture', 483.

[88] See Van Beurden, 'The Art of (Re)Possession', 145.

[89] An early example is a replicated Javanese village at the Chicago World's Fair in 1893.

public. They became part of a market-driven consumerist and voyeuristic culture, promoted through brochures, catalogues, and photographs.[90]

5 Acquisition through forcible expeditions: Selected micro-histories

The histories of objects taken in forcible expeditions as of the mid-nineteenth century provide a vivid account of both the violence of collection, and the processes of cultural conversion of objects.

Forcible operations were common among colonial powers to demarcate colonial boundaries, secure trade privileges, consolidate authority, and counter local resistance. Objects were collected as war booty, signs of power or repression, or to finance colonial expeditions. The building of colonial collections was part of social prestige and competition among colonial powers. In some cases, takings were ordered or commissioned by colonial authorities or museums or encouraged by experts.[91] Some objects became 'symbols of historic moments', colonial ideas, or ideologies.

Some operations were criticized or condemned in hindsight because of their brutality or their inherent friction with the alleged 'civilizing mission', sometimes by collectors themselves. For instance, during the Anglo-Egyptian War (1882) Pitt Rivers, whose own classification of objects was heavily shaped by Darwinian thought, emphasized in a letter to *The Times* on 3 August 1892 that the British expedition was in Egypt 'to civilize and not to rob'.[92] He stated:

> The means of communication are now so easy that all who are interested in Egyptology can see it there … The time has passed when antiquities should be regarded as trophies of war. It is no longer necessary for instruction to hoard up valuable specimens of foreign antiquities in European museums. So long as science has access to the materials of knowledge, that is all which is necessary to bring away, and national museums, with the limited space at their disposal, should more and more become devoted to local collections.[93]

However, such critiques remained an exception, and were not consistently applied. The late nineteenth century witnessed some of the worst forcible expeditions.

---

[90] See MacKenzie, *Museums and Empire*, 11, 265.

[91] According to the Sarr and Savoy Report, the 'targeted and plundered locations' had sometimes 'much more to do with the museums than military plundering stricto sensu', since some museums had already claimed them. See Sarr and Savoy Report, 11.

[92] Augustus Pitt Rivers, Letter to the Editor of *The Times*, 'Scientific Exploration in Egypt' (3 August 1882).

[93] Ibid.

Many of them were formally justified as acts of legitimate retaliation, liberation, or alleged humanization. Large-scale operations such as punitive expeditions against the Chinese Emperor (Beijing 1860), Maqdala (Ethiopia 1868), the Asante (Kumasi, Ghana 1874), and Benin (Nigeria, 1897) share striking similarities in relation to the justification of looting. Rationales of protection, the fight against the slave trade, or human sacrifice or the vindication of 'crimes' committed against envoys, missionaries, or embedded journalists[94] were used as a pretext for invasion or military operations. Cultural objects were inter alia seized as a reward or to recover the costs of operations.

The principle of effective occupation, promoted by the Final Act of the Berlin Conference, provided an indirect incentive for forcible expeditions.[95] It required colonial powers to assume effective control over protectorates in order to have their claims recognized by other colonial powers. This policy encouraged practices of subjugation. For instance, the expeditions in Asante/Ghana (1896, 1900), Douala/Cameroon (1884), or Dahomey/Benin (1892) were guided by such rationales. Cultural objects associated with native rule or former kingdoms were captured or removed in order symbolically to express the ousting of local rulers and demonstrate the assumption of administrative and political control by colonial powers.[96]

In practice, punitive expeditions were used to capture objects that could not be obtained through purchase or consensual transactions. Key decisions to loot or destroy objects were often taken by individuals (e.g. James Bruce, the son of Lord Elgin, Gustave Roze, Garnet Wolseley, or Alfred-Amédée Dodds) who spearheaded the operations. They acted sometimes without express instruction of the metropolis, used ambiguities in colonial policies, or profited from the occasion.

The histories of cultural takings show the close interplay between the taking of objects and colonial violence, as well as the transformation of objects. A recurring technique is what Dan Hicks has called 'white projection',[97] i.e. a reversal of roles through which colonizers presented themselves as 'innocent' agents who were coerced into violent action by their opponents in a situation of crisis, although the underlying context was inflicted through the colonial condition.

---

[94] Kwame Opoku, 'When will Britain Return Looted Ghanaian Artefacts? A History of British Looting of more than 100 Objects', 8–9 https://www.africavenir.org/fileadmin/downloads/occasional_papers/Opoku_Asante_Regalia.pdf ('The scheme is as follows: 1. Existence of lucrative trade in a non-European country or its strategic importance in the region. 2. The British seek to take control over trade in the area and meet resistance. 3. The British send a team or delegation allegedly to negotiate peace, a delegation which is often secretly armed. 4. Some or all of the members of the delegation are attacked and killed. In some cases, the alleged killing of some Europeans, such as missionaries, suffices as justification. 5. Britain sends an army, a punitive expedition army to the non-European country. 6. The non-European country is attacked, government there is deposed, city or main palace there is burnt but before doing that, all treasures, including artworks are looted. What cannot be taken is burnt').
[95] Articles 34 and 35 of the General Act of the Berlin Conference on West Africa (26 February 1885).
[96] The most visible example is the dispute over the 'Golden Stool' of the Asante, the spiritual symbol of the unity of the former kingdom.
[97] Dan Hicks, *The Brutish Museums* (London: Pluto, 2020) 37 ff.

The chapter demonstrates the violence of takings, and the processes of object transformation, through micro histories of ten forcible expeditions that produce continuing effects in contemporary relations: (1) the looting of the Yuanmingyuan Palace (1860); (2) the French punitive expedition to Korea (1866); (3) the Abyssinian Expedition of 1868; (4) the punitive expeditions during the Anglo-Asante Wars; (5) the German expedition against Douala chief Lock Priso (1884); (6) the French expedition to Dahomey (1892); (7) the Dutch Lombok expeditions (1894); (8) the Belgian Force Publique expedition to Lulu (1896); (9) the taking of the Benin bronzes (1897); and (10) looting during the French Dakar–Djibouti mission (1931).

5.1 Looting of the Yuanmingyuan Palace (1860)

The looting of Yuanmingyuan, the country estate of the emperors in Imperial China (the 'Garden of Perfect Brightness', also referred to as the 'Summer Palace') by an Anglo-French expeditionary force in 1960[98] shows the thin line between liberalism, civilization, and 'barbarism' in nineteenth-century colonial ideology. It has been described as 'one of the worst acts of cultural vandalism of all time'.[99] Victor Hugo famously branded it as an act of destruction that (Western) 'civilization has done to barbarism'.[100] It broke the divide between civilized colonizer and the imagined 'inhumane' other.

The looting and destruction occurred in the context of the Second Opium War (1856–1860),[101] which was deemed to maintain free European trade and opium exports from China. The British East India Company had lost its trade monopoly in China in 1833, but made profits through trade of opium delivered by Chinese suppliers. This led to confrontations with the Chinese government, which cut down exports in 1839, and subsequent military hostilities. Following the First Opium War (1839–42), China was required by the Treaty of Nanjing (1842) to open five

[98] Young-Tsu Wong, *A Paradise Lost: The Imperial Garden Yuanming Yuan* (Hawaii: University of Hawai'i Press, 2001); James Hevia, *English Lessons: The Pedagogy of Imperialism in Nineteenth-century China* (Durham and London: Duke University Press, 2003); Greg Thomas, 'The Looting of Yuanming and the Translation of Chinese Art in Europe' (2008) 7 *Nineteenth-Century Art Worldwide* 23–55; Katrina Hill, 'Collecting on Campaign: British Soldiers in China during the Opium Wars' (2013) 25 *Journal of the History of Collections* 227–252; James Hevia, 'Loot's fate: the economy of plunder and the moral life of objects from the Summer Palace of the Emperor of China' (1994) 6 *History and Anthropology* 319–345; Erik Ringmar, *Liberal Barbarism: The European Destruction of the Palace of the Emperor of China* (London: Palgrave Macmillan, 2013); Louise Tythacott, 'Trophies of War: Representing "Summer Palace" Loot in Military Museums in the UK' (2015) 13 *Museum & Society* 469–488.

[99] Ringmar, 'Liberal Barbarism and the Oriental Sublime', 922; see also Hill, 'Collecting on Campaign', 227.

[100] Victor Hugo, 'L'Expédition de Chine: au capitaine Butler' in Victor Hugo, *Oeuvres complètes de Victor Hugo: actes et paroles pendant l'exile, 1852–70*, originally written in 1861 (Paris: J. Hetzel, 1880) 267–270, 269.

[101] Robert Swinhoe, *Narrative of the North China Campaign of 1860* (London: Smith, Elder and Co., 1861).

ports to British merchants and agree to the cession of Hong Kong. The treaty of Tianjin, signed during the Second Opium War in 1858, obliged China to open access to further ports, legalize opium, and allow to access for travellers and missionaries. But China refused to ratify and implement the terms of the treaty. According to British accounts, the Emperor had granted these concessions in order to 'get rid' of the British and did not consider them to 'be permanently binding upon him'.[102] Britain and France created a joint force to secure compliance. The British force operated under James Bruce, 8th Earl of Elgin (1811–1863), the son of the 7th Earl of Elgin, who had taken the Parthenon marbles, and General Hope Grant (1808–1875), who had been involved in British colonial warfare in India. The French force was headed by General Charles Guillaume Montauban (1796–1878).

Subsequent attempts at negotiation failed. On 18 September 1860, the Chinese captured an envoy of thirty-nine soldiers and civilians, including diplomats and an embedded correspondent from *The Times* (twenty-six British and thirteen French men), who were on their return from a mission to negotiate Chinese surrender. They were held as hostages and not allowed to return in order to compel Britain and France to give in.[103] The allied forces regarded the hostage-taking as a treacherous and humiliating act, which signalled the unwillingness of the Chinese side to reach a negotiated settlement.[104] They started their march on Beijing on 3 October 1860. The captives were only gradually released after 9 October—following the attack and pillage of Yuanmingyuan, which took place on 7 and 8 October. Their reports indicated that they had been severely tortured. Only eighteen men returned alive, including Henry Loch, Harry Parkes, and Stanislas d'Escayrac de Lauture.[105] Elgin assumed that they had been held in the palace.

The hostage situation was used as an argument to defend the looting of the palace. The attack on Beijing was presented as a retaliatory measure. It was carried out in order to intimidate the adversary and to respond to perceived public pressure from audiences at home.[106] This rationale did not justify the amount of destruction or looting.[107] British and French troops could have seized the palace and negotiated the surrender of the members of the envoy. Instead, they used the opportunity to carry out an 'orgy of looting' that involved the 'humiliation' of the emperor.[108]

---

[102] Ringmar, *Liberal Barbarism: The European Destruction of the Palace of the Emperor of China*, 114, referring to a correspondence of the Earl of Elgin to Lord J. Russell, dated 7 August 1860, Houses of Parliament, Correspondence, 1857–59, 95.

[103] Ibid, 67.

[104] Ibid, 78.

[105] Hosea Ballou Morse, *The International Relations of the Chinese Empire: The Period of Conflict, 1834–1860*, vol. 1 (New York: Paragon, 1900) 608.

[106] See Ringmar, *Liberal Barbarism: The European Destruction of the Palace of the Emperor of China*, 131.

[107] See Robertson, *Who Owns History?*, 207–208.

[108] Hevia, 'Loot's Fate', 324 and 333 ('What more commanding image could there be for the constitution of colonising subjectivities than the appropriation of the signs of another "sovereign" and the assimilation of these signs to oneself').

The attack was a measure of subjugation. The damage went far beyond any reasonable measure of proportionate response and exceeded the initial purpose of the operation. This was apparent to Elgin, who was not a notorious imperialist, but a rational pragmatist. He later admitted this in hindsight, when commenting that '[w]ar is a hateful business. The more one sees of it, the more one detests it'.[109]

French troops reached Beijing and the Palace on 6 October 1860. They did not receive much resistance. The 'indiscriminate loot' started on 7 October. General Montauban showed initial signs of protest,[110] but failed to prevent troops from looting.[111] Elgin and Hope arrived later. There are conflicting reports about the precise course of events.[112] Neither British nor French commanders wanted to take the blame.[113] However, the degree and systematic nature of the looting clearly indicated a breakdown of military order. Colonel Garnet Wolseley, the quartermaster-general of the expedition, qualified the conduct as 'indiscriminate plunder and wanton destruction'.[114] According to eye-witness accounts, it brought out 'good proof of the innate evil in man's nature'.[115] The palace was like an exotic 'wonderland' to soldiers, open to free plunder. This unleashed unrestrained instincts. The proclaimed 'civilizers' turned into 'savages' themselves.[116]

They plundered 'trophies (military supplies, official dress, and insignia), luxury goods (porcelain and silk), and curiosities (sacred art, pictures, and carvings)'.[117] As Erik Ringmar notes, the looting had a strongly symbolic dimension, conveying outrage, conquest, and revenge, and signs of disrespect against the emperor:

> The soldiers destroyed vases and mirrors, tore down paintings and scrolls, broke into the storehouse of silks and used the precious fabrics for tying up their horses; they draped themselves in the empress's robes, and stuffed their pockets full of rubies, sapphires, pearls and pieces of crystal rock.[118]

The soldiers seized inter alia clothes, jade ornaments, vases, porcelain, statues, and wood carvings, which were carried away by an entire 'train of carts full of loot'.[119]

---

[109] See James Bruce Earl of Elgin, *Extracts from the Letters of James, Earl of Elgin, to Mary Louisa Countess of Elgin, 1847-1862* (Edinburgh: Constable, 1864) 220. He noted that '[p]lundering and devastating a place like this is bad enough, but what is much worse is the waste and breakage'.
[110] He later denied culpability. See Ringmar, *Liberal Barbarism: The European Destruction of the Palace of the Emperor of China*, 74.
[111] Hevia, *English Lessons*, 77–78.
[112] Ibid, 76–78.
[113] Ibid, 78 ('Neither the British nor the French, it would seem, wanted to be held responsible in the eyes of the other').
[114] Garnet Wolseley, *Narrative of the War with China in 1860* (London: Longman, Green, Longman and Roberts, 1862) 224.
[115] Hevia, *English Lessons*, 80.
[116] See also Ringmar, 'Liberal Barbarism and the Oriental Sublime', 932 ('only as barbarians could they effectively spread the blessings of civilisation').
[117] Hill, 'Collecting on Campaign', 248.
[118] Ringmar, 'Liberal Barbarism and the Oriental Sublime', 921–922.
[119] Hevia, *English Lessons*, 79.

They considered these objects as 'trophies', 'specimens', or 'souvenirs'. Montauban, Elgin, and Grant selected particular valuable objects as trophies for their 'sovereigns' at home, i.e. Emperor Napoleon III and Queen Victoria. Following procedures developed in colonial India, Grant organized a war prize auction on 9 October for objects taken by British soldiers.[120] The looting was an act of subjugation, indignation, and 'sovereignty taking'. It left deep scars in Chinese history. It is part of the long century of 110 years of 'national humiliation' (1839–1949).[121]

On 18 October 1860, i.e. nine days after the looting, the palace was completely destroyed. Elgin had learnt from the kidnapped hostages that they had been brutally tortured or murdered. According to reports,

> [t]hey had been bound hands to feet and carried on sticks through Beijing, where people hit them and threw garbage at them as the guards tightened their wet ropes. They then were held in chains at Yuanming Yuan for three days without food or water, and guards stuffed their mouths with human excrement when they signalled for water.[122]

Elgin ordered the palace to be set on fire as a 'solemn act of retribution' and 'punishment'.[123] He pursued two goals: to punish the emperor, rather than his people, for the kidnapping and torture of the negotiating team,[124] and to force the Chinese side to sign the treaty, securing China's submission. He concealed the violence of his own actions by arguing that Chinese torture, rather than the burning of the palace, constituted 'a great crime'.[125] French General Montauban and Marshall Gros remained opposed to the idea, since they feared that this punitive action would end the dynasty and make the emperor more reluctant to sign the treaty.[126] But British forces went ahead. The burning took two days. Garnet Wolseley later argued the destruction of the emperor's palace 'was the strongest proof of our superior strength; it served to undeceive all Chinamen in their absurd conviction of their monarch's universal sovereignty'.[127]

---

[120] Thomas, 'The Looting of Yuanming and the Translation of Chinese Art in Europe', 32.

[121] Alison Adcock Kaufman, 'The "Century of Humiliation" Then and Now: Chinese Perceptions of the International Order' (2010) 25 *Pacific Focus* 1–33.

[122] Thomas, 'The Looting of Yuanming and the Translation of Chinese Art in Europe', 35.

[123] See Theodore Walrond (ed.), *Letters and Journals of James, Eighth Earl of Elgin* (London: John Murray, 1872) 366.

[124] Ibid, 366 ('The army would go there not to pillage, but to mark, by a solemn act of retribution, the horror and indignation with which we were inspired by the perpetration of a great crime. The punishment was one which would fall, not on the people who were comparatively innocent, but exclusively on the Emperor whose direct personal responsibility for the crime committed is established').

[125] Ibid.

[126] Thomas, 'The Looting of Yuanming and the Translation of Chinese Art in Europe', 34–35.

[127] Wolseley, *Narrative of the War with China in 1860*, 280–281.

The *Illustrated London News* described the event in devastating terms in 1861. It stated:

> The loss inflicted cannot be estimated by any money valuation. Treasures of gold and silver, works of the highest Chinese art, which no sums could purchase, the accumulation of ages, the most valuable secret records of the empire, the sacred genealogical tablets of the dynasty, are all gone, and can never be replaced. The solid, indestructible stone, here and there a marble arch or gateway, and massive bronzes too ponderous to be removed, will alone remain to tell to a future generation where the beautiful palace once stood, and to bear undying record of the righteous retribution enacted by the allied armies of the foreigners.[128]

On 24 and 25 October, Prince Gong, the temporary regent and brother of the emperor, signed a treaty on the behalf of the Qing government with Britain and France, represented by Lord Elgin and Marshall Gros. In the treaty, the Emperor accepted the provisions the Treaty of Tianjin (1858), which compelled China to pay compensation to Britain and France for the war, cede part of Chinese territory, legalize the opium trade, and grant trade privileges to foreigners.

The looting and auctioning of objects transformed their nature. They turned from imperial treasures, exotic regalia, and personal possessions into military trophies and prizes of war, and then into market commodities.[129] Over 1,300 objects were sold in auction houses in London and Paris as 'magnificent oriental jars' or Chinese 'art and curiosities'.[130] They acquired new meanings as precious 'works of art'.[131] This representation and rebranding of objects erased their earlier histories and concealed their historical and political past.[132] Their display and collection in Britain and France after 1860 marked a transformative moment for the appreciation of Chinese artefacts. It shaped 'the taste for elaborate eighteenth-century jades, porcelains, and enamels in Europe during the second half of the nineteenth-century'.[133] The violence of the takings created a political economy of loot. Over time, the link of objects to the Imperial Summer Palace 'significantly' enhanced their 'final price' and market value.[134]

Curiously, the plundering also led to the introduction of 'Pekinese dogs' in Britain. British soldiers discovered this rare species of dog, favoured at the royal court, in the palace of the emperor. They found five dogs of this exotic breed, which

---

[128] Zuozhen Liu, *The Case for Repatriating China's Cultural Objects* (Singapore: Springer, 2016) 9.

[129] Hevia, *English Lessons*, 16.

[130] Ibid, 92.

[131] Thomas, 'The Looting of Yuanming and the Translation of Chinese Art in Europe', 41.

[132] On return claims, see Liu, *The Case for Repatriating China's Cultural Objects*; Richard Curt Kraus, 'The Repatriation of Plundered Chinese Art' (2009) 199 *The China Quarterly* 837–842.

[133] Nick Pearce, 'From relic to relic: a brief history of the skull of Confucius' (2014) 26 *Journal of the History of Collections* 207–222, 214.

[134] Ruida Chen, 'Healing the Past: Recovery of Chinese Cultural Objects Lost During the Colonial Era' (2022) 8 *Santander Art and Culture Law Review* 161–184 172.

'belonged to the Empress or to one of the ladies of the Imperial family'.[135] They took them as spoils of war to Britain. Captain John Hart Dunne (1835–1924) gave one of the dogs to Queen Victoria in April 1861. She picked a name, which perfectly captured the origins of the taking: 'Looty'. Looty was presented as 'the smallest and by far the most beautiful little animal that has appeared in [the] country',[136] and was later represented in an oil painting by animal painter Friedrich Keyl (1823–1871), commissioned by the queen.[137]

5.2   French punitive expedition to Korea (1866)

Only six years after the looting of the Yuanmingyuan palace, France launched a punitive expedition to Korea (known as 'Byeongin Yangyo').[138] It occurred in the context of rising atrocities against Christian missionaries in China after the Second Opium War, Korea's reluctance to allow foreign concessions, and France's intent to protect Catholic missionaries 'in order to counterbalance the prestige and influence' of Britain.[139] Korea was formally governed by a young ruler, King Gojong, the first Emperor of Korea (1852–1919), but controlled by his father, the regent Heungseon Daewongun ('Prince of the Great Court', 1820–1898). Daewongun was critical towards opening up to free trade and the expansion of Christian missionary activity, following China's experiences in the Opium Wars ('no treaties, no trade, no Catholics, no West, and no Japan').[140]

At the time, Korea had a growing local Christian community, including more than 20,000 members, also based on movements from China. In 1866, native Korean Christians sought to persuade the Korean leadership to foster an alliance with France and Britain in order to repel threats from Russia, which sought to enforce trading and residency privileges. They named the head of the Catholic Church in Korea, French Bishop Siméon-François Berneux (1814–1866), to lead the discussion at the royal court. Daewongun received Berneux, but killed him, partly based on rumours about anti-Christian outbursts in China.[141] Berneux's execution was followed by the executions of nine French missionaries and the persecution of local Christian Koreans. Three French missionaries managed to escape

---

[135]   J. P. Entract, 'Looty, A small Chinese dog, belonging to her Majesty' (1972) 50 *Journal of the Society for Army Historical Research* 237–238, 237.

[136]   Ibid, 237.

[137]   The other four dogs were given to the Duchess of Wellington and the Duchess of Richmond.

[138]   Daniel Kane, 'Bellonet and Roze: Overzealous Servants of Empire and the 1866 French Attack on Korea' (1999) 23 *Korean Studies* 1–23; Douglas Cox, 'Inalienable Archives: Korean Royal Archives as French Property under International Law' (2011) 18 *International Journal of Cultural Property* 409–423.

[139]   Paul A. Cohen, *China and Christianity: The Missionary Movement and the Growth of Chinese Antiforeignism 1860-1870* (Cambridge, MA: Harvard University Press, 1963) 202.

[140]   Bruce Cumings, *Korea's Place in the Sun: A Modern History* (New York: W.W. Norton & Company, 2005) 91, 100.

[141]   Kane, 'Bellonet and Roze', 3.

and reported the situation to Rear Admiral Pierre-Gustave Roze (1812–1882), the commander of the French Far Eastern Squadron. Roze sought to retaliate in order to 'strike fear into the Korean Court'.[142] He was supported by the French consul in Beijing, Henri de Bellonet, who was of the view that 'the slightest delay in the punishment of this bloody outrage could result in serious endangerment to the 500 missionaries preaching in China'.[143] Bellonet sought to overthrow the leadership in Korea and seize royal treasures and property to secure reparation for the deaths of the missionaries and cover the expenses of the expedition.[144]

This led to the composition of an expedition force, commanded by Roze, on behalf of French Emperor Napoleon III. The mission was branded as an act of retribution, but part of a broader effort to obtain trade concessions from Korea and enhance France's prestige.[145] Roze composed a French fleet with seven warships. The force occupied Ganghwa Island. Roze demanded punishment of those responsible for the massacres against Catholic Christians and sought to negotiate commercial privileges, but did not obtain agreement. He defeated the Korean army, led by general Yang Heon-su (1816–1888). The French army seized silver, jade, and paintings. It also looted 297 volumes of royal manuscripts of the Joseon Dynasty, known as Uigwe, from the Ganghwa branch of the royal library (the Oegyujanggak).[146] The books contained official government records of the dynasty, including illustrations of royal rites and ceremonies, and were listed in UNESCO's Memory of the World register in 2007. It is unclear whether the French forces confiscated the royal protocols, based on the assumption that they contained 'enemy information possibly useful for military operations' or whether they seized them due to their value 'as artistic booty'.[147]

In his final report, Roze openly defended the retributive nature of the operation. He stated:

> The expedition I just accomplished, however modest as it is, may have prepared the ground for a more serious one if deemed necessary ... The expedition deeply shocked the Korean Nation, by showing her claimed invulnerability was but an illusion. Lastly, the destruction of one of the avenues of Seoul, and the considerable losses suffered by the Korean government should render it more cautious in the future. The objective I had fixed to myself is thus fully accomplished, and the murder of our missionaries has been avenged.[148]

---

[142] Ibid, 16.

[143] Ibid, 6.

[144] Hal Swindall, 'When the French Arrived: the 1866 French Punitive Expedition to Korea 150 years on' http://thethreewisemonkeys.com/2016/10/30/french-arrived-1866-french-punitive-expedition-korea/.

[145] Kane, 'Bellonet and Roze', 19.

[146] Cox, 'Inalienable Archives', 411.

[147] Ibid, 419.

[148] New World Encyclopedia, 'French Campaign against Korea, 1866' https://www.newworldencyclopedia.org/entry/French_Campaign_against_Korea,_1866#cite_note-7.

To Koreans, it illustrated 'the basic nefariousness of the Westerners and the virtues of isolation'.[149] The royal manuscripts were stored in the French National Library and returned to Korea in 2011.[150]

5.3 The Abyssinian Expedition of 1868 (Maqdala Pillage)

A notorious example of looting and destruction of cultural property, carried out as punishment for hostage-taking, is the pillage of a fortress of Ethiopian Emperor Tewodros II (1818–1868) in Maqdala (now Amba Mariam) during the Anglo-Ethiopian War (1867–1868).[151] It has become known as the 'Abyssinian Expedition of 1868'.[152] It marks an early example of the industrialization[153] and 'privatization of war'.[154] It was formally launched to free British hostages and missionaries held by the emperor, but had a larger symbolic or performative purpose, namely to signal the force of the British Empire, by using Ethiopia (former Abyssinia) as an example.

Tewodros was an influential ruler (the 'King of Kings') who sought to unify the different kingdoms of Ethiopia, establish royal control over the Ethiopian Church, end the feudal system, and modernize the country. In 1862, he sought friendly relations with Britain in a letter to Queen Victoria, transmitted to the British consul for Abyssinia, Captain Charles Duncan Cameron (1825–1870), and requested British assistance to support his rule and fight against foreign incursions, including interventions from Egypt (which was of strategic importance to Britain). The request remained unanswered. Tewodros was uncertain whether the lack of cooperation reflected official governmental policy or was influenced by Cameron.[155] He imprisoned Cameron and a handful of European missionaries and envoys, whom he suspected of plotting against his reign, and held them in detention in Maqdala. His action was perceived as an insult and caused growing indignation in the British public. As a result, the British government composed a large armed expeditionary

---

[149] Kane, 'Bellonet and Roze', 17.

[150] Cox, 'Inalienable Archives', 409.

[151] See Richard Pankhurst, 'The Napier Expedition and the Loot from Magdala' (1985) 133/ 134 *Présence Africaine* 233–240; Henry M. Stanley, *Coomassie and Magdala: the Story of Two British Campaigns in Africa* (New York: Harper & Bros., 1874).

[152] Clements R. Markham, *A History of the Abyssinian Expedition* (London: Macmillan, 1869); Frederick Myatt, *The Abyssinian War 1868* (London: Leo Cooper, 1970); Volker Matthies, *The Siege of Magdala: The British Empire Against the Emperor of Ethiopia* (Princeton: Markus Wiener Publishers, 2012).

[153] The operation involved '44 elephants, 5,735 camels, 17,934 mules and ponies, as well as 8,075 oxen and 2,538 horses ... shipped from India to East Africa on 75 steamships, 205 sailing ships, and 11 smaller ships'. Matthies, *The Siege of Magdala*, 39–40.

[154] Ibid, 170, referring to embedded journalists, civilian scientific staff, and military attachés from several European countries.

[155] Richard Pankhurst, 'Ethiopia, The Aksum Obelisk, and the Return of Africa's Cultural Heritage' (1999) 98 *African Affairs* 229–239, 230.

force in 1867, headed by Lieutenant General Sir Robert Napier (1810–1890), who had fought in the Anglo-Sikh wars in order to retaliate and secure the release of the detainees from the 'cruel despot'.

As Nini Rodgers has stated, the 'imperial war of 1867-8' was initially 'fought not for the purpose of annexation but in order to extricate Britain, with honour, from the shattered remnants of an unsuccessful policy'.[156] It was deemed to make an example of an African ruler who had 'mocked every human and international law'.[157] The sheer size of the Abyssinian expedition confirms the theory that the purpose of the mission was to vindicate national honour and defend British prestige.[158] It comprised 13,000 British and Indian soldiers, many civilian observers, journalists, or translators and over 40,000 animals, including elephants pulling heavy artillery. It even included archeologist Richard Holmes (1835–1911), an assistant in the Department of Manuscripts of the British Museum, who was sent by the trustees of the museum to excavate or collect antiquities and appointed him as archaeologist to Napier's expedition.[159] Based on reports by Henry M. Stanley, Napier made clear to local chiefs and the population that he regarded the detention as a 'violation of the laws of all civilized nations', but that the expedition was not designed 'to occupy permanently any portion of the Abyssinian Territory, or to interfere with the government of the country'.[160]

Tewodros' influence and support in Ethiopia was declining. During the siege of Maqdala, Napier gave Tewodros II an ultimatum in which he demanded surrender and pledged him to 'submit to the Queen of England'.[161] Napier argued that unconditional surrender was 'essential for the vindication of our national honour, which he has so grossly insulted, that he should be removed for ever from his place'.[162]

---

[156] Nini Rodgers, 'The Abyssinian Expedition of 1867-1868: Disraeli's Imperialism or James Murray's War?' (1984) 27 *Historical Journal* 129–149, 149.

[157] Matthies, *The Siege of Magdala*, 28. Some soldiers were under the impression that the operation pursued broader strategic objectives. For instance, one German participant observed: 'No one … had ever imagined that such a large campaign would be undertaken and millions of pounds willingly expended just to liberate an English consul and a few prisoners unless in addition other, more relevant … grounds had served as the basis for this strategic operation. Even in the army, from the most superior general to the most ordinary soldier, the men were firmly convinced that after Tewodros was subjugated and the Europeans were freed, a golden profit would somehow have to be drawn from the presence of the troops in this African mountain world'. Ibid, 175–176.

[158] Ibid, 137, 144.

[159] This is shown by correspondences between archeologist Charles Thomas Newton (1816–1894), who was in charge of Greek and Roman Antiquities at the British Museum, and the Royal Geographical Society. After receiving notice of the expedition, Newton argued it would be 'desirable that an archaeologist should be sent out with the army'. See letter from Newton to Sir Roderick Murchison dated 3 October 1867, London, The British Library/BL: AM, Murchison papers, III, Add MS 46127, fos. 271–4, F. 271; Lucia Patrizio Gunning and Debbie Challis, 'Planned Plunder, the British Museum, and the 1868 Maqdala Expedition' (2023) 66 *The Historical Journal* 1–23, 11.

[160] Henry Morton Stanley, *Magdala: The History of the Abyssinian Campaign of 1866-1867* (Marston: Sampson Low, 1896) 48–49.

[161] David Appleyard and Richard Pankhurst, 'The Last Two Letters of Emperor Tewodros II of Ethiopia (April 11 and 12 1868)' (1987) 1 *The Journal of the Royal Asiatic Society of Great Britain and Ireland* 23–42, 25.

[162] Ibid, 38, referring to Houses of Parliament, *Further Papers Connected with the Abyssinian Expedition* (1868) 6.

Tewodros agreed to release the European captives, and offered cattle, which according to local traditions implied a 'peace-offering',[163] but refused to surrender unconditionally.

On 13 April 1868, Napier proceeded with the attack on the imperial fortress, which hosted imperial treasures, precious illustrated manuscripts, including Amharic bibles, and paintings. His forces plundered the palace and nearby churches. They seized golden and silver artefacts, over 400 manuscripts, regalia, sacred vessels, including the emperor's golden crown, adorned with images of the Apostles. The spoils were 'transported, on 15 elephants and nearly 200 mules'.[164] The palace was burned down on 17 April 1868. Tewodros committed suicide before the occupation of the fort. British officer Tristram Charles Sawyer Speedy (1836–1910) took custody of the emperor's seven-year-old son, Prince Alamayu (1961–1879), and brought him to the Isle of Wight,[165] in order to protect him from violence by enemies of his father.

Many of the objects were offered for auction in order to cover the costs of the expedition. On 20 and 21 April 1868, the British military authorities organized a two-day auction to raise 'prize-money' for the troops. Richard Holmes was authorized by Napier to select objects for the British Museum. He was celebrated for acquiring a looted crown, belonging to the head of the Ethiopian church, and a solid gold chalice for £4 from a soldier.[166] He also acquired manuscripts and religious objects. Many manuscripts and the king's crown and seal found their way into museums (e.g. the British Museum,[167] the British Library, and the Victoria and Albert Museum).

As Richard Pankhurst, founder and first Director of Addis Ababa University's Institute of Ethiopian Studies, has argued, 'such looting, it may be contended, was in no way justified, either by Tewodros' imprisonment of the European captives, or by his subsequent resistance to the Napier expedition'.[168] The British Prime Minister, William Gladstone, later expressed regret concerning the Maqdala looting, including the taking of the gold crown and chalice. He 'deeply lamented, for the sake of the country, and for the sake of all concerned, that these articles ... were thought fit to be brought away by a British army'.[169] He argued that 'these articles, whatever the claim of the [British] Army, ought not to be placed among the national treasure, and said they ought to be held in deposit till they could be returned to Abyssinia'.[170]

[163]   Henry Blanc, *Narrative of captivity in Abyssinia* (London: Smith Elder, 1868) 405.

[164]   Pankhurst, 'Ethiopia, The Aksum Obelisk, and the Return of Africa's Cultural Heritage', 231.

[165]   See Andrew Heavens, *The Prince and the Plunder* (Cheltenham: History Press, 2022).

[166]   Gunning and Challis, 'Planned Plunder, the British Museum, and the 1868 Maqdala Expedition', 18–19.

[167]   See British Museum, Maqdala collection, at https://www.britishmuseum.org/about-us/british-museum-story/objects-news/maqdala-collection.

[168]   Pankhurst, 'Ethiopia, The Aksum Obelisk, and the Return of Africa's Cultural Heritage' 232–233.

[169]   William Gladstone, Extracts from Hansard (30 June 1871) http://www.afromet.info/about_us_statements.html.

[170]   Ibid. On return see Richard Pankhurst, 'Restitution of Cultural Property: The Case of Ethiopia' (1986) 149 *Museum* 58.

Ethiopia called for the return of the treasures and the human remains of Prince Alamayu, who passed away in 1879 and was buried at Windsor Castle. In 2021, the Scheherazade Foundation, a British non-profit organization, purchased a hand-written Ethiopian religious text, crosses, and an imperial shield seized by British forces from a British auction house and a Belgian collector, and returned them to Ethiopia.[171] Buckingham Palace has denied requests to repatriate Alamayu's remains to Ethiopia, arguing that his exhumation would disturb the 'peace' of others buried at St George's Chapel.

5.4 Punitive expeditions to Kumasi during the Anglo-Asante Wars (1974, 1896, 1900)

The punitive expeditions against the Asante Empire in West Africa (nowadays Ghana) during the nineteenth century illustrate the complex interplay between anti-slavery policy, colonial rivalry, displays of power, and the logic of protection in British imperial policy.[172] They have their origins in a conflict between British, Dutch, and local interests over economic control of the Gold Coast in the Gulf of Guinea, famous for its large gold resources and role in the slave trade.

Britain had exercised economic control over the coastal areas of the Gold Coast through the (British) African Company of Merchants, which recognized the sovereignty of powerful Asante rulers. The decision to end transatlantic slave trading in 1806 due to shifting public opinion in Britain led to a decline of the company and the transformation of the Gold Coast into a British protectorate in 1821, which secured protection of coastal regions, including coastal peoples, such as the Fante, and the inhabitants of Accra. It also affected the trade interests of the Asante, which continued to rely on the slave trade. Britain concluded a peace treaty with the Asante in 1831, who had closer ties to the Dutch. It expanded its influence through the acquisition of the Danish Gold Coast in 1850 and the Dutch Gold Coast in 1872, including the port of Elmina, an important trade outlet claimed by the Asante, for which the Dutch had paid a tribute rent to the Asante. The British failed to recognize the Asante claim. This led to hostilities, i.e. the Third Anglo-Asante War from 1873 to 1874.

The Asante invaded the new protectorate in 1873, took possession of Elmina, and held European missionaries as hostages in order to prevent the loss of the town and to secure future revenues from the post. The British government decided to

---

[171] It constituted one of 'the largest single restitution of Magdala-era artefacts in Ethiopian history'. See Martin Bailey, 'Maqdala treasures looted by British troops returned to Ethiopia in "largest single restitution"' *The Art Newspaper* (10 September 2021).

[172] William David D. McIntyre, 'British Policy in West Africa: The Ashanti Expedition of 1873-4' (1962) 5 *Historical Journal* 19–46; Edward M. Spiers, *The Victorian Soldier in Africa* (Manchester: Manchester University Press, 2018) 20–34.

establish a punitive expedition against the Asante (the 'First Ashanti Expedition') in order to set an example, repel the attack, and secure a peace arrangement. It was led by General Sir Garnet Wolseley (known as Sargrenti in Ghana), who had taken part in the looting of Yuanmingyuan Palace in 1860. Wolseley was mandated to remove Asante from the protectorate and to negotiate a new treaty.[173] Prime Minister Gladstone cautioned against a complete defeat of the Asante in order to enable the negotiation of a peace agreement.[174] But the modalities of the operation were left for Wolseley to determine. The expedition involved 2,500 British and West Indian troops, who were accompanied by famous correspondents, such as Henry Morton Stanley. Wolseley regarded his mission as a mandate to teach a lesson to the Asante ('signal chastisement') and to show that British 'troops could fight in tropical Africa.'[175] He wrote on 3 October 1873 in a letter to Edward Cardwell (1813–1886), the Secretary of State for War:

> There is, Sir, but one method of freeing these settlements from the continued menace of Ashantee invasion, and this is to defeat the Ashantee army in the field, to drive it from the protected territories, and, if necessary, to pursue it into its own land, and to march victorious on the Ashantee capital, and show not only to the king, but to those chiefs who urge him on to constant war, that the arm of Her Majesty is powerful to punish, and can reach event to the very heart of their kingdom. By no means short of this can lasting peace be insured.[176]

The operation is a 'vivid example of how a plan once made gains a certain momentum of its own.'[177] When the troops arrived, the Asante left the protectorate, but failed to agree to negotiate a peace settlement. Wolseley thus decided to enter Asante territory and continue hostilities in order to make the Asante Empire 'submissive' and prompt King Kofi Karikari (1837–c. 1884), the tenth king of the Asante, to enter into an agreement.[178] In a note to Kofi Karikari, dated 2 January 1874, Wolseley demanded 'the return of all captives; an indemnity of 50,000 oz. of gold dust; and a new treaty to be signed.'[179] When his troops were about to cross to Asante territory, the Asante accepted and sent a message that the captives had been released. However, on 24 January 1874, Wolseley posed new additional conditions which were humiliating and unacceptable to Kofi Karikari, namely to provide 'the king's heir, the Queen Mother, and the heirs of the four leading Ashanti kings' as

---

[173] McIntyre, 'British Policy in West Africa', 37–38, 40.
[174] Ibid, 38.
[175] Ibid, 40.
[176] Henry Brackenbury, *The Ashanti War: A Narrative*, Vol. 1 (Edinburgh and London: William Blackwood & Sons, 1874) 187–188.
[177] McIntyre, 'British Policy in West Africa', 44.
[178] Ibid, 40.
[179] Ibid, 41.

hostages.[180] These terms made military hostilities unavoidable. They were turned down by Kofi Karikari. This led to invasion and defeat of the Asante.

The military expedition force was superior to Asante fighters. It obtained victories in hostilities in Amoaful (31 January 1874) and Ordahsu (4 February 1874) and marched on to Kumasi, the capital of the Asante. It occupied Kumasi on 4 February 1874. The city was abandoned. The forces entered the royal palace and seized its treasures, including golden masks, ornaments, and other cultural artefacts.[181] Captain Henry Brackenbury (1837–1914), Wolseley's Secretary wrote:

> Here we found those gold masks, whose object it is difficult to divine, made of pure gold hammered into shape. One of these, weighing more than forty-one ounces, represented a ram's head, and the others the faces of savage men, about half the size of life. Box after box was opened and its contents hastily examined, the more valuable ones being kept, and the others left. Necklaces and bracelets of gold, Aggery beads, coral ornaments of various descriptions, were heaped together in boxes and calabashes. Silver-plate was carried off, and doubtless much left behind. Swords, gorgeous ammunition-belts, caps mounted in solid gold, knives set in gold and silver, bags of gold-dust and nuggets; carved stools mounted in silver, calabashes worked in silver and in gold, silks embroidered and woven, were all passed in review. The sword presented by her Majesty to the king was found and carried off; and thousands of things were left behind that would be worth fabulous sums in cabinets at home.[182]

A famous icon is the royal stool of Afua Kobi I (1834–1884), the queen mother of the Asante empire. This object had important religious, historic, and symbolic value in Asante culture, since it represented the status and spirit of its owner. It was taken from the palace by Sir Archibald Alison (1826–1907), a British commander, and later offered as trophy of war to the Kelvingrove Museum in Glasgow.

The palace and town of Kumasi were burned down. Brackenbury described the nature and intended effects of the burning in vivid terms:

> The town burnt furiously ... the destruction was practically complete. Slowly huge dense columns of smoke curled up to the sky, and the lighted fragments of thatch drifting far and wide upon the wind showed to the King of Ashanti, and to all his subjects who had fled from the capital, that the white man never failed to keep his word.[183]

---

[180] Ibid, 41.

[181] Stanley provides a 'hastily written inventory' of 'valuable, curious and worthless things' taken from the palace. See Stanley, *Coomassie and Magdala*, 233–234.

[182] Henry Brackenbury, *The Ashanti War: A Narrative*, Vol. 2 (Edinburgh and London: William Blackwood & Sons, 1874) 241.

[183] Brackenbury, *The Ashanti War: A Narrative*, Vol. 2, 243–244.

Wolseley later commented on the devastating effects. He noted: 'From all that I can gather I believe that the result will be such a diminution in the prestige and military power of the Ashantee monarch as may result in the break-up of the kingdom altogether.'[184] Formally, the defeat was defended on humanitarian grounds. To home audiences, it was presented as a victory which liberated the Gold Coast from Asante slavery and human sacrifice.[185]

On 13 March 1874, Kofi Karikari, who had left Kumasi, agreed to sign a new peace treaty with the British, the Treaty of Fomena, which replaced the 1831 treaty. The arrangement contained harsh conditions that provided the basis of the decline of the Asante empire over the next decades. It required the king of the Asante inter alia 'to pay the sum of 50,000 ounces of approved gold as indemnity for the expenses he has occasioned to her Majesty the Queen of England by the late war',[186] renounce titles on neighbouring states (Denykyira, Assin, Akim, Adans),[187] rent payments or any claims to Elmina,[188] guarantee 'freedom of trade between Ashanti and Her Majesty's forts' on the Gold Coast,[189] and suppress human sacrifice, a practice deemed 'repugnant to the feelings of all Christian nations'.[190]

The Asante collected gold beads and other jewelry to pay the large indemnity owed under the treaty. Many of the looted or collected items ended up in museums. For instance, a prestigious solid gold mask from the palace became part of the Wallace Collection. Other artefacts were auctioned or found their way into the collections of the British Museum (Museum of Mankind), the Victoria and Albert Museum, or the Pitt-Rivers Museum in Oxford.[191]

Wolseley's victory and the Treaty of Fomena had enduring consequences for the Asante Federation. Kofi Kakari was dethroned. The loss of the slave trade, protracted tribal and secessionist wars with provinces who refused to recognize central control, and the indemnities weakened the kingdom.[192]

The destabilization of the region, fears of decline in trade, and increasing competition from France and Germany led to further tensions twenty years later. Following the Berlin Conference, which determined criteria for colonial expansion (i.e. a settled administration) and growing French and German

---

[184] Edmund Burke (ed.), *The Annual Register: A Review of Public Events at Home and Abroad for the Year 1874* (London: Rivingtons, 1875) 30.

[185] It formed a recurring bone of contention in British-Asante relations. See Clifford Williams, 'Asante: Human Sacrifice or Capital Punishment? An Assessment of the Period 1807-1874' (1988) 21 *The International Journal of African Historical Studies* 433–441.

[186] Treaty of Fomena, Art. 2.

[187] Ibid, Art. 3.

[188] Ibid, Art. 4.

[189] Ibid, Art. 6.

[190] Ibid, Art. 8.

[191] See Gertrude Aba M. Eyifa-Dzidzienyo and Samuel N. Nkumbaan, 'Looted and illegally acquired African objects in European museums: issues of restitution and repatriation in Ghana' (2020) 7 *Contemporary Journal of African Studies* 84–96.

[192] Gus Casely-Hayford, *The Lost Kingdoms of Africa* (London: Bantam Press, 2012) 276–279.

expeditions to West Africa, Britain gradually moved away from a policy of non-interference in 1888/1889 and took initiatives to transform Asante formally into a British protectorate. Sir William Brandford Griffith (1824–1897), Governor of the Gold Coast, extended an offer to the Asante king, Nana Ageyman Prempeh I (1870–1931), to place his country under British protection, but his offer was rejected.[193] In 1894, Griffith wrote that '[Asante] is nothing but a few tribes, with difficulty held together by the power and the recollection of the former influence of Kumasi'.[194] Britain managed to conclude separate treaties of friendship and protection with different Asante states. At the end of 1895, Britain deployed an expeditionary force with 2,500 British and West Indian troops to Asante. It was commanded by Colonel Sir Francis C. Scott (1834–1902). Military action in 1895–96 was justified by a number of grounds, such as protection of the Gold Coast colony, suppression of slavery and human sacrifice, and lack of full implementation of the terms of the 1874 Treaty of Fomena, including partial payment of the indemnities owed, i.e. only two instalments. Major Robert Baden-Powell (1857–1941), a British army officer and founder of the worldwide Scout Movement, who took part in the expedition, described the 'main reasons and objects of the expedition' as follows: 'to put an end to human sacrifice; to put a stop to slave-trading and raiding; to ensure peace and security for the neighbouring tribes; to settle the country and protect the development of trade; to get paid up the balance of the war indemnity'.[195]

The force arrived in Kumasi in January 1896. It occupied the city without encountering significant resistance. Prempeh I had given instruction to retreat. The expedition performed a *coup d'état*. The king was arrested and compelled to sign a treaty of protection. Although he had accepted British conditions, he was deposed and sent into exile in the Seychelles, together with other Asante leaders. British rule was proclaimed. Sir William Maxwell (1846–1897), the governor of the Gold Coast, formally took over control. After the fall of Kumasi, troops seized the gold and other treasures from the palace. Baden Powell stated: '[T]he work of collecting the treasures was entrusted to a company of British soldiers … The 'loot' which we collected was sold by public auction excepting golden valuables which were all sent home to the Secretary of State.'[196] The 1896 expedition created a feeling of resentment and humiliation among the Asante. This was reinforced in 1900, when Frederick Mitchell Hodgson (1851–1928), the new governor-general of the Gold Coast, demanded in a speech delivered to Asante leaders on 28 March 1900, to be

---

[193] Ivor Wilks, *Asante in the Nineteenth Century*, 298.
[194] W. E. F. Ward, 'Britain and Ashanti, 1874–1896' (1974) 15 *Transactions of the Historical Society of Ghana* 131–164, 160.
[195] Robert Baden-Powell, *The Downfall of Prempeh: A Diary of Life with the Native Levy in Ashanti 1895-1896* (London: Methuen & Co., 1900) 11.
[196] Ibid, 45.

seated on the golden stool, the spiritual symbol of the unity of the Ashanti state and its peoples,[197] in his role as representative of the queen of England. For the Asante, the golden stool marked not only a throne, i.e. a symbol of power, but the foundation of 'the Ashanti political and religious system'.[198] It did not belong to a specific king, but the Asante nation. In Asante culture, it was not only regarded as a sacred object, but treated as a 'living being'.[199] Asante rulers did not usually sit on it during their reign. The stool itself was never allowed to sit on the bare ground.[200] Its capture by foreign powers was associated with the demise of the entire Asante nation. Together with the demand for taxes and the ousting of Prempeh I, the claim for the stool led the Asante to believe that 'the British had no desire other than to ruin and to subjugate them'.[201]

Nana Yaa Asantewaa (1850–1921), the queen mother of Edwisu, asked Asante leaders to stand up against the capturing of the golden stool. She delivered a famous address to the Asante Government Council (known as the 'undergarment' speech). It has become a reference point of female anti-imperial resistance.[202] She stated:

> How can a proud and brave people like the Asante sit back and look while white men took away their king and chiefs, and humiliated them with a demand for the Golden Stool. The Golden Stool only means money to the white men; they have searched and dug everywhere for it. I shall not pay one predwan to the governor. If you, the chiefs of Asante, are going to behave like cowards and not fight, you should exchange your loincloths for my undergarment.[203]

She then addressed her fighters:

> We should rise and defend our heritage; it is better to perish than to look on sheepishly while the white man whose sole business in our country is to steal, kill and destroy, threatens to rob us of our Golden Stool. Arise men! And defend the Golden Stool from being captured by foreigners. It is more honourable to perish

---

[197] Alex Kyerematen, 'The Royal Stools of Ashanti' (1969) 39 *Africa: Journal of the International African Institute* 1–10, 4. It was a 'sacrilege for any other person, within or without Ashanti, to make another Golden Stool or to decorate a stool or any other king's seat with gold'.

[198] Samson C. Ukpabi, 'The British Colonial Office Approach to the Ashanti War of 1900' (1970) 13 *African Studies Review* 363–380, 368.

[199] Kyerematen, 'The Royal Stools of Ashanti', 4.

[200] Ibid, 3.

[201] B. Wasserman, 'The Ashanti War of 1900: A Study in Cultural Conflict' (1961) 31 *Africa: Journal of the International African Institute* 167–179, 174.

[202] Harcourt Fuller, 'Commemorating an African Queen: Ghanaian Nationalism, the African Diaspora, and the Public Memory of Nana Yaa Asantewaa, 1952–2009' (2014) 47 *African Arts* 58–71; Tom C. McCaskie, 'The Life and Afterlife of Yaa Asantewaa' (2007) 77 *Africa: Journal of the International African Institute* 151–179.

[203] Agnes Akosua Aidoo, 'Asante Queen Mothers in Government and Politics in the Nineteenth Century' (1977) 9 *Journal of the Historical Society of Nigeria* 1–13, 12.

in defence of the Golden Stool than to remain in perpetual slavery. I am prepared
and ready to lead you to war against the white man.[204]

Asante leaders appointed her as first female commander of the Asante forces
(*sahene*).[205] She established an army of 20,000 warriors, including a battalion of
Amazons, and led the rebellion against British rule in the 'War of the Golden Stool'
(also known as the 'Yaa Asantewaa War').[206] The army started a siege on Kumasi.
During this period, the Asante managed to protect the golden stool. It was hidden
from the British in a forest. It was later discovered by railway builders in 1920, who
stripped it of its golden ornaments. However, the rebellion was ultimately defeated
by a British expedition. On 1 January 1902, the Asante nation became a British
protectorate. Queen Mother Nana Yaa Asantewaa was arrested and exiled to the
Seychelles. A restored version of the golden stool was offered to Ageyman Prempeh
as a private person when he returned from exile in 1924.[207] Since 1974, the Asante
Royal Court has made requests to return regalia and other items removed by British
expeditionary forces in 1874, 1896 and 1900. The V&A and British Museum have
considered the option of a loan of Asante treasures. Such an arrangement has encountered resistance in Ghana, since it implies recognition of British ownership
and comes with financial burdens.

5.5 The canoe prow ornament (tangué) of Lock Priso (1884)

The capture of the canoe prow of Kum'a Mbappé (also known as King Lock Priso)
is a less well known forcible taking. It illustrates, like hardly any other case, the
divergent object understandings in the colonial encounter, the epistemic violence of takings, and the problems that differing object ontologies pose for return
processes.[208]

Lock Priso (1846–1916) was a pro-British chief, who resisted German rule in
Cameroon. Like other Douala chiefs, he owned a vessel with a masterfully carved
wooden ornament, the canoe prow (*tangué*), placed at the tip of the boat. It was
removed in the context of a punitive expedition in 1884 and offered to the ethnographic museum in Munich.

---

[204] Asirifi-Danquah, *The Struggle: Between Two Great Queens, 1900-1901*, Yaa Asantewaa and
Victoria of Great Britain (Ghana: Asirifi-Danquah, 2007) 62.

[205] Adu Boahen, *Yaa Asantewaa and the Asante-British War of 1900-1* (Accra: Sub-Saharan
Publishers; Oxford: James Currey, 2003) 128.

[206] Arhin Brempong, 'The role of Nana Yaa Asantewaa in the 1900 Asante war of resistance' (2000) 3
Ghana Studies 97–110.

[207] Adu Boahen and others (eds.), *The History of Ashanti Kings and the Whole Country Itself and
Other Writings* (Oxford: Oxford University Press, 2003) 50.

[208] On German expeditions, see Paul Nchoji Nkwi, *The German Presence in the Western Grassfields
1891-1913* (Leiden: Africa Studies Centre, 1989).

Canoe prows count among the most spectacular cultural objects of the Douala people on the Cameroonian coast.[209] According to Douala traditions, the *tangué* is not only a material object, but an organism or living instrument, whose powers played an important role in traditional culture.[210] It was considered to be more precious than the canoe itself.[211] Canoe prows, like *tangué*, had social and spiritual meanings. They are symbols of 'power and identity',[212] representing the prestige and economic power of local chiefs and trading families. They served to recognize the owner (e.g. the chief, family) of a canoe. Some prows were considered as royal insignia, while other were deemed to belong to communities.[213] They also carry spiritual functions. They symbolize the connection between the soul of the Douala people and the spiritual forces of the river. Rosalinde Wilcox has described this connection as follows: 'Forces summoned into the carving were used in spiritual healing rites that invoked the water spirits (*miengu*) … When affixed to the dugout, supernatural energies and forces are captured and harnessed in the Tange.'[214] These functions gained particular importance during canoe races and the Ngondo, a water ceremony. Rituals were held to summon the water spirits into the *tangué* before and during races to protect it[215] and influence the outcomes of races.

The *tangué* of Lock Priso was seized during a German military operation in 1884, geared at breaking local resistance to German rule.[216] At the time, the Douala region was the centre of a clash of interests between Britain and Germany. Britain had established trade posts and settlements on the coast. British missionaries and traders had developed strong networks. They faced competition from Germany which sought to turn Cameroon into a German protectorate. The Douala people initially sided with Britain. However, in February 1884, German Chancellor Otto Von Bismarck sent explorer Gustav Nachtigal (1834–1885) to negotiate protection treaties with the Douala kings. Through gifts and promises, Nachtigal managed to persuade Ndumbé Lobé Bell (1839–1897), the king of the Bell lineage, and King Akwa to sign treaties with representatives of the German trading companies Woermann and Jantzen & Thormählen, who acted on behalf of the German State. Local rulers agreed to cede sovereign rights and administration, while keeping property and the right to levy taxes. The treaty arrangement served as basis for

---

[209] Ralph Austen and Jonathan Derrick, *Middlemen of the Cameroons Rivers: The Duala and their Hinterland, c.1600–c.1960* (Cambridge: Cambridge University Press, 1999).

[210] Splettstößer, *Umstrittene Sammlungen*, 252.

[211] Ibid, 241.

[212] Rosalinde Wilcox, *The Maritime Arts of the Duala of Cameroon* (PhD Thesis, Los Angeles: University of California, 1994) 3.

[213] Splettstößer, *Umstrittene Sammlungen*, 249.

[214] Wilcox, *The Maritime Arts of the Duala of Cameroon*, 232.

[215] Ibid, 156.

[216] During an expedition in 1904 to Laikom, German colonial officers acquired sacred statues from the Kom people. The expedition was carried out to make local rulers submissive. The statues could be seized because the king of the Kom fled with all the objects in use that were valuable to him. He left two statues, after removing valuable glass beads. Splettstößer, *Umstrittene Sammlungen*, 132.

Germany to declare a protectorate, but was contested among the natives.[217] Lock Priso, the King of Hickorytown (Bonabéri), who favoured the British, refused to support the German-Douala treaty arrangements of 12 July 1884. He protested against the raising of the German flag in Hickory Town ('We beg you to pull that flag down. No man [can] buy [us]') and encouraged his people to resist expansion of German control.

German consul Max Buchner (1846–1921) requested support from Berlin in order to defeat the rebellion. On 22 December 1884, a German punitive expedition, with 300 men from the warships SMS Bismarck and SMS Olga, launched an attack on Hickory Town in order to break resistance and capture their leadership. Buchner was part of the expedition. Entries of his diary suggest that he was searching for 'ethnographic curiosities'[218] in the course of the operation. He seized Lock Priso's *tangué* when his house was set on fire. He traced the circumstances in his diary:

> Lock Priso's palace is plundered, a colorful and striking image. We set it on fire. But I have asked all the houses to be inspected before to find ethnographic treasures. My main booty is a great wooden carved work, the princely bow (tangué) of Lock Priso, which will be sent to Munich.[219]

The narrative might suggest that he rescued the *tangué* from burning. But the acquisition clearly occurred in a coercive context. The *tangué* turned into war booty, collected as an imperial trophy in the fight against colonial resistance.

One year later, Buchner donated the object to the Royal Ethnographic Collection in Munich. The museum entry recorded it as 'Gift from Dr. Max Buchner', without inquiring into the problematic context of acquisition.

In the twentieth century, the *tangué* became an object of intensive dispute, when Kum'a Ndumbe III, the grandson of Lock Priso, requested its return in the 1990s. The underlying controversy highlights the complexities of the changing biography of cultural colonial objects. The *tangué* blurs traditional categories of property law and ownership. For some, it is a private commodity, which symbolizes family power. For others, it constitutes a royal artefact, a work of art, a symbol of anti-colonial resistance, or sacred object. Kum'a Ndumbe III defined it as the 'sum of spiritual symbols, which connect [the Douala] people to nature, the environment, universe or God'.[220] In traditional circles, the *tangué* is associated with

---

[217] Harry Rudin, *Germans in the Cameroons, 1884-1914: A Case Study in Modern Imperialism* (New Haven: Yale University Press, 1938) 53. For a critique of the treaty practice, see also Bénédicte Savoy et al. (eds), *Atlas der Abwesenheit: Kameruns Kulturerbe in Deutschland* (Berlin: Reimer, 2023) 34–35.

[218] Max Buchner, *Aurora Colonialis: Bruchstücke eines Tagebuchs aus dem ersten Beginn unserer Kolonialpolitik 1884/85* (München: Piloty & Loehle, 1914) 195 ('ethnographischen Merkwürdigkeiten').

[219] Ibid, 195 (translated from German).

[220] See interview with Kum'a Ndumbe III, Postkolonial, 'Aus Kriegsbeute wird Schenkung' (30 November 2009) *Hinterland* 64, 65 (translated from German: 'The tangue is not just a carving, a work of

agency over people. The museum remained reluctant to return it, because it could not determine to whom the *tangué* should be allocated in light of these different meanings: Paul Mbappé, the representative of the royal Bele Bele family, or Kum'a Ndumbe III, the descendant of Lock Priso.

5.6 French expedition to Dahomey (1892)

The expedition against the Dahomey kingdom (1625–1892, nowadays Benin) marks one of the most notorious episodes of French looting from the second half of the nineteenth century. It has become a tipping point for the restitution movement.

The kingdom was deprived of its royal treasures, based on European imperial rivalries between France, Britain, and Germany, economic interests in trade and the fight against slavery and human sacrifice.[221] France had a strategic interest in Dahomey in order to secure trade in palm oil and have access to seaports from the mainland, including the Niger Delta. It was one of the wealthiest and most powerful kingdoms in the region, known for its female warriors (Amazons). Between 1863 and 1882, France managed to transform the neighbouring kingdom of Porto-Novo into a French protectorate, following rivalry with Britain,[222] and secured treaties with King Glélé (1856–1889), the tenth King of Dahomey, placing the port of Cotonou under French control. In 1889, France sought to turn Cotonou into a full French protectorate, including adding the power to collect taxes. It faced resistance from Glélé's son, Kondo (later King Béhanzin) who opposed French influence and declared previous treaty-based concessions void.[223] These controversies led to the First Dahomey War between France, led by General Alfred-Amédée Dodds (1842–1922), and King Béhanzin (1845–1906), who assumed the kingship on 1 January 1890. France occupied Cotonou. Béhanzin agreed to a settlement, which recognized the French protectorate over Porto Novo and French rights in Cotonou in return for an annual rent (20,000 francs) and the power of Dahomey to rule the native Fon inhabitants in the town.[224] However, peace turned out to be elusive. King Béhanzin continued to conduct slave raids into French protectorates, including

---

art, and not just a royal insignia. It is a sum of spiritual symbols that connects a people with nature, the environment, the universe and God. It reflects the soul of our people').

[221] François Desplantes, *Le général Dodds et l'expédition du Dahomey* (Rouen: Mégard et Cie, 1894); François Michel and Jacques Serre, *La campagne du Dahomey, 1893–1894: La réddition de Béhanzin* (Paris: L'Harmattan, 2001).
[222] E. A. Soumonni, 'Porto-Novo, Between the French and the British 1861–1884' (1985) 12 *Journal of the Historical Society of Nigeria* 53–60.
[223] Boniface Obichere, *West African States and European Expansion: The Dahomey-Niger Hinterland, 1885-1898* (New Haven: Yale University Press, 1971) 64–65.
[224] Ibid, 82–83.

Porto Novo, while France sought to secure a land route through Dahomey to the Niger River.

A relatively minor incident triggered the Second Franco-Dahomean War (1892–1894), leading to the fall and plunder of the Royal Palace of Dahomey. A French gunboat, named *Topaz*, sailed from Porto Novo into Dahomean territory to investigate the raids. Dahomey's soldiers opened fire on the boat and injured several Frenchmen. The attack was seen as a provocation and reported in the French press.[225] It provided a convenient pretext for renewed military controversy and a fully-fledged invasion, which was sold to the French public as an operation to bring civilization to a backward kingdom in response to a brutal attack.[226] On 23 April 1892, *Le Petit Journal* published a depiction of King Béhanzin, with human skulls and female Amazon fighters, stating: 'He does not speak any European language … Our country will easily finish him.'[227]

France established an expeditionary force with 3,000 men, including French, Senegalese, and Gabonese soldiers, under the leadership of Dodds. The goal was to march to Abomey and remove Béhanzin from power. Dodds blocked the coast and requested King Béhanzin to surrender, who declined and replied: 'I am the friend of the whites; ready to receive them when they wish to come to see me, but prompt to make war whenever they wish.'[228] In the subsequent hostilities the French expedition was victorious, due to 'superior tactics, more sophisticated weaponry, and outstanding leadership'.[229] Béhanzin's forces retreated. Dodds reached the palace of Abomey on 17 November 1892. In light of the overwhelming French force, Béhanzin fled from Abomey and went into hiding. The palace had political and spiritual power for Dahomey. Before leaving, Béhanzin set the monument on fire in order to prevent Abomey heritage from falling into the hands of the enemy. French troops entered the burning city and looted it. Dodds was involved in the taking of some objects. Within days, his tent was surrounded by a 'bazaar' of plundered items.[230] His troops collected objects of symbolic religious or political importance, including the relief doors of the palace, ancestral altars, silver sceptres, the golden throne of King Béhanzin, and three half-animal statues representing the kings of Dahomey (Guezo, Glélé, and Béhanzin). Other objects, such as a sculpture dedicated to the God of War (Gou)

---

[225] The article claimed that France should not put up with 'the bravado of the bloody and grotesque petty kingdom whose bands periodically came to murder and pillage the little kingdom of Porto-Novo'. William Schneider, *An Empire for the Masses: The French Popular Image of Africa, 1870-1900* (Westport, Connecticut: Greenwood Press, 1982) 48.

[226] Rick Duncan, *Man, Know Thyself: Volume 1 Corrective Knowledge of Our Notable Ancestors* (London: Xlibris Corporation, 2013) 314.

[227] Jean Bayol, 'Behanzin: Roi du Dahomey' *Le Petit Journal: Supplément Illustré* (23 April 1892).

[228] Duncan, *Man, Know Thyself*, 314–315.

[229] Charles Shryer, 'The Roles of the Military in the History of Benin (Dahomey): 1870-Present' (2003) 4 *McNair Scholars Journal of the University of Wisconsin–Superior* 81–118, 90.

[230] Alexandre L. d'Albéca, *La France au Dahomey* (Paris: Librairie Hachette, 1895) 111.

or a further throne, were taken from the city of Ouidah and Cana, the burial site of Dahomey kings.[231]

Dodds donated his finest 'trophies' to the Trocadero Ethnographic Museum (later the *Musée du quai Branly*). Their cultural value was quickly realized.[232] They were exhibited as of 1894 to showcase the 'glory' of the expedition and received a positive reception in the press[233] and among experts. The objects turned from trophies into ethnographic objects and works of art. French anthropologist Maurice Delafosse (1870–1926) already recognized their value in 1894. He wrote:

> One opinion, which is unfortunately quite widespread, tends to see blacks in general and the Dahomeans in particular as inferior beings, incapable of any elevated or artistic feeling. The few objects that we could save from the Abomey fire and which are exhibited at the Trocadero Ethnographic Museum are here to prove the opposite.[234]

Béhanzin surrendered to France on 25 January 1894 and was sent into exile in Martinique. Dahomey was turned into a French protectorate and later became part of French West Africa. In November 2021, France returned twenty-six items from the kingdom of Dahomey, including the iconic depictions of the three kings of Dahomey, to modern-day Benin.[235]

5.7 The Lombok expeditions (1894)

A famous example of Dutch imperialism[236] is the military expedition to the island of Lombok,[237] located east of Bali. It was formally initiated in 1891 by a request from the Sasak Datus chiefs of the east coast of Lombok to the Dutch colonial government, seeking protection against oppression and cruel treatment by the Hindu Balinese rajas of the House of Karang Asem. Like many other punitive expeditions,

---

[231] On the social biography and diffusion of objects taken from Dahomey, see Gaëlle Beaujean-Baltzer, 'Du trophée à l'œuvre: parcours de cinq artefacts du royaume d'Abomey' (2007) 6 *Gradhiva* 70–85.

[232] Julia Kelly, 'Dahomey!, Dahomey!': The Reception of Dahomean Art in France in the Late 19th and Early 20th Centuries' (2015) 12 *Journal of Art Historiography* 1–19.

[233] Guy Tomel, 'Le trône de Behanzin' *Le Monde illustré* (10 February 1894).

[234] Maurice Delafosse, 'Statues des rois de Dahomé au Musée ethnographique du Trocadéro' *La Nature* No. 1086 (24 March 1894) 262–266, 262.

[235] See Chapter 9.

[236] On Dutch imperialism, see Maarten Kuitenbrouwer, *The Netherlands and the Rise of Modern Imperialism: Colonies and Foreign Policy 1870-1902* (New York: Berg, 1991).

[237] Capt. W. Cool, *With the Dutch in the East, an Outline of the Military Operations in Lombok, 1894* (London: Luzac & Co., 1897); Alfons Van der Kraan, *Lombok: Conquest, Colonization and Underdevelopment, 1870–1940* (Singapore: Heinemann Educational Books, 1980); Alfons Van der Kraan, 'Lombok under the Mataram Dynasty, 1839–94' in Anthony Reid (ed.), *The Last Stand of Asian Autonomies* (New York: McMillian, 1997) 389–408.

the operation was based on a mix of rationales, including trade interests, expansion of political control and revenge against humiliation ('the treason of Lombok').

Lombak was a semi-independent kingdom in the 1890s. In 1843, the Government of Dutch East-India had concluded a treaty with the Balinese Raja of Mataram, which made the island the 'property of the Netherlands Indies Government',[238] but left the administration 'entirely under the control of the Rajas of the country'.[239] Despite the treaty, the Dutch regarded Balinese rule on Lombok with suspicion. The Balinese rajas purchased steam boats and weapons from Singapore. The colonial government feared that they would forge alliances with foreign powers, including the British.

The internal conflict between Lombok Sasaks and the Balinese raja provided an opportunity for the Dutch to 'pacify' the island, i.e. to assume control and oust the Balinese aristocracy.[240] Muslim Sasak rebelled against unfair taxation, exploitation and oppression by the reigning Balinese monarch, Anak Agung Gde Ngurah Karangasem. The Dutch Minister of the Colonies submitted the request for Dutch intervention and support to parliament in July 1894. The Dutch first blocked the import of weapons and supplies from Singapore. In a second step, the Dutch Governor-General of the Dutch East-Indies, Carel Herman Aart van der Wijck (1840–1914), deployed a military expedition to Lombok. The force consisted of about 2,500 men, led by Commander-in-Chief Major Jacobus Augustinus Vetter (1837–1907). The intervention was formally designed to combat famine and heed the request of the Sasaks. The Dutch gave Balinese ruler Raja Anak Agung Ngurah Karangasem an ultimatum with several conditions, including handing over power to his son, Anak Agung Petut, who was deemed to be more favourable to Dutch interests, the conclusion of a new treaty arrangement with the colonial government, and the payment of a war indemnity.[241] But the request was not met in time.

The expeditionary force entered Lombok on 7 July 1894 and started to march towards Cakranegara, the royal capital of the island. The Raja then accepted the Dutch demands, and asked his other son, Anak Agung Madé, who opposed Dutch rule and was considered to be the mastermind behind the oppression of Sasaks, to commit suicide. The Dutch felt safe, since Anak Agung Petut, the new Lombok ruler, had committed to the conditions on 12 July 1894. When it became clear that acceptance of the conditions would entail loss of power for the Sasaks and end of independent rule, the Balinese leadership changed its stance. On 25 August, Balinese forces launched a surprise attack on the Dutch contingent near Cakranegara, in

---

[238] Article 1.
[239] Article 7.
[240] See also Van Beurden, *Treasures in Trusted Hands*, 145.
[241] Willard A. Hanna, *Bali Chronicles: Fascinating People and Events in Balinese History* (Singapore: Periplus, 2004), Chapter 10 ('Tragedy in Lombok 1891-1894').

which nearly 100 men were killed and 250 soldiers were injured. Other Dutch forces were imprisoned, tortured, stripped of their uniforms, or brutally murdered. The attack marked one of the most humiliating defeats of the Dutch in the nineteenth century. It was branded as the 'treason of Lombok' in the Dutch press.[242]

This led to the launch of a second expedition, which was visibly guided by retaliatory motives.

It 'pacified' Lombok through brutal violence. An even greater force, led by Major Vetter, captured and destroyed the palace city of Mataram. It then occupied Cakranegara in November 1894, following a siege and intensive bombardments. The raja and Balinese forces surrendered. Some family members of the monarch committed ritual suicide. Dutch forces seized the treasure of the Lombok ruler. They captured over 200 kilos of gold, 7,000 kilos of silver, jewels, including a 75 carat diamond, and other precious items and brought them back to Batavia.[243]

The acquisition and preservation of cultural objects was a premeditated part of the expedition. The philologist Jan Laurens Andries Brandes (1857–1905) was charged by the colonial government to collect valuable artefacts of the Lombok kingdom.[244] He accompanied the second expedition. He took manuscripts and other treasures from the royal library and protected them from looting or burning. He preserved, in particular, the Nagarakretagama, a eulogy written in honour of Javanese King Hayam Wuruk (1350–1389), which provides an account of the Mājapāhit Empire. His mandate reflects the turn towards a professionalization of heritage collection in colonial collecting, providing a more civilized image to cultural takings in violent contexts. This approach has been rightly branded as 'violent rescue'.[245]

The Dutch took over power in Lombok. It was administered from Bali. The remaining family of the Balinese Lombok raja were exiled to Batavia. Many items of the Lombok treasure were brought to the Netherlands. Some were melted. Others became part of collections or museums (Museum Volkenkunde Leiden, Rijksmuseum) and came to be seen as important samples of Buddhist civilization or art. A part of the 'Lombok Treasure' was returned to Indonesia in the 1970s. Based on recommendations by the Dutch Advisory Committee on the Return of Cultural Objects from Colonial Contexts, the Dutch government transferred ownership of the remaining 335 objects of the treasure to Indonesia in July 2023.[246]

---

[242] Willard A. Hanna, *A Brief History Of Bali: Piracy, Slavery, Opium and Guns: The Story of an Island Paradise* (Tokyo, Vermont, Singapore: Tuttle, 2016) 168.

[243] Van Beurden, *Treasures in Trusted Hands*, 145.

[244] Bloembergen and Eickhoff, *The Politics of Heritage in Indonesia*, 125–127.

[245] Ibid, 124.

[246] On the Dutch returns, see Van Beurden, *Inconvenient Heritage*, 82–98, id., 'Hard and Soft Law Measures for the Restitution of Colonial Cultural Collections – Country Report: The Netherlands' (2022) 8 *Santander Art and Culture Law Review* 407-426.

5.8   The acquisition of the male Luba mask during the Belgian Force Publique expedition to Lulu (1896)

The acquisition of the Luba helmet mask[247] with horns and bird, one of the icons in the Tervuren Museum, illustrates some of the coercive features of collection under King Leopold's rule of the Congo Free State (1885–1908).

The mask counts as one of the 'masterpieces' of African sculpture. It is listed under the inventory number as item 'EO.0.0.23470' in the collection of the museum. The object blends 'human and animal attributes', contains references to a 'powerful male buffalo associated with the Luba culture hero Mbidi Kiluwe', and reflects the attributes of a 'sacred ruler', transcending categories.[248] It was most probably used in sacred community rituals, inducing Luba rulers into office.[249]

The mask was acquired at a time when the Congo was administered by King Leopold II (1835–1909) as a private possession. The governance of the Free State posed a significant burden on Leopold. The vast territory was run by direct, rather than indirect rule. King Leopold II relied on the Force Publique, a military force composed of European officers and locally recruited forces from Zanzibar, West Africa, and the Congo, including freed slaves. He encouraged missionaries to facilitate 'the task of administrators and industrialists' and 'evangelize the savages so that they ... never revolt against the restraints they are undergoing'.[250] The discovery of rubber trees saved him from financial ruin in the mid-1890s. The Force Publique started a brutal campaign to secure the extraction of resources, in particular rubber. It carried out forcible expeditions in order to establish effective control, as encouraged by the Berlin Conference, and to maximize profits. The collection of cultural artefacts was a means of subjugation. Following collecting by early explorers of the 1880s, the Tervuren Museum was gradually filled through 'instances of collateral cultural damage, by-products of the frenzy for rubber that had cut a swathe of fire and blood through the villages of the Congo Free State'.[251]

The Luba helmet mask was acquired in this context. The provenance of the mask is incomplete, but the details were later reconstructed. In 1895, a group of locally

---

[247] The Luba people existed as kingdom from the seventeenth to the late nineteenth century. Mary Nooter Roberts notes that 'these groups never referred to themselves homogeneously as "Luba" until Arab traders and later European travelers and colonizers began to call them by that name in the late nineteenth century'. Mary Nooter Roberts, 'The Naming Game: Ideologies of Luba Artistic Identity' (1998) 31 *African Arts* 56–73, 60. See also Mary Nooter Roberts and Allen F. Roberts, 'Luba Art and the Making of History' (1996) 29 *African Arts* 22–35.

[248] Mary Nooter Roberts, 'The King Is a Woman: Shaping Power in Luba Royal Arts' (2013) 46 *African Arts* 68–81, 70.

[249] Allen F. Roberts, 'Why the Hero Lost his Teeth: Reflections on the Great Luba Helmet Mask' in Anna Seiderer (ed.), *Masks Dance, Bodies Exult: Liber Amicorum in Honour of Anne-Marie Bouttiaux* (Tervuren: Royal Museum for Central Africa, 2016) 51–68, 52.

[250] Letter from King Leopold II of Belgium to Colonial Missionaries, 1883.

[251] Debora L. Silverman, 'Diasporas of Art: History, the Tervuren Royal Museum for Central Africa, and the Politics of Memory in Belgium, 1885–2014' (2015) 87 *Journal of Modern History* 615–667, 619–620.

recruited Force Publique soldiers launched a rebellion in Luluabourg (Batetela Rebellion),[252] in order to protest against the execution of their fellow chief Gongo Lutete (1863–1893), who had supported an Arab slave trader (Tippu Tip) in resistance against Leopold in the Arab war of 1892–1894. The mutiny posed a serious threat to the authority of the Free State in the Lomami district. The mask was seized during a counter-insurgency operation of the Free State, conducted by deputy district commissioner Lieutenant Oscar Michaux (1860–1918)[253] with 300 soldiers, between 1 February 1896 and August 1896.[254] It was deemed to reestablish prestige and authority by a 'show of force' and seek retribution against heads of villages who had made common cause with the Batetela insurrection.[255] The expedition went from village to village in order to secure local submission, food, and accommodation. The details were recorded by a Belgian officer, Albert Lapière (1873–1910), who assisted Michaux and kept a diary of events.[256] Lapière's entries illustrate the brutality of the expedition. He noted that 'wherever we stay for several days it is devastation.'[257] He reports how the force used grenades and explosions in order to instill fear among natives, who believed they were dealing with a new enemy hidden underground.[258] An entry from 26 March 1896 traces the acquisition of the Luba helmet mask to Lulu. Lapière notes that the troops occupied the village and seized objects, livestock, and 'fetishes'. Then he mentions the acquisition of an artefact which reflects the features of the mask: 'A lot of fetishes were brought back to us, including a huge head with two large horns serving the fetishist and fitting on the shoulders; it was pierced with a large number of small holes at the eye level.'[259] Many of the diary entries reflect a banalization of violence of colonial collecting. Michaux kept all artefacts. He collected over 716 objects during his service in the Congo. In 1919, the Tervuren museum purchased his collection.

At the beginning of the twentieth century, ethnographers such as Emil Torday (1875–1931)[260] or Joseph Maes (1882–1960), director of Ethnography at the Tervuren Museum, started systematically to collect objects and artefacts during

[252] Rick Ceyssens and Bodhan Procyszyn, *La révolte de la force publique congolaise* (1895): *Les papiers Albert Lapière au Musée de Tervuren* (Paris: L'Harmattan, 2015).

[253] Oscar Michaux, *Au Congo. Carnet de Campagne. Episodes et impressions de 1889-1897* (Bruxelles: Falk, 1907).

[254] Rick Ceyssens, *De Luulu à Tervuren: la collection Oscar Michaux au Musée royal de l'Afrique centrale Royal* (Tervuren: Museum for Central Africa, 2011).

[255] Michel Bouffioux, 'Musée royal de l'Afrique centrale: un masque tellement "emblématique"' *Paris Match* (3 September 2019).

[256] On the story of the diary, see Michel Bouffioux, 'Masque volé de Tervuren: une pièce à conviction aux enchères' *Paris Match* (11 September 2019).

[257] Bouffioux, 'Musée royal de l'Afrique central' (translated from French: 'partout où nous restons plusieurs jours, c'est la dévastation').

[258] Ibid, referring to diary entry from 10 July 1886.

[259] Ibid (translated from French).

[260] John Mack, *Emil Torday and the Art of the Congo 1900-1909* (London: British Museum Publications, 1990).

expeditions in Kasai (1907–1909,[261] 1913–14) for the British Museum and the Royal Museum for Central Africa.

Like other objects, the Luba helmet mask was recontextualized in the course of the twentieth century. It became a cultural icon through exhibition, merchandising, and communication, showcasing the value of the colonial collection. It was listed in the catalogues and guidebooks of Tervuren as of the 1920s and even produced as a stamp. It turned into 'a chef d'oeuvre' of the museum, celebrated 'in a special exhibition' at the world fair in 1958,[262] and was recognized as a 'masterwork' of African sculpture.[263]

5.9 The taking of the Benin bronzes: A hallmark of colonial looting (1897)

The Punitive Expedition to Benin in 1897, leading to the removal of Benin plaques and sculptures (the Benin bronzes), is arguably the most famous example of cultural looting by the British Empire at the end of the nineteenth century.[264] The operation destroyed not only a city, but the cultural history and memory of the kingdom. The removed brass castings, plaques, and artworks constituted historical records or spiritual objects.[265] Some of the statues represented former rulers of the kingdom, dating back to the twelfth century. A memorandum, submitted by Prince Edun Akenzua to the British Parliament in 2000, explains the significance of the objects:

> Benin did not produce their works only for aesthetics or for galleries and museums. At the time Europeans were keeping their records in long-hand and in

---

[261] Melville William Hilton-Simpson, *Land and Peoples of the Kasai; Being a Narrative of a Two Years' Journey Among the Cannibals of the Equatorial Forest and Other Savage Tribes of the South-Western Congo* (London: Constable and Co., 1911).

[262] Silverman, 'Diasporas of Art', 658.

[263] Juliet Moss, 'Exhibition Review: Shaping Power: Luba Masterworks from the Royal Museum for Central Africa Los Angeles County Museum of Art July 7, 2013–May 4, 2014' (2016) 49 *African Arts* 90–91.

[264] For a full account, see Alan Boisragon, *The Benin Massacre* (London: Methuen, 1897); Philip A. Igbafe, 'The Fall of Benin: A Reassessment' (1970) 11 *The Journal of African History* 385–400; Mary Lou Ratté, *Imperial Looting and the case of Benin* (Masters Thesis, Amherst: University of Massachusetts, 1972); Robert Home, *City of Blood Revisited: A New Look at the Benin Expedition of 1887* (London: R. Collings, 1982), Staffan Lundén, *Displaying Loot: The Benin Objects and the British Museum* (PhD: Gothenburg University, 2016); Dan Hicks, *The Brutish Museums* (London: Pluto Press, 2020); Barnaby Phillips, *Loot: Britain and the Benin Bronzes* (London: Oneworld, 2021); Salome Kiwara-Wilson, 'Restituting Colonial Plunder: The Case for the Benin Bronzes and Ivories' (2016) 23 *DePaul Journal of Art, Technology & Intellectual Property Law* 375–426; Charles O. Osarumwense, 'Igue Festival and the British Invasion of Benin 1897: The Violation of a People's Culture and Sovereignty' (2014) 6 *African Journal of History and Culture* 1–5; Thomas Uwadiale Obinyan, 'The Annexation of Benin' (1988) 19 *Journal of Black Studies* 29–40.

[265] See Barbara Plankensteiner, 'Benin—Kings and Rituals: Court Arts from Nigeria' (2007) *African Arts* 74–87, 77–78.

hieroglyphics, the people of Benin cast theirs in bronze, carved on ivory or wood. The Obas commissioned them when an important event took place which they wished to record. Some of them of course, were ornamental to adorn altars and places of worship. But many of them were actually reference points, the library or the archive.[266]

The expedition influenced the approach towards colonial collecting. The discovery of the bronzes set in motion a competitive run for artefacts, based on their cultural value.

The story of the expedition shares striking parallels with the Maqdala Pillage and the Asante expeditions.[267] Britain used a mix of treaty-based, paternalistic, and retaliatory rationales to remove Oba Ovonramwen (1888–1914), the King of Benin, and secure economic interests.[268] His palace was burned, he was exiled, and the treasures of the Kingdom were used to finance the expedition.

5.9.1 Context

Benin was a flourishing kingdom which had entertained trade relations with Portugal or the Dutch since the sixteenth century.[269] It was described as a 'prosperous' and 'civilized' city[270] by travellers, or as 'Great Benin',[271] before being rebranded as 'City of Blood'.[272] In the late nineteenth century, European trading companies took over control. Benin was considered to be within Britain's 'sphere of influence'. The region was administered by the Royal Niger Company. But the Oba of Benin claimed a monopoly over trade, requiring tolls or duties for access to commercial activities, mostly as 'gifts' made through middlemen. The royal monopoly conflicted with British interests in trades of palm-oil, rubber, and ivory. In 1892, Captain Henry Gallwey, the first British Vice-Consul stationed in the Benin River, managed to meet the Oba and brokered a protectorate agreement. The agreement, dated 26 March 1892, recognized British protection[273] in return for freedom of

---

[266] Memorandum submitted by Prince Edun Akenzua to the British Parliament, Appendices to the Minutes of Evidence, Appendix 21, House of Commons, United Kingdom Parliament (March 2000).

[267] It inspired Joseph Conrad's novel *Heart of Darkness*.

[268] Igbafe, 'The Fall of Benin', 388; Obinyan, 'The Annexation of Benin', 32 ('economic interests were the dominant motivation for the expedition against Benin and not the eradication of things "repugnant to natural justice and humanity"').

[269] Alan Ryder, *Benin and the Europeans* (London: Longman, 1969); Peter M. Roese and Dmitri M. Bondarenko, *A Popular History of Benin: The Rise and Fall of a Mighty Forest Kingdom* (Frankfurt am Main: Peter Lang, 2003).

[270] Home, *City of Blood Revisited*, 1.

[271] A Portuguese captain noted: 'Great Benin, where the King resides, is larger than Lisbon, all the streets run straight and as far as the eyes can see. The houses are large, especially that of the king which is richly decorated and has Fine columns. The city is wealthy and industrious. It is so well governed that theft is unknown and the people live in such Security that they have no door to their houses.' See Osarumwense, 'Igue Festival and the British Invasion of Benin', 3.

[272] In 1862, British diplomat Richard Burton noted that Benin 'stinks of death' and contributed to stereotypes in the British public about the kingdom.

[273] Article I.

trade 'in every part of the king's territories'.[274] Its status remained contested.[275] It is unclear to what extent the Oba or his entourage understood the treaty as an instrument giving up royal rights or privileges, rather than as a general commitment to cooperation and trade, when it was explained by the British.[276] Signing a written agreement was unusual in a culture that recorded history in different ways. The Oba had not requested the 'gracious favour and protection' of the Queen, as implied by Article I of the agreement. According to Gallwey's report, the Oba 'refused to touch the pen though he allowed his chiefs to do so and his name to be used'.[277] They put an 'X' in place of a signature. Chief Osuolale Abimbola Richard Akinjide (1930–2020) has explained this reluctance as follows:

> The King of Benin … refused to sign any treaty of protection with Britain since he could see no need for such protection from a foreign power who had been dealing with them for centuries as equals, and in any event, Benin was a great power when Britain was a Roman colony.[278]

The 'lop-sided bargain' was a victory for Gallwey, but 'marked the beginning of the end of the independence of Benin'.[279] It soon became evident that Oba Ovonramwen and the British did not agree on the concept of 'free trade' and the concessions made. The Oba continued to require tolls and duties, and even imposed an embargo when 'gifts' were not paid. This practice hampered trade by British and local African agents, and encouraged plans to overthrow the Oba.

5.9.2 The 'Benin Massacre'

Frustrated by the lack of compliance with the 1892 treaty, Commissioner and Consul-General of the Niger Coast protectorate Ralph Moor (1860–1909) wrote on 14 June1896 to the Foreign Office: '[I]f the efforts now being made continue unsuccessful until next dry season, an expeditionary force should be sent about January or February to remove the King and his Juju men.'[280] These plans were developed by Deputy Commissioner and Acting Consul James Robert Phillips (1863–1897). He sent a dispatch to the Prime Minister on 16 November 1896,

---

[274] Article VI.

[275] See also Obinyan, 'The Annexation of Benin', 36 ('the treaty of 1892 was signed via Gallwey's trickery and deceit'; Igbafe, 'The Fall of Benin', 377–378; Plankensteiner, 'Benin—Kings and Rituals', 77.

[276] Osarumwense, 'Igue Festival and the British Invasion of Benin 1897', 4.

[277] See F. O. 84/2194, Gallwey's Report on visit to Ubini (Benin City), the Capital of the Benin Country (30 March 1892). See also Igbafe, 'The Fall of Benin', 387.

[278] Omo n'Oba n'Edo and Uku Akpolokpolo, 'Opening Ceremony Address' (1997) 30 *African Arts* 30–33, 32.

[279] Igbafe, 'The Fall of Benin', 387.

[280] PROFO, 2/101, Moor to Foreign Office (6 June 1896) 14, cited after Obinyan, 'The Annexation of Benin', 37.

which foreshadowed the underlying motives of the expedition, including the seizure of raw materials or artefacts:

> The King of Benin has continued to do everything in his power to stop the people from trading and prevent the Government from opening up the country ... I therefore ask for His Lordship's permission to visit Benin City in February next, to depose and remove the King of Benin and to establish a native council in his place and to take such further steps for the opening up of the country as the occasion may require. I do not anticipate any serious resistance from the people of the country ... but in order to obviate any danger I wish to take up a sufficient armed Force, consisting of 250 troops, two seven-pounder guns, 1 Maxim gun and 1 Rocket apparatus ... I would add that I have reason to hope that sufficient Ivory may be found in the King's house to pay the expenses in removing the King from his Stool.[281]

The request was denied. But Phillips took matters into his own hands and proceeded without government approval. He composed a smaller team, composed of nine British officials and about 240 carriers in order to try to persuade the Oba to allow unrestricted trade,[282] and depending on the king's answer, build a public case for his removal.[283] The Oba was reluctant to receive him, because the proposed visit coincided with the Igue festival, a sacred period, during which the Oba 'went into spiritual consultation with the ancestors'[284] and visitors were prohibited from entering the city. As Ekpo Eyo explains:

> The Oba requested that the visit be delayed for two months, to enable him to get through the Igue ritual during which time his body is sacred and not allowed to come in contact with foreign elements. Igue ritual is the highest ritual among the Edo and is performed not only for the well-being of the king but of his entire subjects and the land. But Phillips showed no sympathy. He replied [to] the king that he was in a hurry and could not wait because he has so much work to do elsewhere in the Protectorate.[285]

The Oba did not want provoke hostilities with Britain. Phillips was warned, through his messengers, not to approach Benin. But he went ahead. He was ambushed in a

---

[281] CSO 1/13, 6 Phillips to FO no 105 (16 November 1896).

[282] Boisragon, *The Benin Massacre*, 58 ('The object of the expedition was to try and persuade the King to let white men come up to his city whenever they wanted to').

[283] See Hicks, *Brutish Museums*, 93–94 ('The technique was to be seen to want to speak, to be refused a meeting, and so to sign one's own carte blanch for a retributive attack').

[284] Osarumwense, 'Igue Festival and the British Invasion of Benin 1897', 4.

[285] Ekpo Eyo, 'Benin: The Sack that was', *Edo Nation*, https://www.edo-nation.net/articles/benin-the-sack-that-was-1502.

village near Ughoton on 4 January 1897 by Benin soldiers, based on the instructions of Chief Ologbosheri, the Oba's son-in-law, who—as was later shown—acted
without the explicit consent or knowledge of the Oba. The ambush was described
as follows by Lieutenant-General Pitt Rivers:

> In 1896 an expedition, consisting of some 250 men, with presents and mer-
> chandise, left the British settlements on the coast, and endeavored to advance
> towards Benin City. The expedition was conducted with courage and persever-
> ance, but with the utmost rashness. Almost unarmed, neglecting all ordinary
> precautions, contrary to the advice of the neighbouring chiefs, and with the ex-
> press prohibition of the King of Benin to advance, they marched straight into
> an ambuscade which had prepared for them in the forest on each side of the
> road.[286]

The attack has become known as 'the Benin Massacre'.[287] Seven of the nine white
members of the party, including Phillips, were killed and many of the carriers lost
their lives or were detained. The event caused an outcry in Britain. It provided the
prelude to an even bigger massacre, the raid of the city of Benin. The Oba was associated with the attack, even though he was perhaps in reality 'more sinned against
than sinner'.[288]

Historically, the use of the notion of 'Benin Massacre' for the attack on the
Phillips party is an indication of how 'punitive' language was used to justify the
pursuit of colonial interests. It involved a misreading of events. It stylized the Oba
as enemy and mastermind of the attack—a claim that later turned out to be false.
In hindsight, it also reversed history: The much bigger 'massacre' was to follow.
Nigerian and British accounts differ in their terminology used. While British
sources, including eye-witness reports, focused typically on the episode of violence or refused to the use term 'sack' of Benin, Nigerians rather speak of invasion (*Osarumwense*)[289] or even 'annexation' (*Obinya*),[290] drawing attention to
the longer-term consequences. The view that the people of Benin resisted 'British
interference in the affairs of a sovereign and independent nation',[291] which has been
put forward by native voices (Chief Akinjide) but has fallen on deaf ears.

---

[286] A. Pitt Rivers, *Works of Art from Benin, Collected by Lieutenant-General Pitt Rivers, Inspector of Ancient Monuments in Great Britain* (1900; reprint, New York: Hacker Art Books, 1968) iii–iv.

[287] Ekpo Eyo, 'The Dialectics of Definitions: "Massacre" and "Sack" in the History of the Punitive Expedition' (1997) 30 *African Arts* 34–35.

[288] N'Edo and Akpolokpolo, 'Opening Ceremony Address', 33 ('Traditional history is inclined to the view that Oba Ovonramwen was grievously misled and, perhaps, too trusting. He was, as they put it in Shakespeare, "more sinned against than sinner"').

[289] Osarumwense, 'Igue Festival and the British Invasion of Benin 1897'.

[290] Obinyan, 'The Annexation of Benin'.

[291] N'Edo and Akpolokpolo, 'Opening Ceremony Address', 33.

5.9.3 The punitive expedition

The attack on Phillips was used as an opportunity to present Britain as victim of barbaric native practices and to launch the punitive expedition to dispose the Oba, which had already been contemplated by Moor and Phillips months ago.[292] It was officially justified on three grounds: denial of trading rights under the 1892 Gallwey treaty,[293] retaliation for the 'Benin massacre' and the failure of the Oba to suppress human sacrifice. An article in the Illustrated London News from 23 January 1897 described the society of Benin as a 'race of savages' who need to be liberated from 'superstition and ignorance'.[294] The mixture of civilizing and punitive rationales is reflected in a correspondence from Moor to the Marquess of Salisbury, sent on 24 February 1897, after the capture of Benin:

> It is imperative that a most severe lesson be given the Kings, Chiefs, and Ju Ju men of all surrounding countries, that white men cannot be killed with impunity, and that human sacrifices, with the oppression of the weak and poor, must cease. All buildings on this site, saturated as it is with blood of human victims, will be levelled to the ground, and no building of any description will ever again be allowed to be erected thereon.[295]

This justification demonized the Oba and his people and blended out the broader context. The terms of the 1892 treaty did not contain an express obligation to abolish human sacrifice, but only an engagement to 'assist' in the 'general progress of civilization'.[296] The broader aim of the expedition, namely to protect British economic interests through the raid, was left unmentioned.

The expedition, headed by Admiral Harry Rawson (1843–1910), was mandated to occupy the city of Benin, liberate any remaining captives, and punish the Oba. It was composed of 1,200 British and native soldiers, reinforced by carriers. It managed to gain the support of Benin river chiefs, who were opposed to the Oba, and captured the city on 18 February 1897.

---

[292] Ratté, *Imperial Looting and the Case of Benin*, 46 ('The death of Phillips offered proof of the savage character of Benin, proof of the need for a civilizing mission. A humanitarian interpretation, complete with evil leaders and people needing to be saved from them dominated the telling of the Benin story. Hints in the press that another type of expedition had been planned against the king with no Phillips to justify it went unnoticed').

[293] Annie E. Coombs, *Reinventing Africa: Museums, Material Culture and Popular Imagination in Late Victorian and Edwardian England* (New Haven: Yale University Press, 1994) 9.

[294] *Illustrated London News* (23 January 1897) 123.

[295] See Despatch from Consul-General Moor to the Marquess of Salisbury, Benin City (24 February 1897), Great Britain, Vol LX in Ratté, *Imperial Looting and the Case of Benin*, 63–64.

[296] Article V read: 'The King of Benin hereby engages to assist the British Consular or other officers in the execution of such duties as may be assigned to them; and, further, to act upon their advice in matters relating to the administration of justice, the development of the resources of the country, the interests of commerce, or in any other matter in relation to order, and government, and the general progress of Civilization.'

When the soldiers entered the city, the king and other priests had already left the city. According to reports from Felix Roth (1857–1921), a medical officer, the city was paved with 'sacrificed human beings' who were 'lying in the path and bush' and 'even in the King's compound',[297] where 'blood was dripping off the figures and altars'.[298] Such narratives fuelled the initial perception that Benin objects were artefacts of savages. According to British accounts, the soldiers destroyed sacrificial trees and altars, as well as the houses of the Queen Mother and other chiefs.[299] They collected carved ivory stocks and discovered many metal objects, including hundreds of plaques. They removed ceremonial brass heads of former Obas, which were placed on ancestral altars and provided a base for ivory tusks. They also took more than 900 brass plaques, which were found in a storage room of the palace. They traced key historic moments in the history of the kingdom.

The discovery of the diverse artefacts triggered different reactions. Moor described some of the items found as 'hideously-constructed brass heads' and viewed them predominantly as 'trophies' or 'curios'.[300] Others saw their artistic or historical value. Captain Reginald Bacon (1863–1947), who later recorded his account in the book *Benin: City of Blood*, qualified them as 'very antique bronze heads'[301] that bore similarities to Egyptian or Chinese influence. Henry Gallwey wrote:

> Buried in the dust and dirt of centuries, in some of the houses were hundreds of bronze plaques of unique design; castings of wonderful details, and a very large number of elephants' tusks of considerable age … In addition to the tusks and plaques there was a wonderful collection of ivory and bronze bracelets, splendid ivory leopards, bronze heads, beautifully carved wooden stools and boxes, and many more articles too numerous to mention. A regular harvest of loot![302]

The looting was partly inspired by the aim of countering the practices and traces of human sacrifices, but was extended to all valuable objects, including jewelry. Moor was put in charge by Rawson to collect objects, in particular those of the compound of the Oba. The distribution was organized by Moor. He 'allowed trophies to all officers involved in the expedition',[303] as well as the admiralty and the Queen. But his influence was limited, as Mary Lou Ratté notes:

---

[297] Felix Roth, 'A Diary of a Surgeon with the Benin Punitive Expedition' in Henry Ling Roth, *Great Benin: Its Customs, Art and Horrors* (Halifax: King, 1903), Appendix II, x.

[298] Ibid, x–xi.

[299] Gallwey noted that they turned 'the spot where the main crucifixion tree had stood' into the last hole of a nine-hole golf course. Henry L. Galway, 'Nigeria in the "Nineties" (1930) 29 *Journal of the African Society* 221–247, 242.

[300] Dispatch from Consul-General Moor to the Marquess of Salisbury, Benin City (24 February 1897).

[301] Reginald Bacon, *Benin: City of Blood* (London: Edward Arnold, 1897) 87.

[302] Gallwey, 'Nigeria in the "Nineties"', 241.

[303] Ratté, *Imperial Looting and the Case of Benin*, 73.

The control Moor exercised over looting outside the King's compound depended upon the integrity of the individuals involved. Since only the officers received tangible rewards, many of the smaller bronze pieces may have found their way into the pockets of the first sailors or marines to lay eyes upon them, and then gone to England unobserved in sea chest or duffel bag. Since each house had an altar of some kind, and the compound included not only the King's but the large compounds of the chief and the Queen Mother, the pickings would be easy.[304]

Items were picked because of their value or as symbols of trophy. On the third day of the occupation, the palace of the Oba and the city caught fire. It is disputed whether this was accidental or on purpose.[305] It is estimated that at least 3,000 pieces of bronze and ivory works were removed.[306] Between 900 and 1,000 Bronze plaques were captured as official war booty,[307] while the remainder constituted 'unofficial loot'.[308] Some were sold locally. The whole campaign was celebrated as a triumph of 'the white man's rule—equity, justice, peace and security', as Gallwey later put it.[309]

Six months after the destruction of the palace, the Oba surrendered and was forced to kneel down and abdicate. He was treated as a political prisoner and 'tried' for the 'Benin massacre'. The trial was a political 'show trial'. Contrary to the assumptions underlying the expedition, it was shown that the Oba 'had done all he could, as regards issuing orders, to prevent the massacre, but he was overruled by his leading Chiefs, of which the master mind was the head War Chief'.[310] He was found to be 'unfit to rule', and removed since 'the first essential in wiping out for all time the fetish rule of the Benin country was to remove the King'.[311] He was exiled to Calabar. Six other chiefs were found guilty, and two of them were immediately executed. General Ologbosheri, who had staged the attack on Captain Gallwey, according to the testimony by some of the chiefs, was later captured, tried and hanged on 28 June 1897 for 'instigating' the 'massacre of Benin'. He argued in his defence that, according to his information, the 'white men were coming' to Benin to 'fight' the Oba.[312] But this argument was not accepted. The monarchy was replaced by a council of chiefs.

---

[304] Ibid, 74.
[305] According to Roth, the fire was caused unintentionally by two carriers. Roth, 'A Diary of a Surgeon with the Benin Punitive Expedition', xii.
[306] N'Edo and Akpolokpolo, 'Opening Ceremony Address', 30.
[307] Ratté, *Imperial Looting and the Case of Benin*, 80.
[308] William Fagg, 'Benin: The Sack that Never Was' in Flora Kaplan (ed.), *Images of Power: Art of the Royal Court of Benin* (New York: New York University Press, 1981) 20–21, 21.
[309] Gallwey, 'Nigeria in the "Nineties"', 243.
[310] Ibid, 243.
[311] Ibid.
[312] See Benin Expedition 120 years on, 'The Chiefs' Trial Transcript' https://beninexpedition120year son.weebly.com/oba-overami-trial-transcript.html.

Moor, who had long pushed for Benin's opening to trade, if necessary by force,[313] summed up the rationale of the Benin expedition perfectly in his annual report for the Niger Coast Protectorate for the years 1896 to 1897. He noted: '[a] rich country has thus been opened up to the influence of civilization and trade, containing extensive rubber forests, valuable gums, the usual products of palm-oil and kernels and possible many other valuable economic products.'[314] Many of the official justifications for the taking of Benin and the removal of the Oba remained on shaky ground. The argument that the operation was justified based on the breach of the 1892 treaty is weak, in light of the doubts around the signature and the understanding of the content of the terms of the agreement. The rationale to blame and punish the Oba for the attack on Phillips was refuted at trial. As Philip Igbafe has argued, reports about human sacrifice were exaggerated[315] and did not justify a removal of the Oba or destruction of the kingdom—the 1892 treaty failed even to mention them. The operation was ultimately about expanding control to facilitate economic interests. Local norms were blatantly disregarded in the context of the discussion of the legalities of takings.[316]

5.9.4 The afterlife of the bronzes

Soon after their arrival in Europe, the bronzes were quickly dispersed over Europe and North America.[317] Moor noted that the 'greater part of the property of value found was disposed of locally as opportunity offered, or shipped home.'[318] The artefacts, which were originally captured as ritual objects of a savage society, underwent a rapid metamorphosis: they were quickly appreciated for their 'aesthetic merit and antiquity'.[319]

At the beginning, it was questioned whether they originated indeed from the Edo culture. But myths about their link to Portuguese traders were quickly dispelled.[320] Their violent acquisition became secondary. The objects quickly turned into 'the most highly prized of all African art'.[321]

---

[313] A. E. Afigbo, 'Sir Ralph Moor and the Economic Development of Southern Nigeria: 1896-1903' (1970) 5 *Journal of the Historical Society of Nigeria* 371–397.

[314] Niger Coast Protectorate, Annual Report for 1896–97, 14; Obinyan, 'The Annexation of Benin', 31.

[315] See Igbafe, 'The Fall of Benin', 391–392 ('once the consuls identified human sacrifices with the obstruction to trade, it became usual to regard any event in Benin which retarded trade as involving human sacrifice').

[316] See Oluwatoyin Sogbesan and Tokie Laotan-Brown, 'Reflections on the Customary Laws of Benin Kingdom and Its Living Cultural Objects in the Discourse of Ownership and Restitution' (2022) 8 *Santander Art and Culture Law Review* 9–28.

[317] Chika Joseph Ananwa, 'Internationalisation of Benin Art Works' (2014) 2 *Journal of Humanity* 41–53.

[318] 83/1610, Moor to Foreign Office (9 June, 1898); Ratté, *Imperial Looting and the Case of Benin*, 80.

[319] Coombes, *Reinventing Africa*, 43.

[320] Ibid, 44–45.

[321] Elazar Barkan, 'Aesthetics and Evolution: Benin Art in Europe' (1997) 30 *African Arts* 36–41, 36.

The first auctions, in which the bronzes were sold, took place only a few weeks after the expedition. Philip Dark has explained this phenomenon with the rising interest in exotic ethnological objects:

> Benin art was thus not familiar to Europe before the Expedition of 1897, and certainly not the bronze art upon which its fame largely rests. Its sudden appearance in Europe came at a time when objects from exotic cultures were becoming more familiar to European eyes: scholars, particularly in Germany, had been taking a keen interest for some time in assembling ethnographical collections from cultures remote from and unfamiliar to Europe.[322]

Another factor was the unique style and rare nature of the objects, including their origin from a seemingly vanishing culture. Many objects were already antiquities when they were looted. Edward Maunde Thompson, the first director of the British Museum, wrote on 28 December 1897 to the Secretary of State, Robert Gascoyne-Cecil, 3rd Marquess of Salisbury (1830–1903):

> The collection now deposited here shows that at some former time there was in Benin a highly developed art of modelling and casting of metal though the decline of the kingdom during the last hundred years would appear to have led to the abandonment of such crafts.[323]

Collectors expressed interest. Von Luschan offered to 'buy up all available antiquities from Benin, regardless of price'.[324] General Lane Fox Pitt-Rivers acquired a large number of objects privately, which were later placed in the Oxford museum named after him. Many of the objects brought to Britain were sold at public auctions in London as of 1898. The British museum received 203 objects as a donation from the Foreign Office.

Elazar Barkin has rightly qualified the conquest in 1897 as a 'watershed event'.[325] When it became clear that they were indeed from Africa, and not from any other culture, they reinvigorated the hype for colonial collecting and challenged common European stereotypes of Africa. Although individual experts and collectors had appreciated the quality of African works earlier, the discovery of the Benin objects had broader public ramifications. As Neil MacGregor has noted: 'a whole set of stereotypes collapsed; a whole set of hierarchies disintegrated'.[326]

---

[322] Philip Dark, *An Introduction to Benin Art and Technology* (Oxford: Clarendon Press, 1973) 14.

[323] F.O. 83/1539, Edward Maude Thompson to the Secretary of State for Foreign Affairs (28 December 1897).

[324] Ratté, *Imperial Looting and the Case of Benin*, 81.

[325] Barkan, 'Aesthetics and Evolution'.

[326] Neil MacGregor, 'To Shape the Citizens of "That Great City, the World"' in James Cuno (ed.), *Whose Culture? The Promise of Museums and the Debate Over Antiquities* (Princeton & Oxford: Princeton University Press, 2009) 39–54, 52.

Throughout the twentieth century, the objects were considered as works of art and became a source of inspiration for modernist artists. Their violent acquisition was concealed in official narratives. The objects were rebranded as international heritage which belongs to humanity.

More than 120 years after their taking, which triggered a collecting mania, they took on yet another 'life-story'. They have turned into the public face of colonial injustice and shifting attitudes towards return. They symbolize, like hardly any other objects, the cry for justice, acknowledgement of wrong and return. They have triggered a reverse movement, namely a race for return.[327]

5.10   Removal of the Kono boli figure: Looting during the Dakar–Djibouti mission (1931)

A famous example of looting under the umbrella of French authority is the Dakar–Djibouti Mission from 10 January 1931 to 31 May 1933.[328] It was equivalent to the historical 'voyages of discovery' for French ethnography.[329] Formally, the operation was an 'ethnographic and linguistic' mission, rather than a punitive expedition. It was the largest French expedition of this kind.[330] The title (Mission Dakar–Djibouti) suggested that it was a 'heroic' enterprise, guided by benevolent intentions.[331] It was deemed to document the totality of material culture. However, it became notorious for its coercive approach to collection. The methods of acquisition involved not only classical purchase or exchange, but intimidation, forced consent, blackmail, theft, and looting.[332] The techniques bear similarities with the hunt for objects during Napoleon's expeditions. The mission acquired 3,500 ethnographic works and artefacts, many of which entered French collections.[333]

5.10.1   Context

The operation was established in 1931, after the opening of the colonial exhibition in Paris in 1931, which was deemed to reinvigorate the value of the colonial project. It was carried out under the leadership of French anthropologist Marcel Griaule

---

[327] See Chapter 9.

[328] See Jean Jamin, *Le cercueil de Queequeg: Mission Dakar-Djibouti, mai 1931–février 1933* (Paris: Berose, 2014).

[329] See Charlotte Joy, *Heritage Justice* (Cambridge: Cambridge University Press, 2020) 27.

[330] In French collecting, see Alice L. Conklin, *In the Museum of Man: Race, Anthropology, and Empire in France, 1850-1950* (Ithaca: Cornell University Press, 2013).

[331] James Clifford, 'Interrupting the Whole' (1984) 6 *Conjunctions* 282–295, 290.

[332] Ruth Larson, 'Ethnography, Thievery, and Cultural Identity: A Rereading of Michel Leiris's L'Afrique Fantôme' (1997) 112 *PMLA* 229–242.

[333] Jean Jamin, 'Objets trouvés des paradis perdus: A propos de la Mission Dakar-Djibouti' in Jacques Hainard and Roland Kaehr (eds.), *Collections passion* (Neuchâtel: Musée d'ethnographie, 1982) 69–100.

(1898–1956), who had extensively lobbied for it. Its national significance is reflected in the fact that it was supported by a special parliamentary law.

The expedition was partly inspired by a salvage ideology. Research and collecting of objects were understood as a means to understand cultural differences and further ethnographic knowledge in the interests of colonial administration, rather than a means of 'othering'.[334] The mission was seen as a part of a 'humanist' justification of colonial policies. For instance, Albert Charton, the Inspector General of Education in French West Africa, took the position that 'it is unacceptable to allow native works that embody a whole era of humanity to perish without making an effort to collect and conserve them'.[335] Ethnographers were eager to spend longer periods in Africa in order to gain a more organized, comprehensive, and systematic understanding of native cultures. Cubism and the modern movements in art, including surrealism, which took an interest in the magic of non-Western objects, strengthened public interest in the aesthetics, exotic appeal,[336] or artistic value of objects.[337] These factors explain why the mission enjoyed support by a wide range of public and private funders, including several French ministries (Education, Colonies, Agriculture), the Institut Français, the ethnological institute of the University of Paris, the natural history museum, as well as private actors, such as banks, businesses, or art donors.

The mission reflected the desire to collect, categorize, and contain artefacts. Marcel Mauss had cautioned that France was falling behind other colonial powers in terms of ethnographic field work.[338] Griaule portrayed the mission as a scientific undertaking, designed to understand and document native life, and free of interpretive or theoretical bias in the approach towards collection.[339] His instructions encouraged the collection of every-day life objects, ranging from ordinary to aesthetic items. However, the goals of the operation went beyond ethnological field research and were closely intertwined with the 'colonial enterprise'. The objects were collected to expand the Trocadéro Museum, gather knowledge to facilitate colonial administration, catch up with the 'scientific' missions that UK and Germany had undertaken decades earlier,[340] and raise prestige in relation to other colonial powers.

---

[334] On changing French policies, see Gary Wilder, *The French Imperial Nation-State: Negritude and Colonial Humanism Between the Two World Wars* (Chicago: University of Chicago Press, 2005).

[335] Albert Charton, 'Organisation du musée de l'A.O.F. à Dakar' Report to Governor-General Jules Brévié (7 June 1933) dossier 'Organisation et creation du musée' O 606 31, Archives Nationales du Sénégal, Dakar (ANS) 1–3, 5.

[336] Alyce Mahon, *Eroticism and Art* (Oxford: Oxford University Press, 2005).

[337] Phyllis Clarck-Taoua, 'In Search of New Skin: Michel Leiris's L'Afrique Fantôme' (2002) 167 *Cahiers d'Études africaines* 479–498, 484–485.

[338] Griaule was a student of Mauss.

[339] Marcel Griaule, 'Buts et méthodes de la prochaine mission Dakar-Djibouti' in Éric Jolly and Marianne Lemaire (eds.), *Cahier Dakar-Djibouti* (Paris: Éditions les Cahiers, 2015), 101–19. On his approach generally, see Marcel Griaule, *Methode de l'ethnographie* (Paris: PUF, 1957) Marcel Griaule, *Projet de la Mission ethnographique et linguistique Dakar-Djibouti* (Paris: January, 1931).

[340] For instance, Leo Frobenius, undertook six expeditions to Africa between 1904 and 1914 for different German museums.

The different steps of the expedition and the stories behind the acquisition of objects were recorded by writer and ethnographer Michel Leiris (1901–1990), who acted as official secretary-archivist and kept a diary of the twenty-one months of the mission ('Phantom Africa').[341] It bears similarities to Joseph Conrad's novel *Heart of Darkness*, whom Leiris admired. It shows the flagrant contrast between the objectives of the mission and its disempowering or humiliating impact on natives. As Kwame Opoku has noted, it brings out the 'brutal methods which the French ethnologists used to acquire artefacts in Africa',[342] as well as the social psychology of colonial expeditions.

Griaule and his colleagues made efforts to acquire objects with consent.[343] However, Leiris' diary shows the fragile nature of consent and some of the dubious methods used to acquire objects, such as deception, forced sales, intimidation, blackmail, or outright theft. The practices disrespected domestic traditions, local conceptions of ownership, and customary forms of trade and exchange. Some entries show that the 'ethnographers resembled a gang of delinquents on a crime spree', who stole out of 'spite as well as desire and sometimes simply because the opportunity presented itself' and 'often did not know the significance of what they were stealing'.[344]

The expedition benefited from the colonial context of structural violence to acquire objects. Group members carried weapons. They pressured local inhabitants to sell sacred objects, often at ridiculously low prices. They relied on threats or the power of French colonial authorities in order to compel acquisition in cases where natives were reluctant to alienate objects. They captured sacred objects, sometimes in blatant violation of domestic customs, in front of local leaders, who were powerless to resist and prevent such 'sacrilege'.

5.10.2 The removal of the boli figure in Dyabougou

A famous episode, which illustrates the methods of acquisition, is the capture of a boli figure from an altar in the Bamana village of Dyabougou in the region of Ségou in French Sudan, now central southern Mali.[345] The boli is a ritual object, which is covered by different layers of sacrificial material and associated with spiritual force (the *nyama*).[346] The taking is documented in Leiris' entries from 6 and 7 September

---

[341] Michel Leiris, *Phantom Africa* (Brent Hayes Edwards tr, Calcutta, London, and New York: Seagull Books, 2017).

[342] Kwame Opoku, 'Who Is Afraid of Phantom Africa?' *Modern Ghana* (5 September 2017).

[343] Larson, 'Ethnography, Thievery, and Cultural Identity', 925.

[344] Ruth Larson, 'Ethnography, Thievery, and Cultural Identity: A Rereading of Michel Leiris's L'Afrique Fantôme' (1997) 112 *PMLA* 229–242, 234.

[345] John Warne Monroe, 'Of Memory and a "Masterpiece": A Bamana Boli between Mali and France', Academic Paper, 1–20 https://www.academia.edu/20013279/Of_Memory_and_a_Masterpiece_A_Bamana_Boli_between_Mali_and_France_.

[346] Monroe, 'Of Memory and a "Masterpiece"', 2–3.

1931. They read like 'a novel or a thriller instead of a diary of an ethnologist from the field'.[347]

According to his notes, the team had received news about a 'magnificent hut' in Kéméni. It belonged to a secret society, which preserved order in the neighbourhood. Leiris writes that they were 'burning with desire to see' the objects, including a Kono 'fetish'.[348] Women and non-circumcised men were not allowed to come into contact with it. The chief of the Kono told the group that they could only see it if they provided a sacrifice. Leiris and Griaule were asked to sacrifice two chickens. The chickens were brought by an interpreter. But no person was available to carry out the sacrifice. The African 'boys' of the mission were 'terrified' and declined. Griaule pressured the Bamana chief to release the object. He argued that the village 'must hand over the kono as recompense in exchange for 10 francs, or the police supposedly hiding in the truck will take the chief and the village notables to San, where they will have to explain themselves to the administration'.[349] Leiris acknowledged that this was an 'appalling blackmail'. According to his account, the chief agreed to the removal of the 'fetish' 'under these conditions'. However, no one wanted to take the object. Griaule's own men were 'horrified', to 'such a degree that the fumes of sacrilege' were 'beginning to waft around' their heads.[350] Griaule and Leiris then fetched the 'holy object' themselves, 'wrapping' it in 'the tarp and creeping out like thieves while the devastated chief flees'.[351] They gave 10 francs to the chief and left 'in a hurry', 'amid general astonishment', and 'crowned with the haloes of demons or particularly powerful and daring gangsters'.[352]

Leiris recognized that the removal constituted an act of looting. He wrote: 'As soon as we arrive[d] at our stopping-place (Dyabougou), we unwrap[ped] our loot: it is an enormous mask of a vaguely animal form, unfortunately deteriorated but entirely covered with a crust of coagulated blood which gives it the majesty that blood confers on all things'.[353]

On the next day, they removed another Kono boli figure from a hut. Leiris' entry from 7 September 1931 shows that he was still moved by the events at the day before. He noted: 'My heart is beating very loudly because, since yesterday's fiasco, I am more keenly aware of the enormity of our crime'.[354] They cut the object from a 'costume adorned with feather'. Leiris describes it as follows: '[I]t is another one of those bizarre shapes that so strongly intrigued us yesterday—a sort of suckling pig, nougat made of the same brown (i.e. coagulated blood) and weighing at least 15

---

[347] Opoku, 'Who Is Afraid of Phantom Africa?'.
[348] Leiris, *Phantom Africa*, 152–154, entry 6 September 1931.
[349] Ibid.
[350] Ibid.
[351] Ibid.
[352] Ibid.
[353] Ibid.
[354] Ibid, entry for 7 September 1931.

kilos.'[355] He recognized at the same time his own wrongdoing. He continued: 'We quickly carry the whole thing out of the village and return to our cars through the fields. When we leave, the chief wants to return the 20 francs we have given him. Lutten let him keep them, naturally. But this doesn't make things any less ugly.'[356]

In the diary, Leiris provides many other examples in which the mission disrespected or destroyed sacred objects, violated domestic codes, or used minimal payment, deceit, bribes or coercion in order to remove objects, leaving local leaders with limited choice to resist. For instance, the mission extracted sacred and spiritual objects, such as Dogon masks and statues from present-day Mali, like scientific finds. In some cases, natives were not allowed to sell ritual masks. Transactions were branded as gift-giving, rather than purchase in order to prevent conflict with local traditions. The mission offered gifts as 'tokens of friendship', instead of payment for the masks in order to acquire them from local dancers.[357] It used bribes to replace Ethiopian church paintings with replicas[358] and disguised them to customs officials. In a letter to his wife, Leiris recognized the contradictions of takings: He wrote: 'We pilfer from the Africans under the pretext of teaching others how to love them and get to know their culture, that is, when all is said and done, to train even more ethnographers, so they can head off to encounter them and "love and pilfer" from them as well'.[359] Leiris' open acknowledgement of 'collecting' practices led to a falling out with Griaule, who was 'absolutely furious when the book came out'.[360]

The Dyabougou boli figure, which was regarded as a 'bizarre shape' by Leiris, has become a famous object in art history.[361] In 1933, it was reproduced in avant-garde magazine Le Minotaure, which devoted an entire issue to the Dakar–Djibouti expedition.[362] It showed the interconnection between surrealism and ethnography. Man Ray photographed several Dogon masks for the publication.[363] The boli figure was celebrated by surrealists as an object that transcended the classical categories of art or beauty. It became an 'aestheticized commodity'. It was listed as one of the masterpieces in the Musée de l'Homme and exhibited in the Quai Branly as

---

[355] Ibid.

[356] Ibid.

[357] Anny Wynchank, 'In the Wings of the Ethnography Stage: Michel Leiris' Scientific Pursuit and Existential Quest' (2011) 48 Tydskrif vir Letterkunde 186–197, 188.

[358] For instance, in his entry of 3 August 1932, Leiris notes: 'Griaule and Roux are continuing to remove the paintings in Antonios church, replacing them as they go along with dazzling copies executed by Roux. This work began a few days ago, with the agreement of the intendant and the head of the church.'

[359] Michel Leiris, Letter of 19 September 1931, in Michel Leiris, Miroir d'Afrique (Jean Jamin ed., Paris: Gallimard, 1996) 204.

[360] Sally Price and Jean Jamin, 'A Conversation with Michel Leiris' (1988) 29 Current Anthropology 157–174, 171.

[361] Monroe, 'Of Memory and a "Masterpiece"', 9–13.

[362] See Le Minotaure, 'Mission Dakar-Djibouti 1931-1933', No. 2 (1 June 1933) x.

[363] Ian Walker, 'Out of Phantom Africa: Michel Leiris, Man Ray and the Dogon' in Wendy A. Grossman, Man Ray, African Art, and the Modernist Lens (Washington, D.C.: International Arts and Artists, 2009) 113–125.

'primitive art'. It thus developed multiple identities, namely as sacred object in the Kono society, ethnological specimen in the eyes colonial collectors, icon of the surrealistic avant-garde, and object of art in modern museums.

5.10.3 The aftermath

In France, the mission was hailed as a success. The most spectacular objects of 'booty' were exhibited in the Trocadéro Museum. The operation strengthened the belief in the value of the colonial project. It was followed by similar expeditions, such as the Sahara–Sudan mission (1935), the Sahara–Cameroon mission (1936–1937), and the Niger–Lake Iro mission (1938–1939).

The experience promoted a broader culture of collecting in the colonies. It influenced the creation of the Institut Français d'Afrique Noire (IFAN) in Dakar, as well as the establishment of additional local museums in Abidjan (1942) and Bamako (1953). Inspector General of Education Albert Charton promoted the idea of a stronger regional presence in 1933, when the Dakar–Djibouti mission ended. He saw a need for greater coordination of scientific and ethnographic research in the colonies and defended the creation of IFAN as part of a changing colonial culture. He noted:

> We have taken charge of the future and the interests of the native populations of West Africa. We must not overlook anything that concerns them: reviving their past, showing the products of their industry, studying their customs, bearing witness to their level of civilization are not only scientific tasks, but political necessities, occasions for understanding, demonstrations of sympathy. Knowledge of native life in its variety and originality is part of our colonial culture.[364]

On 19 August 1936, Jules Brévié (1880–1964), Governor-General of French West Africa, created IFAN in Dakar by decree.[365] It had its own museum, which received objects as of 1941. The determination of which objects were worthy of 'rescue' or conservation under colonial policies was left to French administrators, rather than African voices.

5.11 Concluding reflections

These histories present only a fraction of the vast amount of forcible expeditions that were undertaken of the mid-nineteenth century. Cultural takings were

---

[364] John Warne Monroe, 'Restitution and the Logic of the Postcolonial Nation-State' (2019) 52 *African Arts* 6–8, 7.

[365] Agbenyega Adedze, 'Symbols of Triumph: IFAN and the Colonial Museum Complex in French West Africa (1938–1960)' (2002) 25 *Museum Anthropology* 50–60.

common among all colonial powers, not only in Africa, but also in South Asia or the Pacific region. They were geared at oppression and subjugation, based on political pretexts, constructed treaty violations, one-sided readings of history, or demonization of native chiefs. Such operations were not considered as formal acts of warfare by colonial powers, but rather as 'legitimate' means to establish power and control over non-Western rulers or societies.[366] They often faced considerable resistance.

The coercive dimensions were justified by questionable civilizing rationales, retributive motives, 'savage warfare' or the protection of colonial agents or traders, merchants and explorers. Colonial powers presented themselves as victims of local acts of violence, such as attacks, hostage-taking, or obstruction of trade. They interpreted attacks against their envoys or forces as uncivilized acts (e.g. the massacre of Benin) or acts of treason ('treason of Lombok'). Such readings disregarded the broader historical context prompting such attacks, such as opposition to conquest and exploitation, or reversed patterns of victimization.

The language and narratives reflected in historical accounts, such as dispatches, letters, or diaries (e.g. Lapière, Leiris) illustrate the marginalization of colonial violence and sometimes open racism or intended humiliation of the imagined 'other'. Colonial archives, diaries, reports, or Western media concealed the violence of collecting and made it seem commonplace. In cases like the Asante (Golden Stool) or Benin, entire campaigns were launched based on cultural misunderstandings, misinterpretations, or misreadings of actions. A striking feature is the almost complete disregard of counter-perspectives. Reports often glorified actions, sometimes with a degree of personal shame, but without contemplating the devastating effects of cultural takings on affected societies or cultures. 'Local' perspectives were not deemed worthy of mention. According to prevailing ideology, source communities were deemed to be in need of salvation and civilization, or portrayed as 'culprits'.[367] The operations are often seen in diametrically opposed perspectives in native narratives. What is described as a 'mission' or expedition in diplomatic correspondence, letters, or media in colonial powers constituted an invasion, aggression, or act of subjugation in the eyes of colonized people.

The taking of cultural objects was not only a by-product, but a means of colonization. The integration of experts, semi-professionals, or collectors into the structure of colonial operations shows that cultural takings were viewed as an inherent part of colonial policics. Punitive expeditions served to acquire objects that could not be gathered through purchase or exchange. Correspondence prior to major operations, such as the raid of Maqdala, suggests that certain cultural takings were anticipated and supported by museums, even if they did not always go according

---

[366] See Chapter 6.
[367] These practices align with one of central premises of the colonial project, namely the claim that the colonized could neither take care of themselves nor speak for themselves.

to plan.[368] The Benin bronzes are not an isolated case, but fit within a broader pattern of brutal campaigns that deployed similar strategies and forms of violence. It is thus artificial to use them as a showcase for colonial looting and the need for return, while ignoring other episodes. Takings included multiple categories of objects: historical objects, royal regalia and treasures, ornaments, ritual, or spiritual objects. Looting extended to the removal of humans, such as Prince Alamayu's transfer to Britain after the Maqdala Pillage, or animals, as shown by the removal of Pekinese dog 'Looty' from China. In some cases, punitive expeditions destroyed local systems of governance under the pretext of rights vindication, 'protection', or combat of slavery and human sacrifice. Colonial doctrines or labels marginalized the impact of forcible interventions on state disfunction in the post-colonial era.

A common feature of both large-scale expeditions and smaller enterprises is their performative nature. The operations were deemed to send messages to local rulers or forces, competing colonial powers, or the wider public at home. Objects were taken as trophies or spoils of war, to demonstrate dominance, express revenge, obtain prestige in the metropole, pay for expeditions, or simply because of human obsession with power and destruction.[369] Appropriation was legitimized through prize procedures, alleged violation of treaty arrangements, rationales of compensation, or shaky forms of consent or local acquiescence.[370] All of these factors make it impossible to assess acquisitions and provenance of objects merely by their recorded history.

With the rising interest in ethnographic items, scientific experts, ethnologists, or collectors became an integral part of colonial missions. The acquisition of certain types of objects was specifically commissioned by collectors or museums. Operations, such as the Dakar–Djibouti mission illustrate that even 'scientific' or 'linguistic' missions could take on violent and coercive features, due to their close entanglement with colonial power structures. Anthropology and racial science was used to present the colonial project in more 'rational' or 'humane' terms, and rationalize takings that would otherwise be seen as violations of professional codes. The rise of film and photography, colonial exhibitions, and magazines or postcards increased the theatrical features of the colonial encounter. Collection of objects was not only a performance of power towards natives or colonial rivals, but a cultural performance, involving 'seeing', 'watching', and 'staging' of objects and people.

---

[368] Gunning and Challis, 'Planned Plunder, the British Museum, and the 1868 Maqdala Expedition', 5–6.

[369] As eyewitness accounts or diary reports demonstrate, objects were sometimes plundered or taken spontaneously, based on group dynamics, prejudices about native cultures, the exotic aura of objects, or mere greed. In other cases, they were deliberately searched or targeted, in full knowledge of their value. See Roger MacGinty, 'Looting in the Context of Violent Conflict: A Conceptualization and Typology' (2004) 25 Third World Quarterly 861.

[370] Some of the objects were never 'owned' in the classical Western sense, but belonged to communities.

Punitive expeditions, such as the looting of the Yuanmingyuan Palace or the Benin takings, show that the distinction between military prize and object of art was often blurred and shaped by cultural stereotypes. Objects were originally treated as prize or trophy or even initially considered ugly or hideous. However, after their taking, they became quickly accepted as part of the art world and its markets. In certain cases, the violence behind the takings was used to enhance the value of objects. It became part of commodification. Exoticism, savagery, and violence were evoked in auction catalogues and marketing strategies in order to demonstrate the rarity (e.g. evidence of perished cultures) or authenticity of objects and increase their value.[371]

---

[371] For a study of Pacific objects, see Donna Yates, 'Violence as a Value Enhancer in the Art Market' *Items* (1 March 2022) https://items.ssrc.org/where-heritage-meets-violence/violence-as-a-value-enhancer-in-the-art-market/.

4

The Scramble for Cultural Colonial Objects: Other Types of Acquisition

1 Introduction

> You cannot see now a mask, an African mask, without seeing the way in which it was also used by Picasso too, as the face of Les Demoiselles d'Avignon at MoMA. It is part of it.
>
> *Souleymane Bachir Diagne*[1]

Histories of collection cannot be reduced to punitive expeditions or military intervention alone. Explorers, traders, and local intermediaries played an important role in the systematization of collection. Colonial structures have facilitated voluntary dispossession and takings through complex networks of power, 'scientific', economic, or ideological incentives for collection, and other structures of 'gifting' or exchange. Colonial officials, missionaries, or explorers collected objects based on orders or requests from the metropole, based on their fascination with objects or monetary or reputational incentives. Collectors often recruited local agents or had to establish some rapport with locals in order to get access to objects, to broker or secure acquisition, and remove cultural artefacts.[2] Local chiefs exercised agency and sometimes developed their own techniques to avoid a breach of customs. Some of them sought to profit from the trade or exchange opportunities and collaborated with collectors. Others protested against cultural takings or showed strong resistance. Some objects were acquired through deceit, simply carried away or removed under exploitation of the circumstances.

Arguments of world heritage were already used in the colonial period in order to encourage local leaders to sell objects of significant importance. For instance, Emil Torday (1875–1931), a self-made anthropologist who collected over 3,000 objects in an expedition on behalf of the British Museum in the Belgian Congo, used this argument in negotiations with the Kuba people in the Kasai region. He

---

[1] See Clark Art Institute, 'A Gesture of Reciprocity': Souleymane Bachir Diagne on Translation & Restitution, Transcript, In the Foreground: Conversations on Art & Writing (14 October 2020).
[2] Donald Simpson, *The Dark Companions: The African Contribution to European Exploration of East Africa* (London: Paul Elek, 1975).

Confronting Colonial Objects. Carsten Stahn, Oxford University Press. © Carsten Stahn 2023.
DOI: 10.1093/oso/9780192868121.003.0004

persuaded elders to sell objects with the argument that 'all the world might see and marvel at them in the museum'.[3] German collector Leo Frobenius (1873–1938)[4] acquired 26,000 objects for the Hamburg Museum of Ethnology during expeditions with the help of local negotiators, sometimes with dubious methods, including threats and bribes.[5] His collection became so vast that 'the museum could not afford to buy them all at the agreed price of ten marks an item'.[6] Many acquisitions were done without a record, or recorded based on the collector's side of the story.

This chapter examines the complex interplay between power, complicity, and resistance in processes of collection. It sets out the diverse methods of acquisition of objects by collectors and their interconnection with colonial structures. It demonstrates how collectors, traders, or missionaries benefited from colonial contexts or links to museum curators or colonial administrations in order to acquire objects. It shows that even voluntary exchanges and transactions or processes of gifting, were often deeply entangled with colonial power relations, which affected conditions of consent. It argues that classical market labels, such as purchase or the idea of a 'gift' do not necessarily reflect the context of colonial transactions. It also traces challenges and forms of resistance to colonial narratives and the social transformation of objects. It demonstrates these different types of entanglement through the study of object histories from different colonial contexts (settler colonialism, extractive colonialism, and colonial occupation), namely: (1) the Māori ancestral house from Tūranga; (2) the Easter Island Moai Hoa Hakananai (1868); (3) the history of the 'Great Zimbabwe Birds'; (4) the acquisition of the Bangwa 'Queen' and the Ngonnso statue; (5) the collection of the grand canoe from Luf in German New Guinea; (6) missionary collecting of *minkisi* power figures in the Congo; (7) the gifting of King Nsangu's throne; (8) the 'sale' and return of the Olokun head from Ife; (9) the removal of Nefertiti from British occupied Egypt; and (10) the acquisition of the Venus of Cyrene and the Axum Obkelisk, which were later returned by Italy. These stories, taken by themselves, present invaluable insights into the close interconnection between cultural takings, colonial narratives, resistance, and political change. They reflect the multiple forms of violence and harm inflicted through different types of acquisition, as well as ongoing colonialities.

---

[3] The exchange was recorded in a publication of his travel companion, Melwille William Hilton-Simpson (1881–1938). Melwille W. Hilton-Simpson, *Land and Peoples of the Kasai; Being a Narrative of a Two Years' Journey among the Cannibals of the Equatorial Forest and Other Savage Tribes of the South-western Congo* (London: Constable, 1911) 209.

[4] Leo Frobenius, *The voice of Africa: being an account of the travels of the German Inner African Exploration Expedition in the years 1910–1912* (London: Hutchinson & Co., 1913).

[5] Penny, *Objects of Culture*, 116–122.

[6] Suzanne Marchand, 'Leo Frobenius and the Revolt against the West' (1997) 32 *Journal of Contemporary History* 153–170, 161.

2 The taking of the Tūranga Meeting House (Te Hau ki Tūranga) (1867)

The removal of the Te Hau ki Tūranga[7] illustrates some of the contestations sur-rounding the removal and return of indigenous cultural objects in Victorian New Zealand. The meeting house, one of the oldest carved houses of the Rongowhakaata people, was constructed in 1840 by Raharuhi Rukupō (c. 1800s–1873), a famous Māori wood carver. It served not only as a meeting place or symbol of commu-nity power, but as illustration of tribal history and ancestral home, i.e. as a ritual space of unification with ancestors. Its name expresses the intimate connection to the 'spirit' or the 'good-tidings from Turanga'.[8] The house was removed by the im-perial government in 1867 as part of a land confiscation campaign by the Crown in Tūranga. The removal was connected to a policy to deter Māori resistance, punish 'rebels', and open land to European settlement. It coincided with a 'history of European collecting of Maori artefacts' and 'imperial practices of collecting, clas-sifying, and displaying artefacts', driven by a fascination with 'indigenous art and objects' and 'savage races'.[9]

The house was taken on the initiative of Native Minister James Richmond (1822–1898), who also served as Acting Director of the Colonial Museum. Richmond instructed Captain John Fairchild (1835–1898) to collect the house with a government steamer, called 'the Sturt'. He told Fairchild that the Māori had agreed to the removal. Upon arrival, the crew faced considerable local opposition. Resident magistrate Reginald Biggs sought to appease the protest, by paying a sum of £100 to Māori.[10] This manoeuvre helped to facilitate the disassembly of the an-cestry house and its transfer to the Colonial Museum in Wellington, where it was reinstalled and exhibited.

The removal continued to spark opposition. On July 1867, Rukupō filed a peti-tion in which he requested the government to return the house. He argued that it was taken without consent. He stated:

Our very valuable carved house has been taken away, without pretext, by the Government: we did not consent to its removal. This is a true account of what took place in reference to the removal of that house: at the time of Mr Richmond's visit here, he asked me to give up the house; I did not consent, but told him, 'No, it is for the whole people to consider.' He then asked me if the house belonged to

---

[7] Deidre S. Brown. 'Te Hau ki Turanga' (1996) 105 *The Journal of the Polynesian Society* 7–26; Kesaia L. Waigth, *Stolen from its people and wrenched from its roots? A Study of the Crown's 1867 Acquisition of the Rongawhakaata Meeting House Te Hau ki Turanga* (Wellington: Victoria University of Wellington, MA thesis, 2009).

[8] Waitangi Tribunal, 'Turanga Tangata, Turanga Whenua: The Report on the Turanganui a Kiwa Claims' Vol. II, Chapter 10, 'Te Hau ki Turanga' (Wellington 2004) 587–607, 589.

[9] Ibid, 598.

[10] Ibid, 590.

them all. I answered, 'No, the house is mine, but the work was done by all of us'. To this Mr Richmond replied, 'That is all; I will cease to urge you'.

The steamer left with Mr Richmond. After having been away a short time, the steamer came back again to take away the house; Captain Biggs came to fetch away the house. He desired me to give it up for the Governor, to be taken to Wellington. I told him I did not agree to it. He said other things, which I have not forgotten. He then went to take down the house, and carried it off, but I did not give my sanction to it.[11]

Richmond defended the acquisition in his testimony before the Native Affairs Committee, which examined the 1867 petition. He claimed that the house was not confiscated. But he offered ambivalent narratives. He no longer claimed that the house was a 'gift', but he took the view that it was purchased with the 'assent of the natives' through Bigg's payment and was in need of repair.[12] The Committee ultimately sided with Richmond, and offered justifications that have become standard pretexts for acquisition in colonial contexts. It noted that the price of £100 was a sizeable amount, that the 'house itself and the land on which it stood belonged to rebel Natives, and were, strictly speaking, forfeited to the Government', and that the purchase rescued the house from decay.[13]

A second petition for return or compensation was filed by Māori leader Wi Pere (1837–1915) in 1878. This time, Fairchild admitted openly that the 'natives objected' to the 'taking the house after the money was paid' and that he had to 'take the house by force'.[14] Biggs confirmed that the sum of £100 was paid to 'ten different natives' on board of the Stuart who 'got £10 each'.[15] The money was thus paid to end the protest, rather than to acquire title from the owner.[16] The Native Affairs Committee ordered that 'a further sum of £300 be paid to the native owners ... in final satisfaction of all claims'.[17] It did not determine whether the initial £100 or the additional £300 were actually paid to the proper owners.

In the Colonial Museum, the Te Hau ki Tūranga became one of the showpieces of the collection. It was called the 'Māori house'. It was initially displayed as a trophy of conquest, but then gradually branded as visual art and a sample of Māori craftsmanship.[18] In the 1930s, some of the wooden panels located underneath the house, illustrating ancestors, were removed in order to fit the house into the premises of a new location, the Dominium museum.[19]

---

[11] 'Petition of Natives at Turanga' (8 July 1867) Appendices to the Journals of the House of Representatives, 1867, G–1, 2.
[12] Waigth, *Stolen from its people and wrenched from its roots?*, 53.
[13] Waitangi Tribunal, 'Te Hau ki Turanga', 593.
[14] Ibid, 594.
[15] Ibid, 595.
[16] Waigth, *Stolen from its people and wrenched from its roots?*, 53.
[17] Waitangi Tribunal, 'Te Hau ki Turanga', 594.
[18] Waigth, *Stolen from its people and wrenched from its roots?*, 66.
[19] Ibid, 68.

The illegality of the removal, namely its breach of the principles of the Treaty of Waitangi, was finally recognized in 2004 in a non-binding opinion by the Waitangi Tribunal, which addressed ownership issues based on a complaint by Rukupō's descendants. It found that the house was 'stolen'.[20] It held that 'Te Hau ki Turanga was removed by force, in the face of objections from local Maori, and without identifying the owners or seeking their consent'.[21] The tribunal argued that 'payment of £300 to the four petitioners did not constitute payment for the whare',[22] and that 'the Crown has been unable to point to any freely given agreement by the traditional owners to transfer the title they held in 1867 to the museum or to the Crown'.[23] It expressly rejected the 'salvage theory' proposed by Richmond and the Native Affairs Committee in 1867:

> Whether Te Hau ki Turanga was in an apparent state of disrepair is … in our view, an irrelevant factor in assessing the Crown's actions in taking or assuming possession of the whare in light of the strong objections by the assembled Maori, the surrounding circumstances of the taking.[24]

In 2011, the museum of New Zealand Te Papa Tongarew agreed to return Te Hau ki Turanga from its Māori collection to the Rongowhakaata people.

3 Removal of the Easter Island Moai Hoa Hakananai by the HMS Topaze (1868)

The acquisition of the 'Moai Hoa Hakananai',[25] one of the most famous Easter Island statues (*moai*) by officers and crew from the British Royal Navy ship *HMS Topaze* in November 1868 highlights the problems surrounding the voluntary nature of transactions in the colonial period and conflicting approaches towards the identities of objects.[26]

---

[20] Waitangi Tribunal, 'Te Hau ki Turanga', 601.
[21] Ibid, 596.
[22] Ibid, 601.
[23] Ibid, 602.
[24] Ibid, 598.
[25] Steven Fischer notes that the 'statue's name Hoa Hakananai'a is not its "ancient name" after all but would have been coined by the Rapanui in 1868 when the British purloined the moai from "Orongo and peremptorily packed it aboard the *Topaze*"'. Steven Fischer, 'Has the British Museum a 'stolen friend' from Rapanui? (1999) 5 *Rapa Nui Journal* 49–51, 50.
[26] See Jo Anne van Tilburg, *Remote Possibilities: Hoa Haka Nanai'a and HMS Topaze on Rapa Nui* (London: The British Museum Press, 2006); Mike Pitts and others, 'Hoa hakananai'a: A new study of an Easter Island statue in the British Museum' (2014) 94 *The Antiquaries Journal* 291–321; Annie Rischard Davis, 'The Cultural Property Conundrum: The Case for a Nationalistic Approach and Repatriation of the Moai to the Rapa Nui' (2020) 44 *American Indian Law Review* 333–367.

Easter Island was 'discovered' by Dutch explorer Jacob Roggeveen (1659–1729) in 1722.[27] The systematic collection of artefacts on the island began with an increased presence of missionary activity, mostly from Tahiti and Mangareva, and collecting expeditions by explorers.[28] Rapa Nui culture changed rapidly, with a dwindling population, ecological factors, and the expansion of Christianity on the island. As of the 1860s, many of the existing *moai* were toppled.[29] In the mid-1870s, the island counted only 110 native people. It was occupied by Chile in 1888 and run under the rule of a company.

The arrival of the *HMS Topaze* and the removal of the Moai Hoa Hakananai in 1868 fell within this context.[30] As Captain Luis A. Lynch, who served on the Chilean ship *O'Higgins*, noted in his diary in 1870,[31] i.e. two years after the landing of the *HMS Topaze*:

> Almost everyone brings objects for swapping, small stone and wooden idols, hens, rabbits, shells, chiefs' scepters, etc., and what the ask the most for exchange are clothes, pants …They show themselves distrustful, not giving away a thing until they receive the exchange. This happens because the crews of warships have frequently deceived them. Evidently, the Topaze, British ship that preceded us, has made them lost.[32]

The *HMS Topaze* was captained by commander Richard Ashmore Powell. Her mission was to conduct a survey of Easter Island. James Cook had already discovered the *moai* during his second voyage in 1774.[33] Powell and his crew captured two *moai*, including the Moai Hoa Hakananai, which John Linton Palmer (1824–1903), surgeon on the ship, called the 'beautifully-perfect one'.[34] Ironically, the name for the statue, revealed by the islanders to the crew, was later translated as 'Lost

---

[27]   See Davis, 'The Cultural Property Conundrum', 339.
[28]   Steven Hooper, *Pacific Encounters: Art and Divinity in Polynesia 1760–1860* (Hawaii: University of Hawaii Press, 2006).
[29]   Carl P. Lipo, Terry L. Hunt, and Sergio Rapu Haoa, 'The 'walking' megalithic statues (moai) of Easter Island' (2013) 40 *Journal of Archaeological Science* 2859–2866.
[30]   Jacinta Arthur, *Reclaiming Mana: Repatriation in Rapa Nui* (PhD, Los Angeles: University of California, 2015) 141–144.
[31]   Luis A. Lynch, 'Diario de Navegación Llevado por el Capitán de Fragata Graduado Don Luis A. Lynch Zaldívar y los Cadetes de la Escuela. En Viaje de Instrucción a la Isla de Pascua y Otros Puntos' (1870) in Rolf Foerster, Sonia Montecino, and Cristián Moreno (eds.), *Documentos Sobre Isla de Pascua (1864–1888)* (Santiago: Cámara Chilena de la Construcción, Pontificia Universidad Católica de Chile y Biblioteca Nacional, 2013) 417–429.
[32]   Foerster, Montecino, and Moreno, *Documentos*, 420.
[33]   Cook noted in 1774: '[T]he gigantic statues, so often mentioned, are not, in my opinion, looked upon as idols by the present inhabitants, whatever they might have been in the days of the Dutch; at least I saw nothing that could induce me to think so. On the contrary, I rather suppose that they are burying-places for certain tribes or families.' See J. C. Beaglehole (ed.), *The Journals of Captain James Cook on his Voyages of Discovery: Volume II* (Cambridge: Hakluyt Society, 1961) 357.
[34]   J. Linton Palmer, 'A Visit to Easter Island, or Rapa Nui, in 1868' (1870) 40 *The Journal of the Royal Geographical Society of London* 167–181, 177.

or Stolen Friend'[35]—a designation that reflects their collecting history. Reports about its discovery carry traces of salvage anthropology. Palmer reports that it was 'found' in a special location, namely in an underground 'stone house called Tau-ra-renga'[36] in the ceremonial village of Orongo near the crater Kau, where it 'was buried waist deep in the ground, and had no crown'.[37] It was excavated by Powell and the crew. The removal was later followed by several other expeditions (Chile, France, Germany),[38] including 'many uncompensated takings of the moai'.[39] It was offered as a gift to Queen Victoria, who donated it to the British Museum.

The precise conditions of acquisition of the Hoa Hakananai remain disputed. The British Museum notes the two *moai* were 'discovered' and 'collected', 'with the intent of bringing them both to Britain'.[40] Jo Anne van Tilburg argues that the British crew 'bartered' for the Hoa Hakananai and 'dragged it to their boat in a procession led by a dancing chief'.[41] Rapa Nui have expressed doubts whether the sculpture was removed with consent. Drawing on the spiritual nature of the *moai*, Geoffrey Robertson questions whether the Rapa Nui would have agreed to 'give away the spirit of an ancestor' as a gift.[42] Jacinta Arthur has even gone so far as to claim that the removal constitutes an 'emblematic case' of 'robbery' which was carried out in a context of concerted strategy to 'rob these and other hiding places'.[43]

Local reports suggest that both missionaries[44] and Rapa Nui assisted in the removal. The German priest Father Gaspard Zumbohm described the transport of the *moai* from the house to the ship in a letter to the director of the Anales des Sacrés-Cœurs. He noted:

A British ship called Topaze had come to spend some days at our bay of Hanga Roa. The commodore of this embarkation wanted to take one of our 'moai' to give it to the museum of London, but it was impossible to transport one of these enormous masses on board. Now, a league from our residency there was the bust of an idol half buried. The British admiral visited this monument and found it to his taste. Despite the reduced dimensions of this piece, the work of 500 crewmen aided by two or three hundred Indians was required to move it. The operation benefitted from the new route that we recently finished, which did not prevent

---

[35] For a critique of this translation, see Arthur, *Reclaiming Mana: Repatriation in Rapa*, 144, arguing that it should be called 'The Friend that Brings Joy'.

[36] Palmer, 'A Visit to Easter Island', 177.

[37] Ibid, 178.

[38] Arthur, *Reclaiming Mana: Repatriation in Rapa Nui*, 145–160.

[39] Davis, 'The Cultural Property Conundrum', 344.

[40] British Museum, *Moai* https://www.britishmuseum.org/about-us/british-museum-story/objects-news/moai.

[41] Alex Marshall, 'British Museum Kept a Statue for 150 Years. Now, Easter Island Wants It Back' *NY Times* (16 August 2018).

[42] Robertson, *Who Owns History?*, 210.

[43] Arthur, *Reclaiming Mana: Repatriation in Rapa Nui*, 142.

[44] Missionaries sought to persuade Rapa Nui to abandon their ancestral beliefs.

the idol from marking with the nose a long line on the land, despite all of our precautions to avoid this accident. Our archaeologists feared that much of the cap-
tive god's face was noticeably disfigured, but the enterprise resulted beyond their
hopes; also to declare their joy they offered us a splendid meal.[45]

This account suggests that the removal involved natives, while leaving unclear
to what extent they consented to the transaction. Although is not entirely certain whether the Hoa Hakananai was 'collected' through purchase or exchange,
it was certainly acquired through exploitation of circumstances. Powell and his
crew vigorously exploited the fact that the Rapa Nui people were facing 'depriv-
ation'. They removed objects from a civilization which formed essential elements
of their ancestral culture and history.[46] Their status in the British museum remained contested, because of their 'unique archaeological value' and 'spiritual
symbolism'.[47]

These concerns and the different conception of the maoi as subjects are reflected
in requests for return, made by Raou Nui leaders in 2008 in cooperation with the
government of Chile. Tarita Alarcón Rapu, governor of the Rapa Nui indigenous
community on Easter Island, said: 'We are just a body. You, the British people, have
our soul.'[48] Anakena Manutomatoma, a member of the island's development commission, explained the role of Hoa Hakananai'a as a 'living person' in Rapa Nui
traditions. She stated:

We want the museum to understand that the moai are our family, not just rocks.
For us [Hoa Hakananai'a] is a brother; but for them it is a souvenir or an attraction … Once eyes are added to the statues, an energy is breathed into the
moai and they become the living embodiment of ancestors whose role is to protect us.[49]

The British Museum has defended the continued retention of the object by arguments of cultural internationalism. It has stated:

Hoa Hakananai'a represents one of the world's great sculptural traditions, and
is a witness to the global significance of Rapanui culture. Its presence increases

---

[45] See Gaspard Zumbohm, 'Anales (de la Congrégation) des Sacrés-Cœurs (de Jésus et de Marie)'
SS.CC. 343–355 in Rolf Foerster, Sonia Montecino, and Cristián Moreno (eds.), *Documentos Sobre Isla
de Pascua (1864–1888)* (Santiago: Cámara Chilena de la Construcción, Pontificia Universidad Católica
de Chile y Biblioteca Nacional, 2013) 146–152, 150–151.

[46] Marshall, 'British Museum Kept a Statue for 150 Years'.

[47] Davis, 'The Cultural Property Conundrum', 345.

[48] Agence France-Presse, 'Easter Island governor begs British Museum to return Moai: "You have our
soul" ' (20 November 2018).

[49] John Bartlett, '"Moai are family": Easter Island people to head to London to request statue back'
The Guardian (16 November 2018).

public understanding of the history of Rapa Nui, its people's artistic achievements past, present and future, and the challenges faced by the community today. The strength of the British Museum's collection is its breadth and depth which allows millions of visitors an understanding of the cultures of the world and how they interconnect—whether through trade, migration, conquest, peaceful exchange or other interactions—both in the past and today.[50]

4 Forced migration: The history of the Great Zimbabwe Birds (1889–1891)

The removal of the so-called Soapstone Birds from the ruins of the ancient city of Great Zimbabwe (House of Stones) by German and British explorers at the end of the nineteenth century demonstrates the transformation of objects through forced migration and colonial interaction.[51]

The stone birds were originally placed on the top of walls and monoliths in the 'Great Zimbabwe'.[52] According to archaeological and historical studies, they represent spiritual objects and metaphors of royal ancestors in the culture of the Shona people of Zimbabwe.[53] They were acquired and displaced through successive excavations by colonial hunters and collectors. They became features of state iconography. In the colonial era, they were falsely attributed to non-African civilizations and viewed as symbols of the superiority of Northern or Eastern cultures over Africa. At independence, they became the national symbol of Zimbabwe.

---

[50] British Museum, *Moai* https://www.britishmuseum.org/about-us/british-museum-story/objects-news/moai.

[51] Thomas N. Huffman, 'The Soapstone Birds from Great Zimbabwe' (1985) 18 *African Arts* 68–73; Edward Matenga, *The Soapstone Birds of Great Zimbabwe: Archaeological Heritage, Religion and Politics in Postcolonial Zimbabwe and the Return of Cultural Property* (PhD: Department of Archaeology and Ancient History, Uppsala University, 2011); Dawson Munjeri, 'The Reunification of the Great Zimbabwe Bird: The Reunification of a National Symbol' (2009) 61 *Museum International* 12–21; Paul Hubbard, 'The Zimbabwe Birds: Interpretation and Symbolism' (2009) 55 *Honeyguide: Journal of Birdlife Zimbabwe* 109–116.

[52] The notion of Zimbabwe is a Shona term, which refers to 'stone houses'.

[53] Gai Roufe, 'Soapstone Birds in Soapstone Nests: Ethnohistorical Interpretation of the Zimbabwe Birds Based on Sixteenth- to Nineteenth-Century Portuguese Documents' (2016) 51 *Azania: Archaeological Research in Africa* 178–196, 182 ('The most prevalent interpretation is that the birds represented the interaction between the ancestral spirits and the ruler. This is based on the symbolic role that certain birds of prey have in Shona cosmology as messengers mediating between the spirits of the ancestors and the people, mainly local chiefs'). See also Huffman, 'The Soapstone Birds from Great Zimbabwe', 68–73. Roufe argues that 'based on the Portuguese accounts of the region' the 'main function' of the soapstone birds between the sixteenth and nineteenth centuries 'was to indicate the presence of a grave or the physical remains, as well as the spirit of a king. As these locations were considered sacred, the birds also functioned as a warning sign'. Ibid, 192.

4.1 Removal through colonial collecting

The history of the removal reveals some of the questionable methods and cultural biases of colonial collecting. The ruins of the Great Zimbabwe were first explored by German geographer Carl Gottlieb Mauch (1837–1875) and German-American hunter and trader Adam Render (1822–1881) in the context of European colonial expansion in Southern Africa. Mauch falsely associated the Great Zimbabwe with the biblical land of Ophir, described in the first Book of Kings in the Old Testament, based on names of chiefs showing a Semitic influence.[54] He searched for artefacts and objects, such as pottery and cedar wood associated with the Queen of Sheba in order to confirm this assumption.

The first stone birds were removed in 1889 by hunter William Posselt, who was on an expedition from South Africa.[55] Posselt discovered the site through locals. He was originally also in search of reminders of King Solomon and the Queen of Sheba. He received permission to inspect the ruins of the city from Chief Chipfunhu Mugabe. He discovered four stone birds on an old ruined wall in the Eastern Enclosure, the 'Sanctum Sanctorum' of the hill (also known as the Sacred Enclosure) on 14 August 1889. He sought to remove the 'best' of the four birds, and but was stopped by the guardian of the site, Haruzivishe Mugabe, the brother of Chief Mugabe, who protested fiercely against the action, presumably based on the sacred nature of the objects.[56] Posselt then decided to acquire the birds through an exchange on the next day in order to 'secure them from the natives'. He reports the acquisition as follows:

> I examined the best specimen of the four 'bird' stones and decided to dig it out; but while doing so, Andizibi [Haruzivishe] and his followers became very excited, and rushing around with their guns and assegais, I fully expected them to attack us. I went on with my work and told, Klaas [his Sotho porter], who had two loaded rifles, to shoot the first man he saw aiming at either of us. By means of a native, who spoke a little Sesuto—as I did not know any Mashona—I was able to tell Andizibi that I had no intention of removing the stone, but that I was quite prepared to buy it. This evidently pacified him, for I was not molested any further. Next day I returned with some blankets, and other articles and in exchange of these received the one 'bird' stone and a round perforated stone. The former was

---

[54] See Carl Gottlieb Mauch, *The Journals of Carl Mauch, His Travels in the Transvaal and Rhodesia, 1869–1872* [ed. E. E. Burke] (Salisbury: National Archives of Rhodesia, 1969) 226 ('All the natives admit that neither they nor the formerly so powerful Balosse were capable of constructing such walls, they even maintain that these could only have been built by white people. Should one not come close to the truth if one assumes that Phoenicians and, possibly, Israelites in their thousands had been working here!').

[55] Matenga, *The Soapstone Birds of Great Zimbabwe*, 70–72.

[56] Joost Fontein, 'Silence, Destruction and Closure at Great Zimbabwe: Local Narratives of Desecration and Alienation' (2006) 32 *Journal of Southern African Studies* 771–794, 782–783.

too heavy to be carried, and I was therefore obliged to cut off the pedestal. I stored the remaining stones in a secure place, it being my intention to return and secure them from the natives.[57]

Posselt cut one of the birds from its column and stored the rest. His account suggests that he 'purchased' the birds through a voluntary commercial transaction. But is doubtful whether Haruzivishe was authorized to 'sell' or exchange sacred items. As Edward Matenga has argued, it is more plausible to interpret the transaction as a deal in which 'Haruzivishe received a bribe' and 'sold the bird' under a 'dereliction of duty'.[58] Haruzivishe apparently later had second thoughts after the transaction.[59] Posselt's reference to the need to rescue the 'birds' from the natives, who were their actual creators, is in line with the ethnological prejudices of 'salvage' theories. His removal arguably violated the customs of Shona people, which prohibit the 'removal of things belonging to shrines and sacred forests'.[60]

Posselt took the bird (the '1889' soapstone bird) to South Africa. He sold it to Cecil John Rhodes, who was at the time Prime Minister of the Cape Colony and had received permission from the British government to create his British South Africa Company. Rhodes, like Mauch and others, thought that 'Great Zimbabwe' was Ophir and was keen to find gold. He relied on this idea to justify the invasion of the area, then known as Mashonaland, by the company's police and settlers.[61] He occupied the area, raised the British flag, and renamed it 'Rhodesia'.

Rhodes was eager to explore 'Great Zimbabwe'. In 1891, the British South Africa Company mandated archaeologist James Theodore Bent (1852–1897) to start excavations. These early excavations were 'unsystematic, without proper registration procedures, and directed by the already given assumption of an earlier white civilization'.[62] Bent retrieved four and a half birds[63] from the sacred Eastern Enclosure, which are presumably those left by Posselt ('1891 birds').[64] Locals protested against the desecration of the ruins, but 'were "pacified" by threats to destroy their

[57] William Posselt, 'The Early Days of Mashonaland' (1924) 2 *Native Affairs Department Annual* (NADA) 74–75.

[58] Matenga, *The Soapstone Birds of Great Zimbabwe*, 72. See also Hubbard, 'The Zimbabwe birds: interpretation and symbolism', 109–116.

[59] Posselt, 'The Early Days of Mashonaland', 75

[60] Matenga, *The Soapstone Birds of Great Zimbabwe*, 225–226.

[61] On the invasion of Mashonaland, see John S. Galbraith, *Crown and Charter: The Early Years of the British South Africa Company* (Berkeley and Los Angeles: University of California Press, 1974) 128–153.

[62] Preben Kaarsholm, 'The past as battlefield in Rhodesia and Zimbabwe: The struggle of competing nationalisms over history from colonization to independence' (1992) 42 *Institute of Commonwealth Studies Collected Seminar Papers* 156–170, 157.

[63] James Theodore Bent, *The Ruined Cities of Mashonaland: Being a Record of Excavation and Exploration* (London: Longmans & Co., 1896) 181, 183, 184.

[64] Richard Nicklin Hall wrote in 1905: 'In 1891 Mr. Bent removed four birds on beams and also the lower portion of another bird, but he did not discover any of them, as the position of all these was well known to settlers both before the occupation and previously to this visit, many attempts having been made to buy these relics from the Mogabe Chipfuno, who persistently refused to part with them'). See Richard Nicklin Hall, *Great Zimbabwe: Mashonaland, Rhodesia* (London: Methuen & Co., 1905) 106.

homesteads'.[65] Based on orders from Rhodes, Bent deposited the birds in the South African Museum in Cape Town, since 'Rhodesia did not have a museum at the time'.[66] They acquired a partly new identity. In 1902, they were listed as part of the 'The Ancient Ruins of Rhodesia' in a publication.[67] Based on false archaeological information, they were originally deemed to form part of the land from which the gold of Ophir was obtained.[68]

Later, other birds were retrieved. In 1903, Richard Nicklin Hall (1853–1914), a journalist, appointed as Curator of the Great Zimbabwe under the 1902 Ancient Monuments Protection Ordinance of Southern Rhodesia, collected another soapstone bird outside the Acropolis ('the 1903 bird'). It was buried upside down in the 'Philips ruin'. He noted: 'This bird and beam are undoubtedly not only in the best state of preservation of any yet found at Zimbabwe, but show evidence of more artistic workmanship having been bestowed upon them than any of those previously discovered.'[69] This bird is the only officially known object which remained in the country.[70] It was shown in the Rhodesia Museum, built in Bulawayo in 1902, based on a request of the Rhodesia Scientific Board, which was later renamed the National Museum (1836) and the Natural History Museum of Zimbabwe (1981). There are suspicions that other birds were taken by 'Austrian scientists'.[71] In 1907, a German missionary, Karl Theodor Georg Axenfield, acquired the pedestal of one bird, which he sold to the Ethnological Museum in Berlin.[72]

4.2 Colonial prejudice and misinterpretation

The acquisitions show how closely cultural appropriation was interrelated with colonial bias or national interests. As Paul Hubbard has argued, both: 'the Rhodesian and Zimbabwean governments have used the Zimbabwe bird, as well as other images of Great Zimbabwe, in a variety of ways to bolster their seemingly separate claims to legitimacy, create a national identity, and assert their version of the past.'[73] Cecil Rhodes had an interest in maintaining the myth about the origins of the 'Great Zimbabwe' and placed science in the service of the colonial endeavour.[74]

---

[65] Hubbard, 'The Zimbabwe birds: interpretation and symbolism', 110.

[66] Matenga, *The Soapstone Birds of Great Zimbabwe*, 73.

[67] Richard Nicklin Hall and W.G. Neal, *The Ancient Ruins of Rhodesia* (London: Methuen & Co., 1902) 142.

[68] Hall and Neal defended the view that certain stone buildings had been erected by the Phoenicians or other people from the Middle East.

[69] Hall, *Great Zimbabwe: Mashonaland, Rhodesia*, 107.

[70] Roger Summers, *Zimbabwe: A Rhodesian Mystery* (Johannesburg: Thomas Nelson and Sons, 1963) 70; Matenga, *The Soapstone Birds of Great Zimbabwe*, 100.

[71] Hall, *Great Zimbabwe: Mashonaland, Rhodesia*, 106–107.

[72] Matenga, *The Soapstone Birds of Great Zimbabwe*, 75.

[73] Hubbard, 'The Zimbabwe birds: interpretation and symbolism', 114.

[74] See Kaarsholm, 'The past as battlefield in Rhodesia and Zimbabwe', 157 ('Cecil Rhodes and the British South Africa Company supported the elaboration of the mythology from the earliest days of

He shared an interest in the stone birds, because he believed they came from an ancient empire in the heart of Africa. He imagined that native Africans were unable to establish such a complex structure. In his view, the occupation and reclaiming of Great Zimbabwe constituted a means to save an ancient civilization from 'native barbarism'. He kept the soapstone bird acquired from Posselt (the '1889 bird') in the personal collection of his Groote Schuur residence in Cape Town. For him the bird, which had been 'liberated' from the ruins, marked 'the symbol of Rhodesia'.[75] He assumed it had special power. He placed it in his library and used it in meetings to guide important decision-making or discussions.[76] This importance is reflected in a statement by him:

> Often in Cape Town when I speak to the people about the Hinterland, some of them take no notice others have no faith in that wild country. But then I take that stone bird you found in the Zimbabwe Ruins; I place it on the table and tell them that where this stone bird came from there must be something else.[77]

According to a guidebook from the Rhodes House, it marked a 'favourite symbol [for Rhodes] of the link between the order civilisation derived from the North or the East and the savage barbarism of Southern and Central Africa before the advent of the European'.[78] He had replicas made and adorned the staircase of the house, based on the belief that the birds were not made by an African civilization.

Bent, who had mostly worked in the Middle East and had limited archaeological experience, thought that the soapstone birds were made by Phoenicians or Arabs, i.e. the ancient Sabæan people of South Arabia.[79] This myth supported the colonial narrative and the cause of the invasion of Mashonaland. It was replicated in published works. For instance, in the preface to the 1904 edition of work on the 'Ruins of Rhodesia', Richard Hall and W.G. Neil write:

> The authors are forced to admit that the theory of the successive occupations of Rhodesia by South Arabians and Phoenicians has, so far as researches have been made, exceedingly strong claims for acceptance. With reference to Rhodesia

colonization for two reasons: the idea of an earlier white civilization in the Rhodesian territory together with the assertion of black African prirnitivity and barbarism served well to justify the return of the Europeans; further, the tradition and the myth of Great Zimbabwe was of interest because it indicated the existence of gold deposits in the region').

[75] Matenga, *The Soapstone Birds of Great Zimbabwe*, 209.
[76] Ibid.
[77] Hubbard, 'The Zimbabwe birds: interpretation and symbolism', 114–115.
[78] Paul Maylam, *The Cult of Rhodes: Remembering an Imperialist in Africa* (Claremont: New Africa Books, 2005) 74.
[79] Hubbard, 'The Zimbabwe birds: interpretation and symbolism', 111 (He believed the birds to be vultures, comparing them to vaguely similar finds from the classical world and Egypt).

being the land from which the gold of Ophir was obtained, it may be noticed that the recent discoveries in Rhodesia of a vast number of massive ruins, beyond the few mentioned either by Mr. Theodore Bent … with additional 'finds' further evidencing the practice by the ancients of Phallic worship, the arguments in favour of the theory of Rhodesia being the source not only of King Solomon's gold, but also of the wealth in gold possessed by the Sabasan nation and the Tyrian and Sidonian kingdoms, references to which are so frequent in Holy Writ, have been very considerably strengthened.[80]

The works by Bent and Hall were financed by Rhodes and the British South Africa Company.

Despite early challenges,[81] the theory of the non-African origins endured at least until the 1930s, when it was corrected by work of Gertrude Caton-Thompson (1888–1985), a leading archaeologist at the time. Caton-Thompson showed through her study of pottery and deposits that the Great Zimbabwe was of African origin.[82] More differentiated interpretations, linking the artefacts to ancestors of the Shona people and other local groups in the area, emerged as of the 1950s.[83]

4.3 Symbols of new national identity

With the path toward independence, the soapstone birds turned gradually from icons of Rhodesia into new symbols of national identity. The symbol of the bird was first used on coins in colonial Rhodesia in the 1930s. After the country's independence as Zimbabwe in 1980, it was reproduced on currency and stamps. As Paul Hubbard has argued:

> The Zimbabwe Bird is perhaps the definitive icon of independent Zimbabwe, for the same reason as the Rhodesians used it: it is a unique icon of the country's rich and varied past, of which we are all a part and should be proud.[84]

---

[80] Richard Nicklin Hall and W. G. Neal, *The Ancient Ruins of Rhodesia*, 2nd edn (London: Methuen & Co., 1904), Preface.

[81] David Randell MacIver had already assumed in 1906 that the Great Zimbabwe was of African origin. See David Randell MacIver, *Mediaeval Rhodesia* (London: Macmillan, 1906).

[82] She was sent to Southern Rhodesia in the 1920s by the British Association for the Advancement of Science and faced opposition for challenging ethnic stereotypes by settlers. See Gertrude Caton-Thompson, *The Zimbabwe Culture: Ruins and Reactions* (Oxford: Clarendon Press, 1931).

[83] Roger Summers, K. R. Robinson, and Anthony Whitty, *Zimbabwe Excavations 1958* (Bulawayo: National Museums of Southern Rhodesia, 1961); Shadreck Chirikure and others, 'New Pathways of Sociopolitical Complexity in Southern Africa' (2013) 30 *African Archaeological Review* 339–366.

[84] Hubbard, 'The Zimbabwe birds: interpretation and symbolism', 115.

The bird became the counter-narrative to Rhodes' 'Rhodesia', namely the symbol of the country's origins in African culture and history.[85] The bird collected by Hall (the '1903 bird') became the inspiration for the coat-of-arms and the national emblem of Zimbabwe.[86] It is now called the 'Zimbabwe Bird'.

Other birds were retrieved, based on requests for return. The South African government returned four of the birds removed by Bent (the '1891 birds') to Zimbabwe in 1981. In 2000, the Prussian Cultural Heritage Foundation returned the fragment of the stone bird which had come into German possession, after it had been taken from Germany by the Russian Army during the Second World War. The underlying memorandum of understanding branded the return as a permanent loan in order to avoid the debate on restitution.[87] President Mugabe handed the birds over to chiefs from Masvingo in 2004.

The bird acquired by Rhodes (the '1889 bird') and placed in his former residence in Capetown (Groote Schuur) has become more closely entangled with his own identity, and also stands as a symbol of his violent past. It has not yet been returned by South Africa, based on provisions in his will, which transferred his estate to a future Federal Government of South Africa and prohibited the alienation of the property, with the exception of 'any furniture or like articles which have become useless'.[88] The will was protected by domestic legislation (The Rhodes' Will Act No. 9 of 1910). It has been invoked as a basis to retain the bird, although this claim is challenged.[89]

5   Acquisition in the shadow of violence: The Bangwa Queen (1899) and Ngonnso, 'Mother of the Nso' (1902)

Many objects were taken in the shadow of violence. Their exact provenance is often difficult to reconstruct in light of competing narratives and rudimentary documentation in museum collections. This is shown by the history of the so-called Bangwa Queen and the Ngonnso figure. The two objects illustrate both the uncertainties

---

[85] As Matenga put it, the 'determination by the Zimbabwean government to reclaim the birds stemmed from a desire to rehabilitate Great Zimbabwe as a cultural symbol of the African people. The desire was inspired by the belief that the potency of Great Zimbabwe as the guardian spirit of the nation lies in its possession of sacred artefacts such as the conical tower and the Zimbabwe Birds. It was imperative to bring back the bird emblems in order to re-equip and revive the shrine of Great Zimbabwe'. See Edward Matenga, *The Soapstone Birds of Great Zimbabwe: Symbols of a Nation* (Harare: Africa Publishing Group, 1998) 57.

[86] Matenga, *The Soapstone Birds of Great Zimbabwe*, 82.

[87] See Folarin Shyllon, 'Repatriation of Antiquities to Sub-Saharan Africa: The Agony and the Ecstasy' (2014) *Art Antiquity and Law* 121–144, 143; William J. Dewey, 'Repatriation of a Great Zimbabwe Stone Bird' (2006) *Bulletin of the Society of Africanist Archaeologists* 30 https://static1.squarespace.com/static/5bd0e66f8d97400eb0099556/t/5bdcda3870a6ad0fe18afb4b/1541200448979/SAFA2006Dewey.pdf.

[88] Matenga, *The Soapstone Birds of Great Zimbabwe*, 217.

[89] For a critique based on potential violations of local customs at the time of taking see ibid, 225–226.

regarding the conditions of takings and their close entanglement with a context of structural colonial violence, as well as the complicity of museum structures. They were taken by German agents from Cameroon.

5.1 The Bangwa Queen

The Bangwa 'Queen'[90] was collected during a period of resistance by chiefs of the Bangwa people in present-day western Cameroon against German expansion to Cameroon's Grassfields region.[91] The sculpture presents perhaps the 'most well-known of all Bangwa works',[92] which later gained recognition in cubism, expressionism, and Man Ray's surrealistic photography in the 1930s.[93] The wooden figure has been called a 'queen' based on her royal appearance.[94] But most likely, she was not a 'queen' in Bangwa culture, but a 'Lefem' figure, i.e. the embodiment of an ancestor with spiritual importance.[95] The object was collected by Gustav Conrau, a German businessman[96] and amateur collector, who travelled in the Cameroon hinterland. He had developed close ties with a Bangwa leader, Chief Fontem Asunganyi of the Kingdom of Lebang (1870–1951) and von Luschan in Berlin, who financed and commissioned the collection of Bangwa works in 1888 and 1889.[97] Conrau noted that the statue was referred to as 'njuindem' by the Bangwa, which means 'woman of God' and associates her with a dancing 'priestess of the earth'.[98] The object was transferred to Berlin's Museum für Völkerkunde. The history of collection shows the close link between private collecting, museum networks, and colonial violence, in particular the German effort to extend control

---

[90] See Andreas Schlothauer, 'Gustav Conrau's Cameroon Collection in the Berlin Ethnological Museum' (2015) 9 *Kunst and Context Humboldt Forum* 20–32, Bettina von Lintig, 'On the Bangwa Collection Formed by Gustav Conrau' (2017) 22 *Tribal Art* 94–114; Julia Lynn DeFabo, *The Bangwa Queen: Interpretations, Constructions, and Appropriations of Meaning of the Esteemed Ancestress Figure from the Cameroon Grassfields* (Annandale-on-Hudson, New York: Senior Projects Spring 2014); Evelien Campfens, 'The Bangwa Queen: Artifact or Heritage?' (2019) 26 *International Journal of Cultural Property* 75–110.

[91] Elizabeth Chilver, 'The Bangwa and the Germans: A Tailpiece' (1967) 4 *Journal of the Historical Society of Nigeria* 155–160. On context and scope of colonial takings from Cameroon, see Bénédicte Savoy et al. (eds), *Atlas der Abwesenheit: Kameruns Kulturerbe in Deutschland* (Berlin: Reimer, 2023).

[92] Robert Brain and Adam Pollock, *Bangwa Funerary Sculpture* (London: Duckworth, 1971) 124.

[93] Man Ray made a number of photographs of the 'Bangwa Queen' between 1933 and 1935, including one entitled 'Helena's Statue "The Bangwa Queen"'. For a survey, see Wendy Grossman and Letty Bonnell, 'Man Ray, African Art, and the Modernist Lens' (2009) 42 *African Arts* 72–83, 76.

[94] Tamara Northern, *Expressions of Cameroon Art: the Franklin Collection* (Beverly Hills, CA: Rembrandt Press, 1986) 20.

[95] Brain and Pollock, *Bangwa Funerary Sculpture*, 123.

[96] Conrau worked as an agent for the company Jantzen & Thormählen, a Hamburg-based firm.

[97] Schlothauer, 'Gustav Conrau's Cameroon Collection in the Berlin Ethnological Museum', 25–27.

[98] Brain and Pollock, *Bangwa Funerary Sculpture*, 124; Alisa LaGamma, *Helden Afrikas. Ein neuer Blick auf die Kunst* (Zürich: Scheidegger & Spiess, 2011) 125. Schlothauer notes that Conrau used the term 'mânyon' in the inventory book. See Schlothauer, 'Gustav Conrau's Cameroon Collection in the Berlin Ethnological Museum', 28.

over the Protectorate from the coast to the populated hinterlands of Cameroon[99] and the evidentiary problems relating to consent-based acquisition more generally.

5.1.1 Conflicting accounts of acquisition

The exact acquisition of the Bangwa 'Queen' remains contested.[100] However, a rough picture emerges from Conrau's travel report and correspondences, as well as the inventory books of the Berlin museum between 1898 and 1890. Conrau was a trader, hunter, and collector, and one of the first white persons who came in contact with the Bangwa. He visited the region in the highlands in December 1898 and wrote that 'no European had yet visited' the land at that time.[101] Through an exchange of gifts, he managed to obtain access to the palace of Fontem in Azi in the Lebang Kingdom, where he made close contact with Assunganyi. During the visit from 11–15 December 1898, he left a lasting impression on Assunganyi. Assunganyi agreed to send 'some of his people to the coast to work there'.[102] Conrau obtained the 'chief's pipe and a fetish suit'.[103] Assunganyi was inter alia interested in guns[104] and ultimately persuaded Conrau to move his main trading post from the Banyang people, who were his competitors, to Lebang. The mutual relations were reportedly sealed by a ritual in which they became 'blood brothers' by drinking 'drops of their blood and water'.[105] Conrau was given local names, namely 'manjikwara' (the road builder) or 'Tanjok' (elephant), which continued to be reported in Bangwa oral traditions.[106]

Conrau started to collect Bangwa artefacts during his subsequent travels in 1899. He had a close relationship with von Luschan, who had bought objects from him in 1898.[107] Luschan expressed particular interest in masks and statues ('fetishes'). He purchased the two Bangwa objects gathered by Conrau during his first visit. In November 1899, he acquired an additional collection with sixty-nine Bangwa objects, including statues and masks.[108]

During this period, Conrau and von Luschau exchanged correspondence. Some of the letters contain information on the strategies that Conrau used to acquire the

---

[99] See Gustav Conrau, 'Im Lande der Bangwa' in (1899) 12 *Mitteilungen von Forschungsreisenden und Gelehrten aus den Deutschen Schutzgebieten* 201–218, 209–210.

[100] See Campfens, 'The Bangwa Queen: Artifact or Heritage?', 81–82.

[101] See Letter from Gustav Conrau to Felix von Luschan, dated 18 February 1899, Acta Africa Vol. 20 E337/99–45, cited after Schlothauer, 'Gustav Conrau's Cameroon Collection in the Berlin Ethnological Museum', 22.

[102] Conrau, 'Im Lande der Bangwa', 205.

[103] Letter from Gustav Conrau to Felix von Luschan, dated 18 February 1899, cited after Schlothauer, 'Gustav Conrau's Cameroon Collection in the Berlin Ethnological Museum', 24.

[104] Von Lintig, 'On the Bangwa Collection Formed by Gustav Conrau', 103.

[105] Ibid, 103.

[106] Elizabeth Dunstan, 'A Bangwa Account of Early Encounters with the German Colonial Administration, Translation of a Text Recorded by the Fon of Fontem' (1965) 3 *Journal of the Historical Society of Nigeria* 403–414.

[107] Schlothauer, 'Gustav Conrau's Cameroon Collection in the Berlin Ethnological Museum', 24.

[108] Ibid, 24.

objects. On 11 June 1899, Conrau wrote: 'Here in Bangwe I have again collected a lot, particularly fetishes. Some are quite beautiful.'[109] He added: 'The Negroes keep the good things carefully hidden and you can only get them if you have their trust, secretly, by chatting with them as friends.'[110] In a letter dated 3 September 1899, he repeated that the 'nice old pieces' were difficult to obtain since they were generally not open to trade.[111] On 1 October 1899, Conrau argued that he obtained statues through gift exchange. He noted in a letter written from 'Victoria':

> I purchased the other fetishes in all parts of the Bangwe region. After he had re-
> ceived very big presents, the chief allowed his people to sell these things. They
> are all old things that people no longer really appreciate today. The new fet-
> ishes, namely those from chief Fontem, are now mostly covered in beads. The
> people supplied me with the names of the objects, but I cannot vouch for their
> accuracy … Since they are most reticent to discuss the fetishes, I think they may
> have intentionally given me incorrect information.[112]

He implied that important acquisitions might not be possible without Assunganyi's consent, and that some objects were traded secretly.[113]

These different passages suggest that Bangwa artefacts were collected through exchange, rather than by coercion. For instance, Bettina von Lintig has argued that Conrau's correspondences imply that he 'obtained these pieces from the people with the assent of their powerful ruler, Assunganyi' and 'did not meddle in the af-fairs of the secret societies while collecting these "rarities," though we have only his word for this'.[114]

This theory is supported by Conrau's good network and relations, the special nature of the objects,[115] and the fact that he did not have direct military support from the colonial administration, but travelled with locals.[116] He even complained about the prices that local chiefs demanded from him for services.[117] It cannot be

---

[109] Letter from Gustav Conrau to Felix von Luschan, dated 11 June 1899, Acta Africa Vol. 21 E1015/99–48, cited after Schlothauer, 'Gustav Conrau's Cameroon Collection in the Berlin Ethnological Museum', 26.

[110] Ibid.

[111] Letter from Gustav Conrau to Felix von Luschan, dated 3 September 1899, Acta Africa Vol. 21 E1015/99–50, cited after Schlothauer, 'Gustav Conrau's Cameroon Collection in the Berlin Ethnological Museum', 26.

[112] Letter from Gustav Conrau to Felix von Luschan, dated 1 October 1899, Acta Africa Vol. 21 E1015/99–54, cited after Schlothauer, 'Gustav Conrau's Cameroon Collection in the Berlin Ethnological Museum', 26.

[113] Ibid.

[114] Von Lintig, 'On the Bangwa Collection Formed by Gustav Conrau', 104.

[115] Schlothauer, 'Gustav Conrau's Cameroon Collection in the Berlin Ethnological Museum', 27 ('The acquisition from the Bangwa can only have been by consensus and was apparently supported by Asonganyi').

[116] Ibid, 27 ('Theft or the use of force would have been fatal for Conrau, since he was on the road without any military escort').

[117] He noted, inter alia: 'I lost a lot of gear to these greedy chiefs, because they required payment for every little service they rendered.' Von Lintig, 'On the Bangwa Collection Formed by Gustav Conrau', 99.

excluded that Conrau acquired Bangwa objects through the trust of sellers and his 'ability to offer appropriate goods in exchange' during his travels in the region.[118] His collections were officially recorded by the museum in November 1899.

However, Conrau profited from the colonial context, namely the imperial and trade structures supporting his collecting activity, and inter-tribal rivalries which made him of interest to Assunganyi. Due to his connection to Luschan, Conrau gradually turned from a trader and explorer into an agent for the empire. Conrau sought to obtain workers from the hinterland to support plantations on the coast. He requested Assunganyi to raise the German flag in Azi. The events following Conrau's death in December 1899 show that the acquisition cannot not be entirely disconnected from the context of policies of subjugation.

Relations with Assunganyi deteriorated over time. In his 1 October 1899 letter, Conrau gave a more hostile account of his 'blood brother'. He wrote:

[The Fotem] is a major slave dealer and acts as a middleman in the slave trade between the northern tribes and those of the forest areas. He sells or kills anyone who gets in his way and weakens his people in this way. He is ... ruthless and greedy, but cunning and not unintelligent.[119]

The growing divide became apparent shortly before Conrau's death. Assunganyi had allowed Conrau to take more than fifty of his men with him to work for the Victoria plantation company. Conrau promised to return them safely. However, he was unable to live up to his promise since many of them had died or turned into forced labourers. This caused tensions when he returned to the Bangwa in November 1899 in order to recruit more men. Assunganyi arrested Conrau and held him hostage in order to secure the return of his men. There are also rumours that Assunganyi had heard about Conrau's acquisition of 'secret objects'.[120] Conrau sent word to bring Assunganyi's men back from the coast to Lebang. He then attempted to flee from detention. He was detected by a group of Bangwa men, shot at them, and was wounded. His subsequent death gave rise to conflicting accounts. According to Assunganyi, Conrau killed himself with the last bullet in order to escape from possible capture, revenge, or torture. German authorities received news that Conrau was murdered, and viewed his death as part of an uprising.[121] This

---

[118] Schlothauer, 'Gustav Conrau's Cameroon Collection in the Berlin Ethnological Museum', 27.

[119] Letter from Gustav Conrau to Felix von Luschan, dated 1 October 1899.

[120] Paul Gebauer, Art of Cameroon, The Portland Museum, Portland, Oregon, in association with the Metropolitan Museum of Art, New York: 1979) 47; Von Lintig, 'On the Bangwa Collection Formed by Gustav Conrau', 106.

[121] The Bangwa offered the following account: '[S]ome tale-bearers went down to Victoria and told the Europeans that the Fon [Assunganyi] had killed Manjikwara [Conrau]. Then the Germans prepared war and they began the journey to Lebang. They sent a message to Foantem, saying, "You have killed one of our people, you must wait for us, for it is a bad thing you have done." Then Foantem said, "Can a person come to my country and say this to me! Manjikwara killed himself." The Germans arrived

misunderstanding contributed to an attack on Lebang, which was part of a broader punitive expedition against native resistance in the hinterland that led to the defeat of the Bangwa.

In February 1900, a forced expedition under the command of Captain von Besser attacked the Bangwa people and captured the palace of Assunganyi. According to some accounts, the Bangwa 'Queen' was captured as part of this broader punitive expedition. For instance, it is reported that some local chiefs blamed the dispossession on 'destruction of their palaces by the Germans in the early 1900s'.[122] According to Evelien Campfens:

> Bangwa historical accounts report that the Bangwa Queen, together with other lefem figures, were looted by German soldiers when they invaded the palace of the then ruling Fontem Asonganyi during their conquest of the Bangwa region in 1899/1900.[123]

This is supported by consultations with contemporary descendants of the Fontem, including defence lawyer Chief Charles Achaleke Taku, who question whether members of the royal family would have given away 'spiritually important objects' such as the Bangwa 'Queen'.[124]

However, the assumption that the Bangwa 'Queen' was looted by military personnel remains difficult to prove. Local accounts of the events do not expressly mention looting.[125] Correspondence between von Luschan and von Besser challenges this argument. Luschan wanted to persuade the expedition to capture certain objects from Assunganyi's palace, based on earlier descriptions from Conrau. This is reflected in a letter dated 10 February 1900, in which he notes:

> From photographs that the murdered Mr. G. Conrau sent here, it is clear that ... Fontem, the Bangwe chief, has a very strange house on stilts, such as has up till now been totally unknown in West Africa ... It is urgently required in the name of science that at least the pillars and horizontal beams which have been carved with statues should be obtained and sent to Berlin.... It is also very much

and there was war and they came into this compound and burnt down houses.' Elizabeth Dunstan, 'A Bangwa Account of Early Encounters with the German Colonial Administration, Translation of a Text Recorded by the Fon of Fontem' (1965) 3 *Journal of the Historical Society of Nigeria* 403–414, 409.

[122] Brain and Pollock, *Bangwa Funerary Sculpture*, 118.
[123] Campfens, 'The Bangwa Queen: Artifact or Heritage?', 80.
[124] Evelien Campfens and Isabella Bozsa, 'Provenance Research and Claims to Bangwa Collections: A Matter of Morality or Justice?' *Verfassungblog* (12 December 2022).
[125] See the Bangwa account reproduced by Dunstan, 'A Bangwa Account of Early Encounters with the German Colonial Administration', 405–413. See also H. Cadman, 'An Assessment Report on the Bangwa Tribal Area in the Mamfe Division of the Cameroon Province' (19 December 1922) Buea Archives File No. Af 13 http://www.lebialem.info/1922%20Bangwa%20Assessment.pdf.

to be desired that the chief's large signal and dance drums, and whatever else in the way of carved 'fetishes' etc is to be found in his possession, not be destroyed but, rather, sent here.[126]

Von Besser later replied that the expedition did not have an opportunity to loot any objects. He wrote:

[W]hen the village of Fontem was burned down, the chief's house was also deliberately burned down, along with other signal drums, dance drums and fetishes, a small number of which were present and were mostly of little value. The expedition could not think about taking even the smallest rarity because no bearers whatsoever were available. Only with great difficulty could the most essential loads and the wounded be transported.[127]

In later punitive expeditions, Assunganyi was captured, sent into exile, and replaced by a German officer, Lieutenant Emil Rausch (1877–1914), who was put in charge of the Bangwa region.[128]

5.1.2 (Re)naissance of the Bangwa 'Queen'

The Bangwa 'Queen' has witnessed a remarkable cultural reinterpretation. As Julia Lynn DeFabo has shown, her history 'in the West exemplifies the ways meaning is imagined, reimagined, constructed, and appropriated for a particular object'.[129] In association with other media, she turned from a spiritual object into an ethnographic curiosity, and then from an 'artefact to art' through the 'Western reception of African cultural production'.[130] The figure was already seen as an object of artistic beauty in the ethnological museum in Berlin. For instance, German expressionist Ernst Ludwig Kirchner relied on African forms in his work. The expression and aura of the Bangwa 'Queen' inspired one of his earliest wooden sculptures, called 'Dancing Woman' (*Tanzende*) (1911).[131]

In the 1920s and 1930s, the Bangwa 'Queen' gained broader recognition as a work of art and as a commodity. She was first bought by a collector from Berlin, Arthur Speyer, and then sold to a French collector, Charles Ratton, and finally

---

[126] Letter from Felix von Luschan to Imperial Government of Cameroon (10 February 1900) *Acta Africa* Vol. 22, cited after Schlothauer, 'Gustav Conrau's Cameroon Collection in the Berlin Ethnological Museum', 27.

[127] Letter from von Besser, in Bettina von Lintig, *Die bildende Kunst der Bangwa* (München 1994) 170, cited after Schlothauer, 'Gustav Conrau's Cameroon Collection in the Berlin Ethnological Museum', 27.

[128] Schlothauer, 'Gustav Conrau's Cameroon Collection in the Berlin Ethnological Museum', 23.

[129] DeFabo, *The Bangwa Queen*, 20–21.

[130] Wendy Grossman, *Man Ray, African Art, and the Modernist Lens* (Washington, DC: International Arts & Artists, 2009) 4.

[131] See 'Tanzende, Ernst Ludwig Kirchner' https://www.stedelijk.nl/en/collection/1171-ernst-ludwig-kirchner-tanzende.

acquired by Helena Rubinstein, who kept her in her apartment and made her available to exhibitions.[132] In modernist discourse, she was viewed through different lenses, such as identity, race, gender, sexuality. The Museum of Modern Art (MoMA) included her in an exhibition on African Negro art in 1935. Man Ray's photography, which featured her next to a white female model, placed greater emphasis on corporality and the female body.[133] She was associated with 'exoticism and sexuality'[134] and connected to the avant-garde. Through photography, she gained a new identity as part of Man Ray's work.[135] She later featured prominently in other exhibitions which characterize her multiple identities: 'Masterpieces of African Art' (1954–1955), 'African Sculpture' (1970), and 'The Art of Cameroon' (1984).[136]

5.2 Ngonnso, 'Mother of the Nso'

The Ngonnso statue ('Mother of the Nso') is a carved beaded sculpture, which is honoured as the founder and Queen Mother of the Nso kingdom in the Bamenda grass fields in Northwest Cameroon. The statue is considered as a 'living representative of Ngonsso'[137] by the Nso people and used in rituals to communicate with gods and ancestors. It was acquired by the German Ethnological museum in 1903 from colonial officer Curt von Pavel (1851–1933), the commander of the Imperial Protection Force in Cameroon. He headed the first expedition that reached the Nso kingdom. The object has become a bone of contention between the museum and Nso representatives because of its significance for the ancestry, culture, and the identity of the Nso people. In June 2022, the Prussian Cultural Heritage Foundation decided to return it based on its entanglement with structural colonial violence and its spiritual meaning, following a campaign by the 'Bring Back Ngonnso' initiative, led by Cameroonian arts manager Sylvie Njobati.

As in the context of the Bangwa 'Queen', there are conflicting accounts as to how the object was obtained. Felix von Luschan acquired it from Pavel in 1903.[138] Pavel donated it to the museum. In the official inventory, it was recorded as a gift.[139] Pavel claimed in a letter to Von Luschan that he had acquired all objects in Cameroon

[132] DeFabo, *The Bangwa Queen*, 37 ff, 43 ff.

[133] Ibid, 72.

[134] Alisa LaGamma, *Heroic Africans: Legendary Leaders, Iconic Sculptures* (New York: Metropolitan Museum of Art, 2011) 127.

[135] Grossman, *Man Ray, African Art, and the Modernist Lens*, 7–8.

[136] DeFabo, *The Bangwa Queen*, 94.

[137] Anne Splettstößer, *Umstrittene Sammlungen: Vom Umgang mit kolonialem Erbe aus Kamerun in ethnologischen Museen* (Göttingen: Universitätsverlag Göttingen, 2019) 334.

[138] Ibid, 290.

[139] See the identification card, reproduced in ibid, 291.

through purchase or barter.[140] However, this story has been questioned. Van Pavel and his subordinates had carried out various punitive expeditions in the region to subjugate local rulers. According to Nso traditions, the statue marks a sacred object, i.e. a personification of the Queen Mother. It belonged to the community, rather than any particular individual and was kept in a place for special rituals (*kikav ke wong*).[141] In light of this status, it is unlikely that it was sold or given away voluntarily. Its acquisition was undoubtedly shaped by a coercive environment of previous punitive expeditions. Some voices have argued that the statue was acquired by Pavel on 15 January 1902, in Kumbo, the capital of the Nso kingdom.[142] Nso historian Verkijika Fanso claims that it was taken on 3 June 1902, when the troops of Lieutenant Heinrich Gerhard Houben (1871–1942) ransacked the palace in Kumbo, because they were offered no food.[143] Both accounts confirm the nexus to structural colonial violence, even if the exact circumstances remain difficult to reconstruct.[144]

For decades, the statue was listed as object 'III C 15017' in the museum. In 2007, it was requested back by the royal house of the Nso in a letter from Fon Sehm Mbinglo I.[145] The museum first offered to return Ngonnso on the basis of a loan for a limited period of time, based on the condition that it is preserved in a museum that conforms to international standards.[146] In 2022, the museum agreed on a return, even without proof that the object was taken in actual hostilities. It listed two factors to motivate the decision, namely the fact that Pavel's stay in Kumbo 'was an expression of unequal power relations and structural, colonial violence', because he was 'accompanied by soldiers and armed porters intending to have an intimidating effect on the Nso', and the fact that 'Ngonnso has a central role for the Nso', since she is considered as a 'mother deity'.[147] This marked a clear shift in attitudes towards return.

---

[140] The letter is from 23 December 1902. Ibid, 288.

[141] Ibid, 284.

[142] According to Splettstößer, it is likely that the statue was acquired on 15 January 1902 during Van Pavel's presence in Kumbo, the capital of the Nso kingdom. Ibid, 284. Pavel mentioned the visit in the *German Colonial Journal*.

[143] Verkijika Fanso, 'The Ngonnso Statue in Berlin, Germany: Efforts at Restitution' (29 November 2018). According to the Bring Back Ngonnso initiative, Houben removed other Nso royal objects which ended in the Linden museum in Stuttgart.

[144] The Prussian Cultural Heritage Foundation came to the conclusion that 'Ngonnso had not been removed from Kumbo … through looting in the course of acts of war'. See Prussian Cultural Heritage Foundation, Press Release, 'Foundation Board clears the way for the return of the Ngonnso to Cameroon' (27 June 2022).

[145] Letter dated 15 August 2007 from Fon Sehm Mbinglo I to the Minister of Culture in Yaoundé in Splettstößer, *Umstrittene Sammlungen*, 303.

[146] Letter dated 17 August 2011 from the Prussian Cultural Heritage Foundation to Fon Sehm Mbinglo I in ibid, 316.

[147] Prussian Cultural Heritage Foundation, Press Release (27 June 2022).

6 The grand canoe from Luf, German New Guinea: Acquisition after destruction (1882/1903)

The close connection between colonial violence, exploitation, and acquisition was not limited to Africa. A compelling example from the Pacific region is the grand canoe from Luf, sometimes also called Agomes boat. It is one of the most illustrious objects of the Oceania collection of the Humbolt Forum in Berlin. It is a large, richly ornamented outrigger boat from the island of Luf in Papua New Guinea, which represents the sophisticated craft and artistic skills of the islanders.[148] It was collected on the Hermit Islands at the edge of the so-called Bismarck Archipelago, which formed part of the former German protectorate of New Guinea (Schutzgebiet Deutsch-Neuguinea).[149] In this case, a punitive expedition preceded the acquisition, and nearly extinguished the local population, which facilitated the acquisition by Max Thiel, director of the German trading company Hernsheim & Co., and its transfer to the Berlin museum.[150] The grand canoe is one of the last testimonies of the naval culture of the islanders, and its decline with colonial expansion. It was designed as a funeral object for Chief Labenan, a local leader on Luf,[151] and was no longer used for navigation purposes, as in previous traditions. It shows how the growing commercial and colonial expansion under the leadership of companies supported the acquisition of artefacts in the Pacific in the shadow of German imperialism.[152] It was driven by a mixture of 'scientific curiosity' and 'aesthetical appeals'.[153]

6.1   Context

New Guinea and its neighbouring Pacific islands had a highly developed trade, exchange, and fishing culture before the arrival of the Europeans. The German

---

[148] Buschmann notes that 250,000 Oceanic objects were collected by German merchants, explorers, and collectors in the colonial era. See Rainer Buschmann, 'Oceanic collections in German museums: collections, contexts, and exhibits' in Lucie Carreau and others (eds.), *Pacific Presences- Volume 1. Oceanic Art and European Museums* (Leiden: Sidestone Press 2018) 197–229, 197–198.

[149] Rainer Buschmann, *Anthropology's Global Histories: The Ethnographic Frontier in German New Guinea, 1870–1935* (Honolulu: University of Hawai'I Press, 2009); Christine Winter, 'The occupation of German New Guinea' in Barry Craig, Ron Vanderwal, and Christine Winter (eds.), *War trophies of curios? The war museum collection in Museum Victoria 1915–1920* (Melbourne: Melbourne Museum, 2015) 14–41.

[150] On the history, see Hans Nevermann, 'Das Agomes-Boot des Museums für Völkerkunde' (1954) 4 *Berliner Museen* 35–38; Götz Aly, *Das Prachtboot: Wie Deutsche die Kunstschätze der Südsee raubten* (Frankfurt: Fischer, 2021); Götz Aly, *The Magnificent Boat: The Colonial Theft of a South Seas Cultural Treasure* (Cambridge, Mass.: Harvard University Press, 2023).

[151] Otto Dempwolff, 'Über aussterbende Völker (Die Eingeborenen der "westlichen Inseln" in Deutsch-Neu-Guinea)' (1904) 36 *Zeitschrift für Ethnologie* 384–415, 396.

[152] For a cautious appraisal of the relationship between 'ethnographic collecting and the colonial edifice', see Buschmann, 'Oceanic collections in German museums', 203.

[153] Buschmann, 'Oceanic collections in German museums', 210.

government was initially reluctant to become involved in the colonization of New Guinea.[154] This left space for merchants and missionaries to determine their own affairs, pursue trade, cultivate land, recruit labour, carry out mining, or collect cultural objects.

The late 1870s marked 'the golden age of German commerce in the Pacific'.[155] Shipping and trading companies, such as J. C. Godeffroy & Co.[156] or Hernsheim & Co. established outputs in the Pacific, in the second half of the 1870s in order to develop commercial agricultural and extractive activities (e.g. copra).[157] They were later followed by the New Guinea Company ('Neu-Guinea Kompagnie'), a chartered company, which became the agent of the German government.[158] Trade policies focused not only on plantations[159] but also extended to acquisition of native artefacts.[160] For instance, Godeffroy established a curated museum in Hamburg and sponsored collectors to send 'shiploads of ethnographic artefacts and anthropological specimens' to Germany.[161]

Hernsheim & Co. developed considerable trade interests in the Bismarck Archipelago. Eduard Hernsheim settled on the island of Matupi in 1879. Islanders on the Archipelago were initially reluctant to trade. Hernsheim noted in his memoirs that in the late 1870s 'business was restricted to barter trade of the humblest kind; the people had no needs, and even if the goods they demanded, clay beads, hoop iron, and empty bottles, were also worthless, it was on the other hand quite impossible to buy any large quantity of the export articles to be found here'.[162]

The company took active measures to create needs and economic dependence. It introduced the islanders to tobacco and created smoking schools, in which pipes

---

[154] Germany started its activities in the Pacific through traders. Stewart Firth, *New Guinea under the Germans* (Melbourne: Melbourne University Press, 1983).

[155] Stewart Firth, 'German Firms in the Western Pacific Islands, 1857-1914' (1973) 8 *The Journal of Pacific History* 10–28, 14.

[156] Alan E. Bollard, 'The Financial Adventures of J. C. Godeffroy and Son in the Pacific' (1981) 16 *The Journal of Pacific History* 3–19.

[157] Firth, "German Firms in the Western Pacific Islands', 13–15.

[158] It was founded in 1884 by leading German merchants and bankers.

[159] In 1883, the firm Godeffroy & Sohn faced bankruptcy and was succeeded by the German South Sea Islands Trading and Plantation Society ('Deutsche Handels -und Plantagen Gesellschaft der Südsee-Inseln', DHPG). It used 'both commercial and colonial connections to acquire collection' under its director Georg Thilenius; see Buschmann, 'Oceanic collections in German museums', 209.

[160] Rainer F. Buschmann, 'Oceanic Carvings and Germanic Cravings: German Ethnographic Frontiers and Imperial Visions in the Pacific, 1870–1914' (2007) 42 *Journal of Pacific History* 299–315.

[161] Hans Ohff, *Empires of Enterprise: German and English Commercial Interests in East New Guinea 1884–1914* (PhD thesis: University of Adelaide, 2008) 28. The Godeffroy company even launched an ethnological journal, called *Journal des Museum Godeffroy*, which was published between 1871 and 1978. Collectors included Eduard Graeffe, Johann Kubary, and Amalie Dietrich. The Leipzig Museum of Ethnography acquired the artefacts after the bankruptcy of the Godeffroy company.

[162] Firth, "German Firms in the Western Pacific Islands', 13.

and tobacco were initially given out free of charge in order to create demand and encourage trade.[163] Hernsheim described this as follows:

> The Tobacco habit first had to be artificially inculcated in the natives in order to create a constant demand for a quickly consumed commodity, in place of goods made of iron which remained serviceable over a long period. The natives who had been to Matupi brought back pipes and tobacco, and soon schools for smoking were set up with the traders as instructors, in which the new pastime was propagated, so that in a few years' time tobacco was the most coveted and indispensable commodity among the natives.[164]

The company expanded over time and assembled a large ethnographic collection. It entertained close links to the German government.

Public interest in collecting increased in the 1880s, when Adolf Bastiau and others saw an opportunity to collect 'authentic artifacts from one of the last untouched areas of the world to our museum'.[165] In 1886, he brokered an agreement with the New Guinea Company to collect ethnographic objects in return for payment.[166] They were collected through 'exchange' (e.g. tobacco') by intermediaries, such as merchants, naval crews, or colonial agents.[167]

6.2 The 1882 punitive expedition and its consequences

The demise of the Luf islanders and the fate of the grand canoe are closely connected to a punitive expedition, sent by German Chancellor Otto von Bismarck at the initiative of Hernsheim.[168] It was carried out in 1882 by two vessels of the German Imperial Navy, *Carola* and *Hyäne*, in response to an attack on Hernsheim's trading ship *Freya* and his traders.

The punitive expedition was deemed to break local resistance against German trade companies. It was deployed after a series of events. In 1878, natives had plundered and burnt one of the Godeffroy ships (*Elisa*), and later killed one of

---

[163] See also Robin Torrence, 'Just another trader?: An archaeological perspective on European barter with Admiralty Islanders, Papa New Guinea' in Anne Clarke and Robin Torrence (eds.), *The Archaeology of Difference: Negotiating Cross-Cultural Engagements in Oceania* (London and New York: Routledge, 2000) 107–145, 111; Brenda Johnson Clay, *Unstable Images: Colonial Discourse on New Ireland, Papua New Guinea, 1875–1935* (Honolulu: University of Hawai'I Press, 2005) 180–181.

[164] Peter Sack and Dymphna Clark, *Eduard Hernsheim, South Sea Merchant* (Boroko: Institute of Papua New Guinea Studies, 1983) 60.

[165] Adolf Bastian, *Inselgruppen in Oceanien: Reiseerlebnisse und Studien* (Berlin 1883) (iv).

[166] Agreement New Guinea Company and General Museum Administration (3 August 1886) SMB-PK, MV, IB Litt C/E 176/86.

[167] Buschmann, 'Oceanic collections in German museums', 214.

[168] Alexander Krug: *Der Hauptzweck ist die Tötung von Kanaken: Die deutschen Strafexpeditionen in den Kolonien der Südsee 1872–1914.* (Tönning, Lübeck und Marburg: Der Andere Verlag, 2005).

Hernsheim & Co.'s agents who was active on the Hermit Islands. The trigger for the expedition was the attack on the *Freya*. The ship ran aground at the entrance to the Hermit Islands. It was attacked by islanders, who feared that the crew sought to carry out retaliatory acts in response to the previous acts of violence.[169] The captain was killed in the incident, and the ship lost its cargo.

This led to the sending of the imperial corvettes *Carola* and *Hyäne*, which were mandated to 'pacify' the island of Luf and to punish those responsible for the killings. More than 300 German forces raided the island, which had around 400 inhabitants. They destroyed sixty-seven huts and fifty-four boats, which were essential for fishing and access to neighbouring islands.[170] They executed two men who were deemed responsible for the killings.

The expedition had disastrous consequences for the people of Luf. Many died based on a lack of shelter and malnutrition.[171] The loss of boats ended their rule over the island of Ninigo, which had secured income and resources for the islanders.[172] When they tried to regain control with four canoes, they were reportedly caught by a storm on sea and lost fifty of their male warriors. The loss of their fleet and male population contributed to their decline. A German medical officer who visited Luf in 1902 observed that the population declined rapidly.[173] These narratives must, of course, be read with caution, since they fit all too well into existing salvage stereotypes.[174] In particular, the claim that the people of Luf had 'lost hope' and were no longer fighting against their extinction,[175] seems to be a far stretch from reality.

The grand canoe from Luf was built in 1885. During the works, Chief Labenan, the last recognized native ruler of Luf, died. The boat was completed in his honour.[176] It was thus not intended for warfare, but rather meant to serve as a ritual object.[177] According to native traditions, the bodies of important leaders were not buried, but sent out to sea.[178] Ultimately, however, the grand canoe never went on this last journey. Based on accounts from German ethnologist Hans Nevermann

---

[169] Nevermann, 'Das Agomes-Boot des Museums für Völkerkunde', 36.

[170] Ibid; Dempwolff, 'Über aussterbende Völker', 415.

[171] Dempwolff, 'Über aussterbende Völker', 396.

[172] Nevermann, 'Das Agomes-Boot des Museums für Völkerkunde', 36.

[173] He reported that the people of Luf had 'lost hope' and were no longer fighting against their extinction. He traced an encounter with an inhabitant who had told him in broken English 'We like dy out'. Only two families were still willing to reproduce. See Dempwolff, 'Über aussterbende Völker', 395.

[174] See Aly, *Das Prachtboot*, 41.

[175] The officer traced an encounter with an inhabitant who had told him in broken English 'We like dy out'. Only two families were still willing to reproduce. See Dempwolff, 'Über aussterbende Völker', 395. Similar accounts about voluntary population decline were reported by Elisabeth Krämer-Bannow, one of the first white female explorers of the South Pacific. See Elisabeth Krämer-Bannow, *Among Art-Loving Cannibals of the South Seas: Travels in New Ireland 1908–1909*, a translation of the 1916 German edition (Adelaide: Crawford House Publishing, 2007).

[176] Nevermann, 'Das Agomes-Boot des Museums für Völkerkunde', 37.

[177] Dempwolff, 'Über aussterbende Völker', 396.

[178] Ibid.

(1902–1982), the people of Luf did not manage to move the fifteen-metre-long boat from the shore into the water.[179] It remained on the beach, and was later spotted there by another explorer, Georg Thilenius.[180]

6.3 Acquisition by Max Thiel in 1903

The conditions of the acquisition of the Luf canoe by Hernsheim and Co. are poorly documented. According to official accounts, the boat was acquired in 1903 by merchant Max Thiel, the main representative of Hernsheim & Co. in the South Pacific, who saw it during a visit to Luf.[181] But the exact details of the transaction remain unclear. Hernsheim noted in his memoirs that the boat 'passed into' his hands, without specifying how.[182] Other historic accounts are visibly shaped by ideas of salvage anthropology, which were prominent at the time and actively promoted by Bastian.

For instance, Richard Parkinson, a Danish explorer and anthropologist, who had collected artefacts for Godeffroy & Co., wrote in his 1907 book on 'Thirty Years in the South Seas' that:

> Mr Thiel on Matupi, at great effort and cost, had this splendid item transported to his main station in the Bismarck Archipelago, at which site I was able to take a number of photographs of this rare piece—the last of its kind still in existence.[183]

Hans Nevermann, who worked for the ethnological museum in Berlin, notes that Thiel found the boat so 'remarkable that he had a new bow and stern decorations carved in the old style' and 'purchased' it from the Luf people.[184]

Both accounts require a degree of critical scrutiny. They present the removal as an act of heroism. They rely on the threat of extinction of the Luf people in order to make the case that Thiel rescued the boat through its removal. Parkinson seems to imply that Thiel made a sacrifice ('at great effort and cost') in order to preserve the object, although Hernsheim & Co. later sold the boat for a considerable price, namely 6,000 German marks,[185] to the ethnological museum in Berlin.

---

[179] Nevermann, 'Das Agomes-Boot des Museums für Völkerkunde', 38.

[180] See Richard Parkinson, *Thirty Years in the South Seas: Land and People, Customs and Traditions in the Bismarck Archipelago and on the German Solomon Islands* [1907] (John Dennison tr, Sydney: Sidney University Press, 2010) 195. Thilenius became director of the Hamburg Ethnographic Museum in 1904.

[181] Reichs-Marine-Amt (ed.), *Forschungsreise S.M.S. Planet 1906/07*, Vol. 5 (Anthropologie and Ethnographie: Beobachtungen und Studien von Augustin Krämer) (Berlin: Karl Siegismund, 1909) 84–85.

[182] Eduard Hernsheim: *Südseekaufmann: Gesammelte Schriften* (ed., Jakob Anderhandt, Münster: MV-Wissenschaft, 2014/15) 66, 68.

[183] Parkinson, *Thirty Years in the South Seas*, 195.

[184] Nevermann, 'Das Agomes-Boot des Museums für Völkerkunde', 38.

[185] Aly, *Das Prachtboot*, 131.

As historian Götz Aly has argued,[186] such readings offer only a partial account. They treat the acquisition as an isolated transaction, without taking into account the broader history of the relationship between Hernsheim & Co. and the islanders. They do not mention that the punitive expedition caused the decay of the Luf people. They conceal the violent context of exploitation, which made natives dependent on trade and the brutal methods by which they were treated. Even though Thiel's transaction in 1903 may have been consensual, the broader context through this acquisition was secured over time, cannot be fully left aside. The boat became the 'last of its kind still in existence' not through self-inflicted destruction by the Luf islanders, but rather through economic exploitation, cultural collecting, and harsh labour conditions inflicted by German merchant companies and protectorate administration.

Both Hernsheim & Co. and Thiel have been criticized for their collection methods on other islands. For instance, von Luschan blamed Thiel for carrying out 'a plundering action unique in the history of ethnography' against the 'Matty islanders'.[187] Parkinson noted in 1904 that Hernsheim & Co. had 'completely depleted Matty and Durour' of artefacts, in an 'ethnographic raid with no equal'.[188] The history of the Luf canoe is thus an illustration of the 'fatal' combination between commerce, cultural collection, and salvage ethnology in German New Guinea.[189] It shows the long-term consequences of colonization and cultural takings, such as dependence, sickness, or destruction of the natural habitat of islanders.

7   Converted objects: The power figures (*Mikinsi*) collected by Father Leo Bittremieux at the Scheut Mission as of 1907

Missionaries played a complex role in colonial collecting.[190] They destroyed cultural objects, which conflicted with their Christian beliefs or ideas of civilization, but also contributed to their preservation or circulation. They collected and documented the history of objects in order to better understand native cultures or follow requests for collection by colonial authorities or museums. This dual role is reflected in the collecting practice of Father Leo Bittremieux (1881–1946), a Belgian missionary, who gathered a wide array of objects of spiritual power

---

[186] Ibid.

[187] Rainer Buschmann, 'Exploring Tensions in Material Culture; Commercialising Ethnography in German New Guinea 1870-1904' in Michael O'Hanlon and Robert L. Welsch (eds.), *Hunting the Gatherers: Ethnographic Collectors, Agents, and Agency in Melanesia, 1870s-1930s* (Oxford, New York: Berghahn Books, 2000) 55–80, 70.

[188] Ibid, 72–73.

[189] Ibid, 73.

[190] See Karen Jacobs, Chantal Knowles, and Chris Wingfield (eds.), *Trophies, Relics and Curios?: Missionary Heritage from Africa and the Pacific* (Leiden: Sidestone Press, 2015).

(*minkisi*) as a member of the Congregation of the Immaculate Heart of Mary in Mayombe (Lower Congo) after 1907.[191] This type of missionary collection shows how deeply even voluntary processes of acquisition may be entrenched with the structural context of epistemic violence, colonial expansion, and commodification of objects.

According to local traditions, *minkisi* embodied personified forces or spirits. They were called upon to heal diseases, protect against witchcraft, or inflict harm on an adversary (*minkisi nkonde*), as illustrated by nails or metal studs.[192] For many early missionaries, they represented merely 'idols' or 'fetishes'. They misinterpreted native recognition of the life force or 'spirit' as worship of the physical object itself. Bittremieux established unique expertise as a linguist and ethnographer of Mayombe culture and collected hundreds of *minkisi*. He collected objects, which he received from locals as signs of conversion, or acquired them through exchange of gifts.[193] He documented their roles and functions, together with Alois Tembe, a local employee of the mission. His documentation and collection later attracted great attention in ethnological research or museums, along with collections by other missionaries (e.g. Karl Edvard Laman). Some objects entered public museums or private collections in Europe and America. Their taking does not fit into classical categories of looting or purchase. They rather constitute 'converted' objects'.[194] Their acquisition is inherently linked to the process of conversion to Christianity, which was supported by colonial structures.

Bittremieux joined the Scheut congregation in Kangu in 1907. He started to collect *minkisi* figures shortly after his arrival. A photograph from 1902 shows that the mission became a popular drop-off point for indigenous objects, including *minkisi*. They were offered as part of the conversion to Christianity.[195] Bittremieux did not consider *minkisi* as fetishes or objects reflecting local religious beliefs. He argued that 'recourse to spirits ... was not their religion' or 'worship of supernatural beings',

---

[191] Hein Vanhee, 'Agents of Order and Disorder: Kongo Minkisi' in Karel Arnaut (ed.), *Re-visions: New Perspectives on the African Collections of* the *Horniman Museum* (London & Coimbra: The Horniman Museum and Gardens & Museu de Antropologia da Universidade de Coimbra, 2000) 89–106; Van Beurden, *Authentically African*, 34–35.

[192] Wyatt MacGaffey, 'The Personhood of Ritual Objects: Kongo "Minkisi"' (1990) 3 *Etnofoor* 45–61; Wyatt MacGaffey, 'Fetishism Revisited: Kongo "Nkisi" in Sociological Perspective' (1977) 47 *Africa: Journal of the International African Institute* 172–84; J. Maes, 'Les Figurines Sculptées du Bas-Congo' (1930) 3 *Africa: Journal of the International African Institute* 347–359; Harrie Leyten, *From idol to art-African 'objects with power': a challenge for missionaries, anthropologists and museum curators* (Leiden: Africa Studies Centre, 2015) 54–57.

[193] This, inter alia, is shown on photographs by Edvard Karlman from 1912, showing local men lining up at the mission in Kingyi to hand over their 'minkisi' power statues as part of their conversion to Christianity.

[194] Nicholas Thomas has coined the notion of 'converted artefacts' in the context of missionary collecting in the Pacific. See Nicholas Thomas, *Entangled Objects* (Cambridge: Harvard University Press, 1991) 67.

[195] Vanhee, 'Agents of Order and Disorder: Kongo Minkisi', 92.

but rather a sign of 'moral decadence'.[196] This led him to support their handover to the mission. He undertook field research on the meanings of the *minkisi* and wrote a book on initiation society of the Bakhimba in Mayombe.[197] In 1910, he sent thirteen objects to the University of Leuven, together with documentation on names and uses.

In 1911, the colonial government requested missionaries of the Scheut mission to collect and purchase ethnographic objects in order to gain information and increase the collection in Tervuren.[198] It financed the mission for these activities. This support facilitated the collection and preservation of *minkisi*. With the knowledge and expertise of Tembe, Bittremieux provided comprehensive documentation on the meanings and categories of *minkisi*. The Scheut mission dispatched a collection of sixty-nine *minkisi* to the Tervuren museum at the beginning of the First World War. It established a comprehensive collection. Tembe counted more than 180 objects. Some went to Tervuren, others to Bittremieux's family and to the 'Fetish Museum' in Kangu ('Musée des Fetishes'), and became touristic attractions in the 1950s.[199] Through the handover or exchange, the *minkisi* were converted from objects of power into 'fetishes' or artefacts. Some objects were acquired by international or private collections and gradually considered as works of 'primitive art'. Some collectors removed the nails or polished the objects in order to increase their aesthetic attraction.[200]

Bittremieux was a contradictory personality whose work illustrates some of the tensions and pitfalls of missionary collecting.[201] Unlike other missionaries, he did qualify *minkisi* as objects of idolatry. He made efforts to understand and preserve their meanings. However, he also became complicit in their transformation and removal as part of missionary activity and collection. He was convinced that native people needed to be civilized and converted. He accepted that the collection of *minkisi* was justified in the name of conversion to Christianity.[202] The objects became also missionary trophies, i.e. evidence of the alleged 'success' of the Scheut mission.

The collections assembled by missionaries, such as Laman or Bittremieux, enhanced the global visibility and circulation of *minkisi*, but also left a cultural void in societies of origin. They transformed their original meaning and led to their decline in local tradition and perception. As a consequence of missionary activity, they are sometimes perceived as expressions of witchcraft in contemporary contexts.

---

[196] Leo Bittremieux, 'Dilemba, de weldoende nkisi van het huwelijk' (1942) 5 *Aequatoria* 51, 51; Leyten, *From idol to art*, 163.
[197] The book was published in 1911.
[198] Vanhee, 'Agents of Order and Disorder: Kongo Minkisi', 91.
[199] The museum was looted in the early 1970s. Ibid, 93.
[200] Leyten, *From idol to art*, 211.
[201] Ibid, 160.
[202] Ibid, 163.

8 Entangled gift: Mandu yenu, throne of King Njoya (1908)

Gifts played an important role in acquisitions at the peak of colonial encounters. For instance, at the beginning of the twentieth century gift-exchange was commonly practised by local rulers in Cameroon to recognize status and establish commercial and political bonds and replicated by colonial officials. A compelling example is the acquisition of King Nsangu's throne (Mandu Yenu Throne), which was offered by his son King Ibrahim Njoya (1860–1933)[203] as a gift to German Emperor Wilhelm II. It is one of the most famous examples of sculpture from the grass fields in Cameroon,[204] which were greatly admired by Von Luschan.[205] It highlights the strong influence of museums on colonial collecting in contexts of unequal power structures[206] and the misunderstanding that may underlie the offering of 'gifts'.

The throne is a symbol of power. It was originally made for King Nsangu, the ruler of Kingdom of Bamum, in the 1880s. It is made out of assembled wood, adorned by glass beads and shells. It contains a carved seat with two-headed serpents, representing royal power and strength in battle, and two striking human figures at the back, who symbolize fertility and carry ritual objects to protect the ruler. It was formally acquired through voluntary exchange, but can be best described as a 'entangled gift'. It entered German possession through active pursuit by German colonial officers, networking and partial misrepresentation, namely superficial interest by Wilhelm II, which prompted King Ibrahim Njoya to offer it as gift.[207]

King Ibrahim Njoya entertained amicable relations with the German colonizers and accepted German rule. He gained a reputation as a loyal subject after the German protective force (Schutztruppe) established administrative and military presence in Bamenda in 1902. He relied on gift exchange and diplomacy in order to forge alliances. In 1906, he benefited from a German expedition, led by Captain Hans Glauning (1868–1908), against his rival, the Nso king, who had killed his father, King Nsangu, and kept his skull as a trophy.[208] A German officer, Lieutenant von Wenckstern, brought the skull back to King Njoya, which enabled a royal burial

---

[203] Alexandra Galitzine-Loumpet, *Njoya et le Royaume Bamoun: Les Archives de la Société des Missions Evangéliques de Paris (1917–1937)* (Paris: Karthala, 2006).

[204] See generally Christraud Geary, 'Bamum Thrones and Stools' (1981) 14 *African Arts* 32–43.

[205] He stated: 'Nowhere else in West Africa is there a larger abundance of big carvings, masks etc. [than in the Cameroon Grassfields]', plateau area in western Cameroon. Felix von Luschan, 'Erwerbungen der Afrikanisch-Ozeanischen Abteilung' (1908) 24 *Amtliche Berichte aus den Königlichen Kunstsammlungen* 87–95, 88.

[206] On the cultural biography of the throne, see Michaela Oberhofer, 'The Appropriation of the Other: Following a Royal Throne from Bamum to Berlin' (2012) 1 *DiARTgonales* 33–38. On colonial collecting, see Christine Stelzig, *Afrika am Museum für Völkerkunde zu Berlin 1873–1919: Aneignung, Darstellung und Konstruktion eines Kontinents* (Herbolzheim: Centaurus-Verlag, 2004).

[207] See Christine Stelzig '"Africa Is a Sphinx: Once She's Taken Hold of You, She Won't Let Go so Easily": The Officer and Collector Hans Glauning' (2006) 55 *Tribus* 155–200.

[208] Geary, 'Bamum Thrones and Stools', 36.

and reinforced Njoya's own legitimation as ruler.[209] This gesture, and the award of a medal of honour by Glauning for his support of the 1906 expedition, reinforced Njoya's loyalty and made him receptive to the idea of offering a valuable gift.

German museums developed an interest in the throne, based on an image taken in 1902 by Captain Hans Ramsay, a representative of the German Society for Northwest Cameroon, during his initial encounter with King Njoya. The photograph showed him sitting on King Nsangu's throne.[210] It was published in a popular journal, named *Globus*, in 1905. The image started a 'hunt for the throne'.[211] Adolf Diehl, a collector of ethnographic objects for collections, in Leipzig and Stuttgart, and von Luschan, in Berlin, were eager to acquire the Bamum throne.[212] Von Luschan charged Glauning, who was himself a collector of artefacts, and had gained King Njoya's trust, to negotiate in order to purchase the throne or exchange it against another valuable object.

Glauning implied that Emperor Wilhelm II had an expressed interest in such objects. He could not convince King Njoya to sell or exchange the throne initially, but managed to persuade him to produce of a copy of the throne. For King Njoya, this was a way to express gratitude and secure its position as a ruler: 'By keeping the throne of his father and at the same time delivering the desired copy to the Germans, he would be serving the interests of both his own people, as well as to those of the German colonial powers.'[213] Ultimately, the copy of the throne was not completed on time. Martin Göhring, a missionary who had become close to King Njoya, advised him to send the original throne of King Nsangu.[214] This news was reported to Von Luschan by his subordinate Bernhard Ankermann, who was on an expedition in Cameroon at the time. He wrote on 8 April 1908:

> Regarding Ndzoya's throne, you will receive the original; he's had an exact copy made for himself, which I have seen here—before it was finished, without the covering of pearls. He wanted very much to give the throne to the governor himself, and because a copy could not be produced in the rush before his departure, he took the original with him, encouraged by the missionary Göhring.[215]

The throne was presented to Emperor Wilhelm II, but was immediately sent to the Berlin museum. It was branded as a message of submission to German sovereignty.

---

[209] Christraud Geary, *The Voyage of King Njoya's Gift: A Beaded Sculpture from the Bamum Kingdom, Cameroon, in the National Museum of African Art* (Washington: National Museum of African Art, Smithsonian Institution, 1994) 23–24.

[210] See Christraud Geary, 'Bamum Two-Figure Thrones: Additional Evidence' (1983) 16 *African Arts* 46–53, 47.

[211] Ibid, 48.

[212] Ibid, 47.

[213] Stelzig 'Africa Is a Sphinx', 188.

[214] Geary, 'Bamum Two-Figure Thrones', 49.

[215] Ibid, 49, translated from the German, referring to the Museum für Völkerkunde, Berlin, Akte Ankermann E1421/08, Letter from Ankermann to Von Luschan (8 April 1908).

This presentation did not match King Njoya's understanding, who viewed the gift as an exchange between equals, 'from ruler to ruler and not from sovereign to subject'.[216] According to a report by another missionary, Anna Rein-Wuhrmann, the king was deeply disappointed by Wilhelm II's return gift, a uniform and a musical apparatus with recordings of Prussian marches.[217] The acquisition of the throne was steered by von Luschan and Glauning, who partly created the false impression that the German Emperor had an interest in the object. As Christiane Stelzig has argued, it is questionable whether King Njoya had agreed to give up the throne of his father, 'if he had known' that the interest was in reality 'based upon the wishes of a museum curator in Berlin'.[218]

In Germany, the Mandu yenu throne was initially viewed as ethnographic object and colonial trophy. But it gained artistic value with the rise of the expressionist movement. In 1912, Emile Nolde, one of the first expressionists and member of Die Brücke, integrated fragments of the throne in his oil painting 'Man, Woman and Cat'.[219] He used the two human figures at the back of the throne as inspiration for the painting, while turning one of the characters into a male figure.[220] This reception illustrates the recognition of Bamum throne sculptures as art in the Western hemisphere. In 2023, the Sultan King of Bamoun, Nabil Mbombo Njoya requested the return of the throne of his ancestor during a visit of the Humboldt Forum in Berlin.

9 The 'sale' and return of the Olokun head from Ife (1910)

The story of the taking of the 'Olukon head', a famous Ife bronze head, shows some of the questionable methods which German ethnographer and traveller, Leo Frobenius,[221] deployed in order to collect artefacts during his expedition in Southern Nigeria.[222]

Frobenius searched for cultural objects in Nigeria, inspired by the British expedition in Benin. He had received news about the bronze head of the god Olokun during his travels in West Africa. In 1910, he started excavations in the Yoruba region in southern Nigeria. He was led to a grove (Olokun Grove), where a priest

[216] Stelzig 'Africa Is a Sphinx', 189.
[217] Geary, 'Bamum Thrones and Stools', 37.
[218] Stelzig, 'Africa Is a Sphinx', 189.
[219] Nolde even joined a colonial expedition to German New Guinea. See Buschmann, 'Oceanic collections in German museums', 214.
[220] Alexandra Loumpet-Galitzine, 'Objets en exil: Les temporalités parallèles du trône du roi Bamoun Njoya (Ouest Cameroun)' Colloque international Les temporalités de l'Exil, Poexil-Université de Montréal (15–17 February 2007) 10–11.
[221] J. M. Ita, 'Frobenius in West African History' (1972) 13 The Journal of African History 673–688.
[222] See Roger Atwood, 'Searching for a Head in Nigeria' (2014) 55 The Massachusetts Review 496–509; Glenn Penny, Objects of Culture: Ethnology and Ethnographic Museums in Imperial Germany (Chapel Hill and London: University of North Carolina Press, 2002) 115–123.

showed him the head. It was buried in the ground, in accordance with local legends, which suggested that gods descend into the earth. The object was occasionally unearthed for offerings. Frobenius was struck by the artistry of the head, but unable to believe that it could be of African origin. He assumed that he had found evidence of the legendary continent of Atlantis and interpreted the head as 'Atlantic Africa's Poseidon'. He described the discovery in his book *The Voice of Africa*. He wrote: 'Before us stood a head of marvellous beauty, wonderfully cast in antique bronze, true to the life, incrusted with a patina of glorious dark green. This was, in very deed, the Olokun, Atlantic Africa's Poseidon!'[223] He used deception and lies to obtain possession. He acquired the head with the assistance of his interpreter and negotiator Bida, who played a key role in his expeditions. He negotiated with the priest, who guarded the object, and offered him 'six pounds, a bottle of whisky and a few other trifles'[224] to purchase the head. According to Frobenius, the priest agreed to the transaction, subject to a 'sacrifice' the next day to 'unsanctify it'.[225]

Later, the priest has second thoughts. He feared that the removal of the head would get him 'into the bad books of the authorities' and cause trouble with the British Resident in Ibadan, Charles Partridge (1872–1955).[226] Frobenius pretended that he was on good terms with the British authorities in order to appease the priest. He wrote: 'I replied there was no need to worry about that, and that the bigwigs there were some of my best friends. (I plead guilty to the only lie I told in the whole of this business, but at the moment I little knew its full extent).'[227] The sons of the priest excavated the head and handed it to Frobenius. He was overjoyed with his acquisition,[228] but encountered additional obstacles. The priest conceded that he 'had no right at all to sell the head', since it 'belonged' to the local king, the Oni' of Ife.[229] Frobenius kept the head and promised to speak to the Oni in order to find an arrangement. He proposed to him to produce a copy.[230] He deceived the Oni, through a false presentation of title over the original and the replica by his interpreter Bida. The king was led to believe that he was entitled to keep the original, while Frobenius would take the copy. But in reality, Frobenius wanted to maintain the original head. He claimed that the misunderstanding was based on a translation error by Bida. He justified the deception as a legitimate negotiation technique. He noted:

[T]he Oni, on his part, agreed that I was to retain the head of the Olokun, but also, in exchange, that he was to have an exact copy of it, to be forwarded through the

---

[223] Leo Frobenius, *The Voice of Africa, Vol. 1* (London: Hutchinson & Co, 1913) 98.
[224] Ibid, 99.
[225] Ibid, 99.
[226] Ibid, 101.
[227] Ibid, 101.
[228] He wrote: 'Sweet was the burden of it in my arms'. Ibid, 102.
[229] Ibid, 102.
[230] Frobenius had produced clay copies from other objects which he had found.

D.C. of Oshogbo. I explained that a replica undistinguishable from the original could be made and I had a galvanic process of reproduction in my mind. I specially insisted on the need of a formal agreement to be drawn up in the presence of us all to the effect that the original was to be our own and its counterpart the property of the Oni. Bida confessed later on that, to save himself a little trouble and to smooth the road of negotiation, he had translated things the other way round in the real "negro" fashion.[231]

When Frobenius sought to leave with the head, the local population lodged a complaint and reported to Partridge that he had taken 'Olokun by violent means'.[232] Frobenius and Bida were summoned for a trial, and ultimately forced by the British authorities to return excavated artefacts, including the Olokun head. The incident became known as the 'Olokun affair'.[233] Frobenius ultimately returned to Germany, and blamed Partridge for obstructing his mission. The head was reportedly returned to the Oni by British authorities. However, the conflicting relation between copy and orginal continued to shape the afterlife of the bronze head.

The head made headlines when it was offered on loan from Nigeria for an international exhibition on Ife treasures at the British Museum in 1948. British curators claimed that the head associated with Frobenius was only a modern replica, since it was sand-casted.[234] The whereabouts of the original Olokun remained a mystery. Over time, the alleged copy in the national museum in Ife came to be treated as the original. Later, the British artist Damien Hirst drew on the image of the Olokun head to produce his sculpture *Golden Heads (Female)* for the exhibition 'Treasures From the Wreck of the Unbelievable'. He was accused of plagiarizing the original.

10 German Elginism: The Bust of Nefertiti (1913)

The removal the bust of Nefertiti is one of the most controversial episodes of colonial collecting on the basis of sharing arrangements (the 'partage' system) under antiquities laws.[235] The 3,500-year-old limestone bust was discovered by German

---

[231] Frobenius, *The Voice of Africa*, 103.

[232] Ibid, 109.

[233] Memorandum concerning the Olokun Affair from the British Foreign Office (15 April 1911).

[234] Atwood, 'Searching for a Head in Nigeria', 501–502.

[235] For a discussion, see Kurt G. Siehr, 'The Beautiful One Has Come—To Return: The Return of the Bust of Nefertiti from Berlin to Cairo' in John Henry Merryman (ed.), *Imperialism, Art and Restitution* (Cambridge: Cambridge University Press, 2006) 114–134; Stephen K. Urice, 'The Beautiful One Has Come—To Stay' in John Henry Merryman (ed.), *Imperialism, Art and Restitution* (Cambridge: Cambridge University Press, 2006) 115–174; Lauren Bearden, 'Repatriating the Bust of Nefertiti: A Critical Perspective on Cultural Ownership' (2012) 1 *The Kennesaw Journal of Undergraduate Research* 1–16; Peter-Tobias Stoll, 'Where should Nefertiti Go? Reflections on International Cultural Law' in Holger Hestermeyer and others (eds.), *Coexistence, Cooperation and Solidarity: Liber Amicorum Rüdiger Wolfrum* (Leiden: Martinus Nijhoff, 2012) 303–316; Kelly Culbertson, 'Contemporary

archaeologist Ludwig Borchardt in 1912 in Tell el-Amarna, the capital of Pharaoh Akhenaten, during the excavation of Amarna (1911–1914), sponsored by the German Oriental Society (Deutsche Orient-Gesellschaft). The object formed part of the workshop of ancient Egyptian sculptor Thutmose, an official court sculptor in the eighteenth dynasty, the Amarna period. It marks one of the most important works of ancient Egypt.[236] The sculpture portrays Queen Nefertiti ('the beautiful one has come'), the royal wife of the Egyptian pharaoh Akhenaten, who played an elevated role in the eighteenth dynasty and is deemed to have served as co-regent and powerful queen, as demonstrated by her blue crown.[237]

The bust marks not only an 'icon of feminine beauty', but a symbol of cultural identity, representing Egypt's unique culture and power in antiquity. It also a 'feminist icon', representing royal power and the important political role of women in ancient Egypt. Nefertiti was presented as a public figure equal to a king in archaeological sites or other depictions, showing her as a warrior, host of foreign dignitaries, or in the traditional role of a king.

The acquisition of the bust is an example of 'German elginism'. Nefertiti was formally awarded as an archaeological find to James Simon, the head of the German Oriental Society. The partage arrangement was made in 1913 by Gustave Lefebvre (1879–1957), a French official, who allocated the lot on behalf of the Egyptian Antiquities Service and the Egyptian Museum in Cairo. Simon later donated the bust to Berlin's Egyptian Museum, where it was displayed in 1923. Both the conditions of the partage, and the context in which it occurred, have been challenged in the aftermath by other officials and Egypt, which never formally consented to the removal. Borchardt, who was later called 'Indiana Jones of the German Empire',[238] knew of the great significance and value of the bust, since its discovery. The removal was formally justified as a legitimate reward for a scientific expedition.[239]

---

customary international law in the case of Nefertiti' (2012) 17 *Art Antiquity & Law* 27–68; Reinhard Mußgnug, *Wem gehört Nofretete?:Anmerkungen zu dem deutsch-deutschen Streit um den ehemals preußischen Kulturbesitz* (Berlin/New York: De Gruyter, 1977); Rolf Krauss, '1913-1988: 75 Jahre Büste der NofretEte/Nefret-iti in Berlin' (1987) 24 *Jahrbuch Preussischer Kulturbesitz* 87–124; Bénédicte Savoy (ed.), *Nofretete. Eine deutsch-französische Affäre 1912–1931* (Köln: Böhlau Verlag, 2011); Matthias Goldmann and Beatriz von Loebenstein, 'Alles nur geklaut? Zur Rolle juristischer Provenienzforschung bei der Restitution kolonialer Kulturgüter' *MPIL Research Paper Series*, No. 2020–19; Gert von Paczensky and Herbert Ganslmayr, *Nofretete Will Nach Hause. Europa -Schatzhaus der "Dritten Welt"* (München: Bertelsmann, 1984).

[236] On return claims generally, see Salima Ikram, 'Collecting and Repatriating Egypt's Past: Toward a New Nationalism' in Helaine Silverman (ed.), *Contested Cultural Heritage* (Berlin: Springer, 2011) 141–154; Aisha Y Salem, 'Finders Keepers? The Repatriation of Egyptian Art' (2005) 10 *Journal of Technology Law and Policy* 173–193.
[237] Joyce Tyldesley contests the theory that Nefertiti was a pharaoh. See Joyce Tyldesley, *Nefertiti's Face: The Creation of an Icon* (Cambridge, Mass.: Harvard University Press, 2018).
[238] Matthias Schulz, 'Re-Examining Nefertiti's Likeness and Life', *ABC News* (7 December 2012) https://abcnews.go.com/International/examining-nefertitis-likeness-life/story?id=17905667.
[239] Urice, 'The Beautiful One Has Come—To Stay', 139.

But it was facilitated by the imperial environment, which excluded meaningful Egyptian input or consent.[240]

10.1 Context

At the time of the acquisition, Egypt's government and administration was determined by foreign powers, in particular colonial rivalry by France[241] and Britain. Egypt was formally part of the Ottoman Empire, but occupied by Britain, which established a protectorate in 1814, i.e. in the year after the partage. Powers were divided. Britain exercised military power. The Antiquities Service was controlled by French officials, who decided on permissions for research and excavation on Egyptian archaeological sites. Neither the British nor the French trusted local Egyptians to have the necessary expertise to make determinations over cultural heritage.[242] No Egyptian sat on the Antiquities Board.[243]

Archaeological finds were governed by a partage system which allowed foreign experts to lead excavations, in return for a share of the finds.[244] The rules on sharing of finds were regulated in Antiquities Laws. On 12 June 1912, i.e. six months before Borchardt's partage arrangement the Khedive of Egypt, Abbas Helmi II, issued the Law No. 14 on Protection of Antiquities.[245] The law stated that Egyptian antiquities are the property of the state and that finds ought to be divided equally into two shares, one for the state and one for the excavator. It delegated the division to the Antiquities Service. Article 11 of the law stated:

> Absent an agreement on amiable partition, the Antiquities Service shall take the objects it intends to keep. For the other objects, the partition into two shares of

---

[240] Claudia Breger, 'The "Berlin" Nefertiti Bust": Imperial Fantasies in Twentieth-Century German Archaeological Discourse' in Regina Schulte (ed.), *The Body of the Queen: Gender and Rule in the Courtly World, 1500–2000* (New York/Oxford: Berghahn Books, 2006) 281–305.

[241] Benedicte Savoy (ed.), *Nofretete: Eine deutsch-französische Affäre 1912–1931* (Köln: Böhlau Verlag, 2011).

[242] Robertson, *Who Owns History?*, 182.

[243] For a critique, see Sharon Waxman, *Loot: The Battle over the Stolen Treasures of the Ancient World* (New York: Henry Holt and Company, 2009) 57.

[244] For a defence, see Urice, 'The Beautiful One Has Come—To Stay', 147 ('Indeed the partage system created under Egyptian law benefited both Germany and Egypt exactly as intended: by offering tangible rewards for the risky investment in an archaeological expedition, Egypt gained knowledge of its own history and collections of antiquities acquired through scientific excavation. Germany gained prestige for discovery, valuable objects for its museums, and standing within the international archaeological community. Accordingly, it is difficult, if not impossible, to find any historical wrong that would be "righted" by return of the bust').

[245] Khedive Abbas Helmy, Law No. 14 of 1912 on Antiquities (Loi n° 14 de 1912, Loi sur les antiquités) *Journal Officiel du Gouvernement Égyptien*, 39th year (15 June 1912) No. 70, 1391–1393, reproduced in Thomas L. Gertzen, *Einführung in die Wissenschaftsgeschichte der Ägyptologie* (Berlin: LIT Verlag, 2017) 211–213.

equal value shall be made by the Service, and the discoverer shall have the right to choose between the two lots.[246]

The law, adopted during British occupation, was deemed to restrict the generous practice of the French Director of the Service of Antiquities, Gaston Maspero (1846–1916).

Two arguments challenge the legitimacy of acquisition: doubts about error or deceit in the partage procedure, and the structural context, in which the acquisition occurred.

10.2   The partage: legal or moral wrong?

Borchardt was intimately familiar with political structures in Egypt and Great power politics.[247] He had worked as a scholarly attaché at the German consulate in Cairo since 1899. He was known for his ambition[248] and was aware of Maspero's generous' partage practices. Correspondences show that the German Oriental Society was eager to acquire it;[249] Simon was even willing to pay for it.[250] Several voices, including the Egyptian archaeologist and egyptologist Zahi Hawass, have claimed that Borchardt obtained the bust through deceit, by concealing its nature as a royal limestone statue and its true value, or through manipulation of the partage process, led by Lefebvre, an unexperienced partage officer.[251]

Borchardt recognized the importance of the bust, but sought to keep a low profile regarding the finds. He encouraged to treat them 'with the utmost secrecy',[252] in order not to compromise the allocation at the partage and further excavation licences. When he discovered 'the life-size painted bust' on 6 December 1912, he noted in his log book of the excavation: 'Really wonderful work. No use describing it, you have to see it.'[253] He used the partage procedure to his favour, but was uncertain about its outcome.[254]

---

[246]   Ibid, Art. 11.

[247]   Olaf Matthes describes him as 'the best-informed man regarding the complex circumstances in Egypt'. Olaf Matthes, 'Ludwig Borchardt, James Simon and the Colourful Nefertiti Bust in the First Year after Her Discovery' in Friederike Seyfried (ed.), *In The Light of Armana: 100 Years of the Nefertiti Discovery* (Berlin: Michael Imhof Verlag, 2012) 427–437, 429.

[248]   British Egyptologist Alan Gardiner blamed him for 'tactless and brusque behaviour' in 1908.

[249]   Siehr, 'The Beautiful One Has Come—To Return', 117.

[250]   Matthes, 'Ludwig Borchardt, James Simon and the Colourful Nefertiti Bust', 431.

[251]   Robertson, *Who Owns History?*, 183 ('acquired by deception, or at least by oversight').

[252]   Matthes, 'Ludwig Borchardt, James Simon and the Colourful Nefertiti Bust', 429.

[253]   Ludwig Borchardt, Excavation Diary (6 and 7 December 1912) Staatliche Museen zu Berlin, Ägyptisches Museum, Archival/Akte/67/43, p. 43 in Friederike Seyfried, 'Die Büste der Nofretete: Dokumentation des Fundes und der Fundteilung 1912/1913' (2011) 46 *Jahrbuch Preußischer Kulturbesitz* 133–201, 141, 161.

[254]   It is reported that members of the excavation team 'made a pilgrimage to the warehouse to bid farewell to the "Colourful Queen"' before the partage. See Matthes, 'Ludwig Borchardt, James Simon and the Colourful Nefertiti Bust', 431.

One of his advantages was that the excavation team was entitled to propose a division of the lots, while the antiquities service had the right to choose. The secretary of the German Oriental Society, Bruno Güterbock, who was an eyewitness, acknowledged later in a confidential letter to Günther Roeder, dated 12 August 1924, that Borchardt knew of Maspero's fondness for depictions of the royal couple Akhenaten and Nefertiti.[255] He managed to place an altarpiece, known as the 'Stele of Akhenaten and his family', which contained such a depiction, at the top of the list of one lot. The bust of Neferiti was placed on top of the other. The object was designated as 'painted plaster bust of a princess' in the partage protocol,[256] although Borchardt's diary referred to a 'colorful queen'.[257] Lefebvre, an epigraphist and papyrologist, who acted on behalf of Maspero, accepted the 'approximate equivalency' of the two halves, in his partage arrangement. The division was later approved by Maspero.

Borchardt was convinced that he managed to obtain Nefertiti based on his talent and persuasive skills. He noted:

[W]e have ... done remarkably well ... When this find is placed side by side with the Abusir objects, then the Berlin Museum will be first after Cairo ... The division was ... extremely difficult. I still don't know how I managed to direct the split in this way ... you will read the results in a couple of days in the journal. In my last letter I had imagined it to be much worse.[258]

However, there are indications that Borchardt used other strategies in order to 'rescue the bust'[259] for the German Oriental Society, as Güterbock put it. This was confirmed later by several sources. According to the account of one of his younger colleagues, Rudolf Anthes 'lured the representative of the Department of Antiquities into choosing the wrong heap' and that he 'could be a fox, after all, when it was called for'.[260]

More details were later given by Güterbock. He reported that Lefebvre carried out a 'superficial inspection' of the originals[261] and that Borchardt used two

---

[255] Confidential Letter from Bruno Güterbock to Günther Roeder (12 August 1924), in Seyfried, 'Die Büste der Nofretete: Dokumentation des Fundes und der Fundteilung 1912/1913', 196–198, 197.

[256] Seyfried, 'Die Büste der Nofretete: Dokumentation des Fundes und der Fundteilung 1912/1913', 176 and 178, reproducing the wording of the French protocol ('Buste en plâtre, peint, dúne princesse de la famille royale').

[257] Ludwig Borchardt, Excavation Diary (20 January 1913) 228 ('bunte Königin'), in Seyfried, 'Die Büste der Nofretete: Dokumentation des Fundes und der Fundteilung 1912/1913', 190.

[258] Matthes, 'Ludwig Borchardt, James Simon and the Colourful Nefertiti Bust', 431.

[259] Confidential Letter from Bruno Güterbock to Günther Roeder (12 August 1924), in Seyfried, 'Die Büste der Nofretete: Dokumentation des Fundes und der Fundteilung 1912/1913', 197.

[260] Letter from Rudolf Anthes to Bernard V. Bothmer (30 January 1965), cited after Krauss, '1913-1988: 75 Jahre Büste der NofretEte/Nefret-iti in Berlin', 105.

[261] Confidential Letter from Bruno Güterbock to Günther Roeder (12 August 1924), in Seyfried, 'Die Büste der Nofretete: Dokumentation des Fundes und der Fundteilung 1912/1913', 197.

tricks in order to influence the outcome.[262] During the partage, the bust lay already wrapped up in a box in a dimly lit room. Borchard presented photographs of Nefertiti to Lefebvre, which presented her in an unflattering way.[263] He later admitted that the picture showed the object from an angle which concealed 'the full beauty of the bust', but was sufficient to 'refute later talk by third parties that anything was kept secret'.[264]

Borchardt arguably misled Lefebvre about the material of the bust. He noted in the protocol that Nefertiti was made out of plaster (gypsum), although he knew that the core was made of limestone. Güterbock noted that he had expressed misgivings to Borchardt about this 'misrepresentation of the material', but that Borchardt maintained his designation, arguing that it could later be qualified as an error, should it be detected.[265] This description enabled a division by which objects made out of stone went to the Egyptian lot, while items made out of plaster went to the German Oriental Society.[266] The consequences of this misrepresentation are disputed. Zahi Hawass has argued that Borchardt's designation affects the legality of the acquisition, since 'Egyptian law at that time prohibited transferring any piece made of limestone outside the country'.[267]

Further doubts about the ethics of Borchardt's behaviour were later raised by Pierre Lacau, the director of the Department of Antiquities in Cairo, who pleaded for a return of Nefertiti. He argued that Lefebvre's protocol was binding on the Antiquities Service and left it 'defenceless' in legal terms, but challenged its legitimacy on moral grounds. He conceded that Lefebvre was misled about the value of the object.[268] He noted:

> I naturally examined closely all the circumstances (of the partage). Mr. Lefebre, a man of unquestionable conscience and competence, without recalling precisely, thinks that the bust must have been shown to him, and that he was mistaken as to its true value. With complete loyalty, he therefore declares that his minutes must be authentic. As he represented us validly, his signature commits us and our

---

[262] See also Siehr, 'The Beautiful One Has Come—To Return', 118.

[263] Confidential Letter from Bruno Güterbock to Günther Roeder (12 August 1924), in Seyfried, 'Die Büste der Nofretete: Dokumentation des Fundes und der Fundteilung 1912/1913', 197.

[264] Schulz, 'Re-Examining Nefertiti's Likeness and Life'.

[265] Confidential Letter from Bruno Güterbock to Günther Roeder (12 August 1924) in Seyfried, 'Die Büste der Nofretete: Dokumentation des Fundes und der Fundteilung 1912/1913', 198.

[266] Ibid, 198.

[267] Mustafa Marie, 'Zahi Hawass: Now is the time to try and retrieve Nefertiti's Head Statue from Germany' Egypt Today (6 October 2020) https://www.egypttoday.com/Article/4/92793/Zahi-Hawass-Now-is-the-time-to-try-and-retrieve.

[268] Kelly Culbertson argues that this would not affect the validity of the title. See Culbertson, 'Contemporary Customary International Law in the Case of Nefertiti', 52 ('While potentially illustrative of Lefebvre's inadequacies as a partage official, any lack of appreciation for the anachronistic realism of the Amarna style on his part does not equate to fraud by the DOG, or impact upon the validity of title passed to it').

Service is legally defenseless. But are we morally defenseless? That's what I didn't believe.[269]

Borkhardt knew that the partage division was hugely favourable to him. His later conduct confirms that he was aware of the risks of the transaction. He was pleased not to exhibit Nefertiti in Berlin in order to avoid further conflict. He realized that a public display would ruin his chances to continue his excavations. He feared that British officials could blame the French members of Antiquities Service for an unfair partage,[270] based on the value of the German 'half' of the finds.[271] This position led to a dispute with Heinrich Schäfer, the director of the Egyptian Museum in Berlin.

The combination of legal and moral concerns regarding the partage arrangement has caused ongoing divide over the acquisition. Germany has relied on a legal formalist interpretation to defend the validity of the partage, arguing that it was done lawfully according to the standards of the time.[272] Egypt has requested the return of Nefertiti. It submitted that 'Borchardt did act unethically with the intent to deceive'.[273]

10.3 Unjust enrichment?

A second problem of the acquisition is the context in which it occurred. Egypt had limited control over the removal of antiquities. It was at the mercy of competing powers. The arrangement was shaped by the *entente cordiale* between Britain and France (1904), according to which France promised not to 'obstruct' British control in Egypt, while Britain allowed France to control Morocco. At the time of the removal, Egypt was effectively governed by Britain, which exercised occupying power. It lacked direct influence over the Antiquities Service, which remained dominated by French officials.

It is controversial to what extent it is legitimate to hold Egypt to arrangements which were made on her behalf by an agency that was formally controlled by Britain. An occupying power has protective duties towards the administered territory. The alienation of archaeological finds that go to the heart of the cultural identity of a nation by the British controlled Antiquities Service conflicts with this duty.[274] Article 43 of the Regulations Respecting the Laws and Customs of

---

[269] Krauss, '1913-1988: 75 Jahre Büste der NofretEte/Nefret-iti in Berlin', 106–107.
[270] Salima Ikram argues that this 'concern on the part of Borchardt implies that Nefertiti might not have been extracted completely legally from Egypt'. See Ikram, 'Collecting and Repatriating Egypt's Past', 147.
[271] Matthes, 'Ludwig Borchardt, James Simon and the Colourful Nefertiti Bust', 434.
[272] On this view, see also Urice, 'The Beautiful One Has Come—To Stay'.
[273] Julie Bloom, 'Seeking Bust's Return, Egypt Cites Diary Entry, *New York Times* (20 December 2009). For doubts, see also Siehr, 'The Beautiful One Has Come—To Return'.
[274] Goldmann and Von Loebenstein, 'Alles nur geklaut?, 19–20.

War on Land, annexed to Hague Convention (II) of 1899 and (IV) of 1907, vests the occupying power with trusteeship obligations, namely to 'take all the measures in his power to restore, and ensure, as far as possible, public order and safety, while respecting, unless absolutely prevented, the laws in force in the country'.[275] The domestic laws adopted in the nineteenth century embraced the idea that national heritage 'belonged to and helped to define the Egypt'.[276] Auguste Mariette (1821–1881), the founder of the Egyptian Department of Antiquities, noted that 'the time when Lord Elgin could remove the bas-reliefs of the Parthenon is past. Egypt possesses the oldest archives that exist in the history of humankind. These are the parchments of her noble antiquity, and Egypt understands she must protect them'.[277] The partage arrangement is also questionable from another perspective. It has parallels with separation of the Elgin marbles. The removal broke up the unity of the finds. As Kurt Siehr has argued:

> It has long been recognized by archaeologists, art historians, museum curators and even politicians that objects of cultural property should not be dismembered and, if this had happened in the past, such a mutilation of objects d'art should be stopped and dispersed pieces of an ensemble should be reassembled.[278]

The division made in 1913 dispersed the objects contained in the workshop of Thutmose. It thereby destroyed the value of the collection as a whole ('Gesamtkunstwerk'),[279] which cultural heritage principles had sought to protect since the eighteenth century.[280]

Egypt never agreed with the removal.[281] It became an independent state in 1922. When Nefertiti was publicly displayed in Berlin in 1923, together with a publication by Borchardt, Egypt protested. Lacau was sent in 1924 to negotiate a return. He argued that the bust should be returned to Egypt based on moral grounds, namely based on the 'mistake' by Lefebvre that had become apparent afterwards.[282] He wanted to show the 'next generation' that the new country has 'tried everything to return this artwork to Egypt's cultural legacy'.[283] He threatened to bar Germans from further excavations, arguing that no permissions would be given to persons

---

[275] Article 43 of the Regulations Respecting the Laws and Customs of war on Land annexed to Hague Convention (II) of 1899 and Hague Convention (IV) of 1907.
[276] Ikram, 'Collecting and Repatriating Egypt's Past', 143.
[277] Ibid, 143.
[278] Siehr, 'The Beautiful One Has Come—To Return', 127.
[279] Ibid, 128.
[280] See Introduction.
[281] Siehr, 'The Beautiful One Has Come—To Return', 118.
[282] Susanne Voss, 'The 1925 Demand for the Return of the Nefertiti Bust, A German Perspective' in Friederike Seyfried (ed.), In The Light of Armana: 100 Years of the Nefertiti discovery (Berlin: Michael Imhof Verlag, 2012) 460–468, 464.
[283] Ibid, 466.

who had taken undue advantage ('joué un mauvais tour') of the Egyptian system.[284] However, Germany refused to agree on a return.

In 1929, Egypt undertook another attempt to 'repatriate' Nefertiti. This time, it proposed to exchange the bust against other objects from the collection in Cairo. Simon supported this exchange in an open letter in a Berlin newspaper in June 1930 in order to resume excavations. Even Egyptologist Heinrich Schäfer (1868–1957), the director of the Egyptian Museum in Berlin, supported the idea of an exchange. However, following public pressure, the plan was abandoned and the request was turned down.

The issue came back in the 1930s under Nazi rule. On this occasion, the initiative came from Germany. Both Hermann Göring, the Prussian Prime Minister, and Joseph Goebbels, the Minister of Propaganda, sought to use Nefertiti as political leverage. They proposed to return the bust in order to win Egyptian King Fuad I as an ally for Germany in Africa.[285] However, Adolf Hitler blocked the initiative. He regarded the queen as a great work of art which should be retained by the Reich[286] and even promised to build a new museum for her (the Museum of Germania), showcasing Berlin's role as capital of the world. Hitler thus relied on the nature of Nefertiti as a cultural icon in order to enhance national glory.[287]

10.4 Cultural reinterpretation

The story of Nefertiti shares many features of 'elginism', not only due to the mode of acquisition, but also in terms of its reception, impact on German society, and reproduction of imperial narratives in discourse on return.

The exhibition of works from Borchardt's Armana excavation in Berlin was a success. It triggered a wider acceptance of Egyptian art in German society. An article in a Berlin newspaper from 15 December 1913 stressed the social bond between German society and Egyptian culture. It acknowledged that there 'are increasing signs that a more definitive spiritual continuity connects us with Egypt than was previously assumed'.[288] According to reports from Borchardt, the German Emperor Wilhelm II compared Nefertiti 'with Renaissance sculptures'.[289]

---

[284] Ibid, 463.

[285] Hannelore Kischkewitz, 'The Thirties: Trouble with Nefertiti' in Friederike Seyfried (ed.), *In The Light of Armana: 100 Years of the Nefertiti discovery* (Berlin: Michael Imhof Verlag, 2012) 474–479, 477.

[286] Hitler wrote in a letter to the Egyptians: 'I will never relinquish the head of the queen.' See Robertson, *Who Owns History?*, 182.

[287] Kischkewitz, 'The Thirties: Trouble with Nefertiti', 477–478. Hitler apparently noted: 'Nefertiti continually delights me. The bust is a unique masterpiece, an ornament, a true treasure!' See http://www.ioltravel.co.za/article/view/3551832.

[288] See Staatliche Museen zu Berlin, 'The Bust Nefertiti: The Reception: Nefertiti as an icon of beauty' https://www.smb.museum/en/museums-institutions/aegyptisches-museum-und-papyrussammlung/collection-research/bust-of-nefertiti/the-reception/.

[289] Matthes, 'Ludwig Borchardt, James Simon and the Colourful Nefertiti Bust', 435.

Neferiti became a celebrity and icon of beauty, even though the bust was at first not publicly shown. Borchardt acknowledged the popularity of the exhibition. He noted: 'So Berlin is on its head, even without the colourful Queen.'[290] Numerous reproductions were made. Her image became popular through merchandising or publicity. Literary references, such as Thomas Mann's account of Nefertiti in *Joseph and His Brothers*,[291] were inspired by statues displayed in the Egyptian museum in Berlin. Nefertiti's image, including her crown, even inspired costumes at gala events in Berlin society.[292]

With the transfer to Berlin, Nefertiti thus gained multiple new identities, including an affiliation with the 'new home culture'. Her presence contributed to greater recognition of Egypt's enlightened past. But the new location also commodified the bust and made her an unofficial cultural symbol of the city, despite Egyptian claims for return. Her history demonstrates how affiliation with a new place can lead to cultural appropriation. German officials later relied on this bond to counter arguments for return to Egypt. They argued that the bust of Nefertiti marks a 'cultural ambassador' of Egypt in Berlin[293], i.e. as an object of art which 'stimulate[s] interest in, understanding of, and sympathy and admiration for' Egypt[294] to the entire world, through its accessibility in Berlin. Of course, her 'duty' station was decided by Germany, rather than Egypt.

In 2003, Dietrich Wildung, the Director of the Egyptian Museum in Berlin permitted two Hungarian artists, András Gálik and Bálint Havas (Little Warsaw), to place the bust in a newly constructed body sculpture for the Venice Biennial in 2003. This new full body visualization of Nefertiti caused protest in Egypt, based on fears of damage to the bust and concerns regarding cultural appropriation, contradicting Egyptian traditions not to display a naked female body.[295] The treatment was perceived as an illustration of double standards by Egypt, since the museum declined to agree on a loan of the bust to Egypt, arguing that Nefertiti was 'unfit' to travel.

These different examples illustrate how exhibition in new contexts, cosmopolitan narratives, and practices of cultural reinterpretation may be used to overcome ambiguities in the acquisition of objects over time.

---

[290] Ibid, 436.

[291] Thomas Mann, *Joseph and His Brothers* (John E. Woods tr, New York: Knopf, 2005).

[292] Staatliche Museen zu Berlin, 'The Bust Nefertiti: The Reception: Nefertiti as an icon of beauty', referring to an article and picture in the *Berliner Illustrierte Zeitung* (20 April 1930) 712.

[293] Hermann Parzinger, the head of the Prussian Cultural Heritage Foundation, said in 2011: 'She is and remains the ambassador of Egypt in Berlin.' See Joanne Bladd, 'Berlin refuses to return priceless artifact to Egypt Arabian Business' (26 January 2011).

[294] On this understanding of art as 'good ambassador', see Paul M. Bator, 'An Essay on the International Trade in Art' (1981) 34 *Stanford Law Review* 277–382, 306.

[295] Eszter Feró, 'The Body of Nefertiti: The Curious Incident of the Little Warsaw at the Venice Biennial' in Adéla Junova Macková, Lucie Storchová, and Libor Jun (eds.), *Visualizing the Orient: Central Europe and the Nearest in 19th and 20th Centuries* (Prague: Academy of Performing Arts in Prague, 2016) 107–118, 109.

11   Removals under occupation or colonial domination: Venus of Cyrene (1913–1915) and Aksum Obelisk (1936)

Throughout the twentieth century, objects continued to be taken in a context of occupation or colonial domination for purposes of prestige or cultural enrichment. Two important examples are the Venus of Cyrene and the Axum stele. Both were removed by Italy, and later returned to their countries of origin (Libya and Ethiopia) after decolonization.

11.1   Venus of Cyrene (1913–1915)

The history of the Venus of Cyrene[296] shows the exploitation of power in a context of structural inequality, divides over legal acknowledgement of colonial wrong, as well as some of risks of returns.

The Venus is a white marble sculpture of the goddess Aphrodite (Venus in the Roman tradition), which was taken from the ruins of the ancient Greek city of Cyrene in Libya in the early years of the twentieth century. It has been described as a 'masterpiece of early Hellenistic art'.[297] It depicts the goddess rising from the sea at the moment of her first appearance to mortals. The value of the 'beautiful Aphrodite from Cyrene' was quickly recognized. In the early 1920s, commentators had already noted that 'the statue, that alone, might, perhaps, suffice to re-pay the expenses and perils of our war'.[298]

It was captured after Italy's colonial awakening, namely following the Italian offensive against the Ottoman Empire in 1911, which led to the occupation of Tripolitania and Cyrenaica in modern-day Libya. In the 1912 Treaty of Peace between Italy and Turkey, the Ottoman Empire agreed to evacuate 'Ottoman officers, troops, and civil functionaries' from 'Tripoli and Cyrenaica',[299] but Libyan resistance to Italian rule continued. Italian troops 'discovered' the statue in the ruins at Cyrene (near present-day Shahhat, East Libya) in 1913 when the region was under occupation.[300] The site has been the object of archaeological excavations since the

---

[296] See Alessandro Chechi, 'The Return of Cultural Objects Removed in Times of Colonial Domination and International Law: The Case of the Venus of Cyrene' (2008) 18 *Italian Yearbook of International Law* 159–181; Tullio Scovazzi, 'The Return of the Venus of Cyrene' (2009) 14 *Art Antiquity and Law* 355–358; Nancy Wilkie, 'Colonization and Its Effect on the Cultural Property of Libya' in James A.R. Nafziger and Ann M. Nicgorski, *Cultural Heritage Issues: The Legacy of Conquest, Colonization, and Commerce* (Leiden: Martinus Nijhoff Publishers, 2009) 169–183.

[297] Ernest A. Gardner, 'The Aphrodite from Cyrene' (1920) 40 *The Journal of Hellenic Studies* 203–205, 205.

[298] Archaeological Institute of America, 'Aphrodite of Cyrene' Art and Archaeology (February 1921) http://figure-drawings.blogspot.com/2009/01/aphrodite-of-cyrene.html/.

[299] See Treaty of Peace between Italy and Turkey, signed in Ouchy, near Lausanne on 18 October 1912, Art. 2.

[300] Scovazzi, 'The Return of the Venus of Cyrene', 356.

1860s.[301] According to reports, a thunderstorm washed away soil from the sanctuary of Apollo and set the statue free.[302] Historian Gilbert Bagnani wrote in 1921:

> On the night of the 27th of December, 1913, a torrential downpour flooded the platform of the Temple of Apollo and broke down part of the retaining wall at the N.E. corner. The next morning the soldiers of the garrison found, still glistening with the element from which she had been born, the beautiful statue of Aphrodite.[303]

Italian agents recognized the cultural value of the object and removed it in order to protect it against risks of ongoing violence, caused by resistance to Italian authority.[304] They 'made an exception to the rule that the works of art should remain in Africa'[305] and transported it to Rome, where it was exhibited in the Roman National Museum (Museo delle Terme) for more than ninety years.

The statue later gained an important role in post-colonial relations between Italy and Libya. It became a symbol of Italy's imperial past and was deemed to showcase 'shifting political attitudes toward empire and history' in Italy,[306] namely to demonstrate the country's 'modernity and flexibility' in addressing its colonial histories.[307] Its return was meant to foster a new bond with Libya. In 1998, Italy 'pledged' in a Joint Communiqué with Libya to 'return ... all manuscripts, archives, documents, artefacts and archaeological pieces transferred to Italy during and after the Italian occupation of Libya in accordance with the UNESCO convention of 14 November 1970 on banning illegal export and transfer of cultural properties'.[308] In 2000, the Venus of Cyrene was designated as one of the objects to be returned. The government adopted a decree in 2002 in order to allow the removal of the object from national patrimony and enable the return. It viewed return as an act of comity, rather than duty. The Italian Undersecretary of Foreign Affairs Alfredo Mantica made this clear in an interview in October 2002. He said: 'The [restitution of the] Venus of Cyrene is ... an act of generosity in that there is no

---

[301] The first excavations were done from 1860 to 1861 by Robert Murdoch Smith and Edwin Augustus Porche, who sent several objects to the British museum. See Monika Rekowska, 'Early photographers of Cyrenaica (19th century)' (2016) 26 *Quaderni Friulani di Archeologia* 291–299, 292–293.

[302] Wilkie, 'Colonization and Its Effect on the Cultural Property of Libya' 176.

[303] Gilbert Bagnani, 'Hellenistic Sculpture from Cyrene' (1921) 41 *The Journal of Hellenic Studies* 232–246, 232.

[304] Scovazzi, 'The Return of the Venus of Cyrene', 356.

[305] Bagnani, 'Hellenistic Sculpture from Cyrene', 233.

[306] Krystyna von Henneberg, 'Monuments, Public Space, and the Memory of Empire in Modern Italy' (2004) 16 *History and Memory* 37–85, 74.

[307] Ibid.

[308] Joint Communiqué of 4 July 1998, signed in Rome on 4 July 1998, by Libya's minister of foreign affairs Umar Mustafa al-Muntasir and his Italian counterpart Lamberto Dini, English text at BBC, 'Libya says Italy apologizes for colonial occupation' (10 July 1998) http://news.bbc.co.uk/2/hi/world/monitoring/130160.stm.

treaty imposing its restitution' … No one can stop me from giving a gift, but and I repeat it would be a gift.'[309] The proposed return triggered divided reactions in Italian society. The NGO Italia Nostra ('Our Italy'), an organization devoted to the protection of Italy's historical and artistic patrimony, challenged the return before Italian courts.[310] It feared that the return would set a precedent. It relied on a hypocritical justification to justify retention. It compared the acquisition of the Venus to a discovery on Italian soil. It argued that the 'statue of Venus was not stolen by the Italians but discovered by chance in Cyrene which was then under Italian rule'.[311]

This position was reversed by the Italian Council of State.[312] It overruled both the government position that return was merely grounded in comity, as well as the claim by the Italia Nostra. It clarified that the Venus did not become part of Italian heritage, since Libya was under occupation, rather than Italian sovereignty, when the statue was collected.[313] It also specified that the Italian government had a duty under customary law to return the Venus to Libya. It argued that the removal violated the principle of self-determination. It held that self-determination protects the cultural heritage of peoples subject to foreign domination.[314] Although one may doubt whether the ruling adequately reflects customary law in 1913, it set an important precedent, by postulating 'the principle of non-exploitation of the weakness of another subject to get a cultural gain' and declaring it applicable to situations of 'colonial domination' or 'foreign occupation'.[315]

The decision paved the way for the conclusion of the Treaty of Friendship, Partnership, and Cooperation between Italy and Libya in Benghazi on 30 August 2008, in the context of which the Venus of Cyrene was returned. The statue became an embodiment of Italy's ambition to put an end to colonial disputes and embark on a chapter of cooperation. After return, it was placed in a small museum in Libya. Here again, it became a victim of the outbreak of violence, namely internal hostilities in Libya. The object vanished in the conflict in 2011.

[309] Interview, Undersecretary of Foreign Affairs Alfredo Mantica (30 October 2002) https://www.esteri.it/mae/en/sala_stampa/interviste/2007/06/intervista_1.html.
[310] Chechi, 'The Return of Cultural Objects Removed in Times of Colonial Domination and International Law', 161.
[311] Gareth Harris and Federico Castelli Gattinara, 'One rule for the Getty, another for Italy? Italian group appeals restitution verdict' Art Newspaper (30 June 2007) https://www.theartnewspaper.com/archive/one-rule-for-the-getty-another-for-italy.
[312] Council of State (Consiglio di Stato) Case No. 3154, Associazione nazionale Italia Nostra Onlus c. Ministero per i beni e le attività culturali et al. (23 June 2008).
[313] Chechi, 'The Return of Cultural Objects Removed in Times of Colonial Domination and International Law', 175.
[314] Council of State, Case No. 3154, para. 4.4.
[315] Scovazzi, 'The Return of the Venus of Cyrene', 358.

11.2 The Aksum stele

The removal and return of the Aksum stele is a spectacular example of the changing life of objects and the way in which they shape behaviour.[316] The 'obelisk' is a monumental 1,700-year stone object, which was created in honour of King Ezane (320s–c. 360 AD) during the height of the ancient Aksumite Kingdom in modern-day northern Ethiopia (Tigray province) and Eritrea. The kingdom existed from the second to the ninth centuries AD and laid the foundation of the Abyssinian empire. It constituted an important African civilization which differed from ancient Greek and Roman traditions,[317] and was compared to empires, such as Rome or Persia. Under King Ezane, the kingdom converted to Orthodox Christianity in the 330s in order to enable a closer connection to Rome or Constantinople.

In the Aksumite tradition, the megalithic stelae had spiritual significance. They represent the 'ancient roots of Ethiopian civilization.'[318] Aksum had more than 1,000 stelae and obelisks. At least, in the early phase, i.e. the First or Second centuries AD, they were created as funerary objects to mark the palaces and burial places of rulers or nobility.[319] The most distinctive objects, the monumental granite stelae, were established in the era of King Ezane. They arguably represented stairways, enabling Aksumite leaders to ascend to heaven. Later, they became symbols of political power. They were made out of single pieces of granite.

The so-called Aksum stele is the second largest of the monumental stelae. It is 24 metres high and weighs 160 tonnes. It became a colonial object,[320] when it was removed from Ethiopia after the Italian invasion in 1935–1936. The removal was part of a broader campaign of colonial exploitation and looting, pursued by Prime Minister Benito Mussolini. Mussolini attacked Ethiopia in order to gain a 'place in the sun' for Italy and replicate the glory of Roman Empire.[321] Italian troops defeated Emperor Haile Selassie (1892–1975)[322] and annexed the territory of Ethiopia in 1936, in violation of treaty obligations (Treaty of Friendship of 1928,[323] Covenant League of Nations) and despite the emperor's famous appeal

---

[316] Tullio Scovazzi,'Legal aspects of the Axum Obelisk case' (2009) 61 *Museum International* 52–60; Lucas Lixinski, 'Axum Stele' in Jessie Hohmann and Daniel Joyce, *International Law's Objects* (Oxford: Oxford University Press, 2018) 130–140; Richard Pankhurst, 'Ethiopia, the Aksum obelisk, and the return of Africa's cultural heritage' (1999) 98 *African Affairs* 229–239.

[317] S. Munro-Hay, *Aksum: An African Civilization of Late Antiquity* (Edinburgh: Edinburgh University Press, 1991).

[318] David Phillipson, 'The Significance and Symbolism of Aksumite Stelae' (2008) 4 *Cambridge Archaeological Journal* 189–210, 210.

[319] Ibid, 191, 209.

[320] Mark Rose, 'Of Obelisks and Empire' (2009) 62 *Archaeological Institute of America Archaeology* 26–30.

[321] Richard Pankhurst, 'We Want Our Looted Artefacts Back', *New African* (November 2008) 36–38, 36.

[322] Alberto Sbacchi, 'Haile Selassie and the Italians 1941-1943' (1979) 22 *African Studies Review* 25–42.

[323] Italo-Ethiopian Treaty of Friendship and Arbitration (2 August 1928).

for assistance by the League of Nations in June 1936.[324] Mussolini relied on cultural dispossession in order to 'crush the spirit of the Ethiopian people',[325] erase reminders of Ethiopia's independence or national identity, and establish the foundations of a new Roman Empire. He replicated the tradition of ancient Roman emperors who had brought statues from Egypt. He confiscated royal objects, such as the crowns of Ethiopian kings, and important historical and cultural objects, such as the statue of the Ethiopian Lion of Judah, which was unveiled for the coronation of Ethiopia's emperor Haile Selassie in 1930 and had been the country's national emblem.[326] He dismantled the statue of Emperor Menilek, who had defeated the Italians in the Battle of Adwa in 1896.[327] The looting was deemed to erase the 'scar of Adwa' and restore Italy's glory.

Italian soldiers found the Aksum stele in 1935 during an archaeological expedition. It was partly buried in the ground and broken into several pieces. Mussolini personally ordered its removal to Italy in order to mark the anniversary of his declaration of the Fascist Empire.[328] It became the largest and heaviest object removed from Africa to Europe. The gigantic stele was divided into five parts, transported to the port of Massawa and shipped to Italy. Its re-establishment in Rome had a highly symbolic nature. It reflected the fascist and colonial ideology and borrowed from the history of empire. As Krystyna von Henneberg has noted: 'The empire was brought home and a certain version of it, at least, was made tangible.'[329]

The 'obelisk' was placed in front of the former Italian Ministry of the Colonies, which later became the headquarters of the FAO. It was finally inaugurated on 28 October 1937, on the day of the fifteenth anniversary of the fascist takeover of power in the 'March on Rome' in 1922 which had suppressed parliamentary democracy. The statue became a symbol of Italy's reimagination as empire. The Mussolini regime sought to benefit from the splendour of a 'lost civilization' in order to demonstrate its own political power and Italy's conquest of Ethiopia.

---

[324] In the address to the League of Nations, the emperor noted: 'I ask the fifty-two nations, who have given the Ethiopian people a promise to help them in their resistance to the aggressor, what are they willing to do for Ethiopia? And the great Powers who have promised the guarantee of collective security to small States on whom weighs the threat that they may one day suffer the fate of Ethiopia, I ask what measures do you intend to take? Representatives of the World, I have come to Geneva to discharge in your midst the most painful of the duties of the head of a State. What reply shall I have to take back to my people?' See Speech by the His Majesty Haile Selassie I, Emperor of Ethiopia, at the Assembly of the League of Nations, at the Session of June–July 1936, at https://www.mtholyoke.edu/acad/intrel/selassie.htm.

[325] Pankhurst, 'We want our looted artefacts back', 36.

[326] The statue was displayed in front of the Termini railway station in Rome.

[327] Pankhurst, 'Ethiopia, the Aksum obelisk, and the return of Africa's cultural heritage', 236.

[328] According to a telegram, 'H.E. the Head of the Government has ordered that instead of the Lion of Judah statue one of the obelisks of Axum should be brought to Rome. The obelisk must reach Rome in time to be inaugurated on May 9, 1937'. See Richard Pankhurst, 'Ethiopia and The Loot of the Italian Invasion: 1935-1936' (1969) 72 *Présence Africaine* 85–95, 89.

[329] Krystyna von Henneberg, 'Monuments, Public Space, and the Memory of Empire in Modern Italy' (2004) 16 *History and Memory* 37–85, 60.

The removal caused outrage in Ethiopia. The occupation faced active resist-ance. It ended in 1941, when the British East African campaign defeated Italian forces and allowed Haile Selassie to return from exile. Claims for the return of cul-tural objects were formalized in the 1947 Peace Treaty with Italy. The Ethiopian delegation insisted on return of the removed objects. This was specified in Article 37 of the Peace Treaty, which obliged Italy to 'restore all works of art, religious objects, archives of historical value belonging to Ethiopia or its nationals and re-moved from Ethiopia to Italy since 3 October 1935' within a period of 'eighteen months' after the entry into force of the treaty.[330] However, Italy remained reluc-tant to implement this obligation. Some looted objects, such as the statue of the Lion of Judah or paintings taken from the Parliament, were returned.[331] Several Ethiopians crowns, taken by Mussolini during his escape to Switzerland, in 1944, disappeared.[332] It took more than fifty-seven years for the Aksum stele to be returned.

Instead of complying with the 1947 Peace Treaty, Italy negotiated a new agreement on 5 March 1956 in which it left the modalities of return open. The agreement was concluded at a time when Ethiopia was facing major economic difficulties. Annex C recognized that the Aksum stele was 'subject to restitution to Ethiopia'. The Italian government undertook to transport it from Rome to Naples, but did not set out who was responsible for its return to Ethiopia.[333] The 1956 agreement stood in contrast to the unconditional return obligation under the Peace Treaty.

The delay in return facilitated cultural appropriation in Italy. The stele became a 'naturalized object' in Italy's urban culture and history.[334] Until the 1970s, ru-mours endured that the 'obelisk was a gift of the emperor to the Italian people' and that Ethiopians 'knew nothing about it and attached no sentimental or cultural, let alone economic, value to its return'.[335] It was considered to extend the site of the FAO premises to include the Axum obelisk as a symbol of humanity.[336]

In 1968, the Ethiopian Parliament adopted a resolution which stated that the lack of return marked an affront to the 'history and honour of the country' and insisted on 'immediate return of the obelisk', including possible sanctions against Italy (travel ban, suspension of trade, break of diplomatic relations).[337] It was fol-lowed by a resolution of 8 February 1996 in which the Parliament reiterated the

---

[330] Treaty of Peace with Italy, Paris (10 February 1947) Art. 37./
[331] Pankhurst, 'Ethiopia and The Loot of the Italian Invasion: 1935-1936', 95.
[332] Ibid, 94–95.
[333] Pankhurst, 'Ethiopia, the Aksum obelisk, and the return of Africa's cultural heritage', 237–238.
[334] Lixinski, 'Axum Stele', 137.
[335] Giampaolo Calchi Novati, 'Re-establishing Italo-Ethiopian Relations after the War: Old Prejudices and New Policies' (1996) 3 Northeast African Studies 27–49, 40–41.
[336] Lixinski, 'Axum Stele', 135.
[337] Pankhurst, 'Ethiopia, the Aksum obelisk, and the return of Africa's cultural heritage', 238.

demand for immediate return, and a public petition by the people of Aksum, which stated:

> We, the people of Aksum, recall that our second largest obelisk was unjustly taken from our city by fascist Italy in 1937 … We are most anxious to see the obelisk, our priceless historical heritage, returned to Aksum as soon as possible, and, supporting the Ethiopian Parliament's unanimous resolution, hereby petition for our obelisk's immediate restitution.[338]

After these moves, Italy gradually viewed return as means to restore relations with Ethiopia and to come to terms with its own past. In a 1997 declaration, Italy recognized the value of the obelisk to the Ethiopian people and their culture. Postcolonial 'healing' became part and parcel of state discourse. During a 1997 visit to Ethiopia, Italian President Scalfora acknowledged the need to overcome the past and committed to return the Aksum stele, based on Italy's own experience as the victim of looted art in the Second World War.[339] On 18 November 2004, Italy signed a bilateral memorandum with Ethiopia in which it agreed to dismantle, transport, and re-erect the Aksum stele at its original site and assume the corresponding costs.

The actual removal in 2005 was one of the most complex returns in the history of cultural objects. The stele marked one of largest objects ever carried by air. It had to be cut into three segments in order to fit into an Antonov cargo plane. Each segment weighed over 60 tons. Conservationists feared that the low temperature in the plane would damage the object. The airport in Axum was too small for the transport and had to expanded. The road to Axum needed to be repaired. The reassembly was supervised by UNESCO. The operation concluded with some ceremony in September 2008.

The return has been praised as a success.[340] It showed that technically, even the most challenging obstacles to return can be overcome through political will, international cooperation, and sharing of expertise. It challenges the argument that objects cannot be returned to places of origin based on logistical concerns (e.g. the Elgin Marbles). It also demonstrated the use of cultural heritage to overcome

---

[338] Richard Pankhurst, 'The Unfinished History of the Aksum Obelisk Return Struggle: The Ethiopian Parliament, and the People, Speak Out' (11 July 1997) http://ethiopiaonline.net/obelisk/tribune/11-07-97.html.

[339] Henneberg, 'Monuments, Public Space, and the Memory of Empire in Modern Italy', 73 ('we Italians have experienced on our own skin what it means to have an occupying army in our home that takes away what it chooses, without later giving it back').

[340] Scovazzi, 'Legal aspects of the Axum Obelisk case', 52 ('The story of the return of the obelisk can be seen as a precedent in the current process of formation of new principles of international law in the field of cultural heritage: namely, the principle of non-impoverishment of the cultural heritage of states of origin, the principle of non-exploitation of the weakness of other countries to obtain cultural gain and the principle of preservation of the integrity of cultural sites').

colonial divides.[341] For instance, Richard Pankhurst has argued that the 'return of the obelisk represents not only the restoration of Ethiopian cultural patrimony, but … will come to symbolize the Ethiopian people's admirable capacity to persist and endure even when faced with overwhelming adversity'.[342] In the end, the return even improved the original *status quo* since the obelisk was properly reconstructed at its place of origin.

However, the long journey has also illustrated the many recurring features of imperialism.[343] The removal of the Aksum stele was not only an annex to the brutality of Italian occupation but intrinsically intertwined with the colonial reimagination of fascist rule. As war booty, the statue was considered as a symbol of Italian sacrifice in Africa and as an incarnation of Mussolini's triumph.[344] The delayed return generated novel meanings. After the Second World War, the object became closely associated with ideas of cultural internationalism, based on its history and physical proximity to the FAO building.[345] In return negotiations, the Aksum became an instrument to present Italy's new face as a benevolent and peaceful nation, which has been both victimizer and victim throughout the twentieth century and makes up for its violent past. The story of the object shows that initiatives to decolonize collections may easily be perceived as an attempt to cancel colonial debts.

12 Conclusions

The biographies of objects presented here show that many objects are closely entangled with structural or epistemic forms of violence and histories of oppression and resistance, even if it cannot be established that they were directly taken in armed hostilities. Such practices include confiscations, deceit, theft, forced sale, missionary takings, or coerced or stolen gifts. Some acquisitions took place under the shade or appearance of legality. Others simply remained undocumented. They serve as evidence of the need to confront the past in novel ways. They demonstrate different faces of colonial violence, the link between racial science and cultural takings, biases in the interpretation and reading of events, complex complicity structures, and lessons about the silence or instrumentalization of law.

There are recurring patterns of rationalizing cultural takings. Takings, such as the Zimbabwe birds, Nefertiti, or the Venus of Cyrene were motivated by rationales of triumph, self-branding, or association with presumed ancient cultures motivated. They illustrate the strong influence of imagined identities or 'othering' on

---

[341] Lixinski, 'Axum Stele', 138.
[342] Richard Pankhurst, 'The Unfinished History of the Aksum Obelisk Return Struggle' https://www.linkethiopia.org/article/the-unfinished-history-of-the-aksum-obelisk-return-struggle/.
[343] Lixinski, 'Axum Stele', 133.
[344] Ibid, 134.
[345] Ibid, 135.

cultural removals, including some of the stereotypes against African civilizations, which were deemed by collectors to be unable to be the creators of cultural treasures of such magnitude (e.g. the Olokun head).

Ideas of salvage and rescue guided not only the taking of historical objects but also the collection of ethnological or spiritual objects of populations, which were deemed to face extinction (e.g. the Luf boat). These justifications were often pretexts for takings which did not lead to salvage but rather to the destruction of native cultures.[346] The context of structural violence challenges the idea of reciprocal dependence, which informs the logic of gift-exchange, or the transfers of objects, which were taken as objects of idolatry or offered as part of a process of conversion to Christianity.

Local chiefs sometimes collaborated in takings. There are no binary victim/perpetrator divides. However, it is important to examine the context of transactions in each individual case. The dependence of natives on colonial agents was not self-inflicted, but often created by conquest, power, exploitation, or missionary structures. The examples of the taking of Ngonnso or the Luf boat illustrate that it is problematic to speak of a purchase or barter when the acquisition occurred in the shadow of a previous punitive expedition, which reversed the power relations. It is unlikely that royal objects or objects with spiritual objects were given up voluntarily in coercive contexts.

Takings caused resistance or protest. This was expressed in different forms: physical resistance,[347] complaints, requests for return, or contestation of colonial narratives. The legal petition of the natives of Tūranga against the taking of their ancestral house shows that Māori did not simply acquiesce in the taking of land, but defended their ownership rights in line with the Treaty of Waitangi. The people of Ife managed to prevent the taking of the Olukon head by Frobenius by appealing to British resident Partridge. Egypt protested early against the partage arrangement regarding Nefertiti. In other contexts, protest was articulated many decades after the original taking, based on the enduring nature of cultural dispossession. For instance, in case of the tangué of King Lock Priso, heirs and family filed claims against the taking. Rapa Nui leaders called for the return of Moai Hoa Hakananai'. In some cases, this has raised fears of reinvention of tradition.

Some objects were marked as 'objects of resistance'. For instance, certain power figures were used by local leaders to keep control over political relations or mobilize local alliances. They were perceived as a threat by colonial powers, and sometimes prohibited because they represented a system of power relations and form of communication over which Europeans lacked control.

---

[346] See also Hicks, *Brutish Museums*, 142, who argues that many operations 'possessed no logic of salvage, or of saving cultures for the world'.

[347] Ashanti queen Yaa Asantewaa became an icon of female leadership in resistance. She openly encouraged Asante leaders to stand up against the taking of the Golden Stool and called for women to take the lead when the men failed defend their people and kingdom. See Chapter 2.

Cultural takings exposed objects to complex processes of conversion and re-invention. Objects were reconceptualized in line with colonial imaginations, Western aesthetics, or visual codes. Ethnological museums became a 'nucleus of modern art'.[348] The new frames of reference or classifications (e.g. ethnographic objects) modified identities and placed objects into hierarchies or knowledge structures that superseded or erased alternative understandings. This process of conversion gave certain iconic objects greater visibility or prominence. Some objects have been co-opted by Western artists. However, it also had negative consequences. The large majority of objects fell into oblivion in Western collections. They were decontextualized, marked by an anonymous collection number, and stored in boxes. Certain ritual objects or masks lost their original meaning through removal from their places or communities of origin. The knowledge structures or modes of engagement with objects, which activated their meanings, gradually vanished. For instance, certain objects of power are now regarded as repugnant objects in societies of origin (e.g. DRC), because of conversion to Christianity or the dominance of material conceptions of culture. This makes it necessary to develop an 'anti-biography'.[349]

In other cases, the absence of objects continues to affect the 'lives of communities and states'.[350] For instance, the history of Ngonnso shows that objects continue to have agency or can serve as a cause for renewal and a break with the colonial habits. The people of Nso created an annual cultural week festival in honour of Ngonnso in the 1950s, i.e. long after the taking. Return may bring objects back to 'speak' in their local context.[351] The example of the Aksum stele provides evidence that even some of the most physically challenging returns can be managed with the assistance of modern infrastructure if they are backed by political will.

---

[348] Splettstößer, *Umstrittene Sammlungen*, 86.
[349] Hicks, *Brutish Museums*, 35, 226–227.
[350] Lixinski, 'Axum stele', 139.
[351] Splettstößer, *Umstrittene Sammlungen*, 356.

5

Collecting Humanity: Commodification, Trophy Hunting, and Bio-colonialism

1 Introduction

A chest of Herero skulls was recently sent by troops from German South West Africa to the pathological institute in Berlin, where they will be subjected to scientific measurements. The skulls, from which Herero women have removed the flesh with the aid of glass shards to make them suitable for shipment, come from Hereros who have been hanged or who have fallen.[1]

This cruel and distanced description of the collection of human remains by Germans in South West Africa forms part of the memoirs of an officer of the German protective force (*Schutztruppe*), published in 1907. It is connected to a popular image, namely a colonial postcard, which shows officers from the notorious Swakopmund camp 'loading the Herero skulls designated for German museums and universities'.[2] The sober tone of the text and the triumphant image, depicting skulls piled up like brick stones, illustrate the dehumanization of human remains in colonial violence and the degrading methods of collection and preservation, creating an entire industry in the trade of body parts.

The mix of colonial ideology and racial science at the peak of the colonial period prompted not only a stark increase in the removal of cultural objects, but also a new era in the collection of human remains.[3] The presentation of people in world fairs and colonial exhibitions was complemented by an active search for body parts. Thousands of remains, in particular from allegedly 'extinct' or

---

[1] Walter von Damm, *Meine Kriegserlebnisse in Deutsch-Südwestafrika* (Minden: Wilhelm Köhler, 1907) 114.

[2] Leonor Faber-Jonker, *More than Just an Object: A Material Analysis of the Return and Retention of Namibian Skulls from Germany* (Leiden: African Studies Centre Leiden, 2018) 57.

[3] Paul Turnbull, *Science, Museums and Collecting the Indigenous Dead in Colonial Australia* (New York: Palgrave Macmillan, 2017). For a US perspective, see Samuel James Redman, *Human Remains and the Construction of Race and History, 1897–1945* (PhD, University of Berkeley, 2012); David Hurst Thomas, *Skull Wars: Kennewick Man, Archaeology, and the Battle for Native American Identity* (New York: Basic Books, 2000).

Confronting Colonial Objects. Carsten Stahn, Oxford University Press. © Carsten Stahn 2023.
DOI: 10.1093/oso/9780192868121.003.0005

'primitive' populations,[4] were collected in colonies and transferred to scientific, anthropological, or military museums and laboratories. Human skulls turned into the 'holy grail' of nineteenth-century race theory.[5] Human remains constituted 'bio-capital,[6] sought by public institutions, private collectors, and colonial administrations, in order to remap the human space.[7] The study of crania, facial angles, or jaws served to investigate human difference through biological criteria.[8] This 'colonial corporeality'[9] was driven by global networks involving physicians and curators, traders and profiteers, colonial officials, military doctors, or missionaries and museums.[10] It was supported by colonial expansion, Darwinist theories,[11] desires of anthropological objectification, strife for national prestige, or 'educational' purposes. It provided an additional incentive for trophy-taking and collection of remains from burial sites, battlefields, prisons, or internment camps. Remains were commissioned, exchanged, and traded as objects between institutions and individuals. In some cases, colonial forces beheaded local chiefs and kings or members of resistance forces and collected the skulls as trophies. This performative use of deceased body parts as a form of 'bio-power' is a most 'violent emblem of colonial conquest'.[12]

The removal of human remains was deeply problematic from a moral and legal point of view.[13] It shows how colonization dehumanized not only the colonized, but also colonizers themselves. Human remains hold a particular status across cultures, based on their link to personhood, their religious and spiritual significance

---

[4] The discourse on disappearing civilizations was part of the grammar of colonialism. See Patrick Brantlinger, *Dark Vanishings: Discourse on the Extinction of Primitive Races, 1800–1930* (Ithaca and London: Cornell University Press, 2003).

[5] Tim Fulford, Debbie Lee, and Peter J. Kitson, 'Exploration, Race Theory and Headhunting: The Skull Beneath the Skin' in Tim Fulford, Debbie Lee, and Peter J. Kitson (eds.), *Literature, Science and Exploration in the Romantic Era: Bodies of Knowledge* (Cambridge: Cambridge University Press, 2004) 127–148, 148.

[6] Kaushik Sunder Rajan, *Biocapital: The Constitution of Postgenomic Life* (Durham: Duke University Press, 2006).

[7] See Joost Van Eynde, *Bodies of the Weak: The Circulation of the Indigenous Dead in the British World, 1780–1880* (PhD, University of Michigan, 2018) 170.

[8] For instance, findings about transformation of European skulls during the nineteenth century attracted far less interest than racialized science.

[9] See Andrew Zimmerman, 'Adventures in the Skin Trade', Adventures in the Skin Trade: German Anthropology and Colonial Corporeality in H. Glenn Penny and Matti Bunzl, *Worldly Provincialism: German Anthropology in the Age of Empire* (Michigan: University of Michigan Press, 2003) 156–178, 172.

[10] Museums were actively involved in the acquisition and trade. See Ricardo Roque, 'Authorised Histories: Human Remains and the Economies of Credibility in the Science of Race' (2018) 44 *Krons* 69–85.

[11] On the concept of 'war' of races, see Robert Knox, *The Races of Men: A Fragment* (Philadelphia: Lea and Blanchard, 1850) 13.

[12] Jesse Bucher, 'The Skull of Mkwawa and the Politics of Indirect Rule in Tanganyika' (2016) 10 *Journal of Eastern African Studies* 284–302, 297.

[13] It constitutes a dignity-taking and act of de-humanization. See Ciraj Rassool, 'Re-storing the Skeletons of Empire: Return, Reburial and Rehumanisation in Southern Africa' (2015) 41 *Journal of Southern African Studies* 653–670.

or family and community bonds. They enjoy special protection in secularized societies, due to the dignity of deceased persons, their social bond to descendants and human communities, or their contribution to living histories.[14] They challenge classical object/subject divides[15] and are typically distinguished from classical property.[16] In many indigenous cultures, human remains are sacred and treated as people, rather than as objects, in light of their connection between past and present. Collectors treated remains as mere 'objects'. Indigenous populations were regarded as 'research material', i.e. as raw material for anthropological classification or as show objects.[17] Many remains were collected without consent (e.g. as war trophies), in violation of local laws, customs, and belief systems,[18] or under asymmetrical power relations. They were reduced to 'scientific' objects or used as commodities to tell stories.

Like cultural objects, human remains developed their own 'social biography', through practices of removal, conservation, classification, or return, and shifting narratives or meanings.[19] The collected remains often became political or public objects through networks of empire and transactions.

This chapter demonstrates the centrality of the human body as a site of colonial violence. It first introduces the context of colonial collecting of human remains. It shows that remains were not only taken as war trophies or collected as items of racial science, but also traded as communities. It illustrates how projections of violence onto non-Western subjects and belief in the objectivity of science served to marginalize ethical constraints and rationalize dehumanization of others. It documents the political dimensions of remains and changing societal attitudes through biographies of remains. It traces inter alia how the Mkwawa head, mentioned in the Treaty of Versailles, was used as a site of inter-colonial rivalries, how the remains of Sarah Baartman turned from a commodified object of racial science into

---

[14] Belgian Advisory Committee on Bioethics, Opinion No. 82 of 9 January 2023 on the Status of Human Remains in Museum, Scientific and Private Collections, 13 https://www.health.belgium.be/sites/default/files/uploads/fields/fpshealth_theme_file/avis_82_-_comite_consultatif_de_bioethique_de_belgique.pdf/.

[15] Larissa Förster, 'The Long Way Home: Zur Biografie rückgeführter Objekte/Subjekte' in Thierry Greub and Martin Roussel (eds.), *Figurationen des Porträts* (Paderborn: Wilhelm Fink, 2018) 637–656.

[16] Jie Huang, 'Protecting Non-Indigenous Human Remains under Cultural Heritage Law' (2015) 14 *Chinese Journal of International Law* 709–734, 731. For instance, under common law, human remains are generally not associated with classical property rights. Robert K. Paterson, 'Maori Preserved Heads: A Legal History' in Peter Mosimann and Beat Schönenberger (eds.), *Kunst & Recht 2017/Art & Law 2017* (Bern: Stämpfli, 2017) 71–85.

[17] Zimmerman qualified this turn as an anti-humanist movement. See Andrew Zimmerman, *Anthropology and Antihumanism in Imperial Germany* (Chicago: University of Chicago Press, 2001) 2.

[18] See Edward Westermarck, *The Origin and Development of the Moral Ideas* (London: Macmillan and Co., 1926) 513–52.

[19] As Janet Hoskins has noted: 'Relocated to museums, catalogues, and archives, these skulls are removed from their historical context in a society where ancestors are important and are turned into evidence of a "timeless" state of primitive savagery'. See Janet Hoskins, 'Introduction: Headhunting as Practice and as Trope' in Janet Hoskins (ed.), *Headhunting and the Social Imagination in Southeast Asia* (Stanford: Stanford University Press, 1996) 16–17.

an icon of post-apartheid identity in South Africa, and how colonial mindsets continue to shape the treatment of the remains of Irish giant Charles Byrne. It also explores how evolutionary science and bio-politics of colonialism drove the chase for a 'neglected category of cultural objects', namely human fossils (e.g. Java Man, 'Taung child').[20] It demonstrates how collecting practices concealed epistemic violence through scientific labels and classification as natural history objects.

2 Colonial systems of collection

The collection of human remains started long before the peak of colonial expansion. Trophy-taking has been inherent part of warfare. Explorers or naturalists collected body parts and specimen as curiosities or commodities since Cook's voyages.[21] Systematic collection of human remains for scientific purposes began in the eighteenth century.[22] With newly emerging scientific disciplines, such as phrenology and craniology, scientific study increased in the nineteenth century.[23] Human skulls were increasingly studied to explain human characteristics, such as ancestry, intelligence, character, or behaviour. Darwin's theories triggered a new fascination with the study of anatomy and the collection of human remains scientific and intellectual circles.[24] They were used to ground historical racial narratives in natural sciences. As Paul Turnbull has explained in relation to indigenous bodily remains:

> Leading Enlightenment observers of man regarded all human beings as possessing an innate if enervated capacity for social and moral progress. By way of contrast, nineteenth-century discourses of race naturalized taxonomic differences, reified notions of gradation and hierarchy between racial types and generally construed so-called savage races as naturally incapable of embracing few or any elements of civilization.[25]

Skulls, bones, and body parts were collected under the umbrella of science to explain differences between nations or classify human races by anatomical difference.

---

[20] Paul P. Stewens, Nussaïbah B. Raja, and Emma M. Dunne, 'The Return of Fossils Removed Under Colonial Rule' (2022) 8 *Santander Art and Culture Law Review* 69–94, 88.

[21] See Chapter 2.

[22] For instance, Dutch physician Petrus Camper (1782–1789) studied human anatomy and found that humans have different facial angles.

[23] On changing discourses in science, see Kim A. Wagner, 'Confessions of a Skull: Phrenology and Colonial Knowledge in Early Nineteenth-Century India' (2010) 69 *History Workshop Journal* 27–51.

[24] A famous British collector is physician Joseph Barnard Davis (1801–1881), who acquired more than 1,500 skulls to explain racial difference, based on polygenetic theories.

[25] Paul Turnbull, 'British Anatomists, Phrenologists and the Construction of the Aboriginal Race, c.1790–1830' (2007) 5 *History Compass* 26–50, 27.

The obsession with the classification led to an increase in exchanges, purchases, or commissions. Human remains were acquired by museums, laboratories, professional societies, or research institutes.[26] Collection and exchange of human remains for anthropological or ethnological purposes became part of a 'global political economy'.[27] Collectors were eager to acquire indigenous remains and anatomical specimens from 'primitive races' in order to enhance their prestige or authority, to satisfy their desire to 'objectify' or know, or to make economic gains. They developed international networks in order to collect bodies for science and expand their collections. Colonies became a prime site for collection by anthropologists, colonial officials, military personnel, or traders. They acquired skulls, bones, or photographs.[28]

In particular, non-European human skulls became 'fetish' objects.[29] They were increasingly collected as evidentiary material in order to support 'scientific' claims for human and racial diversity of native populations.[30] As Andrew Zimmerman has noted, the collection of body parts turned into a scientific obsession, since they were more accurate than photographs.[31] They were easier to examine than living human beings and presumed to carry a greater degree of 'objectivity' for anthropometric measurement:

[H]uman flesh represented a form of subjectivity that anthropologists rejected from their studies. Anthropologists tightened their measuring calipers as much as possible to get to the dimensions of bones, but the pain of accurate measurement limited the extent to which this technique could be employed. Corpses, on the other hand, could be stripped of flesh ... Furthermore, these supposedly objective skulls or skeletons could be assembled into massive collections, presenting a comparative, centralized overview of the world's 'races' that no individual studying living humans could ever have obtained.[32]

Military physicians, explorers, missionaries,[33] or anthropologists were mandated to obtain skulls. They were collected in military operations, detention camps, or

---

[26] For example, British collections recorded a stark increase in human remains in the 1870s and 1880s. See Van Eynde, *Bodies of the Weak*, 95.

[27] Ibid, 26.

[28] On the role of photography, see Paul Bijl, *Emerging Memory: Photographs of Colonial Atrocity in Dutch Cultural Remembrance* (Amsterdam: Amsterdam University Press, 2015).

[29] Frances Larson, *Severed: A History of Heads Lost and Heads Found* (London: Granta, 2014).

[30] See Simon Harrison, *Dark Trophies: Hunting and the Enemy Body in Modern War* (New York: Berghahn Books, 2012); Ann Fabian, *The Skull Collectors: Race, Science, and America's Unburied Dead* (Chicago: Chicago University Press, 2010).

[31] Zimmerman, 'Adventures in the Skin Trade', 163.

[32] Ibid, 166–167.

[33] Jeanne Cannizzo, 'Gathering Soul and Objects. Missionary Collections' in Tim Barringer and Tom Flynn (eds.), *Colonialism and the Object: Empire, Material Culture and the Museum* (New York: Routledge, 1998) 153–166.

hospitals or taken from burial sites. Samuel Redman has spoken of the creation of 'bone empires'.[34]Although some anthropologists or ethnologists continued to defend ideas of 'cultural pluralism' at the peak of colonial collecting,[35] the fields became more closely entangled with national interests in the colonial agenda,[36] commercialized, or even 'gave meaning to the institutions of colonial violence, including prisons, battlefields, and concentration camps'.[37] Craniometry developed into a special scientific discipline.[38] Scientists developed methods in order to determine the average skull size of races or populations (cephalic index). Anthropological research was deemed to objectify belief in human differences. However, such studies did not necessarily confirm colonial narratives about the distinction between 'primitive' and 'civilized' cultures.[39] For instance, studies by ethnographer Otto Finsch (1839–1917) in New Guinea at the end of the nineteenth century concluded that human races are not distinct, but 'merge into one another to such an extent that the difference between Europeans and Papuans becomes completely unimportant'.[40] Dutch anthropological studies in the East Indies found that even populations in remote islands shared mixed ethnicities. Such findings challenged the idea of racial ideal types[41] or classical 'us' versus 'them' divides. During the peak of colonial acquisition, collections often organized human remains by racial or geographic criteria. The focus shifted gradually in the late 1930s, when collections moved away from race-based classifications.

Human remains were acquired through different types of networks. Some were obtained through trade and exchange, while others were taken as war trophies or collected for the 'progress of science'.

3 Human remains as trade items

In the nineteenth century, trade of human remains became a global phenomenon.[42] Colonial structures created new markets for the acquisition of human

---

[34] Samuel Redman, *Bone Rooms: From Scientific Racism to Human Prehistory in Museums* (Cambridge: Harvard University Press, 2016) 6, 72.

[35] Matti Benzl and Glenn Penny, 'Introduction: Rethinking German Anthropology, Colonialism, and Race' in H. Glenn Penny and Matti Bunzl, *Worldly Provincialism: German Anthropology in the Age of Empire* (Michigan: University of Michigan Press, 2003) 2.

[36] Ibid, 17.

[37] Zimmerman, 'Adventures in Skin Trade', 156–157.

[38] Sujit Sivasundaram, 'Imperial Transgressions: The Animal and Human in the Idea of Race' (2015) 35 *Comparative Studies of South Asia, Africa and the Middle East* 156–172, 158.

[39] Cooper and Stoler, *Tensions of Empire*, 14.

[40] Hilary Howes, *The Race Question in Oceania A. B. Meyer and Otto Finsch between Metropolitan Theory and Field Experience, 1865–1914* (New York: Peter Lang, 2013).

[41] Fenneke Sysling, *The Archipelago of Difference: Physical Anthropology in The Netherlands East Indies, ca. 1890–1960* (PhD, Vrije Universiteit Amsterdam, 2013) 227.

[42] See Gareth Knapman and Cressida Fforde, 'Profit and Loss: Scientific Networks and the Commodification of Indigenous Ancestral Remains' in Cressida Fforde, C. Timothy McKeown, and

remains. They promoted trading networks which facilitated exchange, circulation, and the commodification of remains.[43] The 'scientific' interest gradually enhanced their market value. This interplay is inter alia demonstrated by the trade of Māori heads (*toi moko*).[44] In the late eighteenth century, they were mainly collected as 'curiosities'. However, when the Māori faced increasing pressure as a result of inter-tribal wars, i.e. the so-called Musket Wars (1807–1842),[45] and struggles over land in New Zealand in the first half of the nineteenth century, they started to produce heads for trade purposes. They offered preserved heads in exchange for guns and weapons, in order to defend themselves against European settlements and foreign tribes.

In Māori culture, *toi moko* were originally preserved for different purposes.[46] Some heads were created from the skulls of ancestors, in order to preserve the memory of deceased and enable them to continue to be part of the community. Others were made from the skulls of enemies defeated in battle, in order to deter adversaries or facilitate agreements and trade with other tribes. In 1831, General Sir Ralph Darling, the Governor of New South Wales, prohibited the trade of heads in a proclamation and imposed a fine for violations.[47] However, the ban did not prevent the production or export. The Musket Wars supported the commercial trade of heads. The new methods of warfare and weaponry introduced by European traders and settlers created an arms race. The Māori preserved the heads of enemies and slaves,[48] in order to exchange them against guns. These heads had a different purpose than the traditional ancestral heads, preserved for spiritual purposes. They became 'hard cash' ('bio-capital'[49]) in a new economy of indigenous remains. They were commercialized, in order to meet demands by traders and to respond to the growing culture of collection and exchange. They were called *mokomokai*. These commercial structures gradually replaced the traditional, ancestor-based *toi moko* culture.

The scientific collection of skulls started in the 1850s, i.e. after New Zealand had formally become a British colony (1840). It increased in the 1870s, based

Honor Keeler (eds.), *Routledge Companion to Indigenous Repatriation* (New York: Routledge, 2020) 361–380.

[43] For instance, Joseph Banks (1743–1820) facilitated the circulation of indigenous remains, including skulls, after James Cook's voyages.
[44] Colleen Murphy, *Talking Heads: On the Repatriation of Māori Toi Moko* (BA Thesis, University of Michigan, 2016).
[45] During the musket wars, thousands of Māori people were killed. Andrew P. Vayda, 'Maoris and Muskets in New Zealand: Disruption of a War System' (1970) 85 *Political Science Quarterly* 560–84.
[46] Wayne Orchiston, 'Preserved Human Heads of the New Zealand Maoris' (1967) 76 *Journal of the Polynesian Society* 297–329.
[47] Paterson, 'Maori Preserved Heads: A Legal History', 74–75.
[48] Hazel Petrie, *Outcasts of the Gods? The Struggle over Slavery in Maori New Zealand* (Auckland: Auckland University Press, 2015) 147–154.
[49] On this concept, see Kaushik Sunder Rajan, *Biocapital: The Constitution of Postgenomic Life* (Durham, NC: Duke University Press, 2006).

on demand for specimens by anthropologists, anatomists, and other scientists. Preserved Māori heads became collectables, and were increasingly sought for scientific purposes. Museums became actively involved in the trafficking of heads. For instance, the museum in Auckland exported human remains to other parts of the world. Some private collectors, such as General Horatio Gordon Robley, who fought in the New Zealand wars, acquired extensive collections of *mokomokai* from museums or hospitals.[50] Some of them were exhibited as samples of a 'primitive' race facing extinction, feeding into narratives of progress created by colonial masters. The close link between racial science and the justification of the colonial enterprise is well reflected in the report of the New Zealand exhibition at the Saint Louis World's Fair of 1904. It postulates the evolution of the Māori from a lower to a higher level of development. It stated:

> The contrast between the position of the Māori in 1840 and 1904 constitutes a remarkable progress in racial development. Formerly the Māori was a savage, clever and enterprising, but ferocious, cruel, and a cannibal. Today he tills the soil, speaks English, and sends his children to school ... Contact with a highly civilized community has diverted the natural intelligence of the Māori to useful channels, while Christianity has developed the best instincts of a fine race of people. In the today [sic] the Māori stands side by side with the white man, a welcome comrade in the building of a new nation.[51]

In Australia, the uncontrolled trade and export of aboriginal remains became so widespread that it was limited by the Governor-General in 1913.[52] The regulation made export subject to ministerial approval and accreditation by scientific institutions. It led to a decrease of exports.

4 Human remains as trophies of war

In the heydays of colonial collecting, human remains were also actively seized as trophies in warfare.[53]

---

[50] Robley had a collection of more than heads.

[51] The Louisiana Purchase Exposition Commission, *Final Report of the Louisiana Purchase Exposition Commission, 1906* (Washington: Govt. Print Off., 1906) 227.

[52] Cressida Fforde and others, 'Inhuman and Very Mischievous Traffic: Early Measures to Cease the Export of Ancestral Remains from Aotearoa New Zealand and Australia' in Cressida Fforde, C. Timothy McKeown, and Honor Keeler (eds.), *Routledge Companion to Indigenous Repatriation* (New York: Routledge, 2020) 381–399.

[53] For a survey, see Lancelot Arzel and Daniel Foliard, 'Grim Trophies: Objects and Human Remains in Nineteenth-Century Colonial Conquests' (2020) 17 *Monde(s)* 9–31.

Trophy hunting has a long tradition in warfare both before and after the colonial period.[54] It was a recurring feature in colonial wars, which were characterized by unequal power relations and brutal methods of warfare. As Simon Harrison has shown, the practices of colonial powers in colonial warfare 'sometimes came to resemble those of indigenous peoples for whom expeditionary trophy-taking was a normal and accepted part of war'.[55] Racial stereotypes, different methods of warfare against 'savages', punitive considerations and the growing interest in the study of non-Western skulls in Europe and North America, provided a context for the collection of human remains.[56] They were collected as war memorabilia, signs of power and victory, or commodities.

4.1 Practices of trophy hunting and mutilation

The acquisition of human remains constituted 'a markedly violent and common form of colonial subjugation'.[57] It involved not only the mutilation of taking body parts but also the decapitation of enemies. This violence exceeded the limits of human imagination. As Frances Larson has explained, the collection of skulls as trophies explodes existing categories:

> A severed head ... is simultaneously a person and a thing ... it is compelling – and horrific – because it denies one of the most basic dichotomies we use to understand our world: that people and objects are defined in opposition to each other.[58]

Such practices stood in contrast to standards of civilized behaviour and military codes of honour. They are, in many ways, the antidote of military culture and self-perception of the cultivated West. They were morally banned and proscribed, yet practised in colonial warfare, sometimes in alleged response to mutilations of bodies or headhunting by 'non-civilized enemies'.

Colonial powers rationalized brutal methods, including mutilation and taking of skulls as war trophies, through distancing. The 'civilized' other was considered

---

[54] Simon Harrison, 'Skull Trophies in The Pacific War: Transgressive Objects of Remembrance' (2006) 12 *Journal of the Royal Anthropological Institute* 817–836; Alan Morris, 'Trophy skulls, museums and the San' in Pippa Skotnes (ed.), *Miscast: Negotiating the Presence of the Bushmen* (Cape Town: University of Cape Town Press, 1996) 67–79.

[55] Simon Harrison, *Dark Trophies: Hunting and the Enemy Body in Modern War* (Oxford: Berghahn Books, 2012) 10.

[56] Ibid, 4 ('the history of this practice [of trophy taking] has been linked inseparably with the history of racism').

[57] Denver A. Webb, 'War, Racism and the Taking of Heads, Revisiting Military Conflict in the Cape Colony and Western Xhosaland in the Nineteenth Century' (2015) 56 *The Journal of African History* 37–55, 39.

[58] Larson, *Severed: A History of Heads Lost and Heads Found*, 9.

as equal and entitled to humane treatment. The protection of the 'distant' other depended on the nature of the behaviour.[59] This relativist and reciprocity-based understanding of protection in warfare was used by colonial powers to justify brutal methods of colonial warfare, while formally branding themselves as 'civilized'.[60]

The taking of human body parts had a performative nature. It was part of a broader system or interaction or communication with the 'other'.[61] It was undertaken to demonstrate power, respond to violations, repel cruel behaviour, or mirror 'enemy' behaviour ('mimicking'),[62] or tolerated, as a result of dependency on local forces, or to profit from the violence for purposes of colonial rule or power, 'scientific' advancement or reward (e.g. prestige). 'Savage' and 'civilized' were thus 'not so much contrasting categories of enemies', but rather 'contrasting modes of interaction to which encounters between enemies can give rise'.[63] Ricardo Roque has used the concept of 'mutual parasitism' in order to explain this interdependency and entanglement of colonial violence.[64] Trophy-hunting or mutilation were both a cause and a consequence of colonial conflict. There are striking parallels between colonial contexts. Examples may be found under British, Belgian, French, Portuguese, or German colonial rule.

Mutilation of bodies or taking of human remains formed a recurrent, though often 'silenced element of British colonial practice'.[65] When such practices became public, they were often condemned by home audiences. However, they formed part of the rationalization of colonial violence. They were, in particular, used to crush local resistance or insurgencies in Asia or Africa. For instance, during the uprising in 1857 in India, British commanders condemned rebel leaders to death by 'cannonade'. They were executed by cannons. The force of the explosion mutilated bodies and made it impossible to perform funeral rites in the Hindu or Muslim traditions. Sometimes, the skulls were preserved.[66] After the Battle of Magdala in northern Ethiopia in 1868, British troops cut hair from the corpse of ruler Emperor Tewodros II as trophy. It later became part of the National Army Museum in London.

---

[59] See Chapter 5.

[60] Simon J. Harrison, 'Skulls and Scientific Collecting in the Victorian Military: Keeping the Enemy Dead in British Frontier Warfare' (2008) 50 *Comparative Studies in Society and History* 285–303, 289.

[61] Van Eynde, *Bodies of the Weak*, 275.

[62] See in relation to British mutilation of Xhosa fighters in the Cape Colony, Jochen Arndt, 'Treacherous Savages and Merciless Barbarians: Knowledge, Discourse and Violence during the Cape Frontier Wars' (2010) 74 *Journal of Military History* 709–735, 733 ('most of the soldiers rationalized these wartime excesses with the metaphor of the merciless barbarian, arguing that the Xhosa's barbarous mode of warfare forced the British soldiers to adopt these "sufficiently revolting" tactics').

[63] Harrison, 'Skulls and Scientific Collecting', 292.

[64] Ricardo Roque, *Headhunting and Colonialism: Anthropology and the Circulation of Human Skulls in the Portuguese Empire 1870–1930* (Basingstoke: Palgrave Macmillan, 2010) 7.

[65] Van Eynde, *Bodies of the Weak*, 14; Kim A. Wagner, 'Between Science and Savagery: Trophy-skulls and the Practice of Collecting in the British Empire throughout the Nineteenth Century' (2020) 17 *Monde(s)* 135–153.

[66] Kim A. Wagner, *The Skull of Alum Bheg: The Life and Death of a Rebel of 1857* (London: Hurst & Co, 2017).

In the late 1890s, British forces decapitated Zimbabwean resistance fighters who revolted against the administration of the British South Africa Company in the First Chimurenga (1896–1900). Cecil Rhodes sent the heads to Queen Victoria as symbol of victory and trophies of war. They became part of the collection of the Natural History Museum in London.[67]

Some of the most violent atrocities in colonial warfare were committed during the Xhosa wars in the Cape Colony of South Africa.[68] Atrocities on both sides, cultural stereotypes, and misunderstandings, and the succession of frontier wars between 1834 and 1853 created a spiral of violence, which involved mutual demonization, bodily mutilation, and head-taking. During the Sixth Frontier War, British forces captured and killed Xhosa leader Hintsa and mutilated his remains, in order to collect souvenirs and degrade the enemy. In the subsequent Seventh and Eighth Frontier Wars, i.e. the War of the Axe (1846–1847) and the War of Mlanjeni (1850–1853), warfare became 'unlimited'.[69] Although some British soldiers despised excessive imperial violence or considered it be 'un-British', others openly regarded the Xhosa as savages and barbarians, who deserve no quarter or humane treatment.[70] British officers were 'outsavaging the savage' by 'imitating the savagery imputed to them and reciprocating it'.[71] The acquisition of skulls came to be seen as a legitimate form of trophy-taking by both sides. They were hunted like a form of 'prey'. Heads were not only 'collected', but also traded. Medical officers gave instructions to loot battlefields, take heads, and ship them to Europe.[72] British soldiers posed with indigenous skulls or 'Kafir' trophies.[73] Battlefields were used as sites for the collection of human remains after the end of hostilities.[74] The collection of native skulls involved gruesome methods and included heads of women. Stephen Lakeman, a British army captain, has described this in a much cited passage of his reflections on the Xhosa:

> Doctor A—of the 60th had asked my men to procure for him a few native skulls of both sexes. This task was easily accomplished. One morning they brought back

[67] Sinai Fleary, 'Museum in Talks to Return 'War Trophy' Skulls Back to Zimbabwe' *The Voice Online* (10 November 2022).

[68] See Andrew Bank, 'Of "Native Skulls" and "Noble Caucasians": Phrenology in Colonial South Africa' (1996) 22 *Journal of Southern African Studies* 387–403.

[69] Arndt, 'Treacherous Savages and Merciless Barbarians', 735.

[70] Ibid, 710–711.

[71] Simon J. Harrison, 'Skulls and Scientific Collecting in the Victorian Military: Keeping the Enemy Dead in British Frontier Warfare' (2008) 50 *Comparative Studies in Society and History* 285–303, 290.

[72] Several skulls reached the museum of the Royal College of Surgeons in London. See Webb, 'War, Racism and the Taking of Heads', 44: '[E]xamples include the skull of a young Xhosa "taken from a native burial ground by a medical officer attached to the British Army" sometime before 1862; the skull of a chief shot by a party of the Rifle Brigade at Mount Coke during the 1846-7 war; and the skull of a Khoikhoi male "obtained and prepared by the donor when stationed at Whittlesea" in 1851.' See also Bank, 'Of "Native Skulls" and "Noble Caucasians"', 402.

[73] See the illustration in Van Eynde, *Bodies of the Weak*, 294.

[74] Ibid, 297.

to camp about two dozen heads of various ages. As these were not supposed to be in a presentable state for the doctor's acceptance, the next night they turned my vat into a cauldron for the removal of superfluous flesh. And there these men sat, gravely smoking their pipes during the live-long night, and stirring round and round the heads in that seething boiler, as though they were cooking black-apple dumplings.[75]

In 1879, British troops desecrated the grave of Zulu King Mpande after victory in the Anglo-Zulu War. According to native eye-witness accounts, the bones were removed by British medical officers to 'be carried across the sea to be looked at'.[76] Their precise fate remains unknown.

In 1906, colonial forces reportedly took the head of Zulu leader Bambatha (Bhambatha kaMancinza, 1865–1906),[77] after defeating his rebellion against the introduction of a new tax in Battle of Mome Gorge. Bambatha was apparently killed by expanding bullets.[78] The soldiers collected the head as trophy and to obtain proof of Bhambatha's death. The motivation is described in a report by Captain Walter Bosman. He justified it by purposes of 'identification', as well as broader aims of messaging. He wrote:

[T]he head was severed from the trunk and conveyed to the camp, where it was recognized as Bambata's by all those who had been acquainted with him and who were available. The exhibition of the head (to be seen by official permit only) undoubtedly had the effect of dispelling the superstition, deep rooted in the mind of the natives, that Bambata was invulnerable. So long as the belief was held that Bambata was alive, waverers would have thrown their lot in with the rebels and, with them, continued the struggle.[79]

The collection of skulls and human specimen in South Africa constituted a form of punishment or retribution or expressed the exercise of power and ownership over natives.[80] It was supported by increased scientific interest in the study of human remains.[81] Racial science provided a comforting pretext for collection. It helped to present 'trophies' as 'objects of science or art'.[82] As scientific objects in museums

[75] Stephen Lakeman, *What I Saw in Kaffir-Land* (Edinburgh and London: William Blackwood and Sons, 1880) 94–95.

[76] Ian Knight, *Companion to the Anglo-Zulu War* (Barnsley: Pen & Sword Military, 2008) 52.

[77] According to alternative narratives, Bambatha managed to escape and flee to Mozambique.

[78] Ken Gillings, 'The "Death" of Bhambatha Zondi, A Recent Discovery' (2002) 12 *Military History Journal* 133–137, 137.

[79] Walter Bosman, *The Natal Rebellion of 1906* (London: Longmans, 1907) 107.

[80] See Webb, 'War, Racism and the Taking of Heads', 55.

[81] Van Eynde, *Bodies of the Weak*, 36.

[82] Bank, 'Of "Native Skulls" and "Noble Caucasians"', 402.

and collections, they constituted no longer brutal trophies of war, but rather 'a token of British knowledge and civilization'.[83]

Trophy-hunting was applied in other contexts. Another famous example is the beheading of the Mahdi Muḥammad Aḥmad in Sudan in 1898,[84] after the massacre of Omdurman in the Mahdist War (1896–1898).[85] The forces of the Mahdi had led a successful insurrection against Ottoman-Egypt rule.[86] They defeated a British-led garrison in Khartoum in 1885, decapitated the commander, General Charles George Gordon (1833–1885), the former Governor-General of Sudan, and put his head on display. The Mahdi established a religious state, but passed away shortly after his victory. The 'story of Gordon's death' was used to justify 'the morality of the overthrow of the Mahdist'.[87] The British Commander Horatio Herbert Kitchener sought to avenge the brutal killing of Gordon.[88] He led a brutal campaign against the Mahdist forces in 1898. He instructed his forces to open Mahdi Muḥammad's tomb, sever his skull, and collect it as a trophy, in order to erase the memory of the prior 'victory of the savage' over the British and 'mirror' Gordon's cruel death.[89] The skull was supposed to be sent for scientific study to the College of Surgeons in London. However, in Britain, Kitchener's trophy-taking came under critique, despite his successful campaign. He had to apologize to Queen Victoria, who was embarrassed by the post-mortem revenge.[90] The skull was reburied in a Muslim cemetery by the British Consul-General in the city of Wadi Halfa in Northern Sudan.[91]

In 1905, British colonel Richard Meinertzhagen (1878–1967) took the skull of Orkoiyot Koitalel Arap Samoei (1860–1905), the chief of the Nandi people,[92] who resisted British colonization and railway projects in the Eastern Province of the Uganda Protectorate (nowadays Kenya).[93] Meinertzhagen used truce negotiations

[83] Van Eynde, *Bodies of the Weak*, 301.

[84] Daniel Foliard, 'Rabah's Head and the Mahdi's Skull: A Connected History of French and British Colonial Trophies' (2020) 17 *Monde(s)* 111–133.

[85] Donald Featherstone, *Omdurman 1898: Kitchener's Victory in the Sudan* (London: Osprey Publishing, 1993); Michelle Gordon, 'Viewing Violence in the British Empire: Images of Atrocity from the Battle of Omdurman 1898' (2019) 2 *Journal of Perpetrator Research* 65–100.

[86] Peter M. Holt, *The Mahdist State in the Sudan, 1881–1898: A Study of Its Origins, Development and Overthrow* (Oxford: Clarendon Press, 1970).

[87] Douglas Hamilton Johnson, 'The Death of Gordon: A Victorian Myth' (1982) 10 *The Journal of Imperial and Commonwealth History* 285–310, 303.

[88] Harrison, 'Skulls and Scientific Collecting', 290. See also Winston S. Churchill, *The River War: An Historical Account of the Reconquest of the Soudan*, 2 vols (London: Longman's Green, 1899) I, 196.

[89] Gordon, 'Viewing Violence in the British Empire', 81.

[90] Harrison, 'Skulls and Scientific Collecting', 290.

[91] Alan Moorehead, *The White Nile* (London: Hamish Hamilton, 1971) 335–336.

[92] David M. Anderson, 'Black Mischief: Crime, Protest and Resistance in Colonial Kenya' (1993) 36 *Historical Journal* 851–877, 858.

[93] See A. T. Matson, *Nandi Resistance to British Rule, 1890–1906* (Nairobi: East African Publishing House, 1972).

as pretext to kill the Nandi chief.[94] The skull was sent to London for 'scientific' purposes.[95]

Human trophy-taking was also common in the Congo Free State.[96] Belgian forces collected the skulls of local rulers as trophies, in order to signal power and facilitate submission. This was often done through mercenaries or local recruits. For instance, during the expedition to Katanga in 1891–1892,[97] the forces of Captain William Stairs (1863–1892) killed and beheaded Mwenda Msiri Ngelengwa Shitambi (1830–1891), the ruler of the Garanganze kingdom in Katanga.[98] Msiri had cut off the heads of his enemies. Stairs' forces put his skull on a palisade, in order to signal the end of his reign and avenge attacks against the expedition. According to reports by Dan Crawford, a missionary who witnessed the event, Msiri was decapitated by Lieutenant Omer Bodson with the words: 'I have killed a tiger! Vive le Roi!'[99] This episode illustrates the close parallels between trophy-taking and animalistic hunting in colonial imaginations[100] and the mutual imitation of violence in behaviour.

Belgian Lieutenant-General Émile Pierre Joseph Storms (1846–1918) became notorious for his collection of human remains. He brought a whole collection of crania to Belgium. They are known as 'skulls of Emile Storms'.[101] Storms relied on local allies and mercenaries (*rugaruga*) in order to control the region. They collected the heads of local leaders, who posed a threat to Belgian authority. His men beheaded Lusinga lwa Ng'ombe (1840–1884), a Tabwa chief, who was removed because of his role in ivory and the slave trade in the region of Lake Tanganyika. As Allen Roberts has shown in his study of the lives of Lusinga and Storms, both leaders relied on similar methods in order to exercise authority in the region.[102] Storms replaced Lusinga with a rival local chief who was loyal to him. He acquired Lusinga's severed head and a wooden sculpture of a male warrior, which embodied Lusinga, during a raid in December 1884. He also collected the skulls of two other Tabwa chiefs, Maribou and Mpampa, in April 1885. He took the three skulls and

[94] Richard Henry Meinertzhagen, *Kenya Diary 1902–1906* (Edinburgh: Oliver and Boyd, 1957) 232–239.

[95] A mausoleum was built in honour of Samoei in the town of Nandi Hills, Kenya. Some personal items of Samoei were returned by Meinertzhagen's son.

[96] Lancelot Arzel, 'The "Bloody Trophies" of Conquest: Cutting of Bodies and Colonial Wars in the Congo Free State Late Nineteenth Century–Early Twentieth Century' (2020) 17 *Monde(s)* 79–109.

[97] Joseph Moloney, *With Captain Stairs to Katanga: Slavery and Subjugation in the Congo 1891–92* (London: Sampson Low, Marston & Co., 1893).

[98] On Msiri, see David Gordon, 'Owners of the Land and Lunda Lords: Colonial Chiefs in the Borderlands of Northern Rhodesia and the Belgian Congo' (2001) 34 *International Journal of African Historical Studies* 315–338.

[99] Dan Crawford, *Thinking Black: Twenty-Two Years without a Break in the Long Grass of Central Africa* (London: Morgan and Scott, 1912) 308–310.

[100] Sivasundaram, 'Imperial Transgressions', 163, referring to the 'skull as animal trophy'.

[101] Julien Volper, 'À propos de sculptures & de crânes: les collectes d'Émile Storms' (2012) 66 *Tribal Art* 91–95.

[102] Roberts has compared their relation to that of a 'dance'. See Allen F. Roberts, *A Dance of Assassins: Performing Early Colonial Hegemony in the Congo* (Bloomington: Indiana University Press, 2013) 21.

the sculpture with him when he returned to Belgium later in the year. Ironically, Lusinga's head and his sculpture have gained greater popularity than Storms or Lusinga in person.[103] The skull was used by Belgian anthropologist Emile Houzé (1816–1886) to develop controversial theories on craniometry. Storms' widow offered the two items, and other artefacts, to the Royal Museum of Central Africa in 1930. The wooden ancestral figure developed into an artistic icon in the museum, reflecting the twists and turns in the presentation of colonial history and its subjects. The encounter between Storms and Lusinga confirms the relational dimensions of trophy-gathering, namely the constitution of violence through the interplay of domination and resistance.

French officers have used human trophy-taking to repel or punish resistance movements. A famous example is the defeat of the rebellion of Sheikh Ahmed Bouziane against France's occupation of Algeria from 1848 to 1949 (Zaatcha uprising).[104] Sheik Bouziane had declared a 'holy war' against the French, following an increase of taxes. After a fifty-two-day long siege, and the conquest of the desert village of Zaatcha, the troops of French General Émile Herbillon (1794–1866) beheaded members of the Algerian resistance, including Sheikh Bouziane and his sons and lieutenants. The heads were put on pikes and displayed in the market place of the city of Biskra, in order to demonstrate the vulnerability of the resistance and deter future insurgencies.[105] Medical officer Ferdinand Quesnoy included illustrations in his book L'armée d'Afrique depuis la conquête d'Alger (1888).[106] The skulls were sent to France as trophies to demonstrate that French troops could achieve 'real victories' in the fight in Algeria. They were classified and numbered by 'scientists' and kept in the Musée de l'Homme.[107] The museum held a collection of more than 18,000 skulls. The skulls of Zaatcha Revolt were kept in boxes and rediscovered in 2011 by Algerian historian Ali Farid Belkadi. The skulls of Sheikh Bouziane and other resistance fighters were returned in 2020, i.e. 171 years later, after a long repatriation campaign. They were buried at the El Alia cemetery in Algiers on Algeria's independence day.[108]

In 1900, French forces captured the skull of Rābiḥ az-Zubayr (Rabih Zubayr), also called Rabih Fadl Allah[109] (1840–1900), one of 'the last major opponent[s]

[103] Ibid.
[104] See Peter von Sivers, 'Insurrection and Accommodation: Indigenous Leadership in Eastern Algeria, 1840-1900' (1975) 6 International Journal of Middle East Studies 259–275, 266.
[105] Djamel Kharchi, Colonisation et politique d'assimilation en Algérie 1830–1962 (Algiers: Casbah, 2004) 107, referring inter alia to the heads of Sheikh Bouziane and his son.
[106] Ferdinand Quesnoy, L'armée d'Afrique depuis la conquête d'Alger (Paris: Jovet, 1888).
[107] The collection included inter alia the skulls of Cheikh Bouzian (skull number 5941) Si-Moussa Al-Derqawi (skull number 5942), and Mokhtar Al Titraoui (skull number 5944).
[108] Madjid Zerrouky, 'La France remet à l'Algérie vingt-quatre crânes de résistants décapités au XIXe siècle et entreposés à Paris', Le Monde Afrique (3 July 2020).
[109] W. K. R. Hallam, The life and times of Rabih Fadh Allah (Ilfracombe: Stockwell, 1977); Kyari Mohammed, 'Borno under Rabih Fadl Allah, 1893-1900: The Emergence of a Predatory State' (1997) 42 Paideuma: Mitteilungen zur Kulturkunde 281–300.

of the French empire'[110] in the Rabih War (1899–1901) in the Borno region in the south-west of Lake Chad (today's Chad). The incident bears resemblance with the decapitation of the Mahdi by the British.[111] Rabih Zubayr, who had served as lieutenant to a Sudanese slaveholder, took control of Borno in 1893 and ruled it from his capital in Dikwa. His rule was seen as an impediment to trade in the area. France sent an expeditionary force to bring the area under its control. As in many other contexts, the struggle against the African slave trade was used as justification for the operation against the Rabih.[112] In 1899, the Rabih managed to repel an attack led by Lieutenant Henri Bretonnet in the Battle of Togbao, during which Bretonnet and other officers were killed. The French increased their forces. In 1900, Rabih was defeated in the Battle of Kousséri by an expedition organized by Captain Émile Gentil (1866–1914), a French naval officer and explorer, who later became governor of the French Congo. Rabih was killed in the battle. According to several accounts, his head was 'cut off'[113] and carried 'on a pike' to Kusseri.[114] Gentil wanted to 'bury Rabeh's body', but it 'was simply thrown in the Chari River'.[115] The skull became a war trophy. It was photographed and brought back to Europe. Gentil included a depiction of the decapitated head in his memoirs of the mission.[116] The skull was included the collection of the *Musée de l'Homme*.[117] The victory gave France control over Chad and paved the way for colonial administration.

Portugal actively sought to acquire skulls and human specimens in the late nineteenth century. In 1885, the Ministry of Marine and Colonies issued an official instruction, which called upon colonial officers to collect human heads for scientific study and send them to Portugal.[118] Lisbon dispatched 'anthropological' missions to colonies in Angola, Guinea-Bissau, or East Timor.[119] During Portuguese rule over East Timor, colonial authorities accepted headhunting practices by natives for the mutual benefit.[120] Portuguese rule remained heavily dependent on the

---

[110] Bertrand Taithe, *The Killer Trail: A Colonial Scandal in the Heart of Africa* (Oxford: Oxford University Press, 2009) 11.

[111] Daniel Foliard, 'Rabah's Head and the Mahdi's Skull: A Connected History of French and British Colonial Trophies' (2020) 17 *Monde(s)* 111–133.

[112] Taithe, *The Killer Trail*, 141–142, arguing that the 'great enemies of the French conquest were always presented as slave-trading states' (141).

[113] Michael M. Horowitz, 'Ba Karim: An Account of Rabeh's Wars' (1970) 3 *African Historical Studies* 391–402, 397.

[114] John E. Lavers, 'The Awlad Rabih 22 April 1900 - 23 August 1901' (1994) 40 *Paideuma: Mitteilungen zur Kulturkunde* 215–242, 217, fn. 7; Arbab Djama Babikir, *L'Empire de Rabeh* (Paris: Dervy, 1950) 95. Foliard claims that the head was 'exposed for days on the walls of Kusseri'. See Foliard, 'Rabah's Head and the Mahdi's Skull', 111.

[115] Horowitz, 'Ba Karim: An Account of Rabeh's Wars', 398, fn. 13.

[116] The head is depicted in Émile Gentil, *La Chute de l'Empire de Rabah: la mission Gentil du Congo au lac Tchad* (Paris: 1902) 221.

[117] It was listed as inventory 'PV00601090'. See Volper, 'À propos de sculptures & de crânes, Fig. 10.

[118] Geoffrey C. Gunn, 'Timor-Leste (Former Portuguese East Timor): From Colonial Anthropology to an Anthropology of Colonialism' (2009) 32 *Review (Fernand Braudel Center)* 289–337, 293.

[119] Ibid.

[120] Roque, *Headhunting and Colonialism*, 17–39 ('Parasitism in Colonial Interactions').

local political system and alliances with indigenous structures.[121] This context facilitated complicity between the colonial state, racial science, and local rituals and traditions. Portuguese army officers used indigenous forces, which carried out headhunting, in order to combat local resistance.[122] Officially, colonial rulers despised such 'uncivilized' practices. However, they tolerated the application of such methods against their enemies.[123] 'Colonial headhunting' became a mutual enterprise. Local forces benefited from the vulnerability of Portuguese rule, in order to continue to practise indigenous headhunting. Portuguese officials and collectors, in turn, profited from indigenous trophy-taking, in order to acquire skulls and human remains for 'scientific' purposes.[124] Between 1878 and 1882, Portugal sent a collection of thirty-five human skulls from East Timor to the metropolis. It was originally meant for the Universal Expedition in Paris in 1878, but entered the collection of the anthropological section of the University of Coimbra (Portugal). The skulls were treated as 'scientific' objects[125] and used for racial-based science, including the question of whether the Timorese were ethnically closer to Malay-Indonesian or Papuan populations.[126]

4.2 The story of the Mkwawa head

The skull of former Hehe leader Mkwavinyika Munyigumba Mwamuyinga, also called chief Mkwawa (1855–1898),[127] is a famous icon, which was collected as colonial war trophy by German troops in German East Africa (1898). It became a showcase of inter-colonial entanglements through its curious mention in the Treaty of Versailles (1919). It finally turned into a symbol of colonial resistance. Its history is marked by myths. The life story of Mkwawa, the journey of the skull, and its authenticity have

---

[121] Colonial administrators ruled indirectly through local chiefs and kings, who were left in power in exchange for loyalty and military support.

[122] Roque, *Headhunting and Colonialism*, 33.

[123] Colonial officers occasionally participated in local feasts celebrations, following the defeat of adversaries.

[124] Roque speaks of a 'Circulatory System of Colonial Headhunting'. See Roque, *Headhunting and Colonialism*, 70–100.

[125] Ibid, 116 ('scientific things').

[126] Alfred Wallace (1823–1913), one of the leading evolutionists in the nineteenth century, whose work inspired Darwin's *Origin of Species* (1859), had argued in 1867 that 'Timorese are not Malays' but belong to a 'curious race which has close affinities to the Papuan in all moral and physical characteristics except colour'. See Alfred Wallace, 'The Polynesians and Their Migrations' (1867) 4 *Quarterly Journal of Science* 161–166, 163.

[127] See Bucher, 'The Skull of Mkwawa and the Politics of Indirect Rule in Tanganyika', 284; Jeremiah Garsha, *The Head of Chief Mkwawa and the Transnational History of Colonial Violence, 1898–2019* (PhD, University of Cambridge, 2020) https://doi.org/10.17863/CAM.56948; Jeremiah Garsha, 'Expanding Vergangenheitsbewältigung? German Repatriation of Colonial Artefacts and Human Remains' (2020) 22 *Journal of Genocide Research* 46–61; Bettina Brockmeyer, Frank Edward, and Holger Stoecker, 'The Mkwawa Complex: A Tanzanian-European History about Provenance, Restitution, and Politics' (2020) 18 *Journal of Modern European History* 117–139.

remained subject to scientific controversy.[128] However, the various narratives surrounding Mkwawa and the treatment of the topic, including its inclusion in the Versailles Treaty, are an important chapter of colonial history in itself.[129] As Jeremiah Garsha has argued, the story illustrates the different entanglements of human remains and the dual life of the skull as physical object and subject of colonial histories.[130]

Chief Mkwawa, 'the conqueror of many lands',[131] gained recognition in the resistance fight against German colonial forces in the southern highlands of Tanzania between 1891 and 1898. His resistance preceded the famous Maji Maji Revolt of 1905–1907.[132] His warriors ambushed and defeated a powerful German unit, led by commander Emil von Zelewski (1854–1891), in Lugalo, near the town of Iringa in August 1891, and captured their guns. Mkwawa established his main headquarters in Kalenga. In 1894, the town was attacked in a punitive raid by German military officer Tom von Prince.[133] However, Mkwawa managed to escape. He continued to lead guerilla warfare against German authorities with troops who remained loyal to him. His brother, Mpangile, who is mentioned in great detail in Magdalene von Prince's diary,[134] surrendered to German rule. He first managed to gain the trust of the German authorities, was named new Hehe 'sultan', but was then hanged because of his alleged continued collusion with Mkwawa.[135] Mkwawa forces were weakened. He continued to launch attacks against German patrols. Germans were eager to 'devour the land of Mkwawa' in order to end resistance.[136] Mkwawa was branded as an 'enemy of the Reich' ('Reichsfeind') by German Governor Eduard von Liebert (1850–1934) in 1897.[137] German authorities placed a bounty of nearly 8,000 Reichsmark on Mkwawa's head,[138] destroyed his father's ancestral site in order to limit his influence on Hehe followers,[139] and started a massive expedition

---

[128] Garsha, *The Head of Chief Mkwawa and the Transnational History of Colonial Violence*, ix ('The skull itself may be lost to time, may still be sitting in a box in a European collection waiting to be uncovered, or may have always been attached to Mkwawa's body, perhaps buried unmarked somewhere in the southern highlands of Tanzania'). See also Martin Baer and Olaf Schröter, *Eine Kopfjagd: Deutsche in Ostafrika, Spuren kolonialer Herrschaft* (Berlin: Links Verlag, 2001).

[129] Brockmeyer, Edward, and Stoecker, 'The Mkwawa complex', 138.

[130] Garsha, *The Head of Chief Mkwawa and the Transnational History of Colonial Violence*. 24 ff.

[131] This is the Hehe meaning of his name. See generally Alison Redmayne, 'Mkwawa and the Hehe Wars' (1968) 9 *Journal of African History* 409–436.

[132] John Iliffe, 'The Organization of the Maji Maji Rebellion' (1967) 8 *Journal of African History* 495–512; Jamie Monson, 'Relocating Maji Maji: The Politics of Alliance and Authority in the Southern Highlands of Tanzania. 1870-1918' (1998) 39 *Journal of African History* 95–120.

[133] Tom von Prince, *Gegen Araber und Wahehe: Erinnerungen aus meiner ostafrikanischen Leutnantszeit 1890–1895* (Berlin: Ernst Sigfried Mittler und Sohn, 1914).

[134] See Magdalene von Prince, *Eine deutsche Frau im Innern Deutsch-Ostafrikas* (Berlin: Ernst Siegfried Mittler und Sohn, 1908) Chapter 3 on Mpangile's reign as sultan. Mpangile offered Magdalene a girl as a gift.

[135] Redmayne, 'Mkwawa and the Hehe Wars', 423.

[136] See David Pizzo, *To Devour the Land of Mkwawa: Colonial Violence and the German-Hehe War in East Africa* (PhD Dissertation, Chapel Hill, University of North Carolina, 2007) 211.

[137] Brockmeyer, Edward, and Stoecker, 'The Mkwawa complex', 127, fn. 74.

[138] Pizzo, *To Devour the Land of Mkwawa*, 207.

[139] Brockmeyer, Edward, and Stoecker, 'The Mkwawa complex', 127.

(*Vernichtungsfeldzug*),[140] which deprived resistance fighters of food and supplies. After many of his remaining 250 warriors were killed or imprisoned, Mkwawa reportedly committed suicide on 19 July 1898 in his hiding place in the Mlambalasi cave near Iringa town, in order to avoid capture by the Germans. He had reportedly stated earlier that rather than surrendering to German rule, he 'would die by his own gun'.[141]

The precise circumstances of his death,[142] and the fate of his head, remain disputed.[143] Sergeant-Major Merkl from the Iringa Station reported that he found the body of Mkwawa near Mlambalasi close to a fire, along with another body. He noted in his report:

> I thought they were asleep, halted at about thirty yards and then fired. The bodies did not move. On reaching the spot, we found both men dead and cold … I ordered my askari to cut off Mkwawa's head to take along to camp. The body was handed over for burial to Mkwawa's people. Next day we arrived in camp at Iringa, where … Prince took charge of the trophy of Mkwawa's head.[144]

Merkl received the information that the body was Mkwawa from a boy (Lifumika) who had been with him at Mlambalasi, but had fled.[145] Merkl noted that Mkwawa had shot himself, before he arrived.[146] The severed head was delivered to Commander Prince and photographed.[147] Madgalene von Prince described the handover as a cruel but necessary proof of the death of Mkwawa and a victory for her husband. She noted that 'there was no other way' of 'demonstrating the death of our most terrible enemy' in such a way 'that there can be no doubt about its

---

[140] Pizzo, *To Devour the Land of Mkwawa*, 213.

[141] Juliette Desplat, 'The skull of Sultan Mkwawa', UK National Archive Blog (15 August 2019) https://blog.nationalarchives.gov.uk/the-skull-of-sultan-mkwawa/. See also Bucher, 'The Skull of Mkwawa and the Politics of Indirect Rule in Tanganyika', 436 ('Mkwawa's own determination not to surrender was a very important factor in the long struggle').

[142] Garsha, *The Head of Chief Mkwawa and the Transnational History of Colonial Violence*, 54, fn. 192 ('There is some debate … if Mkwawa committed suicide by shooting himself in the head or the stomach, or indeed if he committed suicide by shooting himself').

[143] For inaccuracies and inconsistencies, see Alison Redmayne, 'The War Trumpets and Other Mistakes in the History of the Hehe' (1970) 65 *Anthropos* 98–109.

[144] Feldwebel Merkl, 'Bericht über den Tod des Sultans Quawa' (1898) 9 *Deutsches Kolonialblatt* 645–646; British National Archives, FO CO 822/770 (1954–1955), Return of the skull of the late Chief Mkwawa to Tanganyika. Includes 23 photographs depicting: Hehe Tribe, Tanganyika: Governor Sir Edward Twining's presentation to Chief Adam Sapi (grandson), of Chief Mkwawa's skull which had been severed from his body by the Germans in 1898. Dated 1954.

[145] Merkl, 'Bericht über den Tod des Sultans Quawa', 645; Garsha, *The Head of Chief Mkwawa and the Transnational History of Colonial Violence*, 54 ('We crawled within thirty metres of it. We now saw two figures lying before it, apparently asleep. The boy [Lifumika] pointed out one of them as Mkwawa. Since the stones prevented us getting closer unnoticed, we took aim, fired, and ran forward').

[146] See Prince, *Eine deutsche Frau im Innern Deutsch-Ostafrikas*, 180–181.

[147] Ibid, 61. Magdalene von Prince traced the reception and photograph of the head in her diary. She was convinced that the head brought by Merkl was indeed Mkwawa's head. See Prince, *Eine deutsche Frau im Innern Deutsch-Ostafrikas*, 179, 184.

ultimate extermination.[148] It turned initially into a family 'trophy'.[149] The Princes demonstrably kept the photograph of the head, and a tooth which they turned into a family relic.[150]

Merkl's account fits well within the colonial narrative. As Jesse Bucher has argued:

> At the center of German records on the defeat of the Hehe ... is a prevailing sense of the body's capacity to carry additional meaning. More than defeating the Hehe through military conquest, the German forces in Tanganyika also pursued a symbolic conquest by capturing and saving Mkwawa's head.[151]

This narrative reflects the inclination to symbolically end the rule of Mkwawa and avenge the defeat of Zelewski during the 1891 expedition.[152] However, there is no absolute certainty that the skull collected by Merkl was that of Mkwawa. Mkwawa had managed to avoid contact with colonial forces. His physiognomy was not fully known. According to alternative narratives, Mkwawa only staged the suicide and used a different body in order to avoid his remains falling into the hands of the enemy.[153] The events at Mlambalasi broke the resistance and led to the gradual subjugation of the Wahehe. The region was declared 'pacified' by German authorities.[154] The Hehe sided with the Germans in the subsequent Maji uprising.[155] Some German authorities believed that the taking of the head of Mkwawa would reinforce their authority in the eyes of the Hehe people, since they would be seen as his legitimate successor according to native views.[156]

The head collected by Merkl developed a history of its own, as the 'skull of Mkwawa'. It gained new meanings. The Treaty of Versailles and the change from German to British rule in East Africa provided the context to redefine the meaning of the skull as an object of international importance. It was rebranded from a German war trophy into an international artefact, symbolizing the cruelty

---

[148] Ibid, 179.

[149] Harrison, *Dark Trophies*, 77.

[150] Garsha, *The Head of Chief Mkwawa and the Transnational History of Colonial Violence*, 290.

[151] Bucher, 'The Skull of Mkwawa and the Politics of Indirect Rule in Tanganyika', 288.

[152] Garsha, *The Head of Chief Mkwawa and the Transnational History of Colonial Violence*, 54.

[153] Brockmeyer, Edward, and Stoecker, 'The Mkwawa Complex', 125.

[154] Commander Tom Prince reported in 1899: 'The political circumstances are such that the locations named [various locations in Uhehe] appear in the long term, indeed for all time, to be secure. The jumbe that we have installed are either people that proved themselves to be trustworthy in difficult times or are the descendents of those aristocratic families that have all the reason in the world to hate Quawa and his Wahehe. All of them owe their present position to the station. No jumbe has enough power to manoeuvre on his own, and the unity of the Wahehe has been eliminated for all time. This is all the more important in that the station chief has ruled out the possibility that other tribes near northern and eastern Uhehe could be cultivated as a counterweight.' Report of Tom von Prince, 'Bericht des Stationschefs von Iringa über die dortigen Verhältnisse' (1899) 10 *Deutsches Kolonialblatt* 658.

[155] See Pizzo, *To Devour the Land of Mkwawa*, 216; Redmayne, 'Mkwawa and the Hehe Wars', 432.

[156] Harrison, *Dark Trophies*, 77.

and defeat of German colonial authority. The Paris Peace Conference acted as the 'stage'[157] to frame the taking of the 'the skull of the Sultan Mkwawa' as a matter of global politics and seek its 'hand over to His Britannic majesty's Government'.[158] It was mentioned in the Treaty in the 'Special Provisions' on reparations, together with a clause requiring Germany to restore the 'original Koran of the Caliph Othman' to 'His Majesty the King of the Hedjaz'.[159] The text was based on the premise that the skull was 'removed from the Protectorate of German East Africa and taken to Germany'.[160]

The provision was inserted in the Treaty, based on the initiative of Sir Horace Byatt, the British administrator of former German East Africa. Byatt sought to show gratitude to the Hehe people, facilitate British indirect rule and signal the end of German power. The British believed that the Germans had sent the skull as a wat trophy to museums in Berlin. Byatt wrote in a letter to the Foreign Office on 14 November 1918 that:

> [t]he recovery of the head and its subsequent internment in Mkwawa's grave would undoubtedly give the widest satisfaction among the Wahehe, who have been consistently helpful to us during the war, and would probably be appreciated in the country generally. It would also afford tangible proof in the eyes of the natives that German power has been completely broken.[161]

Byatt pursued several rationales with the insistence on treaty inclusion. He wanted to signal the transition from the brutality of German rule to Britain's civilized colonial authority. The debate over the skull coincided with a narrative battle between Germany and Britain over German violence and crimes in Africa, illustrated by the 1918 British Report on the Natives of South-West Africa and Their Treatment by Germany, the so-called 'Blue Book',[162] and Germany's response, the 'White Book', which justified German methods and sought to pinpoint Britain's brutality.[163] Byatt also pushed for a handover, in order to facilitate British control. The acquisition of the skull, and its potential return to the Hehe for burial, supported his plans to install Mkwawa's son, Sapi Mkwawa, as leader of the new native administration

---

[157] Garsha, *The Head of Chief Mkwawa and the Transnational History of Colonial Violence*, 120.
[158] Article 246 of the Treaty of Versailles.
[159] Article 246(1).
[160] Article 246(2).
[161] 'Byatt to Principal Secretary of State' (14 November 1918) British National Archives FO 608/215/383.
[162] Report on the Natives of South-West Africa and Their Treatment by Germany (South-West Africa: Administrator's Office, 1918). See Jeremy Silvester and Jan-Bart Gewald, *Words Cannot Be Found: German Colonial Rule in Namibia: An Annotated Reprint of the 1918 Blue Book* (Leiden: Brill, 2003).
[163] German Colonial Office, *The Treatment of Native and Other Populations in the Colonial Possessions of Germany and England: An Answer to the English Blue Book of August 1918* (Berlin: Reichskolonialamt, 1919).

under British authority. The express mentioning in the Treaty contributed to a public naming and shaming of Germany's practices of taking heads as trophies. The skull of Mkwawa is the only individualized mentioning of a skull in the Treaty.

Initially, the skull was not deemed important enough to be included separately in the provisions of the 'venerable Peace Treaty'.[164] Its mention distinguishes it from other human remains. Its equation to cultural and artistic objects secured its retention in the negotiations.[165] The British delegation argued that the skull presented an object of scientific interest as a human specimen, i.e. a 'craniological curiosity',[166] and implied that it had carried historical importance since it was taken from a 'sultan'.[167] It was thus included in the special provisions without in-depth discussion.

The final formula adopted in the Treaty is particular in several respects. The skull is the only individualized human remain listed in the Treaty. The Treaty contains general provisions on the transfer of human remains[168] and the protection of graves of 'prisoners of war and interned civilians who are nationals of the different belligerent States and have died in captivity'.[169] However, native resistance leaders killed in colonial warfare were not included in this regime of protection. The way out was to equate the skull to a cultural artefact, given its scientific value, historical interest, and alleged status as a museum object. This rebranding explains why the skull is listed in Article 246 after an object of material culture, i.e. the Koran of the Caliph Othman. The German obligation was framed as an inter-state obligation. The Treaty required Germany to return the Islamic artefact to its original owner, the 'King of Hedjaz', but specified that the skull ought to be transferred to Britain, rather than to the Hehe people or the Mkwawa family. This mediation accommodated the British colonial agenda pursued through the treaty negotiations.

Ultimately, the framing of the Treaty relied on a plausible, but ultimately insufficiently demonstrated fiction, namely the assumption that Mkwawa's skull was transferred from the possession of Prince to a scientific collection in Germany. The skull thus 'existed only in the abstract from 1900 until 1954'.[170] The ethnological museum in Berlin had indeed received several skulls from the Hehe for 'scientific' purposes, including skulls from the burial sites of the Mkwawa' family[171] and the skull of Mpangile, who was executed by the Germans.[172] In 1899, the pathologist Rudolf Virchow (1821–1902) identified a skull (item RV.1487) in the possession of

---

[164] British Foreign Office, Minutes on 'Recovery from Germany of the Skull of the late Sultan Mkwawa' (5 February 1919) FO 608/215/379.

[165] Garsha, *The Head of Chief Mkwawa and the Transnational History of Colonial Violence.*133–134.

[166] This point was made by Colonial Secretary Viscount Milner.

[167] Garsha, *The Head of Chief Mkwawa and the Transnational History of Colonial Violence*, 133.

[168] Article 225.

[169] Article 226.

[170] Garsha, *The Head of Chief Mkwawa and the Transnational History of Colonial Violence*, 291.

[171] Brockmeyer, Edward, and Stoecker, 'The Mkwawa Complex', 130–132.

[172] Ibid, 139.

the Berlin collection as Mkwawa's skull. However, the features did not match the injuries suffered by Mkwawa. Contrary to the account made by the Princes, the teeth were still intact.[173] The record was later corrected, and even the modified theory that the skull was Mkwawa's father was later abandoned. In 1919, von Luschan told the German Colonial Office that Mkwawa's skull 'was not in the Ethnological Museum' and that German museums did not know its precise whereabouts.[174]

In 1920, Germany relied on this argument to deny execution of the British demand for the handover of the skull. The German Ministry noted in a note dated 6 May 1920 that the obligation had become pointless, since the skull could not be reliably retrieved in German official collections. It stated:

> There are no indications whatever of the head having been brought to Germany and the researches made hitherto in the skull collections of Germany have been fruitless. Paragraph 2 of Article 246 of the Treaty of Peace has thus no longer any object.[175]

In 1921, Winston Churchill, then British Secretary of State for the Colonies, advised Byatt not to pursue this matter further. It therefore did not take 'six months', as stipulated in the Treaty, but thirty-five years, until Germany acted pursuant to its commitments under Article 246. In this period, the fate of the skull obtained yet another meaning and interpretation.

As of the 1950s, the skull was no longer merely seen as a 'relic' or as a tool to shame German colonial practice from a comparative perspective, but gradually became a symbol of anti-colonial resistance. Edward Twining (1899–1967), the British governor of Tanganyika from 1949 to 1958, helped to secure possession of a skull from the anthropological museum in Bremen, which he branded as Mkwawa's skull and returned to Tanzania. At this time, the story had almost fallen into oblivion and the symbolic nature of the skull had become more important than its authenticity.

Twining had an interest in the return of the skull, in order to facilitate the rule of Mkwawa's grandson, Adam Sapi, and to keep the Hehe as loyal subjects in the context of Mau Mau uprising in Kenya (1952–1960). In 1951, Twining shared rumours with the British Foreign Office that the skull may have been discovered in Germany. Germany first denied the discovery, but conceded in 1953 that the Bremen museum carried several skulls that might share the necessary characteristics and markings.[176] This reinvigorated a novel hunt for the skull.

---

[173] Ibid, 128.
[174] Ibid, 133.
[175] Copy of 'Letter from Köster, German Foreign Ministry to Foreign Office' (6 May 1920) British National Archives, FO 371/3795, 1919.
[176] Garsha, *The Head of Chief Mkwawa and the Transnational History of Colonial Violence*, 190–191.

Twining went to Bremen to examine the skulls. He looked for a skull which was similar in shape and cephalic index to Adam Sapi. He found a skull which shared sufficient resemblance with Mkwawa, in order to match the story. The skull lacked any teeth. He based the authenticity on information provided by a German police surgeon. He wrote:

> A cephalic surgeon ... reported that it contained a bullet mark fired from a 25 mm rifle which was ... in use by the German military force in Tanganyika at that time, and that the head had been severed by a sharp sabre or sword. This evidence, coupled with that of the cephalic index of the skull being an unusual one but similar to the late Sultan's sister and his living grandson, together with the fact the skull was bleached which probably happened when they boiled the meat off, suggesting that it was indeed the skull we were looking for.[177]

It is uncertain whether the 'Bremen' skull is the authentic Mkwawa skull or how it came to Bremen. The museum lacked the necessary information on provenance. However, Twining was successful in creating the impression that he had found the correct one. In his correspondences, he attributed 'poltergeistic qualities'[178] to the skull and noted its irregular behaviour,[179] in order to reinforce the idea that it was Mkwawa's severed head. He also published a pamphlet on the skull, creating a new episode in the biography of the Mkwawa head.

The Bremen museum handed the skull over to Britain on 16 January 1954. Twining returned it to Adam Sapi, who agreed that this was his 'grandfather's skull' and was 'prepared to accept it as such'.[180] On 19 June 1954, he held a formal ceremony with Sapi in Kalenga in the presence of chiefs of the Hehe tribe and more than 30,000 Wahehe in order to mark the return and place the head in a mausoleum, which later became a memorial museum.[181] His address was marked by colonial rhetoric and designed to counter the threat of increasing African nationalism.[182] The Treaty of Versailles was not mentioned, in order not to embarrass Germany.[183] Twining first praised Mkwawa's qualities as a warrior and a leader, and then used the occasion to pledge alliance to British rule. He asked the Hehe to

---

[177] Twining to Davod (25 November 1953) British National Archives, CO 822/566, Return to Tanganyika of the skull of the late Sultan Mkwawa (1951–1953).

[178] 'Twining to David' (15 February 1954) British National Archives, CO 822/770.

[179] He wrote in March 1954 that the 'skull continued to behave very badly while we were on safari on the train, and we had a series of mishaps which cannot otherwise be accounted for. Our poor old Bandmaster, Gulab Singh, died on the train. My A.D.C. collected a sinus and had to go to hospital. The head boy had a soda water bottle burst in his face, and the cook was struck in the face by a flying saucer. We all got hay fever and we all got very irritable!' See 'Twining to David' (8 March 1954) British National Archives, CO 822/770.

[180] 'Twining to David' (25 November 1953) British National Archives, CO 822/566.

[181] The Memorial Museum in Kalenga, also known as the Mkwawa Museum, containing the skull and other relics.

[182] See Bucher, 'The Skull of Mkwawa and the Politics of Indirect Rule in Tanganyika', 294–295.

[183] Twining's report on the ceremony (6 July 1954) British National Archives, CO 822/770.

'continue to give' their 'unstinted loyalty to Queen Elizabeth II and her heirs and successors', while promising them 'all the benefits of modern civilization and science'.[184] The violence of British rule was not mentioned.[185]

In his report of the ceremony, Twining acknowledged that there were still doubts about the authenticity. He took the position that the skull was now officially 'Mkwawa's head', since it was accepted by the Hehe. He wrote:

> [A]lthough, as was natural, some people doubted that the skull was the genuine article, it can be said convincingly that it has been accepted as such by the Hehe people and a number of old men who remembered Sultan Mkwawa pointed out that it must be the true skull because it had a bump in the middle of the forehead exactly similar to that which Sultan Mkwawa had.[186]

He was persuaded that this provided enough 'circumstantial evidence' in order to put the case to rest.[187] This is true in some sense. The Bremen skull has since then become its own reference object. It became an 'anti-colonial icon'.[188] After Tanzania's independence in 1961, it came to serve as a memorial of resistance against colonialism as such, visible to any interested public. This larger cause is now shaping memorialization practice. As recent archival studies have shown, the severed head of Mkwawa has now multiple biographic lives:[189]

> The skull which was returned in 1954 was almost certainly not Mkwawa's. With Mkwawa's skull or its doppelgänger, one could contend that the object itself ultimately became only a minor matter in its own history.[190]

5 Systematized collecting for science in a colonial context

Acquisition and trade of body parts became part of a new political economy in the late nineteenth century. This increase was driven by the professionalization of

---

[184] 'Speech by His Excellency the Governor at the Ceremony of the Return of the Skull of Chief Mkwawa of Uhehe to Chief Adam Sapi and the People of Uhehe, on Saturday 19th June, 1954', CO 822/770/75.

[185] Garsha, *The Head of Chief Mkwawa and the Transnational History of Colonial Violence*, 215 ('The speech served to remind the Wahehe that they fought the Germans, not the practice of colonialism. It reinforced the notion that British colonialism liberated the Wahehe to become prosperous under British benevolence').

[186] Twining's report on the ceremony (6 July 1954) British National Archives, CO 822/770.

[187] Ibid.

[188] Brockmeyer, Edward, and Stoecker, 'The Mkwawa Complex', 138.

[189] See also Garsha, *The Head of Chief of Mkwawa and the Transnational History of Colonial Violence*, 221–231.

[190] See Brockmeyer, Edward, and Stoecker, 'The Mkwawa Complex', 138. See also Garsha, *The Head of Chief Mkwawa and the Transnational History of Colonial Violence*, 292.

science,[191] increased state involvement, and the rise of salvage and race theory. As Joost Van Eynde has argued, collecting 'indigenous bodies was not only about classifying the dead, it was also about ordering the living'.[192] Collecting changed from a system in which individuals 'benefited from the umbrella of imperialism while traveling, trading, and working outside of Europe'[193] to a structure where 'citizens of a nation-state actively engaged in acquiring lands and peoples for the purpose of political and economic domination'.[194] Museums in France, Germany, Britain, or the US increasingly expanded their collections of rare or unique specimens, including indigenous remains as of the 1860s. Scientists and professionals were eager to gather whole collections of objects from indigenous populations as anthropological evidence or material of study. They sought to distinguish themselves from more commercialized or voyeuristic forms of ethnography, which lacked the necessary scientific 'objectivity',[195] and insisted on clear demonstration of provenance[196] or unmediated representation facilitating objective study. They addressed questionnaires to colonial authorities in order to study the customs and physical traits of indigenous people. Skulls from notorious leaders or indigenous populations facing extinction had particular value. Thousands of remains were collected and sent to laboratories and museums.

The accuracy and method of collection mattered more than ethical constraints; involuntary removal was risky, since it enhanced risks of indigenous resistance.[197] The prevailing scientific view of remains as natural objects made it easier to turn a blind eye to the violence of collection and to rationalize questionable practices such as exhumation of graves or decapitation ('The dead could not protest'). As the German Guidelines on Human Remains acknowledge, it is 'incorrect' to assert that the practices of collection 'were in line with the sense of justice of the

---

[191]   Benzl and Penny, 'Introduction: Rethinking German Anthropology, Colonialism, and Race', 17.

[192]   Ibid, 330.

[193]   Colonial collectors studied skulls or remains in the possession of native chiefs, in order to demonstrate the savagery of indigenous violence or the practice of human sacrifice. For instance, the British explorer Richard F. Burton famously described storage (*juju*) houses in West Africa, with rows of 'fleshless human skulls, often painted or decorated', as evidence of human sacrifice, and the skulls decorating the palace of King Gelele of Dahomey 'in token of respect for some dead enemy', in his account of the 1861 mission to persuade the king to abandon the slave trade. See Richard F. Burton, *Wanderings in West Africa: From Liverpool to Fernando Po* (London: Tinsley Brothers, 1863) vol. 2, 282–283; Richard F. Burton, *A Mission to Gelele, King of Dahome* (London: Tinsley Brothers, 1864) vol. 1, 290 ('a human skull, with thigh bones and other amulets hanging about') and corresponding fn. See also Robin Law, '"My Head Belongs to the King": On the Political and Ritual Significance of Decapitation in Pre-Colonial Dahomey' (1989) 30 *The Journal of African History* 399–415.

[194]   Benzl and Penny, 'Introduction: Rethinking German Anthropology, Colonialism, and Race', 14.

[195]   Sierra A. Bruckner, 'Spectacles of (Human) Nature: Commercial Ethnography between Leisure, Learning, and Schaulust' in H. Glenn Penny and Matti Bunzl, *Worldly Provincialism: German Anthropology in the Age of Empire* (Michigan: University of Michigan Press, 2003) 127–155.

[196]   Ricardo Roque, 'Authorised Histories: Human Remains and the Economies of Credibility in the Science of Race' (2018) 44 *Kronos* 69–85, 76 ('Authenticity was crucial if skulls were to be used for the purposes of racial classification in a museum. In particular, determining the genuine "tribal" and geographical origin of each skull was of major importance').

[197]   Van Eynde, *Bodies of the Weak*, 197.

time'.[198] Remains were often collected in contravention of native customs, protecting the inviolability of the human body, even though scientists insisted on collection in a 'loyal way'. At least 'many of the erstwhile "collectors" were themselves well aware of the injustice of what they were doing, but felt themselves "obliged" in the service of science to appropriate the materials or objects in question'.[199]

The collected remains gained new value as objects in the service of anthropological research or the 'common good'. They became part of the 'biogeography' of empire[200] and also 'political objects' in the wider sense.[201]

5.1 Settler colonial contexts

The increase in collection is visible in settler colonial contexts, such as South Africa,[202] Australia, or the US.

In colonial Australia, the rise of evolutionary science, colonial ideology, and nation-building enhanced the collection and trade of bones and skulls of aboriginals in the nineteenth and early twentieth centuries. Ideas of social advancement,[203] salvage anthropology, and trade interests prompted the search for human remains. Aboriginal races were sometimes viewed as 'an almost exact counterpart of the most ancient men [in Europe]'.[204] For instance, Australian and Tasmanian Aborigines ('Bushmen') were thought to be on the lowest scale of civilization in nineteenth-century anthropological works.[205] They were branded as the 'world's most distinct and morphologically unsophisticated race', under threat of extinction.[206] From the 1860s, their remains were collected as objects of racial science[207] or commodities for exchange,[208] in line with state narratives about the promotion of 'intergenerational' development.

---

[198] German Museum Association, *Care of Human Remains in Museums and Collections* (Berlin: German Museum Association 2021) 113.

[199] Ibid.

[200] Janet Browne, 'Biogeography and Empire' in Nicholas Jardine, James A. Secord, and Emma C. Spary (eds.), *Cultures of Natural History* (Cambridge: Cambridge University Press, 2000) 304–321, 320.

[201] Van Eynde, *Bodies of the Weak*, 331.

[202] Martin Legassick and Ciraj Rassool, *Skeletons in the Cupboard: South African Museums and the Trade in Human Remains 1907–1917* (Cape Town: South African Museum, 2000); Patricia Davidson, 'Human Subjects as Museum Objects: A Project to Make Life Casts of "Bushmen" and "Hottentots", 1907-1924' (1993) 102 *Annals of the South African Museum* 165.

[203] Paul Turnbull, 'Australian Museums, Aboriginal Skeletal Remains, and the Imagining of Human Evolutionary History, c. 1860-1914' (2015) 13 *Museum & Society* 72–87, 73.

[204] Edward Charles Stirling, *Prehistoric Man* (Adelaide: South Australian Registrar,1893) 2.

[205] Alan Barnard, *Anthropology and the Bushman* (Oxford/New York: Berg, 2007) 29.

[206] Paul Turnbull, 'Ramsay's Regime: The Australian Museum and the Procurement of Aboriginal Bodies, c. 1874–1900' (1991) 15 *Aboriginal History* 108–121, 110.

[207] Russell McGregor, *Imagined Destinies: Aboriginal Australians and the Doomed Race Theory, 1889–1939* (Carlton: Melbourne University Press, 1997).

[208] For instance, in the 1860s the Ethnological Museum in Oxford requested skeletons and skulls from aboriginal populations in Tasmania, who were deemed to face extinction.

Museums relied on public officials and paid collectors to acquire remains. They were inter alia collected by police forces or frontier workers. They plundered burial sites (e.g. Hindmarsh Island) or used force to acquire remains as collectable items. Some skulls in museums carried bullet holes. Others were collected from old peoples' homes, hospitals, or asylum morgues. South Australia's Anatomy Act of 1884, co-drafted by Charles Edward Stirling (1848–1919), who later became Director the South Australian Museum between 1884 and 1912,[209] allowed the 'scientific' use of human remains of people who passed away in public institutions and did not expressly object to anatomical examination and commodification. This premise ('silence means consent') facilitated collection.[210] As a result, the bodies of many indigenous people were first defleshed, and then buried.

Edward Pierson Ramsay (1842–1916), the curator of the Australian Museum, openly encouraged such collection practices, including removal from graves, between 1874 and 1894. He was eager to attract the attention of scientists in Europe. He published a manuscript in 1887 entitled 'Hints for the preservation of specimens of natural history', which outlined methods for 'anatomising' heads and skulls and turning them into collectable objects.[211] He specified the monetary value of collected skulls, in comparison to other objects. He noted that 'a Bower-Bird skin in good condition was worth five shillings; a 'racially pure' Aboriginal skull complete with jaw was worth seven shillings.'[212] The museum acquired the remains of several thousand people. Ramsay himself owned a collection of more than 100 skulls, mostly from aboriginal people. Some of the remains were sent to the Royal College of Surgeons at Edinburgh University, which acquired a large number of indigenous remains from Australia. Ultimately, the imagination and scientific branding of aboriginal remains as remnants of a lesser developed race served to cultivate the 'colonial' self.[213]

In the US, the scramble for indigenous remains was influenced by the racial science of ethnologist and collector, Samuel G. Morton (1799–1851), who studied American Indian skulls, in order to determine to what extent distinct races are grounded in physiological processes and geographical conditions.[214] Morton had one of the largest collections of human crania. In his famous work 'Crania

---

[209] Paul Turnbull, 'A Judicious Collector: Edward Charles Stirling and the Procurement of Aboriginal Bodily Remains in South Australia, c. 1880-1912' in Sarah Ferber and Sally Wilde (eds.), *The Body Divided: Human Beings and Human 'Material' in Modern Medical History* (Farnham: Ashgate, 2011) 109–130.

[210] See Helen MacDonald, 'The Anatomy Inspector and the Government Corpse' (2009) 6 *History Australia* 40.1–17, 40.11.

[211] Edward Pierson Ramsay, *Hints for the Preservation of Specimens of Natural History* (Sydney: Trustees of the Australian Museum, 1887).

[212] Turnbull, 'Ramsay's Regime', 116.

[213] Turnbull, 'Australian Museums, Aboriginal Skeletal Remains, and the Imagining of Human Evolutionary History', 73.

[214] On Morton, see Ann Fabian, *The Skull Collectors: Race, Science, and America's Unburied Dead* (Chicago: University of Chicago Press, 2010) Chapters 1 and 3.

Americana' (1839)[215], he analysed differences between five 'races' (Caucasian, Mongolian, American, Malay, and Ethiopian), based on measurements of the form, size, and capacity of skulls. He examined crania from more than forty American Indian populations and contrasted them with Caucasian or Asian crania. His measurements suggested that Native Americans had a smaller internal brain capacity and were thus intellectually inferior.[216] Based on analysis of 52 Caucasian and 147 American skulls, he found that American Indian crania were smaller and had a lower brain volume (80 cubic inches), compared to Caucasian crania (87 cubic inches).[217]

Morton grounded racial differences in the separate origins of races. One of the most contested features of his methodology was that he associated brain capacity with intelligence. In this way, his comparative racial anatomy directly supported prevailing racial stereotypes. He qualified Caucasians as a superior race and characterized Anglo Saxons as 'extraordinary people'. He wrote:

> Inferior to no one of the Caucasian families in intellectual endowments, and possessed of indomitable courage and unbounded enterprise, it has spread its colonies widely over Asia, Africa and America; and, the mother of the Anglo-American family, it has already peopled the new world with a race in no respect inferior to the parent stock.[218]

Morton's findings on racial superiority were challenged by other studies. For instance, German anatomist Friedrich Tiedemann (1781–1861), who had carried out measurements of brain weight in the 1830s, openly refuted the idea that cranial capacity coincides with intelligence. He noted that: 'The principal result of my researches on the brain of the Negro, is, that neither anatomy nor physiology can justify our placing them beneath the Europeans in a moral or intellectual point of view.'[219] However, Morton's studies became highly influential. He was recognized as one of the leading craniologists of his time, and a founder of 'physical anthropology in America'.[220] His measurements and theories on racial differences and inferiority[221] supported policies of racial submission, slavery, and segregation.

---

[215] Samuel G. Morton, *Crania Americana: Or a Comparative View of the Skulls of the Various Aboriginal Nations of North and South America* (Philadelphia: J. Dobson, 1839).

[216] Andrew Gulliford, 'Bones of Contention: The Repatriation of Native American Human Remains' (1996) 18 *The Public Historian* 119–143, 122–123.

[217] Morton, *Crania Americana*, 260. The capacity of American crania was corrected from 82 to 80 cubic inches.

[218] Ibid, 17.

[219] Friedrich Tiedemann, 'On the Brain of the Negro, Compared with that of the European and the Orang-Outang' (1836) 126 *Philosophical Transactions of the Royal Society London* 497–527, 525 https://archive.org/details/philtrans05355391/mode/2up.

[220] Gulliford, 'Bones of Contention', 122.

[221] Stephen Jay Gould, 'Morton's Ranking of Races by Cranial Capacity: Unconscious Manipulation of Data May Be a Scientific Norm' (1978) 200 *Science* 503–509.

He assembled a massive collection of skulls under the umbrella of science. He collected hundreds of crania, including skulls of criminals, native chiefs, or children through his networks or sometimes from unmarked graves. This collecting mania made it socially acceptable to treat human remains as scientific objects. As Andrew Gulliford has noted, the 'supposed link between skulls, brain capacity, intelligence, and race' encouraged the 'wholesale looting of thousands of Indian burials and a brisk, purportedly scientific trade in human remains from the 1830s to the 1930s'.[222] Crania became commodities:

> Indian skulls had a dollar value, and amateur scientists or philosophers collected Indian skulls and relics much as one would collect butterflies or categorize types of birds. It is no accident that vast collections of skeletal remains, grave goods, and Indian artifacts came to repose in the Smithsonian Institution's National Museum of Natural History along with elephant tusks, ostrich eggs, and reptile skins. Indian grave robbing became a fashionable gentleman's avocation in the pursuit of knowledge.[223]

This commodification changed methods of collection in the 1860s. Building on emerging science on the classification of races, natural history museums expanded the collection of indigenous skulls.[224] Collecting became an 'industry'.[225] Collectors searched graves and burial sites for native bones, often in violation of customs of Native American tribes. The Medical Museum of the US Army, which was originally set up in 1862 to study injuries inflicted in warfare, developed an interest in collecting human remains.[226] It built one the first museum collections, with the help of medical officers, drawing on Morton's work on comparative racial anatomy. The museum actively stimulated collection through its appeal to scientific interest in the study of race, humanity, and the human body.

The founder of the museum, Surgeon General William A. Hammond, called on officers to collect 'all specimens of morbid anatomy, surgical or medical, which may be regarded as valuable'.[227] Collection focused on the remains of indigenous groups, and in particular American Indians. According to the understanding of the Surgeon General, this collection was deemed to 'aid the progress of anthropological science by obtaining measurements of a large number of skulls of

---

[222] Gulliford, 'Bones of Contention', 123.
[223] Ibid, 123.
[224] Samuel James Redman, *Human Remains and the Construction of Race and History, 1897–1945* (PhD Berkeley, University of California, 2012) 18.
[225] Gulliford, 'Bones of Contention', 124.
[226] Redman, *Human Remains and the Construction of Race and History*, 20 ff.
[227] William A. Hammond, Surgeon General, circular proclaiming intention to establish the Army Medical Museum (21 May 1862). Document published by Armed Forces Institute of Pathology, 12.

the aboriginal races of North America.[228] Circulars from the mid-1860s indicate that the museum was keen to acquire 'specimens of Indian crania and of Indian weapons and utensils'.[229] The scientific purpose of collection and the public nature of the call triggered a broad reaction. They began to receive shipments with human remains from the US and abroad, often with detailed description of race, tribe, age, or gender. Remains were collected from graves or the battlefield. For instance, provenance records indicate that the museum obtained crania from the battles at Sand Creek or Little Big Horn.[230] Sometimes, officers severed the skulls of deceased American Indians and sent them to the museum.[231] The collection included a significant number of remains of females, acquired from graves or massacres.[232] The museum also began to collect the remains of African Americans and people from other parts of the world. In 1876, it produced a catalogue for the 1876 World's Fair, showcasing the research on comparative anatomy.[233] In 1898, the collection and more than 3,000 remains, including over 2,000 skulls 'representing mainly the Indian tribes, ancient and modern, of North America',[234] were moved to the National Museum of National History of the Smithsonian Institution.

The controversial purposes of comparative racial anatomy pursued by the collection of remains in the nineteenth century were later challenged by influential anthropologists such as Franz Boas or Aleš Hrdlička (1869–1943),[235] the head of the newly established Division of Physical Anthropology at the Smithsonian institution in 1903.[236] Both opposed strict theories of racial classification and argued that human diversity resulted from distinct environments.[237] However, the history of the Army Medical Museum illustrates the close entanglement between racial science, military power, and the suppression and 'othering' of Native Americans. As Samuel Redman has noted, 'the combined work of scholars like Morton and those at the Army Medical Museum' provided the 'foundation for the rapid expansion of museum collections of human remains in the United States'.[238]

[228] Redman, *Human Remains and the Construction of Race and History*, 22, referring to a circular of the Surgeon General from 1867.

[229] Gulliford, 'Bones of Contention', 124, referring to a communication from Madison Mills, Surgeon, United States Army, Surgeon General's Office (13 January 1868).

[230] Redman, *Human Remains and the Construction of Race and History*, 23.

[231] Ibid, 25.

[232] Ibid, 28, fn. 95, referring to relative gender parity in the collection, based on the figures of the Smithsonian Institution.

[233] List of Skeletons and Crania in the Section of Comparative Anatomy of the United States Army Medical Museum for use during the International Exposition of 1876 in Connection with the Representation of the Medical Department U.S. Army (Washington D.C.: Army Medical Museum, 1876).

[234] Redman, *Human Remains and the Construction of Race and History*, 42.

[235] Frank Spencer, *Aleš Hrdlička M.D., 1869–1943: A Chronicle of the Life and Work of an American Physical Anthropologist* (PhD, University of Michigan, 1979).

[236] Redman, *Human Remains and the Construction of Race and History*, 46–47.

[237] Franz Boas, 'Some Recent Criticisms of Physical Anthropology', (1899) 1 *American Anthropologist* 98, 100.

[238] Redman, *Human Remains and the Construction of Race and History*, 18.

The discriminate effect of the search for remains in the name of science on indigenous populations is reflected in the composition of the collection of the Smithsonian Institution. The remains of American Indians represent more than 50 per cent of the more than 30,000 specimens in the collection. This figure is clearly in 'excess of any statistical Indian representation in the American population.'[239]

In other instances, native bodies were collected for medical experiments. For instance, in the 1880s German microbiologist Eduard Arning (1855–1936) exhumed of the bodies of natives on the island of Molokai on Hawaii to curb the spread of epidemic disease brought about by European and US colonial expansion.[240] He ordered the opening of graves and favoured the application of the death penalty in order to carry out autopsies. He also carried out experiments on living subjects. In 1884, he sought permission from His Majesty's Privy Council to test leprosy transmission on a convicted person named Keanu, who had been sentenced to death for murder by Hawaiian courts. The Privy Council agreed to commute his sentence, in order to facilitate the experiment. On 30 September 1884, Arning transferred tissue from a girl infected with leprosy onto Keanu's arm. The experiment was discussed in the *British Medical Journal*. Henry Press Wright, Archdeacon of the Church of England, defended the power of the state to grant or take lives of criminals for the purpose of civilization. He wrote in an article entitled 'The Inoculability of Leprosy': 'The State, which could take life for the terror of evil doers, could also grant life in order to stay, if possible, in some degree, the advance of the most terrible disease that tortures man.'[241] The incident shows how colonial powers embedded violence against native subjects within narratives of reason and scientific progress. Keanu became deaf and blind and died of leprosy on 18 November 1892.[242]

5.2 The story of Sarah Baartman ('The Black Venus')

The close link between human stereotypes and scientific racism is illustrated by the story of the body of Sarah Baartman[243] (mid-1770–1815).[244] Baartman was a

---

[239] Gulliford, 'Bones of Contention', 126.

[240] On the close links between empire and public health, see Sheldon J. Watts, *Epidemics and History: Disease, Power and Imperialism* (New Haven: Yale University Press, 1997).

[241] Henry Press White, 'The Inoculability of Leprosy' (1888) 2 *The British Medical Journal* (1888) 1359.

[242] Kerri A. Inglis, "Cure the Dread Disease": 19th Century Attempts to Treat Leprosy in the Hawaiian Islands' (2009) 43 *Hawaiian Journal of History* 101–124, 111–112.

[243] Yvette Abrahams, 'Disempowered to Consent: Sara Bartman and Khoisan Slavery in the Nineteenth-Century Cape Colony and Britain' (1996) 35 *South African Historical Journal* 89–114; Sadiah Qureshi, 'Displaying Sara Baartman, The "Hottentot Venus"' (2004) 42 *History of Science* 233–257; Pamela Scully and Clifton Crais, 'Race and Erasure: Sara Baartman and Hendrik Cesars in Cape Town and London' (2008) 47 *Journal of British Studies* 301–323; Clifton Crais and Pamela Scully, *Sara Baartman and the Hottentot Venus: A Ghost Story and a Biography* (Princeton: Princeton University Press, 2009).

[244] Scully and Crais, 'Race and Erasure', 306. The exact date of birth remains disputed. Some have argued that she was born in 1789. However, she carried a child in the 1790s. Kirby argues that child was born in 1777. See Percival R. Kirby, 'The Hottentot Venus' (1949) 6 *Africana Notes and News* 55–61, 61.

Khoikhoi woman from the Eastern Cape in South Africa. Her story is complex. She was both a human curiosity and a political figure, showcasing the commodification of the black body, the intersection between gender and racial domination, and the growing resistance against such practices. During her lifetime, her body was commodified. After her death, her remains were used as an anthropological sample for scientific racism. After the apartheid regime, her life story was seen as a reflection of the history of the nation in South Africa. Only after 192 years following her departure from the Cape were her remains returned to her homeland in 2002.

Baartman's indigenous name is not known. She first served as a servant, and was then brought by Dutch farmers to Cape Town (hence the Dutch name Saartjie, 'little Sarah'). She worked as a maid for an entrepreneur, Hendrik Cesars. She had a particularly curvy body shape, with large buttocks, based on a genetic condition known as steatopygia. Cesars presented her in shows for patients in a local hospital to gain additional income. This is where she came into contact with Scottish military surgeon Alexander Dunlop, who exported animal and museum specimens from the Cape. He proposed to display her in shows in Europe. In 1810, she was lured to travel to Britain, attracted by the promise of fame and the option of earning money through cultural performances. Cesars and Dunlop brought her to London, where she became popular as the 'Hottentot Venus'. She was put on display as a human and sexual curiosity in 'freak shows'. She was placed in a cage at the beginning of the performance, portraying her as a savage who needed to be tamed. At the end of the show, spectators were allowed to touch, pinch, or poke her body and curvaceous behind. Baartman passed away from illness in Paris in 1815.

Baartman's story gained significant symbolic importance because it represents both colonial exploitation and misrepresentation, as well as shifting political attitudes towards racism. She was traded as a commodity and treated with racial bias, even beyond her death. Dunlop marketed her 'racialized and sexualized identity'.[245] During her 'shows' in London, and later in Paris, she was represented as an exotic, savage woman, whose fascination lies in her 'otherness', namely her contrast to the 'civilised female'.[246] She was first presented as human curiosity, i.e. a 'freak', like giants or dwarfs.[247] When her presentation caused public protest, narratives shifted and she was shown as ethnographic curiosity from the south of Africa.[248]

Baartman was heavily dependent on her manager Cesars. Her display and treatment conflicted with the campaign against slavery, promoted by the abolitionist movement. Members of the African Institution, i.e. the successor of the

---

[245] Scully and Crais, 'Race and Erasure', 304.

[246] Qureshi, 'Displaying Sara Baartman', 239 ('the typological basis of alterity').

[247] See generally Sadiah Qureshi, *Peoples on Parade: Exhibitions, Empire and Anthropology in Nineteenth-Century Britain* (Chicago: University of Chicago Press, 2011).

[248] Scully and Crais, 'Race and Erasure', 304.

Society for the Abolition of Slave Trade, sought to terminate the spectacle and questioned whether she was acting of her own free will. Zachary Macaulay initiated proceedings against her 'employers' to determine whether she was held as a slave. Dunlop was able to show a contract in which Baartman stated that she was a domestic servant and agreed to shown in public in exchange for money.[249] The case was ultimately dropped by the court of King's Bench.[250] However, doubts remained as to the extent to which she was able to express free and voluntary consent, in light of her dependency, or forced into the arrangement by Cesars through violence.

After her death, her commodification and othering continued. Her body became an object of racial study. French anatomist Georges Cuvier (1769–1832) examined and dissected her remains. He produced a plaster cast of her body. He preserved her brain, genitalia, and skeleton as biological specimens, in order to support the view that Africans had more ape-like features than Europeans. He qualified Baartman as a 'bushwoman' ('Femme de race Boschimanne'),[251] i.e. as a human being on the lowest scale of evolutionary advancement. Her dissected body was put on display as a specimen of humanity in the Natural history Museum in Angers. It was later shown for more than 150 years as a sample of Khoikhoi anatomy in the ethnographic Museum of Man (*Musée de l'homme*).

Over time, the meaning attributed to her remains changed. She was no longer seen as a symbol of racial inferiority or body features, but rather as a personification of the commodification and trafficking of women, the perils of racial science, and the stereotypes and wrongs of the colonial past. In the 1950s, the Khoi people requested the return of her remains from France to South Africa. American palaeontologist Stephen Jay Gould (1941–2002) told her story in his critique of racial science at the beginning of the 1980s.[252] In post-apartheid South Africa, Baartman came to be seen as a symbol of the fate of African people and the violence, oppression, and exploitation caused by colonial domination and apartheid.[253] In 1994, President Nelson Mandela requested the return of her remains and plaster cast. However, France remained reluctant to meet this request, based on Baartman's

---

[249] Ibid, 320–321.

[250] Records regarding the Hottentot Venus (21–28 November 1810) British National Archives: Public Record Office, King's Bench 1/36/4.

[251] Georges Cuvier, '*Extrait d'observations faites sur le cadavre d'une femme connue à Paris et à Londres sous le nom de Vénus Hottentotte*' in Musée d'histoire naturelle, *Mémoires du Muséum d'histoire naturelle*, vol. 3 (Paris: Belin, 1817) 259–274, 264.

[252] Stephen Jay Gould, *The Mismeasure of Man* (New York, London: W.W. Norton, 1981); Stephen Jay Gould, 'The Hottentot Venus' (1982) 91 *Natural History* 20–27.

[253] In his speech at the funeral of Sarah Bartmann on 9 August 2002, South African President Thabo Mbeki said: 'It was not the abused human being who was monstrous but those who abused her. It was not the lonely African woman in Europe, alienated from her identity and her motherland who was the barbarian, but those who treated her with barbaric brutality.' See South Africa, Department of International Relations and Cooperation, Speech (9 August 2002) http://www.dirco.gov.za/docs/speec hes/2002/mbek0809.htm.

importance as national patrimony and continuing scientific interest.[254] In 1998, South African writer Diana Ferrus published a poem in tribute to Baartman, called 'I've come to take you home', in which she brought out the abuse and violence inflicted on her. She wrote:

I have come to wrench you away, away from the poking eyes of the man-made monster who lives in the dark with his clutches of imperialism, who dissects your body bit by bit, who likens your soul to that of Satan, and declares himself the ultimate God![255]

On 6 March 2002, the French parliament National Assembly, agreed to return the remains. She was buried on 9 August 2002 (Women's Day) in the Eastern Cape. President Thabo Mbeki recognized her political importance in a speech regarding the return, burial, and memorialization of Baartman. He said: 'The story of Sarah Baartman is the story of the African people of our country in all their echelons. It is a story of the loss of our ancient freedom. It is a story of our dispossession of the land and the means that gave us and independent livelihood.'[256] Her return was seen not only as a measure to restore her dignity and respect, but as a victory for all South Africans over colonial conquest. Baartman returned as a survivor, rather than as a victim.

5.3   Commodification in British/Irish relations: The body politics of Charles Byrne, 'the Irish Giant'

The commodification of human remains was not limited to non-European bodies, but also occurred in European settings. This is illustrated by the story of 'Irish giant' Charles Byrne (1761–1783), whose remains became a bone of contention in Northern Irish–British relations. Byrne was born in rural Tyrone in Northern Ireland and lived at the time before Ireland's union with Great Britain under the Acts of Union in 1800. He became a human curiosity because of his exceptional height. When he passed away, he was 2.31 metres tall. His physical condition was influenced by a hormonal condition which stimulated abnormal growth. He earned his living as a curiosity and was presented as a 'freak' in Edinburgh and London. He passed away in London at the age of 22. He requested friends to bury him in a sealed coffin at sea in order not to become an object of scientific research.[257] However,

---

[254] A French museum curator stated: 'We never know what science will be able to tell us in the future. If she is buried, this chance will be lost ... for us she remains a very important treasure.' See Qureshi, 'Displaying Sara Baartman', 246.

[255] Diana Ferrus, 'I've come to take you home: A tribute to Sarah Baartman' (June 1998).

[256] See Thabo Mbeki, Speech (9 August 2002).

[257] Len Doyal and Thomas Muinzer, 'Should the Skeleton of "The Irish Giant" Be Buried at Sea?' (2011) 343 *British Medical Journal* 1290–1292.

British surgeon John Hunter (1728–1793), who owned a large collection of anatomical specimens, reportedly bribed Byrne's friends to obtain the corpse before the funeral. He extracted his skeleton for preservation, violating Byrne's 'common right to burial'.[258] The skeleton became a hallmark of Hunt's private museum, and was later displayed for more than two centuries years at the Hunterian Museum in the Royal College of Surgeons, against Byrne's reported wishes.

The presentation of the Irish 'giant' in the Hunterian Museum triggered controversies as to the proper location of Byrne's remains, based on origin and kinship relations, and 'colonial discourses of difference' in the 'political and cultural relations' between the United Kingdom and Ireland.[259] His display evoked 'English colonial discourses of Irish primitivism'.[260] Irish citizens and parliamentarians, including the late novelist Hilary Mantel, have called for the relocation of the remains. Byrne has been equated to an 'imprisoned Irish citizen' by the 'Free Charles Byrne' campaign.[261] Thomas Muinzer has argued that the 'remains of Byrne are the cultural property of the Northern Irish, that the Hunterian Museum ought to divest itself of his skeleton on moral grounds, and that a burial ought to be carried out in Byrne's homeland at, or as near as possible to, the Giant's Grave'.[262]

The Hunterian Museum defended its decision to retain the skeleton, but agreed to remove it from display. In January 2023, the board of trustees of the Hunterian Museum issued a statement that the remains would no longer be shown. They acknowledged that: 'John Hunter (1728–1793) and other anatomists and surgeons of the 18th and 19th centuries acquired many specimens in ways we would not consider ethical today and which are rightly subject to review and discussion.'[263]

5.4 Science as accomplice to genocide: the hunt for skulls and remains in German South West Africa

One of the cruellest examples of the collection of body parts is the systematic collection of skulls in German South West Africa at the beginning of the twentieth century, in particular in the internment camps in Swakopmund and Shark Island in Lüderitz Bay.[264] In this context, entire populations were imprisoned. The camps

---

[258] Thomas Muinzer, 'A Grave Situation: An Examination of the Legal Issues Raised by the Life and Death of Charles Byrne, the "Irish Giant"' (2013) *International Journal of Cultural Property* 23–48, 30.

[259] Catherine Nash, 'Making Kinship with Human Remains: Repatriation, Biomedicine and the Many Relations of Charles Byrne' (2018) 36 *Environment and Planning D: Society and Space* 867–884, 871.

[260] Ibid, 873.

[261] Ibid, 872.

[262] Muinzer, 'A Grave Situation', 41.

[263] Board of Trustees of the Hunterian Collection, 'Statement on the skeleton of Charles Byrne from the Board of Trustees of the Hunterian Collection' (11 January 2023) https://www.rcseng.ac.uk/news-and-events/news/archive/statement-on-the-skeleton-of-charles-byrne/.

[264] Benjamin Madley, 'From Africa to Auschwitz: How German South West Africa Incubated Ideas and Methods Adopted and Developed by the Nazis in Eastern Europe' (2005) 35 *European History*

turned into 'skull production centres'.[265] Racial science served not only as 'a laboratory for genocide', but as 'a reminder of anthropology's complicity in Germany's trajectory'.[266] Dehumanization went beyond traditional trophy-taking, retribution, or expression of power. Scientific interest and demand in the metropolis turned skull production into a systematic practice. It provided an additional layer of meaning and authority to mistreatment, which broke traditional moral codes and military ethics and made soldiers and medical officers voluntary executioners of requests for collection. Women were instructed to remove the flesh from skulls of executed or deceased prisoners. Skulls and body parts were shipped to Germany in boxes as study material. The process was captured by photographs, which showed the skulls piled up as cargo goods. These practices reflected the brutality of the 'colonial corporeality' constituted through the interplay of 'anthropology and imperialism'.[267]

The removal of skulls and human remains from violent contexts was shaped by discriminatory world views on natives and 'Bushmen', which emerged in the 1860s. 'Hottentots' or 'Bushmen' were seen to reflect the lowest stage of advancement, while Europeans were regarded as the hallmark of evolution.[268] In scientific circles, natives and tribes were seen as important resources to trace the past of the human species. For instance, in 1869, German linguist Wilhelm Bleek (1827–1875) argued in his work *On the Origin of Language*, that 'bushmen' were important for scientific study, since they 'stand nearest to the apes'.[269] This position contrasted with the logics of colonial science and views of colonial officials, who argued that natives should either be developed through education or tutelage or eradicated.[270] For example, Paul Rohrbach (1869–1956), Germany's former Settlement Commissary in South West Africa, justified the extermination of the Nama in 1907, arguing that 'the Hottentots [Namas] are generally regarded, in the wider sense, as useless, and in this respect, provide no justification for the preservation of this race'.[271] The concept of the 'bushmen' was thus used in different ways in scientific discourse and (settler) colonial narratives. The 'metropole' shared an

Quarterly 429–464; Faber-Jonker, *More Than Just an Object*; Vilho Amukwaya Shigwedha, 'The Homecoming of Ovaherero and Nama Skulls: Overriding Politics and Injustices' (2018) 4 *Human Remains and Violence* 67–89.

[265] Harrison, 'Skulls and Scientific Collecting in the Victorian Military', 298.
[266] Benzl and Penny, 'Introduction: Rethinking German Anthropology, Colonialism, and Race', 18–19.
[267] Zimmerman, 'Adventures in the Skin Trade', 172.
[268] Christian Fetzer, 'Rassenanatomische Untersuchungen an 17 Hottentottenköpfen' (1913/14) 16 *Zeitschrift für Morphologie und Anthropologie* 95–156.
[269] Wilhelm Bleek, *The Origins of Language* (E. Haeckel (ed.), New York: Schmidt, 1869) 53.
[270] Robert Gordon, 'Gathering the Hunters: Bushmen in German (Colonial) Anthropology' in H. Glenn Penny and Matti Bunzl, *Worldly Provincialism: German Anthropology in the Age of Empire* (Michigan: University of Michigan Press, 2003) 256–82, 261.
[271] Paul Rohrbach, *Deutsche Kolonialwirtschaft*, I (Berlin-Schöneberg: Buchverlag der "Hilf", 1907) 349.

interest in collecting and 'salvaging' their 'relics', while 'many settlers' sought to 'exterminate them'.[272]

In the context of the Nama and Herero, the direct link between the German scientific community and colonial officials and collectors is well demonstrated. Felix von Luschan and Rudolf Virchow, who had studied skulls of American aborigines[273] and founded the German Anthropological Society, actively encouraged naval officers, colonial officials, military doctors, and private collectors to obtain and send anthropological material, including skulls and remains, to Berlin.[274] They collected several thousand skulls between 1885 and 1920, based on purchases, commissions, shipments, or donations from army officers, colonial officials, medical personnel, explorers, or employees of mining companies.[275] They were divided in three collections: the collection of Berlin Anatomical Institute, the skull collection of the Museum for Ethnology (S-collection), and the 'Virchow Collection'.[276] They issued questionnaires and elaborated detailed instructions ('Ethnographic Observation and Collection' pamphlets), in order to facilitate the collection, purchase, or trade of cultural objects and human remains. For instance, Virchow instructed collectors to preserve severed heads in 'zinc containers filled with alcohol'[277] and send them to Germany. The collection was supported by the 'lordly patronage' of the German Emperor and the treasury.[278]

Skulls and human remains were collected from different sources: Colonial prisons, hospitals, battlefields, or other museums or collections.[279] Adolf Bastian, who worked closely with Virchow, admitted openly that the ethnological collections were 'valuably enriched' by military operations and punitive expeditions.[280]

---

[272] Gordon, 'Gathering the Hunters: Bushmen in German (Colonial) Anthropology', 258.

[273] Virchow published his work 'Crania Ethnica Americana: a Choice Collection of American Skulls' in 1892.

[274] The Ethnological Museum in Berlin actively purchased and traded human remains.

[275] Holger Stoecker and Andreas Winkelmann, 'Skulls and Skeletons from Namibia in Berlin: Results of the Charité Human Remains Project' (2018) 4 *Human Remains and Violence* 5–26, 11 ('Collectors, senders and transporters of human remains from German South West Africa to the Berlin collections were in equal measure officers in the Imperial Schutztruppe (Konradin von Perbandt, Philalethes Kuhn, Otto Eggers, Richard Volkmann), colonial administrators (Berengar von Zastrow, Ralph Zürn), Stabsärzte (sta surgeons), government doctors and veterinarians (Albert Schöpwinkel, Anton Lübbert, Franz Goldammer, Karl Borchmann, Hugo Bonger, Hugo Zöllner, Joseph Seibert) as well as directors of mining companies (Heinrich Lotz, Paul Heimann). Likewise, German, Austrian and Swiss travellers and explorers (Waldemar Belck, Hans Schinz, Ludwig Sander, Franz Seiner, Eduard Moritz, Leonhard Schultze(-Jena), Hermann von Wissmann) took part in the transfer of skulls to Berlin. The Director of Deutsche Bank and patron of natural history collections, Arthur von Gwinner, may also be counted among those who delivered human skulls').

[276] Ibid, 8–10.

[277] Zimmerman, 'Adventures in the Skin Trade', 167.

[278] Felix von Luschan, 'Der Kaiser und die Wissenschaft' in Adolf von Aschenbach and Georg Bürenstein, *Unser Kaiser, Fünfundzwanzig Jahre der Regierung Kaiser Wilhelm II 1888–1913* (Berlin: Bong & Co., 1913) 259, 278.

[279] For instance, the museum traded with American museums and traders and acquired a large number of Native American human remains as of the late 1870s. Von Luschan exhumed eighty-three bodies in Hawaii in 1914.

[280] Zimmerman, *Anthropology and Antihumanism in Imperial Germany*, 156.

Von Luschan did not want to encourage collectors to kill 'bushmen' for their skulls[281] or to rob graves. However, he followed colonial violence, including local rebellions, and did not consider it inappropriate to seek the acquisition of skulls of defeated enemies. For instance, in 1906, he communicated with colonial officials in German East Africa about the remains of persons killed in the Maji Maji uprising.[282] Such collection was delicate, since it easily increased tensions with locals and complicated colonial administration. For example, in 1908, von Luschan made a request to the Colonial Office to acquire remains from South West Africa. It was denied, since German authorities considered societal peace ('political calm') in the protectorate more important in the 'current situation' than 'the interests of science.'[283]

Von Luschan used the context of violence, and his network to obtain skulls from the German campaign against the Nama and Herero. This is demonstrated by correspondences with Lieutenant Ralf Zürn, the German commander in Okahandja. Zürn played a key role in the conflict. He had been in charge of transfer of the transfer of ancestral land and had ordered the exhumation of skulls from Herero graves in 1903, which was one of the causes of the rebellion.[284] He interpreted the arrival of 100 Herero in January 1904 as an attack on the German settlement, which set off the subsequent extermination campaign.[285] In April 1905, Luschan requested Zürn to gather 'a larger collection of Herero skulls for scientific investigation.'[286] Zürn consulted his counterpart in Swakopmund and admitted that the conditions were conducive to collection. He wrote:'[I]n the concentration camps taking and preserving the skulls of Herero prisoners of war will be more readily possible than in the country, where there is always a danger of offending the ritual feelings of the natives.'[287] Zürn was recalled from duty later in 1904. However, he donated a skull taken from a Herero grave in Okahandja to the Berlin Museum. Thus, one of the first skulls which entered the collection was offered by a colonial officer, whose actions contributed to the rebellion and initiated the cycle of violence, leading to the historical genocide.[288]

As Zürn predicted, the establishment of the camps at Swakopmund and Shark Island created a whole machinery for the supply of skulls. The number of human remains and specimens traced in German collections grew significantly during

---

[281] Zimmerman, 'Adventures in the Skin trade', 170.

[282] Ibid, 171, fn. 51.

[283] Ibid, 176, referring to correspondence from the Imperial Colonial Office to Felix von Luschan (1 June 1908) MfV, IB 39, vol. 3, 1057/08.

[284] David Olusoga and Casper W. Erichsen, *The Kaiser's Holocaust: Germany's Forgotten Genocide And The Colonial Roots of Nazism* (London: Faber and Faber, 2010) 128.

[285] Ibid, 126.

[286] Zimmerman, 'Adventures in the Skin Trade', 174, referring to Luschan to Oberleutnant Zürn (15 April 1905, 21 June 1905) MfV, IB 39, vol. 1, 775/05.

[287] Ibid, 175, referring to Oberleutnant Zürn to Felix von Luschan (25 June 1905) MfV, IB 39, vol. 1, 775/05.

[288] Faber-Jonker, *More than Just an Object*, 48.

this period. The camps provided an environment for systematic collecting, with easy access to bodies. They led to 'skulduggery'.[289] This is illustrated by a famous photograph taken at Swakopmund between 1905 and 1906, which was turned into a postcard. It shows a group of military officers loading 'Herero skulls designated for German museums and universities' onto a wooden crate.[290]

The camp at Shark Island in Lüderitz Bay became notorious for skull collecting and experiments. It hosted several thousands of Herero and Nama people. It was also called 'The Death Camp', with a mortality rate of 70 per cent. The chief physician at field hospital XII, Hugo Bofinger (1876–1946), was heavily involved in the collection, preservation, and shipment of skulls. He carried out experiments on prisoners. He injected inmates suffering from scurvy, a disease caused by vitamin C deficiency, with different substances, including arsenic and opium in order to test whether the illness was contagious. He also severed the heads of 'several dozen' dead prisoners,[291] and the head of a one-year-old Nama girl, preserved them in alcohol and sent them to Berlin. Several hundreds of bodies were dissected at Shark Island every year. Anatomist Wilhelm von Waldeyer (1836–1921), the Director of the Anatomical Institute, and Paul Bartels (1874–1914), a scientist, received Herero and Nama body parts from the camps.[292] At least twenty skulls from Nama and Herero from Shark Island were officially included and listed in the anatomical collection of the Charité in Berlin.[293] The 'S collection' hosted the remains of at least twenty-nine individuals collected in South West Africa and sent to Berlin between 1896 and 1912.[294] Some documentation was lost. It must thus be assumed that the inventory of both collections was 'originally far more extensive'.[295]

The context provided space for opportunists to become part of the body trade. For instance, Leonard Schultze (1872–1955), a zoologist, who had originally come to South West Africa to collect and preserve animals, turned to the hunt for human remains. He noted in the report of his mission between 1903 and 1905: 'I could put to use the victims of the war and take parts from fresh native corpses, which made a welcome addition to the study of the living body (imprisoned Hottentots

---

[289] Reinhart Kößler, 'Imperial Skulduggery, Science and the Issue of Provenance and Restitution: The Fate of Namibian Skulls in the Alexander Ecker Collection in Freiburg' (2018) 4 *Human Remains and Violence* 27–44.

[290] Walter von Damm, *Meine Kriegserlebnisse in Deutsch-Südwestafrika* (Minden: Wilhelm Köhler, 1907) 114.

[291] Stoecker and Winkelmann, 'Skulls and Skeletons from Namibia in Berlin: Results of the Charité Human Remains Project', 12.

[292] Waldeyer received inter alia preserved brains. Fifty-three preserved larynxes of Herero and Nama people and preserved heads were sent to Bartels. Bartels acknowledged that he obtained a large number of heads of 'prisoners-of-war' in South-West Africa.

[293] Stoecker and Winkelmann, 'Skulls and Skeletons from Namibia in Berlin: Results of the Charité Human Remains Project', 8.

[294] Ibid, 9.

[295] Ibid, 9.

[Nama] were often at my disposal)'.[296] He later published a study on 'the Bodies of the Hottentots and Bushmen'.[297]

The anthropologist Eugen Fischer (1874–1967), who later became director of the Kaiser Wilhelm Institute for Anthropology, Human Hereditary Teaching and Eugenics and was complicit in the eugenic and racial policies of the Third Reich,[298] came to South West Africa to study the phrenology of the Herero and the Nama. He visited the internment camps and carried out experiments on race. He examined and measured the skulls of hundreds of prisoners and studied children, in order to demonstrate that native races (Hottentots) and mixed-race children from white men and native women are of 'lesser racial quality'. He removed native bodies from graves for the purpose of his studies. His research crossed the boundary between physical anthropology (*Rassenkunde*) and scientific racism. It foreshadowed theories on 'racial hygiene' and experiments during the Holocaust. Adolf Hitler reportedly consulted his work on 'The Principles of Human Heredity and Race Hygiene' during his imprisonment in Landsberg. Fischer's ideas influenced eugenicist Otmar Freiherr von Verschuer (1896–1969), who worked at the Kaiser Wilhelm Institute and taught the physician at Auschwitz, Joseph Mengele.

These contacts and networks show how closely colonial violence and racial science were intertwined in the collection of human remains. Indigenous skulls and body parts had different identities. In the logic of collectors, they were both trophies and symbols of the superiority of colonial powers and the 'White man', and at the same time natural objects, with material value and significance for science and prestige. As Andrew Zimmerman has emphasized, this dual character made it easier to justify the violence of collection: 'By donating to 'science' the body parts they perhaps originally took as trophies, Zürn ... and others perhaps sought to exculpate their own barbarism.'[299] In the collections, they became objects of racial study and commodities. However, they remained at the same 'more than objects'.[300] They continued to represent subjects in the eyes of affected native populations. They are also 'witnesses to history', reflecting the violence of German imperial policy and the cruel 'body politics' replicated in the holocaust.

---

[296] Leonard Schultze, *Zoologische und anthropologische Ergebnisse einer Forschungsreise im westlichen und zentralen Südafrika. Ausgeführt in den Jahren 1903–1905, Erster Band: Systematik und Tiergeographie* (Jena: Gustav Fischer, 1908) viii.

[297] Leonhard Schultze, *Zur Kenntnis des Körpers der Hottentotten und Buschmänner* (Jena: Gustav Fischer, 1928).

[298] Eugen Fischer prepared inter alia expert opinions on race for Nazi officials and provided training on 'racial science'. In 1933, he endorsed the 'biological population policy' of the Nazi government, while disputing the inferiority of German Jews. He later joined the Nazi Party and participated in discussion on extermination in 1941. See Richard F. Wetzell, 'Eugenics, Racial Science, and Nazi Biopolitics' in Devin O. Pendas, Mark Roseman, and Richard F. Wetzel, *Beyond the Racial State: Rethinking Nazi Germany* (Cambridge: Cambridge University Press, 2017) 147–175.

[299] Zimmerman, 'Adventures in the Skin Trade', 177.

[300] Faber-Jonker, *More than Just an Object*.

5.5 Bio-colonialism and the collection of fossil remains

Evolutionary theory and racial distinctions shaped not only the collection of human remains in colonial contexts, but also the search for human origins and specimen.[301]

Nineteenth-century narratives about the human past were driven by scientific theories which sought to maintain control over evolutionary history.[302] They portrayed human evolution through migration, group, and hierarchies. Darwin had argued that the origins of the human species lay in Africa.[303] Other evolutionary scientists located these origins in Asia, based on Asia's alleged superiority to Africa ('Out of Asia theory'). German biologist Ernst Haeckel (1834–1919), a strong defender of Darwinism, claimed that there must be intermediate evolutionary stages between apes and humans, i.e. a transitional 'ape-like man'.[304] Colonial expansion in Africa and Asia provided a window of opportunity to explore these origins.

A milestone was the discovery of the so-called 'Java Man' by Dutch naturalist Eugène Dubois (1858–1940). Dubois was obsessed with the idea of finding the connection between human and non-human apes. He sought to encourage the Dutch Colonial Office to carry out an expedition to the Dutch East Indies to search for fossils, and ultimately joined the army as a medical officer for that purpose. He assumed that the Dutch East Indies were an appropriate location for the search in light of the climate conditions and wildlife, including gibbons and fossil apes. He carried out excavations on the island of Java in in 1891 and 1892, with the assistance of the Dutch colonial government, local interlocutors, and forced labourers. In October 1891, his workers unearthed a skullcap at Trinil that differed from traditional apes. Dubois noted the unusual the cranial capacity, which 'was higher and larger than that of the recent chimpanzee and substantially more human-like'.[305] He was persuaded that he had found the 'missing link' between human and ape and referred to it as *Pithecanthropus erectus* ('upright ape-man'), a human-like transitional form from Java, borrowing from Haeckel. He treated the find as his personal property, although it was retrieved by forced labourers, and took it back to the Netherlands in 1895. It became known as the 'Java Man'. The object represented

---

[301] Sheela Athreya and Rebecca Rogers Ackermann, 'Colonialism and Narratives of Human Origins in Asia and Africa' in Martin Porr and Jacqueline M. Matthews (eds.), *Interrogating Human Origins: Decolonisation and the Deep Past* (London: Routledge 2019) 23–42.

[302] Peter Bowler, *Theories of Human Evolution: A Century of Debate, 1988–1944* (Oxford: Blackwell, 1986); Roger Lewin, *Bones of Contention: Controversies in the Search for Human Origins* (Chicago: University of Chicago Press, 1997).

[303] Charles Darwin, *The Descent of Man, and Selection in Relation to Sex* (London: John Murray, 1871).

[304] Ernst Haeckel, *The History of Creation* (London: 4th edn, Kegan Paul, Trench, Trubner & Co., 1892) 397.

[305] John de Vos, 'The Dubois Collection: A New Look at An Old Collection' in Cor Winkler Prins and S. K. Donovan (eds.), VII International Symposium 'Cultural Heritage in Geosciences, Mining and Metallurgy: Libraries, Archives, Museums': "Museums and their collections", Leiden (The Netherlands), 19–23 May 2003, (2004) 4 *Scripta Geologic* 267–85, 271.

the oldest human specimen known at the time. It was later placed in the natural history museum in Leiden.[306] It brought him scientific prestige, but also caused controversy and critique. His theory was contested by other scientists. Some denied the link of the fossils to modern humans and regarded them as an example of a deformed species of ape. Others continued to argue that European ancestry derived from the 'Neanderthal Phase of Man' (Aleš Hrdlička)[307] or from Africa ('Out of Africa theory').

It took more than three decades until the significance of Dubois' excavation was confirmed by other finds and excavations. In the mid-1920s, Australian anthropologist Raymond Dart (1893–1988) and British/South African palaeontologist Robert Broome (1866–1951) qualified the 'Taung child', i.e. a 2.5 million-year-old fossilized skull, as the evidence of the link between African apes and humans in the history of evolution. The skull was collected by a quarryman of the Northern Lime Company in the town of Taung in South Africa. Dart was the first to establish the connection. He argued that the skull exceeded the brain size of apes and interpreted it as confirmation of human ancestry. He qualified it as *Australopithecus africanus*, i.e. an extinct race of 'man-ape of South Africa',[308] tracing human evolution back to Africa. His theories on human origin continued to face resistance in Europe until the 1950s. For instance, British anatomist Arthur Keith (1866–1955), who defended Eurocentric models of human ancestry and segregation of Caucasian, mongoloid, and negroid races,[309] argued that the skull is merely that of a young gorilla.[310]

In 1929, Chinese geologist Péi Wénzhōng (1904–1982) discovered the complete skullcap of another *Homo erectus* at a cave in the village of Zhoukoudian, near to Beijing, as part of an excavation by Western and Chinese scientists.[311] It was qualified as a human fossil and named *Sinanthropus pekinensis* ('Chinese man of Peking' or 'Peking Man') based on its cranial capacity and alleged age.[312] Canadian paleoanthropologist Davidson Black (1884–1934) interpreted it as an indication of a 'new genus of man',[313] following earlier studies of a tooth found in 1927. Its discovery was used to challenge African or European origins. German anthropologist Franz Weidenreich (1873–1948) argued that Peking Man was the direct ancestor of

---

[306] In July 2022, Indonesia requested the return of the remains of the Java Man.

[307] Aleš Hrdlička, 'The Neanderthal Phase of Man' (1927) 57 *The Journal of the Royal Anthropological Institute of Great Britain and Ireland* 249–74.

[308] Raymond Dart, '*Australopithecus africanus*: The Man-Ape of South Africa' (1925) 115 *Nature* 195–199.

[309] Arthur Keith, 'The Evolution of the Human Races' (1928) 58 *The Journal of the Royal Anthropological Institute of Great Britain and Ireland* 305–321.

[310] Arthur Keith, 'The Taungs Skull' (1925) 116 *Nature* 11.

[311] Jia Lanpo and Huang Weiwen, *The Story of Peking Man: From Archaeology to Mystery* (Yin Zhiqi tr, Beijing: Foreign Languages Press & Oxford: Oxford University Press, 1990).

[312] Hsiao-Pei Yen, 'Evolutionary Asiacentrism, Peking Man, and the Origins of Sinocentric Ethno Nationalism' (2014) 47 *Journal of the History of Biology* 585–625.

[313] See 'Peking Man: The New Skulls and the Evolutionary Problem' (1937) 129 *Nature* 261–62, 261.

modern man and the 'missing link'.[314] In 1936, German palaeontologist Ralph von Koenigswald (1902–1982) discovered further skullcaps on Java with the help of locals. Ultimately, evolutionary biologist Ernst Walter Mayr (1904–2005) qualified both Java Man and Peking Man as *Homo erectus* in 1950.[315]

Both the finds of Java Man or the 'Taung child' and the scientific discourse over human fossils by Western scientists were deeply interconnected with colonial structures. As Caroline Drieënhuizen and Fenneke Sysling have argued, such remains are not simply 'scientific' or 'unpolitical objects with universal meanings', but rather political objects with colonial histories and enormous significance for identity.[316] They do not only present objective witnesses of a past natural history, but are the 'creations of modern science' and contemporary rationalities.[317] Their history shows how closely the narratives regarding the origins of human origins were intertwined with racial ideology and stereotypes regarding the inferiority of non-European people.[318]

The evidence relating to the discovery of the Asian or African ancestry of humans faced resistance for decades, since it was partly a challenge to the idea of Europe as cradle of 'mankind'. Authorities such as Ales Hrdlička or Arthur Keith[319] continued to argue that the origins of the modern *Homo sapiens* lie in Europe. Others preferred the 'Out of Asia' theory, based on implicit prejudices against Africa. Henry Fairfield Osburn (1857–1935), director of the American Museum of Natural History, disputed the value of the discovery of the Taung child, because he challenged the very idea that human ancestry could come from Africa.[320]

Later, European superiority continued to be defended by African primitivism and orientalism. The idea that the line of human descent emanated from Africa or Asia was not seen as incompatible with the assumed higher degree of civilization in Western nations. It was argued that people in Africa or Asia had not evolved as quickly as their Western counterparts beyond the early stages of evolution. In this way, colonial powers could concede that the ancestry of human lies in other continents, while maintaining the ethos of the civilizing mission.[321]

---

[314] Franz Weidenreich, '*Sinanthropus pekinensis* and Its Position in the Line of Human Evolution' (1936) 10 *Peking Natural History Bulletin* 1–56.

[315] Ernst Mayr, 'Taxonomic Categories in Fossil Hominids?' (1950) 15 *Cold Spring Harbor Symposium on Quantitative Biology* 109–118; Raymond A. Dart, 'Pithecanthropus and Australopithecus' (1960) 50 *Zeitschrift für Morphologie und Anthropologie* 261–74, 267

[316] Caroline Drieënhuizen and Fenneke Sysling, 'Java Man and the Politics of Natural History: An Object Biography' (2021) 177 *Bijdragen tot de Taal-, Land- en Volkenkunde* 290–311, 307.

[317] W. J. T. Mitchell, 'Objecthood and Empire' in W. J. T. Mitchell, *What Do Pictures Want? The Lives and Loves of Images* (Chicago: Chicago University Press, 2005) 145–168, 167.

[318] Bowler, *Theories of Human Evolution*, 15 ff.

[319] Arthur Keith, 'The Fossil Man of Peking' (1929) 214 *The Lancet* 683–685.

[320] Henry Fairfield Osborn, *Man Rises to Parnassus: Critical Epochs in the Pre-History of Man* (Princeton: Princeton University Press, 1927) 202; Henry Fairfield Osborn, 'Recent Discoveries Relating to the Origin and Antiquity of Man' (1927) 65 *Science* 481–488.

[321] Athreya and Rebecca Rogers Ackermann, 'Colonialism and Narratives of Human Origins in Asia and Africa', 27.

The explanation of human ancestry in evolutionary discourses reflects the role of power within knowledge production. It marked a form of 'scientific imperialism'.[322] Scientists treated people and their ancestors as objects. Colonial narratives shaped the interpretation of fossils. The bio-centric evolutionary model defended in certain Eurocentric scientific accounts supported colonial narratives of racial difference and hierarchy. Personalities, such as Dubois, Von Koenigswald, or Davidson Black benefited from colonial power structures. They relied heavily on local expertise and support to make their discoveries, but marginalized these contributions in historical accounts and built their own reputation and prestige based on the finds. In this way, 'science' also served as a means of disempowerment. It created new hierarchies of knowledge under the umbrella of science.

The human fossils were treated as 'natural history objects'. This label concealed some of the politics and biases of scientific interpretation and the conditions of their original taking. In the second half of the twentieth century, objects such as 'Java Man' or 'Peking Man' became the focal points of national identity politics. For instance, Indonesia has sought the return of the large collection of fossils retrieved by Eugène Dubois between 1887 and 1900, including the remains of the Java Man.

6 Conclusions

The collection of human remains is a particular category of 'colonial violence'.[323] It shows the centrality of the 'raced, sexed, classed' or 'ethnicized' body[324] as a site of colonial power. Body parts were essential to demonstrate 'colonial difference'[325] and to assert 'imperial difference' in connection to other colonial powers. Their treatment illustrates the contradictions of colonial discourse. Violent collecting practices challenged the basis of the alleged evolutionary or moral superiority of colonial powers, namely the imagined divide between civilizer and civilized. They turned civilizers into savages. Native populations became 'victims of progress'.[326] They were reduced to objects, dehumanized or destroyed through the interplay between economics, science, power, and colonial performance.

The collection and trade of remains dissociated body parts from their local cosmology. It involved separation, identity loss, or dehumanization and contributed to the demise or subordination of indigenous value systems or beliefs through

---

[322] Drieënhuizen and Sysling, 'Java Man and the Politics of Natural History: An Object Biography', 298.

[323] Van Eynde, *Bodies of the Weak*, 40.

[324] Lisa Skwirblies, *Theatres of Colonialism Theatricality, Coloniality, and Performance in the German Empire, 1884–1914* (PhD, University of Warwick, 2017) 105.

[325] Walter D. Mignolo and Madina Tlostanova, 'The Logic of Coloniality and the Limits of Postcoloniality' in Revathi Krishnaswamy and John C. Hawley (eds.), *The Postcolonial and the Global* (Minneapolis: University of Minnesota Press, 2007) 109–123, 110.

[326] John H. Bodley, *Victims of Progress* (Lanham, MD: Rowman & Littlefield Publishers, 2014).

global networks. Colonial powers benefited from these transactions in multiple ways. They gained economic benefit from transactions, and practised or tolerated head-taking in order to instil fear, provide retribution, or deter enemies, or otherwise increase their scientific reputation.

Collectors were not only captives of ideological or racial prism of their time. They provided the materials for racial or imperial theories and were complicit in the construction of a new classificatory system which ordered human society along hierarchical lines.[327] They profited from this system.[328] Explorers and traders could justify collection and commercialization in the name of science. Soldiers and medical officers obtained recognition or honour for appropriation of remains. Museums and medical science institutions gained relevance, voice, or power in discourse, through their acquisitions, studies, and systematic collections. Colonial powers enhanced their own standing and prestige through acquisition, or used racial research to gain power over local knowledge systems or shape their own self-understanding.

Human remains gained a new identity through these practices. They were not only transformed from subjects into objects, but recast as emblems of 'a primitive racial type'[329] or 'specimens of racial science'.[330] In many cases, they were anonymized, anatomized, stored in boxes, numbered and registered, and displayed as 'objects of race, species and evolution'[331] or simply forgotten. The remains of historical figures were guarded as trophies of war or awarded new meanings. Today, they have relevance to colonized and colonial societies alike. They stand as witnesses to colonial violence and as a 'means to challenge' the very 'systems of power' that facilitated identity loss and dehumanization.[332]

The human body was not the only site of violent collecting. Cultural and social bonds, indigenous ways of living, and human environments were destroyed through the interplay of different types of collecting: ethnographic collecting, the taking of 'bio-cultural objects',[333] and natural history collecting. The bio-politics of colonial discourse extended to human fossils. Many of them were collected by individuals through a network of colonial structures. They were presented as universal natural history objects, but served to rationalize theories of human differences or establish new hierarchies of knowledge. This makes it necessary to contextualize

---

[327] Van Eynde, *Bodies of the Weak*, 170.

[328] Ibid, 208 ('collecting men saw the acquisition of the indigenous dead as "a means of self-fashioning". They all sought to advance the cause of science, but in the process, they hoped to secure their own financial futures, launch their professional careers, and hone their social personas').

[329] Nicky Rousseau, Riedwaan Moosage, and Ciraj Rassool, 'Missing and Missed: Rehumanisation, the Nation and Missing-ness' (2018) 44 *Kronos* 10–32, 17.

[330] Ibid, 21.

[331] Ibid, 24.

[332] Van Eynde, *Bodies of the Weak*, 337; Rassool, 'Re-storing the Skeletons of Empire', 653.

[333] Danielle L. Gilbert, 'Possessing Natural Worlds: Life and Death in Biocultural Collections' (2022) 25 *Locus-Tijdschrift voor Cultuurwetenschappen* https://edu.nl/d476x.

historical perspectives on scientific collections and revisit their contribution to Western knowledge production, 'biocolonialism', and the epistemic violence of scientific discourses. They may well qualify as cultural objects in contemporary relations, even if they were originally not attached to any particular nationality.[334]

The return of skulls and remains is an important element to reverse colonial legacies. Skulls, human remains, and fossils are more than objects or human biological material. The rich history of return claims shows that they may carry equal or even more importance to nations and communities than cultural objects. This is visibly illustrated by the claims for return of Māori heads, the skulls taken by Germany from Namibia, the stories of the Mkwawa head, or the remains of Sarah Baartman. The debate on return based on colonial relations has also reached prehistoric objects in natural history collections. This is shown by requests for return of human fossils, such as Java Man[335] or the 'Zinjanthropus boisei' skull (Nutcracker Man), one of the most important early fossils found in Africa, which was taken by British archaeologists Mary and Louis Leakey in 1959 from Tanzania to Kenya, and requested back as national heritage.[336]

For a long time, the temporal and physical distance to societies of origin, the anonymity of skulls or body parts, the prioritization of scientific interests, and the collecting mania of museums, institutions, or individuals have impeded discussion of the ethical and legal elements of the treatment of human remains in Western collections and public spaces. However, the tide is turning. As former Zimbabwean President Robert Mugabe noted in 2015, 'keeping decapitated heads as war trophies, in this day and age, in a national history museum, must rank among the highest forms of racist moral decadence, sadism and human insensitivity'.[337]

Issues surrounding the collection, display, and return of human remains have gained greater attention at the end of the twenty-first century. It is increasingly questioned whether museums should hold and study human remains if their acquisition was not based on free and voluntary consent. While some voices contend that repatriation may constrain freedom of scientific inquiry[338] or foster romanticized indigenous world views,[339] many museums have stopped displaying them based on their link to personhood and dignity. Indigenous representatives claim

---

[334] Stewens, Raja, and Dunne, 'The Return of Fossils Removed Under Colonial Rule', 79.

[335] Nina Siegal, 'Dispute Over Java Man Raises a Question: Who Owns Prehistory?' *New York Times* (9 November 2022).

[336] Amy Staniforth, 'Returning Zinj: Curating Human Origins in Twentieth-century Tanzania' (2009) 3 *Journal of Eastern African Studies* 153–173.

[337] David Smith, 'Robert Mugabe Tells Natural History Museum to Return Human Skulls' *The Guardian* (13 August 2015).

[338] Elizabeth Weiss, 'The Bone Battle: The Attack on Scientific Freedom' (2009) 23 *Liberty* 39–45.

[339] See Elizabeth Weiss and James Springer, *Repatriation and Erasing the Past* (Gainesville: University of Florida Press, 2020). For a critique, see Siân Halcrow and others, 'Moving Beyond Weiss and Springer's Repatriation and Erasing the Past: Indigenous Values, Relationships, and Research' (2021) 28 *International Journal of Cultural Property* 211–20.

that retaining their human remains in museums makes them 'second-class' citizens.[340] It is disputed whether it is possible to own the rights to part of a person.[341] Legally, retention and display of human remains conflicts the protection of human dignity, post mortem rights, or the derivative rights of descendants to bury and to mourn.

The World Archaeological Congress has adopted the Vermillion Accord on Human Remains (1989)[342] and the Tamaki Makau-Rau Accord on the Display of Human Remains and Sacred Objects (2006),[343] which emphasize the centrality of the principles of 'respect' and 'agreement' between holders and affected communities. The Code of Ethics of International Council of Museums (ICOM) stipulates that human remains must be 'presented with great tact and respect for the feelings of human dignity held by all peoples' and 'displayed' consistent with professional standards and, 'where known, taking into account the interests and beliefs of members of the community, ethnic or religious groups from whom the objects originated'.[344] There is growing consensus in national frameworks, such as legislation (e.g. NAGPRA, UK Human Tissue Act 2004[345]) or guidelines[346] that human remains from colonial contexts should, in principle, be returned.[347] Repatriation does not necessarily entail a loss of science, but offers new prospects for consultation, collaborative research approaches, and to renew relations affected by postcolonial trauma and structural violence.[348]

Ethical concerns regarding the treatment of human remains extend to Egyptian mummies or prehistoric fossils. Egyptologists are divided as to whether mummies excavated by white explorers and archaeologists should continue be shown in public collections, since they are both bodies and archaeological artefacts.[349] The status of human fossils raises complex questions relating to the link between prehistory and modern cultural identity.[350] In light of their prehistoric origin, human

---

[340] Halcrow and others, 'Moving beyond Weiss and Springer's Repatriation and Erasing the Past', 214.

[341] Some communities even argue that digital reproductions of remains conflict with the personhood of deceased persons. See Sarah Wild, '3D Printing and the Murky Ethics of Replicating Bones' *Undark* (1 October 2020).

[342] World Archaeological Congress, Vermillion Accord, South Dakota (August 1989).

[343] World Archaeological Congress, Tamaki Makau-rau Accord on the Display of Human Remains and Sacred Objects, Osaka (January 2006).

[344] See ICOM Code of Ethics, 2017, section 4.3 'Exhibition of Sensitive Material'. See also ICOM Code of Ethics for Natural History Museums (2013).

[345] Section 47(2) of the Act allows specific national museums to de-accession human remains of persons who are reasonably believed to have died less than 1,000 years before the entry into force of the Act.

[346] E.g. German Framework Principles for Dealing with Collections from Colonial Contexts (13 March 2019).

[347] German Museum Association, *Care of Human Remains in Museums and Collections*, 53.

[348] Halcrow and others, 'Moving beyond Weiss and Springer's Repatriation and Erasing the Past', 216; Amber Aranui, 'Restitution or a Loss to Science? Understanding the Importance of Returning Māori Ancestral Remains' (2020) 18 *Museum & Society* 19–29.

[349] See Angela Stienne, 'The Egyptian Mummy in UK Museums: Cultural Histories and Object Biographies' (2016) 44 *Techne* 40–44.

[350] Siegal, 'Dispute Over Java Man Raises a Question', 15.

fossils lack a direct affiliation to the cultural identity of a specific society. However, they have often become a matter of identity politics over time and are protected by the right to access to culture.[351] The Belgian Advisory Committee on Bioethics has argued that 'the distinction between the historical period and the prehistoric period (human fossils) is neither useful nor ethically relevant, since all human fossils deserve the same level of attention'.[352] This makes contemporary debates on display or return relevant to natural history collections, which have tended to argue that they are non-political, scientific spaces. New forms of consent on ownership, shared stewardship, or display may be warranted if they were acquired through exploitation of colonial conditions or through flawed methods (e.g. coercion, fraud, or deception).

---

[351] Stewens, Raja, and Dunne, 'The Return of Fossils Removed Under Colonial Rule', 85.
[352] Belgian Advisory Committee on Bioethics, Opinion No. 82 of 9 January 2023, 37–38.

6

Law's Complicity in Cultural Takings and Colonial Violence: Double Standards, Discursive Silencing, and Social Transformation

1 Introduction

> No one colonizes innocently ... no one colonizes with impunity either
> (*Aimé Césaire*, 1950)[1]

This insight from Aimé Césaire's 'Discourse on Colonialism' (1950) 'captures not only the facets of the colonial condition, but also the different faces of the law in the colonial encounter.[2] Law in the broad sense, i.e. as a juridical field,[3] had an ambivalent role in the colonial context. It has imperial and counter-imperial features. It served as 'a mode of coercion', a form of discursive power, and catalyst of 'social transformation'.[4] It became 'part of the structure of violence'.[5] It provided a system that constituted colonial relations,[6] defined colonial subjects and subjectivities,[7]

---

[1] Aimé Césaire, *Discourse on Colonialism* (New York: Monthly Review Press, 2001 [1950]) 39.
[2] See generally Antony Anghie, *Imperialism, Sovereignty and the Making of International Law* (Cambridge: Cambridge University Press, 2012); Antony Anghie, 'Towards a Postcolonial International Law' in Prabhakar Singh and Benoît Mayer (eds.), *Critical International Law: Postrealism, Postcolonialism and Transnationalism* (Oxford: Oxford University Press, 2014) 123–142; Bhupinder S. Chimni, 'The Past, Present and Future of International Law: A Critical Third World Approach' (2007) 27 *Melbourne Journal of International Law* 499–515; S. Pahuja, *Decolonizing International Law* (Cambridge: Cambridge University Press, 2011); Tendayi Achiume Report of the Special Rapporteur on contemporary forms of racism, racial discrimination, xenophobia and racial intolerance (21 August 2019) UN Doc A/74/321, para. 18.
[3] Pierre Bourdieu, 'The Force of Law: Toward a Sociology of the Juridical Field' (1987) 38 *Hastings Law Journal* 814.
[4] Sally Engle Merry, 'From Law and Colonialism to Law and Globalization' (2003) 28 *Law & Social Inquiry* 569–590, 578. See also Irene Watson, *Aboriginal Peoples, Colonialism and International Law: Raw Law* (Routledge 2015); Jennifer Balint and others, *Keeping Hold of Justice: Encounters between Law and Colonialism* (Ann Arbor: University of Michigan Press, 2020).
[5] Elizabeth Kolsky, *Colonial Justice in British India: White Violence and the Rule of Law* (New York: Cambridge University Press, 2011) 35; Martti Koskenniemi, *To the Uttermost Parts of the Earth: Legal Imagination and International Power 1300–1870* (Cambridge: Cambridge University Press, 2021) 699–794.
[6] Law has provided a structure and space for colonial relations, which 'served both to enable and to constitute colonialism'. Zoë Laidlaw, 'Breaking Britannia's Bounds? Law, Settlers, and Space in Britain's Imperial Historiography' (2012) 55 *Historical Journal* 807–830, 821.
[7] John Comaroff, 'Colonialism, Culture, and the Law: A Foreword' (2001) 26 *Law & Social Inquiry* 305–314, 312.

Confronting Colonial Objects. Carsten Stahn, Oxford University Press. © Carsten Stahn 2023.
DOI: 10.1093/oso/9780192868121.003.0006

suppressed alternative world views,[8] and facilitated the violence of collecting.[9] As Achille Mbembe has noted, colonial powers acted as if 'the West alone had invented the "rights of people"' or 'succeeded in constituting a civil society of nations'.[10] Treaties, doctrines, and colonial law were used to justify displacement, dispossession, or exploitation within the law,[11] govern and manage foreign populations, and remap identities.

At the same time, law cannot not be reduced to an instrument of oppression. It also served as a means of resistance and contestation.[12] For instance, Frantz Fanon (1925–1961) criticized the totalitarian character of European exploitation and called for a revolt against a law that keeps the colonized in a condition of 'damnation'.[13] Legal anthropologist Sally Engle Merry has examined the complex role of colonial law in colonial relations. She has argued that law had a dual role: '[It] serve[d] as the handmaiden for processes of domination, helping to create new systems of control and regulation. At the same time, it constrain[ed] these systems and provide[d] arenas for resistance'.[14]

This chapter illustrates this dichotomy. It argues that positivist law and legal doctrines were actively used to organize the world along lines of social or racial inclusion and exclusion[15] and to legitimatize domination and suppression, through double standards, discriminatory semantics, silencing or dis-narration and social transformation. It shows how international law constituted colonial conditions through (i) lack of recognition of legal subjectivities, (ii) hybrid frames of governance, and (iii) discriminatory standards regarding colonial violence (e.g. the doctrine of 'savage warfare'). It highlights how colonial laws were used to facilitate cultural takings or erase native heritage. But it also demonstrates the contestations and counter-readings to dominant colonial world views, which call into question the premises of the colonial condition. It claims that international law was more pluralist at the time than admitted. It thereby challenges the argument that takings

---

[8] Makau wa Mutua, 'Why Redraw the Map of Africa? A Legal and Moral Inquiry' (1995) 16 *Michigan Journal of International Law* 1113–1176, 1120.

[9] As Yasuaki Onuma has stated, it 'justified colonization by "treaties" and the principle of effective occupation on one hand, and evaded the problematization of the essential meaning of colonization under international law on the other'. See Yasuaki Onuma, 'When Was the Law of International Society Born? An Inquiry of the History of International Law from an Intercivilizational Perspective' (2000) 2 *Journal of the History of International Law* 1–66, 50.

[10] Achilles Mbembe, *Critique of Black Reason* (Durham: Duke University Press, 2017) 11.

[11] Will Smiley, 'Lawless Wars of Empire: The International Law of War in the Philippines, 1898-1903' (2018) 36 *Law & History Review* 511–550, 533.

[12] Saliha Belmessous, *Native Claims: Indigenous Law against Empire, 1500–1920* (Oxford: Oxford University Press, 2011). Balakrishnan Rajagopal, *International Law from Below: Development, Social Movements and Third World Resistance* (Cambridge: Cambridge University Press, 2003).

[13] Frantz Fanon, *The Wretched of the Earth* (New York: Grove Weidenfeld, 1963 [1961]) 93. The book is entitled 'Les Damnés de la Terre' in its original French version.

[14] Sally Engle Merry, 'Law and Colonialism' (1991) 25 *Law & Society Review* 889–922, 917.

[15] On the dual nature of civilization as 'logic of improvement' and 'logic of biology', see Ntina Tzouvala, *Capitalism as Civilisation: A History of International Law* (Cambridge: Cambridge University Press, 2020).

occurred in a legal vacuum. It develops a theory of legal entanglements in order to enable a differentiated contemporary assessment of cultural colonial takings.

2 Empire's tools: Double standards in the recognition of legal personality

International law served as a means of facilitating conquest, submission, and assimilation throughout the colonial period. Many territories were acquired through a combination of force and formal 'legal' acts, by which local leaders recognized sovereign rights, jurisdictional powers, or trade privileges of Western powers in exchange for protection. The lack of recognition of the legal personality of non-Western entities and the limitation of international law to 'civilized' states were used as argumentative tools to justify colonial empire and 'legalize' colonialism.[16] Only sovereign states qualified as states in the European sense,[17] while 'half-civilized' (e.g. China) or uncivilized entities were not regarded as members the 'legal community of nations'.[18] The identity of other forms of sovereignty or political organization received marginal recognition.[19] It was ignored, set aside, or transformed.[20] This discourse was used to justify the elimination of native sovereignty or indigenous jurisdiction in settler colonial contexts, or the subjugation of native subjects for purposes of colonial exploitation. It was complemented by an evolutionist jurisprudence on rights and culture.[21] Such practices were marked

---

[16] According to 'classical colonial' conceptions of international law, public international law applied 'in relations between European Powers, and unequal domination in relations with the indigenous authorities'. See ICJ, *Sovereignty over Pedra Branca/Pulau Batu Puteh, Middle Rocks and South Ledge (Malaysia v Singapore)*, Judgment of 23 May 2008 [2008] ICJ Rep 12, Declaration by Judge Ranjeva, § 5.

[17] John Westlake, *Chapters on the Principles of International Law* (Cambridge: Cambridge University Press, 1894) 137, 141.

[18] Only a few Western scholars, such as Johann Caspar Bluntschli (1808–1881), have argued that international law also governs relations to entities which do not qualify as a state. Johann Caspar Bluntschli, *Das moderne Völkerrecht der civilisierten Staaten als Rechtsbuch dargestellt* (New York: C. H. Beck, 1868) 66–69.

[19] The General Act of the Berlin Conference formally reserved claims of sovereignty to European powers. Other societies were deemed to constitute themselves after the model of the European sovereign. See General Act of the Berlin Conference on West Africa (26 February 1885) Arts. 34, 35.

[20] The issue as to whether indigenous populations enjoyed legal personality under international law remained controversial among jurists throughout the colonial period. See Mark Frank Lindley, *The Acquisition and Government of Backward Territory in International Law* (New York: Longmans, Green and Co., 1926) 10; Norbert B. Wagner, *Die deutschen Schutzgebiete: Erwerb, Organisation und Verlust aus juristischer Sicht* (Baden-Baden: Nomos, 2002) 104; Jeremy Sarkin, *Colonial Genocide and Reparations Claims in the 21st Century* (Westport: Praeger, 2009) 17.

[21] A striking example is a decision from the Privy Council from 1919, which validated the expropriation of the territory of Southern Rhodesia, occupied by Cecil Rhodes' British South Africa Company. It stated: 'Some tribes are so low in the scale of social organization that their usages and conceptions of rights and duties are not to be reconciled with institutions or the legal ideas of civilized society. Such a gulf cannot be bridged. It would be idle to impute to such people some shadow of the rights known to our law'. See Privy Council, *Re Southern Rhodesia* (26 July 1918) (1919) AC 211, 233–234 (Lord Sumner). Remnants of such an approach endured well into the latter half of the twentieth century. For

by striking contradictions, in both settler colonial contexts and extractive colonial structures. Law was often more pluralist than admitted.[22] Obligations towards colonized peoples existed not only under natural law (e.g. as ethical or moral duties), but also under treaty provisions or international law[23] understood as law of peoples.[24] As political theorists have shown, a different political order, such as indigenous sovereignty (which is in itself a European concept[25]), can exist 'nested' within a sovereign state and prevail 'within and apart' from these governance structures, through indigenous discourse and practices.[26]

2.1 Contradictions in colonial practices

Colonial subjects were subjected to conflicting treatment in colonial practice. Legal interpretations were by no means homogenous. In several settler contexts, native populations were initially treated as sovereigns, but later deemed to be too 'primitive' to hold sovereignty or to qualify as independent legal subjects. For instance, in the US, settler nations relied initially on negotiations and treaties with Native American Nations in order to acquire title over land and people.[27] They accepted that native tribes enjoyed pre-constitutional and extraconstitutional sovereignty and entitlement to their lands.[28] In the treaty-making period between 1778 and 1871, domestic authorities concluded more than a hundred treaties with native nations.[29] They were ratified in the same way as treaties with other

---

instance, some Canadian decisions on aboriginal rights of the Inuit people still required claimants in the late 1970s to show that 'their ancestors were members of an organized society' in order to claim rights. Justice Mahoney determined in *Baker Lake* that the Inuit people have to prove that 'they and their ancestors were members of an organized society' in order to claim a title to hunt and fish. Federal Court (Canada), *Hamlet of Baker Lake v Minister of Indian Affairs and Northern Development* (1979) 107 DLR (3d), 513, 542. This has come to be known as the *Baker Lake* test in the jurisprudence of the Canadian Supreme Court.

[22] Arnulf Becker Lorca, 'Universal International Law: Nineteenth-Century Histories of Imposition and Appropriation' (2010) 51 *Harvard International Law Journal* 475–552, 520; Belmessous, *Native Claims*.

[23] R. Anderson, 'Redressing Colonial Genocide under International Law: The Hereros' Cause of Action against Germany' (2005) 93 *California Law Review* 1155–1189, 1169.

[24] Belmessous, 'Introduction' in Belmessous, *Native Claims*, 3–18, 15.

[25] Taiaiake Alfred, 'Colonialism and State Dependency' (2009) 5 *Journal of Aboriginal Health* 42–60; Glen S. Coulthard, 'Subjects of Empire: Indigenous Peoples and the 'Politics of Recognition in Canada' (2007) 3 *Contemporary Political Theory* 1–29.

[26] Audra Simpson, *Mohawk Interruptus: Political Life across the Borders of Settler States* (Durham, NC: Duke University Press, 2014) 11.

[27] The Royal Proclamation, issued by the British Crown in 1763, implied that title should be conferred through negotiation between Britain and First Nations. See generally Neal Ferris, 'Between Colonial and Indigenous Archaeologies: Legal and Extra-legal Ownership of the Archaeological Past in North America' (2003) 27 *Canadian Journal of Archaeology* 154–190, 157.

[28] On native perspectives, see Robert A. Williams, Jr., *Linking Arms Together: American Indian Treaty Visions of Law and Peace, 1600–1800* (New York: Routledge, 1999).

[29] These treaties often turned inherent sovereign rights to land into use and occupancy rights.

states.[30] Early US Supreme Court decisions recognized that the US was bound to respect tribal sovereignty as a successor to Britain (e.g. *Worcester v Georgia* 1832).[31] However, later decisions reduced the roles of Indian tribes to that of 'wards of the nation' or reserved the right to unilaterally abrogate treaty obligations and allocate land against the terms of a treaty.[32] Some decisions reflected racial and cultural stereotypes of colonialism. For instance, Justice Edward White, who delivered the opinion in *Lone Wolf v Hitchcock*, wrote in 1903 that the relationship of the US to tribal nations 'would be governed by such considerations of justice as would control a Christian people in their treatment of an ignorant and dependent race'.[33]

In New Zealand, the British Crown concluded the Treaty of Waitangi with more than 540 Māori chiefs in 1840 in order to formalize the assumption of sovereignty. The treaty recognized the sovereignty of Māori chiefs. It stated: '[t]he treaty Chiefs ... cede to Her Majesty the Queen of England absolutely and without reservation all the rights and powers of Sovereignty which [they] exercise or possess, or may be supposed to exercise or to possess over their respective Territories as the sole sovereigns thereof'.[34] Later conflicts arose about the meaning of the powers ceded to the British. The notion of 'sovereignty' was translated as 'kawanatanga' in the Māori text, which is understood as 'government' in the Modern English translation of Māori version.[35] It takes into account that chiefs did not understand the notion in the same way as the British, based on their experience or culture. This reading was confirmed by Waitangi tribunal, which found that the term 'kawanatanga' means 'less than the sovereignty ceded in the English text', namely 'the authority to make laws for the good order and security of the country but subject to the protection of Māori interests'.[36]

The Supreme Court of New Zealand adopted a discriminatory interpretation of the treaty[37] in the second half of the nineteenth century in the 'Wi Parata v Bishop of Wellington' case (1877).[38] Chief Justice James Prendergast referred to Māoris

---

[30] The US Congress stopped to recognize natives as sovereign nations in the Indian Appropriation Act of 3 March 1871.

[31] US Supreme Court, *Worcester v Georgia* 31 US 515 (1832).

[32] US Supreme Court, *Lone Wolf v Hitchcock*, 187 US 553 (1903).

[33] Ibid, 567, drawing on Supreme Court of the United States, *Beecher v Wetherby*, 95 US 517 (1877) 525.

[34] Article 1.

[35] Treaty of Waitangi, Agreement between the British Crown and Māori chiefs (6 February 1840) Modern English translation of Māori version https://nzhistory.govt.nz/files/documents/treaty-kawharu-footnotes.pdf, Art. 1, with footnotes by Prof. Hugh Kawharu: 'The Chiefs of the Confederation and all the Chiefs who have not joined that Confederation give absolutely to the Queen of England forever the complete government over their land.'

[36] Waitangi Tribunal 1987, para. 11.11.4(a).

[37] Grant Morris, 'James Prendergast and the Treaty of Waitangi: Judicial Attitudes to the Treaty during the Latter Half of the Nineteenth Century' (2004) 35 *Victoria University of Wellington Law Review* 117–144.

[38] Supreme Court New Zealand, *Wi Parata v Bishop of Wellington* (1877), 3 NZ Jur (NS) 72 (SC).

no longer as 'aboriginal natives' or 'Māori New Zealanders', but qualified them as 'primitive barbarians' and 'savages' who were not able to hold sovereignty. He argued that New Zealand was validly acquired by occupation and discovery since 'there existed amongst the natives no regular system of territorial rights nor any definite ideas of property in land'.[39] He stated: 'So far indeed as that instrument [the Treaty] purported to cede the sovereignty … it must be regarded as a simple nullity. No body politic existed capable of making cession of sovereignty, nor could the thing itself exist'.[40] The *Wi Parata* jurisprudence, which challenged aboriginal title was upheld by the Privy Council[41] and continued to enjoy 'widespread support' in the domestic judiciary for almost a century, until it was reversed in the mid-1980s.[42]

A similar contradiction is visible in the practice of protectorate agreements, which were used to foster colonial submission and extractive practices. According to colonial conceptions, such agreements illustrated the capacity of non-Western entities to transfer or limit their sovereign rights and powers in relation to protective powers, but did not recognize the other contracting party as a sovereign state under international law.[43] As Yasuaki Onuma has noted, this practice shows the inherent conflicts in colonial attitudes. Western powers recognized native leaders or populations for the purpose of forming contractual 'agreements', but eliminated this recognition in their reading of international legal relations.[44]

2.2 Counter-narratives

The limited recognition of the legal subjectivity of local entities in the narratives of colonial powers relied on a one-sided reading of international law, which rendered the identity of others invisible.[45] Colonial entities (tribes, chiefdoms, kingdoms, etc.) had their own organically grown forms of self-government and social rules organizing society (*ubi societas ibi ius*).[46] States accepted the treaty-making power and sovereignty of many rulers in Asia[47] in reciprocal

---

[39] Ibid, 77.

[40] Ibid, 78.

[41] Privy Council, *Nireaha Tamaki v Baker* (1900–1901) NZPCC 371, 383–384.

[42] Morris, 'James Prendergast and the Treaty of Waitangi', 133.

[43] The existence of sovereign rights was implied at the time of the conclusion of agreements to relinquish power, but then erased or denied on the basis of the very same treaties.

[44] See Onuma, 'When Was the Law of International Society Born?', 49.

[45] For instance, following colonization, the 'relationship between the colonial power and the African states' was often regarded as 'a matter of domestic jurisdiction of the former', rather than a matter of international law. Onuma, 'When Was the Law of International Society Born?', 50.

[46] Yasuaki Onuma argues that 'agreements among various independent human societies' create 'intersocietal law'. See Ounuma, 'When Was the Law of International Society Born?', 58.

[47] Charles Henry Alexandrowicz, *An Introduction to the History of the Law of Nations in the East Indies (16th, 17th and 18th Centuries)* (Oxford: Clarendon Press, 1967), 2.

legal arrangements.[48] Indigenous laws and customs determined many rights.[49] Property and land acquisitions were governed by competing sources of law: domestic law, the law of nations, and natural law.[50]

This pluralism is reflected in certain rulings in settler contexts, which countered colonial expansion based on indigenous law and property rights.[51] For instance, in 1706, the Privy Council recognized in a landmark case (*Mohegan Indians v Connecticut*) that the 'Mohegan Indians are a Nation' with treaty rights.[52] In subsequent proceedings, British judges 'were prepared to acknowledge the continuity of aboriginal customary law and government in British colonies'.[53] In 1743, Commissioner Daniel Horsmanden even went a step further. He argued that: 'a matter of property in lands in dispute between the Indians, a distinct people (for no act has been shown whereby they became Subjects) and the English Subjects, cannot be determined by the laws of our land, but by a law equal to both parties, which is the Law of Nature and Nations'.[54] The final Privy Council appeal decision in 1772 confirmed that the 'aboriginal system was independent, in at least some degree, from local colonial governments and courts'.[55]

Later, the pluralism of legal orders was recognized in a Report of the British Parliamentary Select Committee on Aboriginal Tribes from 1837, which examined relations between the empire and indigenous populations. It recognized that the intercourse of Europeans has been 'a source of many calamities to

---

[48]   Certain non-Western societies (e.g. the Ottoman Empire) were recognized as states early on. In the case concerning *Sovereignty over Pulau Batu Puteh, Middle Rocks and South Ledge* (Malaysia/ Singapore), the ICJ confirmed that the Sultanate of Johor, which came into existence in 1512, 'established itself as a sovereign State with a certain territorial domain under its sovereignty in this part of southeast Asia'. See ICJ, *Sovereignty over Pedra Branca/Pulau Batu Puteh, Middle Rocks and South Ledge*, § 52.

[49]   On aboriginal titles and custom, see T. W. Bennett and C. H. Powell, 'Restoring Land: The Claims of Aboriginal Title, Customary Law and the Right to Culture' (2005) 16 *Stellenbosch Law Review* 431–445.

[50]   See Lauren Benton, *A Search for Sovereignty: Law and Geography in European Empires, 1400–1900* (New York: Cambridge University Press, 2009).

[51]   On appeals by native Americans to the British Crown, see Joseph H. Smith, *Appeals to the Privy Council from the American Plantations* (New York: Columbia University Press, 1950); Craig Yirush, 'Claiming the New World: Empire, Law, and Indigenous Rights in the Mohegan Case, 1704–1743' (2011) 29 *Law and History Review* 333–373; Ann Marie Plane, 'Liberator or Oppressor? Law, Colonialism, and New England's Indigenous Peoples' (2004) 43 *Connecticut History* 163–170. In New Zealand, a specialized court, the Māori Land Court adjudicated indigenous land claims by Māori, taking into account customary law. See Christopher Hilliard, 'The Native Land Court: Making Property in Nineteenth-Century New Zealand' in Belmessous, *Native Claims*, 204–222.

[52]   Privy Council, 'Report of the Committee for hearing of Appeals from the Plantations touching ye Mohegan Indians Lands' (21 May 1706) Privy Council Records, Public Records Office 2/81, 204–205.

[53]   Mark D. Walters, 'Mohegan Indians v. Connecticut (1705-1773) and the Legal Status of Aboriginal Customary Laws and Government in British North America' (1995) 33 *Osgoode Hall Law Journal* 785–829, 818.

[54]   Ibid, 820, referring to the majority opinion by Daniel Horsmanden in the 1743 interim ruling on jurisdiction in *Mohegan Indians v Connecticut*. See Privy Council, *Mohegan Indians v Connecticut*, Proceedings Before Commission of Review 1743 (1769) 191–192.

[55]   Walters, 'Mohegan Indians v. Connecticut', 829.

uncivilized nations'.[56] It stated: 'Too often, their territory has been usurped; their property seized, their numbers diminished; their character debased; the spread of civilization impeded'.[57] It then expressly confirmed unwritten rights of native populations:

> It might be presumed that the native inhabitants of any land have an incontrovertible right to their own soil: a plain and sacred right, however, which seems not to have been understood. Europeans have entered their borders uninvited, and, when there, have not only acted as if they were undoubted lords of the soil, but have punished the natives as aggressors if they have evinced a disposition to live in their own country.[58]

In settler colonial contexts, such as the US, Australia or New Zealand, pre-colonial ancestral bonds between land and people are increasingly as viewed a form of 'native sovereignty' (aboriginal sovereignty) that has not been extinguished by colonization.[59] For example, US Courts have held that Indian communities enjoyed 'inherent powers of a limited sovereignty which has never been extinguished'.[60] In 1832, Chief Justice Marshall argued in *Worcester v Georgia* that Indian nations retained 'their original natural rights, as undisputed possessors of the soil'[61] and that the charters granted by the Crown 'asserted a title against Europeans only, and were considered as blank paper, so far as the rights of the natives were concerned'.[62] In Australia, the groundbreaking *Mabo* case[63] recognized aboriginal land titles in Australia. Justice Toohey contrasted materialistic Eurocentric conceptions of sovereignty from 'spiritual' foundations of sovereignty. He relied on Judge Ammoun's argument in the *Western Sahara* case[64] in order to deny the *terra nullius* doctrine, arguing that the 'ancestral tie between the land, or 'mother nature', and the man who was born therefrom, remains attached thereto, and must one day return thither to be united with his ancestors'.[65]

---

[56] Report of the Parliamentary Select Committee on Aboriginal Tribes (London: Aborigines Society, 1837) 3.

[57] Ibid, 3.

[58] Ibid, 4.

[59] See Julie Cassidy, 'Sovereignty of Aboriginal Peoples' (1998) 9 *Indiana International & Comparative Law Review* 65–119.

[60] US Supreme Court, *United States v Wheeler*, 435 US 313 (1978) 326.

[61] *Worcester v Georgia*, 31 US 515 (1832) 559.

[62] Ibid, 544–545.

[63] High Court of Australia, *Mabo and Others v Queensland (No 2)* [1992] HCA 23; (1992) 175 CLR 1, paras. 40–41 (Judge Brennan), para. 19 (Justice Toohey).

[64] In the *Western Sahara Advisory* Opinion, the ICJ found that Western Sahara was not *terra nullius* when it was colonized by Spain in 1844, since the territory was inhabited by people organized in 'tribes'. See ICJ, *Western Sahara*, Advisory Opinion of 16 October 1975 [1975] ICJ Rep 12.

[65] High Court of Australia, *Mabo and Others v. Queensland*, Justice Toohey, para. 19, referring to ICJ, *Western Sahara Case*, Separate Opinion of Vice-President Ammoun, 85–86.

The treaty-making practice with native authorities supports the idea of legal pluralism in extractive colonial contexts.[66] As Judge Dillard has noted: 'You do not protect a *terra nullius*.'[67] Some scholars have already argued, towards the end of the nineteenth century, that agreements with non-Western entities implied the recognition of international legal subjectivity.[68] Many agreements concluded in the colonial expansion of Africa were translated and ratified by local chiefs and contain elements, which suggest that they were meant to be international agreements.[69] They did not necessarily extinguish the 'internal sovereignty' of African rulers. For instance, protectorate agreements only transferred external sovereignty, but did not provide a title for the exercise of 'supreme authority of and over the polity'.[70]

3 Justification and contestation of hybrid legal forms and corporate structures

The dual role of law, as enabler and constraint, of colonial relations is further reflected in the use of hybrid legal forms and corporate identities. As Frantz Fanon has stated, colonial expansion and governance relied on 'a sort of detached complicity between capitalism and the violent forces' in colonial territories.[71] Trade corporations and chartered companies served as of points of interaction with non-European entities, or as means to assume control. These semi-private, semi-public entities and informal networks enabled 'coercion' and 'social transformation'.[72] However, they also encountered significant resistance and critique. Their methods and corporate orientation stood in stark contrast to their governing functions.[73]

---

[66] Article 37 of the UN Declaration on Indigenous Peoples explicitly recognizes the right of indigenous peoples to 'the recognition, observance and enforcement of treaties, agreements and other constructive arrangements concluded with States or their successors, and to have States honour and respect such treaties, agreements and other constructive arrangements'. Art. 37(1) UNDRIP.

[67] ICJ, *Western Sahara*, Separate Opinion Judge Dillard [1975] ICJ Rep 116, 124.

[68] Franz von Holtzendorff, *Die völkerrechtliche Verfassung und Grundordnung der auswärtigen Staatsbeziehungen*, Vol. 2 (C. Habel, 1887) 6–7.

[69] Mamadou Hébié, 'The Role of the Agreements Concluded with Local Political Entities in the Course of French Colonial Expansion in West Africa' (2016) 85 *British Yearbook of International Law* 21–89, 89.

[70] The assumption of colonial rule was thus not necessarily covered by treaty arrangements native subjects. See Mieke Linden, *The Acquisition of Africa: The Nature of Nineteenth-Century International Law* (Oisterwijk: Wolf Legal Publishers, 2014), 245.

[71] Fanon, *The Wretched of the Earth*, 65.

[72] See generally Pepijn Brandon, 'Between company and state: The case of the Dutch East and West India Companies' in Grietje Baars and Andre Spicer (eds.), *The Corporation: A Critical, Multidisciplinary Handbook* (Cambridge: Cambridge University Press, 2017) 215–225; Grietje Baars, 'Corporate Imperialism 3.0: from the Dutch East India Company to the American South Asia Company' in Grietje Baars, *Corporation, Law and Capitalism* (Leiden: Brill, 2019) 343–380.

[73] Both the British and Dutch East India companies came under critique. See Eric Wilson, *The Savage Republic: De Indis of Hugo Grotius, Republicanism and Dutch Hegemony within the Early Modern World-System (c.1600–1619)* (Leiden: Martinus Nijhoff, 2008).

In the early modern period, the British East India Company[74] and the Dutch East India Company[75] served as proxy states.[76] Later, chartered companies became a popular means to secure trade monopolies, facilitate the establishment of protectorates or colonial administration in the race for overseas extension, and foster exploitation and extractive cultures.[77] The use of company-states or chartered companies provided a means to bring colonial encounters outside the realm of interstate relations. It served to outsource responsibilities[78] and avoid accountability.[79] It allowed European states to establish commercial ties or authority over non-European entities, without formally recognizing them as equal states. As Wilhelm Grewe has observed, this practice enabled Western powers to create an 'elastic system of colonial international law', in which 'it was the corporations and not the states themselves, that encountered each other, and that were considered (or at least held out to be) more or less independent'.[80] Companies served as extensions of states, but retained a hybrid status. Their conduct was typically governed

---

[74] Philip Stern, *The Company-State: Corporate Sovereignty and the Early Modern Foundations of the British Empire in India* (Oxford: Oxford University Press, 2011); Andrew Phillips and J. C. Sharman, *Outsourcing Empire: How Company-States Made the Modern World* (Princeton: Princeton University Press, 2020).

[75] On the role of Grotius with respect to the Dutch East India Company, see Martine van Ittersum, *Profit and Principle: Hugo Grotius, Natural Rights Theories and the Rise of Dutch Power in the East Indies, 1595–1615* (Leiden: Brill, 2006).

[76] They exercised territorial control and governmental authority, including regulatory and sovereign powers (e.g. tax collection), which went far beyond the powers of military companies. The British East India Company was described as 'a state in disguise as a merchant'. The Dutch East India Company was compared to a 'corporate sovereign'.

[77] For instance, the creation in the British North Borneo Company in 1881 served as a precedent for British chartered companies in Africa. See John S. Galbraith, 'The Chartering of the British North Borneo Company' (1965) 4 *Journal of British Studies* 102–126, 125. It was a forerunner for entities such as the Royal Niger Company (1886), the Imperial British East Africa Company (1888), or the notorious British South Africa Company (1889), which administered 'Rhodesia' until the 1920s. Otto von Bismarck supported the creation of the New Guinea Company by a consortium of bankers, led by Adolph von Hansemann (1826–1903) in order to administer the Protectorate of New Guinea and the Bismarck Archipelago. The company administered the territory until 1899 on behalf of the German government, and was then transformed into a German colonial company. Bismarck was inspired by the British model. See William Harbutt Dawson, *Bismarck and State Socialism: An Exposition of the Social and Economic Legislation of Germany Since 1870* (London: Swan Sonnenschein & Co, 1890) 150–151. See also Kim Todzi, *Unternehmen Weltaneignung. Der Woermann-Konzern und der deutsche Kolonialismus, 1837-1916* (Göttingen: Wallstein, 2023).

[78] Grietje Baars, '"It's Not Me, It's the Corporation": The Value of Corporate Accountability in the Global Political Economy' (2016) 4 *London Review of International Law* 127–163. The corporate form made it easier to outsource responsibility for the use of force or to recruit mercenaries or local fighters. Company-states protected themselves against accountability or expropriation through colonial law or extraterritorial application of domestic laws. They claimed that they acted as traders, and used military force only to protect trade.

[79] Company actions were difficult to challenge under international law since the respective entities did not enjoy international legal personality at the time. See Janne Elisabeth Nijman, *The Concept of International Legal Personality: An Inquiry into the History and Theory of International Law* (The Hague: TMC Asser Press, 2004).

[80] Wilhelm Grewe, *The Epochs of International Law* (Berlin: De Gruyter 2001) 346.

by domestic law, including colonial law permitting removal of objects from the colony to the metropole.[81]

However, both models came under critique, in the context of abuse or actions conflicting with the liberal ethos in the metropolis. For example, the company-state model was openly challenged in the Impeachment Trial of Warren Hastings.[82] Edmund Burke criticized the outsourcing of responsibilities, which facilitated arbitrary governance and immoral exploitation. He argued that the model established by the British East India Company was based on a selective 'geographical morality' 'by which the duties of men in public and in private situations are not to be governed by their relations to the Great Governor of the Universe, or by their relations to men, but by climates, degrees of longitude and latitude, parallels not of life but of latitudes'.[83] He criticized the theory of cultural relativism, advocated by Hastings, who had argued that his actions mirrored practices in Asia, and pushed for the recognition of universal standards in relation to company behaviour. He argued that:

> [t]he laws of morality are the same everywhere, and that there is no action which would pass for an act of extortion, of peculation, of bribery, and of oppression in England, that is not an act of extortion, of peculation, of bribery, and oppression in Europe, Asia, Africa and all the world over.[84]

Burke accepted that the colonized had a legitimate right of resistance against oppression and aggressive acts by the East India Company or colonizing powers, recognized under their own laws and the law of nations and of nature.[85] He suggested that the House of Lords should serve as impartial arbiter over disputes between the East India Company and Indian society.[86] Burke's approach gained greater attention in nineteenth century practice, in particular in the aftermath of the Indian Mutiny in 1857, which led to the end of the rule of the company.[87]

---

[81]   For example, officials of the British East India refused to submit themselves to the authority of local courts in India. Mithi Mukherjee, 'Justice, War, and the Imperium: India and Britain in Edmund Burke's Prosecutorial Speeches in the Impeachment Trial of Warren Hastings' (2005) 23 *Law and History Review* 589–630, 612.

[82]   Mukherjee, 'Justice, War, and the Imperium', 616.

[83]   Edmund Burke, 'Speech on Opening of Impeachment' (1788) in David P. Fidler and Jennifer Welsh (eds.), *Empire and Community: Edmund Burke's Writings and Speeches on International Relations* (London: Routledge, 2018) 221.

[84]   Ibid.

[85]   Burke contested Hastings' view simplistic that Mughal emperors were simply arbitrary or despotic rulers. He stated: 'those people lived under the Law, which was formed even whilst we, I may say, were in the Forest, before we knew what Jurisprudence was ... it is a refined, enlightened, curious, elaborate, technical Jurisprudence under which they lived, and by which their property was secured and which yields neither to the Jurisprudence of the Roman Law nor to the Jurisprudence of this Kingdom'. See Peter J. Marshall (ed.), *The Writings and Speeches of Edmund Burke, vol. 7, India: The Hastings Trial 1789–1794* (Oxford: Clarendon Press, 2000) 285.

[86]   Mukherjee, 'Justice, War, and the Imperium', 627.

[87]   Ibid, 629.

Later, international lawyers challenged the idea that territories inhabited by 'non-civilized' were *terra nullius* and could be seized by mere occupation, but legitimized colonization through chartered companies or private association through cessions of sovereignty by native leaders.[88]

Travers Twiss (1809–1897),[89] a British lawyer, who was mandated by Leopold II to set up the constitution of the Congo Free State, was instrumental in the framing of legal approaches which facilitated the colonization of Africa through companies.[90] He developed a contractual justification of corporate governance, which accepted that rulers of non-European peoples could transfer sovereign rights, even though they were not recognized as 'civilised states'.[91] The arguments made by Twiss and jurist Egide Arntz (1812–1884), who was Secretary-General of the Institute of International Law and worked for Leopold, were key for the international recognition of private rule by the International Association of the Congo[92] by the US and Berlin

[88] It was disputed whether tribal chiefs could transfer sovereign rights to a private association which lacked the capacity of statehood. Casper Sylvest, 'Our Passion for Legality': International Law and Imperialism in Late Nineteenth Century Britain' (2008) 34 *Review of International Studies* 403–423, 412. For instance Friedrich Martens took the view that only civilized states had the capacity to enter into international treaties. See Friedrich Martens, 'La Conférence du Congo à Berlin et la politique coloniale des Etats modernes' (1886) 18 *Revue de droit international et de législation comparée* 113–150, 147.

[89] Andrew Fitzmaurice, *King Leopold's Ghostwriter: The Creation of Persons and States in the Nineteenth Century* (Princeton: Princeton University Press, 2021).

[90] Andrew Fitzmaurice, 'The Justification of King Leopold II's Congo Enterprise by Sir Travers Twiss' in Shaunnagh Dorsett and Ian Hunter, *Law and Politics in British Colonial Thought* (New York: Palgrave Macmillan, 2010) 109–126.

[91] Twiss drew an analogy to historical associations which had exercised territorial rights, such as the Teutonic Order and the Order of St. John of Jerusalem, and the chartered companies, which had established English colonies in North America. See Travers Twiss, 'La Libre Navigation du Congo' (1883) 15 *Revue de Droit International* 547–563, 552, 553. He noted that chartered companies, such as the North Borneo Company, had acquired sovereign rights from indigenous chiefs through treaty arrangements. Ibid, 553–554. In the 1884 edition of his manual on the 'Law of Nations', Twiss added the example of American Society for Colonizing the Free People of Colour of the United States, which had created the 'Commonwealth of Liberia' (later the Republic of Liberia) in order to show that a purely private association could exercise sovereign rights. See Travers Twiss, *The Law of Nations Considered as Independent Political Communities: On the Rights and Duties of Nations in Time of Peace* (2nd edn, Oxford: Clarendon Press, 1884) xi. He concluded that chartered companies are 'capable of acquiring an international status in cases where they have obtained cessions of territory … from native chiefs' (ibid, x) and that the 'juridical difficulty, which has been suggested to be in the way of private associations forming settlements in Africa, and acquiring … the right of Empire of the territory ceded to them is without justification'. Ibid, xii–xiii. He was rewarded by Leopold through membership in the Supreme Council of the Independent State of the Congo.

[92] The association was a private entity, founded by King Leopold II in 1879, with the support of business men and bankers. It was initially created for philanthropic and scientific purposes, but then vested with the mandate to establish an independent state. It was recognized as legitimate governing authority over the Congo by States represented at the 1884 Berlin Conference 1884 and the US Secretary of State Frederick T. Frelinghuysen ('a friendly Government') and then transformed by royal decree into the Congo Free State. Some states recognized the association as a 'friendly state' (e.g. Austria-Hungary, Belgian, Denmark, Norway, Sweden, the Ottoman Empire Russia, United Kingdom), others qualified it as a 'friendly government' (e.g. Italy, The Netherlands, Spain). Friedrich Martens, who had been sceptical towards the power of African kings to conclude international agreements, ultimately recognized in a memorandum that the International Association had acquired authority over the Congo through peaceful conquest and agreements with indigenous chiefs. See

Conference.[93] They paved the way for the taking of ethnographic objects and human skulls in the Congo Free State by companies such as the Kasai Company[94] or corporate exploitation in the South Pacific.[95] However, such treaty-based justifications did not go unchallenged. They faced critique or resistance by home audiences or native rulers.

For example, British parliamentarian Henry Du Pré Labouchère (1831–1912) openly criticized the way in which the Royal Niger Company used treaties to acquire territory or minerals. The company, led by George Goldie (1846–1925), had concluded thirty-seven treaties with the chiefs in the Niger basin ceding territory to the company. Labouchère challenged the methodology during a parliamentary debate in 1899:

> When you talk of treaties having been made by which land rights and mineral rights are made over to white men, what happens? Someone belonging to one company or another meets a black man. Of course, he has an interpreter with him. He asks the black man if he is proprietor of certain land, and if he will sign a paper he shall have a bottle of gin. The black man at once accepts; a paper is put before him, and he is told to make his mark on it, which he does. And then we say that we have made a treaty by which all the rights in that country of the emperor, king, or chief, or whatever you call him, have been given over to us. That is the origin of all these treaties.[96]

In some cases, it is unclear whether local rulers properly understood the underlying agreements, or whether they were fabricated. A famous example is the concession of mining rights (so-called Rudd concession) by Ndebele King Lobengula of Matabeleland on 30 October 1888 to agents of Cecil John Rhodes (Charles

---

Friedrich Martens, *Etat indépendant du Congo: Mémoire sur les droits dominiaux de l'État indépendant du Congo* (Bruxelles: Hachez, 1892) 4.

[93] Fitzmaurice, *King Leopold's Ghostwriter*, 451–474.

[94] A notorious example is Belgian officer Léon Rom (1859–1924), who took part in multiple punitive expedition in Kasai and collected objects from the Kuba people which were purchased from his widow by the Royal Museum of Africa in 1925. They were designated as objects 'collected by L. Rom' in the museum. Michel Bouffioux, 'Musée royal de l'Afrique centrale: Les non-dits de la collection "Rom"' *Paris Match* (21 December 2019). Rom's inspired the personality of Kurtz, Joseph Conrad's lead character in *Heart of Darkness*.

[95] For example, the New Guinea Company became a major player in the collection and sale of cultural objects. It started to collect and sell artefacts for commercial purposes. Commercial considerations gained greater importance when the company "faced financial difficulties. Company Director Hansemann sold a sizeable collection of objects collected by naturalist and ethnologist Otto Finsch to the museum in Berlin, partly also to attract further settlements in the 'company colony'. See Rainer Buschmann, *Anthropology's Global Histories: The Ethnographic Frontier in German New Guinea, 1870–1935* (Hawaii: University of Hawaii Press, 2009) 35.

[96] Henry Labouchère, House of Commons Debate, Royal Niger Company, Hansard, Vol. 73 (3 July 1899) 1289–1331, 1320.

Rudd, Rochfort Maguire and Francis Thompson), which paved the way for the colonization of Zimbabwe.[97] The illiterate king was persuaded by Rhodes' envoy to sign a far-reaching concession agreement in exchange for weapons (1.000 Martini-Henry breech loading rifles), ammunition and a gunboat.[98] According to the text of the agreement, the king agreed to grant Rhodes' party, in the 'exercise of [his] sovereign powers', exclusive land or mining rights, including:

> [t]he complete and exclusive charge over all metals and minerals situated and contained in [his] kingdoms, principalities, and dominions, together with full power to do all things that they may deem necessary to win and procure the same, and to hold, collect, and enjoy the profits and revenues, if any, derivable from the said metals and minerals.[99]

The text was 'interpreted and explained' to the king by Reverend Charles Helm, a missionary from the London Missionary Society.[100] It is doubtful whether he understood the signed document, which came close to 'selling his country'.[101] The negotiating history suggests that there are discrepancies between the oral and the written version of the agreement. Helm himself admitted later that Charles Rudd had made a number of verbal promises in the negotiations with the king that were not reflected in the written document. He wrote:

> They promised that they would not bring more than 10 white men to work in his country, that they would not dig anywhere near towns, etc., and that they and their people would abide by the laws of his country and in fact be his people. But these promises were not put in the concession.[102]

---

[97] Edward Cavanagh, 'Crown, Conquest, Concession, and Corporation: British Legal Ideas and Institutions in Matabeleland and Southern Rhodesia, 1889–1919' in Edward Cavanagh (ed.), *Empire and Legal Thought* (Leiden: Martinis Nijhoff, 2020) 520–547.

[98] The promised delivery of weapons and ammunition conflicted with General Act of the Brussels Conference (1876) which regulated arms transfers to Africa. See General Act of the Brussels Conference of 1890 or, the Convention Relative to the Slave Trade and Importation into Africa of Firearms, Ammunition, and Spiritous Liquors (2 July 1890).

[99] Treaty between Lobengula, 'King of Matabeleland, Mashonaland, and other adjoining territories', and representatives of Cecil Rhodes (30 October 1888) in William Worger, Nancy Clark, and Edward Alpers, *Africa and the West: A Documentary History, Volume 1: From the Slave Trade to Conquest, 1441–1905* (Oxford: Oxford University Press, 2010) 241.

[100] Ibid. The text stated: 'I hereby certify that the accompanying document has been fully interpreted and explained by me to the Chief Lobengula and his full Council of Indunas and that all the Constitutional usages of the Matabele Nation had been complied with prior to his executing the same.'

[101] The envoy may have disguised the true meaning of the concession. See John Galbraith, *Crown and Charter: The Early Years of the British South Africa Company* (Berkeley: University of California Press, 1974) 72.

[102] Arthur Keppel-Jones, *Rhodes and Rhodesia: The White Conquest of Zimbabwe, 1884–1902* (Montreal, Quebec and Kingston, Ontario: McGill-Queen's University Press, 1983) 77.

African historians have doubted whether King Lobengula gave his consent, since the document did not carry the official royal stamp, the 'Elephant Seal'.[103] The king later argued that he had been deceived. He noted:

> I hear it is published in all the newspapers that I have granted a Concession of the Minerals in all my country to Charles Dunell Rudd, Rochford Maguire, and Francis Robert Thompson ... As there is a great misunderstanding about this, all action in respect of said Concession is hereby suspended pending an investigation to be made by me in my country.[104]

Rhodes relied on the concession to acquire the Royal Charter from Queen Victoria for his company, the British South Africa Company.[105]

4 The legitimation of colonial violence

The complicity of international law in colonial violence is particularly visible in the legitimation of use of force.[106] The law was used to provide structure and discipline in colonial warfare, on the hand, and to legitimate takings and conversion of objects in the frames and language of law, on the other. Colonial wars, interventions and hostilities were not 'lawless'.[107] However, they were treated in different categories and vocabularies than conflicts between civilized or 'half-civilized' states.[108] They were either deemed to be governed by more permissive rules, submerged under blurry categories, such as measures short of war, branded as law enforcement operations or rendered invisible in legal frameworks.[109] Attempts to make colonial warfare more humane did not necessarily call into question the legitimacy of empire or colonial expansion.[110]

---

[103] Tendai Mutunhu, 'Nehanda of Zimbabwe (Rhodesia): The Story of a Woman Liberation Fighter' (1976) 7 *Ufahamu: A Journal of African Studies* 59–70, 60.

[104] Keppel-Jones, *Rhodes and Rhodesia*, 85–86.

[105] It was granted on 29 October 1889 and provided the licence for the expeditions to Mashonaland and Matebeleland, which ultimately ended Lobengula's authority over his subjects and kingdom.

[106] Christopher Szabla, 'Civilising Violence: International Law and Colonial War in the British Empire, 1850–1900' (2023) 25 *Journal of the History of International Law* 1–35.

[107] Smiley, 'Lawless Wars of Empire', 550.

[108] Jochen von Bernstorff, 'The Use of Force in International Law before World War I: On Imperial Ordering and the Ontology of the Nation-State' (2018) 29 *EJIL* 233–260, 245 ff.

[109] Some voices denied the applicability of international legal standards to colonial wars. For instance, Lassa Oppenheim argued native chiefs or tribes were not considered to be part of the 'family of nations' but rather as tribal communities excluded from international law Lassa Oppenheim, *International Law: A Treatise, Vol. 1 (Peace)* (2nd edn, New York: Longmans, Green and Co., 1912) 297. Others accepted its usefulness in colonial encounters, based on pragmatic considerations (e.g. the utility of law to maintain order and structure in hostilities), moral grounds (demonstration of civility or moral superiority regarding the opponent) or operational concerns (e.g. the need to constrain excessive violence to maintain legitimacy in the eyes of locals or prevent retaliation).

[110] Szabla, 'Civilising Violence', 20.

4.1 Specificities of colonial warfare

Colonial warfare was subject to specific doctrines.[111] It encompassed diverse types of operations, ranging from prolonged or successive campaigns of military conflict to shorter or targeted acts of violence.[112] Colonial warfare did not conclude with the defeat of adversary, but was related to subjugation of territory or population.[113] Operations to repress resistance were not branded as acts of 'war', but rather justified by the aim of 'pacification'.[114] Violence was closely associated with dubious pedagogical rationales, such as the desire to discipline colonial subjects or teach lessons through use force.[115] Colonial troops had superior technology, but were often limited in size and struggled with disease and the natural habitat.[116] They applied extreme forms of violence in order to force enemies into submission.[117]

---

[111] Donald Featherstone, *Colonial Small Wars, 1837–1901* (Newton Abbot: David & Charles, 1973); Samson C. Ukpabi, 'British Colonial Wars in West Africa: Image and Reality' (1970) 20 *Civilisations* 379–404; Susanne Kuss, *German Colonial Wars and the Context of Military Violence* (Cambridge, Mass.: Harvard University Press, 2017); Philip Dwyer and Amanda Nettelbeck, *Violence, Colonialism and Empire in the Modern World* (Cham: Palgrave Macmillan, 2017); Jaap de Moor and Henk L. Wesseling (eds.), *Imperialism and war: essays on colonial wars in Africa and Asia* (Leiden: Brill, 1989); Henk Wesseling, 'Imperialism and the Roots of the Great War' (2005) 134 *Daedalus* 100–107; Dierk Walter, *Colonial Violence: European Empires and the Use of Force* (Oxford: Oxford University Press, 2017).

[112] Political scientists Melvin Small and David Singer have distinguished two types of 'extra-systemic wars': imperial and colonial wars. Imperial wars were fought to submit 'an independent political entity that did not qualify for system membership because of serious limitations on its independence, a population insufficiency, or a failure of other states to recognize it as a legitimate member'. See Melvin Small and J. David Singer, *Resort to Arms: International and Civil War, 1816–1980* (Beverly Hills: Sage, 1982), 52. Colonial wars were armed hostilities against an existing colony or protectorate. Small and Singer found that only seventeen operations qualified as full-fledged wars between 1871 and 1914. However, the number of battles, military expeditions and hostilities was much larger. As Henk Wesselink has noted: 'Not a single year passed without a war; in fact, not one month passed without some kind of violent incident or act of repression'. Wesseling, 'Imperialism and the Roots of the Great War', 102.

[113] Henk Wesseling, 'Colonial Wars: An Introduction' in De Moor and Wesseling, *Imperialism and War*, 1–11, 3.

[114] Ibid, 'Colonial Wars: An Introduction', 9. In his famous poem 'The White Man's Burden' (1899), Rudyard Kipling used the term 'savage wars of peace' It expressed the idea 'that savage' or 'primitive' people could only be 'pacified' through force.

[115] In the mind of colonizers, 'violence' was a language that 'savages' could understand. Colonial agents often viewed local adversaries as 'unruly' infants who require coercion to in order to be brought into the realm of humanity. Kim Wagner, 'Savage Warfare: Violence and the Rule of Colonial Difference in Early British Counterinsurgency' (2018) 85 *History Workshop Journal* 217–237, 231.

[116] Colonial officer Charles Callwell qualified colonial operations as 'campaigns against nature'. See Charles Callwell, *Small Wars: Their Principles and Practice* (London: Her Majesty's Stationery Office, 1906) 57.

[117] For instance, Frederick Lugard justified the brutal destruction of towns and villages in Munshi Province in Nigeria during the expedition in 1900 with a perverted sense of humanity. He stated: '[i]t is far more humane, in the event, to inflict a drastic lesson at first and thoroughly subdue people of this kind than to attempt half -measures, which inevitably lead to a further outbreak and a greater eventual loss of life'. See CO 446/10. Report of the Munshi operation by Frederick D. Lugard (1900). General Sir Garnet Wolseley applied this logic in the Ashanti wars in order to justify the attack and destruction of Kumasi, the most important site of the kingdom. German troops used this reasoning to justify attacks against the civilian population and agricultural sites in order to break the resistance of the Maji Maji Rebellion. On extreme violence as a transimperial phenomenon, see Tom Menger, ' "Press the thumb onto the eye": Moral Effect, Extreme Violence, and the

Colonial forces used techniques which they would otherwise not allow in 'civilized' warfare. They relied on warriors from other colonies or recruited native soldiers in order to learn about local tactic, sites or 'play the enemy's own game'.[118] Some of the brutal methods, i.e. to 'awe' indigenous populations into submission, conflicted with the longer-term goals of colonial rule, i.e. to secure stable and peaceful governance and trade after combat and avoid insurgency.[119]

Sociologically, colonial warfare was not only a military, but a cultural encounter. It was marked by racialized violence and rules of colonial difference, i.e. 'othering' of adversaries based on cultural and anthropological hierarchies.[120] Colonial conflicts in Southeast Asia were not only driven by capitalist expansion and exploitation, but also shaped by racial prejudices.[121] Farish Ahmad-Noor and Peter Carey have qualified them as 'wars of civilization', in which the 'adversarial Other was not an equal to the Western colonizer, but an inferior both racially and culturally'.[122] Racial stereotypes permeated British imperial imagination in warfare in Africa. For instance, in the Ashanti Wars Garnet Wolseley instructed his troops that 'every native of Africa' has 'a superstitious awe and dread of the white man that prevents the negro from daring to meet us face to face in combat'.[123] On other occasions,

---

Transimperial Notions of British, German, and Dutch Colonial Warfare, ca. 1890–1914' (2022) 46 *Itinerario* 84–108.

[118] Ukpabi, 'British Colonial Wars in West Africa', 399.

[119] Military theorists, such as Sun Tzu or Clausewitz opposed pillaging based on strategic rationales, such the resentment they may cause by defeated powers in the aftermath of hostilities. French General Thomas Robert Bugeaut recognized this dichotomy in the French war in Algeria in the 1840s. He stated: 'The object is not the present war; victory will be sterile without colonization ... I attach less importance, less glory to victory in battle than to the establishment of something valuable and useful for France'. Hew Strachan, *European Armies and the Conduct of War* (London & New York: Routledge, 1983) 78.

[120] See Wagner, 'Savage Warfare', 231; Catherine Hall, *Civilizing Subjects: Metropole and Colony in the English Imagination, 1830–1867* (2002) 10; Farish Ahmad-Noor and Peter-Brian Ramsay Carey (eds.), *Racial Difference and the Colonial Wars of 19th Century Southeast Asia* (Amsterdam: Amsterdam University Press, 2021); Rotem Giladi, 'The Phoenix of Colonial War: Race, the Laws of War, and the "Horror on the Rhine"' (2017) 30 *Leiden Journal of International Law* 847–875; Robert Knox, 'Civilizing Interventions? Race, War and International Law' (2013) 26 *Cambridge Review of International Affairs* 111–132; Devin O. Pendas, '"The Magical Scent of the Savage": Colonial Violence, the Crisis of Civilization, and the Origins of the Legalist Paradigm of War' (2007) 30 *British Colombia International & Comparative Law Review* 29–53.

[121] Scottish colonial administrator John Crawfurd (1783–1868) defined the strategies of the company in relation to Southeast Asia based on racial-biological distinctions of natives. He argued that there are 'broad' innate 'physical, intellectual, and moral differences' between European and Asiatic races, preventing local populations from reaching the same level of civilization as Western cultures. He distinguished almost civilized natives, from 'semi-civilized' and uncivilized populations, such as savages. See John Crawfurd, 'On the Physical and Mental Characteristics of the European and Asiatic Races of Man' (1867) 5 *Transactions of the Ethnological Society of London* 58–81, 81.

[122] Farish Ahmad-Noor and Peter Carey, 'Introduction: Why Race Mattered: Racial Difference, Racialized Colonial Capitalism and the Racialized Wars of Nineteenth-Century Colonial Southeast Asia' in Farish A. Noor and Peter Carey (eds.), *Racial Difference and the Colonial Wars of 19th Century Southeast Asia* (Amsterdam: Amsterdam University Press, 2021) 9–30, 15.

[123] Henry Brackenbury, *The Ashanti War: A Narrative Prepared from the Official Documents by Permission of Major-General Sir Garnet Wolseley by Henry Brackenbury, Volume 1* (Edinburgh: Blackwood and Sons, 1874) 366.

they were presented as skilled savage warriors.[124] Violence against cultural objects and persons was in itself perceived as a means of civilization, an 'object-lesson in civilization', as Ralph Moor, the British commissioner and consul for the Niger Coast Protectorate, put it in relation to looting of the Benin bronzes.[125]

These premises provided the foundations of 'savage war' doctrine.[126] In 1896, Charles Edward Callwell used the term 'small wars' to characterize colonial interventions and uses of force. It included 'campaigns of conquest when a Great Power adds the territory of barbarous races to its possessions' and 'punitive expeditions against tribes bordering upon distant colonies'.[127] The qualification of these encounter as 'small' wars had a strongly racialized background. The term 'small' referred not to the scope or intensity of warfare, but rather to the inferior and primitive nature of the adversary.[128] Political scientists, such as Quincy Wright (1890–1970), argued that the world was divided in 'three concentric spheres': 'that of civilized humanity, that of barbarous humanity and that of savage humanity entitled respectively to "plenary political recognition, partial political recognition and natural or merely human recognition".'[129] Such divisions led to the justification of double standards in colonial warfare.[130] The doctrine of 'savage warfare' accepted that there are constraints 'against indiscriminate looting and needless

---

[124] In the Anglo-Zulu War, the Zulus were considered as 'unusual savages'. See Catherine Anderson, 'Red Coats and Black Shields: Race and Masculinity in British Representations of the Anglo-Zulu War' (2008) 20 *Critical Survey* 6–28. An article in *The Graphic*, written in 1879 after the British defeat at the battle of Isandhlwana, stated: 'The Zulus may be savages, but they are not as savages usually are—a loose congregation of isolated bands provided with miserable weapons; these men possess enough of the civilised instinct to submit to a stern military despotism, they are, after a primitive fashion, well-drilled, and (as our loss has proved) well led, and, thanks to the unpatriotic enterprise of white traders, they are excellently armed.' Ibid, 15, referring to *The Graphic* (15 February 1879) 16.

[125] Consul-General Moor to the Marquess of Salisbury (24 February 1897) in Papers relating to the Massacre of British Officials near Benin, and the consequent Punitive Expedition presented to both Houses of Parliament by command of Her Majesty (August 1897) (London: Eyre and Spottiswode, 1897) 26–30, 29.

[126] On colonial warfare as 'transimperial phenomenon' and the justification of violence through the racialization of the enemy in British, German, and Dutch military manuals, see Tom Menger, 'Of "Golden Bridges" and "Big Bags": Thinking the Colonial Massacre in British, German and Dutch Manuals of Colonial Warfare, c. 1860–1910' in Noëmie Duhaut and Johannes Paulmann (eds.), *Europe Across Boundaries* (Oldenbourgh: De Gruyter, 2022) 79–97.

[127] Charles Edward Callwell, *Small Wars: Their Principles and Practice* (London: Her Majesty's Stationery Office, 1906) 22.

[128] Wesseling, 'Colonial Wars: An Introduction', 4.

[129] See Quincy Wright, 'The Bombardment of Damascus' (1926) 20 *AJIL* 263–280, 265.

[130] In 1927, Captain Elbridge Colby relied on the concept of 'savage warfare' in order to justify the brutal bombing of Damascus by French troops, following a Syrian revolt in the French protectorate. In his article 'How to Fight Savage Tribes', he argued that 'the laws of war mean nothing' to 'Oriental peoples' since they 'are accustomed to pillaging and being pillaged, accustomed to torturing and flaying alive distinguished prisoners'. Elbridge Colby, 'How to Fight Savage Tribes' (1927) 21 *AJIL* 279–288, 285. He used this argument to justify the discriminatory application of the laws of war in armed conflicts with 'savages'. He stated: 'When combatants and non-combatants are practically identical among a people, and savage or semi-savage peoples take advantage of this identity to effect ruses, surprises and massacres on the 'regular' enemy, commanders must attack their problems in entirely different ways form those in which they proceed against Western peoples.' Ibid, 279.

barbarity', but derived them from 'the internal necessity for military discipline and control, as well as an innate sense of decency'.[131]

4.2 Double standards and racial bias in the laws of war

These double standards are reflected in the history of the laws of war.[132] They gained popularity in the context of guerrilla warfare in Spanish War of Independence (1807–1814).

4.2.1 Historical codifications
Early military manuals and humanitarian codifications are marked by a friction.[133] They sought to humanize warfare and recognized the special importance of the protection of cultural objects in armed conflict. However, they continued to be shaped by classical Western-centred conceptions of cultural property and civilizational divides.

The Lieber Code enhanced protection of cultural objects in wartime. It established a framework for the protection of property in order to prevent destruction and looting in armed conflict. It exempted the property of 'museums of the fine arts' or scientific institutions from the general rules of seizure applying to public property[134] and required conflicting parties to 'secure' certain types of cultural property from injury in the context of sieges or bombardment.[135] However,

---

[131] Ibid.

[132] They may be traced back to scholars, such as Emerich de Vattel, who argued that 'ravaging and burning' may be justified in warfare by the 'necessity of chastising an unjust and barbarous nation, or checking her brutality'. See Emerich de Vattel, *The Law of Nations, Or, Principles of the Law of Nature, Applied to the conduct of Affairs of Nations and Sovereigns*, Book III, § 167. He wrote: 'Who can doubt that the king of Spain and the powers of Italy have a very good right utterly to destroy those maritime towns of Africa, those nests of pirates, that are continually molesting their commerce and ruining their subjects? But what nation will proceed to such extremities merely for the sake of punishing the hostile sovereign?' Johann Bluntschli argued the that the 'removal of items or documents of artistic value' should be limited, since it lacks a 'direct connection' with war aims. Johann Caspar Bluntschli, *Le droit international codifié* (Paris: Felix Alcan, 1895) 42–43.

[133] In East Asia, cultural protection was subordinated to imperial interests in the Sino-Japanese war. Shortly before the war in 1894, Kuki Ryūichi (1852–1931), the Director General of the Imperial Museum in Japan, issued an instruction, which legitimized the collection of Chinese and Korean treasures in warfare. Ji Young Park, 'Kuki Ryūichi: How to Collect Treasures of the Qing Dynasty during the War (1894)' in Bénédicte Savoy, Robert Skwirblies, and Isabelle Dolezalek (eds.), *Beute: Eine Anthologie zu Kunstraub und Kulturerbe* (Berlin: Matthes & Seitz, 2021) 227–231. It was meant to guide public officials and military officers. It specified that it was in Japan's national interest to collect cultural artefacts in imperial warfare, since armed conflict provides an opportunity to collect objects which are difficult to acquire in peacetime. The instruction acknowledged that collection was subject to rules of public international law. But it argued that it is permissible for victorious power to collect enemy property for purposes of preservation and national prestige. The document has been described as an 'anti-civilizational guideline for a civilized nation'. Ibid, 227.

[134] Instructions for the Government of Armies of the United States in the Field, General Order No 100 (Lieber Code) (24 April 1863) Art. 34.

[135] Ibid, Art. 35.

it limited property protection to established public institutions, churches or arts and sciences in the Western sense, namely 'classical works of art, libraries, scientific collections'.[136] It distinguished 'modern regular wars of the Europeans, and their descendants in other portions of the globe' expressly from wars 'fought by barbarians'.[137] It stated: 'Protection was, and still is with uncivilized peoples, the exception'.

The subsequent codifications of the laws of war in the 1899 and 1907 Conventions, which were deemed to constitute customary law, sought to strike a balance between the necessities of war, humanitarian ideals, and cultural protection. They contained traces of progression, but also continued to facilitate histories of oppression and exploitation of non-civilized entities.[138] The Conventions extended war-time protection of cultural property beyond the Brussels Declaration of 1874, initiated by Henry Dunant and the Emperor of Russia.[139] They approached property protection through the distinction between public and private property and the perspective of protected sites.[140] They protected cultural property as a category of civilian property, and more specifically through the Regulations on the laws and customs on war on land, annexed to Hague Convention No. IV (1907).

Protection in hostilities was not framed in absolute terms, but connected to considerations of military necessity, which allowed destruction of cultural sites or objects if required by the exigencies of war.[141] It was generally prohibited to 'destroy or seize the enemy's property', unless 'imperatively demanded by the necessities of war'.[142] Special categories of immovable property, such as 'buildings dedicated to religion, art, science, or charitable purposes' and 'historic monuments' were given special protection. The 1907 Hague Regulations made clear they should be

---

[136] Ibid, Arts. 34–36.

[137] Ibid, Arts. 24, 25.

[138] Amanda Alexander, 'A Short History of International Humanitarian Law' (2015) 26 *EJIL* 109–138, 113. This tension is reflected in the preamble to the Hague Convention No. IV ('Animated by the desire to serve, even in this extreme case, the interests of humanity and the ever progressive needs of civilization'). Only few non-European states participated in the first Peace Conference (US, Mexico, Turkey, Iran, China, Japan, and Thailand (Siam)). African voices were absent. See David D. Caron, 'War and International Adjudication: Reflections on the 1899 Peace Conference' (2000) 94 *AJIL* 4–30, 6.

[139] The Brussels Declaration qualified 'institutions dedicated to religion, charity and education' and 'the arts and sciences' as protected private property and made their seizure or destruction in situations of occupation subject to 'legal proceedings by the competent authorities'. See Project of an International Declaration Concerning the Laws and Customs of War, adopted by the Conference of Brussels (27 August 1874) Art. 8. It also obliged conflicting parties to take 'all necessary steps' to 'spare' such institutions, 'as far as possible' from bombardments and siege, 'provided they are not being used at the time for military purposes'. Ibid, Art. 17. The term 'buildings dedicated to religions', instead of churches, was introduced the Turkish delegate and meant to cover 'Christian and non-Christian' buildings. Jiri Toman, *The Protection of Cultural Property in the Event of Armed Conflict* (UNESCO: Dartmouth, 1996), 11. But the instrument never became formally binding.

[140] Ibid, 13.

[141] Joshua E. Kastenberg, 'The Legal Regime for Protecting Cultural Property During Armed Conflict' (1997) 42 *Air Force Law Review* 277–302, 286.

[142] Article 23(g) of the 1907 Hague Regulations.

spared 'as far as possible' in 'sieges and bombardments'.[143] They also prohibited the pillaging of towns or places more generally.[144] The prohibition of pillage was grounded in an 'imperative to minimize the harms of war and the desirability of restoring peace'.[145]

The Regulations limited the rights of occupying powers in relation to movable or immovable cultural property, in an effort to protect the sovereignty of occupied states over their territory and patrimony. They specified that property of 'institutions dedicated to religion, charity and education' and 'the arts and sciences', should be treated as protected private property, even when it is owned by the state.[146] This cultural property was thus protected from confiscation[147] or pillage.[148] They also awarded special protection to 'institutions of this character', 'historic monuments' and 'works of art and science', by prohibiting their seizure, destruction or wilful damaging and making violations 'subject' to 'legal proceedings'.[149]

The approach towards cultural heritage protection was heavily shaped by Western-liberal conceptions of property.[150] It relied on public-private distinctions, which were shared by 'civilized' nations at the same time, but less common in other societies. It protects cultural property not so much, because of its relevance or importance to humanity as such,[151] but rather through the lens of civil-military distinctions and its value for civilians (in the sense of the laws of war).[152] Due to loosely defined concepts, such as military necessity, the 'line between legal commandeering and illegal looting' remained thin.[153] Cultural protection received considerably less importance in combat with non-civilized entities.[154]

---

[143] Ibid, Art. 27.

[144] Ibid, Art. 28.

[145] Stephen M. Miller and Jessica Miller, 'Moral and Legal Prohibitions against Pillage in the Context of the 1899 Hague Convention and the South African War' (2019) 26 *War in History* 185–203, 195.

[146] 1907 Hague Regulations, Art. 56.

[147] Ibid, Art. 46.

[148] Ibid, Art. 47.

[149] Ibid, Art. 56.

[150] This is reflected in the equation to private property. The concept of private property was used to legitimate protection and the primary point of reference in the laws of war. See Sebastian Spitra, *Die Verwaltung von Kultur im Völkerrecht* (Baden-Baden: Nomos, 2021) 134.

[151] Micaela Frulli has called this the 'cultural-value approach'. See Micaela Frulli, 'The Criminalization of Offences against Cultural Heritage in Times of Armed Conflict: The Quest for Consistency' (2011) 22 *The European Journal of International Law* 203–217, 205.

[152] The Conventions placed considerable focus on the historic, artistic, or scientific relevance role of objects in their conception of culture. The spiritual value of places or objects as such gained lesser attention. See Sigrid Van der Auwera, 'International Law and the Protection of Cultural Property in the Event of Armed Conflict: Actual Problems and Challenges' (2013) 43 *The Journal of Arts Management, Law, and Society* 175–190, 179. Article 16 of the Additional Protocol No. 2 to the Geneva Conventions contains a wider protection. Under the Protocol, it is 'prohibited to commit any acts of hostility directed against historic monuments, works of art or places of worship which constitute the cultural or spiritual heritage of peoples'.

[153] Miller and Miller, 'Moral and legal prohibitions against pillage' 197–198.

[154] John MacDonnell, 'Looting in China' (1901) 79 *Contemporary Review* 444–452, 446–450.

4.2.2 Indeterminacy and contradictory behaviour

The ambiguous approach towards cultural protection became apparent in the immediate aftermath of the 1899 Convention. In practice, looting was not abandoned, but at best renamed or constrained. Prize procedures, which converted plundered property into orderly distributed assets, continued to be applied after the Hague Peace Conferences.[155] They did not prohibit the taking of property as such, but merely constrained it for purposes of discipline and order, namely to prevent uncontrolled takings and to secure transparency and proper distribution for the benefit of the Crown and soldiers. They were sometimes even used as recruitment tools.[156]

States relied on the ambiguities of the Convention in colonial hostilities in order to maintain flexibility in the methods.[157] The pillage of Beijing in 1900, carried out after an allied intervention to defeat the Boxer rebellion in China,[158] showed openly that major powers and allied forces failed to come to an agreement on approaches and applied double standards in hostilities with non-European entities. The amount of loot and plunder carried out after the occupation of Beijing was even larger than the looting of Yuanmingyuan palace in 1860.

The intervention was based on requests from missionaries and businessmen, who called for a punitive response to violations of concessions by members of Boxer rebellion and the Qing government, the killing of Christians, and attacks on foreign property.[159] The allied force was formally led by German commander (Count Alfred von Waldersee). It comprised eight nations (Germany, Japan, Russia, Britain, France, the United States, Italy, and Austria-Hungary). Journalist George Lynch, who accompanied the multinational force, argued that it was 'the

---

[155] The double standards of prize procedures were acknowledged by Mary Hooker in her account of the looting in Beijing in 1900. She wrote: 'The English, although giving their vote for no looting, added they should continue to place "in safe-keeping all valuable things" found in the district given them to police. This, of course, gives them practically the right to loot, although whatever is brought in has to be placed in one place, where they have an auction later, and the officially prescribed amount pro rata is given to the officers and men, so that they are really doing just what the other nations are doing, only in a somewhat more legalized way'. See Mary Hooker, *Behind the scenes in Peking* (London: John Murray, 1911) 191.

[156] Byron Farewell, *Mr Kipling's Army* (New York: Norton, 1981) 211.

[157] For example, during the Boer wars in South Africa, British troops searched and destroyed farms and confiscated property. Lord Frederick Roberts, the Supreme Commander of the British forces, authorized inter alia the looting of homes and the confiscation of cattle. He justified these measures by the ambiguity of the military necessity clause in the Hague convention and the fact that the Boers used guerrilla tactics, which removed moral constraints in warfare. See Miller and Miller, 'Moral and legal prohibitions against pillage in the context of the 1899 Hague Convention and the South African War', 202.

[158] Michael H. Hunt, 'The Forgotten Occupation: Peking, 1900-1901' (1979) 48 *Pacific Historical Review* 501–529.

[159] See James Hevia, 'Looting and Its Discontents: Moral Discourse and the Plunder of Beijing, 1900–1901' in R. Bickers and R. G. Tiedemann (eds.), *The Boxers, China, and the World* (London: Rowman & Littlefield Publishers, 2007) 93–114. He argued that the forcible intervention 'against Chinese "barbarism"' was justified 'either on the grounds of retributive justice or as a timeless feature of warfare'. Ibid, 102.

biggest looting expedition' since Pizarro's conquest of Peru.[160] It was branded as a 'carnival of loot'. The troops of the multinational force engaged in systematic and widespread looting,[161] although many members were signatory to the Hague Convention. James Hevia wrote: '[a] loot fever gripped the armies and Euro-American civilian population in Beijing, and a wild orgy of plunder ensued, one in which few if any could resist temptation'.[162]

Soldiers plundered Qing palaces, private homes or premised, or shops. They searched for jewellery, bronzes, ornaments, or garments. Waldersee has described the practices in an account of events.[163] He reported that 'Indian troops' took 'it as a matter of course that the property of a defeated enemy should be looted'.[164] The French 'looted freely, with the encouragement of General Frey',[165] who sent a bronze lion as trophy to Paris. Japanese soldiers 'plundered with system and discipline'. They were keen to acquire artistic or antique objects, including imperial artefacts, and distinguished objects of historical importance from other trophies.[166] They were not 'permitted to loot for private profit' but 'required to turn over' what they had taken.[167] US troops looted contrary to military instructions, but were allowed by US commander Adna Chaffee (1842–1914) to sell the booty in auctions, which contributed to the recovery of the costs of the US intervention.[168] British soldiers were reportedly 'on the search for articles of value' and 'particularly interested in bronzes'.[169] They removed Buddha statues from temples in Beijing, under the protest from the Chinese, not 'for their historical or artistic value, but merely on account of their metal'.[170]

Russian troops were described as the 'the frankest and most brutal' forces: 'Not only did they plunder on private account but also officially. They were particularly keen for the art objects that were so abundant in the Summer and Winter Palaces, and in the private palaces under Russian protection. Whole wagon-trains of these objects were shipped.'[171] Each contingent followed the rules or instructions from their home government. Several forces introduced auctions or prize procedures to

---

[160] George Lynch, *The War of the Civilizations* (New York: Longmans, Green & Co., 1901) 179.

[161] Waldersee noted that it is 'useless to discuss whether the Russians, Japanese, English, French, or Americans' played the biggest role 'in these exploits': 'All shared in them'. See Alfred Waldersee, 'Plundering Peking' (1923) 317 *The Living Age* 563–569, 565.

[162] Hevia, 'Looting and Its Discontents', 94.

[163] Ibid, based on notes by Heinrich Otto Meisner, who published the account in 'Preussische Jahrbücher'.

[164] Waldersee, 'Plundering Peking', 566.

[165] Ibid, 568.

[166] Hevia, 'Looting and Its Discontents', 98.

[167] Waldersee, 'Plundering Peking', 565.

[168] Waldersee notes: 'For weeks you could buy openly in the American Camps, from officers and privates alike, articles of every kind, and it was not unusual to see American soldiers peddling their booty'. Waldersee, 'Plundering Peking', 565.

[169] Ibid, 567.

[170] Waldersee writes: 'They did not go to museums but to foundries'. Ibid, 567.

[171] Ibid, 567.

control and manage looting. They became a daily occurrence over a period of two months and were 'regularly advertised and published'[172] or even reported in illustrated newspapers. The sale included a wide range of booty: 'porcelains, cloisonnes, bronzes, red-lacquerwares, furs, silks (mostly in bales), embroideries, clocks, real pearls, precious stones, and various ornaments'.[173] The objects were purchased by European or American collectors or Chinese bidders. Some of them went to European or North America markets and museums.[174]

The Beijing loot caused divisive reactions. Waldersee noted that the sales were 'considered strictly regular and legal'[175] under prize law procedures. However, he criticized their 'hypocrisy'.[176] The press in the UK, France, the US, and Japan qualified the plunder as a barbaric act or expressed 'moral shame' and 'barbarism'.[177] The behaviour stood in flagrant contrast to the protection of cultural property under the Hague Conventions. The auctions and prize procedures transformed looted objects 'into private property'.[178] This legal contradiction was only recognized by a few voices.[179]

4.2.3 The divide of the legal protection of 'non-civilized' entities

The divide between humanitarian positions and the rule of colonial difference is reflected in the framing of the two Hague Conventions.[180] Some progressive voices had advocated universal application of minimum protections at the end of the nineteenth century. For instance, Bluntschli argued that 'savages are men' who 'ought to be treated with humanity'.[181] However, such positions were viewed as utopian by delegates who defended colonial warfare or called for the restriction of warfare between European powers at The Hague Conferences.[182] In particular

---

[172] Ibid, 567.

[173] Ibid, 566.

[174] Waldersee notes: 'One of the most eager buyers was Lady MacDonald, who took it exceedingly ill if anybody ventured to bid against her. She bought vast quantities of treasures, naturally at ridiculously low prices'. Ibid, 566.

[175] Ibid, 567. He notes: 'The proceeds were regarded as a sort of prize money, and distributed to the British expeditionaries according to a sliding scale, which must have given the Commanding General a small fortune. Naturally all the loot was not turned into the common stock'.

[176] Ibid, 567.

[177] Hevia, 'Looting and Its Discontents', 102–104.

[178] Hevia, *English Lessons*, 83.

[179] MacDonnell, 'Looting in China', 446–450; Lynch, *War of Civilizations*, 303, 311–316.

[180] Stephen Barcroft, 'The Hague Peace Conference of 1899' (1998) 3 *Irish Studies in International Affairs* 55–68.

[181] See J. Llewelyn Davies, 'International Christianity' (1880) 38 *Contemporary Review* 231–232, 227. Bluntschli argued in 1874 argued that civilized nations should respect the laws of humanity even in case of violations of the laws of war. He wrote: 'The barbarian conduct of the enemy does not authorize similar actions against him. If the savages torture their prisoners and put them to death, civilized troops can at most shoot their prisoners, and under no circumstances torture them'. See Johann Caspar Bluntschli, *Le droit international codifié* (Paris: Guillaumin,1874) 318, para. 567.

[182] Friedrich Martens (1845–1909), the famous 'name-giver' of the Martens clause, was influenced by the divide between 'civilized' nations and 'non-civilized' countries and challenged Bluntschli's 'enlightened cosmopolitanism'. See Lauri Mälksoo, 'The Legacy of F.F. Martens and the Shadow of Colonialism' *Chinese Journal of International Law* (2022). He argued that 'international law is not applicable to the whole human race' and excludes 'dealings with savage or semi-barbarous nations', who ignore

those who had fought in colonial contexts feared that restrictions in the conduct of warfare would 'favour savage nations at the expense of the more highly civilised'.[183] They claimed that relations towards non-civilized nations were governed by natural law, rather than international law[184] or that it would be unfeasible to extend equal protection to colonial subjects, since they were considered to be particularly cruel or violent or unwilling to recognize the limits of 'civilized' warfare and manifest restraint.[185] These stereotypes were coupled with a sense of denial of the cruelty of colonial practices. European atrocities were downplayed or excused by the 'savage' environment.[186] Sometimes, locals were deemed responsible for a decay of Western standards.

4.2.4 The debate on dum dum bullets

At the 1899 Hague Peace Conference, these tensions became apparent in the debate[187] on the contested of use of dum dum bullets[188] in colonial wars. It illustrates

---

'commerce, agriculture and trade' and cannot be expected to comply with the 'principle of reciprocity – a principle beyond the comprehension of barbarians'. See Friedrich Martens, *Russia and England in Central Asia* (London: Ridgway, 1879) 18, 22, 23.

[183] See Admiralty's position paper to the Foreign Office, 'Admiralty to UK Foreign Office' (16 May 1899) in Paul Smith, *Government and Armed Forces in Britain, 1856–1990*, 51. At the 1899 Conference, Vice Admiral Sir John Arbuthnot 'Jacky' Fisher argued that any limitations 'would place civilized peoples in a dangerous situation in case of war with less civilized nations or savage tribes'. See Scott, *Proceedings of The Hague Peace Conferences*, 360.

[184] For Martens claimed that 'in Asia international law is superseded by the law of nature'. See Martens, *Russia and England in Central Asia*, 26. On his view on colonialism, see Friedrich Martens, 'La conférence du Congo à Berlin et la politique coloniale des États modernes' (1886) XVIII *Revue de droit international et de législation comparée* 244–280.

[185] John Stuart Mill had argued in his 'Few Words on Non-intervention' that the 'rules of ordinary international morality' cannot be applied to 'barbarians' since they 'imply reciprocity'. John Stuart Mill, 'A Few Words on Non-intervention' in John Stuart Mill, *Dissertations and Discussions: Political, Philosophical, and Historical*, Vol. 4 (Boston: William V. Spencer, 1867) 157–182, 171–172. In 1899, Theodore Roosevelt defended methods of US expansion (e.g. the war in the Philippines) and submission of 'barbarian' natives in an essay entitled 'Expansion and Peace'. See Theodore Roosevelt, 'Expansion and Peace' in Theodore Roosevelt, *The Strenuous Life: Essays and Addresses* (New York: P. F. Collier & Son, 1900) 23–36, 31.

[186] For instance, when British officials learned about abuses in the Congo Free State, they refused to believe that such 'acts of refined cruelty' could have been committed by 'members of a cultivated people'. See Adam Hochschild, *King Leopold's Ghost: A Story of Greed, Terror, and Heroism in Colonial Africa* (Boston: Mariner Books, 1999) 204. In other cases, they blamed them on the conditions in Africa 'where the European mind disintegrates and regresses into a primitive state' Ania Loomba, *Colonialism/Postcolonialism* (London: Routledge, 2005) 117.

[187] See generally Edward Spiers, 'The Use of the Dum Dum Bullet in Colonial Warfare' (1975) 4 *The Journal of Imperial and Commonwealth History* 3–14; Geoffrey Best, 'Peace Conferences and the Century of Total War: The 1899 Conference and What Came After' (1999) 75 *International Affairs* 619–634; Maartje Abbenhuis, Branka Bogdan, and\ Emma Wordsworth, 'Humanitarian Bullets and Man-Killers: Revisiting the History of Arms Regulation in the Late Nineteenth Century' (2022) *International Review of the Red Cross* 1–24, doi:10.1017/S1816383122000492. Tensions became evident in the debate at the third meeting of the First Commission on 31 May 1899.

[188] Dum dum bullets were developed by the British army in campaigns in India in order to increase the impact of rifle bullets in hostilities with barbarian enemies, and produced in a factory in Dum-Dum, near Calcutta. Their value and necessity was contested by continental surgeons, such as Paul

the conflicting positions on the permissibility of their use against 'non-civilized' entities. One possibility was to take the 'moral high ground' and accept that colonial warfare should, in principle, be subject to the same standards of warfare as 'civilized nations'. This position was supported by the humanitarian ethos of the laws of war, namely to put enemy soldiers outside of combat (*hors de combat*)[189] and reinforced by pragmatic considerations, namely the fear that allowing cruel methods of warfare in colonial warfare could backfire in European contexts.[190] However, the British delegation remained opposed to an open condemnation of the dum dum bullets. It argued that European continental powers misunderstood their effects and that 'that public opinion in England would never sanction the use of a projectile which would cause useless suffering'.[191] The British delegate, General Sir John Ardagh, who had fought in Egypt and served in India, rationalized their use through their effectiveness in colonial wars.[192] Such justifications were promoted by biases and fantasies regarding the physical alterity of natives (e.g. their presentation as 'super-humans'), which were propagated in medical journals.[193]

---

von Bruns, who criticized their excessive destructive potential in comparison to other bullets. Paul von Bruns, *Über die Wirkung der Bleispitzengeschosse (Dum-Dum Geschosse)* (Tübingen: Laupp'sche Buchlandlung. 1898).

[189] Delegates argued that ordinary bullets were 'sufficient for this purpose'. See e.g. Colonel Gilinsky in Scott, *Proceedings of The Hague Peace Conferences*, 279.

[190] Colonel Gilinsky stated that would be improper to 'make a distinction between civilized and savage tribes'. Ibid, 83.

[191] General Sir John Ardagh in Scott, *Proceedings of The Hague Peace Conferences*, 277 ('the erroneous conception formed in Europe').

[192] Ardagh stated at the third meeting of the First Commission on 22 June 1899: 'It has been proven in one of our petty wars in India that a man perforated five times by these bullets was still able to walk a considerable distance to an English hospital to have his wounds dressed. It was proven just recently, after the Battle of Om-Durman, that the large majority of the Dervishes who were able to save themselves by flight had been wounded by small English bullets, whereas the Remington and Martini of the Egyptian army sufficed to disable. It was necessary to find some more efficient means, and to meet this necessity in India, the projectile known under the name of 'dumdum' was made in the arsenal of that name near Calcutta'. Scott, *Proceedings of The Hague Peace Conferences*, 276–277.

[193] For instance, British surgeon Alexander Ogston defended the use of expanding dum dum bullets in 'wars with semi-civilised or barbarous races who practise no humanity in their warfare'. See Alexander Ogston, 'Continental Criticism Of English Rifle Bullets' (1899/1995) *The British Medical Journal* 752–757, 752. He argued that it would be contradictory to prohibit a 'missile that was permissible against a charging tiger, elephant, or buffalo' against a 'charging human enemy, however fierce and tiger-like his onset might be'. Ibid, 752. He criticized that in India or Sudan, 'the injuries produced by the modern bullets were remarkably slight—so slight that a brave and determined enemy was not stopped or disabled in his onset'. Alexander Ogston, 'The Wounds Produced by Modern Small-Bore Bullets: The Dum-Dum Bullet and the Soft-Nosed Mauser' (1898) 2 *The British Medical Journal* 813–815, 814. Surgeon-Major J. B. Hamilton openly argued that natives are less sensitive to injuries than 'white men'. He wrote in the British Medical Journal in 1898: '[C]ivilised man is much more susceptible to injury than savages. As a rule when a 'white man' is wounded he has had enough, and is quite ready to drop out of the ranks and go to the rear; but the savage, like the tiger, is not so impressionable, and will go on fighting even when desperately wounded.' J. B. Hamilton, 'The Evolution of the Dum-Dum Bullet' (1898) 1950 *The British Medical Journal* 1250–1251, 1251.

Initiatives to ban expanding bullets were introduced by the Swiss delegate, Colonel Arnold Künzli,[194] and the Russian delegate, Colonel Gilinsky.[195] Gilinsky argued that there is a gap in the existing law. He referred to a 'hiatus' in the St. Petersburg Declaration of 1868.[196] He stated:

> As to savages, they are of course not guaranteed against the use even of explosive bullets. In the St. Petersburg Declaration of 1868, the contracting Powers decided not to employ these bullets in wars among themselves. It is evident that there is a gap in the St. Petersburg Declaration, a gap which enables not only dumdum bullets but even explosive bullets to be used against savages.[197]

The Russian delegate, Arthur Raffalovich, argued that the defence of dum dum bullets in colonial warfare would be 'contrary to the humanitarian spirit which dominates this end of the nineteenth century'.[198] He stated that would be 'impermissible to make a distinction between a savage and a civilized enemy' because 'both are men who deserve the same treatment'.[199] He added that it would be unfeasible to maintain different standards, since 'soldiers stationed outside of Europe and armed with bullets for use against savages' might 'be called upon to fight against the regular troops of a civilized nation',[200] and could not change bullets overnight.

The counter-position was advocated by General Ardagh. He stated expressly that 'there is a difference in war between civilized nations and that against savages'.[201] He defended the permissibility of expanding bullets by the violence of opponents, i.e. the cruelty of 'fanatical barbarians'. His argument illustrates the racial biases and stereotypes associated with the 'colonial other'. He noted:

> In civilized war a soldier penetrated by a small projectile is wounded, withdraws to the ambulance, and does not advance any further. It is very different with a savage. Even though pierced two or three times, he does not cease to march forward, does not call upon the hospital attendants, but continues on, and before anyone has time to explain to him that he is flagrantly violating the decisions of the Hague Conference,

---

[194] The Swiss proposal stated: 'Prohibition of infantry projectiles such as have the point of the casing perforated or filed, and whose direct passage through the body is prevented by an empty interior or by the use of soft lead'. See Scott, *Proceedings of The Hague Peace Conferences*, 338.

[195] The Russian proposal read: 'The use of bullets whose envelope does not entirely cover the core at the point, or is pierced with incisions, and, in general, the use of bullets which expand or flatten easily in the human body, should be prohibited, since they do not conform to the spirit of the Declaration of St. Petersburg of 1868.' See Scott, *Proceedings of The Hague Peace Conferences*, 338.

[196] Declaration Renouncing the Use, in Time of War, of Explosive Projectiles under 400 Grammes Weight, Saint Petersburg (29 November/11 December 1868). See Colonel Gilinsky in Scott, *Proceedings of The Hague Peace Conferences*, 287.

[197] Colonel Gilinsky in Scott, *Proceedings of The Hague Peace Conferences*, 344.

[198] Mr Raffalovich in Scott, *Proceedings of The Hague Peace Conferences*, 343.

[199] Ibid, 343.

[200] Ibid, 344.

[201] General John Ardagh in Scott, *Proceedings of The Hague Peace Conferences*, 286.

he cuts off your head. It is for this reason that the English delegate demands the liberty to use projectiles of sufficient efficacy against savage populations.[202]

Ultimately, Ardagh was unable to persuade other delegates that wounds inflicted through dum dum bullets are comparable to injuries caused by other ammunition and necessary in colonial warfare. Nineteen countries supported a prohibition of 'bullets which expand or flatten easily in the human body'.[203] Mr. Auguste Beernaert, the Belgian First Delegate and President of the first Commission, gave an indication of the views at the third meeting on 22 June 1899. He stated:

> The President believes that he expresses the opinion of the assembly in saying that there can be no distinction established between the projectiles permitted and the projectiles prohibited according to the enemies against which they fight even in case of savages.[204]

Britain felt that the proposals to limit such warfare were part of a 'crusade against British rule in Africa'.[205] As Historian Arthur Eyffinger reports, the Dutch Vice President of the conference, Abraham Pieter Cornelis van Karnebeek, made a last-minute attempt in an informal meeting on 8 July 1899 to win British support for the majority opinion, by arguing that additional prohibitions to the St. Petersburg Declaration were 'only binding upon signatory and acceding states' and thus not 'applicable to savage warfare'.[206] However, the British side refused to join the majority, since it continued to take the view that the condemned bullets did not inflict unnecessary suffering.[207]

The ambiguity, pointed out by Van Karnebeek, is reflected in the final text. The wording of the Declaration, adopted at the Conference, is far less clear and committal than the Russian argument. It fails to make any mention that a 'savage' and 'a civilized enemy' ought to be treated equally. It simply states:

> The Contracting Parties agree to abstain from the use of bullets which expand or flatten easily in the human body, such as bullets with a hard envelope which does not entirely cover the core or is pierced with incisions.

---

[202] Ibid in Scott, *Proceedings of The Hague Peace Conferences*, 343.
[203] Scott, *Proceedings of The Hague Peace Conferences*, 287 (noting support for the 'Russian formula' by 'Germany, United States of America, Belgium, Denmark, Spain, France, Japan, Netherlands, Persia, Portugal, Italy, Romania, Russia, Serbia, Siam, Sweden and Norway, Switzerland, Turkey and Bulgaria').
[204] President Beernaert, in Scott, *Proceedings of The Hague Peace Conferences*, 287.
[205] Arthur Eyffinger, *The 1899 Hague Peace Conference: The Parliament of Man, the Federation of the World* (Dordrecht: Kluwer, 1999) 227. Ogston later even claimed that the majority stance brands Britain 'as anti-humanitarian and barbarous'. Alexander Ogston, 'The Peace Conference and the Dum-Dum Bullet' (1899) 2(2013) *The British Medical Journal* 278–281, 278.
[206] Eyffinger, *The 1899 Hague Peace Conference*, 231.
[207] Ibid, 231.

The present Declaration is only binding for the Contracting Powers in the case of a war between two or more of them.[208]

The reference to 'war between two or more of them' suggests that the obligation applies in civilized warfare, not in colonial wars against non-civilized entities. Non-civilized entities were not permitted to become 'contracting parties'. This left non-European peoples formally outside the framework of laws of war and, thereby, ultimately kept protective provisions out of the colonies. It provided leeway for a permissive reading in later practice, which made compliance voluntary and subject to the judgment of individual commanders in hostilities, in case of armed hostilities against enemies that were not party to conventions.

4.2.5 The flexible approach towards the laws of war in military doctrines
The ambiguity of international instruments provided space for states to adjust their approach to international legal protections on a case-by-case basis in military strategies of the early twentieth century. Colonial forces used grey zones to their benefit in order to maintain flexibility and discretion. They presented themselves as guardians of the law, if that was in the interest of colonial operations, and considered themselves at liberty to justify extreme violence, if this was deemed necessary for military needs. They interpreted fundamental notions, such as the notion of 'civilian' or civilian objects in different ways in hostilities with irregular armies or tribes. However, warfare was justified 'through the law', rather than through a logic of exclusion.[209]

For instance, in the Philippine-American War in 1899, bringing 'civilization' to the Philippines was one of the main narratives used to justify armed force. Yale academic Theodore Woolsey (1852–1929) argued that the US was not bound by the laws of war in hostilities with local guerrilla forces, since their strategies did not comply with the Hague Convention.[210] The US government and military,[211] by contrast, saw merit in the argument to accept the applicability of the laws of war in principle, subject to their own interpretation in order to maintain claims of moral superiority and civility.[212] If necessary, extraordinary violence was justified by perceived military needs or the need to 'civilize' the enemy.[213]

A similar approach is reflected in Dutch operations in Indonesia. As host of the Hague Peace Conference, the Dutch who were eager to 'bring the colonial military

---

[208] Hague Peace Conference, Declaration No 3 concerning Expanding Bullets (29 July 1899).

[209] Smiley, 'Lawless Wars of Empire?', 544.

[210] Theodore S. Woolsey, 'The Legal Aspects of Aguinaldo's Capture', *The Outlook* (13 April 1901) 855–856; Smiley, 'Lawless Wars of Empire?', 539–540.

[211] Military commanders had an interest in advocating compliance with the law, because army officers were trained to obey the laws of war and structure operations according to these principles. Smiley, 'Lawless Wars of Empire?', 540–543.

[212] Ibid, 548.

[213] Ibid, 548.

ethics into line with the international laws of war'.[214] They argued that military force in operations in Indonesia should be constrained by the law and ethics of war on pragmatic grounds, namely to limit local resistance, or to set a good 'humane' example. They established special rules for colonial warfare, which limited the application of principles, such as the distinction between combatants and non-combatants or the prohibition of collective punishment.[215] No attempt was undertaken to understand various non-European customs which reflect practices similar to modern rules of international humanitarian law.

4.2.6 'Colonial occupations' and the laws of war

The double standards in colonial warfare are further reflected in the law of occupation. The codification of the law of occupation increased the protection of cultural objects since it constrained the rights of victors of war to take property as war booty. It made it clear that an occupant does not acquire sovereignty over foreign territory or ownership of property of the defeated power.[216] However, the 1899 and 1907 Hague Regulations relied on a concept of occupation that is ill-suited to apply to colonial warfare.[217] It was geared at regulating wars between sovereigns, based on the idea that laws of war apply 'within the boundaries of the so-called "civilized" world'.[218] 'Colonial occupations' were not meant to fit into the framing of the laws of war.[219]

Bringing colonial warfare under the umbrella of occupation would have impeded colonial expansion. The General Act of the 1885 Berlin Conference implied that effective occupation was a legitimate means to acquire sovereign powers over the entities in question.[220] The drafters had an interest in distinguishing occupation, which is deemed to be temporary in nature, from colonial subjugation, which is meant to secure long-term control and power or the assumption of sovereignty without constraints.[221]

---

[214] See Petra Groen, 'Colonial Warfare and Military Ethics in the Netherlands East Indies, 1816–1941' (2012) 14 *Journal of Genocide Research* 277–296, 288.

[215] Ibid.

[216] This point was already made by August Wilhelm Heffter in 1844. He noted: 'From a legal perspective, the defeat of the enemy does not immediately bring about the complete subjugation of the enemy's state authority'. See August Wilhelm Heffter, *Das Europäische Völkerrecht der Gegenwart* (Berlin: E. H. Schroeder, 1844) 220–221. See also Spitra, *Die Verwaltung von Kultur im Völkerrecht* 127.

[217] Eyal Benvenisti, 'The Origins of the Concept of Belligerent Occupation' (2008) 26 *Law and History Review* 621–648, 647.

[218] Thomas Graditzky, 'The Law of Military Occupation from the 1907 Hague Peace Conference to the Outbreak of World War II: Was Further Codification Unnecessary or Impossible?' (2019) 29 *EJIL* 1305–1326, 1321.

[219] Yutaka Arai-Takahashi, 'Preoccupied with Occupation: Critical examinations of the historical development of the law of occupation' (2012) 94 *International Review of the Red Cross* 51–80.

[220] In practice, European states continued to rely on treaty practices to support their authority, but invoked the provisions of the Final Act of the Berlin Conference to justify their claims. See Onuma, 'When was the Law of International Society Born?', 47.

[221] Arai-Takahashi, 'Preoccupied with Occupation', 76.

The concept of occupation was designed to protect national sovereignty and not meant to apply to entities which were not recognized as sovereigns. This is inter alia reflected in the framing of the 'conservationist principle' which provides protections to the benefit of civilians and the former sovereign, ousted by occupation, by requiring the occupant to refrain from changes, which compromise the sovereignty of the ousted power.[222] As Nehal Bhuta has stated, this duty loses its essential meaning in conflicts with non-sovereign entities, since it does not make sense to protect 'less civilized' or 'non-sovereign–peoples and territories' against 'fundamental constitutional change by the military occupant'.[223]

This point is further illustrated by the fact that the Hague Conventions rely heavily on understandings of property or social order that are modelled after Western structures of governance. For instance, the strict distinction between public and private property under law of occupation or the predominant role of public authorities in governance, do not necessarily coincide with less ownership-centred approaches to property or alternative conceptions of sovereignty in non-European societies.[224]

4.3 The silencing of violence in the legitimization of the use of force

Colonial violence was reinforced through an ambivalent framing and interpretation of the rules governing recourse to force. Approaches towards the justification of the use of armed force in colonial settings shifted between narrative inclusion and exclusion. Colonial powers sought to justify use of force in the language and rhetoric structures of the law in order to validate their operations in the eyes of home audiences or rival powers and reinforce claims of moral superiority or social advancement of native populations, but used legal silences, ambiguities in the law or legitimizing discourses to rationalize practices of conquest and submission. Certain uses of forces were simply placed out of the umbrella of accepted legal categories of warfare ('measures short of war') in order to reduce legal constraints.[225] Other operations were legitimized through protective or alleged 'humanitarian' rationales (combat of slavery, eradication of human sacrifice), which

---

[222] According to Art. 43 of the Hague Regulations, the occupant 'shall take all steps in his power to re-establish and insure, as far as possible, public order and [civil life], while respecting, unless absolutely prevented, the laws in force in the country'. This framing was a victory of small states, who criticized the more permissive wording of the 1874 Brussels Declaration and pushed for limitations of the powers of occupants. See Benvenisti, 'The Origins of the Concept of Belligerent Occupation', 646.

[223] Nehal Bhuta, 'The Antinomies of Transformative Occupation' (2005) 16 *EJIL* 721–740, 729.

[224] Ibid, 730.

[225] Jochen von Bernstorff, 'The Use of Force in International Law before World War I: On Imperial Ordering and the Ontology of the Nation-State' (2018) 29 *EJIL* 233–260, 248.

disguised broader imperial interests.[226] Smaller military activities were branded as legitimate acts of law enforcement.

Colonial military activities involved different types of the use of force. The notion of 'war' was rarely used in the context of armed hostilities with 'half-civilized' or less 'civilized' states or forcible encounters with indigenous leaders.[227] Such interventions were typically branded as 'measures short of war'.[228] In particular, the use of force within a protectorate, was mostly exempted from classical conceptions of warfare.[229]

In many cases, treaty arrangements, trade interests or protective rationales were invoked to qualify interventions or armed operations as measures below the threshold of war. Labels, such as 'punitive expeditions', 'punishment raids', or 'police operations' reduced use of force to an internal affair or local disturbance and were preferred over the term 'war', which 'smacked of naked aggression'.[230] They presented hostilities against colonial entities or local rulers as legitimate acts of law enforcement, namely as policing or law enforcement operations, geared at ensuring order, respect of legal obligations or sanctioning wrong 'in pluri-political regions of overlapping and uncertain sovereignties'.[231]

The notion of 'measures short of war' provided leeway to legitimize a broad range of acts.[232] It was applied in relation to a diverse spectrum of order-related interventions, such as operations to secure free trade, measures to put an end to the slave trade, human sacrifice or fetish practices, interventions to protect traders or missionaries or the use of force to avenge wrongs committed against colonial

---

[226] The attack on the Yuanmingyuan palace, the 'expeditions' against the Asante, Dahomey or Benin, or German violence in South West Africa were formally justified by alleged violations of bilateral treaty arrangements or acts of aggression or rebellion by local leaders. See Chapter 3.

[227] In British colonial policy, the proper designation of armed violence, i.e. as 'war' or 'expedition' was disputed. The notion of war was used on an exceptional basis. When it was invoked, it was applied to 'fighting on a larger scale', namely 'that against a king or territory (technically or legally) not owing allegiance to the Crown'. See Ukpabi, 'British Colonial Wars in West Africa', 386.

[228] For example, in the context of the armed hostilities over the Golden Stool of the Asante in 1900, Joseph Chamberlain (1836–1914), the British Colonial Secretary, took the view that the operation qualified as a 'war' with the Ashantis, since they were not British subjects and 'could not be tried for rebellion'. By contrast, James Willcocks (1857–1926), the commander of the British forces, preferred to view it as an expedition to fight a rebellion against British rule. Ukpabi, 'British Colonial Wars in West Africa', 386.

[229] For instance, French lawyer Georges Scelles (1878–1961) noted in 1925 that the use of force by France against the Riffian rebels in the protectorate of Morocco fell outside classical rubrics of international law. He wrote: 'The Rif, the Riffians, Abd-el-Krim, have no international personality of any degree. Morocco is a country under protectorate with two protecting States and the League of Nations the League of Nations has no capacity to intervene in the domain of a protectorate ... [L]egally, one cannot even say that there is war'. See Nathaniel Berman, '"The Appeals of the Orient": Colonized Desire and the War of the Riff" in Karen Knop (ed.), *Gender and Human Rights* (Oxford: Oxford University Press, 2004) 195, 202, referring to Georges Scelle, 'Rapport' (1925) 25 *Cahier des Droits De L'Homme* 496.

[230] Ukpabi, 'British Colonial Wars in West Africa', 386.

[231] Laura Benton, 'Protection Emergencies: Justifying Measures Short of War in the British Empire' in Lothar Brock and Hendrik Simon (eds.), *The Justification of War and International Order: From Past to Present* (Oxford: Oxford University Press, 2021) 167–182.

[232] Bernstorff, 'The Use of Force in International Law before World War I', 250.

officials.[233] Colonial discourses were often complicit in the creation of the sense of disorder, which 'measures short of war' were meant to address. They produced an image of chaos or crisis through simplifications, use of stereotypes or one-sided readings or constructions of events. Many acts of insurgency or colonial resistance were simply presented as challenges to law and order, without contemplating the conditions of violence inflicted through colonial rule. The mission to 'protect' Africa from 'slave trade' was a classical rationale to justify the displacement of rulers in West Africa. In Asia, the 'war on piracy' was used as argument to justify armed intervention to secure free trade.[234] Use of force was presented as an act of salvage, which put an end to the alleged problem. It reduced colonial subjects to objects of political action.

4.4 Counter-narratives

The discriminatory application of the laws of war and the broad justification of the use of force in colonial warfare were based on shaky normative foundations. They disregarded alternative normative systems, including perspectives from societies who were 'subjected to European tyranny and imperialism'[235] and conflicted with the self-proclaimed identity of Western powers as 'civilized' nations. As Frédéric Mégret has argued, it was ultimately 'less the "savages" who were "civilized", than the "civilized" who "savaged" ' themselves.[236]

The theory that the laws of war were 'subtly designed to exclude non-European peoples from their protection'[237] undermined the fundamental rationale of humanitarian law to minimize harm and provide protection in conflict, irrespective of compliance. It provided greater leeway for colonial violence, but conflicted with the need to provide structures in conflict or secure local support in colonial warfare and created risks for abuse in warfare between 'civilized' states. It often met criticism by army commanders themselves or was set aside, since it was preferable to motivate operations 'through the law, rather than by emphasizing exclusions'.[238]

---

[233] For example, the multinational military operation, carried out in 1900 in response to the 'Boxer rebellion' in China, was justified by the violation of the rights of Western diplomats and the enforcement of treaty obligations. See above.

[234] Farish A. Noor, 'Hostis Humanis Generis: The Invention of the "Warlike Dayak Race" during the "War on Piracy" in Borneo, 1830–1848' in Farish A. Noor and Peter Carey (eds.), *Racial Difference and the Colonial Wars of 19th Century Southeast Asia* (Amsterdam: Amsterdam University Press, 2021) 73–106.

[235] Mutua, 'Savages, Victims, and Saviors', 204.

[236] Frédéric Mégret, 'From Savages to Unlawful Combatants: A Postcolonial Look at International Law's "Other"' in Anne Orford (ed.), *International Law and Its Others* (Cambridge: Cambridge University Press, 2006) 265–317, 315.

[237] Ibid, 268.

[238] Smiley, 'Lawless Wars of Empire?', 544.

The exclusionary logic was questionable from a normative point of view. It was based on a statist and institutionalist perspective of law. It assumed that other societies were lawless spaces. This assumption conflicted with the 'multiplicity of legal orders', including 'the context of other customs of the time',[239] i.e. non-European practices. Various pre-colonial African customs reflect 'principles' which can be found in modern rules of international humanitarian law.[240] They sometimes formed part of 'a genuine ethics of war which was taught to any young nobleman for his future calling as a warrior'.[241] These customs protected inter alia sacred places (e.g. shrines, trees, ceremonial spaces) and their surroundings.[242] Some societies recognized the prohibition of looting for personal gain.[243] African indigenous law protected ownership and property entitlements, based on communal land tenure schemes or social relationships.

The existence of local customs or native forms of sovereignty challenges the perception that the acquisition of cultural colonial objects occurred in a legal vacuum or was exclusively governed by European standards or colonial law.[244] Justice LeBel applied this logic in a Canadian Supreme Court case concerning land rights of First Nations under aboriginal customary laws.[245] He argued that 'aboriginal conceptions of territoriality, land-use and property' should be taken into account in assessment of the required standard for occupation, including nomadic or semi-nomadic modes of occupation, since '[o]therwise, we might be implicitly accepting the position that aboriginal peoples had no rights in land prior to the assertion of Crown sovereignty' simply 'because their views of property or land use do not fit within Euro-centric conceptions of property rights'.[246] He wrote:

> Aboriginal law should not just be received as evidence that Aboriginal peoples did something in the past on a piece of land. It is more than evidence: it is actually law.

---

[239] Kiwara-Wilson, 392.

[240] Yolande Diallo, 'African Traditions and Humanitarian Law' (1976) 185 *International Review of the Red Cross* 387–401, 400. See also Emmanuel Bello, 'Shared Legal Concepts between African Customary Norms and International Conventions on Humanitarian Law' (1984) 23 *Military Law and Law of War Review* 285–310. See also Taslim Olawale Elias, *The Nature of African Customary Law* (Manchester: Manchester University Press, 1956).

[241] Diallo, 'African Traditions and Humanitarian Law', 394.

[242] Ibid, 395. For example, customs in Mahgreb countries exempted places of worship from attack, based on a rule of conduct laid down by Hannibal in the Punic wars. Mutoy Mubiala, 'International Humanitarian Law in the African Context' in Monica Kathina Juma and Astri Suhrke (eds.), *Eroding Local Capacity: International Humanitarian Action in Africa* (Upsala: Nordiska Afrikainstitutet, 2002) 35–59, 38.

[243] Adamou Ndam Njoya, 'The African Concept' in UNESCO (ed.), *International Dimensions of Humanitarian Law* (Leiden: Martinus Nijhoff, 1988) 5–12, 8.

[244] Elmien du Plessis, 'African Indigenous Land Rights in a Private Ownership Paradigm' (2011) 14 *Potchefstroom Electronic Law Journal* 44–69.

[245] Supreme Court of Canada, *R v Marshall; R v Bernard* [2005] 2 SCR 220, 2005 SCC 43.

[246] LeBel, para. 127.

And so, there should be some way to bring to the decision-making process those laws that arise from the standards of the indigenous people before the court.[247]

Certain constraints in colonial warfare may be derived from concepts such as the 'laws of humanity' and the 'dictates of public conscience'. Positive law and public morality were closely intertwined in nineteenth-century international law. This is reflected in many humanitarian instruments, including the 1880 *Oxford Manual on Laws of War on Land*[248] and the Martens clause, contained in the preamble to the Fourth Hague Convention.[249] They served as universal minimum standards. They departed from the common 'rule of colonial difference'[250] and were deemed to apply in relation to all entities, irrespective of their recognition as 'civilized' states.[251]

Cultural heritage was protected by 'principles that are located somewhere between morality and law'.[252] In particular, punitive expeditions, such as the raid of the Benin palace, conflicted with minimum standards of protection reflected in military manuals[253] and 'principles of justice which guide the public conscience'.[254]

The doctrine of colonial warfare was unable to explain why the colonized had to endure the consequences of forcible action. The justification of colonial use of force as a law enforcement measure or punitive operation conflicted with rights of resistance to foreign domination. Such rights have been recognized in scholastic doctrine and natural law.[255] For instance, Bartolomé de las Casas defended a right of natives to resist conquest and tyranny by the conquistadors already in the sixteenth century. He regarded the conquest of indigenous nations as a violation of

---

[247] Ibid, para. 130.

[248] This is reflected in the preface of the 1880 Oxford Manual. It states: '[I]ndependently of the international laws existing on this subject, there are today certain principles of justice which guide the public conscience'. Institute of International Law, *Manual, The Laws of War on Land* (Oxford: 9 September 1880).

[249] It states that 'inhabitants and the belligerents remain under the protection and the rule of the principles of the law of nations, as they result from the usages established among civilized peoples, from the *laws of humanity, and the dictates of the public conscience* (emphasis added). See generally Theodor Meron, 'The Martens Clause, Principles of Humanity and Dictates of Public Conscience' (2000) 94 *AJIL* 78–89.

[250] Partha Chatterjee, *The Nation and Its Fragments: Colonial and Postcolonial Histories* (Princeton: Princeton University Press, 1993).

[251] See Mégret, 'From Savages to Unlawful Combatants', 283 (' Few for example would have gone so far as to advocate that the clause did not apply to 'savages', and the consensus was that it did').

[252] See Tullio Scovazzi, 'The "First Time Instance" as Regards Restitution of Removed Cultural Properties' (2012) 30 *Agenda Internacional* 9–19, 18.

[253] See e.g. 1880 Oxford Manual, Art. 32.

[254] Alexander Herman, 'Britain's Pillaging of the Benin Bronzes Begs for a Reasonable Resolution' *The Art Newspaper* (21 December 2018) https://www.theartnewspaper.com/comment/law-restitution-and-the-benin-bronzes.

[255] As Arnulf Becker Lorca has argued, law provides native rulers 'limited', but 'important avenues' to resist colonial oppression. See Arnulf Becker Lorca, *Mestizo International Law: A Global Intellectual History 1842–1933* (Cambridge: Cambridge University Press, 2015) 19.

principles of universal justice.[256] He stressed the premise that every human society is free under natural law and entitled to resist foreign authority established without consent of the people. He argued in *Apologia* that a change of religion should not be secured through force and that practices, such as cannibalism or human sacrifice, could not justify foreign oppression.[257] He recognized a right to resistance, arguing that 'the natives in any or all of the regions we have invaded in the Indies have acquired [the] right to make just war upon us'.[258] This position legitimized acts of resistance, such as the rebellion by Inca ruler Túpac Amaru I (1537–1572)[259] against the Spanish conquest and the rule of Viceroy Francisco Álvarez de Toledo (1515–1582) in Peru.[260]

In his work on the Treasures of Peru,[261] Las Casas even argued that the Spanish King should restore Inca sovereignty and return treasures back to natives, since Peru had not consented to conquest. He claimed that plunder of indigenous grave sites and sacred places is impermissible, since it disrupts the spiritual relations between objects, spaces and people and impedes cultural memory in societies. He counts as one of the earliest defenders of the principle that the 'archeological and artistic treasures of a nation are the inalienable property of the people' and should not be seized.[262]

Later, Emer de Vattel challenged the idea that European powers could subject other nations to colonial rule based on arguments of civilization or faith, in his treatise on the Law of Nations (1758). Vattel's conception of natural law had both imperial and counter-imperial features.[263] He defended colonial settlements in the Americas on agricultural grounds, namely based on the argument that land must be cultivated according to the natural order of the world.[264] But he condemned the Spanish 'conquest of the civilized empires of Peru and Mexico' as a 'notorious usurpation'.[265] He distanced himself from Grotius, who had defended the right to

---

[256] Yuri G. Mantilla, 'Francisco de Vitoria's Normative Ideas and the Beginnings of International Law: A Colonial Ethnocentric Discourse, or a Bona Fide Effort to Construct Just International Norms?', (2021) 44 *Loyola of Los Angeles International and Comparative Law* 43–104, 46.

[257] Bartolomé de las Casas, *Apologia* (Madrid, 1975).

[258] Mariano Delgado, *A Stumbling Block: Bartolome de Las Casas as Defender of the Indians* (2017) 95.

[259] Philip Ainsworth Means, 'The Rebellion of Tupac-Amaru II, 1780-1781' (1919) 2 *The Hispanic American Historical Review* 1–25.

[260] David. M Lantigua, 'God, Sovereignty, and the Morality of Intervention outside Europe' in Pamela Slotte and John D. Haskell (eds.), *Christianity and International Law: An Introduction* (Cambridge: Cambridge University Press, 2021) 91–114, 104.

[261] Bartolomé de las Casas, *Los tesoros del Perú* (The treasures of Peru) (Madrid,1958).

[262] Angel Losada, 'Bartolomé de las Casas: Champion on Indian rights in 16th-century Spanish America' in UNESCO, *Courier*, June 1975, Vol. 28, 4–10, 9.

[263] See Antony Anghie, 'Vattel and Colonialism: Some Preliminary Observations' in Vincent Chetail and Peter Haggenmacher (eds.), *Vattel's International Law from a XXIst Century Perspective* (Leiden: Martinus Nijhoff, 2011) 237–253.

[264] He argued that the people of North America 'made no actual and constant use' of land. See Vattel, *The Law of Nations*, Book I, § 209. This understanding of the relationship between people and land justified the dispossession of land of indigenous peoples. See Anghie, 'Vattel and Colonialism', 250. It was used in British doctrine, see David Armitage, *The Ideological Origins of the British Empire* (Cambridge: Cambridge University Press, 2000) 97.

[265] Vattel, *The Law of Nations*, Book I, § 81.

use force to 'chastise' other nations for purposes of punishment, and advocated the non-intervention principle and the right to self-preservation of each sovereign. He wrote:

> Those ambitious Europeans who attacked the American nations, and subjected them to their greedy dominion, in order, as they pretended, to civilise them, and cause them to be instructed in the true religion,—those usurpers, I say, grounded themselves on a pretext equally unjust and ridiculous.[266]

In his view, the 'Spaniards violated all rules, when they set themselves up as judges of the Inca Atahualpa', although that 'prince' had not 'violated the law of nations with respect to them'.[267]

He accepted that no foreign power has the right to sit as judge over another sovereign and recognized a right of resistance against powers that abused their position. He motivated the right to resistance expressly in relation to the 'iniquitous and cruel conditions' imposed by Spain on Mexico. He wrote:

> [W]ill any man pretend to assert that he would not have been justifiable in seizing a convenient opportunity to recover his rights, to emancipate his people, and to expel or exterminate the Spanish horde of greedy, insolent, and cruel usurpers? No! Such a monstrous absurdity can never be seriously maintained. Although the law of nature aims at protecting the safety and peace of nations by enjoying the faithful observances of promises, it does not favour oppressors.[268]

He supported this position by the idea that sovereigns should exercise public authority in the interest of the *salus populi*, i.e. the preservation and welfare of society.

Edmund Burke drew on these arguments in the impeachment trial of Hastings. He invoked the concept of legitimate resistance against the abusive rule and treaty breaches of the East India Company in order to defend Maharaja Chait Singh, the ruler of the Kingdom of Benares, who had refused to pay revenues and provide troops to the company.[269] He qualified Hastings' government as a 'whole system of oppression, of robbery of individuals, of destruction of the public, and of suppression of the whole system of the English government'.[270] Burke defended the Indian rebellion against violence and exploitation of resources. He grounded the right to legitimate resistance against company conduct in natural law, namely in purposes

---

[266] Ibid, Book II, § 7.
[267] Ibid, Book II, § 55.
[268] Ibid, Book IV, § 37.
[269] See Zak Leonard, 'Law of Nations Theory and the Native Sovereignty Debates in Colonial India' (2020) 38 *Law and History Review* 373–407.
[270] Edmund Burke, *The Writings and Speeches of Edmund Burke*, Vol. X, Speech in Opening, Fourth Day (New York: Cosimo, 2008) 136. Hastings claimed that he was entitled to use violence against Indian rulers because he had assumed sovereignty through defeat and treaties.

of self-preservation. He argued that Indian leaders 'had not just a right, but a duty to rebel against sovereign authority if it was tyrannical'.[271]

According to this line of reasoning, native people could not be expected to accept their own 'pacification' through colonial violence, but enjoyed protection against use of force and subjugation under natural law.[272]

Some constraints were contained in legal instruments of the time. For instance, the General Act of the Berlin Conference of 1885 mandated colonial powers to further 'the moral and material well-being of the native populations'[273] and 'to watch over the preservation of the native tribes, and to care for the improvement of the conditions of their moral and material well-being'.[274] Violent campaigns, leading to the extermination of local populations, marked a flagrant violation of these duties. This was sometimes openly recognized by colonial powers. For instance, in 1904, German Imperial Chancellor Count Bernard von Bülow lobbied for the withdrawal of General Lothar van Trotha's controversial extermination order (*Vernichtungsbefehl*), arguing that it would constitute a crime against humanity, 'seriously undermine' the colony's 'potential for development',[275] and 'be demeaning to our standing among the civilized nations of the world'.[276]

Unconstrained violence and looting in punitive expeditions entailed not only 'costs' for the enemy, but also for 'the self'.[277] It broke the very same rules that European powers used in the middle of the nineteenth century to define their own identity.[278] It was condemned as barbaric behaviour at home.[279] This became evident in instances, such as the looting of the Magdala treasures in Ethiopia.[280]

---

[271] Mukherjee, 'Justice, War, and the Imperium', 616.

[272] Formally, the 'waging of colonial wars' was only banned much later, namely with the recognition of the right to self-determination and the adoption of the UN Charter, the Universal Declaration of Human Rights and the Declaration on the Granting of Independence to Colonial Countries and Peoples in the second half of the twentieth century. See UN, Declaration on the Granting of Independence to Colonial Countries and Peoples, GA Res. 1514 (XV) (14 December 1960) para. 1; UN Commission on Human Rights, 'The Right of Peoples to Self-determination and Its Application to Peoples under Colonial or Alien Domination or Foreign Occupation' (25 February 1982) E/CN.4/RES/1982/16, para. 13. In 1970, the UN Declaration on Principles of International Law concerning Friendly Relations and Co-operation among States, UN GA Res. 2625 (1970) (24 October 1970) expressly prohibited use of force against colonial peoples and recognized a right of 'resistance' to 'forcible action' in ''pursuit of the right of self-determination'. It recognizes a right of 'peoples under colonial and racist regimes or other forms of alien domination' to revolt ('struggle') against the use of armed force by oppressors. However, this does not mean that were no legal constraints in the colonial era itself.

[273] General Act of the Berlin Conference of 1885, preamble.

[274] Article 6.

[275] Thomas Pakenham, *The Scramble for Africa: The White Man's Conquest of the Dark Continent 1876–1912* (New York: Random House, 1991) 612.

[276] Ibid.

[277] See Erik Ringmar, '"How to Fight Savage Tribes": The Global War on Terror' (2013) 25 *Historical Perspective, Terrorism and Political Violence* 264–283, 270.

[278] For instance, the eighth edition of Henry Wheaton's treatise on international law recognized that looting and seizure of cultural property contravened civilized principles of warfare. See Henry Wheaton, *Elements of International Law* (London: Sampson Low, Son and Comp., 8th edn, 1866) 449–450.

[279] Lawrence James, *The Savage Wars: British Campaigns in Africa, 1870–1920* (New York: St Martin's Press, 1985) 174.

[280] See Chapter 3.

Certain forcible property takings, undertaken in punitive expeditions, can be regarded as treaty violations, namely as violations of agreements with local leaders.[281] Protectorate agreements typically involved obligations for both colonial powers and local leaders. European powers undertook to extend 'favour and protection' to the protected states, in return for trade concessions or governance rights. For example, in the Treaty between the Queen of England and the King of Benin of 26 March 1892 on the Oil Rivers Protectorate, Britain agreed to 'extend to him, and to the territory under his authority and jurisdiction, her gracious favour and protection',[282] while the Oba of Benin agreed to open up his territory to trade by 'the subjects and citizens of all countries',[283] to 'assist the British Consular or other officers' and to 'act upon their advice in matters relating to the administration of justice, the development of the resources of the country, the interest of commerce, or in any other matter in relation to peace, order, and good government, and the general progress of civilization'.[284] Britain justified the punitive expedition in 1897 based on human sacrifice in Benin and an alleged violation of the obligation to open Benin to trade.[285] However, the terms of the treaty cut both ways. From the perspective of the Oba, the brutal looting of the city and spoliation of the Benin bronzes may qualify as a violation of Britain's general protective duty under the protectorate agreement.[286]

5 Colonial law: The making and unmaking of colonial identities

Colonialism constituted not only means of political and economic submission, but was also a site of legal experimentation.[287] The law served as a space for the making and unmaking of identities.[288] Colonial law provided the intersection between

---

[281] See Mamadou Hébié, 'The Role of the Agreements Concluded with Local Political Entities in the Course of French Colonial Expansion in West Africa' (2016) 85 *British Yearbook of International Law* 21–89, 89.

[282] See Treaty between the Queen of England and the King of Benin (26 March 1892) FO 84/2194/114–116 in Osarhieme Benson Osadolor, *The Military System of Benin Kingdom, c. 1440–1897* (PhD Dissertation, University of Hamburg, 2001) 207–208, Art. 1.

[283] Ibid, Art. 6.

[284] Ibid, Art. 5.

[285] Ibid, Art. 6.

[286] On state responsibility for 'spoliation of national treasures' in violation of protectorate agreements, see 'W. Michael Reisman, 'Reflections on State Responsibility for Violations of Explicit Protectorate, Mandate, and Trusteeship Obligations' (1989) 10 *Michigan Journal of International Law* 231–240, 240.

[287] Laura Benton, *Law and Colonial Culture: Legal Regimes in World History 1400–1900* (New York: Cambridge University Press, 2002).

[288] Catherine Hall, *Civilizing Subjects: Metropole and Colony in the English Imagination 1830–1867* (Cambridge: Polity Press, 2002) 774. John Comaroff associates this process with 'lawfare'. See John Comaroff, 'Colonialism, Culture, and the Law: A Foreword' (2006) 26 *Law & Social Inquiry* 305–314, 306.

colonial interests and local interests.[289] It was both a mode of coercion[290] or domination[291] and an instrument of social transformation. It regulated political and economic order, legitimized colonial rule, and transformed local laws.

5.1 Roles of colonial law

In settler colonialism contexts, colonial law became the dominant framework for social interaction and superseded or suppressed alternative traditions or indigenous law.[292] It provided the frame which defined people as legal subjects,[293] regulated identity, and controlled 'traditional practices'.

In other contexts, colonial law was enacted to support assimilation[294] or indirect rule.[295] It involved the transfer of legal norms and traditions from the metropole to the colony and transformed local systems. It was a hybrid law marked by legal pluralism.[296] Colonial governments often sought to maintain some elements of native law in order to accommodate legal traditions and customs. However, practices were reshaped and adjusted in order to fit into the colonial framework. Colonial administrations determined to what extent customs remained applicable. For instance, British rulers often tolerated domestic customs unless they conflicted with applicable British law or violated standards of public policy or natural justice, defined in repugnancy clauses.[297] This approach created novel legal systems, which were based on cultural difference[298] and dual standards: one for colonial rulers, and a different one for colonized peoples.

Colonial law was also a site of contest, not only between colonial administrations and local subjects, but also between different colonial subjects. For instance,

---

[289] Sally Engle Merry, 'Law and Colonialism' (1991) 25 *Law & Society Review* 889–922; Sally Engle Merry, 'From Law and Colonialism to Law and Globalization' (2003) 28 *Law & Social Inquiry* 569–590.

[290] This was openly admitted by Lord Lugard, who argued that 'law and order depends in every [colony] on the power of coercion by force'. See Sir Frederick Lugard, *The Dual Mandate in British Tropical Africa* (Edinburgh and London: William Blackwood & Sons, 1922) 578. See also Matthias van Rossum, 'The Carceral Colony: Colonial Exploitation, Coercion, and Control in the Dutch East Indies, 1810s–1940s' (2018) 63 *International Review of Social History* 65–88.

[291] Kristin Mann and Richard Roberts, 'Introduction, Law in Colonial Africa' in Kristin Mann and Richard Roberts (eds.), *Law in Colonial Africa* (Portsmouth, NH: Heinemann, 1991) 3–58, 3.

[292] Karolina Kuprecht, *Indigenous Peoples' Cultural Property Claims: Repatriation and Beyond* (Heidelberg: Springer, 2013) 49.

[293] For a critique, see Glen Coulthard, *Red Skin, White Masks: Rejecting the Colonial Politics of Recognition* (Minneapolis: University of Minnesota Press, 2014).

[294] Michael Crowder, 'Indirect Rule: French and British Style' (1964) 34 *Africa: Journal of the International African Institute* 197–205.

[295] Lugard, *The Dual Mandate in British Tropical Africa*, 58.

[296] On early modern empires, see Lauren Benton, *A Search for Sovereignty: Law and Geography in European Empires, 1400–1900* (New York: Cambridge University Press, 2009).

[297] See Melissa Demian, 'On the Repugnance of Customary Law' (2014) 56 *Comparative Studies in Society and History* 508–536.

[298] Martti Koskenniemi, 'Colonial Laws: Sources, Strategies and Lessons?' (2016) 18 *Journal of the History of International Law* 248–277, 274.

certain social elites saw changes in legal culture as a means to brand themselves as 'civilized beings', interact with colonial administrations or benefit from new market opportunities,[299] while others saw them as a challenge to traditional cultures and a form of power. Some colonial laws and practices erased native identities, by prohibiting religious or indigenous cultural practices which were considered to 'primitive' or 'dangerous'[300] or by facilitating the confiscation or removal of ceremonial and cultural objects.

5.2 Cultural transformation, alienation, or destruction

Colonial law transformed conceptions of property and culture.[301] Colonial agents introduced or amended heritage legislation, which allowed the acquisition and removal of objects. They transformed the meaning of heritage sites or banned expression of cultural identity.[302]

These changes were driven by different motivations: national interests, such as identification with the prestige and glory of ancient civilizations, on the one hand, or discourses of 'civilization', on the other.[303] In some cases, colonial powers allowed cultural dispossession in order to foster their own social and cultural identity.[304] They relied on actual or projected images of ancient cultures or civilizations[305] or claimed that they knew ancient civilizations better than societies of origin. In other cases, the alleged lack of development or the primitive nature of other societies was used to justify dispossession or even destruction.[306] Cultural objects were regarded as indicators of degrees of 'civilization'.[307] Spiritual objects and intangible heritage,

---

[299] Sally Engle Merry, 'Law and Colonialism', 918.

[300] Comaroff, 'Colonialism, Culture, and the Law', 306.

[301] Sebastian M. Spitra, 'Civilisation, Protection, Restitution: A Critical History of International Cultural Heritage Law in the 19th and 20th Century (2020) 22 *Journal of the History of International Law* 329–354.

[302] On colonialism and archaeology, see Chris Gosden, *Archaeology and colonialism: Cultural contact from 5000 BC to the Present* (Cambridge: Cambridge University Press, 2004); Bonnie Effros and Guolong Lai, *Unmasking Ideology in Imperial and Colonial Archaeology: Vocabulary, Symbols, and Legacy. Ideas, Debates, and Perspectives* (Los Angeles: Cotsen Institute of Archaeology Press; University of California, 2018).

[303] Cole Harris, 'How Did Colonialism Dispossess? Comments from an Edge of Empire' (2004) 94 *Annals of the Association of American Geographers* 165–182.

[304] For instance, France's takings in Egypt were guided by the idea to 'bring civilization back to its origins'. See Alice Conklin, *A Mission to Civilize: The Republican Idea of Empire in France and West-Africa, 1895–1930* (Stanford: Stanford University Press, 1997) 18–19.

[305] M. Bernal, 'The Image of Ancient Greece as a Tool for Colonialism and European Hegemony' in G. C. Bond and A. Gilliam (eds.), *Social Construction of the Past: Representation as a Power* (London & New York: Routledge, 1994) 119–128.

[306] Bruce Trigger, 'Alternative Archaeologies: Nationalist, Colonialist, Imperialist' (1984) 19 *Man, New Series* 355–370, 363.

[307] For instance, General Augustus Pitt-Rivers (1827–1900) established systematic collections of objects in order to develop an evolutionary theory of material culture and contrast primitive cultures

such as rituals, were viewed as exotic or found to be in conflict with the ethos of assimilation pursued by the 'civilizing mission'.[308]

Colonial law contributed to cultural removal, transformation, or destruction through diverse types of regulation: Property regulation, antiquity laws, protection of monuments or historical sites or outright prohibition of intangible forms of heritage.

5.2.1 Protection as dispossession

In certain contexts, protection was de facto a means of dispossession. For example, in Indonesia, the Dutch administration integrated heritage 'protection' into colonial practices. The system operated on the premise that heritage 'that was not cared for by the local population was taken into national ownership'.[309] Colonial agents regarded themselves as guardians of ruined temple sites on Java. They gave explicit instructions to prevent the plundering of sites by the Chinese and Javanese,[310] but collected items for private possession or shipment to the Netherlands. As of 1842, the Batavian Society was mandated by regulation to decide which objects should stay in Indonesia or which ones should be removed to the metropole. Items that were not adequately preserved were considered to be 'national property'.[311] This triggered paradoxical effects. Local inhabitants started to hide objects to save them from Dutch 'protection'.

5.2.2 The ambivalent role of antiquity laws and regulations

In the nineteenth century, antiquity laws gained significant importance in colonial contexts.[312] They were adopted to regulate archaeological practices and define fundamental legal aspects of heritage protection, such as property definitions, export and division of finds, or control of museums or specialized antiquity services.[313] They provided greater formal protection against theft and looting, but also contributed to the removal of heritage, by facilitating excavation, export or partage

---

with European technological progress and advancement. See David K. van Keuren, 'Museums and Ideology: Augustus Pitt-Rivers, Anthropological Museums, and Social Change in Later Victorian Britain' (1984) 28 *Victorian Studies* 171–189, 175.

[308] Ana Vrdoljak, *International Law, Museums and the Return of Cultural Objects* (Cambridge: Cambridge University Press, 2006) 60. For instance, in Kenya, the Witchcraft Act of 1925 proscribed traditional practices and allowed district commissioners to confiscate and destroy objects. Some of them entered Western collections.

[309] Advisory Committee on the National Policy Framework for Colonial Collections, *Colonial Collection: A Recognition of Injustice* (The Hague: Council for Culture, 2021) 23.

[310] Marieke Bloembergen and Martijn Eickhoff, *The Politics of Heritage in Indonesia A Cultural History* (Cambridge: Cambridge University Press, 2020) 39.

[311] Bloembergen and Eickhoff, *The Politics of Heritage in Indonesia*, 42.

[312] See also Sebastian Spitra, 'The Administration of Culture in International Law since the 19th Century: A New Historical Narrative' (2021) 5 *University of Vienna Law Review* 121–153, 133.

[313] On the Ottoman Empire, see Michael Greenhalgh, *Plundered Empire: Acquiring Antiquities from Ottoman Lands* (Leiden: Brill, 2019).

arrangements.[314] The respective laws were often drafted, written or enacted with the influence of Western agents, who played a dominant role in the development of the field archaeology.[315] This influence is particularly visible in the case of the Ottoman Empire and Egypt.[316] In both cases, antiquity regulation was initially adopted to counter Western cultural imperialism. However, in practice, it ultimately legitimized and facilitated the removal of antiquities, as shown by notorious examples.

The framing of the first antiquity law of the Ottoman Empire contributed to the removal of ancient Greek treasures. For a long time, the excavation of antiquities has been governed by a mere system of administrative permits (*firman*). This opened the door for abuse.[317] The Ottoman Empire sought to limit the flow of antiquities from the Empire to Western powers. It created the Imperial museum in Constantinople. In 1874, Anton Philip Dethier (1803–1881), a German-born former high school principal, who served as Director of the museum from 1872 to 1881,[318] was mandated to prepare the first antiquities law. The new law was intended to strengthen protection and to defend 'Ottoman claims against foreign excavators such as Cesnola in Cyprus or Schliemann in Troy'.[319] However, it failed to secure sufficient state control and continued to support European removal of heritage.[320] The most famous example is the removal of the Pergamon Altar by Carl Humann (1839–1896).

The altar frieze was excavated by Humann, a German road engineer employed by the Turkish government, in the town of Bergama in Anatolia.[321] He first carried out unofficial excavations, but managed to persuade German museums to support the excavation of the altar at a time when Germany was eager to expand its museum collections, in particular Greek works of art in order to compete with the British Museum or the Louvre.[322] Humann discovered the acropolis and claimed to rescue it from robbery and decay. The framing of the 1874 Law of Antiquities facilitated the export of the monument. The law provided for an equal division of finds between the Ottoman state, the landowner, and the excavator (each one third). It implied that excavators, who purchased the land, acquire the right to two thirds of the finds. Humann used

[314] Spitra, 'Civilisation, Protection, Restitution', 341.

[315] Sarah Griswold, 'Locating Archaeological Expertise: Debating Antiquities Norms in the A Mandates, 1918-1926' in Philippe Bourmaud and others (eds.), *Experts et expertises dans les mandats de la Société des Nations: Figures, champs et outils* (Paris: Presses de l'Inalco, 2020) 141–158.

[316] See also Jürgen Gottschlich and Dilek Zaptcioglu-Gottschlich, *Die Schatzjäger des Kaisers: Deutsche Archäologen auf Beutezug im Orient* (Berlin: C. H. Links, 2021).

[317] This is shown by the controversy over the removal of the Parthenon marbles. See Chapter 3.

[318] Edhem Eldem, 'The Archaelogy of a Photograph: Philipp Anton Dethier and His Group for the History of Greek Art' (2013) 128 *Jahrbuch des Deutschen Archäologischen Instituts* 499–530, 504.

[319] Ibid, 504.

[320] Peter Magee, 'The Foundations of Antiquities Departments' in Daniel T. Potts, *A Companion to the Archaeology of the Ancient Near East* (Malden and Oxford: Blackwell, 2012) 70–86, 73–74.

[321] Humann had participated in the search of Troy.

[322] Can Bilsel, *Antiquity on Display: Regimes of the Authentic in Berlin's Pergamon Museum* (Oxford: Oxford University Press, 2012) 45–57.

this opportunity and was entitled to two thirds. In 1878–1879, the German side ne-gotiated the acquisition of full ownership with the support of Bismarck.[323] A German banker in Izmir oversaw the division of finds between the Berlin Museum and the Ottoman Museum. Humann was able to remove the full altar in exchange for 20,000 Mark, 'using his personal connections in the Ottoman government, applying Prussia's diplomatic pressure, and concealing the true value of the finds.'[324]

He legitimized the acquisition as an act of salvage[325] and victory for humanity in line with nineteenth-century rhetoric. He stated: 'Such a great and magnificent work had been given back to the world and crowned our efforts.'[326] In Germany, the frieze was welcomed as a cultural icon of the empire, and later inspired the design of the large grandstand of the Nazi party rally grounds (Zeppelin Field) in Nuremberg by Albert Speer. In 1991, the mayor of Bergama, Sefa Taşkın, chal-lenged the legitimate acquisition of the altar and made a request for return 'to the site where it was constructed and where it stood for thousands of years.'[327]

Humann's 'archeological coup' contributed to the adoption of a more effective new law in the Ottoman Empire in 1884, based on the initiative of Director Osman Hamdi Bey (1842–1910) in 1884. Mehmet Tahir Münif Pasha (1828–1910), the Minister of Education, justified the new regulation by a dual rationale, critique of European practices and the strife for greater recognition in the eyes of Western audiences. He stated:

> Until now, Europeans have used various means to take the antiquities of our country away, and they did this because they did not see an inclination toward this in us. For a long time this desire has been awakened among Ottomans and recently even a law was passed concerning antiquities. Since the foundation of the Imperial Museum is the greatest example of this, we can now hope that the Europeans will change their opinions about us.[328]

The removal of heritage from Egypt during the nineteenth and early twentieth centuries is another striking example demonstrating how cultural exploitation was facilitated through antiquity regulation. European explorers, excavators, and archaeologists benefited from governance structures in order to collect antiquities

---

[323] Max Kunze, *The Pergamon Altar: Its Rediscovery History and Reconstruction* (Mainz: Staatliche Museen zu Berlin Preußicher Kulturbesitz Antikensammlung, 1995) 10–11.

[324] Bilsel, *Antiquity on Display*, 98.

[325] Alexander Conze, who headed the sculpture collection of Berlin's museum at the time, argued that the altar was rescued from destruction, decay, and stone robbers.

[326] Bilsel, *Antiquity on Display*, 95.

[327] Sefa Taşkın, *Sürgündeki Zeus: Bergama'dan Berline, Berlin'den Bergamaya* (Izmir: Bergama Belediyesi, 1991) 51.

[328] Wendy M. K. Shaw, *Possessors and Possessed: Museums, Archaeology, and the Visualization of History in the Late Ottoman Empire* (Berkeley and Los Angeles: University of California Press, 2003) 93–97.

for Western museums. They were able to gain ownership over antiquities through their archeological knowledge and skills, their resources and foreign control over Egyptian institutions, the Antiquities Service, and partage regulation.

The protection of Egyptian antiquities was first regulated in 1835 by Ottoman ruler Muhammad Ali Pasha. His decree prohibited the export of archaeological treasures from Egypt. It was designed to prevent the plunder of Egyptian antiquities by European collectors and excavators. The text of the ordinance openly addressed the contradictory collecting behaviour of Europeans. It criticized Europeans for collecting and acquiring antiquities abroad wherever they can, often for little money, while refusing to allow removal of antiquities from their own home countries.[329] It proposed the creation of a national museum in Cairo in order to present Egyptian antiquities to audiences from all nations and increase the prestige of Egypt.[330] However, the political context of the nineteenth century impeded these objectives. Egypt remained heavily dependent on foreign political power and European explorers, who excavated sites and claimed title to finds. European excavators competed to acquire Egyptian antiquities. British archaeologist John Gardner Wilkinson (1797–1875) wrote in his *Handbook for Travellers in Egypt* in 1847:

> The impediments raised against the removal of antiquities from Egypt does an injury to the world … The excavations are made without knowledge or energy, the Pasha is cheated by those who work, and no one there takes any interest in a museum.[331]

The Egyptian Antiquities Service was under French control from 1858 to 1952, first under Ottoman rule, then under French authority and the Anglo-French Entente of 1904, which granted France the right to determine the head of Egyptian Service of Antiquities. This regime facilitated the removal of antiquities and the establishment of comprehensive Egyptian collections in museums, such as the Louvre, the British Museum, or the Berlin Museum. Excavation and export were heavily determined by the authority of two French officials: Archaeologist Auguste Mariette (1821–1881), who was appointed as Director of the Antiquities Service by Ottoman viceroy Said Pasha (1822–1863) from 1858 until 1881 and founded the Boulaq Museum, and French Egyptologist Gaston Maspero (1846–1916), who served as director from 1881 to 1886 and 1899 to 1914 and introduced the partage system, which allowed a division of finds between excavators and the Egyptian museum in Cairo.

---

[329] See Decree Mehmet Ali Pasha (15 August 1935) in Savoy, Skwirblies, and Dolezalek, *Beute: Eine Anthologie zu Kunstraub und Kulturerbe*, 188.

[330] Donald Malcolm Reid, *Whose Pharaohs? Archaeology, Museums, and Egyptian National Identity from Napoleon to World War I* (Berkeley: University of California Press, 2002) 55–56.

[331] John Gardner Wilkinson, *Handbook for Travellers in Egypt* (London; John Murray, 1847) 123.

Both men had considerable influence on both the conservation and the removal of antiquities. They strengthened efforts to preserve antiquities in Egypt, but also facilitated ongoing excavations and export. Mariette had originally been sent to Egypt by the Louvre to collect Coptic manuscripts.[332] Prior to his appointment by Said Pasha, he had already sent almost 6,000 works to the Louvre between 1852 and 1853, including the famous Seated Scribe, which earned him a title of Chevalier de la Legion d'Honneur in France.[333] He used the establishment of the new museum to argue that Egyptians were able to take care of their own heritage and to reinforce protection and the ban of exports. However, he also continued to contribute to removals.[334] He used his power to reserve excavation sites for himself and his allies and organized large labour forces for excavation. Not all the objects, which he excavated 'ended up in the first Egyptian Museum of Antiquities in Boulaq'.[335]

In 1883, one year after Egypt became a British protectorate, Mariette's successor, Gaston Maspero updated the terms of the partage system, which provided incentives for foreign expeditions to compete for excavation.[336] The system replaced the export bans under the 1835 decree and a later ordinance from 1869, and developed a system of division of ownership in case of excavations, drawing on an ordinance from 1874.[337] At the time, excavations were carried by Western experts under the control of Egyptian inspectors.[338] The new system was initiated by British archaeologist William Flinders Petrie (1853–1942), who had developed a field methodology to excavate objects for collections, placing particular emphasis on their contextualization.[339] Petrie worked for the British Egypt Exploration Fund (EEF) and offered his services to the Bulaq Museum to be able to acquire 'smaller antiquities' with the authorization of the museum.[340] The partage system allowed the excavator to retain a portion of the excavated objects, in agreement with the antiquities service. Duplicates could be more exported more easily. This system was beneficial to the EEF and other excavating institutions. It enabled the EEF to secure sponsors

[332] Tim Murray, *Milestones in Archeology* (Santa Barbara: ABC-CLIO, 2007) 226.

[333] Ibud., 227.

[334] For instance, obelisks continued to be exported during his service. See Magee, 'The Foundations of Antiquities Departments' 71.

[335] Shadia Mahmoud, *The development of archaeological and historical museums in Egypt during the nineteenth and twentieth centuries: Imperialism, nationalism, UNESCO patronage and Egyptian museology today* (PhD, Texas Tech University, 2012) 67 https://ttu-ir.tdl.org/handle/2346/45592.

[336] Alice Stevenson, 'Artefacts of excavation: The British Collection and Distribution of Egyptian Finds to Museums, 1880–1915' (2014) 26 *Journal of the History of Collections* 89–102.

[337] Dalia N. Osman, 'Occupier's Title to Cultural Property: Nineteenth-Century Removal of Egyptian Artifacts' (1999) 37 *Columbia Journal of Transnational Law* 969–1002, 989–990. The 1874 decree provided for a division between excavator, land owner and government.

[338] Mahmoud, *The development of archaeological and historical museums in Egypt*, 98.

[339] Petrie wrote: 'A specimen may be inferior to others already in a museum, and yet it will be worth more than all of them if it has its history; and it will be the necessary key, to be preserved with the better examples as a voucher of their historical position'. William Flinders Petrie, *Tanis II* (London: Egypt Exploration Fund, 1888) vii.

[340] Margaret S. Drower, 'Gaston Maspero and the Birth of the Egypt Exploration Fund (1881-3)' (1982) 68 *Journal of Egyptian Archaeology* 299–317, 315–316.

for excavations and export thousands of artefacts, after the museum's right of first refusal.[341] It was applied in a relaxed way by Maspero.[342]

Antiquity laws and regulations were selectively enforced, and influenced by 'colonial and interpersonal negotiations'.[343] Maspero's partage system facilitated the removal of the bust of Nefertiti by Ludwig Burckhardt in 1913.[344] The Egyptian government only learnt about the transaction in 1920s. This shows to what extent 'European Egyptologists possessed the upper hand in the field of Egyptology'.[345] Egyptian heritage was redefined through the development of Egyptology, including men like Maspero and Petrie. It was dislocated, narrated through Western frames, and presented in Western collections.[346] Egyptians 'existed both within and outside of the Europeans' world of museums filled with the treasures they excavated'.[347]

5.2.3 Cultural transformation and alienation through monument protection

In other cases, colonial heritage legislation contributed to cultural alienation, by separating local inhabitants from cultural sites or destroying intangible heritage. Colonial law extended regulation for the protection of cultural sites from the metropole to administered territories.[348] While practices such as looting removed cultural objects from their physical location, 'colonial norms of preservation disconnected other vital links between the object and its larger cultural milieu'.[349] Such regulation protected ancient monuments or sites, but changed the status or access to sites and suppressed cultural traditions. It often served the interests of colonial administration or preserved heritage for European audiences.

For instance, Lord George Curzon (1859–1925), Governor General of India, introduced the first comprehensive law on protection of historic monuments, the Ancient Monuments Preservation Act, in India in 1904. The Act was designed to ensure the protection and preservation of ancient monuments and 'objects of

---

[341] Ibid, 316 ('This plan worked smoothly … In subsequent years so much was allowed to the excavators that exhibitions could be mounted in London').

[342] Ibid, 316 ('as Maspero felt more secure in his office, he was able to interpret the law more liberally in terms of what was or was not a duplicate. As well as small objects, some fine sculptures found their way to the museums of Europe and America').

[343] Stevenson, 'Artefacts of excavation', 91. For example, in 1942, German archaeologist Richard Lepsius was allowed by a firman to excavate and collect objects, which entered the collection Egyptian Museum in Berlin, despite the 1935 decree prohibiting exports.

[344] See Chapter 3.

[345] Mahmoud, *The development of archaeological and historical museums in Egypt*, 98.

[346] Heba Abd el-Gawad and Alice Stevenson, 'Egypt's dispersed heritage: Multidirectional storytelling through comic art' (2021) 21 *Journal of Social Archaeology* 121–145, 123.

[347] Wendy Doyon, 'The History of Archaeology through the Eyes of Egyptians' in Bonnie Effros and Guolong Lai (eds.), *Unmasking Ideology in Imperial and Colonial Archaeology* (Los Angeles: Cotsen Institute of Archaeology Press, 2018) 173–200, 180.

[348] Paul Basu and Vinita Damodaran, 'Colonial Histories of Heritage: Legislative Migrations and the Politics of Preservation' (2015) 226 *Past & Present* 240–271.

[349] Mrinalini Rajagopalan, 'From Loot to Trophy' (2011) 57 *The Newsletter* 24–25, 25.

archaeological, historical or artistic interest'.[350] It marked a stark departure from the looting or sale of cultural objects under the regime of the East India Company, but approached cultural heritage protection largely through the lens colonial administration.

Curzon had explained his vision of Indian cultural heritage in his remarks on 'Archaeology and Ancient Monuments' before the Asiatic Society of Bengal on 7 February 1900. He stated that 'the majority of Indian antiquities ... do not represent an indigenous genius or an Indian style'.[351] He defended British protection from a position of cultural superiority:

> [a] race like our own, who are themselves foreigners, are in a sense better fitted to guard, with a dispassionate and impartial zeal, the relics of different ages and of sometimes antagonistic beliefs, than might be the descendants of the warring races or the votaries of the rival creeds.[352]

He viewed monument protection under the 1902 Act as a means to recover 'buildings from profane or sacrilegious uses'.[353] In his address before the Legislative Council, he noted that visibility and attraction to audiences, in particular visitors, was an important rationale of protection under the new legislation.[354]

The Act institutionalized protection, but also distanced monuments from their cultural context and transformed the meanings of objects. For instance, monuments like the mausoleum of Mughal emperor Akbar I (1556–1605) were used for veneration, pilgrimage, or memorial ceremony.[355] The new regime limited access, by fences if necessary. As Mrinalini Rajagopalan has argued, it transformed 'living spaces' into museums: 'From objects of aesthetic beauty as well as religious sites, memorial institutions, burial grounds, festive spaces, etc., preservation turned Indian cultural heritage into fixed objects that were valued merely for their historical and artistic import'.[356]

In Africa, colonial legislation transformed sacred sites into archeological spaces, administered by colonial authorities, and thereby extinguished cultural practices

---

[350] An Act to provide for the preservation of Ancient Monuments and objects of archaeological, historical, or artistic interest, Act No. VII of 1904 (18 March 1904).

[351] See Lord Curzon, Address before the Asiatic Society of Bengal, 7 February 1900 in *Lord Curzon in India: Being a Selection From His Speeches as Viceroy and Governor-General of India 1898–1905* (London: MacMillan & Co., 1906) 185.

[352] Ibid, 185.

[353] Ibid, Address before the Legislative Council, Ancient Monuments Bill (18 March 1904) in *Lord Curzon in India*, 200.

[354] Ibid, 202 ('Objects of archaeological interest can best be studied in relation and in close proximity to the group and style of buildings to which they belong, presuming that these are of a character and in a locality that will attract visitors').

[355] Rajagopalan, 'From loot to trophy', 25.

[356] Ibid, 25.

and references.[357] A prominent example is the site of the Great Zimbabwe.[358] It was traditionally regarded as homes of ancestors and used for spiritual purposes. The search for gold and resources by Rhodes' British South Africa Company as of the 1870s and the colonial myth of its non-African origins (e.g. its Semitic or European history), spread by archaeologists, such as Karl Mauch (1837–1875) or James Theodore Bent (1852–1897), transformed the use of the site and cultivated a novel cultural history, favourable to white settlements.[359]

In 1895, the Rhodesian Ancient Ruins Company was authorized by the British South Africa Company to search for gold and treasures in ancient ruins.[360] Rhodes claimed the right of first purchase.[361] The activity of the Ancient Ruins Company included grave robbing and caused great damage to ruins. In 1902, the legislative council of Southern Rhodesia passed the Ancient Monuments Protection Ordinance in order to protect antiquities, including the great Zimbabwe.[362] It was the first heritage legislation in the territory. It made archaeological excavation dependent on permissions.[363] Richard Nicklin Hall (1852–1914), a journalist with close links to Rhodes, was appointed as Curator of the Great Zimbabwe. He played a crucial part in the 1902 Great Zimbabwe Excavation. He engaged in excavations in order to clear the site 'from the filth and decadence of the Kaffir occupation'.[364] They contributed to the destruction of the site.

The 1902 ordinance had schizophrenic effects. It was formally meant to protect heritage. However, it contributed actively to efforts to transform the cultural meaning of the site through colonial archaeology and separated locals from their 'living heritage'.[365] It turned the monument into a state, rather than a community property.[366] As Kundishora Chipunza has stated, the regulation is 'deeply rooted in a colonial philosophy that believes that "sites and monuments" must be "preserved rather than used"'.[367] It ignored local ways of knowledge and restricted cultural practices, such as the role of the ruins as seat of ancestral power or

---

[357] Gilbert Pwiti and Webber Ndoro, 'The Legacy of Colonialism: Perceptions of the Cultural Heritage in Southern Africa, with Special Reference to Zimbabwe' (1999) 16 *The African Archaeological Review* 143–153, 150.

[358] Shadreck Chirikure, *Great Zimbabwe: Reclaiming a 'Confiscated' Past* (Oxford and New York: Routledge, 2021) 8–11.

[359] See Chapter 4.

[360] It was dissolved in 1900.

[361] Peter Garlake, *Great Zimbabwe* (London: Thames and Hudson, 1973), 70.

[362] It was complemented in 1912 by the 'Bushmen Relics Protection Ordinance', which protected rock paintings.

[363] Basu and Damodaran, 'Colonial Histories of Heritage', 247.

[364] Garlake, *Great Zimbabwe*, 72.

[365] See generally Shadreck Chirikurea and others, 'Unfulfilled Promises? Heritage Management and Community Participation at Some of Africa's Cultural Heritage Sites' (2010) 16 *International Journal of Heritage Studies* 30–44.

[366] Chirikure, *Great Zimbabwe: Reclaiming a 'Confiscated' Past*, 9.

[367] Kundishora Chipunza, 'Protection of immovable cultural heritage in Zimbabwe: An evaluation' in Webber Ndoro and Gilbert Pwiti (eds.), *Legal Frameworks for the Protection of Immovable Cultural Heritage in Africa* (Rome: ICCROM, 2005) 42–45, 43.

sacred site.[368] Locals were used as a labour force to support excavation. The Land Apportionment Act of 1930 displaced the local population.[369]

The history of the Great Zimbabwe provides an example as to how colonial heritage legislation became complicit in the 'alienation' of local people 'from the administration of their natural and cultural heritage':

> Prior to colonization, the custody of both the tangible and intangible heritage of African societies was vested in the elders, special custodians, chiefs or/and kings. With the coming of colonization however, the African Customary legal systems were destroyed and replaced with European legal systems which … only recognized and therefore protected the tangible heritage to the exclusion of the intangible heritage.[370]

Such practices had long-term consequences. For instance, George Abungu and Webber Ndoro found in their study on immovable cultural heritage that many English-speaking countries in Sub-Sahara Africa (with the exception of South Africa) remained 'reliant on colonial legislation' and failed to recognize 'tradition and community management mechanisms' or 'intangible heritage' in their legislation.[371]

5.2.4 Prohibiting intangible heritage

In certain settler contexts, ruling powers introduced discriminatory laws prohibiting 'living heritage' of indigenous populations. A famous example is the Indian Act (1876), which was adopted by the Canadian government to assimilate First Nations into the settler population.[372] John Alexander Macdonald (1815–1891), the first prime minister of Canada, formulated this rationale quite blatantly: 'The great aim of our legislation has been to do away with the tribal system and assimilate the Indian people in all respects with the other inhabitants of the Dominion as speedily as they are fit to change.'[373] The Act outlawed various religious ceremonies and expressions of indigenous culture. It was used to ban the 'potlatch',[374] a

---

[368] Chirikure, *Great Zimbabwe: Reclaiming a 'Confiscated' Past*, 9.

[369] The 1930 Act reserved large parts of the land to use by European settlers.

[370] Webber Ndoro and Herman Kiriama. 'Management mechanisms in heritage legislation' in Webber Ndoro, Albert Mumma, and George Abungu (eds.), *Cultural Heritage and the Law: Protecting Immovable Heritage in English-Speaking Countries of Sub-Saharan Africa* (Rome: ICCROM, 2009) 53–62, 53–54.

[371] George Abungu and Webber Ndoro, 'Introduction' in Ndoro, Mumma, and Abungu, *Cultural Heritage and the Law*, viii.

[372] Aziz Rahman, Mary Anne Clarke, and Sean Byrne, 'The Art of Breaking People Down: The British Colonial Model in Ireland and Canada' (2017) 49 *Peace Research* 15–38, 24.

[373] John Alexander Macdonald, Memorandum (3 January 1887) in *Sessional Papers*, Vol. 16, First Session of the Sixth Parliament of the Dominion of Canada, 20B (Ottawa: Parliamentary Printers, 1887) 37.

[374] Franz Boas, 'The Potlatch' in Tom McFeat (ed.), *Indians of the North Pacific Coast* (Toronto: McClelland and Stewart Limited, 1966) 72–80.

communal ceremony of First Nations, involving gift-giving and expression of sol-idarity, often practised to confer a certain status, right, or claim during marriages, births, or funerals. The ceremony was prohibited in 1884 at the request of gov-ernment officials and missionaries who regarded it as a wasteful or anti-Christian tradition. In 1885, the ban was extended to other First Nations dances and cere-monies, including the sun dance, a sacred ritual, involving regeneration, healing, and self-sacrifice for the benefit of family and community. The practice was contra-dictory since it prohibited the use of sacred objects which officials and mission-aries continued to collect or sell. In some cases, agents seized ceremonial objects or masks (e.g. Potlatch objects of the Kwakwaka'wakw), in return for a promise not to prosecute violations of the ban of the potlach.[375] This practice had detrimental effects, since it destroyed the basis of community relations. This is reflected in con-temporary accounts of community members:

> [T]he Indian Act took our culture away and as a result of that we are in the situ-ation that we're in right now, which is we have unhealthy members in our com-munity. We have lost our culture. We have sad families because it took that ability to be a family away. So it's probably the worst thing that ever happened to the First Nations people in Canada.[376]

Overall, the colonial experience shaped how cultural heritage ought to be under-stood. As Nicholas Thomas has emphasized, 'the circulation of objects, especially across the edges of societies, civilizations, and trading regimes' is not 'merely a physical process but is also a movement and displacement of competing concep-tions of things'.[377] Many objects acquired new meanings through the colonial en-counter, i.e. through removal to the metropolis, trade relations or conservation in colonized societies. Cultural artefacts were predominantly understood as material objects or representations, rather than as sources or mediators of relationships.[378] They came to be appreciated for their aesthetics, style, or artistic value, their an-thropological or historical significance in the eyes of collectors, or their sheer market value, based on their pedigree (e.g. list of previous owners) or recognition as work of art. In some cases, protection and defence of cultural heritage became

---

[375] Gloria Cranmer Webster, ' Repatriation and Protection of First Nations Culture in Canada: The Potlatch Collection Repatriation' (1995) 29 *University of British Columbia Law Review* 137–142, 138.

[376] Catherine Bell and Heather McCuaig, 'Protection and Repatriation of Ktunaxa/Kinbasket Cultural Resources: Perspectives of Community Members' in Catherine Bell and Val Napoleon (eds.), *First Nations Cultural Heritage and Law: Case Studies, Voices, and Perspectives* (Vancouver: University of British Colombia Press, 2008) 312–365, 354.

[377] Nicholas Thomas, *Entangled Objects: Exchange, Material Culture, and Colonialism in the Pacific* (Cambridge, Mass.: Harvard University Press, 1991) 123.

[378] Anthony Forge, 'Introduction' in Anthony Forge (ed.), *Primitive Art and Society* (London: Oxford University Press, 1973) xiv–xviii.

part of the identity of 'civilized' nations as good colonial powers or guardians of heritage protection.[379]

6 Entangled legalities

The complex role of law as both enabler and constraint of the colonial condition challenges binary understandings of legality in colonial contexts. Colonial takings do not fit into generic categorizations of legal, illegal, or immoral, but encompass a spectrum of shades of illegality. They are governed by contradictions. Colonial agents and networks developed methods of cultural dispossession that were formally undertaken under the disguise of the law, but in reality were cultural takings. The underlying frames themselves were grounded in an exclusionary or discriminatory conception of law that failed to take into account the pluriversality of legal systems. It is necessary to broaden perspectives on legality in contemporary assessments in order to take into account existing contestations at the time and avoid the trap of reproducing false dichotomies.

6.1 Multi-normative frames of reference

Historical jurisprudence and practice, as well as resistance to takings, show that the relevant frames of reference for assessment of legality are more diverse and complex than portrayed in contemporary discourse. They exceed positivist law. The colonial world view on justification of conquest, trade expansion, or cultural takings in the name of salvage, 'science', or civilization of humanity was not simply accepted, but contested. Indigenous communities have challenged takings of human remains and cultural property in petitions to museums or courts since the nineteenth and early twentieth centuries.[380]

The Eurocentric conception of law and order was presented 'as if' it was universal law.[381] In reality, it silenced the plurality of legal systems and overlapping

---

[379] In 1899, Charles Normand proposed the creation of an international league of 'civilized nations' for the protection and defence of cultural heritage in his opening remarks to the International Congress on the Protection of Works of Art and Monuments, held at the Trocadero Palace. He noted: 'The protection and the safeguard of monuments, or more general, of artworks, which cover the memory and the history of all civilised nations, must be in the mind of everybody who knows, loves and respects the traditions and the glory of his fatherland ... United in one thought, we intend to provoke a compassionate current, an international league to constitute, even in the midst of the violence of war, an effective defense of cultural heritage inherited by all generations.' See Falser, 'Cultural Heritage as Civilizing Mission', 11.

[380] C. Timothy McKeown, 'Indigenous repatriation: The rise of the global legal movement' in Cressida Fforde, C. Timothy McKeown, and Honor Keeler (eds.), *The Routledge Companion to Indigenous Repatriation* (London: Routledge, 2020) 23–43.

[381] Mbembe, *Critique of Black Reason*, 11.

sovereignties. Lauren Benton has used the notion of 'interpolity law' to recognize this diversity.[382] It implies that international law itself was produced by a 'broader range of historical actors in places across the globe'.[383] It is necessary to go beyond codified norms and rules, and take into account practices by a variety of polities (e.g. indigenous norms, customs) in order to understand legalities. This approach does not necessarily involve a modern rereading of law in the past, but a fuller recognition of historical plurality.[384] It addresses the problem of the voice in colonial relations, namely the fact that alternative conceptions were not translated into the written law by colonial powers, who acted as self-appointed guardians of international law.

The multi-normative perspective is essential to assess cultural takings.[385] It challenges the argument that takings were acceptable according to the 'standards of the time'.[386] The protection of cultural objects was not only governed by treaty protections and 'hard' customary rules of the laws of war, but informed by natural law, minimum standards of behaviour and military ethics. This is reflected in the Martens clause and military practices. Law in itself was deeply intertwined with morality. Concepts of public conscience and morality were not only moral categories, but part of legal frameworks designed to ensure protection. The assessment of cultural takings thus requires a broader vision of legality, including its nexus to natural law concepts. Non-Western practices and unwritten norms, including pre-existing customary law, that have been disregarded in positivist international law, may provide standards for the assessment of behaviour.[387] For instance, the prohibition of grave robbing and the protection of human remains are common to Western and many non-Western traditions. As Bartholomé de las Casas has argued, indigenous norms, institutions, and customs have relevance for the assessment of cultural takings. In 2020, the Expert Mechanism on the Rights of Indigenous Peoples stressed the need for a multi-normative perspective in its report on 'Repatriation of ceremonial objects, human remains and intangible cultural heritage':

> a determination of whether an item is 'illicit' or 'stolen' property must include analysis not only of State laws, but the laws of indigenous peoples that set out

---

[382] Lauren Benton and Adam Clulow, 'Empires and protection: Making interpolity law in the early modern world' (2017) *Journal of Global History* 74–92.

[383] Lauren Benton, 'Made in Empire: Finding the History of International Law in Imperial Locations: Introduction' (2018) 31 *LJIL* 473.

[384] Thomas Duve, 'What is global legal history?' (2020) 8 *Comparative Legal History* 73–115, 104.

[385] German Museums Association, *Guidelines for German Museums: Care of Collections from Colonial Contexts* (Berlin: Deutscher Museumsbund, 2021) 167 ('we should acknowledge that objects were acquired in a situation of legal pluralism').

[386] Paul Turnbull, 'The ethics of repatriation: reflections on the Australian experience' in *The Routledge Companion to Indigenous Repatriation*, 927–949.

[387] Kuprecht, *Indigenous Peoples' Cultural Property Claims*, 49.

standards of alienability, ownership, treatment and custody of ceremonial objects, human remains and spiritual, intellectual and other properties.[388]

The discussion of normative protection of cultural objects in the colonial era is often limited to wartime protections against property taking and looting. However, the legality of takings is also governed by norms and standards applicable in peacetime. Some takings may not only stand in contrast to local laws or practices, but constitute violations of protectorate agreements or duties undertaken for the protection of the welfare of native populations under colonial administration, or even violate colonial law.

The reports and justifications offered by collectors to justify acquisition show that some form of consent was deemed necessary to legitimize a change of ownership in peacetime. Collectors sought to cover up flaws in contractual transactions, such as deception (Nefertiti), lack of title (Parthenon Marbles) or forced consent in order to bring takings within the realm of legality. During the Dakar-Djibouti expedition, Marcel Griaule offered locals a few coins or goods in return for the taking of objects in order to legitimize the acquisition. Their acceptance was interpreted as a form of consent to the transaction.[389] Missionaries had incentives to present the acquisition of objects as voluntary disposals in the context of conversion to Christianity.

Legally, it is wrong to qualify all takings of cultural objects as looted art or theft. In certain contexts, objects were specifically produced and offered for trade with European counterparts. But it is equally wrong to state that colonial acquisitions were lawful, simply because they involved some type of consent, exchange, or compensation. Instead, legality must be regarded as a spectrum, with different degrees of legality or illegality ('entangled legalities') and certain grey zones, which require moral judgment. The degree of legality depends on multiple frames of reference and the nature of the object. For instance, the removal of sacred objects, historical objects, or dignity objects (e.g. human remains) is difficult to justify by legitimate considerations. Other colonial takings may qualify as abuses of rights.[390]

---

[388] Report of the Expert Mechanism on the Rights of Indigenous Peoples, Repatriation of ceremonial objects, human remains and intangible cultural heritage under the United Nations Declaration on the Rights of Indigenous Peoples, A/HRC/45/35 (21 July 2020) para. 88.

[389] Philippe Baqué, *Un novel or noir: Le pillage des objets d'art en Afrique* (Marseille: Agone, 2021) 20.

[390] This doctrine goes back to Cicero's maxim 'summum ius, summa iniuria' which implies that law itself can become the locus of greatest injustice. See Friedrich Kratochwil, 'Summum ius, summa iniuria: Critical reflections on the legal form, inter-legality and the limits of law' in Jan Klabbers and Gianluigi Palombella (eds.), *The Challenge of Inter-Legality* (Cambridge: Cambridge University Press, 2019) 42–68. The doctrine is based on the premise that rights of actors are limited by the rights and interests of others.

6.2   Contextualized assessment of circumstances of acquisition

The traditional logic, according to which the legality of acquisition is taken for granted, unless involuntary dispossession can be positively shown, is subject to critique in colonial contexts. It faces not only challenges in relation to the proof of non-consensual acquisition, but disregards the structural nature of colonial injustice. It banalizes the structural and epistemic violence inherent in colonial relations. It assumes that the taking was acceptable according to the standards of the time, as long as no proof to the contrary is offered. It supports a market-driven agenda, which places protection of guardianship, ownership, or circulation of objects over ongoing effects of colonial violence. It reduces returns to moral acts, i.e. voluntary acts of exculpation, which demonstrate ethical behaviour.

This approach to consent overlooks the entanglements caused by the colonial condition. It recognizes certain formal impediments to the legality of acquisition (coercion, lack of consent), but makes them irrelevant by virtue of the passage of time, the existence of grey zones, gaps in provenance or difficulties of proof. The very histories of objects presented here show that the context cannot simply be blended out in legal assessments. In many instances, the colonial context creates ongoing legal entanglements. A nuanced assessment of colonial legalities requires a contextualized assessment, which takes into account the colonial structure and the unequal power relations that characterize the colonial system.

There are at least, three common forms of 'entanglement', which have occurred on a repeated basis in the past and continue to produce effects in the present: Coercion, 'entangled consent' and 'entangled authority'.[391] They involve legal wrongdoing or 'unconscionable takings', conflicting with 'principles of equity'.[392]

6.2.1   Coercion

The most obvious form of entanglement, which affects legality, is coercion. Objects which have been removed by force remain contested. Coercion itself comes in many forms. Some operations were related to military campaigns, others were linked to economic exploitation. Punitive expeditions, carried out with brutal force and the intent to foster subjugation or enrichment, are on the maximum spectrum

---

[391] For a similar typology in relation to unjust acquisitions, see Karin Edvardsson Björnberg, 'Historic Injustices and the Moral Case for Cultural Repatriation' (2014) 18 *Ethical Theory and Moral Practice* 461–474, 464. The German Guidelines adopt these criteria in relation to human remains. They distinguish (i) '[a]cquisitions in which the donors were put under pressure or compulsion or where they acted out of desperation'; (ii) '[a]cquisitions that were carried out without the consent of the owners/guardians and/or descendants, such as grave robbery, theft and looting'; and (iii) '[a]cquisitions in which consent was given but not by the person entitled to give or refuse consent'. See German Museum Association, *Guidelines: Care of Human Remains in Museums and Collections* (Berlin: German Museum Association, 2021) 18.
[392] Geoffrey Robertson, *Who Owns History?* (London: Biteback, 2019) 169–170.

of coercion. However, there are many other, more subtle forms of coercion, which may affect the legality of colonial takings. For instance, a taking of objects may be facilitated by mere threats of force or the structural context of force. During colonial expeditions, objects were given away because of fear of retaliation. In such contexts, lack of resistance cannot be qualified as act of consent. The simple taking of objects (e.g. Benjarmasin Diamond, Luf boat), or their offering to colonial administrators and their entourage, may be conditioned by the structural context of colonial violence. The fact that colonial officers were allowed by local leaders to remove objects does not mean that dispossession was voluntary. Other takings were carried out in a context of subjugation or exploitation maintained through force (e.g. Aksum obelisk). Such conditions cannot be disregarded in the assessment of the legalities of takings.

6.2.2 Entangled consent

Entangled consent, i.e. circumstances where consent was not freely given or provided under conditions of inequality, is a second flaw in modes of acquisition. Forced consent is an obvious example of entanglement. It was commonly used to validate the acquisition of royal regalia, treasures, or historical objects after military defeat, such as the Koh-i-Noor or the Rosetta stone. Surrender instruments gave the acquisition a formal stamp of legality, although it was procured through force.[393] In other instances, consent was vitiated by deceit, misrepresentation or concealing of facts. For instance, Prince Diponegoro was lured into peace negotiations which led to his arrest and handover of his dagger. Lord Elgin used bribes and exceeded the authority given to him for excavations. King Njoya was misled about the interest of the German Emperor in the throne of his father. Ludwig Borchardt concealed the value of Nefertiti in the partage lot in order to facilitate export. In New Zealand and Australia, indigenous human remains were exported in violation of indigenous customary norms and export prohibitions at the beginning of the twentieth century.[394]

Gifts were not necessarily made voluntarily or based on 'generous friendship'. Some of them were coerced or 'stolen'. Gifts were made to avoid subjugation (Atztec treasures) or to express loyalty in the context of local uprisings or after punitive expeditions.[395] Others were tribute payments to colonial rulers. Missionary

---

[393] In contemporary international law, this practice is challenged by Art. 52 of the Vienna Convention on the Law of Treaties (23 May 1969) 1155 UNTS 331, which states that 'a treaty is void if its conclusion has been procured by the threat or use of force in violation of the principles of international law embodied in the Charter of the United Nations'.

[394] Cressida Fforde, Amber Aranui, Gareth Knapman, and Paul Turnbull, 'Inhuman and very mischievous traffic: Early measures to cease the export of Ancestral Remains from Aotearoa New Zealand and Australia' in *The Routledge Companion to Indigenous Repatriation*, 381–399, 396 ('While in New Zealand and Australia the various legal measures to regulate export certainly had some impact, it is clear that many individuals sought ways, sometimes (perhaps often) successfully, to disregard the law').

[395] On skull drums obtained from the king of Kpandu in Togo, see Jan Hüsgen, 'Colonial Expeditions and Collecting – The Context of the "Togo-Hinterland Expedition" of 1894/1895' (2020) 1 *Journal for Art Market Studies* 1–12, 8–9.

collecting often benefited from colonial power structures to collect ritual objects, with or without the permission of local communities.[396]

Such types of acquisitions, where consent was not free, but driven by coercive circumstances or deceit, remain the subject of debate. An indication of exploitation of coercive circumstances is the acquisition of objects below price or with marginal compensation. Such practices were common in the large ethnographic missions carried out in the twentieth century.[397] Even ethnographers and private collectors profited from the coercive circumstances of colonial contexts, which prompted natives to 'accept the offers made'.[398] Such acquisition may be legal in form, but can only be explained by the irregular context in which they were made.

6.2.3 Entangled authority

A third factor affecting the acquisition is the authority to alienate objects. In certain cases, it is doubtful whether the agent allowing the purchase or removal of objects enjoyed the authority to dispose of them (*nemo dat quod non habet*). For example, reports from the Dakar-Djibouti mission or the story of the 'sale' and return of the Olokun head show how colonial officers or collectors pressured natives, including priests, to sell objects they were not authorized to give away.[399] This includes sacred objects or objects that were deemed to belong to the community. These objects were hard to acquire. Collectors often knew that they would not be able to acquire them under regular conditions. They were removed in secret or under dubious circumstances.

The authority to grant permission to remove historical objects is problematic in contexts of occupation. For instance, the Ottoman Empire has been criticized for allowing the alienation of ancient Greek artefacts (Parthenon marbles, Pergamon altar). French and British authorities paid limited attention to the interests of Egyptians in excavation and regulation of the export of antiquities.

The authority to dispose of objects may be limited by the inalienable nature of cultural property. This argument has particular relevance in relation to indigenous objects. It may compromise the acquisition of objects that are 'not subject to individual ownership by anyone, and thus cannot justly be transferred by any individual, including a person who belongs to the relevant culture'.[400] Such an argument

---

[396] On missionary collecting in the Congo carried out with 'force and under pressure', see Independent Group of Experts, *Ethical Principles for the Management and Restitution of Colonial Collections in Belgium*, June 2021.

[397] For instance, the Sarr and Savoy report mentions the acquisition of a mask from the Ségou region which the Dakar-Djibouti mission purchased for 7 francs, although the average market value at auctions was 'around 200 francs'. See Sarr and Savoy Report, 56.

[398] Sarr and Savoy Report, 57.

[399] See Chapters 3 and 4.

[400] Erich Hatala Matthes, 'Repatriation and the Radical Redistribution of Art' (2017) 4 *Ergo* 931–953, 936; Janna Thompson, 'Cultural Property, Restitution and Value' (2003) 20 *Journal of Applied Philosophy* 251–262, 255.

has been made by the Colombian Constitutional Court to challenge the validity of the donation of the Quimbaya Treasure by Colombian President Holguín Jaramillo to Spain in 1893. The Court questioned whether an executive agent is authorized to 'gift away' national treasures without parliamentary approval. It regarded the transfer as an unlawful alienation of the public patrimony of Colombia to the detriment of its own people, which violated the Constitution and self-determination, namely the right to ancestral cultural patrimony.[401]

6.3 Legalities as a spectrum involving law and ethics

This contextualized assessment of acquisition, and the different forms of entanglement, make it necessary to take a differentiated look at legality and consent. The legality of acquisition of objects cannot be simply presumed, with reference to the different normative standards applicable at the time, or a presumption of consent. The multi-normative frame and the structural context of colonial relations need to be taken into account in the evaluation of practices. The spectrum ranges from lawful to unlawful or unethical acquisitions. Some takings contravened applicable obligations under international law (e.g. punitive raids) or domestic law (illegal export, excavation). Others conflicted with principles of equity, which are commonly recognized in many legal systems (e.g. duress, undue influence, lack of authority) or minimum standards of humanity (e.g. grave robbing, taking of human remains). Again other acquisitions were made under lawful procedures, but affected by an illegitimate context. Some of them may qualify as abuses of rights.

The prohibition of the abuse of rights is recognized by a large number of national legal systems, including civil and common law systems. It is part of the general principles of international law.[402] It has particular relevance to colonial structures, which relied on the rudimentary and indeterminate character of positivist international law to create an uneven body of law, which marginalized non-Eurocentric legal orders. It corrects the unfettered application of law through standards of good faith, fairness, or reasonableness. It recognizes that the exercise of rights may become abusive if it is arbitrary and causes annoyance, harm, or injury to others.[403] This doctrine may set limits to the acquisition of ownership rights in contexts of colonial exploitation or abuses of colonial laws and procedures (e.g. antiquity laws, prize law procedures, instructions for colonial collecting) to gain custody over objects.

---

[401] Diego Mejía-Lemos, 'The "Quimbaya Treasure"', Judgment SU-649/17, (2019) 113 *AJIL* 123–130, 124. See Chapter 2.

[402] Michael Byers, 'Abuse of Rights: An Old Principle, A New Age' (2002) 47 *McGill Law Journal* 389–431, 431.

[403] For instance, Hersch Lauterpacht has argued a state violates the doctrine when it 'avails itself of its right in an arbitrary manner in such a way as to inflict upon another State an injury which cannot be justified by a legitimate consideration of its own advantage'. See Lassa Oppenheim, *International Law: A Treatise* (8th edn, H. Lauterpacht (ed.), London: Longmans, Green & Co., 1955) 345.

It is, of course, difficult and problematic to assess standards of morality and public conscience in retrospect. This is why a contextualized assessment of colonial takings requires both legal and ethical criteria. It involves legal determinations, evaluating illegality or legal flaws in acquisitions from a multi-normative perspective, and broader ethical categories to capture structural injustice. This dual lens reflects the pluralist structure of law at the time. It makes it necessary to search for 'just and fair' solutions. In controversial cases, ownership may require a new basis of consent.[404] As Victoria Reed has argued, traditional legal categories applied in museum practice or treaty semantics, such as loot, theft ('stolen', 'illegally exported') or duress, do not suffice to capture the complexities of legality in the context of colonial transactions.[405] The determination, as to whether an object was validly acquired, i.e. without coercion or contrived consent, requires a consideration of the context and period of colonization, an assessment of political economies and trading schemes, and critical evaluation of the laws or authorities which permitted removal.[406] In case of legal grey zones or provenance gaps, it is necessary to look beyond the immediate act of acquisition. The nature, function and use of objects may provide important indicators. For instance, it is important to consider the ontology, societal function or status of the object in its original context (e.g. whether the object was individually or collectively held or subject to ownership at all), relevant ritual or spiritual functions, whether it could be alienated according to local rules or customs, and/or whether it was meant to be preserved.[407]

The fluid structure of international law, and the contestations of the Eurocentric vision articulated in discourse, have major implications for the contemporary debates on return and restitution. It is wrong to state that such claims simply apply today's standards of justice to distant historical realities. The interplay between law and morality, which governs these claims today, is a reflection of the past. As Charlotte Joy has noted:

> Principles of justice have … always existed in parallel to the laws at any given time. Repatriation claims do not, as some people claim, rely on applying today's moral norms to a very different past as … norms have always been heterogenous and contested.[408]

---

[404] See Chapter 9.
[405] Victoria S. Reed, 'American Museums and Colonial-Era Provenance: A Proposal' (2023) *International Journal of Cultural Property*, 1–21, doi:10.1017/S0940739123000036.
[406] Ibid, 8.
[407] Ibid, 9.
[408] See Charlotte Joy, *Heritage Justice* (Cambridge: Cambridge University Press, 2020) 24.

7

Colonial and Post-colonial Continuities in Culture Heritage Protection: Narratives and Counter-narratives

1 Introduction

> We might ask ourselves if the time has not come to 'liberate' international law (*Mohammed Bedjaoui*, 1979)[1]

The twentieth century witnessed a novel turn to cultural heritage protection. It recognized not only the material value of objects,[2] but also their social and intergenerational importance. Post-Second World War instruments have extended the protection of cultural property in armed conflict. Human rights frameworks have offered new visions on the link between communities and objects and claims for access and return. However, the dual face of law as an instrument of complicity and frame of resistance[3] endured. International legal instruments simultaneously acknowledged and challenged the traces of colonial injustice.

The acquisition and removal of objects from former colonies to the metropole or market countries[4] triggered an urge for conservation and market protection. More and more objects were recognized as works of art throughout the twentieth century, based on their aesthetics, craftsmanship or artistic language. Their exchange and trade contributed to commodification and changing reference systems. The qualification as 'art' brought objects closer within market schemes and ownership-based property categories, i.e. tangible property that is materially owned and carries a monetary value.[5] The market value of objects increased. Objects, such as the

---

[1] Mohammed Bedjaoui, *Towards a New International Economic Order* (Paris: UNESCO, 1979) 109–110.

[2] Stefan Groth, Regina F. Bendix, and Achim Spiller (eds.), *Kultur als Eigentum: Instrumente, Querschnitte und Fallstudie* (Göttingen: Göttingen University Press, 2015).

[3] See Chapter 6. See also Carsten Stahn, 'Reckoning with Colonial Injustice: International Law as Culprit and as Remedy?' (2020) 33 *LJIL* 823–835.

[4] On one-dimensional flow, see Lyndel V. Prott, 'The International Movement of Cultural Objects' (2005) 12 *International Journal of Cultural Property* 225–248, 228.

[5] Charity Gates, 'Who Owns African Art? Envisioning a Legal Framework for the Restitution of African Cultural Heritage' (2020) 3 *International Comparative, Policy & Ethics Law Review* 1131–1162, 1156.

Benin bronzes, which did not constitute market objects in pre-colonial Benin, have been auctioned for high prizes in contemporary settings.[6] Philippe Baqué compared ethnological objects from Africa as the 'new black gold'.[7] This created new colonialities, less along degrees of civilization, but rather around ownership, belonging and economic exploitation.

The taking of objects, and the framing of their value and meaning, demonstrates the close entanglement of art and culture and practices of 'racial capitalism',[8] i.e. the process of 'deriving social and economic value from racial identity'.[9] Many objects were first extracted from colonized populations based on colonial power relations and racialized divisions of human populations, grounded in ethnicity, indigeneity, language, culture, or religion. They were used as spectacle to demonstrate power, wealth, or superiority over inferior or less 'civilized' people, and then gradually transformed into commodities through new systems of classification, generating and expanding market value and profits, based on their artistic and commercial value.[10] This transformation and accumulation of value served to make continuing possession and exploitation more socially acceptable in the eyes of holding objects. Many cultural heritage codifications protected the interests of possessors more than those of claimants.[11]

Colonial inequalities returned in new forms in the debate on restitution. Colonization favoured the creation of cultural elites.[12] The independence and decolonization movement in late 1950s and 1960s reinvigorated claims for return of objects.[13] The issue of return was inherently linked to economic inequalities between market countries and requesting states. Colonized states started to reclaim objects more systematically. Countries, such as Benin, Nigeria, or Indonesia, made demands for the return of their cultural heritage. Individuals, such as anthropologist Ekpo Eyo (1931–2011),[14] the head of the Nigerian service of antiquities

---

[6] Auction prices for Benin Bronzes have increased rapidly in the twentieth century, reaching up to £10 million paid by a private collector in 2016.

[7] Philipe Baqué, *Un nouvel or noir: Le pillage des objects d'art en Afrique* (Marseille: Agone, 2021) 360.

[8] Anna Arabindan-Kesson, *Black Bodies, White Gold: Art, Cotton, and Commerce in the Atlantic World* (Durham, NC, and London: Duke University Press, 2021) 114

[9] Nancy Leong, 'Racial capitalism' (2013) 126 *Harvard Law Review* 2151–2226, 2152.

[10] On the re-'invention of the non-Western artifact as art', see Shelly Errington, 'What Became Authentic Primitive Art?' (1994) 9 *Cultural Anthropology* 201–226, 213.

[11] See also Jos van Beurden, *Inconvenient Heritage* (Amsterdam: Amsterdam University Press, 2020) 227.

[12] Pan-African Cultural Manifesto, 26.

[13] The Pan-African Cultural Manifesto stated in 1969: 'Cultural domination emphasized the depersonalization of a part of the African peoples, falsified their history, systematically denigrated and opposed their religious and moral values, progressively and officially replaced their language by that of the colonizers in order to devitalize them and to deprive them of their raison d'etre'. See Organization of African Unity, Pan-African Cultural Manifesto, Algiers (July 1969) (1970) 17 *Africa Today* 25–28, 26. See also Folarin Shyllon, 'International Standards for Cultural Heritage: An African Perspective' (2000) 5 *Art Antiquity & Law* 159–176.

[14] Babatunde Lawal, 'Eye Du Ke Esit Nyin Ke Nsinsi!: Remembering Ekpo Okpo Eyo (1931–2011) Administrator, Archaeologist, Scholar, Teacher, Mentor, and Friend' (2017) 50 *African Arts* 48–61.

between 1968 to 1979, pushed for the creation of museums and heritage institutions in non-Western contexts in order to facilitate returns. However, such claims encountered significant opposition. For decades, Western collections were only prepared to offer works on loan, sell them back, or agree to return them on a voluntary basis. Museums argued that objects were validly acquired or had become inalienable national heritage over time. Holding States preferred to present returns as act of gratitude[15] or cooperation.[16]

Economic imbalances and competing interests between source countries or communities and market countries, who shared an interest in holding and trading objects as 'art', influenced the negotiation of cultural heritage instruments. With growing representation in international institutions, newly independent countries pushed to include restitution in novel multilateral frameworks. In the 1970s, lawyers, like Algerian jurist Mohammed Bedjaoui, advocated a new 'international cultural order'.[17] However, major twentieth century codifications, such as the UNESCO Convention on the Means of Prohibiting and Preventing the Illicit Import, Export and Transfer of Ownership of Cultural Property (1970 UNESCO Convention) or the 1995 UNIDROIT Convention on Stolen or Illegally Exported Cultural Objects (UNIDROIT Convention), evaded the issue rather than addressing it.[18]

Treaty instruments have created an 'international limbo'.[19] International legal instruments have partly cemented existing inequalities through codification. They have largely failed to recognize the wrong of cultural removals or exploitation in the colonial encounter or to address its ongoing effects.[20] Historian Michel-Rolph Trouillot has argued that silence is a constructed process, i.e. a way to create history.[21] This applies not only to fact-creation or attribution of historical meaning, but also to legal sources. Law served as a means of distancing, i.e. an instrument to separate past and present. Many legal regulations silenced or excluded cultural colonial objects from the scope of legal protection, created impediments to return, or defined relationships to objects in terms of distinctions (e.g. cultural versus natural objects) or property or ownership categories that do not necessarily coincide with non-Western perspectives.

Legal frameworks were used as a means to protect market countries, rather than as mechanisms to remedy past injustices. Colonial objects were vested with

---

[15] In 1957, the UK offered an Ashanti stool to Ghana as a 'gift'.

[16] For instance, Belgium agreed to return over 100 objects to Zaire between 1976 and 1981 as gifts, rather than acts of restitution, in order not to set a legal precedent.

[17] Mohamed Bedjaoui, Special Rapporteur, Eleventh report on succession of states in respect of matters other than treaties, A/CN.4/322 and Corr.1 & Add.1 & 2, 1979, para. 46.

[18] See Folarin Shyllon, 'The Recovery of Cultural Objects by African States through the UNESCO and UNIDROIT Conventions and the Role of Arbitration' (2000) 5 *Uniform Law Review* 219–242.

[19] Lyndel Prott, 'The Ethics and Law of Returns' (2009) 61 *Museum International* 101–106, 103.

[20] Ibid, 103.

[21] Michel-Rolph Trouillot, *Silencing the Past: Power and the Production of History* (Boston: Beacon Press, 1995).

greater international protection, with their growing recognition as works of art and increased appreciation of their material and cultural value. However, international codifications curtailed restitution claims through colonial clauses, non-retroactivity or vocabulary concealing past wrongdoing. The approach differs considerably from the treatment of cultural objects acquired under Nazi occupation. Legal regulation was used to maintain ownership in Western collections or impede returns through legal norms and concepts, such as the intertemporal rule, statutes of limitation or the inalienability of public property. As Sarah van Beurden has cautioned, even benevolent ideas, such as the protection of objects as 'world heritage', may have critical repercussions for countries or societies of origin, since they empower holder countries:

> Casting objects from former colonies as 'world heritage' weakened claims for repatriation and restitution since it allowed museums to argue for the universal value of the material they possessed, and therefore their continued custodianship of the objects was in the best interest of the materials.[22]

The grand vision of UNESCO Director-General Amadou-Mahtar M'Bow, who had pleaded for the 'return of cultural assets to their countries of origin' in 1978,[23] was reduced to symbolic action in the UN and the facilitation of bilateral negotiation on return in the International Committee for Promoting the Return of Cultural Property to its Countries of Origin (ICPRCP). Cultural takings were largely treated as a problem of ethics and morality. Returns were framed as acts of solidarity or comity, grounded in political convenience or the ambition to maintain amicable international relations. Removals of objects in the colonial period were not brought under the formal umbrella of restitutions under the 1970 UNESCO or the 1995 UNIDROT Convention, governing looted, stolen or illegally exported objects, but rather treated under the more neutral and flexible regime of 'return', or under the concept of 'repatriation', which covers return of 'human remains and cultural or religious artefacts to indigenous or native communities'.[24]

Modern cultural heritage and human rights-based instruments have challenged state-centred and protectionist visions of cultural colonial objects, and the assimilation of indigenous peoples and their culture into settler societies.[25] However,

---

[22] Sarah van Beurden, 'The Pitfalls of "Shared" Heritage' https://blog.uni-koeln.de/gssc-humboldt/the-pitfalls-of-shared-heritage/.

[23] Amadou-Mahtar M'Bow, 'A Plea for the Return of Cultural Heritages to Those Who Created Them' (1979) 6 *Annals of Tourism Research* 199–201.

[24] See Pierre Losson, 'Opening Pandora's Box: Will the Return of Cultural Heritage Objects to Their Country of Origin Empty Western Museums?' (2021) 51 *The Journal of Arts Management, Law, and Society* 379–392 381.

[25] See Paul Turnbull and Michael Pickering (eds.), *The Long Way Home: The Meanings and Value of Repatriation* (Oxford & New York: Berghahn Books, 2010).

practices continued to be marked by colonial and post-colonial continuities.[26] Concepts, such as guardianship, shared heritage or the universality of objects have been used to legitimize continuing ownership. Delays or lack of returns have been justified by knowledge gaps about the provenance of objects, doubts about continuing cultural bonds to objects or disputes over the proper recipient of returns. Digital return has become a new frontline of controversy. Transformation has only occurred incrementally, with the rise of de-colonial movements, shifting public consciousness and museums ethics, experiences in settler colonial contexts and new policy or 'soft law' instruments.

This chapter traces the development and contrasting faces of legal frameworks throughout the twentieth century, including their interplay with market economies. It argues that the political economy of takings and the market value of objects contributed to patchwork regulation of entangled cultural objects, which protected the *status quo* and left decisions on the future of objects largely within the power of holding states. It shows that legal instruments in the (i) inter-war period, the (ii) post-Second World War era, and (iii) decolonization have strengthened protection, but also upheld unequal power relations or legitimized the retention of objects in collections. It illustrates how states created silences relating to colonial takings in legal frames and how they were perpetuated over time. It investigates (iv) the extent to which indigenous rights and human rights law serve as frames to challenge historical gaps and blind spots and promote resistance to cultural extraction and epistemic violence. It examines lessons from national repatriation practices in settler colonial contexts, including the Native American Graves Protection and Repatriation Act (NAGPRA), for return of cultural colonial objects. It identifies alternative property and object conceptions which are able to accommodate different world views on cultural colonial objects.

2 Silences and continuities in the inter-war period

The inter-war period was marked by both colonial continuities and novel impulses to protect cultural objects. It recognized the importance of culture objects for 'humanity' and promoted the creation of new instruments and international institutions to safeguard culture in times of war and peace, but replicated double standards and embedded cultural protection in colonial discourses of civilization or guardianship. Archeological sites and cultural objects were branded as patrimony of humankind. This qualification has conflicting implications. It increased the case for protection, but also legitimized continuing exploitation. It served to

---

[26] Wazi Apoh and Andreas Mehler, 'Mainstreaming the Discourse on Restitution and Repatriation within African History', Heritage Studies and Political Science' (2020) 7 *Contemporary Journal of African Studies* 1–16, 12.

reduce colonial rivalry and to promote 'free trade and equal access to cultural re-sources',[27] including market access of European excavators or collectors.

2.1 Double standards under mandate administration

The mandate system of the League of Nations did not constrain European colo-nialism per se, but established a new framework for administration of cultural heritage in former colonies of the Ottoman and German Empire. It created a supervisory mechanism, administered by the Permanent Mandate Commission of the League. The system reflected the discriminatory division of the world into different scales of civilization. It fed into narratives that civilized nations have a 'moral obligation' to 'raise' and advance lesser developed peoples and that colo-nial rule itself is an act of benevolence. The 'communities formerly belonging to the Turkish Empire', including Palestine, Syria/Lebanon and Iraq ('A' mandates), were provisionally recognized as 'independent nations', subject to the 'rendering of administrative advice and assistance' by mandatory powers, while German ter-ritories in Central Africa ('B' mandates) and South West Africa and the South Pacific ('C' mandates) were placed under foreign administration or the 'laws of the Mandatory', subject to certain safeguards supervised by the League. Colonies outside the mandate system remained under the sovereignty of their colonial powers.

This system created double standards in relation to treatment of cultural ob-jects. Mandatory powers enacted legislation for cultural heritage, in particular the protection of archaeological sites in 'A' mandates, which were considered to be cul-turally 'civilized', while failing to adopt rules for 'B' and 'C' mandates, which were considered to be less developed. The classical antique heritage in the territories of the former Ottoman Empire was regulated and protected under the umbrella of League, while collection of ethnological objects was unconstrained.[28] Cultural protection in colonies outside the mandate system remained governed by the laws of colonial powers,[29] which were often shaped by paternalistic motivations.[30]

The mandate system restricted the freedom of mandated territories to determine how to protect their own cultures. However, even the legal regimes in 'A' mandates, supervised by the Mandates Commission followed a colonial logic. They were often designed to secure market access to cultural resources and guarantee equal treat-ment of foreign excavators, instead of ensuring protection of local interests. For

---

[27] Ana Vrdoljak, *International Law, Museums and Return of Cultural Objects* (Cambridge: Cambridge University Press, 2006) 116.

[28] Sebastian Spitra, *Die Verwaltung von Kultur im Völkerrecht* (Baden-Baden: Nomos, 2021) 241.

[29] Vrdoljak, *International Law, Museums and Return of Cultural Objects*, 107.

[30] Spitra, *Die Verwaltung von Kultur im Völkerrecht*, 270–271.

instance, the antiquities regulation for Iraq, approved by the League, allowed foreign missions to 'take away objects which ought to have been kept for Baghdad'.[31]
In 1935, Leonard Woolley (1880–1960), the director of the Joint Expedition of the
British Museum and of the Museum of Pennsylvania to Mesopotamia, defended
the liberal stance of the regulation against change by Iraqi authorities. He argued
that this flexibility was 'essential to encourage foreign missions by conceding to
them a fair proportion of objects', even when such concessions were 'grudgingly
made'.[32] They would be 'amply' repaid by 'the gains from future work'.[33]

The Executive Committee of the Syro-Palestinian Congress filed a petition to
the Permanent Mandate Commission, in which it flipped the argument of the
'standard of civilization' around. It alleged that France failed to comply with its
duty to protect cultural heritage in Syria under the mandate agreement, namely
enact antiquities regulation, ensuring 'equality of treatment in the matter of excavations and archaeological research to the nationals of all states members of the
League of Nations'.[34] In 1925, the Syro-Palestinian Congress addressed an appeal
to the Sixth Assembly of the League of Nations, in which it criticized the lack of
influence of local authorities on the approval of expeditions and the granting of
concessions. It stated:

[M]andatory authorities are alone competent in all that concerns antiquities.
They deliver permits to make excavations to whom they wish without previously
asking the opinion or consent of the local authorities ... we do not know what
treasures were removed from our soil the excavations having been carried out
without any supervision.[35]

The petition led to the enactment of a new regulation, which continued to be favourable to foreign excavators. It allowed France to decide which finds should be
ceded to the excavation mission, and which objects ought to remain in the mandated territory.[36] The system placed the interests in cultural exploitation over the
interests of the local population. Antiquities were treated as a commodity, which
was open to appropriation with the consent of the mandatory power.[37]

---

[31] Leonard Woolley, 'Antiquities Law, Iraq' (1935) 9 *Antiquity* 84–88, 85.
[32] Ibid.
[33] Ibid.
[34] League of Nations, Mandate pour la Syrie et le Liban, O.528.M.313.1922vi (12 August 1922).
[35] Executive Committee of the Syro-Palestinian Congress, Appeal addressed to the 6th Assembly
of the League of Nations in Permanent Mandates Commission, Minutes of the Eighth session, C. 174.
M. 65. 1926. VI (8 March 1926) 173–194, 183.
[36] See Decree No. 207 on the regulation of antiquities in Syria and Lebanon (26 March 1926) Art.
19. It stated: 'The State may decide that all or part of the objects resulting from the excavations will be
alienated free of charge or in return for payment, subject to the formal reservation that such alienations
shall not prejudice the interest of its collections' (Eng. tr). See Spitra, *Die Verwaltung von Kultur im
Völkerrecht*, 233.
[37] Ibid, 234.

2.2 Codification efforts

The League of Nations promoted the internationalization of cultural property protection through codification efforts and cooperation.[38] It stressed the universal
character and educational role of cultural resources held in public collections and
the need for accessibility to all states. However, the emerging legal regimes continued to be marked by divides between Western and non-Western societies. They
built on traditional patterns of 'civilization discourse' and legitimized Western
models of possession and trade of cultural objects. For instance, a resolution on the
Protection of Historical Monuments and Works of Art, adopted by the Assembly of
the League in 1932, recognized that artistic and archaeological objects are not only
governed by concepts of national ownership, but part of a 'heritage of mankind'.[39]
Preservation was entrusted to 'the community of states, which are the guardians of
civilization'.[40] This reference entrenched divides between 'civilized' and less 'civilized' in relation to cultural protection. It understood 'civilized' nations as guardians of the common artistic and archaeological patrimony of humankind, while
excluding nations that did not meet this definition.[41]

The International Museums Office (IMO) prepared several new legal instruments protecting cultural objects in times of war and peace, under the guidance of
Belgian international lawyer Charles de Visscher.[42] These draft conventions sought
to reconcile two conflicting imperatives, namely the universal nature of works of
art and their significance to humanity, and the interests of states to preserve 'national heritage to which any civilized nation is closely attached'.[43] A 1936 IMO
draft, International Convention for the Protection of National Historic or Artistic
Treasures, even extended protection to 'objects of remarkable palæontological,
interest'.[44] However, these codification projects replicated civilizational divides
and largely ignored colonial acquisitions.[45] They did not address the issue of colonial returns. The regulation of the relationship between metropolis and periphery

---

[38] For a survey, see Ana Vrdoljak, 'International Exchange and Trade in Cultural Objects' in Valentina
Vadi and Bruno de Witte (eds.), *Culture and International Economic Law* (London: Routledge, 2015)
124–141.

[39] League of Nations, Preservation of Historical Monuments and Works of Art, C.L.176.1932.XII[A]
(23 November 1932) adopted by the International Committee on Intellectual Co-operation, based
on recommendations drawn up by the Athens Conference concerning the preservation of historical
monuments and works of art.

[40] Ibid.

[41] Spitra, *Die Verwaltung von Kultur im Völkerrecht*, 252.

[42] See generally Joe Verhoeven, 'Charles De Visscher: Living and Thinking International Law' (2000)
11 *EJIL* 887–904.

[43] Charles de Visscher, 'International Protection of Works of Art and Historic Monuments' in
Documents and State Papers (Washington: Department of State, 1949) 822–871, 858.

[44] Draft International Convention for the Protection of National Historic or Artistic Treasures,
Art. 1.

[45] Sebastian Spitra, 'Civilisation, Protection, Restitution: A Critical History of International Cultural
Heritage Law in the 19th and 20th Century' (2020) 22 *Journal of the History of International Law* 329–
354, 340.

was left within the discretionary power of colonial powers. For instance, the 1939 (draft) 'International Convention for the Protection of National Collections of Art and History' contained both a non-retroactivity provision[46] and a colonial clause, allowing colonial powers to declare provisions inapplicable to 'colonies, protectorates, overseas territories, territories placed under its sovereignty or territories for which a mandate has been entrusted to it'.[47] The draft left it thus to colonizing states to determine cultural protection and restitution in colonial contexts. It maintained different spheres of violence, one among Western powers, and another one in the colonies. It ultimately failed to be adopted by the League.

The Treaty on the Protection of Artistic and Scientific Institutions and Historic Monuments (Roerich Pact), initiated by the 'Roerich Museum' in the United States and adopted by members of the Pan-American Union on 15 April 1935, was the first targeted convention on the protection of cultural property in conflict.[48] It reinforced global protection and was referred to as the 'Red Cross of Culture'.[49] It introduced a distinctive protective sign for cultural objects and strengthened protection of 'historic monuments, museums, scientific, artistic, educational and cultural institutions' beyond the Hague Regulations.[50] It protected cultural property because of its intrinsic value, rather than its civilian or public character. It stated that such entities shall only lose protection by virtue of military necessity if they are used 'for military purposes'.[51] According to US President Roosevelt, the treaty carried 'a spiritual significance' that is 'far deeper than the text of the instrument itself'.[52] It made the Americas the guardians of 'standards of civilization' in relation to cultural objects.[53]

3 Post-Second World War codifications

The codifications adopted after World War II marked a decisive step away from 'cultural Darwinism' towards the recognition of 'cultural pluralism',[54] but continued to uphold double standards in relation to past colonial violence.

---

[46] Draft International Convention for the Protection of National Collections of Art and History (1939) Art. 2 (3).

[47] Ibid, Art. 12.

[48] Treaty on the Protection of Artistic and Scientific Institutions and Historic Monuments (26 August 1935) 167 LNTS 289. It goes back to the efforts of Russian painter Nicholas Roerich (1874–1947), who had witnessed cultural destruction in Russo-Japanese war (1904–1905) and the First World War.

[49] Roerich Pact and Banner of Peace Committee, 'Call To World Unity' (1947) in (2018) 20 *Labyrinth* 168–170, 170.

[50] Article 1.

[51] Article 5.

[52] Lewis Elbinger, 'The Neutrality of Art: The Roerich Pact's Quest to Protect Art from the Ignorance of Man' (1990) 67 *Foreign Service Journal* 16–20, 17.

[53] Spitra, *Die Verwaltung von Kultur im Völkerrecht*, 267.

[54] Vrdoljak, *International Law, Museums and Return of Cultural Objects*, 130.

The post-war period marked a shift away from civilizational divides. The holocaust and the crimes committed during World War II marked a rupture in the self-proclaimed image of civilization of West. Historian Dan Diner has qualified it as a 'civilizational rupture' (*Zivilizationsbruch*).[55] It became unacceptable openly to apply discriminatory standards of 'civilization'. This is partially reflected in the regime of the Geneva Conventions of 12 August 1949.[56] They 'brought the whole of humanity, at least theoretically, into the fold of the laws of war'.[57] The application of international humanitarian law to colonial conflicts was a major battlefield in the drafting of Common Article 3 of the Geneva Conventions. Colonial powers remained reluctant to bring colonial conflicts fully within the realm of the rules governing international armed conflicts in order to maintain the possibility to fight colonial resistance and criminalize opposition and unrest[58] and distinguish colonial warfare from Nazi atrocities.[59] But they agreed to apply minimum humanitarian standards in internal conflicts. The adoption of Common Article 3 left colonial governments considerable leeway in the application of the law.[60] However, it departed from the logic of cultural difference and broke 'absolute state sovereignty in wartime colonial affairs'.[61] States from the Global South partly adhered to the conventions in order to be able invoke them in future conflicts with colonial powers. However, they did not apply retroactively to past colonial warfare.

In terms of protection and restitution of cultural heritage, the Holocaust formed the centre of attention. The conditions for return of objects looted by the Nazi regime were addressed even before the end of the war.[62] For instance, in 1943, signatory powers of the Inter-Allied Declaration Against Acts of Dispossession Committed in Territories Under Enemy Occupation or Control (London Declaration), expressly reaffirmed their right to invalidate transfers or dealings, irrespective of whether they had 'taken the form of open looting or plunder, or of transactions apparently legal in form, even when they purport to be voluntarily

---

[55] Dan Diner (ed.), *Zivilizationsbruch: Denken nach Auschwitz* (Frankfurt am Main: Fischer, 1988).

[56] Gilad Ben-Nun, *The Fourth Geneva Convention for Civilians: The History of International Humanitarian Law* (London: Bloomsbury, 2020).

[57] Frédéric Mégret, 'From Savages to Unlawful Combatants: A Postcolonial Look at International Law's "Other"' in Anne Orford (ed.), *International Law and Its Others* (Cambridge: Cambridge University Press, 2006) 265–317, 297.

[58] Fabian Klose, 'The Colonial Testing Ground: The International Committee of the Red Cross and the Violent End of Empire' (2011) 2 *Humanity* 107–126.

[59] Boyd van Dijk, 'Internationalizing Colonial War: on the Unintended Consequences of the Interventions of the International Committee of the Red Cross in South-East Asia, 1945–1949' (2021) 250 *Past & Present* 243–283, 279.

[60] Boyd refers to advantage of 'vagueness' articulated by the UK delegate in the negotiations. See Boyd van Dijk, *Preparing for War: The Making of the Geneva Conventions* (Oxford: Oxford University Press, 2022) 116–117.

[61] Van Dijk, 'Internationalizing Colonial War, 281.

[62] On restitution efforts from the 1940s to the 1990s, see Michael Marrus, *Some Measure of Justice: The Holocaust Era Restitution Campaign of the 1990s* (Madison: University of Wisconsin Press, 2009). See also Bianca Gaudenzi and Astrid Swenson, 'Looted Art and Restitution in the Twentieth Century: Towards a Global Perspective' (2017) 52 *Journal of Contemporary History* 491–518.

effected'.[63] It covered objects removed from public collections and restitution of individuals who had been dispossessed through confiscation, forced loans, donations or forced sales, including sales far below market value. The Declaration marked an important 'precedent for the resolution' of disputes over property return, since it gave 'advance warning to third parties' that their acquisitions might be 'declared invalid'.[64] It established the principle that good faith acquisition would not be accepted in light the structural inequality of power and the discriminatory laws during Nazi occupation.[65] The purchaser has to establish that cultural property was acquired in regular circumstances. Many states, including countries which were neutral in the Second World War (e.g. Sweden, Switzerland, and Portugal), adopted corresponding legislation, overturning the protection of 'good faith' acquisition. No parallel system was envisaged for objects looted in colonial contexts.[66]

The 1954 Hague Convention for the Protection of Cultural Property in the Event of Armed Conflict[67] (1954 Convention), and its Protocols, reframed norms regarding cultural takings in armed conflict in response to the destruction of cultural heritage in the Second World War. They cover both international and non-international armed conflicts, including situations of occupation.[68] The 1954 Convention adopted a more inclusive understanding of cultural protection by recognizing the contribution of 'each people' 'to the culture of the world'.[69] It deviates from the previous Hague Regulations, by untying cultural property protection from the classical distinction between public and private property. The conception of cultural property as 'cultural heritage of peoples' implies that it is protected by virtue of the cultural value of object and their context.[70] However, the instrument is less progressive than the Roerich Pact. Protection from destruction or damage in armed conflict is constrained by a much criticized qualifier,[71] which limited the obligation to refrain 'from any act of hostility' against cultural property[72] in cases

---

[63] Declaration of the Allied Nations Against Acts of Dispossession Committed in Territories Under Enemy Occupation or Control (5 January 1943) 1943 8 Dept of State Bulletin 21.

[64] Lyndel Prott, 'The History and Development of Processes for the Recovery of Cultural Heritage' in Lyndel Prott (ed.), *Witnesses to History: A Compendium of Documents and Writings on the Return of Cultural Objects* (Paris: UNESCO, 2009) 2–18, 10.

[65] Vrdoljak, *International Law, Museums and Return of Cultural Objects*, 141.

[66] According to the logic of the Declaration, 'gifts' to colonial agents might also be suspect. See Prott, 'The History and Development of Processes for the Recovery of Cultural Heritage' 11.

[67] Anthi Helleni Poulos, 'The 1954 Hague Convention for the Protection of Cultural Property in the Event of Armed Conflict: An Historic Analysis' (2000) 28 *International Journal of Legal Information* 1–44.

[68] Article 33(3) makes clear that protections apply to objects obtained 'before or after the beginning of hostilities or occupation'.

[69] See preamble 1954 Hague Convention.

[70] Roger O'Keefe, *The Protection of Cultural Property in Armed Conflict* (Cambridge: Cambridge University Press, 2009) 95.

[71] See generally Kevin Chamberlain, *War and Cultural Heritage* (Leicester: Institute of Art and Law, 2013).

[72] Article 4(1).

'where military necessity imperatively requires a waiver'.[73] It was only constrained in 1999 by a Second Protocol, which specified that the waiver is only permissible if 'cultural property has, by its function, been made into a military objective' and if 'there is no feasible alternative available' to 'that offered by directing an act of hostility'.[74]

The preamble embraces traces of cultural internationalism,[75] which have their origins in the codifications of the League. It reflects the idea that states should preserve 'cultural heritage' that 'is of great importance for all peoples of the world' as guardians of humanity.[76] It specifies that 'damage to cultural property belonging to any people whatsoever means damage to the cultural heritage of all mankind'.[77] This understanding breaks with the old idea that only 'civilized nations' are trustees of cultural heritage. However, the idea of trusteeship on behalf of humanity or the 'civilization of the world' also has an alternative aspect. It may easily become a new label or placeholder for significance to 'Western civilization'.[78] The fact that the convention protects movable or immovable property due to its 'great importance to the cultural heritage of every people', rather than its value to a particular community, introduced an implicit hierarchy in terms of the worthiness of protection. It provided some leeway for market countries to argue that they are entitled to retain removed cultural objects as guardians of universal heritage, in cases where countries of origin may be less capable of preserving them.[79]

Like other conflict-related instruments, the 1954 Convention and its protocols captured colonial violence of the past only marginally. For instance, the 1954 Hague Protocol contains an absolute obligation to return cultural objects removed from occupied territory after the end of hostilities, without statutes of limitation or protection of good faith acquisition.[80] It specifies that protected cultural property 'shall never be retained as war reparations'.[81] However, it is of limited use for return claims of objects removed in the colonial era or indigenous claims.[82] The respective instruments contain express restrictions which left it to administering powers of colonial territories to determine to what extent obligations and protections should apply to colonial entities.[83] The Protocol did not address return obligations in

---

[73] Article 4(2).
[74] Second Protocol to the Hague Convention of 1954 for the Protection of Cultural Property in the Event of Armed Conflict, The Hague (26 March 1999) 2253 UNTS 172, Art. 6.
[75] It has been branded as a hallmark of 'cultural internationalism'. See John Henry Merryman, 'Two Ways of Thinking About Cultural Property' (1986) 80 *AJIL* 831–853, 837.
[76] Preamble 1954 Hague Convention.
[77] Ibid.
[78] Erich Hatala Matthes, ' "Saving Lives or Saving Stones?" The Ethics of Cultural Heritage Protection in War' (2018) 32(1) *Public Affairs Quarterly* 77.
[79] Spitra, *Die Verwaltung von Kultur im Völkerrecht*, 313.
[80] See Art. I(3) and (4) of the Protocol for the Protection of Cultural Property in the Event of Armed Conflict (14 May 1954) 249 UNTS 358 (1954 Hague Protocol).
[81] Ibid, Art. I(3).
[82] Vrdoljak, *International Law, Museums and Return of Cultural Objects*, 150.
[83] See Art. 35 of the 1954 Convention and Arts. 12 and 13 of the 1954 Hague Protocol.

relation to non-international armed conflicts.[84] In this way, colonial wrong was largely placed outside the binding framework of international treaty instruments protecting cultural property in times of conflict, and left within the grey zone of ambiguity and discretion. The US and the UK, two major players in the debate on restitution, did not ratify the 1954 Hague Protocol enshrining the duty to return cultural property removed from occupied territories.

4 UN decolonization: Law as a fortress

The period of UN decolonization was marked by contradictions in terms of heritage protection.

The UN condemned the 'colonialist political order' in 1960 in Resolution 1514 (XV).[85] Newly independent states started to file claims for return of cultural objects since the 1960s. Indigenous communities started to challenge acquisition of objects through colonial policies.[86] The move towards political decolonization was accompanied by a strong claim to reorder economic relations. States of the Global South argued that the wealth of developed nations had been built on exploitation of former colonies and that developed countries continued to benefit from it.[87]

Societies in newly independent states struggled to acquire objects or even receive them as loans. The faced an 'empty museum' dilemma. Ekpo Eyo has described the situation in Nigeria, which had 'lost more than half of their cultural property through the advent of foreign religions and governments':[88]

By the end of the 1960s, the prices of Benin works had soared so high that the Federal Government of Nigeria was in no mood to contemplate buying them. When, therefore, a National Museum was planned for Benin City in 1968, we were faced with the problem of finding exhibits that would be shown to reflect the position that Benin holds in the world of art history ... We tabled a draft resolution at the General Assembly of the International Council of Museums (ICOM) ... appealing for donations of one or two pieces from those museums which have large stocks of Benin works ... We circulated the adopted resolution to the embassies and high commissions of countries we know to have large Benin

---

[84] Obligations in non-international armed conflicts are addressed by the Second Protocol to the Hague Convention of 1954.

[85] The Declaration on the Granting of Independence to Colonial Countries and Peoples states that 'subjection of peoples to alien subjugation, domination and exploitation constitutes a denial of fundamental human rights'. See Declaration on the Granting of Independence to Colonial Countries and Peoples (14 December 1960) Art. 1.

[86] Vrdoljak, *International Law, Museums and Return of Cultural Objects*, 226.

[87] Universal Declaration of the Rights of Peoples (4 July 1976) (Algiers Charter), preamble ('Imperialism, using vicious methods, with the complicity of governments that it has itself often installed, continues to dominate a part of the world').

[88] Ekpo Eyo, 'Nigeria' (1979) 31 *Museum* 18–21, 18.

holdings but up till now we have received no reaction from any quarters and the Benin Museum stays 'empty'.[89]

Representatives from the Global South criticized that 'museums in Europe and the United States' piled up 'good quality objects from the four corners of the world' in their storages to depict the 'culture of the human race', while rarely exhibiting them to the public.[90] Some made a distinction between cultural 'appropriation', which 'colonization allows' and 'ownership, which remains inalienable from the colonized country'.[91]

The UN became a forum to promote new ideals of justice among and within nations.[92] In 1973, Mobuto Sese Seko, the President of Zaire, initiated a campaign for the return of objects with his famous speech before the General Assembly.[93] It has been branded as the origin of the restitution movement in the UN.[94] At the Algiers Summit in September 1973, the heads of State or Government of Non-Aligned Countries adopted an Economic Declaration, in which they emphasized 'the need to reaffirm national cultural identity and eliminate the harmful consequences of the colonial era, so that … national culture and traditions will be preserved'.[95]

This call was reinforced by the push for a new international political and economic order. The claim was most vigorously formulated in legal terms by Algerian diplomat and jurist Mohammed Bedjaoui, who emphasized that a new international order was the 'very condition of decolonization'.[96] He argued that international law should 'serve—and not just to be subject to—the world's economic development'.[97] He criticized the 'venality' of the international legal system, which required newly independent states to apply the 'rules and principles which were approved' before they 'came into existence',[98] but saw international law as a transformative instrument.[99] He noted:

---

[89] Ibid, 21.

[90] Pilippu Hewa Don Hemasiri de Silva, 'Sri Lanka' (1979) 31 *Museum* 22–25, 23.

[91] Tayeb Moulefera, 'Algeria' (1979) 31 *Museum* 10–11, 11.

[92] In a speech delivered on 22 April 1964 at the Sorbonne, UNESCO Director-General Rene Maheu stated: 'The decisive change comes about when the struggle against underdevelopment is envisaged from the viewpoint of mankind as a whole, and the idea of world organization based on justice replaces the present idea of individual and more or less arbitrary assistance'. See UNESCO, In-Depth Studies Conducted by the Special Committee on the Basis of the Report by the Director-General on the Activities of the Organization in 1984–1985', UN Doc. 127 EX/SP/RAP.1, Paris (14 August 1987) 21.

[93] See Introduction.

[94] Bénédicte Savoy, *Afrikas Kampf um Seine Kunst* (München: C. H. Beck, 2021) 45.

[95] Fourth Conference of Heads of State and Government of Non-Aligned Countries (5–9 September 1973) Economic Declaration, XIV (Preservation and Development of National Cultures).

[96] Bedjaoui, *Towards a New International Economic Order*, 86. He argued that 'decolonization, considered as a complete structural revolution, is bound to lead to a new legal and economic order, which is why decolonization and the new order are necessarily linked to one another'. Ibid, 88–89.

[97] Ibid, 113.

[98] Ibid, 101.

[99] Ibid, 109.

Traditional international law was an obstacle to decolonization, although decolonization today represents a stimulus to the transformation of that law ... the impetus which decolonization has given to international law can be seen in the reinforcement of this new law which is being established, in an international development law, in tolerance for wars of liberation, in the condemnation of colonialism and racism, in the drafting of a law on equitable relations, in the relation established between decolonization and the maintenance of peace and security, in the right to development and, finally, in the demand for a new international economic order.[100]

The role of international law to address inequalities in the international legal order is most visibly reflected in the Charter of Economic Rights and Duties of States, developed under the auspices of the United Nations Conference on Trade and Development. It was adopted by the UN General Assembly in resolution 3281 (XXIX) on 12 December 1974, with 115 votes to 6,[101] with 10 abstentions.[102] The Charter was originally envisaged as legally binding instrument, designed to 'to codify and develop rules for the establishment of the new international economic order',[103] but was watered down in the negotiation process.[104] It addresses the economic inequalities created by colonialism in Article 16. It states expressly that it is the 'duty of all States, individually and collectively, to eliminate colonialism ... neocolonialism ... and the economic and social consequences thereof, as a prerequisite for development'.[105] It then adds:

States which practise such coercive policies are economically responsible to the countries, territories and peoples affected for the restitution and full compensation for the exploitation and depletion of, and damages to, the natural and all other resources of those countries, territories and peoples.[106]

However, the Charter remained vague on the socio-cultural dimensions of development, and in particular 'cultural decolonization'. It framed cultural development as an individual state duty and matter of international cooperation.[107]

---

[100] Ibid, 62.
[101] Belgium, Denmark, German Federal Republic, Luxembourg, United Kingdom, and the United States voted against the resolution.
[102] Austria, Canada, France, Ireland, Israel, Italy, Japan, the Netherlands, Norway, and Spain abstained.
[103] Charles N. Brower and John B. Tepe, 'The Charter of Economic Rights and Duties of States: A Reflection or Rejection of International Law?' (1975) 9 *The International Lawyer* 295–318, 300.
[104] According to the preamble, the General Assembly 'solemnly adopts the present Charter of Economic Rights and Duties of States' and 'promote[s] the establishment of the new international economic order', while the reference to codification was dropped.
[105] GA Resolution 3281(XXIX) (12 December 1974) Art. 16.
[106] Ibid.
[107] See Art. 7.

In 1974, UNESCO recognized in a resolution that 'establishment of a new international economic order' depends 'on socio-cultural factors'[108] and that the activities of the organization 'should be guided by the principles of a new international economic order'.[109] Later, Bedjaoui made efforts to link the movement towards a new international economic and legal order with a new 'international cultural order'.[110] He argued that the 'right of peoples to a cultural identity' constitutes 'the very basis of their national identity'.[111] He used an innovative argument. He connected it to a 'right to a cultural memory'[112] and framed restitution of cultural property as an issue of 'lost collective memory'.[113] However, this argument caused tensions and resistance.[114] The grounding of the right to return in a 'country's cultural memory and identity' conflicted with the interests of holder countries, who argued that works of art had acquired a universal nature.[115]

In 1976, the heads of state and government of the Organization of African Unity adopted a Cultural Charter for Africa, which recognized that cultural domination under colonialism 'led to the depersonalization of part of the African peoples' and 'falsified their history'.[116] It stressed both cultural identity as a 'concern common to all peoples of Africa' and 'African cultural diversity'.[117] It called on African States to take steps, through the General Assembly and UNESCO 'to put an end to the despoliation of African cultural property and ensure that cultural assets, in particular archives, works of art and archeological objects, which have been removed from Africa, are returned there'.[118] The Algiers Charter of 4 July 1976, a document prepared by the non-governmental actors, even qualified violations of the right of 'every people' to its 'artistic, historical and cultural wealth'[119] as 'a breach of obligations towards the international community as a whole'.[120]

Ultimately, the forces of market power and protection prevailed. Former colonial powers and states hosting collections remained reluctant to accept an obligation to return objects to countries of origin. The debate on 'restitution' involved many arguments that recurred in new forms in contemporary contexts.[121]

---

[108] UNESCO, 'Unesco's contribution to the establishment of a new international economic order', Resolution adopted at the thirty-seventh plenary meeting on 19 November 1974, para. 3.

[109] Para. 4.

[110] Mohamed Bedjaoui, Special Rapporteur, Eleventh report on succession of States in respect of matters other than treaties, A/CN.4/322 and Corr.1 & Add.1 & 2, 1979, para. 46.

[111] Ibid, para. 46.

[112] Ibid, para. 46

[113] Ibid, para. 46.

[114] Ibid, para. 49.

[115] Ibid, para. 49.

[116] Organization of African Unity, Cultural Charter for Africa, Resolution CM/Res.371 (XXIII) (5 July 1976).

[117] Ibid, preamble,

[118] Ibid, Art. 28.

[119] Algiers Charter, Art. 13.

[120] Ibid, Art. 22.

[121] See Savoy, *Afrikas Kampf um Seine Kunst*.

The choice of the proper term (restitution versus return) caused strong semantic divides. In the framework of UNESCO, states refused to brand returns as restitutions in order to avoid an acknowledgement of the illegality of historical takings. Return was largely treated as a political issue, governed by diplomacy, negotiation, and inter-state cooperation. In bilateral returns, countries such as Belgium or the Netherlands replaced the term 'restitution' by the term 'transfer' in order to maintain interpretive authority over the legal qualification of the past, brand individual returns as acts of cultural development or cooperation and maintain their image as legitimate guardians of objects acquired in colonial contexts.[122]

Some voices acknowledged that certain arguments, 'such as bad conditions prevailing in the museums of the demanding countries' are not necessarily valid counter-arguments to return since museums could be 'built in the Third World and equipped in conformity with international standards.'[123] However, market countries invoked other objections against restitution, such as concerns regarding the 'depreciation of collections in the restituting countries' or the fear that 'objects might appear on the international art market' after their restitution due to lack protection or the absence of heritage legislation in requesting countries.[124] Options, such an 'exchange of objects under a long-term loan contract' or 'interchanging exhibits' were proposed to deal with cases of 'insolvable' ownership issues (e.g. Nefertiti).

Some states from the Global South sought to provide reassurances against these concerns, including the fear of 'empty museums' in the West. For instance, the Director of National Museums of Sri Lanka noted:

> I believe I am voicing the opinion of several others in the 'deprived' Third World countries that we are not requesting the return of every single object, document, etc., taken away. We think that the cultural image of our countries abroad is as important as it is in our own countries. We are asking for the restitution of only those unique and specially significant items which express to the world and to our own countrymen the unique cultural heritage that is ours and our craftsmanship par excellence.[125]

He acknowledged the corresponding responsibilities of states receiving objects:

> The receiving countries must also realize that with the restitution of their cultural treasures their responsibility is doubled, for these nations must keep in

---

[122] On the Belgian approach, see Sarah van Beurden, 'Restitution or Cooperation? Competing Visions of Post-Colonial Cultural Development in Africa' Käte Hamburger Kolleg/Centre for Global Cooperation Research, *Global Cooperation Research Paper* No. 12 (2015). On the Dutch approach, see Jos van Beurden, *Treasures in Trusted Hands* (Leiden: Sidestone Press, 2017) 122–170.

[123] Herbert Ganslmayr, 'Germany' (1979) 31 *Museum* 12–14, 12–13.

[124] Ibid, 13.

[125] De Silva, 'Sri Lanka', 23.

mind that these 'priceless' objects are also the cultural legacy of the entire human race.[126]

However, market countries were eager to treat the 'problem of the restitution of cultural objects' as 'a political one with regard to its causes as well as to a possible solution'.[127]

In practice, non-retroactivity and the inter-temporal rule became the legal instruments to maintain the *status quo*, distance the colonial period from its aftermath, and preserve the integrity of colonial collections. They created a legal barrier between past and present. They disassociated works of art from their historical contexts and provided room for market states to refute claims by newly independent states as acts of cultural nationalisms and present case-by-case returns as benevolent acts. Ana Vrdoljak has rightly spoken of a process of 'decolonization without restitution'.[128]

4.1 The battle over retroactivity of the 1970 Convention

The conflict between competing interests is reflected in the drafting of the Convention on the Means of Prohibiting and Preventing the Illicit Import, Export and Transfer of Ownership of Cultural Property. The Convention marked a turn towards the protection of States and national heritage.[129] Article 1 recognizes 'illicit import, export and transfer of ownership of cultural property is one of the main causes of the impoverishment of the cultural heritage of the countries of origin'.[130] The preservationist attitude is represented in the definition of the categories of objects which are deemed to form 'part of the cultural heritage of each State'.[131] It places considerable emphasis on consensual methods of acquisition. It includes 'cultural property acquired by archaeological, ethnological or natural science missions, with the consent of the competent authorities of the country of origin of such property', cultural property 'which has been the subject of a freely agreed exchange' and 'cultural property received as a gift or purchased legally with the consent of the competent authorities of the country of origin of such property'.[132]

The controversy over the return of colonial objects was most visible in the battle over temporal application. Newly independent States were eager to create

---

[126] Ibid.
[127] Ganslmayr, 'Germany', 13.
[128] Vrdoljak, *International Law, Museums and Return of Cultural Objects*, 197.
[129] On the impact, see Brigitta Hauser-Schäublin and Lyndel V. Prott, *Cultural Property and Contested Ownership: The Trafficking of Artefacts and the Quest for Restitution* (London: Routledge, 2016).
[130] Article 1 of the 1970 Convention.
[131] Ibid, Art. 4.
[132] Ibid.

a mechanism for the return of cultural colonial objects on the international level. States holding objects were opposed to regulating events relating to the colonial past in order to preserve existing collections.[133] This led to a dispute with diametrically opposed positions. An early draft of the Convention sought to confirm the validity of past acquisitions. It required that states adhering to the Convention were required to accept ownership acquired by other states parties prior to the entry of the Convention.[134] This position went directly against the interests of former colonized states. It was rejected by an expert group in 1970.[135] China made a proposal, which went to the opposite direction. It favoured retroactive application. It stated that:

> any State party which, when the Convention comes into force, is in possession of important cultural property, illicitly acquired, inalienable to, and inseparable from, the history and civilization of another State, shall, in the interest of international goodwill, endeavour to restore such property to that State.[136]

This position, however, was unacceptable to market countries, who were not prepared to accept challenges to ownership acquired before 1970. As a result, the Convention remained silent on the issue.[137]

Newly independent states succeeded in negotiating a prevision, which prohibited the 'transfer of ownership of cultural property under compulsion arising directly or indirectly from the occupation of a country by a foreign power'.[138] But an initiative by Iraq to extend this prohibition to 'any ... action in the past' was rejected.[139]

The Convention contributed to greater protection of the cultural heritage of indigenous people in settler contexts through its focus on the duty of states to 'prohibit and prevent the illicit import, export and transfer of ownership of cultural property' within the territories 'for which they are responsible'.[140] But it fell short of meeting the interests of formerly colonized states to address injustices of the past. It did not confirm the validity of past acquisitions, nor acknowledge the

---

[133] Vrdoljak, *International Law, Museums and Return of Cultural Objects*, 210.
[134] Prott, 'The History and Development of Processes for the Recovery of Cultural Heritage', 12; UNESCO Doc SHC/MD/3 Annex, Art. 4(f).
[135] UNESCO Doc 16 C/17 Annex II, 4.
[136] UNESCO Doc SHC/MD/5 Annex II, 10.
[137] According to Art. 28 of the 1969 Vienna Convention of Law Treaties, the 1970 Convention is in principle non-retroactive.
[138] Article 11.
[139] Iraq proposed the following wording: 'The export of cultural property arising directly or indirectly from pressure exerted by a foreign power in an occupied country, including any such action in the past, shall also be regarded as illicit.' See UNESCO, Final Report, Doc SHC/MD/5, Paris (27 February 1970) 10; Vrdoljak, *International Law, Museums and Return of Cultural Objects*, 209.
[140] Article 12. Vrdoljak, *International Law*, 209.

existence of any duties of return.[141] Instead, it left the problem unsolved. Article 15 of Convention allowed states parties to negotiate the terms of restitution regarding restitution of cultural property acquired before the entry into force of Convention, but made this dependent on special agreement to that effect.[142]

This solution marked a compromise between market and source countries, but ultimately accommodated the interests of former colonial powers. It did not validate any illegal takings or transactions before the entry into force of the Convention, but also failed to provide an express basis for return requests of newly emerging states.

The failure to take into account the specific difficulties of colonial returns is reflected in some of the substantive provisions. For instance, the Convention requires countries of origin to designate specific objects and support their case for return by 'documentation and other evidence necessary to establish its claim for recovery and return'.[143] This specification is often difficult in relation to colonial artefacts, which have been acquired through plunder or dispersed without documentation, or items whose presence in Western collections is unknown to societies of origin.[144] Technically, the Convention gave newly independent states the option to claim return of objects illicitly exported or acquired after 1970. This excluded most colonial takings. Article 7 required these countries to compensate the good faith purchaser in case of returns.[145] Unlike an earlier draft from 1969,[146] the final Convention does not contain a reference to the analogous application of the criteria of the 1943 London Declaration to the cultural takings from extra-metropolitan territories.

The outcome was disappointing for colonized states.[147] It indirectly favoured market countries. These countries, in turn, remained reluctant for a long time to

---

[141] This reflected in the UNESCO Operational Guidelines for the Implementation of the Convention on the Means of Prohibiting and Preventing the Illicit Import, Export and Transfer of Ownership of Cultural Property (May 2015) para 102, at https://en.unesco.org/sites/default/files/operational_guidel ines_en_final_final.pdf ('the Convention does not in any way legitimize any illicit transaction of whatever nature which has taken place before the entry into force of this Convention nor limit any right of a State or other person to make a claim under specific procedures or legal remedies available outside the framework of this Convention for the restitution or return of a cultural object stolen or illegally exported before the entry into force of this Convention'). See also Katja Lubina, *Contested Cultural Property: The Return of Nazi Spoliated Art and Human Remains from Public Collections* (PhD Thesis, Maastricht, 2009) 124 https://cris.maastrichtuniversity.nl/ws/files/961360/guid-fddba8e0-3478-4062-bf6b-49537780efc7-ASSET1.0.

[142] Article 15.

[143] Article 7(b)(ii) 1970 UNESCO Convention.

[144] See also Teresa McGuire, 'African Antiquities Removed during Colonialism: Restoring a Stolen Cultural Legacy' (1990) 1990 *Detroit College of Law Review* 31–70, 58.

[145] Article 7(a)(ii) of the Convention.

[146] Article 9 of the 1969 draft Convention regulated protection of cultural property transferred from extra-metropolitan territories. It contained an analogy to the London Declaration. It stated: 'Such transfers should be regarded as illicit even where, in the terms of the London Declaration of 5 January 1943, they have taken the form of "transactions apparently legal in form, even when they purport to be voluntarily effected"'. See UNESCO, Preliminary Report, Doc SHC/MD/J, Paris (8 August 1969) para. 67.

[147] Prott, 'The History and Development of Processes for the Recovery of Cultural Heritage', 13.

ratify the 1970 Convention.[148] The battle over restitution continued at the political level at the UN.

4.2 The UN General Assembly as vehicle for restitution

The UN General Assembly became a vivid platform for the debate on returns. It had acknowledged since the 1960s that the voices of formerly colonized countries should enjoy special attention in matters of decolonization, since they had been excluded from participation in international rules.[149] In the early and mid-1970s, the Assembly adopted several Resolutions,[150] which condemned the removal of cultural objects as 'a result of colonial or foreign occupation'[151] or called for the return of cultural heritage.[152] They reflect the clash between different approaches, namely claims of colonized states for return and control over heritage grounded in arguments of historical injustice, and opposition by marked countries to the return of 'their' collections, based on the universal importance and protection of objects.

The most famous resolution, Resolution 3187 (XXVIII), contains the word 'restitution' in the title. It is called 'Restitution of works of art to countries victims of expropriation'. It openly deplored 'the wholesale removal, virtually without payment, of objets d'art from one country to another, frequently as a result of colonial or foreign occupation'[153] and contained a reference to Resolution 1514 (XV) on the Granting of Independence to Colonial Countries and Peoples. It switched the market logic and placed the emphasis on justice and unjust enrichment.

The operative part of the resolution expresses what could not be stipulated in the 1970 Convention. It '[r]ecognizes the special obligations' of countries which have acquired 'access to … valuable objects only as a result of colonial or foreign occupation'.[154] It challenged the idea that former colonized societies had to pay for the return of objects removed. The text '[a]ffirm[ed] that the prompt restitution to a country of its objets d'art, monuments, museum pieces, manuscripts and documents by another country, without charge' is not only a means 'to strengthen international cooperation', but 'just reparation for damage done'.[155] It was of particular

---

[148] The US became a state party in 1983. France, the United Kingdom, Germany and the Netherlands only joined as of the mid-1990s.

[149] UN GA Res 1765 (XVII) of 20 November 1962, Resolution 1902 of (XVIII) of 18 November 1963.

[150] See Douglas N. Thomason, 'Rolling Back History: The United Nations General Assembly and the Right to Cultural Property' (1990) 22 *Case Western Reserve Journal of International Law* 47–95.

[151] GA Res 3187 (XXVIII) of 18 December 1973, Restitution of works of art to countries victims of appropriation, preambular para. 8.

[152] See GA Resolution 3391 (XXX) of 19 November 1975, 'Restitution of works of art to countries victims of expropriation'.

[153] GA Res 3187, preambular para. 8.

[154] Ibid, para. 2.

[155] Ibid, para. 1.

relevance to African countries and Pacific states whose objects were predominantly in the possession of collections in market countries.

This open language came at a price. The resolution was seen as an affront by
market countries. It was adopted by 113 votes, with 17 abstentions. Many states,
who were deemed to have special obligations, abstained, including Belgium,
Canada, France, Germany, Italy, Japan, the Netherlands, the United Kingdom, the
United States, and apartheid South Africa.

Later resolutions were more reserved. For instance, GA Res. 3391 (XXX)
adopted in 1975 noted with interest 'the steps taken by certain States towards the
restitution of art to countries victims of expropriation.'[156] It merely called upon
'those states who have not already done so to proceed to the restitution of objets
d'art, monuments, museum pieces, manuscripts and documents to their countries
of origin' and the spirit of 'international understanding and cooperation'.[157] The
focus shifted on the limitation of illicit traffic of cultural objects[158] and the development of targeted mechanisms under the umbrella of UNESCO to facilitate returns.
The resolutions themselves turned into 'narrative norms' about the colonial past.

4.3 The UNESCO Intergovernmental committee
as political back-up

As a follow up to the GA resolution 3187, UNESCO mandated the International
Council of Museums (ICOM) to devise 'principles, conditions and means for the
restitution or return of cultural property'.[159] The ICOM study framed the removal
of colonial objects as a global problem. It qualified it as a 'problem of solidarity
which concerns not only States at war or former colonial powers, but all countries
which have directly or indirectly, and more often by means that were legal at the
time, profited from and sometimes taken undue advantage of the dispersion of
these patrimonies'.[160] It presented the cooperative structure of UNESCO as a suitable forum to solve disputes.

The study identified main obstacles related to returns, including the 'changing
of national boundaries and State succession'[161] after cultural takings, difficulties
to determine 'whether an object belongs to a certain culture or not',[162] claims that
objects may have become part of 'the inalienable and imprescriptible heritage' of

---

[156] GA Res 3391 (XXX) (19 November 1975) Preamble.
[157] Ibid, para. 6.
[158] Vrdoljak, *International Law, Museums and Return of Cultural Objects*, 213.
[159] International Council of Museums, 'Study on the Principles, Conditions and Means for the
Restitution or Return of Cultural Property in View of Reconstituting Dispersed Heritages' (1979) 31
Museum 62–66.
[160] Ibid, para. 2.
[161] Ibid, para. 14.
[162] Ibid, para. 13.

holding countries,[163] 'information gaps' in relation to objects,[164] problems of requesting States to pay compensation[165] or inadequate resources in countries of origin.[166] It sought to accommodate the interests of newly independent states and holder countries, based on two major principles: the 'reassembly of dispersed heritage' through targeted return of objects 'which are of major importance for the cultural identity and history of countries'[167] and interests in the protection of objects, including preservation, accessibility to the public and protection under the law.[168]

The committee engaged openly with the reservations expressed by market countries, in particular concerns relating to preservation and conservation of objects and fears relating to the recognition of illegality of takings. It conceded that difficulties in relation to 'conservation conditions' in countries of origin 'could not justify a refusal to restitute property', but would require 'training of specialized personnel' and the establishment 'of adequate facilities', if need be, through international assistance.[169] It acknowledged that reservations towards return were partly driven by 'psychological difficulties' related to the 'incriminating aspects of the act of restitution', such as feelings of guilt.[170] It summed up the position by market countries as follows:

> A good number of countries and private owners would accept with difficulty to be placed in the position of the accused, since the objects in question were added to their collections by means that were legal and legitimate at the time, and since they could well, it seems, invoke the principle of non-retroactivity.[171]

The study supported a political solution. It stated that such fears might be overcome by UNESCO's 'direct intervention in the process of restitution or return'[172] and recommended the creation of an 'international committee for the reconstitution of dispersed patrimonies' under its auspices.[173]

Subsequent UNESCO reports identified the basis and Statute of the ICPRCP.[174] The committee was mandated to fill the gaps of the 1970 Convention relating to

---

[163] Ibid, paras. 18, 34–36.
[164] Ibid, para. 23.
[165] Ibid, para. 36.
[166] Ibid, para. 25.
[167] Ibid, para. 38.
[168] Ibid, para. 20.
[169] Ibid, para. 20.
[170] Ibid, para. 27.
[171] Ibid, para. 27.
[172] Ibid, para. 36.
[173] Ibid, para. 37.
[174] UNESCO, Committee of Experts on the Establishment of an Intergovernmental Committee concerning the Restitution or Return of Cultural Property, Dakar (1978) CC.78/CONF.609/6, CC.78/CONF.609/COL.5; UNESCO Committee of Experts on the Establishment of an Intergovernmental Committee Concerning the Restitution or Return of Cultural Property, Final Report, Dakar (20–23 March 1978).

colonial objects.[175] It compensated the absence of a retroactivity clause in the Convention, by facilitating return through dialogue, meditation, or conciliation. It is marked by compromises.

Its long title ('Intergovernmental Committee for Promoting the Return of Cultural Property to its Countries of Origin or its Restitution in Case of Illicit Appropriation') reflects the ambition to reconcile competing positions on legality of takings. European states, such as France or Germany, sought to avoid any reference to the word 'restitution', and preferred to use the term 'return' in order to avoid any recognition that their actions during the colonial period were invalid or improper, while newly independent states wanted to use the vocabulary used in GA Resolutions. As a compromise both terms were used, but the words 'in case of illicit appropriation' were added to 'restitution' to safeguard the position of former colonial powers.[176] This was a concession to museums in market states, which shared an interest in 'de-politicizing' or 'de-historicizing' the provenance of their collections.[177]

The powers of the ICPRCP are limited. It provides an institutional forum to address return of colonial objects, as advocated by former colonized states, but it does not create a binding dispute settlement mechanism. It combines support for essential returns with a commitment to multi—and bilateral cooperation. It serves as an advisory body, with a mandate to facilitate mediation and conciliation,[178] exercise moral pressure, and adopt recommendations. This structure marginalized legal engagement with past takings. It allowed the ICPRCP to avoid a clear determination as to whether or not the objects or collections have left countries of origin 'legally'. The Committee stated that its work is governed by 'moral and ethical', rather than 'legal' principles.[179] It fell short of meeting some of the ambitious goals of GA Resolution 3187, which sought to promote legal and ethical accountability, or UNESCO Resolution 3.428 (1974), which drew attention to the legal regime of the 1943 London Declaration.[180]

Some the biases and dichotomies of the methodology are reflected in the ICPRCP's understanding of returns, articulated in the Guidelines for the Use of the

---

[175] James A. R. Nafziger, 'The New International Legal Framework for the Return, Restitution or Forfeiture of Cultural Property' (1983) 15 *New York University Journal of International Law and Politics* 789; Vrdoljak, *International Law, Museums and Return of Cultural Objects*, 211 ff; Folarin Shyllon, 'The Recovery of Cultural Objects by African States through the UNESCO and UNIDROIT Conventions and the Role of Arbitration' (2000) 5 *Uniform Law Review* 219–240, 222 ff.

[176] Prott, 'The History and Development of Processes for the Recovery of Cultural Heritage', 15; Vrdoljak, *International Law, Museums and Return of Cultural Objects*, 216.

[177] Vrdoljak, *International Law, Museums and Return of Cultural Objects*, 216.

[178] Article 4(1) of the Statute. This was expressly clarified in 2005. See Recommendation No. 3 adopted by the 13th session of the Intergovernmental Committee for Promoting the Return of Cultural Property to its Countries of Origin or its Restitution in case of Illicit Appropriation, Paris (7–10 February 2005).

[179] Vrdoljak, *International Law, Museums and Return of Cultural Objects*, 215.

[180] UNESCO, Res 3.428, Contribution of UNESCO to the return of cultural property to countries that have been victims of de facto expropriation in Records of the General Conference, 18th Session, Paris (17 October–23 November 1974) 60–61.

'Standard Form Concerning Requests for Return or Restitution' from 1986.[181] The text shows how the Committee replicated certain colonial logics, while marginalizing the role of law and reducing cultural takings to matters of ethics. It stated:

> The term 'return' should apply to cases where objects left their countries of origin prior to the crystallization of national and international law on the protection of cultural property. Such transfers of ownership were often made from a colonized territory to the territory of a colonial power.[182]

This passage reflects a misguided and one-sided understanding of the role of law in the colonial period. It implies that cultural takings took place in a legal vacuum. It reduced removals to mere property takings ('transfer of ownership'). It then bought into the classical narrative of the legality of takings, while qualifying certain takings as illegitimate, based on their context. It stated:

> In many cases, they were the result of an exchange, gift or sale and did not therefore infringe any laws existing at the time. In some cases, however, the legitimacy of the transfer can be questioned. Among the many variants of such a process is the removal of objects from a colonial territory by people who were not nationals of the colonial power. There may have also been cases of political or economic dependence which made it possible to effect transfers of ownership from one territory to another which would not be envisaged today.[183]

It used the removal of the Olokun head from Ife by Leo Frobenius in 1910 as an example.[184] It motivated the lack of legitimacy by the fact that it occurred 'against the wishes of the British colonial administration',[185] without any mention of the deception or 'property' of the local ruler (the 'Oni') to whom the head belonged.[186]

The mandate relates to return of selected colonial objects, namely 'cultural property which has a fundamental significance from the point of view of the spiritual values and cultural heritage of the people of a Member State or Associate Member of UNESCO'.[187] One limitation is its interstate-nature. A request must be triggered by a state.[188] This excludes return claims by indigenous groups. The ICOM study promoted a 'campaign' to promote 'the ethical and cultural value' of the return in 'countries holding possession of objects' and to 'inform' countries of origin

---

[181] ICPRCP, Guidelines for the use of the 'Standard Form Concerning Requests for Return or Restitution' (30 April 1986) CC86/WS/3.
[182] Ibid, 11.
[183] Ibid.
[184] See Chapter 4.
[185] ICPRCP 1986 Guidelines, 11.
[186] See Chapter 4.
[187] Article 3(2) of the Statute.
[188] Ibid.

'of existing solutions' and 'difficulties implied by their claim'.[189] UNESCO printed generic forms in three languages to help restitution requests that were largely distributed throughout the end of the 1970s. However, the Committee failed to attract a large buy-in from states. The inter-state nature of procedures and unequal power relations prevented it from assuming a greater role.[190] Many of those countries who had initially advocated for a return mechanism never presented a request to the Committee.[191] Former colonial powers dealt with return claims on a bilateral basis or through mechanisms of economic and cultural cooperation. The ICPRCP facilitated only a limited number of requests, such as claims from Zaire against Belgium and Indonesia against the Netherlands and Zaire, and later the dispute between Greece and the UK over the Parthenon Marbles.

The existing limitations make it unlikely that the ICPRCP will play a significant role in future returns of colonial collections, beyond raising awareness, promoting mediation or conciliation, recording legislation or cases, or providing ethical recommendations.

4.4 Gaps and silences in the 1983 treaty regime on state succession

The divisions between former colonial powers and colonized states over cultural property continued in the negotiation of the 1983 Convention on State Succession in respect of State Property, Archives and Debts.[192] Newly independent states intended to capture lost cultural patrimony, build their own national collections, and gain greater access to colonial archives, while their former rulers sought to preserve objects in their possession and the integrity of archives. The Convention contains special rules in favour of newly independent states, but deals only to a limited extent with issues concerning removal of cultural objects, namely through provisions on succession of public property and archives.

Its drafting was shaped by Bedjaoui, who served as Special Rapporteur of the ILC on state succession. Given Bedjaoui's intellectual stance and the interests at stake for newly independent states in Africa or Asia, one might have expected that the transfer of cultural heritage would play a prominent role in the Convention. However, the final text deals with it only partially. This has been criticized as a lost opportunity.[193] It may be explained by legal and political considerations.

---

[189] ICOM study, para. 23.

[190] Alessandro Chechi, *The Settlement of International Cultural Heritage Disputes* (Oxford: Oxford University Press, 2014) 103.

[191] Prott, 'The History and Development of Processes for the Recovery of Cultural Heritage', 15.

[192] Andrzej Jakubowski, *State Succession in Cultural Property* (Oxford: Oxford University Press, 2015); Gerard Farrell, *The Vienna Convention of 1983: Context, Failure and Aftermath* (Thesis, Uppsala University, 2021).

[193] Ana Vrdoljak argues that this limitation is 'inexplicable'. Vrdoljak, *International Law, Museums and Return of Cultural Objects*, 202.

One reason is the special nature of cultural heritage, which does not fit fully into the traditional frames of state succession. Principles on state succession are traditionally based on territoriality, i.e. the location of property at the time of succession, and its nexus to the predecessor state. These prerogatives do not always coincide with principles on access or return of cultural heritage, which may be grounded in provenance or the cultural importance of the object to specific communities. In certain circumstances, protection of cultural heritage may conflict with or prevail over the allocation of property under regimes of state succession.[194] The recognition of certain objects as universal heritage[195] defies traditional categories used in state succession, such as nationality or territoriality.

In addition, path-dependency and previous political choices, such as the creation of a special regime for return of cultural property under UNESCO, played a role in the approach towards colonial cultural objects. When the 1983 Vienna Convention was adopted, the ICPRCP was in operation and UNESCO had a targeted role.[196] In previous reports, Bedjaoui had recognized the special property problems arising from the withdrawal of colonial countries from dependent territories, which were not always carried out 'in accordance with the canons of justice, morality and law'.[197] Former colonial powers preferred to deal with such issues on a case-by-case basis and through cooperation, rather than through legal commitments under the law of state succession.[198]

Cultural property was only selectively covered through provisions on the allocation and distribution of state-owned property, namely property owned by the predecessor state according to its internal law at the date of state succession. The regime was partly favourable for newly independent states. The Convention recognized that newly independent states are entitled to movable property which 'belonged' to their territory before and during dependence, as well as property to which they 'contributed'.[199] Theoretically, they could claim title to cultural property located on their territories, such as collections of local museums or other institutions established by the former colonial power. However, the restriction to public property excluded property of private persons, non-state actors or religious

---

[194] For instance, claims of self-determination have been used to reclaim objects lost and removed under colonial rule. See <IBT>Jakubowski, *State Succession in Cultural Property*</IBT>, 17. Rules prohibiting pillage or plunder in armed conflict may trigger duties of return, which clash with rules of state succession. See 1954 Hague Protocol. Ibid, 144.

[195] UNESCO, Recommendation on International Principles Applicable to Archaeological Excavations, New Delhi (5 December 1956) UNESCO Doc.9C/Resolution; UNESCO Convention Concerning the Protection of the World Cultural and Natural Heritage (16 November 1972).

[196] Jakubowski, *State Succession in Cultural Property*, 164.

[197] Mohammed Bedjaoui, Eighth report on succession of States in respect of matters other than treaties, A/CN.4/292 (8 April 1976) 83.

[198] Jakubowski, *State Succession in Cultural Property*, 135.

[199] Vienna Convention on Succession of States in respect of State Property, Archives and Debts (8 April 1983) 22 ILM 306 (1983), Art. 15(e) and (f).

organizations, including many objects or collections acquired by private collectors and dispersed around the world.[200]

The Vienna Convention established special rules for state archives, including colonial archives removed from the dependent territories ('migrated archives'). Both the 1954 Hague Convention and the 1970 UNESCO Convention recognized archives as cultural property, i.e. as an essential element of the heritage of a national community. Many colonial powers wanted to protect them from newly independent governments. They invoked the principle of archival integrity to maintain ownership. Newly independent states sought to recuperate archival heritage in order to develop national awareness and cultural identity. The sensitivity of access to archival material has become evident in cases, such as the litigation of UK responsibility for violations during the Mau Mau uprising in Kenya (1952–1960).[201]

The treaty contained a wide definition of archival documents ('documents of whatever date and kind, produced or received by the predecessor State in the exercise of its functions'), but made the qualification depended on the 'internal law' of the predecessor state.[202] This narrow focus was criticized for its Western bias in the ILC drafting process. In its oral comments, a delegation noted in 1979:

> If the expression 'documents of all kinds' was to be interpreted in the widest sense ... all documents relating to the cultural heritage of a people, whether written or unwritten, should be regarded as falling within it. a definition which excluded works of art and culture presupposed that all civilizations used only writing as their means of expression. Yet, in Africa, the cradle of civilization, documents had also been expressed through the medium of objects of art ... the definition should include inscriptions on wood and stone.[203]

The provisions on state archives responded partly to claims from newly independent states, who regarded the right to cultural heritage as an essential part of political and cultural self-determination. This is reflected in a safeguard clause which states that agreements between the predecessor State and the newly independent State on state archives 'shall not infringe the right of the peoples of those States to development, to information about their history, and to their cultural heritage'.[204]

Succession was regulated in light of the organic link between the archives and the territory. Bedjaoui had distinguished three types of archives: Historical archives,

---

[200] Jakubowski, *State Succession in Cultural Property*, 7.
[201] See Caroline Elkins, 'Looking beyond Mau Mau' (2015) 120 *American Historical Review* 852–868, 860
[202] Article 20.
[203] See Mohammed Bedjaoui, Special Rapporteur, Thirteenth report on succession of States in respect of matters other than treaties, A/CN.4/345 and Add.1–3, 6 (29 May, 5 and 16 June 1981) 32, para. 227.
[204] Article 28(7).

which belonged to the territory prior to colonization; colonial archives relating to colonial governance or policy during colonization, and administrative and technical archives concerning the administration of the territory.[205] He argued that it would be 'unreasonable to expect the immediate return of all' colonial archives,[206] but insisted on transfer of all removed historical or administrative archives to former colonies. The 1983 Vienna Convention followed this approach in principle. It specified that historical archives, colonial archives concerning the 'normal administration of the territory' and archives relating 'exclusively or principally to the territory' should pass from the predecessor State to the newly independent State.[207] It also established a cooperation duty in relation dispersed historical archival material. It imposed an express obligation on the predecessor State to cooperate with the successor state 'in efforts to recover any archives' which 'belonged to the territory to which the succession of states relates', but 'were dispersed during the period of dependence'.[208] It is regarded as an expression of the principle of equity in relation to cultural heritage.[209] One limit to the rights of newly independent States in the Convention is the recognition of the indivisibility ('integral character') of state archives.[210] It is visibly a concession to former colonial powers.

The biggest limitation is non-retroactivity. Except 'otherwise agreed', the Convention applies only 'in respect of a succession of States which has occurred after the entry into force of the Convention'.[211] This means that it excluded a large amount of successions in colonial history that were completed before or during decolonization.

The outcome of the Convention was a partial disappointment for both former colonies and colonial powers. Many Western states regarded the provisions on newly independent states as a 'progressive' development of the law and remained critical of the text. For the latter, the Convention did not go far enough, due its non-retroactivity and limited regulation of losses of cultural heritage during colonial occupation. It failed to receive the necessary approval. At the Vienna Conference, only seventy-six out of ninety-two participating states voted on final text. The Convention was adopted by fifty-four votes to eleven, with eleven abstentions. Both settler colonial states (Canada, US) and important former colonial powers, such as Belgium, France, Germany, the Netherlands, or the UK voted against the Convention. It did not reach the required threshold of fifteen ratifications to enter

---

[205] Mohammed Bedjaoui, Special Rapporteur Third report on succession of States in respect of matters other than treaties, A/CN.4/226, 158. He stated that historical archives 'are the product of the land and spring from its soil; they are bound up with the land where they came into existence and they contain its history and its cultural heritage'.

[206] Ibid, 158.

[207] Article 28(1).

[208] Article 28(4).

[209] Vrdoljak, *International Law, Museums and Return of Cultural Objects*, 203.

[210] Article 25.

[211] Article 4(1).

into force.[212] In 2007, the Regional Administrative Tribunal of Lazio relied partly on the Convention as a matter of customary law in the Venus of Cyrene case. It argued that Italy had a duty to transfer the statue back to Libya according to Article 15, since it constituted movable property transferred from the territory prior to independence.[213]

5 Advances and divides of the UNIDROIT Convention

The divide between market countries, favouring trade of objects, and states with interest in returns continued in the UNIDROIT Convention.[214] The Convention reinforced protection for cultural objects against theft and illegal exportation.[215] It addressed in particular, the status and return of objects acquired by private individuals. Based on initiatives of States with indigenous peoples and UNESCO,[216] the treaty takes into account the cultural heritage interest of 'national, tribal, indigenous or other communities'.[217] The Sarr and Savoy Report has described it as 'the only legal instrument with the potential to redress the imbalance [between European 'holding' States and non-European claimant States]', provide 'a common law for restitution', and guarantee the 'permanence of the process undertaken for the cultural objects stockpiled during the colonial period'.[218] However, it faced considerable opposition by art market countries, who feared that protection would constrain the benefits of free circulation of objects.[219] The removal of objects during the colonial period was left unresolved through the non-retroactivity clause. UNESCO addressed this dilemma in its comments in the drafting process:

> [M]any delegations would have liked the draft to cover objects taken in the past. However, while there was a widespread consensus that agreement could be reached on co-operation to stop the present and future illicit trade, there was no such agreement on the return of objects previously taken.[220]

---

[212] Article 50.

[213] Regional Administrative Tribunal of Lazio, *Associazione Nazionale Italia Nostra Onlus v Ministero per i Beni le Attività Culturali et al.*, No. 3518 (28 February 2007) (2007) 17 *Italian Yearbook of International Law* 277–280.

[214] UNIDROIT Convention on Stolen or Illegally Exported Cultural Objects (24 June 1995).

[215] On the importance in the African context, see Folarin Shyllon, 'Why African States Must Embrace the 1995 UNIDROIT Convention' (2012) 17 *Art Antiquity and Law* 135–146.

[216] Diplomatic Conference for the Adoption of the Draft UNIDROIT Convention on the International Return of Stolen or Illegally Exported Cultural Objects, Rome, (7–24 June 1995) Acts and Proceedings, Comments UNESCO, 96.

[217] UNIDROIT Convention, Preamble. See also Art. 5(3).

[218] Sarr and Savoy, 85.

[219] Lyndel Prott, 'The UNIDROIT Convention on Stolen or Illegally Exported Cultural Objects: Ten Years On' (2009) 14 *Uniform Law Review* 215–237.

[220] UNIDROIT Convention, Acts and Proceedings, Comments UNESCO, 106.

The Convention is geared towards 'the future', without conferring 'any approval or legitimacy upon illegal transactions of whatever kind which may have taken place before the entry into force of the Convention'.[221] Following earlier legal instruments, past takings were meant to be addressed through 'diplomatic means, inter-institutional arrangements or through the procedures of the UNESCO Intergovernmental Committee'.[222]

5.1 Concerns of market countries

Some market countries expressed their concerns openly in the drafting process. For instance, France feared that the adoption of the convention would trigger 'a considerable increase in claims for the return of objects of minor importance as well as a deterrent effect on purchasers to the detriment of the market and international trade in works of art'.[223] Germany criticized the idea of a comprehensive limitation of international trade in cultural objects, based on the value of open markets. The German delegation argued that a stricter application of the 'restitution norm' would 'seriously impair the legal trade in such items'.[224] It defended the 'global circulation' of objects, because it 'serves to promote understanding of cultural diversity' and 'to strengthen cross-border relations between peoples and nations'.[225] It claimed that far-reaching restrictions 'promote the formation of black markets'.[226] The US stated that 'the Convention should explicitly make clear that it does not deal with prior occurrences'.[227] The Convention therefore embodies compromises to address 'conflicting interests' of States in 'maximum freedom of trade' and protection of 'endangered cultural heritage'.[228]

5.2 Innovations and drawbacks

The Convention establishes 'common, minimal legal rules' for the restitution and return of stolen or illegally exported cultural objects.[229] It offers protection against outright theft of objects and removal of 'unlawfully excavated or lawfully excavated but unlawfully retained' objects, based on the law of the state where the object was excavated.[230] It goes in several ways beyond the state-centric focus of

---

[221] Ibid, Preamble.
[222] Ibid, Acts and Proceedings, Comments UNESCO, 107.
[223] Ibid, Comments France, 80.
[224] Ibid, Comments Germany, 77.
[225] Ibid.
[226] Ibid.
[227] Ibid, United States of America, 82.
[228] UNIDROIT Convention, Acts and Proceedings, Comments UNESCO, 87.
[229] Ibid, Preamble.
[230] Article 3(2).

the 1970 Convention.[231] It intentionally covers not only objects 'specifically designated' by a contracting state as 'cultural property', but all categories of cultural objects listed in the Annex,[232] whether in private or in public hands. It enables claims filed by private individuals for restitution of stolen cultural objects, in addition to claims of states for return of illegally exported objects, and provides procedures for contracting states to seek recovery through domestic courts, rather than relying on diplomatic cooperation.[233] Finally, it protects 'sacred or communally important cultural objects' of indigenous communities, including their traditional or ritual use. It thereby marks a precedent for the 2003 UNESCO Convention for the Safeguarding of the Intangible Cultural Heritage.

The UNIDROIT Convention covers 'claims of an international character'.[234] One of its most important innovations is the departure from the rule of the good faith acquisition, which facilitated the circulation of stolen, illegally excavated or illegally exported objects.[235] The Convention replaces the concept of bona fide acquisition by a 'due diligence' obligation, requiring purchasers of cultural objects to be diligent in investigating provenance. This aspect was one of the most contested issues, in light of the discrepancies between common law systems which tend to emphasize the lack of title for the transaction under the *nemo dat quod non habet* principle, and some civil law systems which protect the good faith of the purchaser. UNESCO explained this dilemma as follows:

> Most Continental European States, which are not at present Party to the [1970] UNESCO Convention, are being asked to make a fundamental change by returning stolen cultural property and some illicitly exported cultural objects rather than protecting the *bona fide* purchaser (as defined previously in their national systems); in return they will also profit by being able to claim cultural property stolen or illegally exported from their territory.[236]

The 'due diligence' principle was retained in order to increase market ethics. It complemented 'market economy' by 'moral economy'. As Elazar Barkan has argued, 'the agreement underscores a global view of justice that places objects not with the collector but with the originator'.[237] Mere lack of knowledge does not protect the

---

[231] Nina R. Lenzner, 'The Illicit International Trade in Cultural Property: Does the UNIDROIT Convention Provide an Effective Remedy for the Shortcomings of the UNESCO Convention?' (1994) 15 *University of Pennsylvania Journal of International Business Law* 469–500.

[232] UNIDROIT Convention, Annex.

[233] Ibid, Art. 5(3).

[234] Article 1.

[235] Vrdoljak, *International Law, Museums and Return of Cultural Objects*, 275.

[236] UNIDROIT Convention, Acts and Proceedings, Comments UNESCO, 86.

[237] Elazar Barkan, 'Amending Historical Injustices: The Restitution of Cultural Property—an Overview' in Elazar Barkan and Ronald Bush (eds.), *Claiming the Stones, Naming the Bones: Cultural Property and the Negotiation of National and Ethnic Identity* (Los Angeles: Getty Research Institute, 2002) 16–46, 26.

person acquiring the object against a duty to return stolen or illegally excavated objects. The possessor is only entitled to receive 'fair and reasonable compensation' in case of basic precautions, namely if he or she 'neither knew nor ought reasonably to have known that the object was stolen and can prove that it exercised due diligence when acquiring the object'.[238] The Convention specifies that due diligence must be assessed in light of 'all the circumstances of the acquisition'.[239] They include the 'character of the parties, the price paid, whether the possessor consulted any reasonably accessible register of stolen cultural objects, and any other relevant information and documentation which it could reasonably have obtained' in case of 'stolen objects', and the 'absence of an export certificate required under the law of the requesting State' in case of illegally exported objects. These criteria are not directly applicable to colonial acquisitions, and are constrained by distinctive time limitations under the Convention,[240] but might be used by way of analogy as guidance for a contextualized assessment of acquisitions.[241]

The provisions on non-retroactivity highlight the strong trend not to address objects 'stolen' or unlawfully removed in colonial contexts through judicial recovery, but through alternative procedures (diplomatic channels, bilateral treaties, ad hoc negotiations), as contemplated in the 1970 Convention. The safeguard clause in Article 10 (3) reflect a compromise between countries who sought to avoid the risk of declaring 'an amnesty in respect of such illegal acts and set a seal of legitimacy upon them',[242] and countries who faced 'insurmountable legal problems' regarding retroactivity, in light of 'guarantees of property rights', 'principles of non-retroactivity of legislation' or incompatibility with 'fundamental provisions of their civil law'.[243]

5.3 Continuing divides

The UNIDROIT Convention has received mixed support in practice. It has attracted less than 60 ratifications, many of which come from 'source countries'. It was partially seen as a threat to the art market by Western countries and did not go far enough for other countries.[244] Major market countries of cultural property trade, have either not signed the Convention (the US, the UK, Belgium, or Germany) or not ratified it (France, NL). The turn from good faith acquisition to due diligence sparked critique from art professionals.[245] For instance, in 2000,

---

[238] Article 4(1) of the Convention.
[239] Articles 4(4) and 6(2) of the Convention.
[240] See Arts. 3(3), 3(5), and 5(5).
[241] See Chapter 6.
[242] UNIDROIT Convention, Acts and Proceedings, Comments UNESCO, 107.
[243] Ibid, 108.
[244] Egypt and Turkey have not signed the Convention.
[245] James Fitzpatrick, 'The Misguided Quest: The Clear Case against UNIDROIT' (1996) 4 *Journal of Financial Crime* 54–59.

when France contemplated ratification, the Convention was falsely presented as a threat to the survival of the art market in an alarming call by National Union of Antique Dealers in Le Monde.[246] From a (post-)colonial perspective, it is unsatisfying, because it did not reverse the one-dimensional flow of objects from the Global South to market countries. It continued to allow the 'white-washing' of looted or illegitimately acquired colonial objects through auction houses,[247] despite its attempt to increase due diligence. The costs associated with legal proceedings in 'art market' countries constituted another impediment.

6 The Emperor's new clothes

The silences and market-oriented logic, which increased the commodification of objects before and during decolonization, have come under challenge with new cultural heritage instruments, the transformation of cultural rights and the turn to protection of indigenous rights. They do not openly challenge non-retroactivity, past injustices, or the inter-state based regime of the 1970 Convention, but place greater emphasis on the continuing effects of cultural takings, the social importance of objects to communities and avenues to facilitate returns.

Cultural protection has been marked by both the 'humanization' of cultural heritage law[248] and the 'culturalization of human rights'.[249] This development builds on the non-severability between people and objects[250] and positive obligation of states 'to take steps to protect cultural groups and communities in their exercise of [cultural] freedoms'.[251] It counters state-driven and protectionist logic of twentieth century frameworks and serves as an important constraint on cultural nationalist agendas, such as attempts by state leaders to utilize rights-based claims to cultural heritage to cement their own power.[252]

The repatriation movement gained new momentum in the 1980s.[253] Former settler states, such as Australia, New Zealand, the United States or Canada have

---

[246] 'Alarme! La Convention UNIDROIT: L'art gravement menacé' Le Monde (3 April 2000) in Prott, 'The UNIDROIT Convention on Stolen or Illegally Exported Cultural Objects', 221.

[247] Baqué, Un nouvel or noir, 325.

[248] Francesco Francioni, 'The Human Dimension of International Cultural Heritage Law: An Introduction' (2011) 22 EJIL 9–16.

[249] Federico Lenzerini, The Culturalization of Human Rights Law (Oxford: Oxford University Press, 2014).

[250] See Chapter 1.

[251] Francesco Francioni, 'Beyond State Sovereignty: the Protection of Cultural Heritage as a Shared Interest of Humanity' (2004) 25 Michigan Journal of International Law 1209–1228, 1213.

[252] For instance, President Robert Mugabe used the cultural rebranding of the Great Zimbabwe as a way to consolidate his own power. On the role of national identity in Latin American claims, see Pierre Losson, Reclaiming the Remains of the Past: The Return of Cultural Heritage Objects to Colombia, Mexico and Peru (PhD, City University of New York, 2019).

[253] Cressida Fforde, C. Timothy McKeown, and Honor Keeler, 'Introduction' in id, Routledge Companion on Indigenous Repatriation (London: Routledge, 2020), 1–20, 3–4.

enacted national legislation to recognize the cultural heritage rights of their indigenous communities and facilitate legal claims for the return of human remains and cultural objects. Instruments, such as the 1989 ILO Convention on Indigenous and Tribal Peoples openly recognized that the 'laws, values, customs and perspectives' of indigenous populations 'have often been eroded' in settler contexts and sought to counter the 'assimilationist orientation' of 'earlier [international] standards'.[254] These developments have brought a number of important innovations for the discourse and practice of colonial returns.

The move from cultural property to heritage-based rationalizations[255] has widened perspectives on subject-object relations. It has enabled a broader classification of cultural objects, depending on their specific social function and heritage value, including engagement with alternative perspectives on ownership or the identity of objects, beyond commodity, source of historic knowledge or artistic value. It has diversified relations towards objects, by viewing ownership not only as a property relation, but as connection between people, things, and immaterial world ('belonging').[256]

Rights-based language and discourses have moved the discussion on return from the mere confines of morality and cooperation, where claims are dependent on good will, comity, solidarity, or state attitudes, to more complex normative inquiries about the intersectionality of justice, ethics, and human rights. The traditional logic, according to which law serves as a fortress impeding returns, based on intertemporal law or global protection of objects, contrasts with a broader, bottom-up driven movement for restitution or return, grounded in 'the relationship between ... sites, objects, and artefacts and human beings'.[257] Non-state actors have gained a greater voice in debates through the recognition of individual and group rights.[258] The recognition of the rights of indigenous prompted a movement towards intra-national 'repatriation' claims.[259]

However, these various initiatives do not entirely break with the contradictions of the colonial past. They also created novel dichotomies. The notion of 'indigenous' may create distances or continue to feed 'civilizatory divides'. The concept of heritage poses complex questions about recognition and exclusion of identities,

[254] See ILO Convention No. 169 on Indigenous and Tribal peoples (27 June 1989) 1650 UNTS 383, preamble.
[255] See Derek Fincham, 'The Distinctiveness of Property and Heritage' (2011) 115 *Penn State Law Review* 641–684
[256] Brian Noble, 'Owning as Belonging/Owning as Property: The Crisis of Power and Respect in First Nations Heritage Transactions with Canada' in Catherine Bell and Val Napoleon (eds.), *First Nations Cultural Heritage and Law* (Vancouver/Toronto: UBC Press, 2008) 465–488.
[257] Lucas Lixinski, 'A Third Way of Thinking about Cultural Property' (2019) 44(2) *Brooklyn Journal of International Law*, 582.
[258] Vrdoljak, *International Law, Museums and Return of Cultural Objects*, 302.
[259] NAGPRA defines repatriation as 'the transfer of physical custody of and legal interest in Native American cultural items to lineal descendants, culturally affiliated Indian tribes, and Native Hawaiian organizations'.

cultural representation, or political voice, which may entrench colonial classifica-tions (e.g. ethnic divisions, tribal classifications). The requirement of heritage com-munities to demonstrate continuing 'cultural affiliation' may create impediments to return or repatriation based on obstacles created by colonial borders or condi-tions. In some contexts, museums have remained opposed to returns of human re-mains, based on their value for the scientific community (e.g. Kennewick Man[260]). Reliance on the 'universal value' of objects or their guardianship in the interests of humanity became a means to justify retention of cultural objects, based on their importance to 'Western civilization'.[261]

6.1 Conception of cultural objects

An important challenge to the commodification and market-oriented view of cultural objects is the recognition of holistic conceptions of object identities. The notion of cultural property is based on partly opposed paradigms: the asso-ciation with culture, which is based on 'distinctive spiritual, material, intellectual and emotional features that characterize a society and social group',[262] and the concept of property, which is related to ownership.[263] Cultural objects establish 'direct connections to events, places, and people from the past'.[264] They cannot be viewed only through property notions, but are 'vehicles of identity, values and meaning', as the 2005 UNESCO Convention on the Protection and Promotion of the Diversity of Cultural Expressions put it.[265] Many non-Western societies have challenged the idea of a separation between tangible and intangible heritage, based on the argument that all heritage involves non-material aspects elements (memory,

---

[260] The US Army Corps of Engineers and North America scientists refused to return the Kennewick Man ('The Ancient One'), one of the oldest skeletons found in the US, to first nations under NAGPRA, based on rationales of scientific study. US Courts initially held that the remains could not be sufficiently linked to 'Native Americans' under NAGPRA. In *Bonnichsen*, the Ninth Circuit Court of Appeals held that NAGPRA was not applicable to return claims, since the 'the statute unambiguously requires that human remains bear some relationship to a presently existing tribe, people, or culture to be considered Native American'. See US Court of Appeals, Ninth Circuit, *Bonnichsen v United States*, 367 F.3d 864, 875. The remains were only returned when DNA findings from Danish scientists confirmed oral histories and showed that they were genetically related to Native North Americans.

[261] Erich Hatala Matthes, '"Saving Lives or Saving Stones?" The Ethics of Cultural Heritage Protection in War' (2018) 32 *Public Affairs Quarterly* 67–84, 77.

[262] William Logan, 'Cultural Diversity, Cultural Heritage and Human Rights: Towards Heritage Management as Human Rights-based Cultural Practice' (2012) 18 *International Journal of Heritage Studies* 231–244, 234.

[263] Patty Gerstenblith, 'Identity and Cultural Property: The Protection of Cultural Property in the United States' (1995) 75 *Boston University Law Review* 559–668, 567.

[264] Caroline Drieënhuizen, 'Objects, Nostalgia and the Dutch Colonial Elite in Times of Transition, ca. 1900-1970' (2014) 170 *Bijdragen tot de Taal-, Land—en Volkenkunde* 504–529, 506.

[265] UNESCO Convention on the Protection and Promotion of the Diversity of Cultural Expressions, Paris (20 October 2005) Art. 1(g).

identity).[266] In their view, this dichotomy has 'served hegemonic, "Eurocentric" interests in international cultural policy-making in the past'.[267]

6.1.1 From property to heritage

The 1954 Hague Convention and the 1970 UNESCO Convention have approached cultural objects through the lens of 'cultural property'. This designation has limitations from the perspective of subject-object relations and the idea of agency of objects. It frames the relation towards objects in terms of ownership and exclusion. It relies on the idea that human beings own objects, rather than the other way around.[268] Property is primarily treated as an end in itself. It is associated with a sense of entitlement and enduring ownership, which governs the circulation and exchange of objects over time. It creates 'in-groups' and 'out-groups'.

Many Western theories have defined ownership through rights and exclusions, which determine control over and the use of objects. For instance, John Locke has associated property with relations between producer and product and rights of exclusive use, such as rights to possess reproduce, display or transfer.[269] Wesley Hohfeld has viewed ownership as a 'bundle of rights'.[270] Anthony Maurice Honoré has defined as a 'special relation' between the 'holder of the right' and the object.[271] These approaches treat objects as assets or commodities. They place the emphasis on the material value of object and protection of the rights of the owner, rather than the social relations that have shaped, and continue to shape objects. Property-related conceptions of cultural objects offer a powerful basis for claims for ownership and return. However, they also carry significant limitations in relation to cultural colonial objects since they define modern-day relationships to these objects through the knowledge system and legal categories of those who have appropriated them.

The view of property as ownership and possession faces evident limits in relation to cultural property. The classical property approach is unable to reflect the multiple ways in which others may relate to them. Non-Western cultures use a more diverse set of rights and relations to objects than exclusive ownership bonds. They

---

[266] See Helaine Silverman and D. Fairchild Ruggles, 'Cultural Heritage and Human Rights' in Helaine Silverman and D. Fairchild Ruggles (eds.), *Cultural Heritage and Human Rights* (New York: Springer, 2007) 3–22, 12: 'It is not enough for things and monuments to exist on a landscape: in order to be cultural heritage they must be remembered and claimed as patrimony, even if their original meaning is lost or poorly understood.'

[267] Janet Blake, 'Taking a Human Rights Approach to Cultural Heritage Protection' (2011) 4 *Heritage & Society* 199–238, 203.

[268] See Brigitta Hauser-Schäublin and Lyndel Prott, 'Introduction: Changing Concepts of Ownership, Culture and Property in Brigitta Hauser-Schäublin and Lyndel Prott (eds.), *Cultural Property and Contested Ownership: The Trafficking of Artefacts and the Quest for Restitution* (Oxford, New York: Routledge, 2016) 1–20.

[269] John Locke, *Two Treatises of Government* (1689) (New York: Hafner, 1947).

[270] Wesley Hohfeld, 'Fundamental Legal Conceptions as Applied in Judicial Reasoning' (1913) 23 *Yale Law Journal* 16–59.

[271] Anthony M. Honoré, 'Ownership' in Anthony Gordon Guest (ed.), *Oxford Essays in Jurisprudence: A Collaborative Work* (Oxford: Oxford University Press, 1961).

recognize that objects can be non-human subjects, governed by unique ancestral bonds, traditional knowledge systems or continuing spiritual or ceremonial relations, detached from the materiality of objects. For instance, in Māori culture, the concept of guardianship (*kaitiakitanga*) is used as an alternative to ownership concepts. It defines the relations to things in terms of consultation and collaboration. Other communities, including First Nations in the US, view cultural property as a means to enable peoples 'to participate in dialogue' over their heritage, 'without acquiring fixed property rights'.[272]

Such understandings are captured by sociological theories, which pay greater attention to the social, emotional, or political dimensions of property. For instance, Margaret Jane Radin has defended a personhood-related conception of ownership,[273] which challenges the traditional liberal conceptions,[274] based on the inherent connection between persons and objects, including the nexus between objects, individuality, and 'selfhood'. According to Radin, some types of property are so directly to identity that they transcend ordinary market logics, such as universal commodification, alienability, or exchange. This theory is particularly relevant to objects which carry meaning beyond their materiality (e.g. sacred objects).[275] It is able to explain why these objects are not subject to classical market-driven rationales, but protected because of their contribution 'human flourishing'.[276]

Kristen A. Carpenter, Sonia Katyal and Angela Riley have defended a peoplehood-based account of cultural property, which acknowledges that the connection between land and identity of indigenous people, including indigenous cultural property claims, goes beyond traditional categories of ownership.[277] They argued that property relations may be understood through a 'stewardship'-based lens of cultural property,[278] which 'prioritizes service to the organization or group over self-interest' and recognizes its 'pluralistic', rather than 'individualistic' nature.[279] This theory is able to recognize the diverse relationships to objects that are placed in the care of collections.[280] Brian Noble has distinguished 'owning as property' from 'owning as belonging'.[281]

---

[272] Ibid, 1111.

[273] Margaret Jane Radin, 'Property and Personhood' (1982) 34 *Stanford Law Review* 957–1015.

[274] Margaret Jane Radin, *Contested Commodities* (Cambridge, MA: Harvard University Press, 1996).

[275] What appears to be an 'ordinary' object in terms of market-related conceptions of property may qualify as a 'sacred' object and cultural property from the perspective of indigenous people. See Karolina Kuprecht, *Indigenous Peoples' Cultural Property Claims: Repatriation and Beyond* (Heidelberg: Springer, 2014) 41.

[276] Margaret Jane Radin, 'Market-Inalienability' (1987) 100 *Harvard Law Review* 1849–1937, 1851.

[277] Kristen A. Carpenter, Sonia K. Katyal, and Angela R. Riley, 'In Defense of Property' (2009) 118 *Yale Law Journal* 1022–1125, 1065.

[278] The idea of 'stewardship is deemed to take into account the 'fiduciary responsibilities' of indigenous people towards multiple constituencies: 'current members, future generations, and past members now deceased'. Carpenter, Katyal, and Riley, 'In Defense of Property', 1074.

[279] Ibid, 1072.

[280] See Haidy Geismar, 'Cultural Property, Museums, and the Pacific: Reframing the Debates' (2008) 15 *International Journal of Cultural Property* 109–122, 115.

[281] On relationships of 'belonging', see Noble, 'Owning as Belonging/Owning as Property'.

Logically, a cultural object can 'belong' to a person or a culture irrespective of ownership.[282] The concept of heritage is better equipped to reflect the diversity of relations toward cultural objects.[283] It relies on a bond between cultural objects and people, which is focused more on social, rather than economic ownership.[284] It emphasizes the link between objects and identity, including their intergenerational value. It has gained express recognition in several instruments. For instance, the 1972 Convention Concerning the Protection of the World Cultural and Natural Heritage stresses the need for preservation and 'an effective system of collective protection of the cultural and natural heritage of outstanding universal value'.[285] More recent instruments, such as the 2003 Convention for the Safeguarding of the Intangible Cultural Heritage, the 2005 Council of Europe Framework Convention on the Value of Cultural Heritage for Society, the UNESCO Convention on Diversity of Cultural Expression, or the 2007 UN Declaration on the Rights of Indigenous Peoples[286] protect cultural heritage for the sake of present and future generations[287] and broader societal interests, such as 'respect for cultural diversity and human creativity'[288] or the value of cultural expression 'at the local, national and international levels'.[289] They stand in direct contrast to the colonial ideology of justifying cultural takings for purpose of cultural assimilation, and sometimes seek to reverse these effects.[290]

Heritage-based models of protection are conservative in the sense that they are focused on the safeguarding, preservation, and conservation of cultural objects, rather than their transformation.[291] However, they offer greater flexibility and creativity in the balancing and resolution of competing claims than property-based approaches. They determine where objects belong based on the social nexus between cultural objects and people. This allows greater differentiation in the value of objects and the recognition of cultural significance to multiple stakeholders. They

---

[282] Anthony Appiah has explained this broader sense of belonging as follows: 'One connection—the one neglected in talk of cultural patrimony—is the connection not through identity but despite difference. We can respond to art that is not ours; indeed, we can only fully respond to 'our' art if we move beyond thinking of it as ours and start to respond to it as art'. See Anthony Kwame Appiah, 'Whose Culture Is It?' in James Cuno (ed.), *Whose Culture? The Promise of Museums and the Debate over Antiquities* (Princeton: Princeton University Press 2009) 71–86, 85.

[283] Kuprecht, *Indigenous Peoples' Cultural Property Claims*, 42.

[284] See Evelien Campfens, *Cross-Border Claims to Objects: Property or Heritage?* (The Hague: Eleven Publishers, 2021) 238.

[285] 1972 Convention Concerning the Protection of the World Cultural and Natural Heritage, preamble.

[286] UNDRIP, Art. 31.

[287] Ibid, Art. 11 ('right to maintain, protect and develop the past, present and future manifestations of their cultures') and Art. 13.

[288] See Convention for the Safeguarding of the Intangible Cultural Heritage, Art. 2(1).

[289] Convention on the Protection and Promotion of the Diversity of Cultural Expressions, Art. 1(e).

[290] UNDRIP, Arts. 11, 12.

[291] One sociological critique of the inter-generational nature of heritage is the socially constructed nature of culture. This argument presumes that cultural object can be passed on from one generation to the next. It fails to take into account the changing meaning and value of objects over time.

also offer a wide spectrum of remedies. They approach restoration of 'ownership' in broader ways than property models, namely through options of access or control, rather than rigid property categories.[292] The ability to take into consideration different ownership conceptions in source communities is essential for the success of return practices.[293]

6.1.2 Diversifying subject-object relations

One of the continuing challenges of legal instruments is to reflect the multiple ontologies of objects.[294] In many cases, material object conceptions do not correspond to the perspectives of those from whom objects were taken. As Nicky Rousseau, Riedwaan Moosage, and Ciraj Rassool have argued, certain objects may be 'simultaneously themselves and something else', such as 'ancestors', 'living people, embodiments or extensions of those who are missed'.[295] The exercise of ownership or their treatment as objects is perceived as an inappropriate condition, namely as an act of 'imprisonment' or detention, by those who regard them as 'subjects'. This is reflected by multiple object stories.

For instance, in the case of the canoe prow of Lock Priso the spiritual nature associated with the tangué, i.e. its role as mediator of power, has been important element in understanding the return claims filed against the ethnological museum in Munich.[296] Prince Kum'a Ndumbe III contested the argument that the prow was validly acquired through the taking of the material object. He argued: '[Y]ou can't steal the souls of whole peoples, and then claim to bring them civilization.'[297] Māori leaders requested return of the Tūranga Meeting House, based on it ancestral bonds.[298] The Rapa Nui relied on the nature of the Hoa Hakananai as a 'living person' in order to justify their case against the British Museum.[299]

The return of the Dahomey Royal figures (Glèlè, Ghézo, Béhanzin) to modern-day Benin in November 2021 highlight the subject qualities of objects.[300] In his speech at the Quai Branly museum Felwine Sarr compared the figures to 'ancestors' and argued that they are more than objects, namely 'beings inhabited by the soul and spirit of the cultures that gave them life'.[301] He said:

---

[292] Campfens, *Cross-Border Claims to Objects*, 238.

[293] Gates, 'Who Owns African Art?', 1158.

[294] Martin Skydstrup, 'What Might an Anthropology of Cultural Property Look Like?' in Paul Turnbull and Michael Pickering (eds.), *The Long Way Home: The Meaning and Values of Repatriation* (Oxford: Berghahn Books, 2010) 59–81.

[295] Nicky Rousseau, Riedwaan Moosage, and Ciraj Rassool, 'Missing and Missed: Rehumanisation, the Nation and Missing-ness' (2018) 44 *Kronos* 10–32, 28.

[296] See Chapter 3.

[297] Elizabeth Grenier, 'Colonial Art: The Case of a Piece Stolen from Cameroon' (2 September 2020) https://www.dw.com/en/colonial-art-the-case-of-a-piece-stolen-from-cameroon/a-54783942.

[298] See Chapter 4.

[299] Ibid.

[300] See Chapter 9.

[301] Felwine Sarr, 'Les ancêtres repartent, les ancêtres reviennent' *Le Point Afrique* (21 October 2021).

For the ancestors, it took stainless courage and patience to nourish the sap of absence and to pierce the secret of the waiting that does not make one grow old. They held on. They refused to die and to be petrified ... Today, they leave again where the dreams lie.[302]

In Cotonou, they were welcomed as 'ancestors'. Local leaders asked in which language they should be addressed, since they had been in exile for more than 120 years. The President of Benin, Patrice Talon, said: 'The symbolism of the return to Benin is about our soul, our identity'.[303] The returns have been celebrated as an act of 'liberation' and a 'rebirth'.

In contemporary scholarship, several theories have been developed to reflect the multiple identities of objects and take into multiple world views. They include dignity approaches, new relational models (e.g. analogy to missing persons), and agency-related concepts, such as the idea of object-persons, which claim that it is wrong to treat 'persons' as objects and exercise ownership over them.

Personhood-related theory of property (e.g. *Radin*) acknowledge that removal of certain categories of objects causes human loss, because of the inherent connection between material objects and the identity of persons.[304] Bernadette Atuahene has extended this idea to the removal of cultural property. She has argued that certain types of cultural takings may constitute 'dignity takings'.[305] She qualifies dispossessions as 'dignity takings' in cases where 'the state takes property from a class of people that it considers sub persons'.[306] This theory provides a frame to qualify certain property takings in systems of injustice as a violation of identity or personhood, such as the dispossessions in settler colonial contexts (US, Canada, Australia, New Zealand) or property confiscations or expropriations in the Holocaust or in apartheid—South Africa,[307] where Jewish people, minorities or persons of color were regarded as subordinate classes of human beings.

Atuahene's rationale has direct relevance to colonial contexts, where removal of cultural objects was intrinsically linked to the classification of non-white people as savages or lesser races.[308] It is able to able to qualify cultural takings as an attack on personhood, rather than solely a property violation. It also has ramifications for returns and 'repatriations' of objects. It reflects the idea that return is not only an

---

[302] Ibid.
[303] Shannon McDonagh and Theo Farrant, 'Elation on the Streets of Benin as France Returns Stolen Bronze Treasures' *EuroNews* (11 November 2021).
[304] Radin, 'Property and Personhood', 957–1015.
[305] Bernadette Atuahene, 'Dignity Takings and Dignity Restoration' (2016) 41 *Law and Social Inquiry* 796–823.
[306] Bernadette Atuahene, *We Want What's Ours* (Oxford: Oxford University Press, 2014) 23.
[307] Ibid, 23.
[308] Saby Ghoshray has relied on the idea of dignity taking to justify the case for the return of the Kohi-Noor diamond. See Saby Ghoshray, 'Repatriation of the Kohinoor Diamond: Expanding the Legal Paradigm for Cultural Heritage' (2007) 31 *Fordham International Law Journal* 741–780, 780.

act of material recovery or repossession, but also about the recognition of human harm and loss, or the restoration of dignity more broadly.[309]

A second approach to take into account the person-related attributes of objects is their treatment as objects and subjects. The recognition of agency and person-hood has an established tradition in the area of human remains.[310] They are not only objects, but continue to carry traces of living subjects which are protected by the concept of human dignity. Their 'objectification' causes harm to descendants or indigenous communities.[311] For instance, in Māori culture or the tradition of certain Australian native communities, living generations have kinship obligations towards their ancestors.[312] According to Native Hawaiian traditions, the living have an intergenerational responsibility (*kuleana*) to care for their ancestors in physical and spiritual forms, i.e. to bury and protect human remains.[313] Under this conception, the appropriation of ancestral remains disturbs the existing relation between ancestors and the living. Return is thus a means to enable individuals or communities to fulfil their ongoing duties of care, or an act of 'rehumanization'.[314]

Ciraj Rassool has proposed to equate 'human remains' to 'missing persons'[315] in order to recognize the relational bond between the deceased body and the person

---

[309] Atuahene speaks of 'dignity restoration'. See Atuahene, 'Dignity Takings and Dignity Restoration', 796–823.

[310] The personhood and dignity of human remains is one the main justifications of duties of return under UNDRIP or national legislation, such as NAGRA.

[311] Their public display is often perceived as discriminatory and may violate religious beliefs or customs of indigenous people, prohibiting the display bodies of the deceased (e.g. Inuit, Australian Aboriginal people). See Margaret Clegg, 'Other Belief Systems and the Care of Human Remains' in Margaret Clegg, *Human Remains Curation, Reburial and Repatriation* (Cambridge: Cambridge University Press, 2020) 82–92, 83. It is increasingly limited in museums, based on dignity consideration and protection of indigenous rights and cultures. For instance, New Zealand has become reluctant to display Māori remains in public collections.

[312] Clegg, 'Other Belief Systems and the Care of Human Remains', 87.

[313] Edward Halealoha Ayau, 'I Mana I Ka 'Ōiwi: Dignity empowered by repatriation' in Cressida Fforde, C. Timothy McKeown, Honor Keeler (eds.), *The Routledge Companion to Indigenous Repatriation: Return, Reconcile, Renew* (London: Routledge, 2020) 63–82. See also Report of the Expert Mechanism on the Rights of Indigenous Peoples, 'Repatriation of ceremonial objects, human remains and intangible cultural heritage under the United Nations Declaration on the Rights of Indigenous Peoples', A/HRC/45/35 (21 July 2020) para. 17.

[314] This point is made expressly in a 2020 conference report on 'New Ethics for Museums in Transition' by the Goethe Institute in Tanzania. It states: 'From an African perspective, 'human remains' should no longer be called in this Eurocentric way, as it degrades them to scientific objects or museum exhibits. Instead, they should be treated as human individuals, family members and community leaders, whose absence is in some cases deplored until this very day. It is therefore more appropriate to talk about this theft as dehumanisation of the ancestors rather than of their objectification, so that we remain in the human's logic.' Goethe-Institut, MARKK Hamburg and Berlin Postkolonial, Conference Report, *Beyond Collecting: New Ethics for Museums in Transition* (March 2020) 11 https://www.goethe.de/resources/files/pdf212/beyond-collecting-new-ethics-for-museums-in-transition-public-conference-report2.pdf.

[315] The concept of 'missing persons' builds on the legal framework surrounding memory and the political disappearance of persons, which has been recognized as international human rights violation and crime. It recognizes the ongoing harm arising from the uncertainty about the whereabouts of remains in Western collections. See J. Edkins, *Missing: Persons and Politics* (Ithaca, NY: Cornell University Press, 2011).

or community who is missing the 'body' and 'post-mortem' identity of human remains.[316] This analogy challenges the de-personalization of remains in collecting practices and their ongoing presentation as objects in collections. It approaches the return of human remains as a return of human beings or citizens, rather than objects[317] (e.g. by restoring names or enabling burial rites[318]), and encourages the search for 'the truth' regarding the provenance and identity of remains in order to allow descendants to know about their whereabouts and enable them to make claims for return.

The most far-reaching recognition of personhood is the equation of cultural objects to subjects or ancestors. It treats objects like persons or agents in their own right. It is recognized by theories which admit that objects are carriers of meaning (e.g. signs or symbols[319]) and may speak a language, i.e. a language of things.[320] For example, Alfred Gell's theory of agency goes beyond object-subject divides, by acknowledging that people ascribe 'social agent' status to objects in their social relations, even though they are well aware of the distinction between things and human beings.[321] This approach accepts that the nature of a thing or its recognition of personhood is created through social practices. It has a tradition in relation to certain sacred or ceremonial objects,[322] which are associated with spiritual force or power, or objects, which are connected to former ancestors. The objects may be both objects and agents at the same time. Birgit Meyer has explained this in relation to religious images:

> [P]eople are taught to approach, value, treat, and look at pictures in specific ways, and this ensues a process of animation through which pictures may (or may not) become agents who impress themselves on their beholders ... In this way, spirits and the spiritual are made to materialize in a picture, and thus become approachable.[323]

---

[316] Ciraj Rassool, 'Human Remains, the Disciplines of the Dead, and the South African Memorial Complex' in Derek R. Peterson, Kodzo Gavua, and Ciraj Rassool (eds.), *The Politics of Heritage in Africa: Economies, Histories, and Infrastructures* (Cambridge: Cambridge University Press, 2015) 133–156; Ciraj Rassool, 'Re-storing the Skeletons of Empire: Return, Reburial and Rehumanisation in Southern Africa' (2015) 41 *Journal of Southern African Studies* 653–670, 669.

[317] Rousseau, Moosage, and Rassool, 'Missing and Missed', 22, 29.

[318] On the case of Sarah Baartman, see Chapter 5.

[319] Mieke Bal and Norman Bryson, 'Semiotics and Art History' (1991) 73 *The Art Bulletin* 174–208.

[320] Harrie Leyten, *From idol to art* (Leiden: African Studies Centre, 2015) 27.

[321] Alfred Gell, *Art and Agency. An Anthropological Theory* (Oxford: Clarendon Press, 1998) 123. Bruno Latour has shown that the origin of the subject-object divide is often linked to the difference between society and nature. See Bruno Latour, *Politics of Nature: How to Bring the Sciences into Democracy* (Cambridge, Mass: Harvard University Press, 2004) 237-238.

[322] The use of the term 'fetish' in colonial language conveys the idea that objects may dominate persons through their power. Tomoko Masuzawa, 'Troubles with Materiality: The Ghost of Fetishism in the Nineteenth Century' (2000) 42 *Comparative Studies in Society and History* 242–267.

[323] Birgit Meyer, '"There Is a Spirit in that Image": Mass-Produced Jesus Pictures and Protestant-Pentecostal Animation in Ghana' (2010) 52 *Comparative Studies in Society and History* 100–130, 104.

Others have emphasized that the notion of 'person' as such is not confined to human persons, but can be ascribed to entities, which are 'animated', such as statues or objects (e.g. 'statue-persons', 'rock –persons' etc.) For instance, Crispin Paine has argued that such types of personhood are relational, and emerge through the interaction of communities with such objects as 'persons'. He has noted:

> An object-person is only 'alive' when interacting with a human-person—the act of relating is what does the animating. This 'relationality' means that every encounter is different, and any attempt to define the 'true nature' of the non-human person involved is doomed. It also gives added emphasis to the importance of performance.[324]

According to this conception, certain objects may be qualified as object-persons, because they exist as 'persons' in specific cultures.[325]

The equation of objects to ancestors challenges the appropriation, commodification, and retention of objects, since it is impossible to 'own' persons in same way as 'we can own, buy and sell, destroy, rebuild or preserve the tangible heritage of places and artifacts'.[326] It draws attention to the harm caused by the reduction of subjects to objects in ownership and display practices.

6.2   The diversification of cultural heritage law

A second important innovation of human rights approaches to cultural heritage is their ability to address some of the existing impasses and biases of the past, by placing the emphasis on contemporary relations toward objects, rather than past wrongdoing, and extending claims and returns beyond inter-state relations.

6.2.1   From past to present: Cultural rights as means to transform the future
From a human rights perspective, cultural rights mark an expression of the equality and dignity of all cultures and the right of individuals or groups to affirm and maintain their own cultural identity. They contribute to the preservation of cultural diversity, which has been qualified as a 'common heritage of humanity' for 'the benefit of present and future generations'.[327]

---

[324] Crispin Paine, *Religious Objects in Museums: Private Lives and Public Duties* (London: Bloomsbury, 2013) 9.

[325] A good example is the Hoa Hakananai. It was viewed as living face of ancestors and used in rituals and ceremonies before its removal. See Matías Cornejo González, 'Museum Performativity and the Agency of Sacred Objects' (2019) 47 *ICOFOM Study Series* 73–87.

[326] Logan, 'Cultural Diversity, Cultural Heritage and Human Rights', 236.

[327] UNESCO, Universal Declaration on Cultural Diversity (2 November 2001) Art. 1.

Historically, they can be derived from identity-related collective rights, which protect the ability of cultural groups to preserve, develop or maintain their culture, such as the right to self-determination, which secures the cultural identity of a people, or the cultural protection of minority groups[328]. More recently, the right of access to culture has been developed as a part of the right to participate in cultural life under the Universal Declaration of Human Rights[329] and the International Covenant on Economic, Social and Cultural Rights.[330] It involves the right of access to cultural heritage, and the possibility to create, practice, or transmit such heritage within communities. It is prominently reflected in the UN Declaration on the Rights of Indigenous Peoples[331] and the 2005 Council of Europe Framework Convention on the Value of Cultural Heritage for Society (Faro Convention),[332] which clarifies that cultural heritage exists 'independently of ownership.'[333] It ties cultural life particularly to a concept of 'heritage communities', comprising 'people who value specific aspects of cultural heritage which they wish, within the framework of public action, to sustain and transmit to future generations.'[334] Other UNESCO instruments have recognized cultural rights as an 'enabling environment for cultural diversity',[335] a component of human dignity[336] or an element of solidarity rights and human development.[337]

As Janet Blake has argued, legally, cultural rights entail a dual obligation of states: an obligation not interfere with the right of cultural communities to enjoy their own culture and refrain from conduct which destroys, damages or alters 'cultural objects or spaces that are of significant importance for the practice and enactment of a people's culture'[338] and an obligation to 'protect cultural groups and communities against the risk of destruction or damage to religious or historical property that is indispensable for those communities' cultural practices and indeed for their 'continuing existence as a cultural group.'[339]

---

[328] See e.g. Art. 27 ICCPR.

[329] Article 27 .

[330] Article 15 ICESCR. See also Committee on Economic, Social and Cultural Rights, General Comment No. 21, UN Doc E/C.12/GC/21 (21 December 2009); Human Rights Council, Report of the independent expert in the field of cultural rights, Farida Shaheed, UN. Doc. A/HRC/17/38 (21 March 2011) para. 78.

[331] Article 11.

[332] Framework Convention on the Value of Cultural Heritage for Society, CETS No. 199 (27 October 2005) Art. 6. It states that 'rights relating to cultural heritage' are 'inherent in the right to participate in cultural life' (Art. 1(a)) and includes 'the right to benefit from the cultural heritage and to contribute towards its enrichment' (Art. 4).

[333] Ibid, Art. 2 (a). It encompasses 'resources inherited from the past which people identify ... as a reflection and expression of their constantly evolving values, beliefs, knowledge and traditions'.

[334] Ibid, Art. 2(b).

[335] UNESCO, Universal Declaration on Cultural Diversity, Art 5.

[336] Ibid, Art. 4 ('The defence of cultural diversity is an ethical imperative, inseparable from respect for human dignity').

[337] Convention on the Protection and Promotion of the Diversity of Cultural Expressions (20 October 2005) Art. 1(l).

[338] Blake, 'Taking a Human Rights Approach to Cultural Heritage Protection', 216.

[339] Ibid, 216.

This approach reframes perspectives on access and return of cultural colonial objects. From a cultural rights perspective, removals of cultural heritage create a separation between objects and people, which ought to be remedied in contemporary relations. The novelty of this perspective lies in the fact that it ties return to 'the acknowledgement of a right to possess, access, or control certain involuntarily lost cultural objects on the grounds of their intangible heritage interests for specific people, independent of ownership'.[340] It seeks to build and reinforce relationships of respect and responsibility between people, by recognizing the importance of culture heritage communities.[341] It thereby goes beyond cultural nationalist approaches, which link return to sovereignty interests, such as rights of states to have a 'key to their own history'.[342] The guiding criterion is thus not so much, to whom objects belonged in the past or where they are most visible, but rather where they 'belong' culturally and socially. The case for access or return is grounded in the need to preserve cultural diversity and the duty to ensure that objects are accessible to cultural communities in order to enable them to enjoy and exercise their cultural rights. This logic avoids debates over the legality of past takings, intertemporal law, or non-retroactivity. It does not necessarily outlaw past wrongs, but provides a means to transform the future.

6.2.2 Extending heritage relations beyond the state

Human rights-based approaches to culture heritage recognize that the lack of access to heritage may impair the cultural rights of individuals and communities in countries and communities of origin. This has implications for voice, participation and representation in return claims and negotiations. It becomes artificial to mediate interests of heritage communities solely through inter-state based processes, such as those contemplated in the 1970 UNESCO Convention. Individuals or communities need to be given a possibility to make claims or have a voice in negotiations. Museums should cooperate with 'indigenous peoples as constituents, employees and stakeholders'.[343]

This logic makes it easier to accommodate the interests of sub-state actors, such as 'source communities', 'local communities' or individuals in returns, since it links cultural heritage to access and participation more broadly, rather than ownership,[344] and acknowledges different degrees of access and enjoyment, depending

---

[340] Evelien Campfens, 'The Bangwa Queen: Artifact or Heritage?' (2019) 26 *International Journal of Cultural Property* 75–110, 106.

[341] Article 2(b) Faro Convention.

[342] Geoffrey Robertson, *Who Owns History?* (London: Biteback, 2019) 30 ('sovereign right of a people to hold and study the keys of its own history').

[343] Report Expert Mechanism on the Rights of Indigenous Peoples, 'Repatriation of ceremonial objects, human remains and intangible cultural heritage under the United Nations Declaration on the Rights of Indigenous Peoples', para. 61.

[344] It is often difficult to 'attribute ownership' in classical property models or to return objects to their original 'owner', as a result of the transformation or geographic dispersal of communities of origin. See Gates, 'Who Owns African Art?', 1157. In many contexts, state structures reflect configurations of power that have been created through colonial conditions. In settler colonial contexts, communities are

on the relationship to objects. It is able to accommodate multiple or collective titles to cultural objects,[345] facilitate a balancing of competing interests[346] or envisage new ways of 'owning' or 'sharing' which take into account the different functions of objects in their respective contexts. As Felwine Sarr has stated:

> It is up to African communities to define their vision of cultural heritage … According to the different functions attributed to objects, they can find their place in art centers, university-museums, schools or even in the heart of communities for ritual uses, with the possibility of back and forth of objects between museums and communities.[347]

However, human rights-based approaches to culture heritage should not be 'romanticized'. They may also bring new antinomies.[348] They open new debates as to who should control heritage, and why. They are vulnerable to abuse by both 'leaders of hegemonic majorities', who may use 'official' versions of heritage to promote 'political stability' or 'social cohesion'[349] or glorify national history, and/or 'minorities' or groups,[350] who present 'the anti-colonial resistance of their ancestors, their sacrifice and their suffering'.[351] They may perpetuate stereotypes about

---

often dominated by majority groups which have become to represent the state or imposed their understanding of nationhood.

[345] Article 4(a) Faro Convention.

[346] For instance, UNDRIP provides that: 'States shall seek to enable the access and/or repatriation of ceremonial objects and human remains in their possession through fair, transparent and effective mechanisms.' See UNDRIP, Art. 12(2). The Faro Convention establishes a duty to 'deal equitably with situations where contradictory values are placed on the same cultural heritage by different communities'. See Art. 7(b) Faro Convention. The Principles for Cooperation in the Mutual Protection and Transfer of Cultural Material, adopted by the International Law Association (ILA) in 2006, contain cooperative duties, including 'good faith negotiation'. See ILA, Principles for Cooperation in the Mutual Protection and Transfer of Cultural Material, Report of the International Law Association Seventy-second Conference, 2006, Annex, Principle 8. It lists criteria such as 'the significance of the requested material for the requesting party, the reunification of dispersed cultural material, accessibility to the cultural material in the requesting state, and protection of the cultural material'. See James A. R. Nafziger, 'The Principles for Cooperation in the Mutual Protection and the Principles for Cooperation in the Mutual Protection and Transfer of Cultural Material' (2007) 8 *Chicago Journal of International Law* 147–167, 166.

[347] Felwine Sarr, 'Restitution of African Heritage: History, Memory, Traces, ReAppropriation' Geneva (24 September 2021) 5.

[348] Certain cultural traditions applied by religious or ethnic groups may contravene individual human rights or have disempowering effects on specific segments of society. The 2003 UNESCO Convention on Intangible Heritages recognizes this tension. It states that, for the purposes of the Convention, 'consideration will be given solely to such intangible cultural heritage as is compatible with existing human rights instruments, as well as with the requirements of mutual respect among communities, groups and individuals, and of sustainable development'. Art. 2.

[349] Logan, 'Cultural Diversity, Cultural Heritage and Human Rights', 237.

[350] Thomas Hylland Eriksen, 'Multiculturalism, Individualism and Human Rights: Romanticism, the Enlightenment and Lessons from Mauritius' in Richard Wilson (ed.), *Human Rights, Culture and Context: Anthropological Perspectives* (London: Pluto Press, 1997) 49–69, 54.

[351] Wazi Apoh and Andreas Mehler, 'Mainstreaming the Discourse on Restitution and Repatriation within African History, Heritage Studies and Political Science' (2020) 7 *Contemporary Journal of African Studies* 1–16, 6.

identity, reproduce colonial knowledge structures or create new divides in political or economic terms.[352] The balancing of different legally-protected interests can create novel social hierarches among groups or communities.[353] Finally, cultural returns may be a convenient or 'cheap' way for governments to appease communities, sideline issues of political reform or conceal broader claims for corrective justice, particularly in settler colonial contexts.[354] It is thus important to remain aware of the potentially disempowering side effects of human rights discourses.

6.3 The turn to indigenous rights

One of the most important frames to challenge cultural takings in the colonial era is the recognition of indigenous rights.[355] They gained new momentum in many settler contexts as of the 1970s, when Indigenous communities requested return of human remains and sacred objects. For instance, in New Zealand, museums began to take a more active role in the return of human remains to Māori after the establishment of the Waitangi Tribunal in 1975.[356] In the US, a study of the Interior Federal Agencies Task Force, openly criticized the acquisition of objects from First Nations made though trade or coercive practices in 1979. It found:

> Museum records show that some sacred objects were sold by their original Native owner or owners. In many instances, however, the chain of title does not lead to the original owners. Some religious property left the original ownership during military confrontations, was included in the spoils of war and eventually fell to the control of museums. Also in times past, sacred objects were lost by Native owners as a result of less violent pressures exerted by federally sponsored missionaries and Indian agents. Most sacred objects were stolen from their original owners. In other cases, religious property was converted and sold by Native people who did not have ownership or title to the sacred object.[357]

---

[352] For example, the recognition of certain communities as 'source communities' in return claims may reproduce anthropological stereotypes, narratives or vocabulary created through colonial 'science' or practice. Apoh and Mehler, 'Mainstreaming', 7.

[353] Logan, 'Cultural Diversity, Cultural Heritage and Human Rights', 237–239.

[354] For a critique of US repatriation policies, see Liv Nilsson Stutz, 'Claims to the Past: A Critical View of the Arguments Driving Repatriation of Cultural Heritage and Their Role in Contemporary Identity Politics' (2013) 7 *Journal of Intervention and Statebuilding* 170–195.

[355] Such rights were for a long time sidelined by the divide over cultural nationalism versus cultural internationalism. See Russell L. Barsh, 'Indigenous Peoples in the 1990s: From Object to Subject of International Law?' (1994) 7 *Harvard Human Rights Law Review* 33–86.

[356] Amber Aranui, 'Restitution or a Loss to Science? Understanding the Importance of Returning Māori Ancestral Remains' (2020) 18 *Museum & Society* 19–29, 22.

[357] US Secretary of the Interior Federal Agencies Task Force, American Indian Religious Freedom Act Report (August 1979) in Jack F. Trope and Walter R. Echo-Hawk, 'The Native American Graves Protection and Repatriation Act: Background and Legislative History' (1992) 24 *Arizona State Law Journal* 35–76, 44.

It strengthened calls for national legislation on return of remains or cultural objects or new museum policies by indigenous communities.[358] The Federal Museum of History in Canada decided in the late 1970s to return ceremonial objects taken from Kwakwaka'wakw First Nations in 1922 during the ban of the potlatch.[359] In Australia, relations with indigenous Australians started change as of the 1980s, when indigenous groups filed heritage claims against museums (Victoria, Tasmania, Australian museum).[360]

These moves towards greater ownership and control by indigenous groups were only gradually reflected in inter-state relations[361] and international legal documents.[362] The 1995 UNIDROIT Convention contains an important reference to the return of illegally exported indigenous heritage, but does not apply retroactively. The 2003 and 2005 UNESCO Convention require states to protect intangible cultural heritage and the diversity of cultural expressions. However, they lack express return obligations. The main international legal instrument is UNDRIP, adopted by the General Assembly after two decades of negotiations in 2007. It marked partly an 'extension of the process of decolonization' to settler contexts through 'the path of human rights' rather than 'the language of decolonization'.[363] It defines 'minimum standards for the survival, dignity and well-being of the indigenous peoples of the world'.[364] It mandates ('shall') states to 'take the appropriate measures, including legislative measures, to achieve the ends' of the Declaration,[365] but is technically non-binding.[366]

UNDRIP enjoys relatively wide support. It was adopted with the vote of 143 states, and eleven abstentions. Initially, settler states, which were most directly affected by the Declaration (U.S., Australia, Canada, and New Zealand), objected to the Declaration. They feared that the declaration would interfere with domestic legislation or fail to recognize 'lawfully' acquired rights of non-Indigenous

---

[358] Jennifer L. Dekker, 'Challenging the "Love of Possessions": Repatriation of Sacred Objects in the United States and Canada' (2018) 14 *Collections: A Journal for Museum and Archives Professionals* 37–62, 40.

[359] Stacey Jessiman, 'The Edgy State of Decolonization at the Canadian Museum of History' (2014) *UBC Law Review* 889–926, 903.

[360] Vrdoljak, *International Law, Museums and Return of Cultural Objects*, 250.

[361] For instance, in 2003 the government of New Zealand developed an international programme for the programme for the return of Māori and Moriori ancestral remains. See Aranui, 'Restitution or a Loss to Science?', 22.

[362] States have remained reluctant to adopt binding international legal instruments on indigenous heritage, since it relates not only to cultural objects or human remains, but also to issues of a control over land, natural resources, or intangible heritage more broadly.

[363] Asbjørn Eide, 'The indigenous peoples, the Working Group on Indigenous Populations and the adoption of the UN Declaration on the Rights of Indigenous Peoples' in Claire Charters and Rodolfo Stavenhagen (eds.), *Making the Declaration Work: The United Nations Declaration on the Rights of Indigenous Peoples* (Copenhagen: IWGIA, 2009) 32–46, 40–41.

[364] Article 43.

[365] Article 38.

[366] Some scholars have argued that the Declaration is legally binding. See Louis Rodriguez Pinero Royo, 'Where Appropriate: Monitoring/Implementing of Indigenous Peoples' Rights under the Declaration' in Charters and Stavenhagen, *Making the Declaration Work*, 316–317.

citizens.[367] For instance, Canada argued that new legal regime discounted 'the need to recognize a range of rights over land' and possibly called into question 'matters that have been settled by treaty' in Canadian law.[368] Australia claimed that the Declaration failed to recognize the 'rights of third parties to access indigenous land, heritage and cultural objects where appropriate under national law' and made 'indigenous customary law' prevail over domestic law.[369] New Zealand argued that the provisions on lands and resources[370] and on redress[371] were 'fundamentally incompatible with New Zealand's constitutional and legal arrangements, the Treaty of Waitangi, and the principle of governing for the good of all its citizens'.[372] It criticized the text for failing to take into account 'that land might now be occupied or owned legitimately by others, or subject to numerous different or overlapping indigenous claims'.[373] The US objected to the Declaration, arguing that it was 'confusing, and risked endless conflicting interpretations and debate about its application'.[374] However, over time, the four countries came to endorse the document.[375] In 2009 and 2010, the governments of Australia,[376] New Zealand,[377] Canada,[378] and the United States[379] all expressed their support for the Declaration. The UN Permanent Forum on Indigenous Issues recognized it as a landmark document, which 'provides a detailing or interpretation of the human rights enshrined in other international human rights instruments of universal resonance—as these apply to indigenous peoples and indigenous individuals'.[380] Some of its provisions have been qualified as reflecting international customary law.[381]

---

[367] Permanent Mission of Australia to the United Nations Office at Geneva to the Office of the UN High Commissioner for Human Rights Note verbale (2 August 2006), UN Doc A/HRC/2/G/1 (24 August 2006) arguing that the Declaration (Art. 26) would 'require the recognition of indigenous rights to lands now lawfully owned by other citizens, both indigenous and non-indigenous'.

[368] Department of Public Information, 'General Assembly Adopts Declaration on Rights of Indigenous Peoples' UN Doc GA/10612 (13 September 2007).

[369] Ibid.

[370] Article 26.

[371] Article 28.

[372] UN Doc GA/10612.

[373] Ibid.

[374] Ibid.

[375] Federico Lenzerini, Cultural Identity, Human Rights, and Repatriation of Cultural Heritage of Indigenous Peoples (2016) 23 *The Brown Journal of World Affairs* 127–141, 132.

[376] Statement on the United Nations Declaration on the Rights of Indigenous Peoples, Parliament, House Canberra (3 April 2009) https://www.un.org/esa/socdev/unpfii/documents/Australia_official_s tatement_endorsement_UNDRIP.pdf.

[377] Announcement of New Zealand's Support for the Declaration on the Rights of Indigenous Peoples (20 April 2010) https://www.beehive.govt.nz/release/supporting-un-declaration-restores-nzs-mana.

[378] Canada's Statement of Support on the United Declaration on the Rights of Indigenous Peoples (12 November 2010).

[379] White House, Remarks by the President at the White House Tribal Nations Conference (16 December 2010) https://obamawhitehouse.archives.gov/the-press-office/2010/12/16/remarks-presid ent-white-house-tribal-nations-conference.

[380] UN Permanent Forum on Indigenous Issues, Declaration on the Rights of Indigenous Peoples— Frequently Asked Questions' https://www.un.org/esa/socdev/unpfii/documents/faq_drips_en.pdf.

[381] ILA, Conclusions and Recommendation of The Committee on the Rights of Indigenous Peoples (2012) Resolution No. 5/2012.

The Declaration has both de-colonial and neo-colonial features.[382] It serves as an important frame to recognize rights of access and control of indigenous people in relation to human remains and cultural objects. It has promoted return claims and changing lenses towards indigenous rights in government and museum policies. But it fails to provide a full 'right' to return of cultural objects or a concrete 'legal framework or mechanism for the repatriation of ceremonial objects, human remains and cultural heritage directly to the indigenous peoples involved'.[383] In practice, returns remain heavily dependent on national heritage regulation and state behaviour.

6.3.1 The dual face of UNDRIP

UNDRIP has a dual face. It serves as an instrument to challenge colonial assimilation and promote indigenous world views, ways of life and approaches to heritage, but also maintains colonial continuities[384], through its affirmation of state sovereignty over indigenous people, its stance on cultural identity and its ambiguities in relation to return of cultural objects.[385]

The Declaration enhances the status and protection of indigenous populations, by recognizing them not only as 'communities' or minorities, but as 'peoples' with rights to self-determination.[386] It recognizes that indigenous people 'have suffered from historic injustices as a result of, inter alia, their colonization and dispossession of their lands, territories and resources'[387] and condemns colonial doctrines 'advocating superiority of peoples or individuals on the basis of national origin or racial, religious, ethnic or cultural differences' as 'racist, scientifically false, legally invalid, morally condemnable and socially unjust'.[388] It breaks partly with colonial traditions, by acknowledging the value of pluralist cultural identities[389] and the potentially 'international character' of 'rights affirmed in treaties, agreements and other constructive arrangements between States and indigenous peoples'.[390] It upholds at the same time the consequences and status created by colonial practices, by accepting the integration of indigenous peoples into the 'territorial integrity or political unity' of existing nation-states.[391]

---

[382] Shea Esterling, 'One Step Forward, Two Steps Back: The Restitution of Cultural Property in the United Nations Declaration on the Rights of Indigenous Peoples' (2013) 18 *Art Antiquity and Law* 323–344.

[383] Expert Mechanism on the Rights of Indigenous Peoples, 'Repatriation of ceremonial objects, human remains and intangible cultural heritage', para. 51.

[384] Malreddy Pavan Kumar. '(An)other Way of Being Human: "Indigenous" Alternative(S) to Postcolonial Humanism' (2011) 32 *Third World Quarterly* 1557–1572.

[385] Charmaine Whiteface and Zumila Wobaga, *Indigenous Nations' Rights in the Balance: An Analysis of the Declaration on the Rights of Indigenous Peoples* (Minnesota: Living Justice Press, 2013).

[386] Article 3.

[387] Preamble, para. 6.

[388] Ibid, para. 4.

[389] Esterling, 'One Step Forward, Two Steps Back', 324.

[390] Preamble, para. 14.

[391] Article 46(1).

This affirmation confirms the prerogatives of 'White settlers' and stands in contrast with the idea of the 'sovereignty' of First Nations. The text makes the interpretation of provisions subject to 'principles of justice, democracy, respect for human rights, equality, non-discrimination' or 'good governance'.[392] This caveat has been criticized by indigenous scholars for maintaining a 'Euro-centric framework' and 're-inscrib[ing] the civilising mission and the colonial project of assimilation'.[393] The framework is ambivalent in relation to return of cultural heritage. It enhances the prospects of indigenous people to makes claims, but constraints them, by preserving state discretion[394] or tying cultural property claims to 'fixed cultural identities',[395] which may be at odds with the hybridization of cultures through colonial settlements. The enactment of national heritage legislation may alter indigenous relations to objects. For instance, in New Zealand, the Protected Objects Act 1975 brought Māori cultural objectives under the auspices of the cultural heritage of New Zealand and considered it as shared national heritage.[396] Governmental policies can entail a 're-indigenization' or re-enactment of a tribal past which is rejected by community members.[397]

The link between colonialism and 'indigeneity' was contested. Based on pressure by indigenous groups, the Declaration does not contain a definition of 'indigenous peoples'. In 1986, José Martínez Cobo, former Special Rapporteur of the Sub-Commission on Prevention of Discrimination and Protection of Minorities, had linked the notion to 'indigenous communities, peoples and nations' which have 'a historical continuity with pre-invasion and pre-colonial societies'.[398] This understanding was criticized for its Western bias, namely its strong link to colonialism and European settlement or invasion. It posed problems in relation to non-settler contexts, such populations in Africa or Asia, where it is difficult to decide whether certain communities 'would be more "aboriginal" or "native"' than others.[399] In a landmark opinion on the Declaration, the African Commission on Human and Peoples' Rights stated that the 'pre-colonial' or 'pre-settler' requirement would not make sense in relation to Africa, since Africans were continuously 'natives' and not defined in contradistinction to settler majorities. It stated:

---

[392] Article 46(3).

[393] Irene Watson, 'First Nations and the Colonial Project' (2016) 1 *Inter Gentes* 30–39, 33.

[394] Shea Esterling, 'Legitimacy, Participation and International Law-Making: "Fixing" the Restitution of Cultural Property to Indigenous Peoples' in Karen N. Scott and others (eds.), *Changing Actors in International Law* (Leiden: Brill, 2020) 158–184, 179–180.

[395] Naomi Mezey, 'The Paradoxes of Cultural Property' (2007) 107 *Columbia Law Review* 2004–2046, 2005–2006.

[396] Geismar, 'Cultural Property, Museums, and the Pacific', 119.

[397] Jeremy Beckett, 'Returned to Sender: Some Predicaments of Reindigenisation' (2012) 82 *Oceania* 104–112.

[398] José Martínez Cobo, 'Study on the Problem of Discrimination against Indigenous Populations' (7 July 1986) E/CN.4/Sub.2/, para. 379.

[399] Jérémie Gilbert, 'Indigenous peoples' human rights in Africa: The pragmatic revolution of the African Commission on Human and Peoples' Rights' (2011) 60 *International and Comparative Law Quarterly* 245–270, 250.

[I]n Africa, the term indigenous populations does not mean 'first inhabitants' in reference to aboriginality as opposed to non-African communities or those having come from elsewhere. This peculiarity distinguishes Africa from the other Continents where native communities have been almost annihilated by non-native populations.[400]

The definition of who counts as 'indigenous peoples' under the Declaration is thus derived from certain criteria (self-identification, historical continuity, special relationship with ancestral land, distinctiveness, non-dominance, perpetuation),[401] which may apply to a variety of contexts.[402] This approach offers flexibility, but leaves recognition of 'indigeneity' in many contexts de facto still in the hands of states.

UNDRIP contains a number of advances in relation to 'cultural indigeneity'.[403] It pursues a holistic vision of culture, which acknowledges that trade and economic interests find limits in the way of life of indigenous people[404] and 'collective rights which are indispensable for their existence, well-being and integral development as peoples'.[405] Cultural rights are not only linked to specific rights, such as the 'right to maintain, control, protect and develop … cultural heritage, traditional knowledge and traditional cultural expressions',[406] but underpin notions of property, self-determination and other rights under the Declaration.[407] They reflect an indigenous conception of culture.[408] As the Inter-American Court of Human Rights has emphasized, this vision of culture is connected

[t]o a particular form of life of being, seeing, and acting in the world, constituted through their close relationship with their traditional lands and the resources that are found therein, not only since these are their primary means of subsistence, but

---

[400] African Commission on Human and Peoples' Rights, Advisory Opinion on the UN Declaration on the Rights of Indigenous Peoples', 41st Ordinary Session, Accra, Ghana (May 2007) para. 13.

[401] UN Permanent Forum on Indigenous Issues, Fact Sheet, (21 October 2007).

[402] In the Endorois case, the African Commission relied on four elements: '[T]he occupation and use of a specific territory; the voluntary perpetuation of cultural distinctiveness; self-identification as a distinct collectivity, as well as recognition by other groups; an experience of subjugation, marginalisation, dispossession, exclusion or discrimination.' See African Commission on Human and Peoples' Rights, *Centre for Minority Rights Development (Kenya) and Minority Rights Group International on behalf of Endorois Welfare Council v Kenya,* Communication 276/2003, 4 February 2010, para. 150.

[403] Kuprecht, *Indigenous Peoples' Cultural Property Claims,* 91.

[404] Ibid, 52.

[405] UNDRIP, preamble.

[406] Article 31.

[407] Siegfried Wiessner, 'The Cultural Rights of Indigenous Peoples: Achievements and Continuing Challenges' (2011) 22 *EJIL* 121–140, 129.

[408] The International Law Association noted in its 2012 Resolution on Rights of Indigenous Peoples that cultural rights form the 'the core of indigenous cosmology, ways of life and identity, and must therefore be safeguarded in a way that is consistent with the perspectives, needs and expectations of the specific indigenous peoples'. See ILA Resolution No. 5/2012, Rights of Indigenous Peoples, para. 6.

also because they constitute an integral element of their cosmic vision, religion, and, therefore, of their cultural identity.[409]

The Declaration provides space for a distinct understanding of cultural property of indigenous peoples.[410] It respects alterity, namely the right of indigenous peoples to 'consider themselves different'.[411] It recognizes the inherent rights of indigenous peoples deriving 'from their political, economic and social structures and from their cultures, spiritual traditions, histories and philosophies, especially their rights to their lands, territories and resource'[412] and requires states to give 'due consideration to the customs, traditions, rules and legal systems of the indigenous peoples concerned' in the assessment of 'infringements of their individual and collective rights'.[413] This makes it possible to consider different world views in relation to cultural property, such as communal or spiritual bonds, rather than material or individual ownership relations, common in market mechanisms.[414] Such an understanding, enabling *sui generis* approaches towards restitution of indigenous cultural property, based on links between culture and natural resources, has inter alia been recognized in the jurisprudence of the Inter-American Court of Human Rights.[415]

UNDRIP challenges the idea that cultural takings from indigenous people can be justified by structures of subordination. It does not require indigenous people to establish classical ownership relations in order to seek 'restitution' of 'cultural, intellectual, religious and spiritual property taken without their free, prior and informed consent or in violation of their laws, traditions and customs'.[416] However, the regime governing return of cultural property remains marked by concessions and compromise. Indigenous people advocated for the recognition of a full-fledged right to restitution of indigenous people.[417] An initial draft article, affirmed a 'right to repatriation' of all 'cultural, intellectual, religious and spiritual property taken without their free and informed consent or in violation of their laws, traditions and customs'.[418] It was 'watered down' in the negotiations. The final text of the

---

[409] See IACtHR, *Yakye Axa Indigenous Community v Paraguay*, Judgment of 17 June 2005, (Series C) No 125 (2005), paras. 131, 135.

[410] Kuprecht, *Indigenous Peoples' Cultural Property Claims*, 45, 46.

[411] Preamble, para 2.

[412] Ibid, para. 7.

[413] Article 40.

[414] Kuprecht, *Indigenous Peoples' Cultural Property Claims*, 54.

[415] See IACtHR, *Mayagna (Sumo) Awas Tingni Community v Nicaragua*, Judgment (31 August 2001) (Series C) No. 79 (2001), paras. 149, 151.

[416] Article 11(2). See also Kuprecht, *Indigenous Peoples' Cultural Property Claims*, 68.

[417] They proposed an article recognizing the 'right to full restitution of and reparation for cultural, artistic, religious and spiritual property, including the mortal remains of their ancestors of which they have been deprived without their free consent and in violation of their customary law'. Luis-Enrique Chávez, Report of the working group established in accordance with Commission on Human Rights resolution 1995/32, UN Doc E/CN.4/2001/85, Annex III, 38.

[418] Draft United Nations Declaration on the Rights of Indigenous Peoples, UN Doc E/CN.4/Sub.2/1994/56, Art. 12.

Declaration differentiates between different categories of objects. It reflects earlier prioritizations by Special Rapporteur Erica-Irene Daes, who had distinguished a firm duty ('must') to return 'human remains and associated funeral objects' to 'their descendants and territories' from a more flexible return obligation ('wherever possible') of other 'moveable cultural property' to its traditional owners.[419] The provisions of the Declaration on return and repatriation remain ambiguous in relation to state obligations.[420]

UNDRIP explicitly recognizes a 'right' of indigenous people to 'the repatriation of their human remains'[421] and a 'right to the use and control of their ceremonial objects'.[422] They are part of a general right 'to manifest, practise' or 'develop' their 'spiritual and religious traditions, customs and ceremonies'.[423] But the corresponding state obligation is weak. It requires states merely to 'seek to enable the access and/or repatriation of ceremonial objects and human remains in their possession'.[424] It leaves leeway for states to adopt other approaches in relation to ceremonial objects, such as loans or joint forms of ownership.[425]

For other types of cultural objects, such as cultural artefacts, and non-material cultural property, the Declaration does not mention an explicit right to return. An earlier reference to a right of restitution of cultural property was dropped. The Declaration provides states discretion on how to remedy takings of 'cultural, intellectual, religious and spiritual property' which were carried without 'free, prior and informed consent' or in violation of the 'laws, traditions and customs' of indigenous people.[426] It mentions 'restitution' as a possible form of redress, but lists it only as one of a number of potential measures, which states may take to comply with the 'right' of indigenous peoples 'to practise and revitalize their cultural traditions and customs'.[427] This approach highlights colonial continuities with previous instruments. It requires indigenous people to 'rely on the good will of states' to obtain restitution.[428]

In practice, UNDRIP is selectively referenced in restitution of cultural property to indigenous peoples, or sometimes misrepresented. For instance, The 2021 German guidelines on 'Care of Human Remains in Museums and Collections'

---

[419] Final report of the Special Rapporteur, Mrs. Erica-Irene Daes, in conformity with Sub-commission resolution 1993/44 and decision 1994/105 of the Commission on Human Rights, E/CN.4/Sub.2/1995/26 (21 June 1995) Revised text of the Principles and Guidelines for the Protection of the Heritage of Indigenous People, 11, paras. 21–22.

[420] Kuprecht, *Indigenous Peoples' Cultural Property Claims*, 77.

[421] Article 12(1).

[422] Ibid.

[423] Ibid.

[424] Article 12(2).

[425] Karolina Kuprecht, 'Human Rights Aspects of Indigenous Cultural Property Repatriation' NCCR Trade Working Paper No. 2009/34, 1–24, 24.

[426] Article 11(2).

[427] Article 11(1).

[428] Esterling, 'Legitimacy, Participation and International Law-Making', 173.

adopted by the German Museum Association, argue that UNDRIP does 'not provide a sufficient basis for actionable claims for restitution'[429] and that 'customary law has so far not established a right to the return of human remains in international law either'.[430] Such findings illustrate the trend to frame broader international obligations in non-committal terms. It marks a 'retrogression' in relation to human rights jurisprudence on repatriation of cultural property[431] and emerging customary law obligations of states to provide cultural restitution to indigenous peoples living on their territory.[432] It introduces a differentiated regime according to classification of objects. It favours repatriation of human remains, where return is often the only viable ethical option, while leaving states greater flexibility of means how to secure access to sacred or cultural objects.

6.3.2 National practices, including lessons from NAGPRA

Return practices have been significantly shaped by national practices and case-by-case approaches. Factors, such as the rise of civil rights movement the 1970s, indigenous activism, or growing acceptance of UNDRIP, have supported claims and returns to indigenous groups.[433] They have stimulated domestic legislation and policies, as well as repatriation practices in settler colonial contexts (e.g. Australia,[434] Canada,[435] New Zealand,[436] South Africa,[437] or the

---

[429] German Museum Association, Guidelines: Care of Human Remains in Museums and Collections (Berlin: German Museums Association, 2021) 105.

[430] Ibid, 106.

[431] Esterling, 'One Step Forward, Two Steps Back', 343.

[432] Kuprecht, *Indigenous Peoples' Cultural Property Claims*, 87–88. See also ILA Resolution No. 5/2012, Rights of Indigenous Peoples, para. 10 which specifies that: 'States must comply with their obligations—under customary and applicable conventional international law—to recognise and fulfil the rights of indigenous peoples to reparation and redress for wrongs they have suffered, including rights relating to lands taken or damaged without their free, prior and informed consent.' On the customary nature of these obligations, see Dalee Sambo Doriugh and Sigfried Wiessner, 'Indigenous People and Cultural Heritage' in Francesco Francioni and Ana Vrdoljak, *Oxford Handbook of International Cultural Heritage Law* (Oxford: Oxford University Press, 2020) 407–430, 425–426.

[433] Cressida Fforde, C. Timothy McKeown, and Honor Keeler (eds.), *The Routledge Companion to Indigenous Repatriation* (London: Routledge, 2020).

[434] Australian institutions developed new policies and approaches towards repatriation of the Ancestral Remains of Aboriginal People and Torres-Strait-Islanders since the 1980s. The Aboriginal Cultural Heritage Act of 25 June 1984 recognized aboriginal ownership of human remains and sacred objects. In 1990, the government established the Aboriginal and Torres Strait Islander Commission. Later, it extended strategies for international repatriation. According to government information, more than 2,700 First Australian ancestors and 2,000 sacred objects have been returned to local communities through repatriation programmes. See Paul Turnbull, 'International Repatriations of Indigenous Human Remains and Its Complexities: the Australian Experience' (2020) 18 *Museum & Society* 6–19.

[435] Canada established a policy on repatriation of human remains and objects of cultural significance in 1992.

[436] In New Zealand, the Protected Objects Act of 19 September 1975 regulates ownership and protection of Mäori culture, history, or society (*ngä taonga tüturu*), as well as return of unlawfully exported or stolen protected cultural objects.

[437] In South Africa, the work of the Truth and Reconciliation Commission drew attention to the fate of human remains and missing persons. See Nicky Rousseau, 'Identification, politics, disciplines: missing persons and colonial skeletons in South Africa' in Élisabeth Anstett and Jean-Marc Dreyfus (eds.), *Human Remains and Identification: Mass Violence, Genocide, and the 'Forensic Turn'*

US[438]). However, successes vary. In cross-border contexts, i.e. claims against states other than settler societies, the lack of international legal frames has impeded returns.[439] States remained reluctant to modify their property law frameworks to take into account perspectives of indigenous peoples. International repatriations have continued to face obstacles, based on national heritage interests, political considerations, countervailing museum interests, or costs associated with return. The UK and European countries have more reluctance to establish frames and processes for returns to indigenous communities and are slower in reacting to claims.

(i) Mixed comparative experiences
In New Zealand, the Museum of New Zealand (*Te Papa Tongarewa*) developed a successful reparation programme (the Karanga Aotearoa Repatriation Programme) for return of Māori and Moriori ancestral remains. It led to over 420 international repatriations from overseas institutions between 2003 and 2017, including museums in Australia, Austria, Canada, France, Germany, Sweden, the United Kingdom, and the US. However, an estimated number of 600 remains are still awaiting decision.[440] In some cases, repatriations were impeded by national legislation. For instance, the French Civil Code states that 'the human body, its elements, and its products cannot be the object of proprietary rights'.[441] However, French Courts held that Māori Head could not be deaccessioned without the consent of the National Scientific Commission on Collections or national legislation.[442] In 2008, the British Museum agreed to return several Māori bones to New Zealand, but refused to repatriate seven tattooed heads (Toi moko) claimed by the museum. It argued that it had a title to retain the heads, since they were produced for trade, and thus 'modified for a purpose other than mortuary disposal'.[443] As Tristram Besterman has noted in his Report to the Board of Trustees of the British Museum, this logic disregarded the context of 'inter-tribal violence that fed the trade':

(Manchester: Manchester University Press, 2015) 175–202. Heritage legislation did not explicit provision for the repatriation of human remains. However, the South African Heritage Resources Agency (SAHRA) was established in 1999 to deal with the repatriation of heritage removed from South Africa.

[438] See Nicole Watson, 'The Repatriation of Indigenous Remains in the United States of America and Australia: A Comparative Analysis' (2003) 8 *Australian Indigenous Law Reporter* 33–44.
[439] Kathryn Whitby-Last, 'Legal Impediments to the Repatriation of Cultural Object to Indigenous Peoples' in Paul Turnbull and Michael Pickering (eds.), *The Long Way Home: The Meaning and Values of Repatriation* (Oxford: Berghahn Books, 2010) 35–47.
[440] Museum of New Zealand, The Karanga Aotearoa Repatriation Programme https://www.tepapa.govt.nz/about/repatriation/karanga-aotearoa-repatriation-programme.
[441] Article 16–1 of the French Civil Code.
[442] Marine Bel, Michael Berger, and Robert K. Paterson, 'Administrative Tribunal of Rouen, Decision No. 702737 (27 December 2007) (Māori Head case) (2008) 15 *International Journal of Cultural Property* 223–226.
[443] Tristram Besterman, 'Why the British Museum Should Give Back Maori Human Remains if It Wants to Take a Truly Enlightened Approach' (2008) 108 *Museum Journal* 17.

The source iwi from whom such trophies were taken not only never consented, but suffered as a result an appalling violation of their beliefs as well as straightforward bloody violence. No-one would be taken seriously today who argued that the sale of slaves from West Africa more than two centuries ago was done with their consent merely because their Black brothers colluded willingly in the trade by procuring the human merchandise. By analogy, the fact that one Māori tribe traded willingly the Toi moko of their vanquished (or enslaved) brother should not obscure the underlying dispossession and lack of consent of the source iwi.[444]

The argument was part of a broader strategy not to set a precedent for other returns, which is a common pattern in practices concerning return of cultural colonial objects.

The Haida First Nation of British Columbia in Canada managed to secure the repatriation of more than 466 ancestral remains, which were removed in the twentieth century from gravesites in their villages, from museums in Canada and the US. For instance, the American Museum of Natural History returned 34 ancestral remains, which had been taken from Haida graves by British botanist and ethnographer Charles F. Newcombe (1851–1924) between 1897 and 1901. However, repatriations from European museums and private citizens proved to be far more burdensome, in light of the lack of international regulation.

A paradigm example of legal gaps and ambiguities is the dispute over the auctioning of a collection of seventy sacred masks and headdresses of Hopi Native Americans (*katsinam* masks) in France.[445] The collection was assembled by a French collector between 1970 and 2000. The objects were arguable acquired in contravention of the rules and customs of the Hopi, i.e. the Hopi Constitution of 1936. The Hopi people argued in case before the High Court of Paris that their 'tribe' is 'their collective owner' and that the 'objects are inalienable since they are considered by the Hopi as vectors through which the spirits of ancestors communicate with the living'.[446] The judges found that the objects are not inalienable under French law and permitted the auction. The 1970 UNESCO Convention was not considered relevant, based on its non-retroactivity. The Court held that UNDRIP does not prevent the sale by auction because it 'cannot be the legal basis of action taken against a commercial auction house hired by an individual to sell goods that the latter claims to own'.[447] It declared that US law prohibiting the sale of ritual

---

[444] Tristram Besterman, Report to the Board of Trustees of the British Museum (April 2007) 18–19 https://www.britishmuseum.org/sites/default/files/2019-11/00%2022%20Tristram%20Besterman%20 report%20dated%20April%202007.pdf.

[445] Marie Cornu, 'About Sacred Cultural Property: The Hopi Masks Case' (2013) 20 *International Journal of Cultural Property* 451–466.

[446] High Court of Paris, Survival International, V. Nret-Minet, Tessier & Sarrou, RG No. 13/52880, 12 April 2013 in (2013) 20 *International Journal of Cultural Property* 460–465, 461.

[447] Ibid, 464.

objects cannot be invoked, since it is not applicable in France. It declined to equate the masks to human body parts or remains. It stated:

> [W]hile the masks in question may, for people claiming to belong to the Hopi Tribe or practicing the traditional religion to which they are related, have sacred value, be of a religious nature, or embody the spirits of the ancestors of those persons, it is clear that they cannot be likened to human bodies or pieces of the bodies of living or dead persons ... The mere fact that the objects can be described as religious objects, symbols of a faith, or divine or sacred representations does not give them the status of inalienable goods.[448]

The Court disregarded the fact that the masks constituted collective property according to the traditions of the Hopi people. As a result, the only way to break the impasse was to buy some of the masks back. This outcome is open to critique, because it forced the Hopi people to recognize their objects as market commodities and become complicit in their transaction. Such an approach does not empower indigenous groups, 'but rather the trade in cultural artifacts and those who profit from it'.[449] It highlights recurring economic dilemmas in the protection of indigenous rights. Although UNDRIP and domestic legal frameworks have strengthened rights of access and control of indigenous heritage, they are often compromised by 'lack of economic independence' and 'conditional on government funding or development capitalism'.[450]

The repatriation of a Ghost Dance Shirt,[451] taken from the Sioux at the Wounded Knee Massacre on 29 December 1890, counts among the first returns of a European museum to a Native American nation. It was displayed for more than a century in the Kelvingrove museum in Glasgow. The Wounded Knee Survivors Association argued that repatriation was 'the honourable thing to do under the circumstances', because such shirts 'were stolen off dead bodies from a civilian massacre'.[452] The legal case for return was weak, due to the inapplicability of NAGPRA and the 1970 UNESCO Convention. The museum first argued that 'preservation should be continued' since 'the Museum can perform this key educational task both for our local citizens on whose behalf we own the object and for our many British and international visitors'.[453] It later decided to return it to the Lakota people in August 1999, based on the meanings of the shirt to survivors.[454]

---

[448] Ibid, 464.
[449] Matthew H. Birkhold, 'Cultural Property at Auction: The Trouble with Generosity' (2014) 39 *The Yale Journal of International Law Online* 87–93, 90.
[450] Ian J. McNiven and Sean P. Connaughton, 'Cultural Heritage Management and the Colonial Culture' in Claire Smith (ed.), *Encyclopedia of Global Archaeology* (Berlin: Springer, 2018) 1–9, 7.
[451] Sam Maddra, 'The Wounded Knee Ghost Dance Shirt' (1996) 8 *Journal of Ethnography* 41–58.
[452] Ibid, 55.
[453] Ibid, 52.
[454] Christian Feest, 'Glasgow Ghost' (2000) 14 *European Review of Native American Studies* 50–52, 52.

(ii) NAGPRA

Some important lessons for repatriation may be drawn from NAGPRA. It is one of
the first legislative instruments that made the return of human remains binding. It
was enacted in 1990 to enable Native Americans to regain access and control over
human remains and cultural artefacts. It has a double purpose, namely to provide
First Nations with an 'opportunity to redress the wrongs of past centuries perpetrated by the dominant culture and to regain control over the past so as to build a future', and to encourage museum to re-examine past collection practices and revisit
'methods for continuing to collect data'.[455]

NAGPRA regulates the repatriation of Native American human remains and
objects (funerary objects, sacred objects, or objects of cultural patrimony) held by
US Federal agencies and museums.[456] It makes it clear that takings of human remains and cultural objects cannot be judged according to historical titles applicable during their acquisition, but require new solutions. It obliged agencies and
museums to make an inventory of Native American human remains and associated funerary objects and determine their 'cultural affiliation'[457] and has incentivized the creation of compliance structures.[458]

NAGPRA builds on the findings of the 1979 study of the Interior Federal Agencies
Task Force, which found that many indigenous objects were stolen or acquired
from persons who lacked title or authority to alienate them.[459] The legal framework
stands in the tradition of the 'civil rights' movement in support of First Nations.[460]
The main innovation of NAGPRA is that it treats human remains, 'objects of cultural
patrimony' and 'sacred objects' in principle as items which are inalienable from their
original owners. It starts from the premise that there is a general duty ('shall') 'to repatriate remains, funerary objects, sacred objects or objects of cultural patrimony
to culturally affiliated Native Americans or Native Hawaiian organizations'.[461] It
thereby takes into account that historical transactions were flawed and that 'culturally affiliated persons or groups remained the rightful owners of Native American
objects, despite any transfer and until proven otherwise'.[462] It forced agencies and
museums to explore the cultural history of objects. Consultation and integration of
Native American perspectives play a central role in the repatriation process.[463]

---

[455] Fred A. Morris, 'Law and Identity: Negotiating Meaning in the Native American Graves
Protection and Repatriation Act' (1997) 6 *International Journal of Cultural Property* 199–230, 203.

[456] NAGPRA, § 3005.

[457] Ibid, § 3003.

[458] Agencies or museums which do not comply with obligations may face civil penalties or fines.

[459] US Secretary of the Interior Federal Agencies Task Force, American Indian Religious Freedom
Act Report (August 1979).

[460] Karolina Kuprecht, 'The Concept of Cultural Affiliation in NAGPRA: Its Potential and Limits
in the Global Protection of Indigenous Cultural Property Rights' (2012) 19 *International Journal of
Cultural Property* 33–64, 44.

[461] NAGPRA, § 3005(1) and (2).

[462] Kuprecht, 'The Concept of Cultural Affiliation in NAGPRA', 42.

[463] NAGPRA, § 3005(3).

Through its reliance on 'cultural affiliation', NAGPRA has placed strong emphasis on the ongoing connection between objects and Native American culture, namely a 'relationship of shared group identity that may be reasonably traced historically or prehistorically between a present-day Indian tribe or Native Hawaiian organization and an identifiable earlier group'.[464] It requires (i) the 'existence of an identifiable present-day Indian tribe or Native Hawaiian organization', (ii) 'evidence of the existence of an identifiable earlier group' and (iii) 'evidence of the existence of a shared group identity that can be reasonably traced between the present-day Indian tribe or Native Hawaiian organization and the earlier group'.[465] Claims relating to cultural patrimony have thus primarily, though not exclusively, depended on demonstration of an 'ongoing historical, traditional, or cultural importance central to the Native American group or culture itself'.[466] The protection of sacred objects, other than funerary objects, was linked to 'ceremonial use' by 'present day adherents'.[467]

This application of the 'cultural affiliation' criterion has posed obstacles in practice. It has impeded repatriation of human remains which were deemed to be culturally unidentifiable by, including funerary objects, which were often retained by museums. Initially, NAGPRA did not provide a solution for cases in which no cultural affiliation is possible.[468] This gap became evident in the case of the Kennewick Man. It was closed through later regulation. Museums and agencies were obliged to transfer control to 'tribes that are recognized as aboriginal to the area' or to 'other Indian tribes or Native Hawaiian organizations'.[469] NAGPRA enabled Native Americans to request repatriation of 'sacred objects and objects of cultural patrimony' based on previous ownership or 'control'[470] over the object.[471] It identified several principles of allocation for repatriation to 'lineal descendants of the Native American'.[472]

NAGPRA sought to mitigate problems of 'cultural affiliation' through flexible means of proof to establish. It involves a partial reversal of the burden of proof, in light of the context. It enabled Native Americans to make a prima facie case of cultural affiliation, but then shifted the burden to the relevant agency or museum. It specified that these entities are obliged to 'return such objects' unless it

---

[464] Code of Federal Regulations, Title 43, § 10.14(c).

[465] Ibid.

[466] Ibid, § 3001(3)(D).

[467] NAGPRA, § 3001(3)(C).

[468] Sarah Harding, 'Bonnichsen v. United States: Time, Place, and the Search for Identity' (2005) 12 *International Journal of Cultural Property* 249–263.

[469] Code of Federal Regulations, Title 43, § 10.11(c).

[470] See Kuprecht, *Indigenous Peoples' Cultural Property Claims*, 67.

[471] NAGPRA, § 3005(5).

[472] It clarified that funerary objects, sacred objects, and objects of cultural patrimony, and remains whose descent cannot be identified, should in principle be allocated to tribes and organizations on 'whose tribal land such objects or remains were discovered' or those with 'the closest cultural affiliation'. NAGPRA, § 3002 (a).

'can overcome such inference' and 'prove that it has a right of possession to the objects'.[473] Rationales of scientific study can be invoked to postpone repatriation, but do not provide a justification to deny return.[474]

NAGPRA shows a general openness to establish proof through indigenous customs and traditions.[475] In practice, 'cultural affiliation' can be shown through 'oral tradition' or different types of bonds, including geographical proximity, kinship, anthropological, or linguistic relations, or folklore.[476] It does not have be established by 'scientific certainty', but merely requires 'preponderance of the evidence'.[477] This approach allowed reliance on hearsay evidence. It enabled repatriation even in cases where the bond was not yet recognized in scientific study. However, it has encountered challenges in situations where First Nations remained reluctant to share religious beliefs and customs publicly,[478] or in cases of conflicting oral histories.[479]

The resolution of competing claims has posed difficult issues of prioritization and evaluation of evidence in the determination of cultural affiliation. NAGPRA allows the agency or museum to retain such objects, if their allocation cannot be determined by consent, through dispute resolution or a court ruling.[480] But they are first required to determine the 'most appropriate claimant'[481] based on an 'overall evaluation of the totality of the circumstances and evidence pertaining to the connection between the claimant and the material being claimed'.[482] This is a politically sensitive issue. It requires public entities to decide claims, based of competing versions of oral histories and their persuasiveness.

The challenges became evident in the dispute over the repatriation of three painted Buffalo shields, found in 1926 by entrepreneur Ephraim Portman Pectol in Capitol Reef National Park in Utah (so-called 'Pectol Shields').[483] Their origin was disputed since their discovery. The Pectol family sought to preserve the shields in the museum of the Capitol Reef National Park for the common benefit.[484] However, in 2001, the Navajo Nation claimed their repatriation, based

[473] Ibid, §3005 (c).

[474] Ibid, § 3005 (b).

[475] Kuprecht, *Indigenous Peoples' Cultural Property Claims*, 57.

[476] Code of Federal Regulations, Title 43, § 10.14(e). On jurisprudence, see Rachel Awan, 'Native American Oral Traditional Evidence in American Courts: Reliable Evidence or Useless Myth?' (2014) 118 *Dickinson Law Review* 697–727.

[477] Code of Federal Regulations, Title 43, § 10.14(f).

[478] Robert Paterson, 'Ancestral remains in Institutional Collections' in Catherine Bell and Robert Paterson (eds.), *Protection of First Nations Cultural Heritage: Laws, Policy, and Reform* (Vancouver: UBC Press, 2009) 155–180, 173.

[479] Debora L. Threedy, 'Claiming the Shields: Law, Anthropology, and the Role of Storytelling in a NAGPRA Repatriation Case Study' (2009) 29 *Journal of Land, Resources & Environmental Law* 91–119.

[480] NAGPRA, § 3005(e).

[481] Ibid.

[482] Code of Federal Regulations, § 10.14(d).

[483] Threedy, 'Claiming the Shields', 91.

[484] Robert S. McPherson, 'Seeing Is Believing: The Odyssey of the Pectol Shields' (2008) 76 *Utah Historical Quarterly* 357–376, 374–375.

on their nature as sacred ceremonial objects. This request triggered similar claims by other Native American communities, namely the Ute and Paiute, and the Southern Ute. The Park found the Navajo had the strongest claim. It relied on the testimony of Najavo singer and healer John Holiday, who argued that the shields served to offer protection 'against all things that can harm a person'[485] and were hidden by his grandfather 'Man Called Rope' when the Navajos were under threat of war. The repatriation caused controversy, in light of the limited corroborating evidence for the proof (e.g. 'storytelling')[486] and the refusal of Navajos to agree to their continued display in light of their use in traditional ceremonies.[487] Navajo archaeologists argued that NAGPRA expressly allows oral history as valid form of evidence under NAGPRA, even if it is not backed by recognized scientific evidence in order to take into account Native American practices and diverse forms of knowledge.[488]

In 2022, the Department of the Interior proposed significant changes to address NAGPRA critiques by Native American communities.[489] The proposals are meant to strengthen the role of indigenous way of knowing. They require museums and Federal agencies to 'defer to the customs, traditions, and Native American traditional knowledge of lineal descendants' in the definition of 'sacred' and 'cultural patrimony'.[490] They expressly recognize collectively held objects as Native American cultural patrimony. Based on comments and preferences by local stakeholders,[491] they also propose to replace the problematic notions of 'cultural affiliation' and 'culturally unidentifiable' by a broader concept of 'affiliation', based on geographical connection (e.g. proximity to an area inhabited by ancient Native American communities).[492]

Although NAGPRA seeks to remedy historical wrongs inflicted on Native Americans, it has several limitations. Its scope of application is focused on the

---

[485] John Holiday and Robert S. McPherson, *A Navajo Legacy: The Life and Teachings of John Holiday* (Norman: University of Oklahoma Press, 2005) 352–353, note 22.

[486] Threedy, 'Claiming the Shields', 110–115.

[487] McPherson, 'Seeing Is Believing', 374.

[488] Andrew Curry, 'Tribal Challenges: How the Navajo Nation is Changing the Face of American Archaeology' (2005) 58 *Archaeology* 57–67, 67.

[489] US Department of the Interior, Office of the Secretary, RIN 1024-AE19, Native American Graves Protection and Repatriation Act Systematic Process for Disposition and Repatriation of Native American Human Remains, Funerary Objects, Sacred Objects, and Objects of Cultural Patrimony, 43 CFR Part 10, Proposed Rule, Federal Register, Vol. 87, No. 200 (18 October 2022) 63202–63260, at https://public-inspection.federalregister.gov/2022-22376.pdf.

[490] Proposed Rule, Subpart A, § 10.1(a) Federal Register Vol 87, No. 200, 63237. 'Native American traditional knowledge' is deemed to include 'cultural, ecological, religious, scientific, societal, spiritual, and technical knowledge'.

[491] Jenna Kunze, 'Department of Interior Proposes Overhaul of NAGPRA' *Native News Online* (13 October 2022).

[492] US Department of the Interior, Office of the Secretary, RIN 1024-AE19, arguing that the definition of affiliation 'without the qualifier of "cultural" better aligns with Congressional intent, and addresses concerns raised during consultation with Indian Tribes and NHOs about implementing the term "geographical affiliation" separately from cultural affiliation'. For a critique, see *Cultural Property News*, 'NAGPRA: Major Changes Proposed for 2023 to Native American Repatriation Law' (8 January 2023).

'unique relationship between the Federal Government and Indian tribes and Native Hawaiian organizations'. It is not construed 'to establish a precedent with respect to any other individual, organization or foreign government'.[493] It does not cover acquisitions by private entities. This means that historical takings of 'objects', which found their way in private property, are largely left unaddressed, except in the case of trafficking of human remains.[494] The legal regime is tied to the particular context of US settler injustice[495] and the relationship between the US legal order and First Nations. It can thus only be transposed to a limited extent to repatriation claims in relation to objects held outside the United States or general practice under UNDRIP. NAGPRA's focus on tribal nations has raised problems of double standards in relation to the treatment of the human remains of African Americans, including former slaves and their descendants, whose bodies were taken from graves and used for scientific purposes.[496]

Inevitably, NAGPRA has faced critiques from multiple perspectives. Archaeologists have argued that NAGPRA created 'an archaeology without people'.[497] NAGPRA required First Nations to review large inventories of objects and material and revive ceremonies for reburial of remains. This prolonged returns and created spiritual conflicts. Some voices continue to question the validity and objectivity of tribal oral histories.[498] They claim that that reliance on indigenous ontologies or returns may compromise 'objective' knowledge production[499] or entail a reinvention or fabrication of traditions, which romanticize the past, by presenting 'pre-contact America' as 'a paradise'.[500]

---

[493] NAGPRA, § 3010.

[494] NAGPRA protects 'native' ownership over competing private property titles in cases where remains or protected objects were 'excavated or discovered on Federal or tribal lands' after 16 November 1990. See NAGPRA, § 3002. US law penalizes the trafficking of Native American human remains without rights of permission (18 US Code § 1170 (a)) without any time bar. It thereby transforms 'human remains of Native Americans' effectively into inalienable objects. Kuprecht, 'The Concept of Cultural Affiliation in NAGPRA', 51. It also prohibits the trafficking of cultural objects which were obtained in violation of NAGPRA's ownership or repatriation provisions. See 18 U.S. Code, § 1170(b). US courts have found that these two criminalizations cover 'violations by individual traders' in 'an effort to eliminate the profit incentive perceived to be a motivating force behind the plundering of such items'. US Court of Appeals, *United States v Kramer*, 168 F.3d, 1196 (10th Cir., 1999), 1201–1202.

[495] NAGPRA does not grant jurisdiction over international claims. International claims of tribes are facilitated unofficially.

[496] Justin Dunnavant, Delande Justinvil, and Chip Colwell, 'Craft an African American Graves Protection and Repatriation Act' (2021) 593 *Nature* 337–340.

[497] Frances Madeson, 'The Excruciating Legacy of NAGPRA', *Indian Country Today* (13 September 2018).

[498] For instance, in *Zuni Tribe of New Mexico v United States*, the US Court of Claims found that the oral transmission of history and religious observation by the Zuni were of 'evidentiary probity'. See US Court of Claims, *Zuni Tribe of NM v United States*, 12 Cl. Ct. 607 (1987) 616, note 12.

[499] Elizabeth Weiss and James W. Springer, 'Repatriation and the Threat to Objective Knowledge' (2021) 34 *Academic Questions* 64–73.

[500] Elizabeth Weiss and James W. Springer, *Repatriation and Erasing the Past* (Gainesville: University of Florida Press, 2020) 95. See also Ron McCoy, 'Is NAGPRA Irretrievably Broken?' *Cultural Property News* (19 December 2018).

Despite its gaps and challenges, NAGPRA provides valuable experiences for the broader debate on returning cultural objects. It marked a change in consciousness, which 'has helped transform Indian bones from archeological specimens to the remains of human beings'.[501] It challenged the prejudice that the affirmation of the unjust context of historical takings and the recognition of duties of repatriation, based on cultural affiliation, would necessarily lead to a presumed emptying of public collections. The projected 'tabula rasa' effect has not occurred. Repatriations take time.[502] Requests have been filed with care. NAGPRA practices have demystified stereotypes about indigenous traditions, such as the idea that all objects are communally owned or requested back by communities.[503] In some cases, Native Americans have preferred not to request repatriation or to leave objects in the care of public collections.

NAGPRA has provided benefits for museums and federal agencies through the interaction between curators and professionals with First Nations.[504] For instance, the material, information, and histories provided as part of the compilation of inventories or repatriation based on cultural affiliation has increased knowledge or challenged conventional methodologies of provenance research.

NAGPRA has also prompted American museums to take more progressive stances surrounding repatriations or to consider international repatriations.[505] For instance, the National Museum of the American Indian has adopted a repatriation policy which allows the museum to repatriate human remains and cultural items an ad-hoc basis to 'Indian tribes that are not federally recognized and Indigenous communities outside of the United States'.[506] Fears that returns would lead to a loss of objects under the care of Indigenous communities have been countered through stewardship models. One of the successes of NAGPRA is that repatriation has contributed to the emergence of cultural centres and tribal museums, which represent alternative accounts of history or nationhood and strengthen living traditions and cultural practices of Native Americans.[507] In some cases, objects are meant to degrade according to native traditions and communities have been allowed to do so.

---

[501] See Friends Committee on National Legislation, 'Reclaiming Identity: The Repatriation of Native Remains and Culture' (29 September 2016).

[502] Some museums are still finding remains and objects. Complete return would take decades.

[503] Simon Schaffer, 'Get Back: Artifices of Return and Replication' in Adam Lowe (ed.), *The Aura in the Age of Digital Materiality* (Milan: Silvana Editoriale, 2020) 93–100.

[504] Kuprecht, *Indigenous Peoples' Cultural Property Claims*, 66.

[505] One example is the Smithsonian Institution. See Chapter 7.

[506] National Museum of the American Indian, 'Repatriation Policy' (June 2020). It has facilitated returns to Canada, Chile, Cuba, Ecuador, and Peru. See National Museum of the American Indian, '2020 Annual Report, Repatriation Activities of the Smithsonian Institution', 8.

[507] Jennifer Dekker, 'Challenging the Love of Possessions: Repatriation of Sacred Objects in the United States and Canada' (2018) 14 *Collections* 37–62, 42.

7 Conclusions

Throughout much of the twentieth century, legal frameworks governing the taking and return of cultural colonial objects have been marked by colonial and post-colonial continuities. While countries and societies of origin have pushed for re-turn of objects, former colonial powers have actively defended the maintenance of the *status quo* created by the colonial condition. They have relied on techniques of 'distancing', i.e. the separation of the colonial past from present-day relations through temporal barriers, notions concealing wrongdoing, legal gaps and ambi-guities or obstacles to return. 'Distancing' operated in several ways. Legal instru-ments created temporal, spatial, and linguistic boundaries to the past (i) through silencing and exclusion, (ii) rebranding of objects as universal patrimony, and (iii) maintenance of colonial conditions based on market rationales. They indir-ectly perpetuated certain 'structural features of racial capitalism' in relation to cultural colonial objects,[508] namely racialized systems of reference (e.g. 'negro art',[509] 'primitive art'[510]) and continued 'profit-making' throughout decolonization, preserving the wealth and power of Western collectors, art holding countries, or auction houses.

International codification concealed colonial continuities through active silen-cing, limited channels for claims, and framing debates on return in terms of dip-lomacy and ethics, rather than cultural justice, as advocated in GA Resolutions. The inter-state nature of claims made return contingent on negotiation or comity. Countries of origin lacked information on objects in possession in Western collec-tions. Ironically, many objects eligible for return were kept in storages and archives and not actually exhibited, based on the encyclopedic understanding of museums. These practices confirm Trouillot's claim that silences regarding historical injust-ices are not just omissions, but actively constructed through presentations of facts or legal actions.

Legal approaches were influenced by market logics. The very branding of things as 'cultural objects' embodied the ontologies of Western culture. Through removal and public and private collections, many objects were gradually considered as assets, valuable goods, or art, protected for the common benefit of 'civilizations'. The commodification and value increase of objects provided incentives for holder countries to privilege possessors of objects over claimants. Objects were regulated in property categories. They were protected against illicit trafficking or excavation *pro futuro* in order to protect existing collections and trade. Issues relating to the

---

[508] Carmen G. Gonzalez and Athena D. Mutua, 'Mapping Racial Capitalism: Implications for Law' (2022) 2 *Journal of Law and Political Economy* 127–201, 127.

[509] André Salmon, 'Négro Art' (1920) 36 *The Burlington Magazine for Connoisseurs* 164–167, 170–172; James Johnson Sweeney, *African Negro Art* (New York: Museum of Modern Art, 1935) 11.

[510] In the early twentieth century, the notion was associated with authentic objects, 'uncontaminated' by Western civilization or history. See Errington, 'What Became Authentic Primitive Art?', 201.

colonial past were largely left to negotiation and self-regulation. Instruments, such as UNIDROIT, which started to introduce constraints regarding private transactions, were criticized for interfering with economic interests of market countries. Museums asserted duties of care and preservation towards objects in their collections. The market-oriented logic supported deregulation. It facilitated the turn to ethics and soft law instruments, such as resolutions, declarations, guidelines, or codes of conduct (ICOM).

These conservationist approaches and post-colonial continuities have been challenged by non-aligned states and individuals, who articulated alternative visions in regional forums or in the UN in the process of decolonization and the indigenous rights movement, which gained global recognition beyond individual settler colonial contexts since the campaigns in the 1980.[511] It transformed professional practices in museums. It has inter alia drawn greater attention to enduring epistemic violence, such as the racialization of objects in collections.[512] The changes are beginning to affect museum culture and market behaviour. While the violent origin of objects used to enhance their value, it now becomes a form of stigma, which constrains the markets for certain iconic objects, such as Benin bronzes or treasures taken in the Maqdala or Dahomey punitive expeditions.[513]

The limits of economic lenses, and the diversity of interests at stake, are reflected in turn to heritage instruments and the rise of human rights-based protections of cultural objects, which gave new contours to cultural rights and obligations enshrined in universal instruments (Universal Declaration, International Covenant on Economic, Social and Cultural Rights). Cultural heritage law and indigenous rights provided a new vocabulary, language, and legal frame to assert rights of access, control, or return. This is reinforced by regional instruments and practices, which seek to diversify approaches towards heritage and encourage return of objects or human remains.[514] For instance, the Charter for African Cultural Renaissance, adopted in 2006 by the AU, is designed to counter the 'depersonalization of part of the African peoples' and the falsification of African histories through cultural domination in the colonial era[515] and to develop a pan-African perspective on cultural heritage protection. It encouraged African states to promote African cultural values and to 'put an end to the pillage and illicit traffic of

---

[511] Timothy McKeown, 'Indigenous Repatriation: The Rise of the Global Legal Movement' in *Routledge Companion to Indigenous Repatriation*, 23–43.

[512] Paul Turnbull, 'Collecting and Colonial Violence' in *Routledge Companion to Indigenous Repatriation*, 452–468.

[513] See Barnaby Philipps, 'Dealers Say They're Struggling to Sell Looted Art from Africa These Days' *Vice World News* (13 March 2023) https://www.vice.com/en/article/k7ze5n/looted-artefacts-benin-bronzes.

[514] Fiona Batt, 'The Repatriation of African Heritage: Shutting the Door on the Imperialist Narrative' (2021) 5 *African Human Rights Yearbook* 328–350.

[515] See the preamble of the African Charter for Cultural Renaissance, adopted by the Sixth Ordinary Session of the Assembly of the African Union in Khartoum, Sudan (24 January 2006).

African cultural property and ensure that such cultural property is returned to their countries of origin.'[516] It obliged states to take the necessary measures to ensure that 'archives and other historical records which have been illicitly removed from Africa are returned to African Governments.'[517] It has been followed by an ECOWAS Regional Action Plan for the Return of African Cultural Artefacts to their Countries of Origin (2019–2023),[518] the AU Model Law on the Protection of Cultural Property and Heritage[519] and a framework for action for the negotiations of the return of 'illicitly trafficked cultural property from the continent.'[520]

Despite such advances, contemporary frameworks and practices continue to be marked by double standards or gaps. International legal instruments have marginalized the treatment of the taking and return of cultural colonial objects, upheld double standards in relation to Nazi-looted art, and left a considerable amount of discretion and flexibility to states in handling returns (UNDRIP).

There is a striking discrepancy between repatriation of objects to indigenous communities in settler contexts and international repatriation,[521] which is often subject to strict national conditions and governed by state-centric processes. International law provides rights and incentives for return claims, but pays far less attention to the resolution of claims and the implementation of returns. Communities often continue to face obstacles in relation to standing or representation in international repatriation processes. This may lead to reappropriation of cultural heritage by political elites on different sides of the spectrum. Returning states or entities may use return or repatriation as an act of guilt relief in which objects become 'props in a wider redemptive ritual.'[522] States on the receiving end may reappropriate objects to reaffirm their national political agendas. For instance, in some cases, Latin American states have claimed the return of objects on behalf of indigenous communities from former colonial powers in order to serve national, rather than indigenous interests.[523] Both the filing of claims and the success of return claims are conditioned by factors, such as the significance of objects, their nexus to violence, political pressure or the existence of related cases.

At the same time, existing frameworks embody a number of valuable approaches, which may provide guidance for newly emerging practices on restitutions and

---

[516] Ibid, Art. 26.
[517] Ibid, Art. 27.
[518] ECOWAS, Validation of ECOWAS 2019/2023 action plan for the return of African cultural property to their countries of origin (12 April 2019) https://ecowas.int/validation-of-ecowas-2019–2023-action-plan-for-the-return-of-african-cultural-property-to-their-countries-of-origin/.
[519] AU, Draft Concept Note for the Continental Consultations on the Restitution of Cultural Property and Heritage (21 December 2021) para. 5 https://au.int/sites/default/files/newsevents/conceptnotes/41219-CN-HHS51640_E_Original.pdf.
[520] Ibid, para. 8.
[521] McKeown, 'Indigenous Repatriation', 23–43.
[522] Philip Batty, 'White Redemption Rituals: Repatriating Aboriginal Secret-Sacred Objects' (2005) 23 Arena 29–36, 35.
[523] Losson, Reclaiming the Remains of the Past, 318–321.

returns. For instance, UNIDROIT's shift from good faith acquisition (*possession vaut titre*) to due diligence duties in case of 'stolen objects' has relevance for colonial contexts.[524] It might be used to set limits on the acquisition of ownership over 'looted objects' in auctions, based on dubious provenance and failure to take necessary precautions. UNDRIP's protection of 'cultural indigeneity' provides a compelling justification to require the return of sacred objects and human remains, based on their special significance to affected communities or descendants. Based on the rise of rights of access to culture, returns to sub-state groups are no longer merely a matter of ethics. NAGPRA shows that a shifting of the burden of proof in cases of demonstrated cultural affiliation does not necessarily lead to an emptying of collections or the disappearance of Western museums. It may have positive spin offs in terms of knowledge and understanding or incentivize re-engagement with objects in colonized societies.

The dynamics of return are shaped not only by legal or ethical, but also by economic factors. The economic value of objects, which has partly contributed to the scramble for objects, gains a new role in the contemporary debate on return. For many decades, holding countries have benefited from the cultural and the economic value of objects taken in the colonial period. The current debate on the future of objects is a way to mitigate ongoing economic inequalities caused by colonial exploitation.[525] It may inter alia contribute to the establishment of new heritage collections or infrastructure in the Global South, or generate benefits from tourism or intellectual property rights, which have thus far been reserved to holding countries. In certain cases, restitution or return may constitute a means to counter the process of commodification that objects faced through their taking, display, or commercialization.[526]

---

[524] Campfens, *Cross-Border Claims to Cultural Objects*, 239.

[525] Jen Snowball, Alan Collins, and Enyinna Nwauche, 'Ethics, Values and Legality in the Restoration of Cultural Artefacts: The Case of South Africa' (2021) 28 *International Journal of Cultural Policy* 1–18, 4.

[526] Sara Gwendolyn Ross, 'Res Extra Commercium and the Barriers Faced When Seeking the Repatriation and Return of Potent Cultural Objects' (2016) 4 *American Indian Law Journal* 297–389.

8

Acknowledging the Past, Righting the Future: Changing Ethical and Legal Frames

1 Introduction

> You whispered to me, 'Take me back where I belong', Amongst my kith and kin, Away from the soft whispers, Of words spoken in German, French, Dutch and ... Words spoken too often and yet still unfamiliar.
>
> Peju Layiwola, 'I have come to take you home'[1]

'I have come to take you home'. This is the title of a performance delivered by Nigerian artist Peju Layiwola in November 2021 at the Rautenstrauch-Joest-Museum in Cologne during the exhibition 'RESIST! The Art of Resistance'. The title is borrowed from Diana Farrus' poem in honour of Sarah Baartman,[2] whose remains were returned from France in 2002 after 170 years of display in anthropological museums. This time, the call for return referred to the Benin bronzes taken in 1897 from the Oba of Benin in modern-day Nigeria.

Such calls are representative of a 'paradigm shift' in relation to the treatment of specific cultural colonial objects.[3] In the past years, attitudes towards restitution and return have undergone a quiet revolution. Drawing on data from Google Scholar, Google Search, and Twitter, Open Restitution Africa has traced a significant growth of discourse on African Heritage Restitution in professional and public media between 2016 and 2021, which has contributed to a 'more affirmative response to returns'.[4] Traditional justifications for retaining objects obtained through colonial violence 'are beginning to wear thin'.[5] The shift in practices is a result of a number of

---

[1] Peju Layiwola, 'I Have Come to Take You Home' Rautenstrauch Joest Museum, Cologne (24 November 2021).

[2] See Chapter 5.

[3] Alexander Herman, *Restitution: The Return of Cultural Artefacts* (London: Lund Humphries, 2021); Sylvester Okwunodu Ogbechie, 'Momentum Builds for the Restitution of African Art' (2019) 118 *Current History* 194–196.

[4] Molemo Moiloa, Open Restitution Africa, *Reclaiming Restitution* (August 2022) 12.

[5] Herman, *Restitution: The Return of Cultural Artefacts*, 15.

Confronting Colonial Objects. Carsten Stahn, Oxford University Press. © Carsten Stahn 2023.
DOI: 10.1093/oso/9780192868121.003.0008

factors: not only change 'from within museums',[6] but enduring resistance to racial injustices[7] and ongoing effects of colonial takings by states and diaspora communities, greater publicity and public consciousness, generational change, and processes of 'multidirectional memory',[8] opening new space for debates on decolonization, and bottom-up institutional approaches promoting social transformation. Social media and digital imagery make it harder to hide objects in collections, silence violent histories of taking or invoke pretexts or delay tactics. Transparency makes the continuing nature of violence more apparent. The possibility to reconnect to objects is crucial for both the identities and histories in the Global South and the transformation of knowledge and the confrontation of the colonial past in European societies. Countries, such as France, the Netherlands, Germany, or Belgium have started to issue new guidelines or principles on the treatment of objects acquired in colonial contexts, while others (e.g. Austria) are contemplating regulatory reform to deal with returns. These developments are complemented by changing ethical policies of museums in the US[9] or Europe.[10] With the establishment of museums, like the Museum of Black Civilizations in Dakar, the National Museum in Kinshasa, or the planned Edo Museum of West African Art in Benin City and the Great Museum of Africa in Algiers, traditional cultural internationalist objections to return, such as the absence of museums or lack of a proper maintenance culture, become more difficult to sustain.[11] The relational approach to ethics,[12] promoted in the Sarr and Savoy report, has challenged traditional objections to return, resulting from divides between cultural nationalism and cultural internationalism. It has defined 'restitution' as a 'way to open a pathway toward establishing new cultural relations' based on a new ethical relation.[13] For some objects, like the Benin bronzes,

---

[6] Tifany Jenkins, 'From objects of enlightenment to objects of apology: why you can't make amends for the past by plundering the present' in Jill Pellew and Lawrence Goldman (eds.), *Dethroning Historical Reputations: Universities, Museums and the Commemoration of Benefactors* (London: Institute of Historical Research, 2018) 81–92, 84.

[7] In June 2020, protesters sought to 'liberate' objects from the Quai Branly Museum in order to return them. See also Wazi Apoh and Andreas Mehler, 'Introduction: Issues of Restitution and Repatriation of Looted and Illegally Acquired African Objects in European Museums' (2020) 7 *Contemporary Journal of African Studies* ix–xii, ix ('The ideologies that underlie the #BlackLivesMatter also buttress the quest to free and regain the looted African objects that are currently held in Euro-American museums').

[8] Michael Rothberg, *Multidirectional Memory: Remembering the Holocaust in the Age of Decolonization* (Stanford: Stanford University Press, 2009.)

[9] For example, the Smithsonian Institution has developed a new ethical policy. The US-based Arts Council of the African Studies Association has established a working group related to restitution and return.

[10] See later in this chapter.

[11] Fiona Batt, 'The repatriation of African heritage: shutting the door on the imperialist narrative' (2021) 5 *African Human Rights Yearbook* 328–350.

[12] The turn to ethics has an established tradition in relation to holocaust restitution. See Karin Edvardsson Björnberg, 'Historic Injustices and the Moral Case for Cultural Repatriation' (2015) 18 *Ethical Theory and Moral Practice* 461–474.

[13] Felwine Sarr and Bénédicte Savoy, *The Restitution of African Cultural Heritage: Toward a New Relational Ethics* (Drew S.Burk tr, Paris: Ministère de la culture, 2018) 29, at https://www.about-africa. de/images/sonstiges/2018/sarr_savoy_en.pdf

there is almost a race for return across museums,[14] in order to make up for decades of lack of transparency, indifference, or inaction.

The turn to ethics has enjoyed support on the international plane since it offers certain advantages over legal frames in relation to the treatment of historical injustices.[15] Ethical categories provide an opportunity take a broader perspective on justice than legality. They are important since only a small number of objects in public collections are officially recorded as looted or acquired under duress.[16] They are able take into account structural injustices exceeding law, apply more flexible procedures and facilitate broader solutions, including approaches which accommodate interests in colonized societies and former colonial powers.[17] They may enable the return of objects in cases where *bona fide* arguments protect the title of acquisition of objects under national law against former owners. At the same time, ethical criteria have drawbacks from the perspective of reparative justice.[18] They may conceal responsibility for historical wrongdoing, perpetuate power inequalities or post-colonial continuities in the framing and narratives of return policies, treat returns as cosmetic rituals of self-purification and guilt relief or sideline continuing epistemic dilemmas, such as the silences or memory loss caused by the hiding of objects in inaccessible storerooms or boxes[19], the presentation of objects through their colonial collectors, rather than their authors, or the failing identification of human remains.[20]

---

[14] In the UK, the University of Aberdeen and Jesus College at the University of Cambridge were the first institutions which officially restituted Benin bronzes. In the US, the Metropolitan Museum of Art and the Smithsonian Institution in Washington agreed to return Benin objects. See Carsten Stahn, 'Beyond "To Return or Not To Return"—The Benin Bronzes as a Game Changer?' (2022) 8 *Santander Art and Culture Law Review*.

[15] Law operates in binaries. It uses either/or distinctions (lawful/unfawful), prescriptive criteria or produces winners and losers.

[16] Many collections claim their objects were lawfully acquired. For instance, in Belgium or the Netherlands, only a fraction of objects were marked as looted, based on available evidence.

[17] Ethical frames make it easier to take into account uncertainties regarding 'the legal validity of the acquisition', see German Museums Association, *Guidelines for German Museums: Care of Collections from Colonial Contexts* (Berlin: Deutscher Museumsbund, 2021) 153. They may consider structural violence in the taking of objects or contemplate dispute resolution mechanisms, such as restitution committees. See Marie Cornu and Marc-André Renold, 'New Developments in the Restitution of Cultural Property: Alternative Means of Dispute Resolution' (2010) 17 *International Journal of Cultural Property* 1–31.

[18] They have provided a convenient option for states and museums in countries hosting colonial objects to preserve the integrity of their collections, respond to restitution claims on a case-by-case basis and present themselves as moral agents through political returns while avoiding legal recognition of wrong or setting of binding precedents. See Chapter 6. As George Abungu, former director general of the National Museums of Kenya, has argued, the 2002 position on the 'universal museum' plea for universal protection of cultural object marked in fact a refusal 'to engage in dialogue around the issue of repatriation'. George Abungu, 'The declaration: A contested issue' (2004) 57 *ICOM News* 5. It 'remind[ed] the rest of the world of the fact that they have been defeated, oppressed and stripped of their rights'. See Zacharys Gundu, 'Looted Nigerian Heritage – An Interrogatory Discourse around Repatriation' (2020) 7 *Contemporary Journal of African Studies* 47–66, 56.

[19] Fernando Domínguez Rubio, 'Storage as a Form of Violence' (2021) 19 *British Art Studies*, at https://www.britishartstudies.ac.uk/issues/issue-index/issue-19/death-writing-in-the-colonial-museums.

[20] See Chapter 6.

With the growing diversification of cultural heritage law,[21] the status of object is not only governed by ethics, but also by process-related norms and legal requirements in relation to return. They approach protection not merely from the perspective of ownership or legal title, but take into account the structural relation between objects and people, including inter-generational bonds or 'identity' relationships with certain objects.[22] It is thus appropriate to speak not only of an emerging 'moral duty to return the colonial heritage', but 'an ethical responsibility heard in law'.[23] The strict application of the inter-temporal rule, requiring assessment of the legalities of takings solely based on the international law in force at the time of cultural dispossession, has come under challenge.[24] Ethical decision-making processes have become more legalized through greater consideration of procedural justice principles, such as fairness, transparency, access to justice or engagement with claimants. For instance, the criteria for return proposed in new frameworks on cultural colonial objects, such as contexts of acquisition or the cultural significance of objects to countries or communities of origin, are not only grounded in morality or ethics, i.e. the inclination to 'do the right thing', but have a basis in law.[25]

Critics of restitution have challenged the turn to cultural justice based on the argument that atonement for the past may politicize material culture, detract from the original meaning of artefacts, or sensationalize looted objects to the detriment of less visible items. For example, Tiffany Jenkins has argued that justice-related perspectives may reduce artefacts to 'objects of tragedy and apology' and focus perspectives on 'objects and museums as the source of domination, rather than seeing them as institutions and artefacts that reflect wider political and social events of their times'.[26] Some of these risks may be mitigated through by the application of transitional justice principles[27] (e.g. historical truth-seeking,

---

[21] See Chapter 7.

[22] Human rights and indigenous approaches (e.g. UNDRIP) protect the interests of communities to certain objects, irrespective of legal title. They establish consultation requirements or duties to provide access and control to communities, based on their relations to objects or human remains. See Chapter 7.

[23] Independent Group of Experts, 'Ethical Principles for the Management and Restitution of Colonial Collections in Belgium' (June 2021) § 2.3 (Belgian Ethical Principles), at https://restitutionbelgium.be/en/report.

[24] The Dutch 2021 expert report openly questioned whether the 'legal rules made by colonial authorities which were based on a dualistic principle which kept the local populations in conditions of inequality should be the reference point for requests for return assessed today'. Council for Culture, Report, Advisory Committee on the National Policy Framework for Colonial Collections, Guidance on the way forward for colonial collections, 22 January 2021, 60.

[25] The 2021 Belgian Ethical Principles recognizes that the 'return of colonial cultural property to its country of origin not only responds to an ethical requirement of reconciliation, but also constitutes a fundamental legal issue, insofar as this return allows access by the people and communities of origin to their heritage'.

[26] Jenkins, 'From objects of enlightenment to objects of apology', 91.

[27] See Padraig McAuliffe, 'Complicity or Decolonization? Restitution of Heritage from 'Global' Ethnographic Museums' (2021) 15 *International Journal of Transitional Justice* 678–689. On transitional justice and colonialism, see also Ingrid Samset, 'Towards Decolonial Justice' (2020) 14 *International*

access to justice, recognition of the harm, memory or non-repetition) to processes of restitution and return. They are inherently reflected in some reports and principle.[28]

This chapter traces the complex dialectics between ethics, law, and transformation in approaches towards return of cultural colonial objects. It demonstrates how developments in ethics and law challenge the 'standards of the time' argument, i.e. the claim that takings were acceptable according to the ethics or laws of the time. It starts with (i) an analysis of changing ethical frames, including the turn to relational ethics and practices of the International Council of Museums (ICOM), before presenting (ii) different legal models to engage with past and ongoing injustices. It argues that legally return claims may be based on at least three different macro arguments: responsibility for past wrong, complicity in ongoing structures of colonial injustice, and contemporary duties to provide access to cultural heritage, based on subject/object relations. It shows that the dual focus on acknowledgement of the past, and righting the future, challenges the 'fatalistic view' which 'sees the people of today as forever imprisoned by a past that pre-dates their own existence, and encourages them to find refuge in enduring victimhood'.[29] It then proposes (iii) a rethinking of semantics and narratives in order to address continuing elements of epistemic violence caused by colonialism and cultural takings. It claims that the social biography of objects may turn museums into spaces of transitional justice, which have to navigate the violence of the past and the present. It illustrates at the same time some of the inherent limits of law and transitional justice strategies, including their difficulty in confronting certain structural features of colonial violence,[30] as well as critiques of existing frameworks, such as the risk of neutralizing violence or seeking ritual guilt relief and atonement through guidelines.[31]

Journal of Transitional Justice 596–607; Jennifer Balint, Julie Evans and Nesam McMillan, 'Rethinking Transitional Justice, Redressing Indigenous Harm: A New Conceptual Approach' (2014) 8 *International Journal of Transitional Justice* 194–216; Report of the Special Rapporteur on the Promotion of Truth, Justice, Reparation, and Guarantees of Non-Recurrence, 'Transitional justice measures and addressing the legacy of gross violations of human rights and international humanitarian law committed in colonial contexts' UN Doc A/76/180 (19 July 2021).

[28] Some of them make express references to ideas of social transformation or restorative justice, including reconciliation.. For instance, the Executive summary of the Belgian Ethical Principles qualifies restitution as 'part of a wider reconciliation and reparation process'.

[29] Jenkins, 'From objects of enlightenment to objects of apology', 89.

[30] Mohamed Sesay, 'Decolonization of Postcolonial Africa: A Structural Justice Project More Radical than Transitional Justice' (2016) 22 *International Journal of Transitional Justice* 1–18, 8 arguing that even relational accounts of transitional justice 'assume that there is an acceptable normative order to be restored or introduced'.

[31] Dan Hicks, 'UK Welcomes Restitution, Just not Anti-Colonialism' *Hyperallergic* (26 August 2022) https://hyperallergic.com/756241/uk-welcomes-restitution-just-not-anti-colonialism/.

2 Transformation of ethics

Ethical frameworks have a long-standing tradition in the debate on restitution or return. They have shifted considerably over past decades. In the 19th century, individuals, such as Lord Byron or William Gladstone, have challenged the inclusion of cultural important objects in Western collections in the context of the Parthenon marbles or the Maqdala looting.[32] In the twentieth century, ethical-decision-making was for a long time determined by the interests of holders of objects. Some returns were made by colonial representatives or museum professionals prior the 1970s.[33] They were largely based on strategic grounds. With growing critiques of the preservation of artworks in the 'solitude of museums'[34] and the recognition of culture as important means of 'resistance to colonial intrusion' and social and economic development,[35] calls for return increased in the 1970s. ICOM has postulated in 1979 that the 'reassembly of dispersed heritage through restitution or return of objects which are of major importance for the cultural identity and history of countries' is 'now considered to be an ethical principle recognized and affirmed by the major international organizations.'[36] Although anti-colonial ethics were officially promoted in UN circles,[37] the return of colonial objects was largely left to diplomacy, cooperation and professional self-regulation.[38] Returns continued to be approached on an ad hoc basis. They were partly a therapeutic measure for former colonial powers, pursued cultural diplomacy and bilateral negotiations.[39] No ethical principles were developed for colonial collections. The 'Never Again' culture associated with the Holocaust was not transposed to colonial injustice. The treatment of colonial objects was carefully separated from the ethical framework governing cultural takings in the Second World War.[40] Codes of conduct and self-proclaimed ethical guidelines have filled the vacuum left by the absence of

---

[32] See Chapters 2 and 3.

[33] Lars Müller, *Returns of Cultural Artefacts and Human Remains in a (Post)colonial Context* (Magdeburg: Deutsches Zentrum für Kultverluste, 2021) 55–56.

[34] Organization of African Unity, 'Pan-African Cultural Manifesto' (July 1969) (1970) 17 *Africa Today* 25–28, 26.

[35] Ibid, 27.

[36] International Council of Museums, Study on the principles, conditions and means for the restitution or return of cultural property in view of reconstituting dispersed heritages, UNESCO Doc.CC-78/CONF.609/3, Annex 1, para. 38.

[37] See Elazar Barkan argues that UN became the 'basis for a new international morality'. See Elazar Barkan, 'Amending Historical Injustices: The Restitution of Cultural Property—an Overview' in Elazar Barkan and Ronald Bush (eds.), *Claiming the Stones, Naming the Bones: Cultural Property and the Negotiation of National and Ethnic Identity* (Los Angeles: Getty Research Institute, 2002) 16–46, 24.

[38] Cynthia Scott, *Cultural Diplomacy and the Heritage of Empire: Negotiating Post-Colonial Return* (London: Routledge, 2020).

[39] On restitution as therapy, see Elazar Barkan, 'Restitution and Amending Historical Injustices in International Morality' in John Torpey (ed.), *Politics and the Past: On Repairing Historical Injustices* (Lanham: Rowman & Littlefield 2003) 91–102.

[40] See e.g. American Association of Museums, 'Guidelines Concerning the Unlawful Appropriation of Objects during the Nazi Era' (November 1999),

international regulation.[41] Returns were often granted based on self-interest (e.g. honour, benevolence) or convenience, rather than engagement with past wrongs. Former colonial powers returned objects to countries of origins as gifts, in exchange for economic or political cooperation. Morally, such returns provided a means for states to show some good will or foster new relations with former colonized states. However, this action was largely symbolic. The majority of objects was preserved in Western collections.[42]

The idea of the Washington Principles on Nazi-Confiscated Art to ground return in rationales of cultural justice, namely the need to find 'just and fair' solutions to cultural takings in a context of structural injustice, even in the absence of clear international legal norms,[43] was only gradually extended to colonial injustice.[44] It is reflected in legislation on repatriation of indigenous objects[45] or in new national guidelines or specific museum codes on colonial collections. These instruments reflect a broader ethical lens. They often incorporate return criteria, which go beyond moral ideas of honour, solidarity, or compassion, such as acknowledgement of the wrongfulness of past cultural takings or recognition of the link of cultural objects to societies of origin. They include certain common principles in relation to provenance research, relevant return criteria, or approaches towards display. They display more 'victim-centred' methods and frames.

2.1 Divergent approaches

Throughout the twentieth century, many returns have been marked by an absence of recognition of moral or legal responsibility. They were framed as benevolent acts and often driven by geo-political or economic interests of returning states. In this sense, Western powers and holder countries applied some of the 'master's tools' to conceal the detrimental effects of colonial takings. Through voluntary returns of

---

[41] Manlio Frigo, 'Ethical Rules and Codes of Honor Related to Museum Activities: A Complementary Support to the Private International Law Approach Concerning the Circulation of Cultural Property' (2009) 16 *International Journal of Cultural Property* 49–66.

[42] Mireille Lamontagne, 'Museums and Restitution: New Practices, New Approaches' (2015) 30 *Museum Management and Curatorship* 169–171.

[43] The Washington Principles encourage the use of contextualized methods (e.g. consideration of the 'passage of time and the circumstances of the ... era' (Principle 4) and leave space for value judgment in handling claims or alternative dispute resolution for ownership issues. See Principle 11. They have been rightly qualified as a form of 'narrative norm'. See Erik Jayme, 'Narrative Norms in Private International Law: The example of Art Law' (2015) 375 *Collective Courses of the Hague Academy* 9–52.

[44] Jos van Beurden has suggested a similar logic for colonial objects, based on the argument that the relationship to the past requires openness towards 'different interpretations or conceptions of cultural heritage', the roles of museum, the presentation and circulation of objects, and most generally, ' the nature and quality of relations between people and nations'. See Jos van Beurden, *Treasures in Trusted Hands* (Leiden: Sidestone Press, 2017) 241–243, 252–253.

[45] On justifications of NAGRA returns, see Sarah Harding, 'Justifying Repatriation of Native American Cultural Property' (1997) 72 *Indiana Law Journal* 723–774.

objects, they presented themselves as responsible guardians or generous 'givers' of cultural objects, rather than as wrongdoers.

2.1.1 Cultural diplomacy and cooperation

An early illustration is the dispute over the removal of an alligator sculpture by German documentary filmmaker Hans Schomburgk (1880–1967) from the Gola territory in Liberia. Schomburgk argued that he had bought it for a fee of £1,[46] while local chiefs claimed that they had merely authorized him to use it in his movies. When Momolu Massaquoi (1870–1938), the first indigenous Liberian Minister and Consul General in Hamburg started a newspaper campaign to seek return,[47] Schomburgk agreed on return in a court settlement in 1924, in order to protect his professional reputation. In return, he requested to be deemed innocent of all wrongdoing.[48]

On other occasions, returns were offered as symbolic 'gifts' or to protect colonial interests. For instance, in 1907, 1913, and 1938, the Netherlands returned regalia which had been taken during the South Sulawesi expeditions of 1905 in military campaigns against the sultanates of Gowa and Bone.[49] The government decided to return the objects gradually over time to recognize the authority of the new rulers of the sultanates and to facilitate local governmental rule.[50] In 1954, Britain returned the alleged 'Mkwawa head' to modern-day Tanzania in order to secure loyalty for its own colonial administration.[51] In 1957, the UK returned an Asante stool to Ghana in order to honour the country's access to independence.[52] But this was followed by decades of inaction. In the mid-1970s, Belgium and the Netherlands were among the few states which started to return objects more systematically from their collections to former colonies. They framed them as voluntary transfers in order to bring them under the umbrella of cultural cooperation or development aid. Both countries expressly dropped the notion of 'restitution' in bilateral agreements with the Congo and Indonesia and replaced it with the more neutral concept of transfer, in order avoid a fundamental discussion about legal wrong in the

---

[46] Hans Schomburgk, *Zelte in Afrika: eine autobiographische Erzählung* (1931) 412.

[47] Jeff Pearce, *The Gifts of Africa: How a Continent and Its People Changed the World* (Lanham: Prometheus, 2022) 280.

[48] Lars Müller, *Returns of Cultural Artefacts and Human Remains in a (Post)colonial Context* (Magdeburg: Deutsches Zentrum für Kulturverluste, 2021) 18–19.

[49] The objects were placed in the Museum of the Batavian Society and the ethnological museum in Leiden.

[50] Hari Budiarti, 'Taking and Returning Objects in a Colonial Context: Tracing the Collections Acquired during the Bone-Gowa Military Expeditions' in Pieter J. ter Keurs (ed.), *Colonial Collections Revisited* (Leiden: CNWS Publications, 2007) 124–144. On later returns, see Jos van Beurden, 'Hard and Soft Law Measures for the Restitution of Colonial Cultural Collections – Country Report: The Netherlands' (2022) 8 *Santander Art and Culture Law* 407–426.

[51] See Chapter 5.

[52] Sarr and Savoy, *The Restitution of African Cultural Heritage*, 17.

colonial period. In this way, they were able to present themselves as 'well-meaning colonial powers' or legitimate guardians of cultural heritage.

Congo started to request the return of objects after an exhibition of the Tervuren Museum in 1967 on the 'Art of the Congo', which was also shown in museums in North America. In 1976, Congo accepted to receive objects from the reserves in the museum as 'gifts' in order to break the impasse with Belgium which sought to pre-empt any allegation of unlawful removal.[53] Between 1976 and 1982, Belgium offered 114 objects from the Tervuren Museum as gifts to the museum in Kinshasa,[54] without recognizing the contested heritage. The Netherlands agreed with Indonesia in the 1975 joint Recommendations to 'transfer' objects back in order to 'promote cultural cooperation'.[55] This language presented the Netherlands as a 'liberal and generous giver of colonial cultural objects'.[56] The returns included the Prajñāpāramita figure from Singosari and 243 objects taken during the 'punitive expedition' in Lombok in 1894.[57] They were presented as 'successful' examples of returns, but did not openly confront colonial legacies. This future-oriented approach provided a means to move ahead, despite divergent approaches in the past, and to promote future development aid.[58]

Similar economic or geostrategic rationales played a role in iconic returns, such as the return of the Axum Obkelisk.[59] In the 1990s, former French President François Mitterand offered to return ancient royal Korean manuscripts, looted by France in the 'punitive expedition' in 1866,[60] in the context of negotiations of the sale of a French high-speed train (TGV) to South Korea.[61]

Wrongdoing was mainly recognized in processes involving quasi-judicial or judicial settlement, such as the return of the Tūranga Meeting House or the Venus of Cyrene.[62]

The Benin Dialogue Group, a consortium of European museums created in 2010, has spent over a decade negotiating the ownership and display of objects taken from the Oba of Benin. It has for a long time struggled to express a clear commitment to restitution.[63] For instance, the Leiden Statement, issued in 2018, separated the issues of loans and ownership. It stated:

---

[53] Placide Mumbembele Sanger, 'Le restitution des biens culturels en situation (post)colonials au Congo' (2019) 120 *Volkskunde* 459–472.

[54] Van Beurden, *Treasures in Trusted Hands*, 183.

[55] Van Beurden, *Treasures in Trusted Hands*, 155.

[56] Ibid, 168.

[57] Report Advisory Committee on the National Policy Framework, 43.

[58] Scott, *Cultural Diplomacy and the Heritage of Empire*, 170.

[59] See Chapter 4.

[60] See Chapter 3.

[61] Tae-jin Yi and Choong-Hyun Paik, 'The Korean Archives (The Oe-kyujanggak Books)' in Prott, *Witnesses to History*, 300–302.

[62] See Chapter 4.

[63] Folarin Shyllon, 'Benin Dialogue Group: Benin Royal museum—Three Steps Forward, Six Steps Back' (2018) 23 *Art Antiquity and Law* 341–346.

This event occurs within a wider context and does not imply that Nigerian part-ners have waived claims for the eventual return of works of art removed from the Royal Court of Benin, nor have the European museums excluded the possibility of such returns ... Questions of return are bilateral issues and are best addressed with individual museums within their national systems of governance.[64]

2.1.2 Professional self-regulation through ICOM

The 1970 UNESCO Convention encouraged the development of museum ethics. It stated that 'cultural institutions, museums, libraries and archives should ensure that their collections are built up in accordance with universally recognized moral principles'.[65] Ethical parameters for the treatment of cultural objects were not framed through state action in the classical sense, but rather through transnational private regulation. Initiatives to set ethical rules and codes of conduct go back to the first half of the twentieth century.[66] They are not formally legally binding, but operate through 'group pressure' or professional censure.[67] They have played a cen-tral role in regulating market behaviour, establishing obligations towards the pro-fession, nationally and internationally, or consolidating legal standards, beyond national legislation or treaties.[68] They are living documents and continue to be adapted to changing circumstances.

The most famous example is the ICOM Code of Ethics for Museums, which was adopted in 1986 by the General Assembly of the International Council of Museums and periodically updated.[69] It set 'minimum' standards for museums through prin-ciples and guidelines for 'desirable professional practices',[70] which complement international frameworks or fill gaps.[71] ICOM principles established a form of global ethics for the use of collections, including acquisition and de-accessioning of objects. The Code states that museums have 'stewardship' of their collections[72] and an obligation to acquire, preserve and exhibit objects in an ethical way. It stressed the importance of 'rightful ownership'[73]. It requires museums to exercise

---

[64] Statement Benin Dialogue Group, Leiden (19 October 2018) https://www.volkenkunde.nl/en/about-volkenkunde/press/statement-benin-dialogue-group-0.

[65] 1970 UNESCO Convention, 6th preambular paragraph.

[66] An early example is the Athens Charter for the Restoration of Historic Monuments, adopted at the First International Congress of Architects and Technicians of Historic Monuments, Athens 1931.

[67] See Janet Marstine, 'The contingent nature of the new museum ethics' in Janet Marstine (ed.), *Routledge Companion to Museum Ethics: Redefining Ethics for the Twenty-First Century Museum* (London: Routledge, 2011) 3–25, 7.

[68] See Manlio Frigio, 'Codes of Ethics' in Francesco Francioni and Ana Vrdoljak (eds.), *The Oxford Handbook of International Cultural Heritage Law* (Oxford: Oxford University Press, 2020) 787–897, 788.

[69] See ICOM Code of Ethics for Museums (ICOM, 2017).

[70] ICOM Code of Ethics, Preamble.

[71] Art. 7 (2) contains an express reference to obligations under the 1970 UNESCO Convention and the UNIDROIT Convention.

[72] Principle 2.

[73] Art. 2.2.

due diligence in verifying the object's history and provenance, including 'the full history of the item since discovery or production'.[74]

The ICOM framework promoted greater attention to subaltern voices, by recognizing the central role of the interests of source communities in the interpretation and presentation of objects.[75] It mandated museums 'to work in close collaboration with the communities from which their collections originate, as well as with the communities that they serve',[76] through the 'sharing of knowledge, documentation and collections' and 'partnerships with museums in countries or areas that have lost a significant part of their heritage'.[77] The Code sought to decouple return from the political or economic rationales, which have characterized practices in the 1970s. It encouraged an open discussion on the issue. It distinguished returns from restitutions, i.e. objects acquired in 'violation of the principles of international and national conventions'.[78] It states that museums 'should be prepared to initiate dialogue for the return of cultural property to a country or people of origin'.[79] This mandate contrasts with the strict framing of the principle of inalienability of collections in certain jurisdictions (e.g. France, Belgium). It expressly promotes distance from national politics, by clarifying that returns

> should be undertaken in an impartial manner, based on scientific, professional and humanitarian principles as well as applicable local, national and international legislation, in preference to action at a governmental or political level.[80]

The Code preserved at the same time divergent national interests, by leaving museums considerable discretion as to how to handle returns.[81] It specified a number of criteria for the acquisition and care of objects, but failed to define concrete substantive criteria to guide the return of cultural objects or human remains.[82] For instance, it merely states that requests for the return of 'human remains or material of sacred significance from the originating communities' must 'be addressed expeditiously with respect and sensitivity', but does not list criteria and leaves the process up to museums.[83]

---

[74] Art. 2.3. The Code discourages the display of 'unprovenanced' material in order not to 'condone and contribute to the illicit trade in cultural property'. See Art. 4 (5).

[75] See also Arts. 3 (7), 4 (3), and 6 (5).

[76] Art. 6.

[77] Art. 6 (1).

[78] Art. 6 (3).

[79] Art. 6 (2).

[80] Art. 6 (2).

[81] Udo Gößwald, 'ICOM statement on reclaiming cultural property' (2009) 61 *International Museum* 87–90, 88 ('The ICOM Code of Ethics for Museums does not pre-judge any outcomes of cultural property disputes or repatriation claims – except in the case of looting, theft and illicit trafficking, on which its demands for just return are firm and clear').

[82] On the diverse practices, see Louise Tythacott and Kostas Arvanitis (eds.), *Museums and Restitution: New Practices, New Approaches* (Farnham: Ashgate, 2014).

[83] See Art. 4(4) ('Requests for the return of such material should be addressed similarly. Museum policies should clearly define the process for responding to such requests').

In case of objects 'exported or otherwise transferred in violation of the principles of international and national conventions', the Code states that the museum concerned should 'take prompt and responsible steps to cooperate in its return', under the proviso that it is 'legally free to do so'.[84] This has contributed to a perception among former colonized states that 'restitution' is mostly talk without action.

The Code was supplemented in 2013 by a separate ICOM Code of Ethics for Natural History Museums.[85] It provides standards for human remains or sensitive ethnographical material held in such collections, including palaeontological objects.[86] Both instruments prompted multiple national museums to develop their own ethical codes. In some cases, ethical regulation gradually contributed to stricter domestic legislation on illegal traffic of objects.[87]

2.1.3 Paradoxes and contradictions of the 'Universal Museum'

One of most divisive documents is the Declaration on the Importance and Value of Universal Museums. It was signed in 2002 by 18 of the world's leading museums and galleries. It reproduced many of the objections that were voiced against restitution in 1970s curatorial ethics. It establishes a 'firewall' between colonial takings and modern return practices, based on fears regarding the emptying of collections. The Declaration postulates that 'objects acquired in earlier times' cannot be validly judged by contemporary return criteria, since they 'were acquired under conditions that are not comparable with current ones'.[88] It thereby perpetuates colonial amnesia, contrary to the 'agreement not to agree' enshrined in the 1970 UNESCO Convention and the UNIDROIT Convention.[89] It uses a questionable argument to defend the maintenance of objects in 'universal museums'. It derives a title to retention from guardianship and the changing meaning of objects. It states that 'over time' such objects, including those acquired 'by purchase, gift, or partage', have 'become part of the museums that have cared for them, and by extension part of the heritage of the nations which house them.[90] This position prioritizes collective national memory in holder countries over claims relating to return or restitution. It indirectly legitimates the colonial 'salvage' doctrine which justified the title to remove colonial objects by the need to preserve 'dying cultures' from their own demise. It disregards the fact the 'rescue' of an object does not necessarily provide a title for guardian to keep it. It uses the argument of

---

[84] Art. 6(3).
[85] The code was adopted on 16 August 2013 by the 23rd General Assembly of ICOM in Rio de Janeiro. Art 1(g) specifies that repatriation of human remains is 'appropriate where objects still confer a spiritual and/or cultural significance, or where they can be irrefutably demonstrated as being stolen'.
[86] See Chapter 4.
[87] For instance, the adoption of the UK Act on Dealing in Cultural Objects (Offences) of 30 October 2003 was influenced by the due diligence duties under the ICOM Code of Ethics.
[88] Declaration on the Importance and Value of Universal Museums, 2002.
[89] See Chapter 7.
[90] Ibid.

the changing biography of objects to defend contemporary ownership. As Nana Oforiatta-Ayim has powerfully argued, such an approach may entail a double indignation of those affected by cultural takings: 'You kill my parents, and then take objects from me ... when I come to you and say this has been a really traumatic event for me and I want those objects back you say to me, "well they are mine now maybe I'll lend them to you"'[91]

The signing institutions subscribed to the view that 'universal' museums are best placed to decide what 'is best for the subaltern'. This argument stands in conflict with the mandate under the ICOM Code to 'engage in dialogue' and to establish solutions in cooperation with affected communities. As Kavita Singh has noted, the respective museums used universality largely as pretext to 'idolise' themselves and protect their 'own heritage, not the world's'.[92] They defined themselves as the guardians of the past. In what has been labelled as 'cosmocharlatanism',[93] 'High priests' of universalism, such as Neal MacGregor, former director of the British Museum or Philippe de Montebello, former director of the Metropolitan Museum of Fine Arts in New York invoked criteria of access and care to serve the interests of a narrow community of museums,[94] while ignoring that these principles distanced the same objects from many people in the developing world. The Declaration implied that return would conflict with the mandate of museums to 'serve not just the citizens of one nation but the people of every nation'.[95]

In practice, states like France or the UK have used domestic laws protecting national patrimony in order to evade ethical conflicts. The interplay between national patrimony laws and 'universalist' approaches causes moral paradoxes. A compelling example is the dispute over the return of 11 sacred altar tablets, looted by British soldiers during the Maqdala punitive expedition in 1868.[96]

The altar tablets carry spiritual importance in the Ethiopian Orthodox Church. They are replicas of the stone tablets containing the 10 commandments. According to Ethiopian Orthodox tradition, they are only allowed to be viewed by senior clergy. In 2002, St John's Episcopal Church in Edinburgh decided to return one of the carved wooden tabots taken during the Maqdala expedition to

---

[91] Nana Oforiatta-Ayim in Nosmot Gbadamosi, 'Stealing Africa: How Britain Looted the Continent's Art' *Aljazeera* (12 October 2021) https://www.aljazeera.com/features/2021/10/12/stealing-africa-how-britain-looted-the-continents-art.

[92] See Kavita Singh, 'Universal Museums: The View from Below' in Lyndel V. Prott, *Witnesses to History* (Paris: UNESCO, 2009) 123–129, 126.

[93] Andrew McClella, 'Cosmocharlatanism' (2009) 32 *Oxford Art Journal* 167–171.

[94] For instance, Neil MacGregor has argued that exhibition in universal museums 'would allow truths to emerge that could not emerge if the objects were studied only in the context of the objects like them; that is, among only objects from the same culture'. See Neil MacGregor, 'To Shape the Citizens of "That Great City, the World"' in James Cuno (ed.), *Whose Culture?: The Promise of Museums and the Debate Over Antiquities* (Princeton, NJ: Princeton University Press, 2012) 42

[95] It states: 'Although each case has to be judged individually, we should acknowledge that museums serve not just the citizens of one nation but the people of every nation'.

[96] See Chapter 2.

the Ethiopian Orthodox Church.[97] However, the tabots in the British Museum have been locked in a special storage room of the museum for decades. The location has been closed to the public and museum staff. It can be visited only by Ethiopian Orthodox priests. The inaccessibility of the objects runs counter to the mission of the British museum, which justifies its value through transparency and accessibility of objects. Although the tabots are of limited use to the public, the British Museum has opposed a permanent return of these objects. It based its position on the de-accession prohibition in the British Museum Act of 1963, which serves to preserve 'the integrity and global public value of the Collection'.[98] The official museum policy, approved by trustees, established a 'strong legal presumption' against de-accession,[99] except in cases of human remains[100] or Nazi looted art,[101] where de-accession was authorized by law. The museum also refrained from considering a loan to Ethiopia, due to security concerns or fears of seizure.[102]

The moral dilemmas of this position became evident in a parliamentary debate on return in the House of Lords on 30 March 2022. It reflects divisions, which go back to the nineteenth century. Five lords intervened to support the return of the tabots. They correspond to the position of former Prime Minister Gladstone, who had already 'lamented' the taking of the tabots in 1871, because Britain was not 'at war with the people or churches of Abyssinia' and had only an 'insignificant connection' to these 'sacred and imposing symbols'.[103] The moral position in favour of return was most forcefully articulated by Labor Party politician Lord Boateng.

[97] The tabot was taken during the Maqdala expedition from a nearby Christian church (Madhane Alam) and donated to St John by Captain William Arbuthnot (1838–1892), General Robert Napier's Military Secretary, based on its religious importance. It was returned to the Ethiopian Orthodox Church on 27 January 2002. See Returning Heritage, 'Ethiopian Tabot Returned by Edinburgh Church' (3 September 2019) https://www.returningheritage.com/ethiopian-tabot-returned-by-edinburgh-church.

[98] British Museum policy, De-accession of objects from the collection, approved by the Trustees of the British Museum on 29 September 2018, § 2(1).

[99] Ibid, § 3(2).

[100] Section 47 of the Human Tissues Act of 15 November 2004 recognizes the power to de-accession certain human remains to descendants or other persons with sufficient kinship claims.

[101] In 2005, the High Court of Justice has decided in a case concerning Nazi-looted art that moral considerations of trustees cannot override the de-accessioning provisions under the British Museum Act. See High Court of Justice, *Attorney General v Trustees of the British Museum*, [2005] EWHC 1089, 27 May 2005. The government therefore created the Holocaust (Return of Cultural Objects) Act 2009, which allowed the return of certain 'cultural objects on grounds relating to events occurring during the Nazi era' (§ 3).

[102] It envisages a possibility to lend the objects to an Ethiopian Orthodox Church in the UK.

[103] See Mr Gladstone, UK Parliament, 'Abyssinian War- Prize', Hansard, Vol. 207, 30 June 1871. In 2022, this argument was used by Lord Bishop of Worcester. He stated: '[T]hese tabots mean very little to anyone here except as stones of limited historical value, and no one is able to see them anyway, they are of profound religious significance in Ethiopia. Would not the Minister agree that they should therefore be returned to those who understand them to be holy and will cherish them as such?'). See Lord Bishop of Worcester, UK Parliament, 'British Museum: Ethiopian Sacred Altar Tablets', Hansard, Vol. 820, 30 March 2022.

He admitted that the tabots 'were stolen after a brutal, punitive expedition'.[104] He then asked:

> Given that reality and given the fact that they are not able to be seen, venerated or studied by anybody, would it not be the right thing to do—the moral thing to do—and would it not enhance the moral position of the trustees and the British Government in their discussions with the Ethiopian Government about human rights, if they were to be returned without delay?

Lord Parkinson of Whitley Bay, the Parliamentary Under-Secretary of the State for Digital, Culture, Media and Sport (Conservative Party) defended the *status quo* based on their 'complicated provenance'.[105] He conceded that the objects were 'indeed taken by British troops after the expedition', but noted that 'some of the items in the collection were themselves stolen by Tewodros II to assemble the collection in the first place'.[106] This argument reflects the thinking of some British officers at the time of taking. It seems to imply that that it is permissible to 'loot' objects, which have been forcefully acquired by others. He then added: 'The British Museum is looking at the complexity of this issue, talking sensitively to the Ethiopian Church and others to decide the best way of caring for them and reflecting that complex past.'[107]

The exchange shows not only striking historical continuities, but also the disempowering effects of the universalist position. It operates on the assumption that the 'universal museum' is best placed to decide how the objects should be cared for, and how their past can be reflected. This often causes stalemate or paralysis. It becomes a novel means to 'civilize' postcolonial societies.

2.2 The turn to relational ethics

Ethics have taken a new turn with changing visions of the role of museums. Throughout the nineteenth and twentieth centuries, many museum collections ordered and represented objects according to classifications that represented Western-liberal categorizations or perspectives (e.g. individual agency, reason), including colonial world views of civilization in order to define modernity. Tony Bennet has called this the 'exhibitionary complex'.[108] Cultural artefacts were objectified and presented in large and varied collections according to initial colonial knowledge structures, names of colonial missions or collectors or artistic criteria

---

[104] See Lord Boateng, UK Parliament, 'British Museum: Ethiopian Sacred Altar Tablets', Hansard, Vol. 820 (30 March 2022).
[105] Lord Parkinson of Whitley Bay, Hansard, Vol. 820 (30 March 2022).
[106] Ibid.
[107] Ibid.
[108] Tony Bennett, 'The Exhibitionary Complex' (1998) *New Formations* 73–102.

shaped by Western discourses. Museums represented different objects in order to develop particular narratives on peoples and practices or enable connections or comparisons between cultures. The classical idea of the 'universal' or 'encyclopedic' museum,[109] which views the museum as a space to create knowledge and define difference, goes back to the Enlightenment. It has been challenged by critical museum studies,[110] which have questioned the underlying rationales and methodologies to structure ideas of culture, community or race and proposed novel ethical commitments and methods. They have highlighted the dynamic, relative, and 'contingent' nature of ethics[111] which is shaped by a plurality of applied practices,[112] including departures from a 'Western, scientifically based museology'[113] through mixed indigenous/professional curatorial practices, respect of traditional care methods (e.g. in relation to sacred objects), or recognition of the connectivity and interrelatedness of things in cultures of the Americas, the Pacific or the African continent.

2.2.1 Changing conception of the role of museums

The rise of anthropological[114] and post-colonial critiques[115] of museums and increased collaboration between museums and indigenous communities in settler colonial contexts, has inspired moves towards a more reflexive museology in the 1980s and 1990s.[116] This movement has challenged the Eurocentric idea that museums spread and preserve knowledge through collection, storing and description of the role of material objects. It seeks to promote a more inclusive museology, by redefining the museum as space for mutual encounter, engagement, and debate.[117] Christina Kreps has spoken of an 'Age of Engagement'.[118] This strand places greater emphasis on the relational dimensions of education and truth-production and the role of cultural and human rights in curatorial ethics. It reflects greater anthropological sensitivity towards objects and post-colonial critiques of museums.[119] It

---

[109] James Cuno, *Museum Matters: In Praise of the Encyclopedic Museum* (Chicago: University of Chicago Press, 2011); Donatien Grau, *Under Discussion-The Encyclopedic Museum* (2021).

[110] Joshua M. Gorman, 'Universalism and the new museology: impacts on the ethics of authority and ownership' (2011) 26 *Museum Management and Curatorship* 149–162.

[111] Marstine, 'The contingent nature of the new museum ethics', 3–25.

[112] Christina Kreps, 'Appropriate museology and the "new museum ethics"' (2015) 2 *Nordisk Museologi* 4–16, 7.

[113] Ibid, 12.

[114] Richard Handler, 'An Anthropological Definition of the Museum and its Purpose' (1993) 17 *Museum Anthropology* 33–36.

[115] See Iain Chambers, Alessandra De Angelis, Celeste Ianniciello and Mariangela Orabona (eds.), *The Postcolonial Museum: The Arts of Memory and the Pressures of History* (London: Routledge, 2017); Christina Kreps, 'Changing the Rules of the Road: Post-colonialism and the New Ethics of Museum Anthropology' in Marstine, *The Routledge Companion to Museum Ethics*, 70–84.

[116] Adam Kuper, *The Museum of Other People: From Colonial Acquisitions to Cosmopolitan Exhibitions* (London: Profile Books, 2023).

[117] The sixth principle of the ICOM Code of Ethics states that museums should 'work closely with both the communities from which their collections originate and those they serve'.

[118] Christina Kreps, *Museums and Anthropology in the Age of Engagement* (New York: Routledge, 2020).

[119] Kreps, 'Changing the Rules of the Road', 72.

promotes broader curatorial responsibility in order ensure greater representation of stakeholders in the management, use, and presentation of objects[120] and reduce the complicity of collections in the perpetuation of colonial knowledge structures and inequalities. As Tristram Besterman has noted, in this context, museum ethics is increasingly viewed an 'expression of social responsibility' which 'defines the relationship of the museum with people, not with things' and 'helps the museum to navigate through contested moral territory'.[121]

This approach emerged with the growing protection of indigenous culture through instruments, such as the UN Declaration on the Rights of Indigenous People (UNDRIP) or the Native American Graves Protection and Repatriation Act (NAGPRA), which prompted changes in the attitudes toward indigenous people[122] and initiatives to promote the 'decolonization' of museums. They have created greater consciousness regarding the importance of responsible ethical practices.[123] In the late 1990s, James Clifford has challenged the vision of museums as mere 'storage rooms' for colonial artefacts. Building on Mary Louise Pratt's 'concept of contact zones',[124] he has defined museums as space of engagement and promotion of cross-cultural contacts[125] in order to limit one-sided cultural appropriation, counter 'particular histories of dominance, hierarchy, resistance, and mobilization', and support other cultures.[126] In a similar vein, Laura Peers and Alison Brown have pushed for greater recognition of the importance of relational dimensions to source communities in museum practices. They have qualified objects as 'contact zones', namely 'as sources of knowledge and as catalysts for new relationships - both within and between these communities'.[127] This understanding takes into account that indigenous curatorial practices do not necessarily regard cultural

---

[120] Raymond Silverman (ed.), *Museum as Process: Translating Local and Global Knowledges* (London & New York: Routledge, 2014).

[121] Tristram Besterman, 'Museum Ethics' in Sharon Macdonald (ed.), *A Companion to Museum Studies* (Malden: Blackwell Publishing, 2006) 431–441, 431.

[122] In Canada, changes were recommended in a report issued in 1992 entitled 'Turning the Page: Forging New Partnerships between Museums and First Peoples'. It was prepared by the Canadian Museums Association together with an Assembly of First Nations members. It supported better access and participation of Aboriginal people in museums, as well as return of human remains and sacred objects. Repatriation to First Nations is regulated by national guidelines.

[123] Kreps, 'Changing the Rules of the Road', 70.

[124] In 1991, Mary Louise Pratt used the concept of contact zones to define 'social spaces where cultures meet, clash and grapple with each other, often in contexts of highly asymmetrical relations of power, such as colonialism, slavery, or their aftermaths as they lived out in many parts of the world today'. See Mary Louise Pratt, 'Arts of the Contact Zone' (1991) *Profession* 33–40, 34.

[125] Critics note that concepts such as contact, collaboration, or partnering, promoted by the 'contact zone' idea, do not necessarily eliminate hierarchies, but may replicate cultural appropriation. See Tony Benett, *Culture: A Reformer's Science* (London: Sage, 1998) 213; Robin Boast, 'Neocolonial Collaboration: Museum as Contact Zone Revisited' (2011) 35 *Museum Anthropology* 56–70; Amy Lonetree, 'Missed Opportunities: Reflections on the NMAI' (2006) 30 *American Indian Quarterly* 632–645.

[126] James Clifford, 'Museums as Contact Zones' in James Clifford (ed.), *Routes: Travel and Translation in the Late Twentieth Century* (Cambridge, MA: Harvard University Press, 1997) 188–219, 213.

[127] Laura Peers and Alison Brown, 'Introduction' in Laura Peers and Alison Brown (eds.), *Museums and Source Communities* (London: Routledge, 2003) 3–16, 4.

artefacts as 'passive, inanimate objects' or evidence about past traditions.[128] It has strengthened the case for the establishment of indigenous museums[129] or reform of museum structures.[130] For instance, in New Zealand, indigenous governance structures became part the national museum culture through the 'Mana taonga principle',[131] which gave Māori communities the rights to decide how objects should be cared for, managed presented or reproduced.

Rodney Harrison has advocated greater sensitivity to the political and ethical issues surrounding 'ownership of culture and its products', including the 'affective weight of things'. These affective dimensions include the ability of objects to influence human behaviour or take on 'person-like qualities',[132] and their 'political weight', i.e. the effects of their presence in museum collections[133] and the imperial and colonial histories they symbolize. Drawing on 'assemblage' theory,[134] he has defined museums as 'material and social assemblages',[135] which are constituted through relationships between people, things, and institutions. This vision sheds a new light on curatorial responsibilities. It implies that museums are bound by ethical obligations that arise from 'collaborations between researchers and indigenous and other minority community groups',[136] and from 'obligations that stem from the historical, physical, and political "weight" of objects',[137] including their 'relations with those who have made, traded, received, collected, curated, worked with, and viewed them in the past'.[138] Nicholas Thomas has invoked the idea of 'museums as method'.[139] He has argued that the value of museums lies in their ability to tell the stories of different approaches towards material culture through the encounters in collections. Margareta von Oswald has shown in her ethnography of the ethnological Museum in Berlin how curatorial practices have become more

---

[128] Kelley Hays-Gilpin and Ramson Lomatewama, 'Curating communities at the Museum of Northern Arizona' in Rodney Harrison, Sarah Byrne, and Anne Clarke (eds.), *Reassembling the Collection: Ethnographic Museums and Indigenous Agency* (Santa Fe: School of Advanced Research Press, 2013) 259–284, 260–261.

[129] Nick Stanley (ed.), *The future of indigenous museums: Perspectives from the Southwest Pacific* (Oxford & New York: Berghahn Books, 2007).

[130] Ruth Phillips, *Museum Pieces: Toward the Indigenization of Canadian Museums* (Montreal and Kingston: McGill-Queen's University Press, 2013).

[131] Haidy Geismar, *Treasured Possessions* (Durham: Duke University Press, 2013) 134.

[132] Rodney Harrison, 'Reassembling Ethnographic Museum Collections' in Harrison, Byrne, and Clarke, *Reassembling the Collection*, 3–36, 5.

[133] Ibid.

[134] Bruno Latour, *Reassembling the Social: An Introduction to Actor-Network-Theory* (Oxford: Oxford University Press, 2005); Jane Bennett, *Vibrant Matter: A Political Ecology of Things* (Durham: Duke University Press, 2010).

[135] Harrison, 'Reassembling Ethnographic Museum Collections', 4.

[136] Ibid, 13.

[137] Ibid, 14.

[138] Ibid, 35.

[139] Nicholas Thomas, 'The Museum as Method' (2010) 33 *Museum Anthropology* 6–10; Nicholas Thomas, *The Return of Curiosity: What Museums Are Good for in the 21st Century* (London: Reaktion Books, 2016).

'research-focused', 'audience-oriented' and multidimensional, i.e. open to sharing of interpretative authority.[140]

The efforts to develop a museology for the twenty-first century are reflected in ICOM's attempts to formulate a novel museum definition. In 2019, the Executive Board of ICOM proposed a new definition, which deviated from the classical focus on collection, preservation, and access to the heritage to humanity. Earlier ICOM museum definitions have come under critique[141] for failing to take into account the 'ethical, social or political place'[142] of museums and leaving an 'ethical vacuum' in relation to 'colonial or other legacies of power and wealth, which have been constitutive for the principles of how Western museum collections were formed'.[143] The new proposal advocated a social justice-related agenda, which includes the role of museums 'to contribute to human dignity and social justice, global equality and planetary wellbeing'.[144] It stressed the importance of critical dialogue over the past, the intergenerational responsibilities of museums, and a more express role to redress past wrongs. It stated:

> Museums are democratising, inclusive and polyphonic spaces for critical dialogue about the pasts and the futures. Acknowledging and addressing the conflicts and challenges of the present, they hold artefacts and specimens in trust for society, safeguard diverse memories for future generations and guarantee equal rights and equal access to heritage for all people.[145]

The 2019 definition triggered mixed reactions. It has been criticized for associating museums with a political agenda that does not coincide with the mandate of all museums.[146] Critics have noted that the definition offers 'useful recommendations for civic action that fit well with the museum form', but should not be part of a 'definition of what museums are', since it might imply that museums, such as the British Museum or the Louvre might be forced to 'desist from calling

---

[140] Margareta von Oswald, *Working Through Colonial Collections: An Ethnography of the Ethnological Museum in Berlin* (Leuven: Leuven University Press, 2022) 241–244.

[141] The 2007 ICOM definition stated: 'A museum is a non-profit, permanent institution in the service of society and its development, open to the public, which acquires, conserves, researches, communicates and exhibits the tangible and intangible heritage of humanity and its environment for the purposes of education, study and enjoyment.'

[142] Jette Sandahl, 'The Museum Definition as the Backbone of ICOM' (2019) 71 *Museum International* 1–9, 5.

[143] Ibid, 8.

[144] The definition was agreed by the ICOM Executive Board, at its 139th board meeting in Paris on 21 and 22 July 2019. See ICOM, 'ICOM announces the alternative museum definition that will be subject to a vote' (25 July 2019) https://icom.museum/en/news/icom-announces-the-alternative-museum-definition-that-will-be-subject-to-a-vote/.

[145] Ibid.

[146] It has been qualified as an 'ideological manifesto', which fails to distinguish museums from cultural centers. For a discussion of the positions, see Bruno Brulon Soares, 'Defining the museum: challenges and compromises of the 21st century' (2020) 48 *ICOFOM Study Series* 16–32.

themselves museum.[147] The proposal failed to reach consensus at the ICOM General Conference in Kyoto in 2019, which decided to defer the decision.[148] This vote resulted in the establishment of a new standing committee and several resignations from ICOM's executive board.[149] On 24 August 2022, the 26th ICOM General Conference adopted a more cautious museum definition. It refers to the mandate of museums' to 'foster diversity and sustainability',[150] without engaging with issues of decolonization or restitution.

Others have proposed more fundamental change or argued.that the very idea of the museum needs be rethought more radically in order pay greater attention to respect of alterity and indigenous or community relations to objects. For instance, Robin Boast has insisted that museums should conceptualize their authority and politics of representation and adapt a new stance on returns, namely to 'learn to let go of their resources, even at times of the objects, for the benefit and use of communities and agendas far beyond its knowledge and control'.[151] Ciraj Rassool has questioned whether museums or archives are best places to encounter these objects. He stated:

Transforming the museum means embarking on projects of restitution, not just as return but also as a methodology of rethinking what we mean by museum ... The museum needs to be reconceptualized outside evolutionary frames and the impulses of preservation and atonement. The postcolonial museum may indeed require the inauguration of the postmuseum itself.[152]

2.2.2 Evolving curatorial responsibilities

The debate on the changing identity of museums has shifted perspectives on curatorial ethics and methods in relation to cultural colonial objects. Jette Sandahl, former chair of the ICOM Standing Committee for the Museum, has openly acknowledged that museums have a role in addressing historical wrongs. She stated: 'Critiquing and protesting the way museums, monuments and sites perpetuate traditions of power is not an attempt to rewrite history, but a demand, in the present time, to right historic wrongs.'[153] She has pleaded for an ethical framework, which recognizes the social responsibilities of museums and equal cultural rights, through 'processes of repatriation', recontextualization of collection, and 'methods of cooperation and consultation'.[154]

---

[147] John Fraser, 'A Discomforting Definition of Museum' (2019) 62 *Curator The Museum Journal* 501–504, 504.
[148] See Brulon Soares, 'Defining the museum', 23.
[149] Museums Association, 'ICOM in turmoil after resignations', 17 July 2020, at https://www.mus eumsassociation.org/museums-journal/news/2020/07/icom-museum-definition-row-rumbles-on/.
[150] ICOM, 'ICOM approves a new museum definition', *ICOM News*, 24 August 2022.
[151] Boast, 'Neocolonial Collaboration', 67.
[152] Rassool, 'Rethinking the Ethnographic Museum', 56–66, 65.
[153] Sandahl, 'The Museum Definition as the Backbone of ICOM', 8.
[154] Ibid.

Others have argued that museums should act as beacons of 'cultural equity', and apply principles of fairness and justice in order to recognize the broader context of colonial relations. Besterman has defended an 'intergenerational equity' approach, according to which museums are accountable to stakeholders in the past, present and future.[155] Charlotte Joy has supported an ethic of social justice, based on the 'link between human dignity and material culture'.[156] She has argued that return of cultural colonial objects is not only a 'curatorial or art historical concern', but 'a matter of economic and social justice',[157] necessary to forge 'new futures predicated on the ethical insights of the consequences of past events'.[158]

Janet Marstine has proposed three contemporary macro principles for museum ethics, based on the social justice role of museums. The first one is 'social responsibility'. It involves social inclusion, sharing of authority and power in decision-making processes and openness to new agendas or methods.[159] The second one is 'radical transparency'. It seeks to embrace greater 'self-reflexivity' and 'accountability, acknowledgement and assumption of responsibility for actions',[160] such as the grounding of museum practices in post-colonial approaches.[161] The last one is the 'ethics of guardianship'.[162] It seeks to define relations to objects[163] in terms of 'care-taking' and 'partnership' with multiple stakeholders, including source communities, rather than classical ownership bonds, reflected by the notion of cultural property.[164] It understands heritage as 'something animate, to be respected, and communal, to be shared'.[165] It offers new ways to approach repatriation and return through arrangements recognizing the plural relations to objects, sharing of heritage or processes of consultation and collaboration.

One common feature of these ethical models is their recognition of the role of museums as political spaces and sites of power, with social responsibilities associated with the heritage of their collections. Curators and trustees are not merely guardians or arbiters of collections, charged with preservation or authentication or objects, but moral agents who need to take important decisions how to engage with the historical and political significance of objects, including accession, provenance

---

[155] Besterman, 'Museum Ethics', 435.
[156] Charlotte Joy, *Heritage Justice* (Cambridge: Cambridge University Pres, 2020) 53
[157] Ibid, 14.
[158] Ibid, 53.
[159] Marstine, 'The contingent nature of the new museum ethics', 10–14.
[160] Ibid, 14.
[161] Ibid, 15.
[162] It is inspired by the Māori notion of *kaitiakitanga*, which recognizes the collaborative relationships in the care of objects. See Haidy Geismar, 'Cultural Property, Museums, and the Pacific: Reframing the Debates' (2008) 15 *International Journal of Cultural Property* 109–122, 115.
[163] It promotes a relational understanding of the links between people and things, which takes into account their 'fluidity and complexity of identity'. Marstine, 'The contingent nature of the new museum ethics', 19.
[164] Ibid, 18.
[165] Ibid, 19.

and de-accession of objected associated with structural violence.[166] This role in relation to the past makes them agents of transitional justice in the large sense, namely moral actors involved in the transformation from unjust to just relations. They become part of a broader agenda to address historical injustices through efforts of truth-seeking, repair of harm, mitigation of enduring consequences or strategies to ensure non-repetition, including memorialization.

2.2.3 Synergies with transitional justice

The taking and retention of certain categories of objects is not only a property taking or means of artistic or commercial exploitation, but a form of structural violence against people. The role of museum policies and practices in relation to 'heritage justice'[167] carries multiple synergies with principles and concepts of transitional justice,[168] which support transitions from unjust to just relations. Transitional justice concepts have relevance for the treatment of what Sara Ahmed has called 'sticky objects',[169] namely cultural colonial objects, where violence against 'objects' intersects with attacks on human identity, culture, or dignity. Metaphorically speaking, objects themselves may be 'victims of more or less forcible displacements'.[170] Cultural objects play an important affective and symbolic role in processes of memorialization.[171] Sometimes, the 'value and meaningfulness' of heritage 'are revealed ... within the forces of—sometimes violent—contestation'.[172]

Key transitional justice principles, such as 'establishing the facts and conditions that made such violations possible', 'the acknowledgement of responsibility and public apology' or 'the memorialization and restoration of dignity'[173] are relevant

---

[166] Geismar, 'Cultural Property, Museums, and the Pacific', 119.

[167] Joy, *Heritage Justice*.

[168] The field has emerged in the context of violence against persons. However, if cultural heritage embodies more than the materiality of objects, namely a reflection of human identity or a form of social agency, it is only consequential to extend some of its principles to violence against objects. See Johanna Mannergren Selimovic, 'The Stuff from the Siege: Transitional Justice and the Power of Everyday Objects in Museums' (2022) 16 *International Journal of Transitional Justice* 1–15, Alessandro Chechi, 'The return of cultural objects displaced during colonialism. What role for restorative justice, transitional justice and alternative dispute resolution?' (2023) 6 *International Journal of Restorative Justice* 95–118, 107–111.

[169] Sara Ahmed, 'Happy Objects' in Melissa Gregg and Gregory J. Seigworth (eds.), *The Affect Theory Reader* (Durham: Duke University Press, 2010) 29–51

[170] Paul Basu, 'Object Diasporas, Resourcing Communities: Sierra Leonean Collections in the Global Museumscape' (2011) 34 *Museum Anthropology* 28–42, 37.

[171] Brandon Hamber, 'Conflict Museums, Nostalgia, and Dreaming of Never Again' (2012) 18 *Peace and Conflict: Journal of Peace Psychology* 268–281; Cynthia E. Milton and Anne-Marie Reynaud, 'Archives, Museums and Sacred Storage: Dealing with the Afterlife of the Truth and Reconciliation Commission of Canada' (2019) 13 *International Journal of Transitional Justice* 524–554.

[172] Annalisa Bolin, 'Violent Encounters: Cultural Heritage and Contemporary Dynamics of Violence', 1 February 2022, at https://items.ssrc.org/where-heritage-meets-violence/violent-encounters/. See also Sandra Dudley and others (eds.), *The Thing about Museums: Objects and Experience, Representation and Contestation* (Abingdon: Routledge, 2017).

[173] Report of the Special Rapporteur on the promotion of truth, justice, reparation and guarantees of non-recurrence, 'Transitional justice measures and addressing the legacy of gross violations of human rights and international humanitarian law committed in colonial contexts', UN Doc. A/76/180, (19 July 2021) para. 11.

to curatorial ethics and practices and emerging ethical frames regarding colonial collections. For instance, in the context of cultural colonial objects, provenance research is not only an empirical inquiry into the origins and acquisition of objects, but a form of truth-seeking into the life story of the object and a process shaping future engagement. It cannot be confined the establishment of 'ownership' relations and the chain of transactions, but needs to involve critical inquiry into the context of acquisition, the classificatory schemes applied and alternatives frames or epistemologies.[174] It is crucial to involve 'affected communities'[175] in this process, and to 'examine the reasons and ways in which policies of discrimination, oppression, dispossession and marginalization'[176] affected consent to takings or object histories. This focus radically changes the static conception of the museum as place of storage.[177] It requires openness to listening and engaging with communities.

Return or restitution are often not able to redress wrong, but perform a broader role of social repair or reconnection. This is recognized by relational ethics, which acknowledge that the importance of restitution extends far beyond physical act of return:[178] It is an 'ethical and creative act of contrition',[179] which challenges past positionalities and distinguishes returns from acts of generosity and good will.[180] It also has a forward looking dimension. It offers a possibility for re-engagement with objects, which are constantly in motion from a point of view of material culture.[181]

The preservation and display of cultural colonial objects involves memory politics. From the perspective of source communities, objects can be equated to 'diaspora' objects[182] or 'missing' subjects. Museums themselves are 'witnesses to history', with important ethical responsibilities. They need to 'preserve the memory of . . . events'[183] and facilitate critical engagement. They face an important task to educate present and future generations. Memorialization plays a key role in the representation and display of objects. But it also has important repercussions for the ethical debate on returns. As Mamaga Ametor Hoebuadzu II and Togbui Opeku V have noted in relation to the looting of royal objects from the Asante:

---

[174] Larissa Förster, 'Provenance: An essay based on a panel with Ciraj Rassool, Paul Basu, and Britta Lange' in Centre for Anthropological Research on Museums and Heritage, *Otherwise: Re-thinking Museums and Heritage* (Berlin: CARMAH, 2018) 16–23, 18–19.

[175] Report of the Special Rapporteur, 'Violations of human rights and international humanitarian law committed in colonial contexts', para. 50.

[176] Ibid, para. 49.

[177] Förster, 'Provenance', 23.

[178] Report of the Special Rapporteur, 'Violations of human rights and international humanitarian law committed in colonial contexts', paras. 67, 99.

[179] Joy, *Heritage Justice*, 54.

[180] For a corresponding critique of development aid as a form of colonial reparation, see Report of the Special Rapporteur, 'Violations of human rights and international humanitarian law committed in colonial contexts', para. 60.

[181] Basu, 'Object diasporas, resourcing communities', 37.

[182] Ibid, 37.

[183] Report of the Special Rapporteur, 'Violations of human rights and international humanitarian law committed in colonial contexts', para. 110.

When a cultural object is lost or looted, a significant part of our history is also lost with it. What remains is a memory. When that memory fades out of the oral history then that cultural object, its traditions, its performances and its relevance to the people are also lost forever.[184]

This statement reaffirms that memory is essential to secure what Gerald Vizenor has called 'survivance' in Native American studies, namely 'an active sense of presence', instead of 'victimry'.[185] The hiding of objects in storage rooms and collections directly contravenes this objective. It contributes not only to preservation, but also to the gradual 'loss' of objects.[186] Return can make important contributions to 'survivance' through collective reremembering, including maintenance of past traditions or memory of resistance to cultural dispossession, which challenges 'victimry'. This is reflected in a comment made by Shayne Williams, a Gweagal Dharawal elder from the Botany Bay region, on the significance of the Gweagal shield[187] during the Encounters exhibition at the National Museum of Australia. He noted:

What it reminds me of is Aboriginal resistance. And not just resistance back then, but resistance to the destruction of our culture right up until now ... that we're continuing to resist the infringements and impacts and the decimation of our cultures and our identities. I feel it's going to be a great source of pride for a lot of Aboriginal people.[188]

It is also important to preserve critical memory of the past conduct in former colonial powers. This is often possible in alternative ways, such as through replicas, digital images, or education.[189]

According to transitional justice principles, social repair of past injustice is closely linked to measures preventing the recurrence of structural violence.[190] This imperative is also essential for responsible ethical engagement with colonial collections. It provides incentives to reform museum structures in order to ensure that colonial stereotypes or discriminatory practices are not reproduced in current practices or to highlight continuities between past cultural injustices and

---

[184] Mamaga Ametor Hoebuadzu II and Togbui Opeku VI, 'Restitution and return of looted royal heritage: the role of Ghanaian chiefs and queens in sustaining heritage traditions' (2020) 7 *Contemporary Journal of African Studies* 116–122, 120.

[185] Gerald Vizenor, *Manifest Manners: Narratives on Postindian Survivance* (Lincoln: Nebraska, 1999) vii.

[186] See Domínguez Rubio, 'Storage as a Form of Violence'; Dan Hicks, *The Brutish Museums* (London: Pluto Press, 2020) 153.

[187] See Chapter 2.

[188] National Museum of Australia, *Encounters: Revealing Stories of Aboriginal and Torres Strait Islander Objects from the British Museum* (Canberra: National Museum of Australia Press, 2015) 50.

[189] See Chapter 9.

[190] Report of the Special Rapporteur, 'Violations of human rights and international humanitarian law committed in colonial contexts', para. 112.

contemporary ones. Drawing on this logic, Wayne Modest has compared museums as 'investments in critical discomfort'.[191]

2.2.4 Relational ethics principles in the Sarr and Savoy report

This turn to justice and social responsibility is clearly reflected in the Sarr and Savoy report. It acknowledges that the relationship to the past requires openness towards 'different interpretations or conceptions of cultural heritage', the roles of museum, the presentation and circulation of objects, and most generally, 'the nature and quality of relations between people and nations'.[192] It states:

> To openly speak of restitutions is to speak of justice, or a re-balancing, recognition, of restoration and reparation, but above all: it's a way to open a pathway toward establishing new cultural relations based on a newly reflected upon ethical relation.[193]

The relational approach corresponds to a longer tradition in anthropology (e.g. *Marcel Mauss, Alfred Gell*) which has associated historical practices of gift exchange or trade with the creation of relationships.[194] The Sarr and Savoy report applied this logic to processes of return. It identified key elements of re-engagement, which namely (i) process-related considerations, (ii) contextualized criteria to assess the justice of returns, (iii) reconstruction of memory and resocialization of objects, and (iv) measures to prevent recurrence, such as law reform.

The report acknowledges that truth-seeking is essential to renew social relations from an ethical perspective. It states that bringing out 'truth' is necessary to 'understand the context' in which these objects were 'taken, spoiled, or transferred'[195] and to establish a 'historiography' departs from the 'idea of a single narrative' and assumes 'a plurality of perspectives'.[196] It thereby clarifies that return of knowledge is an important part of relational processes.

It advocates a wide restitution approach. It recommends the return 'of any objects taken by force or presumed to be acquired through inequitable conditions' without 'any supplementary research regarding their provenance or origins'.[197] It uses a periodization as guidance, which includes objects taken by 'military personnel' or colonial 'administrators' in Africa during the 'colonial period (1885-1960)' or by 'scientific expeditions prior to 1960'.[198] This approach must be understood in

---

[191] Wayne Modest, 'Museums are Investments in Critical Discomfort' in Margareta von Oswald and Jonas Tinius (eds.), *Across Anthropology: Troubling Colonial Legacies, Museums, and the Curatorial* (Leuven: Leuven University Press, 2020) 65–74.
[192] Sarr and Savoy, *The Restitution of African Cultural Heritage*, 29.
[193] Ibid.
[194] Förster, 'Provenance' 19.
[195] Sarr and Savoy, *The Restitution of African Cultural Heritage*, 36.
[196] Ibid.
[197] Ibid, 61.
[198] Ibid.

light of the mandate given to the authors, which was to facilitate temporary or permanent returns and new forms of circulation of objects and to examine the 'how', rather than the 'if' of returns.[199] It has been criticized for a lack of sufficient differentiation between modalities of taking, and in particular the broad space given to the 'disparity of power between seller and buyer', in addition to classical forms of looting or theft, in order to motivate returns.[200]

The authors paid particular attention to dilemma of a 'truncated history'[201] and the loss of memory caused by the 'absence' of objects.[202] They argued that restitution requires a process of 'reactivating a concealed memory' and restoring the 'signifying, integrative, dynamic, and mediating functions' of cultural heritage within contemporary societies.[203] They cautioned at the same time that return to 'original geo-cultural environments' is not the only legitimate form of approaching restitution and that practices should remain open to novel ideas of circulation.[204]

The commitment to relational ethics breaks not only with many of the questionable premises of the 'universal museum', but addresses many fears or concerns associated with cultural returns. It provides safeguards against the often-repeated critique that greater openness towards return would lead to a complete loss of objects in colonial collections, by recognizing the importance of memory in colonized societies and former colonial powers and accepting that return to source communities is not the only feasible solution to renew social relations or repair harm. It leaves room for intermediary solutions, new forms of partnership, or collaboration in provenance research or display of objects or novel approaches towards circulation and engagement with objects.[205] It has gone hand in hand with appeals to strengthen cultural heritage protection in domestic and regional contexts in order to overcome the paternalistic objection that requesting states are unable or unwilling to take care of culturally significant objects.

2.3 Formalizing ethics: The turn to national guidelines and policies, including common principles

The move towards a new museology and calls for a repositioning of museums have inspired a trend towards the adoption of new guidelines or policy documents

---

[199] See Letter of Mission by President Macron, ibid, 107.
[200] Kate Fitz-Gibbon, 'Arts Council England: Guidelines for Museum Repatriation' (8 April 2020) https://culturalpropertynews.org/arts-council-england-guidelines-for-museum-repatriation-policy/ ('if artistic wealth is "stolen" if not acquired in an absolutely symmetrical power relationship, then most transfers of art (and other goods) could be so classified').
[201] Sarr and Savoy, *The Restitution of African Cultural Heritage*, 36.
[202] Ibid, 35.
[203] Ibid, 39.
[204] Ibid, 39–40.
[205] See Chapter 9.

on colonial collections by a number of 'specially affected' countries, such as the Netherlands,[206] Germany[207] or Belgium,[208] the Arts Council in England[209] or particular museums (e.g. the Smithsonian institution[210]). These instruments seek to establish ethical criteria to deal with the complexity of colonial histories and to fill the gap left by the absence of internationally agreed frameworks, such as the Washington principles. They differ in format and approach, but represent a novel effort to identify 'fair and just' solutions in relation to cultural colonial objects.

This attempt is more complex than the identification of common principles for Nazi-looted art, since colonialism spreads over 400 years, involves very different types of colonization and touches uncomfortable questions of colonial guilt and identity, which have been marginalized in the history, politics, and education of many former colonial powers for decades.

The German Museum Association adopted practical guidelines for both cultural colonial objects[211] and human remains[212] collected in colonial contexts. They are not formally legally binding, but contain a mandate for all public museums and collections. In the Netherlands, the National Museum of World Cultures (NMVW), which compromises the Tropenmuseum in Amsterdam, the Museum Volkenkunde in Leiden, and the Afrika Museum in Nijmegen, first established guidelines for its collections in 2019.[213] They were later complemented in 2020 by the National Policy Framework for Colonial Collections, which is guiding executive decisions on returns.[214] In the UK, some museums, such as Oxford, have established their own guidelines.[215] The Arts Council England has developed a practical guidance to support museums in the restitution and repatriation of cultural objects.[216] In Belgium, an Independent Group of Experts has prepared 'Ethical Principles for the Management and Restitution of Colonial Collections' in 2021.[217] It was complemented by a Belgian Law on the Legal Framework for Restitution

---

[206] See e.g. National Museum of World Cultures, 'Return of Cultural Objects: Principles and Process' (2019).

[207] German Museums Association, *Guidelines for German Museums: Care of Collections from Colonial Contexts* (Berlin: German Museums Association, 3rd edn, 2021) (Guidelines for German Museums 2021).

[208] Independent Group of Experts, *Ethical Principles for the Management and Restitution of Colonial Collections in Belgium* (June 2021) (Belgian Ethical Principles).

[209] Arts Council England, *Restitution and Repatriation: A Practical Guide for Museums in England* (August 2022) (Arts Council England Guidance).

[210] Smithsonian Ethical Returns Working Group, Values and Principles Statement (3 May 2022).

[211] Guidelines for German Museums 2021.

[212] German Museums Association, *Recommendations for the Care of Human Remains in Museums and Collections* (Berlin: Deutscher Museumsbund, 2021).

[213] National Museum of World Cultures, 'Return of Cultural Objects: Principles and Process', 2019 (NMVW Principles).

[214] Council for Culture, Report, Advisory Committee on the National Policy Framework for Colonial Collections, Guidance on the way forward for colonial collections (22 January 2021).

[215] Procedures for claims for the Return of Cultural Objects from Oxford University Museums and Libraries, 13 July 2020 (2020 Oxford Procedures).

[216] Arts Council England Guidance.

[217] See Belgian Ethical Principles.

and Return, which creates an exception to the inalienable character of public cultural property in order to facilitate the return of cultural heritage acquired after the Berlin Conference by Belgian collections.[218] It opens new space for negotiations of the return of objects to the Democratic Republic of the Congo, Burundi or Rwanda.

One common premise of contemporary initiatives that they rely on is the premise that law alone is inadequate to address challenges of colonial injustice. They embrace a flexible, bottom-up driven methodology, which seeks to identity criteria guiding decision-making processes by public agents. They recognize that collecting practices of the past were grounded in structural inequalities and suggest new ethical parameters to accommodate conflicting interests. They go beyond legal standards. For example, the 2021 German Guidelines stress that there is a 'broad political consensus that … returns can be appropriate on ethical grounds' even though there is 'no legally enforceable rights to the return of items from collections from colonial contexts' in 'most cases'.[219] The Dutch NMVW Principles seek to establish 'just and fair solutions', based on 'standards of respect, cooperation and timeliness'.[220] The 2020 Oxford Procedures for claims for the Return of Cultural Objects rely on 'relevant international and national conventions and codes of ethics', in cases of doubt regarding return.[221] The Belgium principles speak of a 'moral duty to return the colonial heritage', based on 'demands for equity and reconciliation', which go 'beyond the limitations of the existing legal framework'.[222] They apply not only 'direct colonial relationships' in the nineteenth and twentieth centuries, but include 'post-colonial situations that mirror the extractivism and inequality of active colonialism'.[223] The Arts Council guidance combines ethical ('the right thing to do') and legal criteria.[224]

These guidelines and policies go beyond the general parameters of the ICOM Code of Ethics. They apply elements of the Washington principles to cultural colonial objects and pay greater attention to the structural nature of colonial violence Some of them leave greater room for different epistemologies and object ontologies and mark an attempt to rethink institutional practices. They reflect, at least, three important elements, which are in line with transitional justice concepts (truth-seeking, repair and access to justice), namely (i) a more structured commitment transparency and what Larissa Förster has called 'post-colonial provenance

---

[218] The law was adopted on 30 June 2022 by the Belgian Parliament. It received royal support on 3 July 2022. See See Law of 3 July 2022 Recognizing the Alienability of Goods Linked to the Belgian State's Colonial Past and Determining a Legal Framework for Their Restitution and Return, *Le Moniteur Belge*, No. 2022042012 (28 September 2022). It provides a basis for the restitution policy of the Royal Museum for Central Africa. For a discussion of the background, see Bert Demarsin and Marie-Sophie de Clippele, 'Georganiseerde terugkeer van koloniaal erfgoed' (2021) 449 *NjW* 706–715.

[219] Guidelines for German Museums 2021, 162.

[220] NMVW Principles, § 1.3.

[221] See 2020 Oxford Procedures, Section 4.4.

[222] Belgian Ethical Principles, 2.3.

[223] Ibid, 1.

[224] Arts Council England Guidance, 14.

research,[225] (ii) justice and equity-based criteria for return, and (iii) and the enhancement of voice and equality in processes and procedures in order to address inequalities in power relations. They highlight the need to establish a new basis for the legitimation of ownership over objects, not only in light of past wrongdoing or flaws in acquisition (e.g. involuntary loss of objects, fragile nature of consent in consensual transactions), but also in light of contemporary relations towards objects.

2.3.1 Transparency and post-colonial provenance research

Provenance research carries special significance in the field of historical injustice. It is to some extent the cultural heritage equivalent of public inquiry and access to truth in the context of transitional justice, and a means to confront colonial amnesia.[226] Thousands of objects are in archives or storage. Source countries or communities cannot meaningfully engage with their heritage if there is no transparency about the whereabouts and location of objects. Provenance research is a key to the history of objects. It involves 'better knowledge of the history of an object/collection' and its nexus to the colonial era, such as the 'circumstances under which an object was collected, sold, acquired or appropriated,'[227] as well as general questions about the function, context and 'materiality of artefacts and ethnographic objects.'[228]

In the past, provenance research has often been carried in an ad hoc, rather than in a systematic fashion, in relation to colonial objects. It has been limited to specific objects, based on resource constraints, or has been used to delay returns.[229] Modern practices acknowledge that responsible engagement with the colonial past require more transparency and novel approaches towards provenance research, i.e. cultural and historical contextualization of objects and collections,[230] proactive provenance research and new methods. .

---

[225] Larissa Förster, Iris Edenheiser and Sarah Fründt, 'Eine Tagung zu postkolonialer Provenienzforschung' in Larissa Förster and others (eds.), *Provenienzforschung zu ethnografischen Sammlungen der Kolonialzeit* (München: Arbeitsgruppe Museum der Deutschen Gesellschaft für Sozial—und Kulturanthropologie, 2018) 13–27; Larissa Förster and others, 'A Conference on Postcolonial Provenance Research: An Introduction to the Conference Anthology' http://www.carmah.ber lin/wp-content/uploads/2018/09/A-conference-on-postcolonial-provenance-research.pdf.

[226] The more past takings of cultural objects are grounded in wrong, the more compelling it becomes to link resolution of claims and return practices to concepts, such as access to truth, requiring transparency and access to the history of objects.

[227] Guidelines for German Museums 2021, 64.

[228] Ibid, 49.

[229] See Belgian Ethical Principles, § 4.2. Museums have relied on information provided by donors or market actors, rather than obtaining additional documentation. Uncertainty about the acquisition and provenance of objects has been used as argument to delay debates on return or justify continued guardianship. Wazi Apoh and Andreas Mehler, 'Mainstreaming the Discourse on Restitution and Repatriation within African History, Heritage Studies and Political Science' (2020) 7 *Contemporary Journal of African Studies* 1–16, 12.

[230] For instance, the German guidelines qualify provenance research 'as a moral obligation and as a prerequisite for handling their collection items responsibly'. See Guidelines for German Museums 2021, 64.

New approaches extend beyond the general provenance provisions in ICOM[231] and follow the direction of the Washington principles, which promote a proactive role of possessors in relation to objects. They involve three elements: Proactivity, diversification of methods, and greater transparency in relation to inventories and object histories.

(i) Proactive approach to provenance research

A proactive approach to provenance research involves not only research on request, but inquiries based on an entity's own motion. It is essential to establish the context of collections and to provide access to information to actual or potential claimants.[232] It concerns, both 'the cultures of the communities' from which objects were taken, and the role which colonial powers 'played in those territories at the time'.[233] It is reflected in several guidelines.[234] For example, the German Guidelines stress that provenance research should be carried out 'proactively and on an ongoing basis', irrespective of whether or not claims for restitution have been made.[235] This commitment to transparency seeks to prevent that mere lack of knowledge about artefacts in collections bars potential claims. The Guidelines add that 'knowledge and expertise of people from countries of origin or communities of origin' form not only 'an important source', but also 'a relevant perspective on the object' and 'a starting point for transnational cooperation in provenance research'.[236] The NMVW principles treat provenance research as part of a commitment to develop new ethical possibilities for collections.[237] They instruct museums to apply the 'principle of reasonable doubt' in cases where claims for return are not sufficiently documented.[238] The Dutch advisory Report on the National Policy Framework for Colonial Collections suggested the creation of an Expert Centre for the Provenance of Colonial Cultural Objects.[239] The Belgium principles go into the same direction. They stress the need for a 'proactive'[240] and 'new type of provenance research', which should go beyond previous ownership or circulation,[241] and propose the establishment of an 'independent and interdisciplinary provenance

---

[231] See ICOM Code of Ethics, Principle 3 ('Museums have particular responsibilities to all for the care, accessibility and interpretation of primary evidence collected and held in their collections').

[232] Belgian Ethical Principles, § 3.2.

[233] Report Dutch Advisory Committee on the National Policy Framework, 79.

[234] Guidelines for German Museums 2021, 64. The 2020 Oxford Procedures are restrictive and leave provenance research in the discretion of museums. See 2020 Oxford Procedures, Section 4.2 ('This may include information from the University's collections and records; any additional research carried out by the University or other academic institutions; consultation with other parties (including, where relevant, the donor of the object or funder of its acquisition); and expert advice').

[235] Guidelines for German Museums 2021, 64.

[236] Ibid, 64.

[237] NMVW Principles, § 1.4.

[238] Ibid, § 5.4

[239] Report Dutch Advisory Committee on the National Policy Framework, 7 (Recommendation 9).

[240] Belgian Ethical Principles, § 1.

[241] Ibid, Executive Summary.

research institute' in order to carry out such research.[242] They also clarify that, for ethical and moral reasons, returns of human remains originating from colonial relations or contexts should be an 'absolute priority' and not be made dependent on a precondition of 'exhaustive provenance research'.[243] The Arts Council guidance recommends 'proactive action' to 'build relationships with originating communities, to open up dialogue around contested items' and to create opportunities for discourse and discussion around cultural heritage.[244]

(ii) Diversifying evidence and perspectives

The complex provenance histories of colonial objects can only be understood through a critical reading of sources.[245] As the Belgium principles note, many 'materials in colonial archives were produced by agents of colonial powers and relate either directly or indirectly to various aspects of the colonial project'.[246] These records often contain biased narratives or representations. False provenance information was used to conceal problematic conditions of acquisitions or to enhance the commercial value of objects.[247] It is thus essential to diversify the pool of information to contextualize objects[248] and to make the process of provenance research itself more 'inclusive'.[249] Greater inclusivity can be sought through reliance on 'oral sources of information', and in particular, 'local sources from the contexts of origin of these object', rather than exclusive consultation of written records.[250] This approach is in line with commitments by museums to recognize the rights of peoples to be included in and consulted about the 'representation and preservation of their heritage'.[251] Oral histories are essential to tell counter-histories. Societies of origins cannot be reduced to 'footnotes in history' or information provides. It is of key importance to develop joint or 'reversed provenance research'. This may require consideration of different or even competing interpretations the local level[252] and transparent motivation of choices in contested cases. Another technique to diversify perspectives on provenance is to give greater weight to circumstantial or contextual evidence. This may help to deal with gaps. For instance, museums may 'on a combination of sources in order to determine a reasonable assumption of origin'.[253]

---

242 Ibid, § 4.1.
243 Ibid, § 4.2.
244 Arts Council England, 2.
245 Ibid, 149.
246 Ibid, § 4.2.
247 Guidelines for German Museums 2021, 67.
248 Guidelines for German Museums 2021, 47, 64–65.
249 Belgian Ethical Principles, § 4.2.
250 Ibid, § 4.2.
251 Guidelines for German Museums 2021, 48.
252 Ibid, 48.
253 Belgian Ethical Principles, § 3.2.

(iii) Open access inventories and digitalization of collections

Proactivity and creativity in relation to methods need to go hand in hand with broader transparency in order to address the invisibility of objects (e.g. their hiding in storage rooms or boxes), reveal their histories and facilitate new engagement with colonial collections. This requires not only the making of inventories, but digitalization of collections and sharing of information communities and countries of origin. The process of open access inventories and digital reconnection with objects is not a substitute for return, but an important step to provide greater transparency and contribute to the emergence of a community of practice.

In many communities, knowledge about objects may be lost. Sharing digital images is an important aspect of reconnecting. For instance, the German guidelines states that museums 'have an ethical responsibility to open up access to the collections for representatives of communities of origin'.[254] They established a centralized platform for information with regard to colonial collection. The Belgian principles support more transparent online inventories, including a 'proactive approach to communication and data sharing'[255] to share knowledge and increase collaboration and dialogue.[256]

A pioneering example is the 'Digital Benin' project.[257] It is an online platform, which connects data from the diverse national and international museum databases on the Benin bronzes with local knowledge.[258] It has been supported by countries of the Benin Dialogue group, including the British Museum, the Weltmuseum in Vienna, Oxford University's Pitt Rivers Museum and Berlin's Ethnology Museum. It reassembles objects from public collections worldwide in a common digital environment. It is not a 'pro-restitution' platform as such, but a space to trace the identity and histories of objects in new ways, by taking into account Edo perspectives. It is designed to provide greater transparency and enable future generations in Africa to 'reconnect with their history'.[259]

2.3.2 Justice and equity-based criteria for return

The most innovative development is the emergence of ethical criteria to deal with requests for the return of objects. They provide more guidance than the vague provisions of the ICOM Code of Ethics, which merely stated that museums should be 'prepared to initiate dialogue for the return of cultural property'[260] and, 'if legally

---

[254] Guidelines for German Museums 2021, 47.
[255] Belgian Ethical Principles, § 3.2.
[256] Ibid, § 4.1.
[257] Catherine Hickley, 'Digital Benin: A Milestone on the Long, Slow Journey to Restitution' *The Art Newspaper* (8 June 2020).
[258] See Museum am Rothenbaum, Press Release, 'Digital Benin, Reconnecting Royal Art Treasures', 16 April 2020.
[259] Barnaby Philips, 'Can Digital Benin Reconnect Future Nigerians with Their History?' *Art Review* (16 November 2022) https://artreview.com/can-digital-benin-reconnect-future-nigerians-with-their-history/.
[260] ICOM, Code of Ethics, § 6.2.

free to do so', take 'prompt and responsible steps to cooperate in its return' in case of requests for restitution.[261] Individual guidelines and policies differ in their precise formulation, and balancing criteria. However, in general, they recognize the importance of standards of 'reasonableness' or 'fairness', which are reminiscent of the Washington Principles. They acknowledge that return may be justified, even in circumstances where complicity in wrongdoing by states or museums cannot be shown.

Many instruments follow the Sarr and Savoy report by recognizing colonialism as a context of structural injustice, but adopt distinct approaches to come to terms with the past. The German guidelines use a wide definition of 'colonial contexts', which is based on an 'an ideology of cultural superiority to colonised or ethnic minority populations and the right to oppress and exploit'.[262] They stress that 'political power imbalances' and 'colonial dependency relationships' have also developed in countries that were 'never, only informally, or only partially formally colonized', such as China in the nineteenth century.[263] They stay at the same time rather general in relation to consequences. They state that return should 'be considered' when the 'circumstances of acquisition appear wrong from today's point of view', and when items were of 'special religious or cultural significance' to communities of origin at the time of their removal and have 'maintained' or 'regained' this significance today.[264]

The report of the Dutch Advisory Committee expresses a clear commitment to 'the principle of redress of a historic injustice'.[265] It states that the 'readiness to 'rectify' a 'historical injustice' which is 'still perceived as an injustice today' should be the 'key principle of the policy on dealing with colonial collections'.[266] It recognizes the importance of the policy as such as a measure of 'acknowledgement and redress' of injustice, beyond 'actual return'.[267] In substance, the Dutch approach places considerable emphasis on conditions affecting consent. It distinguishes an unqualified commitment to redress in cases of involuntary loss of possession from more discretionary approaches to return in cases where 'objects are of particular cultural, historical or religious importance for the source country'.[268] It accepts that in instances of involuntary dispossession, the case for return should be assessed independently of 'the object's cultural nor its scientific value for the Netherlands' or 'the source country's future plans for the object'.[269] It uses the

---

[261] Ibid, § 6.3.
[262] Guidelines for German Museums 2021, 26.
[263] Ibid, 74.
[264] Ibid, 83.
[265] Dutch Advisory Committee Report on the National Policy Framework, 68.
[266] Ibid, 6, Recommendation 2.
[267] Ibid, 6, Recommendation 5.
[268] Ibid, 6, Recommendation 6 ('the case of these requests the fundamental argument is not one of rectifying an injustice, but of honouring a particular interest of the source country').
[269] Ibid, 68.

principle of redress as a baseline, even in cases where objects were not taken under Dutch rule, but by other colonial powers.[270] It thus acknowledges a responsibility for unjust enrichment.[271]

The Belgian principles support a transitional justice approach, grounded in law. They regard 'restitution' as part 'of a wider reparation and reconciliation process'[272] and support the establishment of a new legal framework for restitutions. They acknowledge that 'colonial era collections were gathered' in 'contexts of deep structural inequality' which 'reduced or nullified individual and group agency'.[273] They postulate that 'heritage institutions must be willing to relinquish the gains they made owing to these unequal relationships'.[274] The document places considerable emphasis on the importance of human and cultural rights. It derives a 'moral duty to return cultural heritage' from 'the recognition of the right of people (individuals and groups) to cultural heritage'.[275]

The Arts Council guidance fails to qualify colonialism as a context of structural injustice. However, it states that 'museums must be especially sensitive to countries or communities of origin, and to past owners, in relation to cultural objects' which were 'originally taken in ways' which are 'considered unethical today'.[276] It lists several factors which may compromise: 'war, conflict or occupation', or a 'transaction entered into under duress or without consent (even if it occurred long ago)'.[277]

The guidelines contain some common ground in relation to justifications of returns. They reflect at least two main principles: (i) return based on the context of acquisitions, including wrongful taking, and (ii) criteria related to cultural importance of object and right of access of communities to culture. These criteria openly challenge the traditional 'salvage logic' that was used to justify the taking of objects, namely the idea that objects were simply rescued from dying populations or from decay, based on lack of care. They make a compelling case for the argument that retention in modern collections requires a novel and more inclusive basis of consent.

(i) Context of acquisition

The first justification legitimizes return based on past conduct, namely wrongdoing that is unacceptable according to modern ethical standards. The most far-reaching model is the 'structural injustice approach', reflected in Sarr and Savoy report. It extended the NAGPRA logic of a presumption of unjust acquisition beyond

---

[270] Ibid, 7, Recommendation 7.
[271] The report states that the 'guiding principle must be the redress of an injustice' regardless 'of whether the Netherlands itself played a part in causing the original injustice, as the current owner of the cultural object it is the only party capable of rectifying that injustice'. Ibid. 7, Principle 7.
[272] Belgian Ethical Principles, Executive summary.
[273] Ibid, § 1.
[274] Ibid, § 3.2.
[275] Ibid, § 2.3.
[276] Arts Council England Guidance, 15.
[277] Ibid.

indigenous people to colonial contexts. It supported a reversal of the burden of proof in relation to colonial missions and scientific 'raids' in Africa between 1885 and 1960, according to which the irregular nature of the acquisition should be presumed in this period, unless the museum is able to demonstrate that an item was acquired in Africa pursuant to a free, equitable and evidenced transaction.[278] This approach transposes the model of the Washington Principles to colonial contexts. It has been challenged for its generalized treatment of colonial acquisitions and transactions.

Several instruments have expressly distanced themselves from the reversal of the burden of proof, suggested in the report and supported a case-by-case assessment. For instance, the German guidelines refuse to adopt a general presumption that 'any acquisition during the era of colonialism was wrongful'.[279] The document states:

> Ever since contact was first made, objects were manufactured especially for Europeans because of the demand that was identified. Moreover, transfers of objects where all those involved were on equal terms took place even in the colonial setting, with its structural inequality, sometimes embedded in an indigenous system of exchange and the reciprocal presenting of gifts. The authors consider it to be problematic to deny that the communities of origin had any agency and to declare them all to be victims.[280]

A similar critique is echoed in the Dutch guidance. It states that a reversal of the burden of proof would 'not do justice to the fact that many colonial cultural heritage objects were also acquired legitimately even if this can no longer be evidenced'.[281] It links the principle of 'redress of historic injustice' expressly to involuntary losses of possession. However, it reflects a certain opening towards the Sarr and Savoy report, by allowing flexible standards of proof. It states that 'an object should be unconditionally returned' if it can be 'demonstrated with a *reasonable degree of certainty* that involuntary loss of possession has taken place'.[282] It requires 'sufficiently concrete and convincing indications' of lack of consent.[283] It acknowledges that even 'the gifting and selling of objects' during a 'period of fundamental inequality' can be 'an expression of subjugation' and does not necessarily imply a 'voluntary transfer of ownership'.[284]

---

[278] Sarr and Savoy, *The Restitution of African Cultural Heritage*, 58.
[279] Guidelines for German Museums 2021, 83.
[280] Ibid, 83.
[281] Dutch Advisory Committee Report on the National Policy Framework, 70.
[282] Ibid, emphasis added.
[283] Ibid.
[284] Ibid.

Most guidelines or policies rely to a greater extent on agency and demonstration of flaws in acquisitions in order to establish a justification for return. They make reference to established legal forms of wrongdoing.

For instance, the 2020 Oxford Procedures, which apply to cultural objects taken after January 1601,[285] take into account whether the 'object was taken under duress (including military violence, looting or theft), or other apparently legal transactions that involved use of force or coercion' or 'communal property acquired from a person or persons of that community not authorised to give or sell it'.[286] The Dutch NMVW principles allow return in cases where cultural objects were 'collected/acquired in contravention of the standards of legality at the time'[287] or in circumstances, where 'the claimants were involuntarily separated' from the objects, due to lack of consent, duress ('forced sale') or lack of authority of the former 'possessor' to 'dispose' of the object (e.g. 'inalienable communal property').[288]

The report of Dutch Advisory Committee made unconditional returns dependent on proof (e.g. through provenance research) that 'objects came into Dutch possession against the owner's will' with 'reasonable degree of certainty'.[289] It lists 'theft, looting, extortion or seizure of cultural heritage objects as spoils of war' as examples.[290] It adds that in grey areas, such as gifts or sales in 'contexts of power inequality', it is 'necessary to rely on the available information to assess the degree to which the transfer of possession was voluntary'.[291]

The German guidelines take into account whether 'the legal and ethical standards of the time were already violated when the object was acquired, or if the circumstances under which it was acquired fundamentally contravene today's ethical standards for museum acquisitions'.[292] Relevant factors include whether the 'object was taken from the original owner by the use of direct violent force'[293] or as 'a result of the colonial situation', for example because 'members of the communities of origin acted on behalf of the colonial masters'.[294] The document recognizes that the 'wrongful act' does not necessarily 'have to have been committed by the staff of the museum itself or by German citizens'.[295]

The Belgian Law on the Legal Framework for Restitution and Return lists coercion or force as main examples of illegitimately acquired objects which should be

---

[285] 2020 Oxford Procedures, Section 1.4.
[286] Ibid, Section 2.2.
[287] NMVW Principles, § 4.2.
[288] Ibid, § 4.3.
[289] Dutch Advisory Committee Report on the National Policy Framework, 68.
[290] Ibid, 55.
[291] Ibid, 55.
[292] Guidelines for German Museums 2021, 83.
[293] Ibid, 83.
[294] Ibid, 84.
[295] Ibid, 84.

returned *ex officio*,[296] while determining that objects whose status cannot be determined should remain in Belgian possession.[297]

The Arts Council guidance is more evasive. It states that a museum may 'have to return an object for legal reasons' if 'the claimant can demonstrate a stronger right of ownership to the object than the museum's', such as cases where the object 'was stolen or otherwise misappropriated' or 'removed without authorisation', provided there was a law at the time 'vesting' the antiquities in the state.[298] However, it lists unethical circumstances of removal as one of four ethical criteria, which museums need consider in their decision on restitution or return.[299]

(ii) Cultural significance

The second common justification relates to the role or value of the object to countries or communities of origin. It justifies return not based on past wrongdoing or injustice, but based on contemporary relations to objects, such as the cultural, religious, or sacred nature of the object and its special significance to the former owners or guardians.[300] The scope and conditions of this criteria differ across national contexts.

Dutch guidelines make such returns dependent on a balancing on interests. The NMVW-Principles support return in cases where cultural objects are 'of such value (cultural, heritage or religious) to nations and/or communities of origin that continued retention' cannot be justified.[301] They includes objects whose 'sacred purpose' render them 'unsuited to public display and continued scientific research' and objects 'whose relative national historical significance' or 'influence on continuous cultural wellbeing outside the Netherlands' outweighs 'all benefits of retention' in the Netherlands.[302]

The report of Dutch Advisory Committee recognizes the option of return for objects which are of 'particular cultural, historical or religious importance for the source country'.[303] It allows requests for return of such objects, 'regardless of whether the source country was a Dutch colony or a colony of another European power'.[304] But it distinguishes this process from redress of injustice, since it deals with the 'honouring a particular interest of the source country'.[305] It specifies that

---

[296] See Belgian Parliament, 'Draft law recognising the alienable character of goods linked to the colonial past of the Belgian State and determining a legal framework for their restitution and return', Doc. 55 2646/001, 25 April 2022, 15. The law adopted on 3 July 2022 puts the emphasis on the illegitimate nature of the acquisition, in particular acquisition under duress or as a result of coercive violence.

[297] Ibid.

[298] Arts Council England Guidance, 16.

[299] Ibid, 14–15.

[300] It is inter alia reflected in cultural heritage protections of indigenous people, such as the 'cultural affiliation' requirement under NAGPRA (see Chapter 6,) or Art. 11(2) UNDRIP.

[301] NMVW Principles, § 4.4.

[302] Ibid.

[303] Dutch Advisory Committee Report on the National Policy Framework, 6, Recommendation 6.

[304] Ibid, 71.

[305] Ibid, 6, Principle 6.

the interests of the source country 'should be weighed against other relevant interests on the basis of reasonableness and fairness'.[306] The report acknowledges that the 'importance of retaining an object for the Netherlands' is an important factor, including the ability to tell colonial history in Dutch museums 'through engaging objects, from the perspectives of both the former colonizer... and those who were formerly colonized'.[307] It argues that the assessment may also include conditions in the source country, such as 'storage conditions', 'the scope for academic research' and public accessibility.[308] It distances itself at the same time expressly from the 'universal museum' ideology. It states:

> [U]niversal museums are not always readily accessible to the population of countries whose key cultural heritage objects are there on display. Moreover, it cannot be assumed that an object will be shown to better advantage among objects from other cultures and periods than in the source country among objects which together amount to a comprehensive and historically meaningful presentation of its culture.[309]

The German guidelines adopt a 'community'-based approach. They allow returns of objects which were 'of special religious or cultural significance' to the 'community of origin'. They specify that the items must have enjoyed such cultural importance at the time of their 'removal', and should have 'maintained this significance until today or even regained it'.[310] An exception is recognized for human remains which 'should always be repatriated when the community of origin so desires'.[311] The 2020 Oxford Procedures are more restrictive. They require both illegitimate circumstances of acquisition[312] and 'a genuine link or cultural continuity with the object(s)' by the 'claimant community'.[313] The Arts Council Guidance mentions the 'significance of the object to the claimant' as one of the ethical criteria of assessment of return claims.[314]

The express requirement of continuing link has been exposed to critiques. Experiences with NAGPRA have shown that communities evolve and migrate. Some communities may have lost connection to the objects based on their removal. Knowledge that has been passed over generations may have gone lost. It is cynical to require such a link to be shown, if that same link was disrupted by

---

[306] Ibid.
[307] Ibid, 71.
[308] Ibid.
[309] Ibid.
[310] Guidelines for German Museums 2021, 83.
[311] Ibid, 84.
[312] 2020 Oxford Procedures, s 2.2.
[313] Ibid, Section 4.3.
[314] Arts Council England Guidance, 14. It includes the 'genealogical, cultural, spiritual or religious link between the claimant and the object's original creator or past owner'. Ibid, 15.

colonial structures.[315] Kwame Opoku has openly questioned the relevance of the cultural significance requirement in cases of looting:

> Why should I as African, Ghanaian and Asante have to explain to an Englishman why an Asante sword in any British museum is significant for my people? Would a British official ask a Western claimant such a question?[316]

(iii) Addressee of returns

A commonly recurring problem, both in the context of international returns or repatriation practices, is to decide to whom objects should be returned. This issue may trigger controversies between source countries and communities, or between different communities, and produce stalemate or 'winners and losers' in restitution processes.[317] For instance, royal objects are often subject to competing claims in a source community. A pertinent example is the story of the canoe prow of Prince Lock Priso Bell. The ethnological museum in Munich (*Museum Fünf Kontinente*) found itself unable to return it to Cameroon, because it could not determine whether it should be returned to Lock Priso's grandson, Kum'a Ndumbe, or to Paul Mbappe, the official head of the royal Bele Bele family.[318]

In other cases, community interests may conflict with state interests. Source communities may perceive returns to state entities as an attempt to 'highjack' or rewrite colonial histories to the benefit of ruling authorities. For example, the return of the Bible and whip of Nama resistance leader Hendrik Witbooi (1834–1905) to Namibia caused divided reactions in the Nama community, since it reinforced sentiments of marginalization.[319] Witbooi refused to surrender to the authority of the German Empire, arguing that Nama and Herero are sovereign and independent kingdoms.[320] The objects were taken from him as war trophies by German forces after a surprise attack at Hornkranz in 1893.[321] The negotiation of return by the Namibian government provoked concerns among Nama leaders and the Witbooi household that the state would take credit for Nama resistance and sacrifice and portray Witbooi as a national resistance hero, while marginalizing the role of the Nama, which remain a minority in contemporary political

---

[315] It may have to be newly re-established, as the Sarr/Savoy Report has emphasized.

[316] Kwame Opoku, 'Will the New Guidelines of the Arts Council England Help Restitution of Looted Asante Gold and Benin Bronzes'? *Modern Ghana* (15 September 2022) https://www.modernghana.com/news/1183469/will-the-new-guidelines-of-the-arts-council-englan.html.

[317] Apoh and Mehler, 'Mainstreaming the Discourse on Restitution and Repatriation', 7.

[318] See Chapter 2.

[319] Reinhart Kößler, 'The Bible and the Whip: Entanglements surrounding the restitution of looted heirlooms', ABI Working Paper No. 12 (Freiburg: Arnold Bergstraesser Institute, 2019).

[320] Ibid, 3 ('Damaraland [Hereroland] belongs to the Herero nation alone and is an independent kingdom on its land, and Namaland belongs solely to all the red coloured nations, and these are also independent kingdoms just as it is said of the White man's countries, Germany and England and so on').

[321] Piet van Rooyen, 'The German Attack on the Witboois at Hornkranz, Namibia, April 1893' (2021) 49 *South African Journal of Military Studies* 57–73.

structures.[322] The Nama Traditional Leaders Association (NATLA) requested to be represented in negotiations in its own right, rather than through the Namibian government ('Not about us without us'), and even took legal action to suspend restitution, until ownership issues are settled.[323] The objects were returned to Namibia in a ceremony in 2019. They became initially part of the national archives, until completion of a museum in Witbooi's hometown of Gideon.

Museums and holders of objects seek to avoid to become 'embroiled in domestic disputes in a country of origin'[324] or to be 'drawn into any disputes within a group of claimants'.[325] This is reflected in the framing of guidelines and policies. The Sarr and Savoy report stated that return is in principle an inter-state process. It determined that the decision to whom the object should be returned falls within the responsibility of the requesting state.[326] For instance, in the case of the return of Maori remains, France treated the government of New Zealand as representative of source communities.[327] The same approach was followed by the Constitutional Court for the State of Baden-Württemberg in the *Witbooi* case. It held that the dispute over ownership of the whip and the bible falls within the internal jurisdiction of Namibia.[328]

The Dutch guidance on colonial collections reflects a similar principle. It reaffirms that redress of historic injustice is generally 'directed towards state representatives of the source country' and that in case of returns, the 'ownership passes to the State which has authority over the area from which the cultural heritage object originated'.[329] It then falls within the responsibility of that state to ensure that 'the cultural heritage object reaches the appropriate place'.[330] The guidance mentions at the same time the dilemmas that may arise if the respective state fails to return the object to the community which is deemed to benefit from it. It states that the principle of inter-state return does not detract from the need 'to enter into dialogue … with other parties in the source countries and with the diaspora communities' on the 'possibility of return' and the ways in 'which objects came into Dutch possession'.[331] The difficulties became apparent in the case of the Banjarmasin Diamond.[332] Family descendants of the Sultanate of Banjarmasin requested the return, but remained suspicious of inter-state negotiations, since they feared that the

---

[322] Apoh and Mehler, 'Mainstreaming the Discourse on Restitution and Repatriation', 6.
[323] See Constitutional Court for the State of Baden-Württemberg, Nama Traditional Leaders Association, Order, 1 VB 14/19 (21 February 2019) https://www.disputeresolutiongermany.com/wp-content/uploads/2019/03/190221_1VB14-19_Nama-Leaders.pdf.
[324] Guidelines for German Museums 2021, 88.
[325] Ibid, 89.
[326] Sarr and Savoy, *The Restitution of African Cultural Heritage*, 82.
[327] Ibid.
[328] See Nama Traditional Leaders Association, Order, 21 February 2019.
[329] Dutch Advisory Committee Report on the National Policy Framework, 72.
[330] Ibid, 72
[331] Ibid, 73.
[332] See Chapter 2.

Indonesian government would place it in the National museum in Jakarta. This created an impasse blocking restitution.[333]

In legal terms, the framing of returns as an inter-state act accommodates the preferences of states, which often prefer to place politically sensitive colonial heritage in a supposedly 'neutral' national collection. But it is at odds with the recognition of the legal personality of sub-state entities in international law, such as rights of people under the law of self-determination or the special protection of indigenous people or minorities under international human rights law. Such non-state actors are not always recognized as distinct legal entities under existing heritage instruments, but may enjoy a right of participation in decision-making processes affecting their cultural rights.[334] For instance, the UN Committee on Economic, Social and Cultural Rights has affirmed that the two Covenants include 'the right of minorities and of persons belonging to minorities to take part in the cultural life of society, and also to conserve, promote and develop their own culture'.[335] The right of everyone to take part in cultural life is not confined to participation in cultural activities, but also covers participation in the 'definition, elaboration and implementation of policies and decisions that have an impact on the exercise' of cultural rights.[336] UNDRIP grants indigenous people an express right to act collectively to 'maintain, control, protect and develop their cultural heritage, traditional knowledge and traditional cultural expressions'.[337] It recognizes the right of indigenous peoples 'to participate in decision-making in matters which would affect their rights'.[338] As UN Special Rapporteurs have recognized in the context of the dispute over the participation of Ovaherero and Nama during the German-Namibian interstate negotiations, such participatory rights in decision-making processes may create obligations for states deciding on returns to involve collective sub-state entities, such as representatives of minority groups or indigenous people, in negotiations on return.[339]

---

[333] See Jos van Beurden, *Inconvenient Heritage* (Amsterdam: Amsterdam University Press, 2021) 223–224.

[334] Belgian Ethical Principles, § 2.3.1 ('It is no longer just a question of cultural heritage law, but also of the right to cultural heritage as an "inherent right to participate in cultural life"').

[335] Ibid, General Comment No. 21, 8, with reference to Art. 15 ICESCR and Art. 27 ICCPR.

[336] Ibid, General Comment No. 21, 4.

[337] UNDRIP, Art. 31. See also UN Committee on Economic, Social and Cultural Rights, General Comment No. 21, Right of Everyone to Take Part in Cultural Life (Article 15), UN Doc E/C.12/GC/21, 21 December 2009, 9.

[338] UNDRIP, Art. 18.

[339] On 23 February 2023, seven UN Special Rapporteurs noted in a joint communication to the governments of Germany and Namibia that 'the legal status of the Ovaherero and Nama peoples and their representatives as indigenous peoples under international and national law is different and separate from that of the Namibian Government itself, and thus requires a place of its own in the negotiations'. See UN OHCHR, Joint Communication from Special Procedures, AL DEU 1/2023, 23 February 2023, 8, at https://spcommreports.ohchr.org/TMResultsBase/DownLoadPublicCommunicationFile?gId=27875. See also Jochen von Bernstorff and Jakob Schuler, 'Wer spricht für die Kolonisierten? Eine völkerrechtliche Analyse der Passivlegitimation in Restitutionsverhandlungen' (2019) 79 ZaöRV 553–577, 576.

UNDRIP expressly challenges the logic of exclusive inter-state returns in relation sacred objects, regalia, or cultural objects, which are essential to the cultural or political self-determination of indigenous groups. It suggests that indigenous peoples, rather than states should be beneficiaries of the return of objects, which form part of their cultural traditions and customs. This is further supported by the Mātaatua Declaration on Cultural and Intellectual Property Rights of Indigenous Peoples, adopted by the Commission on Human Rights Working Group on Indigenous Populations in 1993. It states that 'indigenous cultural objects held in museums and other institutions must be offered back to their traditional owners'.[340]

The English Arts Council Guide lists the ability 'to properly care for the object' as one of the ethical criteria.[341] It expresses a clear policy preference for return to 'a collecting institution (e.g. museum) with a track record in storing and caring for this type of material'.[342] This insistence on 'capacity' replicates colonial power relations. It reflects a classical Western perspective on objects, which is reminiscent of the Universal Museum logic. The generalized focus on protection or care may conflict with different object conceptions in communities of origin, who may view them as spiritual or living objects that should not be placed in a museum, or the fact that return is simply owed.[343]

2.3.3 Participatory approaches

The prospects of new relational ethics are inherently connected to the establishment of structures of dialogue and interaction. This idea is reflected in the ICOM Code of Ethics, which mandates museums to work in close collaboration with the communities from which their collections originate as well as those they serve.

The newly emerging guidelines on colonial collections go beyond ICOM, by specifying the need for structural conditions enabling dialogue, in particular a commitment to equality. For instance, the NMVW principles acknowledge that returns can only be successful if they are 'made in a context which allows for consultation and open dialogue'.[344] They specify that return of cultural objects should be treated 'according to standards of respect, transparency and timeliness'.[345] The German Framework Principles for collections from colonial contexts acknowledge the need for 'dialogue in a spirit of partnership, understanding and reconciliation with the societies affected by colonialism'.[346] The German guidelines clarify that

---

[340] Mātaatua Declaration on Cultural and Intellectual Property Rights of Indigenous Peoples, E/CN.4/Sub.2/AC.4/1993/CRP.5, 26 July 1993, Art. 2.14.

[341] Arts Council England Guidance, 16.

[342] Ibid.

[343] As Chimamanda Ngozi Adichie noted in her address at the opening of the Humboldt Forum on 22 September 2021: 'It does not matter whether Africans or Asians or Latin Americans can take care of the art stolen from them. What matters is that it is theirs.'

[344] NMVW Principles, 2.

[345] Ibid, § 1.4.

[346] See Framework Principles for dealing with collections from colonial contexts agreed by the Federal Government Commissioner for Culture and the Media, the Federal Foreign Office Minister of

dialogue should be based on the principles of 'mutual respect' and equality, i.e. 'communication on equal terms'.[347] The Belgium Principles define 'equality' as 'the starting point for renewed collaboration and relations among heritage institutions and between heritage institutions and communities of origin'.[348]

This principled recognition of the principle of equality reflects an attempt to correct inequalities of the past. It is reflected in practices of provenance research and cultural cooperation. For instance, some museums have developed inter-rogative working methods and initiatives, enabling curators to work jointly with representatives from source countries or communities in order to revisit object biographies, challenge colonial narratives, and determine appropriate methods of display. However, in negotiations on return or repatriation, the conditions of dialogue often remain uneven. They are constrained by existing ownership relations, which give holding institutions the power to determine the status of objects, and the inter-state nature of return processes, which mediate the cultural interests of communities through the voice of colonial successor states.

Some guidelines express a more fundamental commitment to device return principles and policies in consultation with source countries or affected communities. For instance, the Dutch guidance recognizes that policies regarding return of colonial cultural heritage objects cannot be based on a 'supply-driven' approach defined by former colonial powers, but require 'a common policy that is supported by both the Netherlands and the source countries' in order to avoid 'neocolonial mimicry'.[349] But existing instruments remain inconclusive in relation to certain ongoing challenges, such as the representation of local community interests in negotiations or the resolution of conflicting claims.[350]

3 Legal avenues: Three models of responsibility

One of the critiques of existing guidelines is that they marginalize the legal foundations of decision-making processes. The strong emphasis on ethics presents returns as a moral question. This limits their ability to express acknowledgement of wrong and provide redress for historical injustice. For instance, the German Framework Principles for Dealing with Collections from Colonial Contexts specify that '[i]dentifying cultural objects from colonial contexts which were appropriated in a

---

State for International Cultural Policy, the Cultural Affairs Ministers of the Länder, and the municipal umbrella organizations (13 March 2019) 1 https://www.auswaertiges-amt.de/blob/2210152/b2731f8b5 9210c77c68177cdcd3d03de/190412-stm-m-sammlungsgut-kolonial-kontext-en-data.pdf   (German Framework Principles).

[347] Guidelines for German Museums 2021, 86.
[348] Belgian Ethical Principles, § 1.
[349] Report Dutch Advisory Committee on the National Policy Framework, 81.
[350] Apoh and Mehler, 'Mainstreaming the Discourse on Restitution and Repatriation', 4–6.

way which is no longer legally and/or ethically justifiable and enabling their return is a moral and ethical obligation and an important political task for our age.[351] The report of the Dutch Advisory Committee on the National Policy Framework for Colonial collections states expressly that 'the handling of requests to return cultural objects is not so much a legal as an ethical question', due to the application of statute of limitations, the non-retroactivity of international conventions and the imprecision of 'standards and principles of international humanitarian law'.[352] It sometimes even claimed 'that there are no rules under international law which prohibited the acquisition of cultural goods during colonial rule'.[353]

Such assertions tend to overlook that ethical criteria in relation to colonial injustice are grounded in fundamental legal concepts. This is expressly reaffirmed by the Belgian Ethical Principles. They acknowledge that the 'return of colonial cultural property to its country of origin' responds not only 'to an ethical requirement of reconciliation', but also 'constitutes a fundamental legal issue', since it enables 'people and communities of origin' to get access to 'their heritage' in line with international human rights law.[354]

A recurring obstacle in the legal assessment of return claims is the intertemporal rule. It prohibits the retroactive application of international law and requires that facts should be assessed according to the standards of the time when they occurred.[355] It protects stability, legal certainty, and fairness by providing a safeguard against the risk of arbitrary decision-making or 'reading history backwards'.[356] However, it is neither absolute[357] nor a bar to forward-looking models of responsibility for colonial takings.

Heritage takings enjoy special features which make it appropriate to apply relational approaches towards intertemporality, which take into account some of

---

[351] Framework Principles for dealing with collections from colonial contexts agreed by the Federal Government Commissioner for Culture and the Media, the Federal Foreign Office Minister of State for International Cultural Policy, the Cultural Affairs Ministers of the Länder, and the municipal umbrella organizations (13 March 2019) Principle 7 (emphasis added) https://www.auswaertiges-amt.de/blob/2210152/b2731f8b59210c77c68177cdcd3d03de/190412-stm-m-sammlungsgut-kolonial-kontext-en-data.pdf (German Framework Principles).

[352] Report Dutch Advisory Committee on the National Policy Framework, 59.

[353] Guidelines for German Museums 2021, 160.

[354] Belgian Ethical Principles, § 2.3.1.

[355] See the famous dictum of arbitrator Max Huber in the 1928 *Island of Palmas* award, Permanent Court of Arbitration, *Island of Palmas (Netherlands v USA)* (1928) 2 RIAA 829, 845 ('a juridical fact must be appreciated in the light of the law contemporary with it, and not of the law in force at the time when a dispute in regard to it arises or falls to be settled'). The rule is reflected inter alia in Art. 28 of the Vienna Convention on the Law of Treaties and Art. 13 of the 2001 ILC Articles on Responsibility of States for Internationally Wrongful Acts. It is generally qualified as representing customary law. See Taslim O. Elias, 'Doctrine of Intertemporal Law' (1980) 74 *American Journal of International Law* 285–307.

[356] Jenkins, 'From objects of enlightenment to objects of apology', 90.

[357] For a discussion, see Carsten Stahn, 'Confronting Colonial Amnesia' (2020) 18 *JICJ* 793–824, 803–807. See also Karina Theurer, 'Germany Has to Grant Reparations for Colonial Crimes: UN Special Rapporteurs Get Involved Right on Time', *Völkerrechtsblog*, 2 May 2023, doi: 10.17176/20230502-204347-0.

the intergenerational harms of past violations,[358] allow contextualization of the intertemporal rule or provide leeway for justice-related exceptions to the application of past norms and time-bars in litigation ('let bygones be bygones').[359]

Theorists in multiple fields have developed new responsibility models, which offer pathways to provide reparatory justice and overcome traditional objections to redress (e.g. passage of time, multiplicity of causes, impossibility of compensation or redress), dilemmas of inter-generational justice and blame for past wrong. For instance, Mari Matsuda has shown that traditional concepts, such as wrong, causation or remedy require a differentiated understanding in relation to types of historical injustice which continue to produce stigma and economic harm.[360]

Political philosopher Iris Young has advocated a social connection model of responsibility,[361] which grounds responsibility in the connection to structural injustice, ongoing harm or unjust conditions, and shared responsibility towards others. This theory is able to accommodate the collective and intergenerational dimensions of colonial injustice. Contemporary agents are not per se blamed for all the wrong the past (e.g. guilty of wrong), but rather held responsible for remedying present injustices that are enduring.[362] This model opens doors for forms of responsibility that are not grounded in agency-based liability (e.g. responsibility without culpability) and oriented towards future-oriented redress. For instance, Olúfẹ́mi O. Táíwò has justified reparatory justice as a future-oriented project, aimed at building a better social order.[363]

Michael Rothberg has developed the notion of 'implicated subject' in holocaust studies in order to emphasize the enduring responsibility of 'those who have inherited or who have otherwise benefited from histories of perpetration'.[364] This concept offers new ways to go beyond simple victim/perpetrator divides and acknowledge that a single subject can be implicated in multiple histories.

---

[358] The argument that cultural takings cause intergenerational harm may be traced back to the Congress of Vienna settlements (Lord Viscount Castlereagh). In 1988, Justice Finlay of the Supreme Court of Ireland held in *Webb v Ireland* that cultural takings deprive people of the 'keys to their history'. See Supreme Court of Ireland, *Webb . Ireland* (1 January 1988) [1988] IR 353, 383, para. 61 ('[i]t would … now be universally accepted, certainly by the People of Ireland, and by the people of most modern States, that one of the most important national assets belonging to the people is their heritage and knowledge of its true origins and the buildings and objects which constitute keys to their ancient history'). Indigenous rights instruments recognize that the retention of human remains or sacred objects marks an ongoing dignity-taking, which may cause spiritual harm and intergenerational trauma.

[359] Stahn, 'Confronting Colonial Amnesia', 823.

[360] Mari J. Matsuda, 'Looking to the Bottom: Critical Legal Studies and Reparations' (1987) 22 *Harvard Civil Rights-Civil Liberties Law Review* 323–399.

[361] Iris Young, 'Responsibility and Global Justice: A Social Connection Model' (2006) 23 *Social Philosophy and Policy* 102–130.

[362] See also Catherine Lu, *Justice and Reconciliation in World Politics* (Cambridge: Cambridge University Press, 2017) 161. On the concept of enduring justice, see Jeff Spinner-Halev, *Enduring Justice* (Cambridge: Cambridge University Press, 2012).

[363] Olúfẹ́mi O. Táíwò, *Reconsidering Reparations* (Oxford: Oxford University Press, 2022).

[364] Michael Rothberg, *The Implicated Subject: Beyond Victims and Perpetrators* (Stanford: Stanford University Press, 2019) 83.

Others again build on insights from transitional justice and argue that colonial injustice should be addressed in dialogical terms,[365] namely through open and transparent structures of discourse that allow for contestation, debate, and diverse perspectives, including non-Western views. They acknowledge that social interaction may not necessarily bring closure about the past, but provide a voice to unheard communities, transform the way in which the past is narrated,[366] or promote recognition, empowerment, or mutual engagement through a process in which each side has to give way in an effort to reach 'fair and just solutions'.[367]

There are, at least, three main models to establish contemporary responsibility for cultural takings: (i) recognition of wrong and return, based on past wrongdoing, (ii) returns grounded in a broader structural relationship to wrong, and (iii) human rights based lenses, aimed at transforming relations towards the objects. These three approaches correspond to different types of justice. The first approach relies on an interactional justice model. It grounds in responsibility for human agency, such as the removal of cultural objects. The second approach is based on looser forms of responsibility. It ties responsibility to implication in structural types of injustice. The third approach follows a relational justice model. Responsibility is derived from the link between agents and cultural objects.

3.1 Interactional justice: Remedying wrong

Interactional justice is based on the premise that colonial injustice entails responsibility for past wrong, which needs to be recognized and remedied.[368] It determines where artefacts 'belong' in light of 'past wrongs'.[369] Under this model, return is owed as a form of material and/or symbolic reparation. It follows a torts model, based on wrongdoer-victim schemes. The wrongdoer, i.e. former colonial powers owe responsibility to the former colonized subject. Remedial action recognizes violations of rights of formerly colonized peoples, strengthens recognition of wrong and empowers claimants.

This model is inter alia reflected in the redress approach, envisaged by the Dutch Advisory Committee, and acquisition criteria used to establish an unjust context. The guidelines establish past wrong in different ways: establishment of wrongfulness according to the standards of the time, and according to contemporary standards.[370]

---

[365] See Anthony Bottoms and Justice Tankebe, 'Beyond Procedural Justice: A Dialogic Approach to Legitimacy in Criminal Justice' (2013) 102 *Journal of Criminal Law and Criminology* 119–169.

[366] See also Iris Young, *Responsibility for Justice* (Oxford: Oxford University Press, 2011) 182.

[367] See Nicole Immler, How to Acknowledge Colonial Injustice?, Interview 26 February 2019, at https://www.ind45–50.org/en/how-acknowledge-colonial-injustice-interview-nicole-immler.

[368] See also Vrdoljak, *International Law, Museums and the Return of Cultural Objects*, 300.

[369] See also generally, Evelien Campfens, 'Whose Cultural Objects? Introducing Heritage Title for Cross-Border Cultural Property Claims' (2020) 67 *Netherlands International Law Review* 257–295.

[370] See e.g. Guidelines for German Museums 2021, 83.

3.1.1 Wrongfulness according to the standards of the time

Legally, there are at least two ways to establish past legal wrong, despite the ambiguous or discriminatory nature of positivist law at the time.[371] One possibility is to argue that certain cultural takings contravened the 'principles of justice which guide the public conscience', even in the absence of express general prohibitions.[372]

As noted earlier,[373] applying on-positivist doctrines and concepts such as principles of humanity, fairness, or equity, to assess the context of removal of cultural objects is not necessarily in conflict with standards of the time.[374] The increasing codification and protection of cultural property suggests that colonial powers were governed, at least, by a 'pre-modern realm' of natural law[375] and by greater positive law obligations in the nineteenth century. Certain cultural takings conflicted with the expected standards of behaviour under minimum principles of humanity, and with the principles of cultural protection and integrity asserted among 'civilized' nations, such as the universalist arguments made by Antoine-Chrysostome Quatremère de Quincy (1755–1849),[376] the *Marquis de Somerueles* case,[377] or professional codes and practices.[378] A clear-cut example is the forcible taking of objects in punitive expeditions (theft and looting) or 'skullduggery' (e.g. grave robbery), which is a form of dignity-taking. Other forcible property takings violated protective duties under protectorate agreements.[379]

Another way to establish legal wrong is to look at cultural takings not only from a purely Western perspective on law, but also from the perspective of the colonized. This argument takes into account the pluriversality of legal orders at the time.[380]

---

[371] For a different view, see Afolasade A. Adewunmi, 'Possessing Possession: Who Owns Benin Artefacts' (2015) 20 *Art Antiquity and Law* 229–242, 240.

[372] See Alexander Herman, 'Law, Restitution and the Benin Bronzes', Institute of Art and Law (23 December 2018) https://ial.uk.com/law-restitution-and-the-benin-bronzes/ ('while the looting of African stores was not legally forbidden at the time, the actions were nonetheless of questionable morality, even back then').

[373] See Chapter 5.

[374] Andreas Buser, 'Colonial Injustices and the Law of State Responsibility: The CARICOM Claim to Compensate Slavery and (Native) Genocide' (2017) *ZaöRV* 409–446, 432–433.

[375] Frédéric Mégret, 'From Savages to Unlawful Combatants: A Postcolonial Look at International Law's "Other"' in Anne Orford (ed.), *International Law and Its Others* (Cambridge: Cambridge University Press, 2006) 265–317, 283.

[376] Antoine-Chrysostome Quatremère de Quincy, *Letters on the Plan to Abduct the Monuments of Italy* in Antoine-Chrysostome Quatremère de Quincy, *Letters to Miranda and Canova on the Abduction of Antiquities from Rome and Athens* (C. Miller and D. Gilks trs, Los Angeles: Getty Research Institute, 2012) 9.

[377] British Court of Vice-Admiralty at Halifax, 'The Marquis de Someruelos' (21 April 1813) in James Stewart, *Reports of Cases Argued and Determined in the Court of Vice-admiralty at Halifax in Nova-Scotia* (London: Butterworth and Son, 1814) 482–486, 483.

[378] One difficulty is the vagueness of notions of 'humanity' and 'public conscience' which makes them vulnerable to divergent interpretations. Their application may thus easily apply contemporary interpretations to past actions. See also Andreas von Arnauld, 'How to Illegalize Past Injustice: Reinterpreting the Rules of Intertemporality' (2021) 31 *EJIL* 401–432, 419.

[379] See Chapter 6.

[380] See Chapter 6.

It may face methodological problems in relation to cultures which relied on unwritten norms and customs.

3.1.2 Wrongfulness according to contemporary standards

A second option is to challenge past legalities based on the contemporary application of principles of justice and equity.[381] This reasoning acknowledges that the intertemporal rule has limits. It takes into account that the application of the standards and constructs of the time may lead to a perpetuation of injustice and make contemporary agents complicit in the consolidation of discriminatory norms.

The jurisprudential foundations of this doctrine have been formulated by German jurist Gustav Radbruch in 1946, who argued that the very idea of legality is tied to an expectation of minimal justice. He claimed that positive law 'must yield to justice' if the 'conflict between statute and justice reaches such an intolerable degree' that the statute itself constitutes 'flawed law' (*Radbruch* formula).[382]

Radbruch's idea is reflected in reflected in the Washington principles and some WWII documents relating to cultural property, such as the 1943 Inter-Allied Declaration Against Acts of Dispossession Committed in Territories Under Enemy Occupation or Control, which affirmed the right of Allied powers not to recognize legal titles over cultural property acquired under Nazi occupation or control.[383] Logically, the argument may be extended to structural injustice in colonial contexts.[384] It may be argued that 'some acts or omissions are so horrendously unjust that no reasonable State, and notably not those States that saw themselves as particularly "civilized", may rely on their legality'.[385]

---

[381] See Report Dutch Advisory Committee on the National Policy Framework, 68: '[A] law prevailing at a time of injustice cannot serve as a guide for assuming responsibility for the past ... The Committee believes the basic principle must be whether loss of possession would be qualified as unlawful or unethical in the present day'.

[382] Gustav Radbruch, 'Statutory Lawlessness and Supra-Statutory Law' (1946) (B. Litschewski Paulson and S. L. Paulson trs) (2006) 26 *Oxford Journal of Legal Studies* 1–11, 7.

[383] It states: 'Governments making this Declaration and the French National Committee reserve all their rights to declare invalid any transfers of, or dealings with, property, rights and interests of any description whatsoever which are, or have been, situated in the territories which have come under the occupation or control, direct of indirect of the Governments with which they are at war, or which belong, or have belonged to persons (including juridical persons) resident in such territories. *This warning applies whether such transfers of dealings have taken the form of open looting or plunder, or of transactions apparently legal in form, even when they purport to be voluntarily effected*' (emphasis added). See also UNESCO Draft Declaration of Principles relating to Cultural Objects Displaced in Connection with the Second World War, Principle 2(iv).

[384] For instance, Jos van Beurden has formulated Principles for Dealing with Colonial Cultural and Historical Objects, encouraging a 'just and fair solution' for objects 'taken without just compensation' or 'lost involuntarily in the European colonial era'. See Van Beurden, *Treasures in Trusted Hands*, 242–243. For an application of the spirit of the 1943 London Declaration to colonial objects, opening prospects of return for objects acquired 'apparently legal in form', see Vivek K. Hatti, India's Right to Reclaim Cultural and Art Treasures from Britain under International Law (2000) 32 *George Washington Journal of International Law & Economics* 465–487, 471.

[385] Buser, 'Colonial Injustices and the Law of State Responsibility', 432–433.

In contemporary litigation, Dutch Courts have relied on this reasoning in order to justify the non-applicability of statutes of limitations in relation to colonial crimes committed in the war of independence of Indonesia between 1945 and 1949. They have argued that a state may be prevented from invoking such bars to responsibility in good faith, if it has been complicit in grave violations and barred victims from claims. Judges have relied on criteria of 'reasonableness and fairness' in order to establish that victims have valid claims against the former colonial power.[386] They provided redress in circumstances where victims have been precluded from making claims under colonial structures and were able to demonstrate continuing harm.[387]

In legal doctrine, this argument has been used to challenge the retention of looted cultural objects, such as the Benin bronzes. For example, Salome Kiwara-Wilson has questioned whether a legal title for acquisition may be derived from 'the nineteenth century international law on spoils',[388] which discriminated among 'civilizations', turned non-Western entities into 'objects of international law'[389] and left them little authority or legal recourse to challenge lootings. She has argued that the legality of acquisition of the bronzes should be assessed based on legal standards applicable between European powers, rather than on the basis of racially biased law, which excluded an entire 'group of people from the protection of the law'.[390]

In the case of the Quimbaya Treasure,[391] the Constitutional Court of Colombia went even a step further. It rightly acknowledged that non-retroactivity is not an absolute principle,[392] but then decided to set aside international law applicable at the time by duties of return under contemporary human rights law and the 1970 UNESCO Convention. The ruling is problematic from a legal point of view because it applied contemporary standards on return of cultural objects retroactively,[393] based on shaky constructions of *jus cogens*.[394]

---

[386] The Hague Court of Appeal, *Children of Executed Men in South-Sulawesi v The Netherlands*, Case No. 200.243.525/01 (1 October 2019); The Hague Court of Appeal, *Heirs Java Torture Victim v The Netherlands*, Case No. 200.247.634/01 (1 October 2019).

[387] For a similar approach in relation to historical injustice, see Matsuda, 'Looking to the Bottom', 379–382.

[388] Salome Kiwara-Wilson, 'Restituting Colonial Plunder: The Case for the Benin Bronzes and Ivories' (2013) 23 *DePaul Journal of Art, Technology & Intellectual Property Law* 375–425, 390.

[389] Ibid, 391.

[390] Ibid, 392.

[391] See Chapter 2.

[392] Diego Mejía-Lemos, 'The "Quimbaya Treasure," Judgment SU-649/17' (2019) 113 *AJIL* 122–130, 125.

[393] Ibid, 125–126.

[394] Ibid, 128–129.

3.2 Structural injustice: Responsibility grounded in the contemporary relationship to wrong

The method of assessing wrongfulness according to contemporary standards has been criticized on a number of grounds: 'interpreting history through the eyes of the present',[395] projecting 'contemporary moral sensibilities' into the consideration of diverse contexts of acquisition[396] or unfairly blaming 'people living today' for the wrong of the past'.[397] Some of these problems may be addressed by an alternative model, namely structural justice theories. They link responsibility to ongoing structural relations and the duty to put an end to the reproduction of injustices, such as exploitation or unjust enrichment. Under this approach, historic injustice needs to be addressed because it is still ongoing and perceived as a 'living injustice'.

Important theoretical foundations have been developed by Young's social connection model of responsibility.[398] It recognizes the identity-related nature of the removal of cultural objects, grounds responsibility to a contemporary relationship towards wrong and may overcome some of the problems of non-retroactivity or intertemporal law caused by classical agent-related models.[399] It enables restitution or return in cases, in which conduct may have been permitted under formal structures of law applicable at the time. In holocaust studies, it is inter alia reflected in Rothberg's conceptualization of the enduring responsibility of implicated subjects.[400] This approach transcends binary victim-perpetrator schemes inscribed in classical models of responsibility and ties responsibility to wider forms of participation than agency, such as contributing, witnessing, or benefiting from social histories.[401]

In cultural heritage law, this argument has been supported by the inherent link between cultural heritage, national identity, or self-determination. For instance, Italian international lawyer Tullio Scovazzi, has argued that cultural heritage law cannot be limited to existing treaties. He has defended the view that principles, such as the preservation of the 'the integrity of cultural contexts' or 'non-exploitation

---

[395] Jenkins, 'From objects of enlightenment to objects of apology', 91.

[396] Martin Skrydstrup, 'Righting Wrongs: Three Rationales of Repatriation and What Anthropology Might Have to Say About Them' in Mille Gabriel and Jens Dahl (eds.), *Utimut: Past Heritage-Future Partnerships, Discussions on Repatriation in the 21st Century* (Copenhagen: International Work Group for Indigenous Affairs and Greenland National Museum & Archive, 2008) 56–63, 59.

[397] Jenkins, 'From objects of enlightenment to objects of apology', 90.

[398] Young, 'Responsibility and Global Justice: A Social Connection Model', 102–130. See also Magali Bessone, 'The Colonial Slave Trade, Slavery and Structural Racial Injustice in France: Using Iris Marion Young's Social Connection Model of Responsibility' (2019) 20 *Critical Horizons* 161–177.

[399] See generally Taslim Olawale Elias, 'The Doctrine of Intertemporal Law' (1980) 74 *AJIL* 285; Rosalyn Higgins, 'Time and the Law: International Perspectives on an Old Problem' (1997) 46 *ICLQ* 501.

[400] Rothberg, *The Implicated Subject*, 83.

[401] Ibid, 1.

of the weakness of another for cultural gain'[402] form part of practices of the field, which are necessary to address 'shortcomings of multilateral treaties' regarding the return of cultural objects[403] and 'reach an equitable solution for each particular case'.[404] He has applied the prohibition to 'exploit weakness of another subject to get a cultural gain' not only to WW II contexts, but also to peoples subjected to colonial or foreign occupation.[405]

This approach extends options of return beyond forcible acquisition or wrongdoing to colonial exploitations. It makes it possible to take into account ethical and historical considerations which taint the acquisition of such objects, based on their current implications, irrespective of whether or not the underlying transactions were legal in form in the past.[406] It captures transactions, in which colonial officials, museums or private collectors exploited unequal bargaining power in colonial contexts or deliberately closed their eyes to the history or conditions of taking of objects. It facilitates proof of returns since it does not require a determination as to whether the particular action was legal or illegal according to the standards of the time.

The unjust enrichment argument also has an economic underpinning. Holders and collections are benefiting from the cultural value of objects.[407] Many culturally significant objects are generating economic benefits for museums in the Western world, based on 'cultural tourism' or property rights. These forms of cultural exploitation, to the exclusion of source countries and communities, are difficult to sustain in case of cultural colonial objects taken through force or in contexts of structural injustice. They require critical reconsideration from a contemporary perspective, through return, novel forms of consent or regimes ensuring sharing of assets and benefits.[408]

This logic is inter alia reflected in the Dutch principles and the German museum guidelines. They recognize a commitment to return, irrespective of whether the country holding the collections played a part in the unlawful taking or unjust taking of objects. The focus is placed on the involuntary nature loss in countries or communities of origin, caused by the structural conditions. This perspective takes into account the collective nature of colonial injustice, caused through the complex interplay of networks and agents. It is also part of the 'Values and Principles' statement of the Smithsonian Institution in Washington. It recognizes that 'ethical

---

[402] Tullio Scovazzi, 'The "First Time Instance" as Regards Restitution of Removed Cultural Properties' (2012) 30 *Agenda Internacional* 9–19, 18.

[403] Ibid, 18.

[404] Ibid, 19.

[405] Ibid, 18.

[406] Tullio Scovazzi, 'Diviser c'est détruire: Ethical Principles and Legal Rules in the Field of Return of Cultural Property' (2011) 94 *Rivista di Diritto Internazionale* 341, 370.

[407] See Chapter 7.

[408] Pierre Losson, 'Opening Pandora's Box: Will the Return of Cultural Heritage Objects to Their Country of Origin Empty Western Museums?' (2021) 51 *The Journal of Arts Management, Law, and Society* 379–392, 384.

norms and best practices at the Smithsonian and in the museum profession have changed over time'.[409] It then adds:

> We acknowledge that the Smithsonian has collected from individuals and communities in a manner that has caused harm or benefited from unequal power relationships. Such practices may be reflected in collections we hold today, but they must have no part in our future interactions and collecting.[410]

3.3 Relational justice: Human rights-based approaches towards cultural heritage

The third and most contemporary model, grounds responsibility in the relationship between people and objects, and rights of access to culture.[411] It is less concerned with the allocation of blame or culpability for past wrong. It deals with the contemporary connection to objects. It is grounded in cultural heritage law, which has recognized the non-severability between people and objects since the nineteenth century,[412] and modern strands in human rights law, which create 'a positive obligation to take steps to protect cultural groups and communities in their exercise of [cultural] freedoms'.[413] This approach recognizes requests for return as identity claims by communities.[414] The guiding criterion is not so much, to whom objects belonged in the past or where they are most visible, but rather where they 'belong' culturally and socially.

The novelty is this approach lies in the fact that it ties return to 'the acknowledgement of a right to possess, access, or control certain involuntarily lost cultural objects on the grounds of their intangible heritage interests for specific people, independent of ownership'.[415] It seeks to build and reinforce relationships of respect and responsibility between people, by recognizing the importance of culture heritage communities. It thereby goes beyond cultural nationalist approaches, which link return to sovereignty interests, or self-determination and minority rights. It is able to address the problem of the lack of retroactivity of many contemporary treaty instruments and facilitates return to non-state actors.

---

[409] Smithsonian Ethical Returns Working Group, Values and Principles Statement (3 May 2022) https://www.si.edu/newsdesk/releases/smithsonian-adopts-policy-ethical-returns.

[410] Ibid.

[411] See Chapter 7.

[412] See Vrdoljak, *International Law, Museums and the Return of Cultural Objects*, 23, 26–27.

[413] Francesco Francioni, 'Beyond State Sovereignty: the Protection of Cultural Heritage as a Shared Interest of Humanity' (2004) 25 *Michigan Journal of International Law* 1209–1228, 1213.

[414] For example, ownership and physical possession shape the way how objects are used or represented.

[415] Evelien Campfens, 'The Bangwa Queen: Artifact or Heritage?' (2019) 26 *International Journal of Cultural Property* 75–110, 106.

The important link between objects and people was first recognized in the context of self-determination. In the case concerning the return of the 'Venus of Cyrene',[416] Italian Courts held that self-determination provides a customary law basis for the duty to return cultural objects removed as a result of colonial domination.[417] Ana Vrdoljak has argued that the rationale for the "restitution of cultural objects held by museums of former metropolitan and national capitals" is intimately linked to the right to self-determination under international law, including 'a people's ability to maintain, revitalize and develop their collective cultural identity'.[418] According to this logic, returns of cultural artefacts or human remains are a way of returning the dignity and culture of their past.[419]

This model provides a legal foundation for the 'cultural significance' criterion, contained in several national guidelines or policies. It is expressly mentioned in the Dutch guidance, which recognizes that 'depriving a community of access to objects essential to its culture is a violation of human rights and therefore constitutes an argument in favour of return'.[420] It also underpins the call for a legal framework for return in the Belgian Ethical Principles. The Principles acknowledge that the recognition of 'a fundamental right to cultural heritage opens the debate on the return of collections'.[421] They ground the legal foundation of return in 'access by the people and communities of origin to their heritage'.[422]

3.4 Intersectionality

The three approaches cannot be viewed in isolation of each other. They all add different angles to the complex debate on restitution and return. The interactional justice lens recognizes wrong in processes of acquisition and relations between agents. It reflects a logic of restitution. It entails a need for inquiry into provenance histories and acknowledgement of wrong, which are necessary to come to terms with colonial wrong. The structural injustice model enables a broader consideration of contextual factors enabling inequalities and ongoing harms created through colonial conditions. It provides a basis to seek new forms of consent for objects contained in colonial collections and procedures to facilitate dialogue.[423] The relational perspective extends claims beyond inter-state relations and supports

---

[416] See Chapter 4.

[417] See Alessandro Chechi, 'The Return of Cultural Objects Removed in Times of Colonial Domination and International Law: The Case of the Venus of Cyrene' (2008) 18 *Italian Yearbook of International Law* 159–181.

[418] Vrdoljak, *International Law, Museums and the Return of Cultural Objects*, 300.

[419] Ciraj Rassool, 'Re-storing the Skeletons of Empire: Return, Reburial and Rehumanisation in Southern Africa' (2015) 41 *Journal of Southern African Studies* 653–670.

[420] Report Dutch Advisory Committee on the National Policy Framework, 63.

[421] Belgian Ethical Principles, § 2.3.1

[422] Ibid.

[423] See Chapter 9.

return and negotiation based on rights of access to culture in contemporary relations.

Taken as a whole, the three models challenge the traditional assumption that cultural colonial takings operate in a legal vacuum. The justice and cultural significance criteria contained in guidelines and notions, such as items from 'colonial contexts' (German Guidelines)[424] or acquisition under 'inequitable conditions' (Sarr and Savoy report)[425] are not only ethical criteria, but correspond to responsibility models and general principles of cultural heritage law. The three models establish a differentiated basis for responsibility, based on past and contemporary relations.

4 Revisiting narratives and semantics

The harms inflicted through cultural takings go far beyond physical removal or cultural dispossession. They encompass ongoing forms of epistemic violence, which may perpetuate stereotypes or divides, entrench inequalities, or marginalize alternative modes of knowledge. Re-considering narratives and semantics is an important element of responsible engagement with the past and 'righting' the future.

Museum terminology and professional discourses continue to rely on concepts and language that have been shaped by the colonial experience.[426] For instance, Native Americans objects or objects from Africa or Latin America are often classified through anthropological or ethnic lenses (e.g. ethnographic or 'tribal' artefacts), while the terms art or antiquities are reserved to objects from Western provenance, the Middle East or certain parts of the 'Far East'. Political narratives, seemingly neutral or technocratic scientific classifications or descriptions, and legal notions may contribute to the silencing of colonial violence, stifle alternative histories, or reproduce cultural hierarchies. They may alter or erase past meanings (e.g. the 'animated' nature objects) or constitute new identities, almost like a 'birth certificate'.[427] Professional and scientific language easily creates an illusion 'that the methods, motivations and impact of this knowledge production are also somehow objective and neutral'.[428] Terms of art, such as or 'primitive art' or 'First Arts', may reproduce developmental myths or cultural inequalities. It is thus

---

[424] Guidelines for German Museums 2021, 23.

[425] Sarr and Savoy, *The Restitution of African Cultural Heritage*, 61.

[426] They are reflected in classifications, provenance research and labelling or display of objects. See Claire Smith, 'Decolonising the Museum: The National Museum of the American Indian in Washington, DC' (2005) 79 *Antiquity* 424–439.

[427] Ciraj Rassool, 'Museum Labels and Coloniality' in Robin Lelijveld and Wayne Modest (eds.), *Words Matter: An Unfinished Guide to Word Choices in the Cultural Sector* (Amsterdam: NMVW, 2018) 20–24, 21.

[428] Hodan Warsame, 'Mechanisms and Tropes of Colonial Narratives' in Lelijveld and Modest, *Words Matter*, 78–85, 85.

critically important to revisit and challenge conscious and unconscious biases created through narratives and labels.

Some of the new guidelines or policy instruments openly address this dilemma. For instance, the Belgian Ethical Principles expressly stress the need for more inclusive forms of display and management practices, with 'careful attention to a context of structural power imbalances'.[429] They encourage 'new labelling practices with deepened provenance, inclusive and critical displays, and self-reflexive approaches to the histories of colonialism and racism'.[430] The Dutch National Museum of World Cultures Research Center for Material Culture has created an 'Unfinished guide to word choices within the cultural sector',[431] in order to promote more inclusive knowledge frames and avoid a perpetuation of discriminatory or racist language. Wayne Modest, the Director of Content National Museum of World Cultures, has argued persuasively argued that this initiative is an essential element of decolonial museum strategies, geared at confronting the past and promoting relational ethics:

> Paying attention to words means acknowledging that the language we use affects whether a person or a group feels excluded or included, whether they feel a sense of belonging to society. This is about representation, recognition and respect.[432]

4.1 Classifications

A first form of epistemic violence, which needs to be addressed, is the replication of colonial classifications and categorizations.[433]

Cultural division into ethnicities and tribes was an inherent part of colonial governmentality. Sometimes museum collections group objects across certain ethnic lines that were defined through the colonial encounter and thereby determine who belongs to a particular culture. This way of classification may perpetuate 'white projection'. Ciraj Rassool has drawn attention to the problem of 'museum entribement' whereby collections attribute works 'to a group or tradition or "tribe" rather than to an individual'.[434] Such practices contribute to the process of 'inventing tribes and classifying groups and artifacts with tribal labels'.[435] Similar problems may arise when museums have to decide on returns based on criteria

---

[429] Belgian Ethical Principles, Executive Summary.
[430] Ibid.
[431] Lelijveld and Modest, *Words Matter*.
[432] Wayne Modest, 'Words Matter' in Lelijveld and Modest, *Words Matter* 12–17, 17.
[433] Hannah Turner, *Cataloguing Culture: Legacies of Colonialism in Museum Documentation* (Vancouver: University of British Columbia Press, 2020).
[434] Rassool, 'Museum Labels and Coloniality', 21.
[435] Ibid, 23.

of cultural affiliation. Such determinations may entrench forms of 'othering' that 'decoloniality seeks to dismantle'.[436]

This problem is acknowledged in the German Guidelines. They confirm that ethnic labels must 'be handled with caution' and 'subjected to critical analysis', even when they 'form the only clues to identify a community of origin', since the 'ethnicities' or 'ethnic groups' recorded in museum holdings may reflect European colonial categorizations, which were assigned without 'sufficient heed to artistic variations and processes of social change and exchange' and therefore 'do not reflect the complexity and changing nature of historical and contemporary social identities'.[437]

It is equally important to reflect the close connection between cultural takings and racial science and salvage anthropology,[438] which have played an important part of the rationalization of the acquisition of objects, including cultural objects, and taking of human remains from the battlefield, detention camps, medical hospitals, or graves.[439] As the Belgium guidelines note, 'discriminatory and racist' notions embedded in colonial rule do not have to be erased in all cases. They also constitute evidence of colonial histories, which form part of historical memory. But where used, they should be presented as 'quotations', with additional clarification 'in footnotes or between brackets'.[440]

In terms of legal categorizations, the choice between the neutral term 'return' and the notion of 'restitution' deserves closer attention.[441] The notion of return may silence colonial violence, since it 'simply acknowledges the fact that an object was removed and is returned to its original place' and thereby erases 'the memory of the object or part of its biography'.[442] Some guidelines seek to counter this implication. For instance, the Sarr and Savoy speaks of 'criteria for restitutability'.[443] The Dutch guidance explicitly distinguishes return and 'redress'. The Belgian Ethical Principles deliberately use the word 'restitution' rather than 'return or repatriation'.[444] It is sometimes even suggested that the notion of 'restitution' is too limited and reflects a Eurocentric approach, centred on illegalities of takings. For instance, in the context

---

[436] Aria Danaparamita, 'Repatriation: One Mode of Decolonial Deaccessioning?' in Recollecting and Reallocation: Collection Assessment, Ethical Deaccessioning and Multiple Stakeholders (Amsterdam: National Museum of World Cultures, 2020) 50–57, 56.

[437] Guidelines for German Museums 2021, 22.

[438] Belgian Ethical Principles, § 5.7, arguing that discussions surrounding human remains 'should engage with the broader ethics and historical legacies of the "scientific" racism that shaped these collections'.

[439] See chapters 2 and 4.

[440] Belgian Ethical Principles, § 5.3.

[441] In the UNESCO context, it has become common to use return in order to avoid the assumption that the original acquisition was unlawful. See Chapter 6.

[442] Emery Patrick Effiboley, 'Reflections on the Issue of Repatriation of Looted and Illegally Acquired African Cultural Objects in Western Museums' (2020) 7 Contemporary Journal of African Studies 67–83, 69.

[443] Sarr and Savoy, The Restitution of African Cultural Heritage, 61.

[444] Belgian Ethical Principles, § 3.1 ('"Restitution" refers to guilt: the rectification of a past mistake … This history illustrates the importance of language, and the importance of the word "restitution" rather than return or repatriation').

of the Belgian negotiations, Congolese Prime Minister Jean-Michel Sama Lukonde has preferred to use the term 'reconstitution', rather than 'restitution' in order to reflect the idea that return is both a cultural and a spiritual act, aimed at reconstituting heritage, re-establishing history, and reconnecting objects with their 'ancestors'.[445]

4.2 Narratives and labels

A second imperative is greater sensitivity to narratives and labels used in display practices. This is a recurring problem across collections.

The vocabulary used to categorize acquisitions in museum archives often fails to reflect the unjust power relations in colonial contexts. Sometimes, the terms suggest that objects were just there and open to takings or purchase or they convey myths about the acceptability of colonial behaviour or tropes about the heroic nature of collection, based on stories of 'discovery or exploration of the unknown and the exotic'.[446] For instance, collection histories in ethnographic museums often feature an innocent or 'heroic White man, an Indiana Jones-like protagonist', such as an 'explorer, scientist, artist, photographer or a missionary', someone 'who bravely went where few other White people had gone before' and returned with objects or photographs.[447] In certain cases, objects are grouped or categorized according to the identity of the 'heroic' collector, rather than their creators. This logic reverses patterns of agency and victimization.[448] The collector becomes the historical source of reference, the creator a passive or anonymous footnote in history.

The terms used to describe individual acquisition may replicate colonial histories through distancing, role reversal or heroization. For instance, the term 'punitive expedition' attaches an appearance of legality to operations which were aimed at suppressing colonial resistance. It is an epitome of 'white projection' since it presents colonial forces as victims of force, provoked by colonial subjects. It contains a psychological reversal of blame. It turns the perpetrators into victims in order to justify the imposition of colonial order, and ignores the structural context of resistance. From a structural perspective, it is not an act of law enforcement, but a forcible method of colonial subjugation.

The term 'protective force' (*Schutztruppe*) is built on a similar logic. It hides colonial violence under the umbrella of the concept of protection.[449] The concepts of

---

[445] Michel Bouffioux, 'Restitution au Congo: Thomas Dermine détaille un dispositif ambitieux' *Paris Match* (7 March 2022) https://parismatch.be/actualites/societe/544638/restitution-au-congo-thomas-dermine-detaille-un-dispositif-ambitieux.

[446] Warsame, 'Mechanisms and Tropes of Colonial Narratives', 84.

[447] Ibid, 84.

[448] Ibid, 84 ('The adventurer in these narratives is the one who has agency, the one who is doing the "doing"').

[449] Another critical example is the use of the word 'battle'. It is inherently entangled with notions of triumph, heroism, or honour on the battlefield. It singles out specific events, and reduces the colonial

'war booty' or 'military prize' reflect a similar dilemma. They are used to legitimize cultural takings, while concealing the forcible and non-consensual nature of acquisition. They silently accept that taking of war booty was an accepted right of the victor (*jus praedae*) at the time, although practices differed across colonial powers. The use of word 'fetish' is derogatory and reflects racial or missionary ideologies.

Some guidelines or policies draw attention to this problem. For instance, the Belgian principles recognize that using verbs, such as 'collecting' objects may mask the violence behind the takings.[450] Reversing epistemic colonialism requires greater efforts and consciousness to understand how the vocabulary used in collecting histories includes or exclude colonial narratives and replicates historical biases. The neutral and objective language used in official archives and documentation requires critical scrutiny, since it may detach artefacts from their social history. What is officially recorded as a 'purchase', 'gift' or exchange may constitute a 'forced' purchase' or gifts, according to closer contextual analysis.

The use of the word 'object' needs to be set in context.[451] Lessons from the display or return of 'spiritual objects' or the repatriation of artefacts or human remains to indigenous people suggest that it is important to reflect and accommodate a counter-perspective which regards objects as 'animate' or carriers of 'reciprocal relationships with humans' in terms of their 'force, personhood, emotions, kin, life cycle, and function'.[452] This is expressed by their equation to 'ancestors' or 'missing persons' in the voices of communities of origin.[453]

New notions, such as 'shared heritage' carry ambivalent meanings. To holder countries, they express the noble idea that cultural heritage is guarded by museums in the name of humanity.[454] However, for countries or societies of origin this form of sharing remains detached from their reality, needs and interests. For them, the concept may be perceived as a placeholder for a novel civilizatory divide, defining who is considered worthy enough to be a proper guardian of this heritage.[455] The notion should only be used if this sharing is mutually agreed. It must be based on participation, mutual involvement, and co-responsibility. It requires involvement

---

encounter to a military contest, while dis-narrating the aggressive and structural context of colonial violence.

[450] Belgian Ethical Principles, Executive Summary ('The term "collecting" is deceptively neutral').

[451] It embraces a one-sided view of material culture, which separates mind and matter. It defines items 'by the absence of mind or spirit and, by extension, by their inability to embody agency and to act as agents in social relations'. See Harrison, 'Reassembling Ethnographic Museum Collections', 15.

[452] Ibid, 33.

[453] See Chapter 7.

[454] Hermann Parzinger, 'Shared Heritage', Konrad Adenauer Stiftung, *The Political Opinion*, Issue 561 (1 April 2020) https://www.kas.de/en/web/die-politische-meinung/artikel/detail/-/content/shared-heritage.

[455] It represents a novel cultural re-possession, a second taking, in the name of humanity, which confirms that objects have also become part of the identity of those countries who have removed or purchased them.

of curators or representatives from countries of origin or societies of origin, including collaboration in displays and activities, representation of 'traditional knowledge' and openness to question entrenched interpretive hierarchies.[456] Ultimately, the concept of sharing and equal partnership needs to include the option of return.

5 Conclusions

In 1978, Amadou-Mahtar M'Bow qualified objects taken in colonial contexts as 'witnesses to history'.[457] More than for decades later, the removal of objects continues to reflect ongoing trauma and inequality. Objects remain 'witnesses to the past'.[458] They are carriers of multiple histories: histories of art and culture, displacement, colonial identity, or anti-colonial movements.[459] Some of them have become objects of apology. However, they also have a transformative role. They open spaces for new forms of engagement, in both societies of origin and holder countries.[460] They highlight the contradictions and double standards of defensive heritage discourses and innovate museology, including the very conception of the museum.

One of the most significant changes is that discourse on return moves gradually from discussions of preservation of legal ownership or universal protection to ethical obligations, transparency of collections and relational engagement with historical responsibilities and some epistemic dimensions of colonial violence. This process is driven by bottom up approaches and social networks (e.g. activists, civil society, social media movements, individual museum, universities, and supporters of restitution). It has led in some cases to the adoption of individual national guidelines and policies on colonial collections, which are beyond UNESCO structures

---

[456] Certain lessons can be learned be from settler colonial contexts, such as New Zealand, where museums apply Māori-specific concepts, such as *kaitiakitanga* (mandated traditional guardianship) or *Kaupapa Māori* (Māori ways of action and decision-making) in curatorial practice. See Charles Royal, *Mātauranga Māori and Museum Practice: A Discussion. Report prepared for National Services Te Paerangi* (Wellington: Museum of New Zealand Te Papa Tongarewa, 2004). They recognize multiple forms of ownership, including forms of stewardship and care which differ, but co-exist with classical forms of legal titles. Jane Legget, 'Shared heritage, shared authority, shared accountability? Co-generating museum performance criteria as a means of embedding 'shared authority' (2018) 24 *International Journal of Heritage Studies* 723–742, 731.

[457] Amadou-Mahtar M'Bow, 'A Plea for the Return of an Irreplaceable Cultural Heritage to those who Created It' (7 June 1978) ('They bore witness to a history, the history of a culture and of a nation whose spirit they perpetuated and renewed').

[458] See Lyndel Prott (ed.), *Witnesses to History: A Compendium of Documents and Writings on the Return of Cultural Objects* (Paris: UNESCO, 2009).

[459] Some objects 'emplot' different visions of national history. others tell communal or family histories.

[460] They are thus more than objects of 'enlightenment' or 'apology', as suggested by Jenkins, 'From objects of enlightenment to objects of apology'.

and international treaty. They have encouraged greater calls and coordination of return claims in countries of origin and changes in museum ethics. They deviate from the comity-related attitudes towards return in the 1970s, but offer at the same time more flexibility than classical legal restitution processes.

Emerging guidelines and policies avoid to a large extent generalized qualifications of colonial injustice, such as the branding of all takings as looting or theft. They encourage a case-by case assessment, based on criteria, which draw on the interplay between accountability for wrongdoing, ethical responsibilities, and cultural heritage rights. Several instruments reflect the idea that the assessment of return claims is not only about ownership relations, but also about access to culture and the transformation of broken social relations through objects.

The process of confronting colonial heritage changes the role of museums. They have traditionally contributed to the preservation and display of objects, but also their invisibility or *amnēsía* through the erasure of subject/object identities or their 'burial' of objects in storage. The turn to relational ethics implies a shift from what Dan Hicks has called a 'model of curatorial authority and innocence' towards 'one of curatorial implication and responsibility'.[461] It encourages curators to 'unlearn' existing epistemologies[462] and to develop new collaborative strategies in order to overcome existing biases and limitations. Museums become to a certain extent spaces of transformative justice. Some museums implicitly apply transitional justice concepts, such as accountability, truth-finding or social repair to discourses on restitution and return, even though they might not be formally aware of the nexus.

The Sarr and Savoy Report has made it clear that return is not only a means of 'coming to terms with the past', but also a process of transforming relations towards objects, in both holding countries and societies of origin. New ethical frames acknowledge that provenance research requires more common and inclusive forms inquiry and truth-seeking into object histories, including engagement with local oral histories, counter-factuals or complicity of racial science in takings. Certain instruments express a principled commitment to the recognition of injustice and redress as an overarching principle. Such an approach is inter alia reflected in the Dutch principles,[463] the Belgian guidelines, which recommended the adoption of a new legal framework on restitution and return,[464] and the German guidelines, which state that the principles in the instrument 'bear witness to a value system in which, on the basis of an assumed superiority, colonial powers placed themselves

---

[461] Dan Hicks, 'Das Jahrzehnt der Rückgaben: Ausstellungspraxis nach der Epoche der Universalmuseen' (21 September 2022) https://markk-hamburg.de/veranstaltungen/the-brutish-muse ums-the-benin-bronzes-colonial-violence-and-cultural-restitution/.

[462] Stephanie Endter, Nora Landkammer, and Karin Schneider (eds.), *The Museum as a Site of Unlearning: Materials and Reflections on Museum Education at the Weltkulturen Museum*.

[463] Report Dutch Advisory Committee on the National Policy Framework, 6, Recommendation 5.

[464] Belgian Ethical Principles, § 2.3.

above other states and their populations or parts of the population, exploiting and oppressing them.[465]

However, there are also less progressive counter-examples. Some guidelines or policies disguise the violent underpinnings of takings or conceal responsibility through technical language or bureaucratic procedures. For instance, the Arts Council England guidance has been criticized for its technical approach towards restitution and return, i.e. its lack of engagement with structures of injustice and histories colonial objects, and its insufficient distinction between unconditional and conditional returns. The guidelines do not refer to colonial violence, loot, or racist underpinnings of takings.[466] They use the more neutral terms of 'war', 'conflict', 'occupation', or 'duress'.[467] They fail to provide concrete object histories from colonial contexts. The case-by-case focus on objects reduces systematic patterns of violence to single incidents or episodes.[468] In this way, the instrument creates distances to colonial injustice and un-narrates the past. It also fails to engage with non-Western concepts of ownership or property.[469]

The application of transitional justice concepts does not necessarily suffice to address structural dilemmas of colonial injustice, such as epistemic violence, racism, or ongoing economic inequalities. However, it may facilitate creative approaches to restitution. For instance, return practices may benefit from lessons regarding the value of intangible heritage, restorative justice[470] or cultural revitalization after conflict,[471] the importance of the 'right to know' the fate of colonial objects or remains[472] or the value of dignity approaches and ceremonial features in repatriation processes.[473] Transitional justice lenses provide space to broaden object ontologies beyond classical property conceptions,[474] set scientifically oriented heritage interests (e.g. value for science) into a broader historical context or illustrate the limits of the museum as site of public memory in politically divided societies. Most fundamentally, transitional justice ideas suggest that it is important

---

[465] Guidelines for German Museums 2021, 12.

[466] Dan Hicks, 'UK Welcomes Restitution, Just not Anti-Colonialism' Hyperallergic (26 August 2022) https://hyperallergic.com/756241/uk-welcomes-restitution-just-not-anti-colonialism/.

[467] Arts Council England Guidance, 15.

[468] Opoku, 'Will the New Guidelines of the Arts Council England Help Restitution'.

[469] Ibid.

[470] Moira Simpson, 'Museums and Restorative Justice: Heritage, Repatriation and Cultural Education' (2009) 61 Museum International 121–129.

[471] Lucas Lixinski, 'Cultural Heritage Law and Transitional Justice: The Law and Politics of Tragedy Corpses and Atrocity Museums' University of Milano, Bicocca School of Law Research Paper No. 20–02 (2020).

[472] On transitional justice and missing persons, see Monique Crettol and Anne-Marie La Rosa, 'The missing and transitional justice: the right to know and the fight against impunity' (2008) 88 International Review of the Red Cross 355–362.

[473] Chip Powell, Plundered Skulls and Stolen Spirits (Chicago: University of Chicago Process, 2017) 121–122, arguing that processes under NAGPRA con contribute to societal healing.

[474] Some cultural objects have been qualified as 'object diasporas', similar to human diasporas' or as 'missing' ancestors or persons .See Paul Basu, 'Object diasporas, resourcing communities: Sierra Leonean collections in the global museumscape' (2011) 34 Museum Anthropology 28–42, 30

to understand restitution in complex ways, i.e. beyond the naïve belief that giving back alone would provide social repair.[475]

Legally, there are different models, which are emerging in relation to returns. The first a 'justice model'. It takes into account legal and ethical arguments for return. It approaches cultural takings from the perspective of redress for injustice. It is closely linked to historical injustice approaches. It involves acknowledgement of wrong. Decisions on return depend less on the characteristics of the object itself, rather than its modalities of acquisition. The appropriate remedy to address wrong is typically return of ownership or rights relating to the object. This approach towards injustice is visibly influenced by the ongoing debate on racism, discrimination, and inequality, which places the emphasis on continuing and ongoing effects of colonialism in everyday structures. It promotes redress of collective wrong, in line with the structural nature of colonial violence. For instance, both the Dutch and the German guidelines promote return based on injustice, even if the wrong was committed by others. The taking of the Benin objects is a case in point. It has prompted initiatives for return even by bystanders. For instance, the National Museum of African Art of Smithsonian Institution in Washington, which has acquired Benin objects, has pledged their return and removed them from display based on past injustices. It has stated:

> The historical artworks from the Benin kingdom (in present-day Nigeria) that were looted by British soldiers in the 1897 raid on the royal palace have been removed from display. We recognize the trauma, violence, and loss such displays of stolen artistic and cultural heritage can inflict on the victims of those crimes, their descendants, and broader communities.[476]

The second model (cultural significance model) places greater emphasis on the cultural or spiritual significance of objects. It is grounded in contemporary relations to objects and rights of access to culture under human rights instruments. The specific nature of the objects thus plays a greater role. This model is more access-based, rather than ownership-based. It is geared towards the future, rather than acknowledgement of past wrong. It is thus less directly grounded in transitional justice concepts, such as access to truth or restitution.

Both models have certain limits. The justice model poses problems in relation to return of objects that did not form part of cultural property of a specific community at the time when they were taken or acquired their value only much

---

[475] On repair as a 'process of working through', see von Oswald, *Working Through Colonial Collections*, 63.

[476] See Smithsonian Institution, National Museum of African Art, 'The Raid on Benin, 1897' https://africa.si.edu/exhibitions/current-exhibitions/visionary-viewpoints-on-africas-arts/the-raid-on-benin-1897/.

later.[477] For instance, Janna Thompson has cautioned that justice criteria should not be used to create 'cultural property' 'retrospectively'.[478] In this case, return is not necessarily an act of restitution in the strict sense. The cultural significance model faces limits if the community of origin from whom the object was taken no longer exists. One of its weaknesses is that it may be used to support 'claims by cultural groups that acquired an object unjustly' and by communities that are 'culturally distant from its original maker and cultural context', in cases in which 'they value it highly enough'.[479] This may require difficult balancing decisions[480] or even encourage colonial powers to claim that they may be entitled to retain objects because they have become part of their 'cultural affiliation'.[481] Both models have limits in relation to prehistoric objects, such as human fossils (e.g. Java Man), which predate contemporary cultural identities, but have become important means to trace the origins of civilization, challenge colonial or racial stereotypes or illustrate the historical past and scientific importance of formerly colonized nations.[482] It is thus important not to understand the two models as a straightjacket. As Lea Ypi has argued, it is necessary to leave space for returns based on considerations, which are not grounded in 'amends' for 'past wrongful behaviour',[483] nor mere acts of generosity.

An inherent risk of the contemporary restitution movement is its selectivity and focus on spectacular objects. Return may easily become a performative, rather than a transformative act. For instance, the Benin bronzes have triggered a race for return, while objects looted during other episodes of violence, such as the Boxer rebellion[484] have enjoyed far less attention. Generally, objects that are looted or stolen gain more prominence than other objects—not because of their artistic value, but rather due to their colonial history. This may create an artificial hierarchy of restitution. Restitution Africa warned that the turn to cultural justice in relation to particular categories of objects, such as the Benin bronzes, 'has the potential to silence discussion around subjects that do not as easily meet the more comfortable standards of lengthy European record, violence, royalty, and artistic merit'.[485]

---

[477] Janna Thompson, 'Cultural Property, Restitution and Value' (2003) 20 *Journal of Applied Philosophy* 251–262, 255, 256, 259. Thompson provides the example of historic manuscripts of the Norse people, which were written in the thirteenth century, taken from Iceland by Danes in the eighteenth century, when Iceland was a Danish colony, and gained value after Iceland's independence.

[478] Ibid, 256.

[479] Janna Thompson, 'The Ethics of Repatriation: Rights of Possession and Duties of Respect in Geoffrey Scarre and Robin Coningham (eds.), *Appropriating the Past: Philosophical Perspectives on the Practice of Archaeology* (Cambridge: Cambridge University Press 2013) 82–97, 89.

[480] NAGRA allows return to contemporary tribes, based on a priority order, including title to tribal or aboriginal land. See Chapter 7.

[481] Waldron has argued that the right to restitution may be superseded in the course of time. See Jeremy Waldron, 'Superseding Historic Injustice' (1992) 103 *Ethics* 4–28.

[482] Fenneke Sysling and Caroline Drieenhuizen, 'Java Man and the Politics of Natural History: An Object Biography' (2021) 177 *Journal of the Humanities and Social Sciences of Southeast Asia* 290–311. See Chapter 5.

[483] Lea Ypi, 'What's Wrong with Colonialism' (2013) 41 *Philosophy & Public Affairs* 158–191, 187.

[484] See Chapter 6.

[485] Restitution Africa, *Reclaiming Restitution*, 15.

Some institutions may seek to rebrand their own reputation or reconstruct national identity through selective returns and changing vocabulary (transparency, shared heritage collaboration), rather than confronting colonial pasts. Return procedures should facilitate practices which go beyond both rituals of self-purification by former colonial powers and cultural nationalist reappropriation of objects in countries of origin.

9

Beyond to Return or Not to Return: Towards Relational Cultural Justice

1 Introduction

'The master's tools will never dismantle the master's house'

Audre Lorde[1]

For decades, the debate over cultural colonial objects has been framed in terms of a modern Shakespearian either/or question, namely a choice between return or not to return.[2] This binary vision is grounded in the divide between cultural nationalism[3] and cultural internationalism.[4] It has created an 'argumentative loop', which has polarized the debate and led to stalemate and antagonism.[5] It fails to capture the complexity of the underlying issues. Restitution is neither a Marxian 'spectre', which entails a threat of 'empty galleries',[6] nor a magical tool, which suffices to

---

[1] Audre Lorde, 'The Master's Tools Will Never Dismantle the Master's House' in Audre Lorde, *Sister Outsider: Essays and Speeches* (Berkeley: Crossing Press 1984) 110–113.

[2] Philippe de Montebello, 'And What Do You Propose Should Be Done with Those Objects?' in James Cuno (ed.), *Whose Culture? The Promise of Museums and the Debate Over Antiquities* (Princeton: Princeton University Press, 2012) 55–70; Tiffany Jenkins, *Keeping Their Marbles: How the Treasures of the Past Ended Up in Museums—And Why They Should Stay There* (Oxford: Oxford University Press, 2018).

[3] Cultural nationalism focuses on the national value of objects. It is criticized for marginalizing claims of intra-national communities or groups. See Joe Watkins, 'Cultural Nationalists, Internationalists, and 'Intra-nationalists': Who's Right and Whose Right? (2005) 12 *International Journal of Cultural Property* 78–94.

[4] Cultural internationalism relies on universal value of cultural objects, based on their meaning to human culture. The focus on the meaning of objects towards humanity has been invoked to challenge arguments in favour of return. See Chapter 8.

[5] See Pauno Soirila, 'Indeterminacy in the Cultural Property Restitution Debate' (2022) 28 *International Journal of Cultural Policy* 1–16, 12, Jérémie Eyssette, 'Restitution vs. Retention: Reassessing Discourses on the African Cultural Heritage' (2023) 66 *African Studies Review* 101–126, Thomas Laely, Marc Meyer, and Raphael Schwere, 'Restitution and beyond in contemporary museum work: re-imagining a paradigm of knowledge production and partnership' (2020) 7 *Contemporary Journal of African Studies* 17–37.

[6] The NAGPRA experience has falsified the initial fear by museums, archaeologists, or scientists perception that the recognition of the option of repatriation would lead to a wholesale emptying of collections. See Patty Gerstenblith, 'Museum Practice: Legal Issues' in Sharon Macdonald (ed.), *A Companion to Museum Studies* (Oxford: Wiley-Blackwell, 2011) 442–456, 453.

Confronting Colonial Objects. Carsten Stahn, Oxford University Press. © Carsten Stahn 2023.
DOI: 10.1093/oso/9780192868121.003.0009

reverse harms of takings or dismantle colonial continuities. It is not always sought,[7] nor necessarily the 'gold standard' for all cases.[8]

Cultural colonial objects sit in 'a space of contested, entangled relationality'.[9] The complexity of colonial violence and object identities make it necessary to rethink approaches towards cultural takings beyond restitution and return. Heritage discourses may be hijacked by considerations of economic benefit or post-colonial self-fashioning. Addressing past wrongdoing and reversing ongoing inequalities require mutual encounter, learning, and remembering. Mutual engagement needs to extend beyond the physical act of return or beyond what is due[10] in order to confront history and epistemic violence. Centuries of colonial past will not simply disappear. The challenge is how to move beyond debates on return or restitution towards social repair. This requires engagement with the trajectories that led to the present, hidden complicities, or uncomfortable truths.[11] Objects represent 'unfinished' events and 'also some form of outstanding debt'.[12] New engagement is not necessarily a loss, but an opportunity for museums and public collections to confront past racial tropes, enable new collaborations, or ensure fairer economic burden-sharing. Return may itself be a means to decommodify objects.[13]

Return itself is not an event, but a process. It concerns not only objects, but relations between people and the development of object possibilities, even in the post-return phase. One of the most significant changes is the broadening of options to deal with objects. Engagement encompasses a spectrum of responses.[14]

---

[7] In practice, African or Native American claimants have only sought the return of a fraction of objects held in collections.

[8] As Kwame Opoku has argued: 'Many source countries do not want to receive any objects from European museums, others have interest in a certain group of objects, for example, religious objects or the restitution is disputed within the relevant circles. Sometimes, there is a wish for long-term access to the objects, capacity building or that the digitalized objects be made available to them rather than the restitution of the physical object.' See Kwame Opoku, 'Revised Guidelines on Colonial Collections: Germany Not Advanced with Restitution of Looted African Artefacts' *Modern Ghana* (28 July 2019) https://www.modernghana.com/news/947508/revised-guidelines-on-colonial-collections-german.html.

[9] Wayne Modest, 'In Search of a Space for the Process of Working Through' in Margareta von Oswald, Bonaventure Soh Bejeng Ndikung and Wayne Modest, 'Objects/Subjects in Exile' *L'Internationale Online* (9 March 2017) 10–19, 17.

[10] Dan Hicks, 'UK Welcomes Restitution, Just not Anti-Colonialism' *Hyperallergic* (26 August 2022) https://hyperallergic.com/756241/uk-welcomes-restitution-just-not-anti-colonialism/ ('cultural restitution must be about what we give up, not just what or how we give back').

[11] Wayne Modest has argued that objects may have value as 'ghostly presences' in Europe, which 'remind us of the trajectories to the present', produce discomfort, or leave scars. See Modest, 'Objects/ Subjects in Exile', 17.

[12] Dan Hicks, 'Conversation Piece: Necrography: Death-Writing in the Colonial Museum' (2021) 19 *British Art Studies* 1-37 https://www.britishartstudies.ac.uk/issues/issue-index/issue-19/death-writing-in-the-colonial-museums.

[13] See Sarah Harding, 'Culture, Commodification and Native American Cultural Patrimony' in Martha M. Ertman and Joan C. Williams (eds.), *Rethinking Commodification: Cases and Readings in Law and Culture* (New York: New York University Press, 2005) 137–155.

[14] There is no 'one-size-fits-all' solution. See also Jen Snowball, Alan Collins, and Enyinna Nwauche, 'Ethics, Values and Legality in the Restoration of Cultural Artefacts: The Case of South Africa' (2021) 28 *International Journal of Cultural Policy* 1–18, 14–15.

In certain cases, it may be in the interest of source countries or communities to retain objects in Western collections. They may serve as 'cultural ambassadors' of societies and/or create a culture of critical memorialization in holding states. In other cases, return of ownership of objects may be the most appropriate way to redress wrong, acknowledge past injustice, or express changing attitudes towards behaviour in contemporary society in a tangible way. In again other cases, access to objects, modified ownership relations[15] or epistemic restitution, such as the return of knowledge, may represent the most feasible option.

With the rise of new technologies, evolving ownership models or means of sharing objects, the relation between an object and cultural identity is becoming less dependent on physical possession.[16] This opens perspectives for new relational spaces and object mobility, including the flow and reinvention of knowledge and ideas.[17] For instance, Germany and Belgium have experimented with novel approaches, separating legal ownership from physical possession.[18] Paul Basu has made a case in favour of a more 'translocational' and flexible museology facilitating object mobility, based on the multiplicity of meanings and forms of cultural significance attached to objects.[19] Such an approach may accommodate the idea that certain cultural objects do 'not really belong to anyone' in the classical Western sense.[20]

Future approaches towards restitution and return are inherently linked to changes in the role and conception of museums. It is increasingly debated whether the value of the museum lies predominantly in their ability to display authentic objects and preserve them for future generations, or in their capacity to share knowledge and histories and provide a space for different forms of encounter with objects. For instance, Jesmael Mataga has argued that the 'future of museums in Africa lies in moving away from big, state-sponsored encyclopaedic museums to museums or heritage sites steeped in the local communities' ideas of themselves.'[21] This fundamental choice informs the degree of flexibility and openness towards

---

[15] For instance, the social and cultural significance of objects to specific communities may be recognized through mutually beneficial agreements, specialized provisions on access and circulation of objects, or changes in museum governance structures.

[16] Sarah Harding, 'Justifying Repatriation of Native American Cultural Property' (1997) 72 *Indiana Law Journal* 723–774, 751.

[17] Felix Driver, Mark Nesbitt, and Caroline Cornish, 'Introduction: mobilising and re-mobilising museum collections' in Felix Driver, Mark Nesbitt, and Caroline Cornish, *Mobile Museums* (London: UCL Press, 2021) 1–20, 2.

[18] In both cases, return of ownership rights marked a first step to find new agreement on the status and future handling of objects. This was done through bilateral agreements or consensual arrangements with source countries and communities of origin.

[19] Basu has encouraged 'new ways of reassembling, remediating, recirculating, and reconfiguring collections so that a wider range of stakeholders and communities can access them on their own terms'. See Paul Basu, 'Re-mobilising colonial collections in decolonial times: exploring the latent possibilities of N. W. Thomas's West African collections' in Driver, Nesbitt, and Cornish (eds.), *Mobile Museums* 44–70, 66–67.

[20] Harding, 'Justifying Repatriation of Native American Cultural Property', 760.

[21] Jesmael Mataga, 'Museums in Africa: Reflections on Recent Histories, Emergent Practices and Decolonial Possibilities' (2021) 43 *South African Museums Association Bulletin* 18–25, 24.

new forms of display or circulation of objects in museum policies, or alternative forms of engagement after return of objects. In some cases, museums may not offer the most appropriate space to facilitate an encounter. Placing objects in museums may carry certain disadvantages for those who are at the receiving end of these processes. It may limit access to social elites, conflict with religious, sacred, or ceremonial functions of objects, or bring back colonial déjà vus.[22]

This chapter argues in favour of a more pluralistic culture justice model, in order to overcome some of the traditional dichotomies and impasses of restitution discourses. It takes the view that the main point about recognizing past injustice or 'righting the future' is not necessarily physical return of objects in all cases, but the establishment of new forms of consent regarding the contemporary status, use, display, or benefits derived from such objects.[23] It first traces (i) some lessons from contemporary return practices, including the historical Dahomey returns and Benin bronzes. It then develops (ii) elements of a relational cultural justice approach in order to confront ongoing dilemmas. It introduces ethical and legal foundations of new forms of consent regarding the status of objects. It examines (iii) relational dimensions of procedures and (iv) the merits and limits of the concept of object mobility to break existing divides. It shows that new relations can be facilitated in a number of ways, such as return of ownership, modification of ownership relations, establishment of new forms of access and guardianship, participatory governance models, loan arrangements, ceremonial access, digital access, or transfer of rights. It argues that the different types of value associated with objects may provide important guidance in this process. It concludes with (v) some recommendations to rethink normative structures in domestic and international contexts and (vi) principles of relational cultural justice.

2 Some object lessons

Approaches towards restitution and return have undoubtedly witnessed a renaissance in inter-state relations in past years. Bénédicte Savoy has qualified the French restitutions to Benin as a 'watershed moment' for restitution, with a historical 'before and after'.[24] Others have spoken new of 'a decade of returns', in which the conversation is 'about how to return, not whether to return'.[25] However, upon closer examination, the picture is more diverse, showing light and shadow.

---

[22] For instance, some museums on the continent were founded by colonial powers. One example is the Museum of Human Sciences in Harare.

[23] See Chapter 8.

[24] Farah Nayeri and Norimitsu Onishi, 'Looted Treasures Begin a Long Journey Home from France' *New York Times* (28 October 2021).

[25] Ayodeji Rotinwa, 'Slowly but Surely, Africa's Plundered Artifacts Are Coming Home' *World Politics Review* (3 May 2022).

Although returns and repatriation of human remains have increased, the total number of inter-state returns of cultural objects remains low, compared to the thousands of objects which remain in Western collections. Existing practices remain selective. Restitutions have gained an important role in settler colonial contexts, but remain less common in extractive colonial settings.[26] In this setting, they have been used as a 'tool of soft power' to change images and perceptions of colonial powers.[27] Some episodes of colonial violence attract particular attention and facilitate negotiation with states.[28] Other takings are much less in the focus of debate.[29] Country approaches vary. Some states, such as the Netherlands, Belgium, or Germany have opened new prospects for a more systematic return. Other institutions prefer to see objects in circulation, delay returns, or seek face-saving strategies through loans.

Regional practices differ in light of the nature of the objects. For instance, Latin American countries have largely filed targeted requests focused on the return of specific objects (e.g. rare objects, regalia, objects carrying special meanings). Restitution requests in settler colonial contexts have been more systematic and encompassed a broader number of objects.[30] The chances of success international returns or repatriations depend on a number of factors, such as civil society support, international pressure, related cases[31] or domestic cultural heritage protections. The mobilization of support for the return of Benin bronzes has incentivized voluntary returns. However, at closer look, even some of the alleged success stories, such as the Dahomey returns or work of the Benin Dialogue Group, have light and shadow.

Statements, such as President Macron's famous 2017 speech at the University of Ouagadougou[32] or the position of the Benin Dialogue Group continue to foreground the centrality of the perspectives of former colonizing powers. They challenge the alleged status of Europe as guardian of universal heritage, but also partly maintain it, by defending the legitimacy of collections or past holdings and presenting return as political gesture or act of gratitude. Actual return processes have been slower than anticipated and have faced obstacles. As Nigerian lawyer Folarin

---

[26] Ingrid Samset, 'Towards Decolonial Justice' (2020) 14 *International Journal of Transitional Justice* 596–607.

[27] See Felwine Sarr and Bénédicte Savoy, *The Restitution of African Cultural Heritage: Toward a New Relational Ethics* (November 2018) 31.

[28] For example, returns are frequently discussed in contexts such as Nigeria, Benin, Ethiopia, or the Democratic Republic of Congo.

[29] See e.g., objects from Cameroon or Ivory Coast.

[30] Pierre Losson, *Claiming the Remains of the Past: The Return of Cultural Heritage Objects to Colombia, Mexico, and Peru* (PhD, City University of New York, 2019) 290.

[31] The struggle over the return of the Quimbaya treasures illustrates these obstacles. See Chapter 1.

[32] See Élysée, 'Emmanuel Macron's speech at the University of Ouagadougou' (28 November 2017) https://www.elysee.fr/en/emmanuel-macron/2017/11/28/emmanuel-macrons-speech-at-the-university-of-ouagadougou.

Shyllon has argued, 'countries seeking the return of cultural objects must have the endurance of the long distance runner'.[33]

2.1 Dahomey returns

The movement towards French returns started with an ambitious pledge. In his Ouagadougou speech, French President Macron stated that he could not 'accept that a large share' of the cultural heritage in African countries is kept in France and pledged to create conditions for 'temporary or permanent returns of African heritage to Africa' within five years.[34] In practice, this commitment proved to be overambitious. It has encountered strong domestic resistance.[35]

The historic return of twenty-six royal objects taken by French colonial forces in the Kingdom of Dahomey in 1892 from the Musée du quai Branly to modernday Benin marked the long-awaited first step in the commitment towards a new relational ethics, pledged in the Sarr and Savoy report. The return was celebrated as an act of renaissance. Jean-Michel Abimbola, the Minister of Culture of Benin, said: 'With this exhibition, we are returning to the Beninese people part of their soul, part of their history and their dignity'.[36]

The return of the objects was not followed by a broad and principled opening towards return.[37] Rather, France continued to assess each return on its merits.[38] The National Assembly adopted a specific law in December 2020 to facilitate the return to Benin, without committing legally to an overarching policy.[39] Roselyn Bachelot, the French Minister of Culture, stated on 30 September 2020 in the French National Assembly:

> This is not an act of repentance or reparation: it is the possibility of opening a new chapter in the cultural link between France and Africa. It is a new starting point, which opens the field to new forms of cooperation and circulation of works. It

---

[33] Folarin Shyllon, 'Repatriation of Antiquities to Sub-Saharan Africa: The Agony and the Ecstasy' (2014) 19 *Art, Antiquity, and Law* 121.

[34] See Élysée, 'Emmanuel Macron's speech at the University of Ouagadougou' (28 November 2017).

[35] An initial request for return was rejected in 2016 by former French Minister of Foreign Affairs, Jean Marc Ayrault, who argued that the objects had become part of French heritage. See generally Clara Cassan, 'Should They Stay or Should They Go? African Cultural Goods in France's Public Domain, Between Inalienability, Transfers, and Circulations' (2021) 31 *Fordham Intellectual Property, Media and Entertainment Law Journal* 1248–1301.

[36] Carol Ann Dixon, 'Benin Art: Yesterday and Today, Palais de la Marina, Cotonou, February-May 2022', Museum Geographies (23 February 2022) https://museumgeographies.com/2022/02/23/benin-art-yesterday-and-today-palais-de-la-marina-cotonou-february-may-2022/.

[37] Jonathan Paquette, 'France and the restitution of cultural goods: the Sarr-Savoy report and its reception' (2020) 29 *Cultural Trends* 302–316.

[38] Philippe Baqué, *Un nouvel or noir: Le pillage des objects d'art en Afrique* (Paris: Agone, 2021) 338.

[39] See Law No. 2020–1673 of 24 December 2020 on the restitution of cultural property to the Republic of Benin and the Republic of Senegal.

takes into account the exceptional nature of the works and objects that we wish to return to these two countries, which have requested them.[40]

The law was not deemed to set a general precedent for a more liberal return policy. The justification of return repeated some of the false stereotypes about the legalities of past takings, suggesting that objects could just be taken in an alleged legal void.[41] Bachelot noted:

> It should be noted that the bill is not general in scope: it applies only to the specific set of objects it expressly lists. Thus, even if the objects in question were considered to be taken in war, the passage of this bill will not have the effect of calling into question the legality of our country's ownership of any property acquired in the context of an armed conflict. This mode of acquisition, which is completely excluded today, was not prohibited by any rule at other times, either in France or in any other country in the world. The rules of law and the moral principles which, fortunately, are now in force cannot therefore be applied to past cases.[42]

This position echoed some of the critiques of the Sarr and Savoy report among certain members of the French museum and professional community, who qualified the approach as an attack on 'cultural universalism' and preferred circulation of objects over restitutions.[43]

At the 'farewell ceremony' at the Quai Branly museum on 27 October 2021, President Macron expressed support for a more 'universal' approach towards objects and targeted returns of those artefacts 'whose absence is psychologically the most intolerable'.[44] In 2022, the French Senate adopted a law, which foresees the creation of a new national expert commission, the National Council of reflection on the circulation and return of extra-European cultural goods, composed of up to twelve members.[45] This interdisciplinary body is mandated to give advice on return claims and methodologies on provenance research concerning objects in

---

[40] National Assembly, Minutes, Committee on Cultural Affairs and Education, Examination of the bill on the restitution of cultural property to the Republic of Benin and the Republic of Senegal (No. 3221) (30 September 2020) https://www.assemblee-nationale.fr/dyn/15/comptes-rendus/cion-cedu/l15cion-cedu1920063_compte-rendu.

[41] For a contrary position, see Chapter 6.

[42] Ibid.

[43] Paquette, 'France and the restitution of cultural goods' 309–310, with reference to the reactions by Jean-Jacques Aillagon, former Minister of Culture, and Stéphane Martin, former president of the Musée du quai Branly. For a critical take, see also Emmanuel Pierrat, *Faut-il rendre des œuvres d'art à l'Afrique?* (Paris: Gallimard, 2019).

[44] Vincent Noce, 'Why Macron's radical promise to return African treasures has stalled' *The Art Newspaper* (3 February 2022).

[45] See Draft Law No. 4877, adopted by the Senate, on the circulation and return of cultural property belonging to public collections (11 January 2022) Art. 1; Draft Law No. 133, adopted by the Senate, on the circulation and return of cultural property belonging to public collections (12 July 2022) https://www.assemblee-nationale.fr/dyn/16/textes/l16b0133_proposition-loi#.

public collections. The law also foresees an accelerated procedure for the return of human remains in public collections without the need for a specific law.[46] However, the law does not establish a separate legislative framework regarding return of cultural objects, which would enable museums to decide on deaccessioning of objects. The government has remained reluctant to adopt plans for a general framework legislation. Rapporteur Catherine Morin-Desailly openly criticized the contradiction between the government's 'manifest refusal to take part in the debate' and 'the President of the Republic's desire to define a doctrine on restitution'.[47] French heritage legislation has thus navigated between distinct approaches: a casuistic approach towards return, supported by the Senate, which reflects the traditional logic that return remains a voluntary act,[48] and proposals for a general framework, expressing a stronger commitment to returns, based on definition of criteria.

Both the Sarr and Savoy report and source countries have supported a more permissive legal framework on return. For example, the President of Benin, Patrice Talon, has pushed for more comprehensive restitutions, including the return of an iron sculpture dedicated to the god Gou, a 'double trophy' first seized by King Glèlè and then donated to the Musée d'Ethnographie du Trocadéro by Captain Eugene Fonssagrives, who allegedly 'found' it in a town nearby after the conquest of Dahomey.[49] It was qualified as the 'pearl of the Dahomean' collection and one of the 'most graceful' works of art in Paris in 1912 by French surrealist Guillaume Apollinaire,[50] shown at the notorious exhibition of 'African Negro Art' at the Museum of Modern Art in New York in 1935, and displayed in the Louvre (Pavillon des Sessions).

In 2022, Ivory Coast requested the return of a 'talking drum', the *djidji ayôkwé* ('panther-lion'), which was used by local chiefs as a secret means of inter-village communication in warfare and to support the boycott and resistance against the French colonial administration.[51] The drum was captured by French administrators

---

[46] Ibid, Art. 2. It concerns human remains 'belonging to living human groups whose cultures and traditions are active', whose presence in public collections conflicts with 'the principle of human dignity', and which 'have not been the subject of scientific research for at least ten years'.

[47] Senate, Press Release, 'Le Sénat adopte un cadre pour le retour des biens culturels dans leur pays d'origine' (10 January 2022) https://www.senat.fr/presse/cp20220110a.html.

[48] See Xavier Perrot, 'Colonial Booty and Its Restitution: Current Developments and New Perspectives for French Legislation in This Field' (2022) 8 *Santander Art and Culture Law Review* 295–310, 308.

[49] See Kerstin Schankweiler, 'Double Trophy: Gou by Akati Ekplékendo' in Eva-Maria Troelenberg, Kerstin Schankweiler, and Anna Sophia Messner (eds.), *Reading Objects in the Contact Zone* (Heidelberg: Heidelberg University Publishing, 2021) 140–147, 145; Julia Kelly, '"Dahomey!, Dahomey!": The Reception of Dahomean Art in France in the Late 19th and Early 20th Centuries' (2015) 12 *Journal of Art Historiography* 1–19.

[50] Guillaume Apollinaire, 'Exotisme et ethnographie' *Paris-Journal* (10 September 1912) in Guillaume Apollinaire, *Oeuvres en prose complètes*, vol. II (Pierre Caizergues and Michel Décaudin eds. Paris: Gallimard, 1991) 473.

[51] David Sadler, 'Restitution of Works to Africa: The Process Of Returning the Djidji Ayôkwé, Ivorian Drum, Is Launched' *Globe Echo* (14 November 2022) https://globeecho.com/news/africa/restitution-of-works-to-africa-the-process-of-returning-the-djidji-ayokwe-ivorian-drum-is-launched/.

in 1916, placed in the garden of the French governor until 1930, and finally hosted by the Quai Branly. Its taking had a detrimental effect on societal organization and communication across villages. In the context of negotiations over return, the Ivorian Minister of Culture reiterated the call for a framework law in order to expedite and facilitate return processes.

The French approach has thus been marked by a striking paradox. What started as an ambitious return agenda by President Macron and the recommendations of the Sarr and Savoy report has gradually been narrowed down through parliamentary debates, resistance in the museum world and the constraints of *Realpolitik*. Within a period of five years, Macron's 2017 speech has produced more visible changes in Germany, the Netherlands, or Belgium than at home. In April 2023, Jean-Luc Martinez, former president of the Louvre, has presented a report on restitution policy[52] which follows up on the critiques of the Sarr and Savoy report. It supports a faster administrative procedure, based on advice of a bilateral scientific committee, but places stricter constraints on returns, based on a bilateral approach, tighter admissibility criteria (e.g., illegal or illegitimate acquisition) and conditions, including the duty of the requesting State to preserve the heritage nature of objects and present them in public, the targeted nature of requests, and the exclusion of any financial compensation.[53] One innovation is the creation of a new intermediate option between restitution and non-return for objects that do not meet all of the restitution criteria, entitled 'shared heritage'. This proposal is deemed to address problems relating to the determination of ownership through alternative arrangements, including long-term loans and circulation objects through bilateral agreements specifying rights and uses.[54] The statue of Gou is expressly listed as example. However, as it is framed, the 'shared heritage' concept replicates some of the existing dilemmas ('he who controls the objects controls the story') since it pre-supposes a common understanding of shared history and conditions of taking. It creates the risk that objects may be unilaterally qualified as shared heritage, because they have conquered a space in the European canon of art (e.g., by inspiring Western artists).[55]

---

[52] Jean-Luc Martinez, 'Shared Heritage: Universality, restitutions and circulation of works of art' (Paris: Ministry of Culture, 25 April 2023), https://www.culture.gouv.fr/fr/Espace-documentation/Rapports/Remise-du-rapport-Patrimoine-partage-universalite-restitutions-et-circulation-des-aeuv res-d-art-de-Jean-Luc-Martinez.

[53] Ibid, 54–58.

[54] Ibid, 71.

[55] Kwame Opoku, 'Does The Martinez Report Constitute A Pre-Announced Burial Of African Cultural Artefacts In French Museums?' *Modern Ghana* (14 May 2023), https://www.modernghana.com/news/1230672/does-the-martinez-report-constitute-a-pre-announce.html.

2.2 The movement towards return of Benin bronzes

The road toward the return of Benin bronzes has been paved with lots of good intentions. It is symptomatic of changing attitudes.[56] Notably, return is not only contemplated in countries which were involved in forcible takings, but also by institutions which acquired objects through market transactions. However, ongoing discussions have also shown divergent view points and the risk of secondary conflicts in societies of origin. Most openness and flexibility has been expressed at the micro-level, i.e. by curators and museums holding objects.[57] The strong proactive stance of certain individuals and institutions has triggered a certain domino effect. Inter-state processes have proved to be more complex and cumbersome.

The Benin Dialogue Group[58] operated for a long time on the premise that Western collections would maintain legal ownership and lend Benin bronzes to Nigeria on a rotating loan basis.[59] The 'Benin Plan of Action', signed in 2013 by the National Commission for Museums and Monuments of Nigeria (NCMM) and museum professionals in Europe with holdings of Benin objects, did not provide for restitution, but merely contained an agreement to 'create an enabling environment for an increased exchange of touring/travelling exhibitions for the Benin art objects and other art traditions'.[60] The focus was initially on the 'sharing of the cultural heritage through loans or common exhibition projects'.[61] A breakthrough occurred at the 2019 meeting in Benin, which envisaged the establishment of 'a new Royal Museum to reunite in Benin City the most significant of Benin's historical artefacts'.[62] It led to the creation of a Legacy Restoration Trust (LRT), under the umbrella of the Edo State Government, whose main project is the construction of the planned Edo Museum of West African Art (EMOWAA) in Nigeria. It is partly financed by contributions from Germany and projects of the British Museum.

The plan for the new museum paved the way for coordinated talks on return and transfer of ownership. It alleviated concerns by holding institutions regarding the safety and preservation of objects. On 1 July 2022, by which Germany agreed to transfer ownership to Nigeria 'of all Benin Bronzes held in public museums

---

[56] See Carsten Stahn, 'Beyond "To Return or Not To Return": The Benin Bronzes as a Game Changer?' (2022) 8 *Santander Art and Culture Law Review* 29–68.

[57] Institutions like the MET, the Smithsonian Institution, the Universities of Aberdeen and Cambridge, the City Council of Glasgow, and the Rautenstrauch-Joest-Museum and Humboldt Forum in Berlin have publicly committed to returns. In 2022, the Smithsonian Institution agreed to return 29 Benin bronzes. The universities of Oxford and Cambridge have pledged to return 200 Benin objects. The Horniman Museum undertook a commitment to return 72 objects.

[58] It was created in 2010. See Chapter 8.

[59] Gareth Harris, 'Looted Benin Bronzes to be lent Back to Nigeria', *Art Newspaper* (16 October 2017).

[60] 'Benin Plan of Action' (21 February 2013) http://www.elginism.com/similar-cases/the-benin-plan-of-action-for-restitution-and-what-it-means-for-the-return-of-disputed-artefacts/20130228/6897/.

[61] Folarin Shyllon, 'Benin Dialogue Group: Benin Royal Museum—Three Steps Forward, Six Steps Back' (2018) 23 *Art Antiquity and Law* 341–346, 341.

[62] Press Statement of the meeting of the Benin Dialogue Group (11 July 2019).

and institutions in Germany', i.e. more than 1,130 objects in total.[63] However, the implementation of these initiatives was delayed by disputes between the Oba of Benin, the Governor of Edo State, and the Federal Government. They highlight the ongoing tension between cultural nationalism, internationalism, and the interests of the Benin royal court.

The Oba of Benin, Oba Ewaure II, remained opposed to the LRT. He argued that he is the proper owner of the cultural heritage of the Benin Kingdom and that the objects should be placed in a 'Benin Royal Museum' at his court. He stated:

> There is no alternative native authority and custodian of the cultural heritage of the Benin Kingdom outside the Oba of Benin as constituted by the Royal Palace. I do not believe that the move by a privately registered company, the Legacy Restoration Trust Ltd. and the purported establishment of Edo Museum of West African Arts are in consonance with the wishes of the people of Benin Kingdom.[64]

Godwin Obaseki, the Edo State Governor, sought their transfer to the state government, in line with the plans for the creation of the EMOWAA, supported by the Benin Dialogue Group. The Nigerian government, in turn, argued that the Benin bronzes are national heritage, that it is internationally entitled to receive the objects, and that the NCMM has the right to determine where arts and monuments are kept, in consultation with the Edo State government and the Royal Benin Palace. Alhaji Lai Mohammed, the Minister of Information and Culture, stated:

> Nigeria is the entity recognized by international law as the authority in control of antiquities originating from Nigeria. The relevant international Conventions treat heritage properties as properties belonging to the nation and not to individuals or subnational groups …The Federal government will take possession of these antiquities, because it is its duty to do so, in line with the extant laws. [W]e have always exercised this right in cognizance of that culture that produced the art works.[65]

These conflicting positions have caused delays in the progress toward returns.[66] On 23 March 2023, outgoing Nigerian President Muhammadu Buhari signed a

---

[63] Joint Declaration on the Return of Benin Bronzes and Bilateral Museum Cooperation Between the Federal Republic of Germany and the Federal Republic of Nigeria (1 July 2022) https://www.auswa ertiges-amt.de/blob/2540404/8a42afe8f5d79683391f8188ee9ee016/220701-benin-bronzen-polerkl-data.pdf.

[64] Statement at the Meeting of His Royal Majesty Omo N'Oba N'Edo, Ewuare II, Oba of Benin with Palace Chiefs and Enigies on the Repatriation of the Looted Benin Artifacts in Kwame Opoku, 'Oba of Benin speaks on the Return of Artefacts', *Modern Ghana* (12 July 2021) https://www.modernghana. com/news/1092994/oba-of-benin-speaks-on-the-return-of-artefacts.html11.

[65] Kwame Opoku, 'Benin Bronzes Belong To Oba Of Benin', Modern Ghana (20 September 2021) https://www.modernghana.com/news/1105713/benin-bronzes-belong-to-oba-of-benin.html.

[66] This dispute came as a surprise to the Benin Dialogue Group, which had assumed that Nigerian actors agreed on a common plan of action. It caused delays in the progress of returns. For instance,

declaration which designated the 'Oba of Benin as the original owner and custo-dian of the culture, heritage and tradition of the people of the Benin kingdom in the Edo State of Nigeria'.[67] It vested Oba Ewuare II with 'ownership of the artefacts looted from the ancient Palace of the Oba and other parts of the Benin kingdom' and granted him custody and management rights over repatriated looted Benin Artefacts. This move came as a surprise to governments and museums who had ne-gotiated with the government of Nigeria, represented by the NCMM,[68] and agreed to transfer ownership based on the assumption that the bronzes would become public property (e.g. in the Edo Museum of West African Art). It contributed to de-lays in restitution by museums and caused backlash by Western voices, who argued that the transfer of bronzes from public to private property showcases the risks and failures of restitution policy. However, the Presidential declaration contained im-portant safeguards to address concerns. It stressed the duty to keep the bronzes in the Palace of the Oba or other locations that are considered 'secure and safe by the Oba and the Federal Government of Nigeria', and stated that the 'Oba shall work jointly with any recognized national or international institution to ensure the pres-ervation and security of the repatriated artefacts for the benefit of humanity'.[69]

One of the lessons of the format of the Benin Dialogue Group and the Benin re-turns is that it is imperative to establish structures for consultation and dialogue which go beyond the State-centric frame of the 1970 UNESCO Convention on the Means of Prohibiting and Preventing the Illicit Import, Export and Transfer of Ownership of Cultural Property.[70] From an international perspective, the broad support in favour of return was significantly shaped by underlying socio-economic factors, including the envisaged creation of the Edo museum. Such commitments may lack in other cases.

3 New approaches towards consent

Attempts to address such impasses and divides and move beyond a selective ad hoc logic require a more radical rethinking of underlying policies and practices. Changing ethical and legal frameworks[71] support the development of a relational

German guidelines encourage institutions to retain objects, if claimants are in dispute amongst themselves.

[67] Notice of Presidential Declaration on the Recognition of Ownership and an Order Vesting Custody and Management of Repatriated Looted Benin Artefacts in the Oba of Benin Kingdom, Federal Republic of Nigeria Official Gazette, Vol. 110, No. 57 (28 March 2023), Art. 8 (b), https://www.modernghana.com/news/1227999/does-affirmation-of-the-rights-of-the-oba-in-benin.html.
[68] See Agreement on the Return of Benin Bronzes between Stiftung Preußischer Kulturbesitz and the Federal Republic of Nigeria (25 August 2022), https://www.preussischer-kulturbesitz.de/fileadmin/user_upload_SPK/documents/presse/pressemitteilungen/2023/Agreement_Benin_Bronzes.pdf.
[69] Presidential Declaration, Art. 8 (e).
[70] UNESCO Convention (14 November 1970) 823 UNTS 231.
[71] See Chapter 8.

cultural justice approach, which places particular emphasis on the connection of people to objects, facilitates encounter with objects beyond imperial lenses, and goes beyond the binary choice between return or not to return. This approach provides a means to take a step back from the moral high ground, claimed over centuries by colonial powers, and to address continuing biases and post-colonial continuities. It takes into account that this connection to objects can be realized through a spectrum of options.[72] It relies on three elements: (i) the need to find a new contemporary basis of consent for 'entangled objects';[73] (ii) the development of more inclusive procedures in line with rights of access to culture; and (iii) strategies to enable new object possibilities and engagement, including in the post-return stage. It facilitates a move from a rights-based framework toward a needs-based consideration of returns.

3.1 Ethical and legal foundations

The establishment of new forms of consent regarding the status of objects is the foundation of a relational cultural justice model.[74] As has been rightly noted in critical scholarship:

> [f]raming returns as a gesture of good will may be seen today, from a postcolonial perspective, as a tentative means to evade responsibility for the damage done in the name of European civilization during the colonial rule.[75]

The need to establish new forms of consent may be derived from both responsibility towards past violations and contemporary rights of access of culture. It is a direct consequence of the ongoing effects of historical wrongs in contemporary relations. It is a means to restore equality in discourse, address past wrongdoing and involuntary loss of objects, or compensate for the fragile nature of consent in colonial contexts. It takes into account the methodological dilemmas of determining past illegalities. It does not imply that all objects were 'looted' or that everything needs to be returned, but establishes a procedural duty to seek a new contemporary basis of consent in relation to different types of heritage objects, whose status can be challenged under existing legal models in relation to historical injustice, namely

---

[72] Pierre Losson, 'Opening Pandora's Box: Will the Return of Cultural Heritage Objects to Their Country of Origin Empty Western Museums?' (2021) 51 *The Journal of Arts Management, Law, and Society* 379–392.

[73] See Chapter 6.

[74] See Chapter 8.

[75] See Pierre Losson, 'Review of Scott Cynthia, Cultural Diplomacy and the Heritage of Empire: Negotiating Post-Colonial Returns' (2021) 28 *International Journal of Cultural Property* 325–328, 326.

(i) objects which were acquired through past wrongdoing, (ii) objects whose reten-tion marks a form of unjust enrichment without sufficient legitimation from a con-temporary point view, based on their procurement through colonial occupation or exploitation, and (iii) objects whose retention conflicts with contemporary rights of access to culture.[76]

Ethically, this approach has a basis in the ethics of care of museums, in particular an ethical model of trusteeship ('trust as entrusting').[77] For instance, Andreas Pantazatos has argued that the obligation of museums to guard objects as trustees is a living duty linked to the 'biography of objects'. It involves participatory and inter-generational duties of care, which make it necessary to regard 'stakeholders' as 'equals in the negotiation of what is transferred to the future'.[78] It requires mu-seums to 'negotiate the transit from past to future of the objects in their care' in a way which secures 'their significance'[79] and takes into account the interests of 'stakeholders who can shape the transit of an object from past to future'.[80] Other scholars, such as Janna Thompson[81] or Erich Hatala Matthes[82] have stressed that the idea of the universal value of objects, which is often used to justify retentionist policies, does not exclude returns, but may be require a fairer distribution based on distributive justice principles. As Matthes has argued: '[i]f we take seriously the claim that art and artifacts have a kind of universal value, then it seems that we need to think carefully about the just distribution of such cultural goods'.[83] Such an ap-proach challenges the argument that the idea of the museum as space of 'common humanity'[84] simply serves a shield to protect national collections.

Legally, the duty to seek new forms of consent in relation to 'entangled' objects is in line with previously discussed justice models: past wrongdoing, contemporary relationship to wrong, and rights of access to culture.[85] It may be founded on dif-ferent legal sources: the requirement of 'prior and informed consent' in relation to indigenous heritage,[86] general principles of cultural heritage law, and contem-porary human rights obligations.

---

[76] See Chapter 7.

[77] Andreas Pantazatos, 'The Ethics of Trusteeship and the Biography of Objects' (2016) 19 *Royal Institute of Philosophy Supplements* 179–197, 179.

[78] Ibid, 196.

[79] Ibid, 182.

[80] Ibid, 197. For instance, from the perspective of local stakeholders, an object like the Gweagal shield in the British museum (see Chapter 2) is not just a material object or curiosity collected during Cook's voyages, but a symbol of the encounter between white men and aboriginal Australians and indigenous resistance. This plural identity underpins the duty of care and its dynamic relations.

[81] Janna Thompson, 'Art, Property Rights, and the Interests of Humanity' (2004) 38 *The Journal of Value Inquiry* 545–600, 558–559.

[82] Erich Hatala Matthes, 'Repatriation and the Radical Redistribution of Art' (2017) 4 *Ergo* 931–953.

[83] Ibid, 940.

[84] See Speech by George Osborne Chair, Annual Trustees Dinner, British Museum (2 November 2022)) https://www.britishmuseum.org/sites/default/files/2022-11/Speech_by_George_Osborne_Annual_Trustees_Dinner_British_Museum_2022.pdf.

[85] See Chapter 8.

[86] See Art. 11 (2) UNDRIP.

Cultural takings in the colonial period involved different forms of legal entangle-ment, ranging from takings under force[87] or without consent to 'objects whose acquisition was in breach of the colonial legal concepts and morality of the pe-riod'.[88] It is compelling to seek new forms of consent for objects obtained through theft, force or coercion, which violated past laws and standards of humanity. For instance, Andreas von Arnauld argued that the violation of ethical principles in cases of historical injustice creates a contemporary obligation to negotiate with the victims of historical injustice or their descendants, i.e. 'meaningful negotiations in order to come to an agreed solution'.[89] In case of established wrongdoing, the premise should be on remedying past injustices.

The argument may also be applied to certain objects acquired in contexts of co-lonial oppression, which entangled voluntary consent. The importance of 'free, prior and informed consent'[90] may be extended beyond settler colonial contexts, based on the application of general principles of cultural heritage law,[91] such as the prohibition of loot and plunder or the duty not to benefit from exploitation of peo-ples subjected to colonial or foreign occupation for cultural gain.[92]

The need to establish new forms of consent may also arise from contemporary relations towards objects, namely human rights-based duties to provide access to culture.[93] Such obligations may be derived from the right of people and commu-nities to maintain and develop cultural identity and enjoy access to their culture,[94] the principle of 'cultural integrity'[95] or the protection of 'intangible cultural heri-tage'. They may trigger a procedural duty to seek a new contemporary basis of con-sent in relation to the status of contested colonial objects.[96] The Prussian Cultural Heritage Foundation applied this logic in the context of return the statue of Ngonso

---

[87] See Jos Van Beurden, *Inconvenient Heritage* (Amsterdam: Amsterdam University Press, 2022) 19, 71.

[88] Guidelines for German Museums, 58.

[89] See Andreas von Arnauld, 'How to Illegalize Past Injustice: Reinterpreting the Rules of Intertemporality' (2021) 32 *EJIL* 401–432, 426, 432.

[90] Article 11(2) UNDRIP.

[91] Francesco Francioni, *General Principles Applicable to International Cultural Heritage Law* in Mads Andenas and others (eds.), General Principles and the Coherence of International Law (Leiden: Brill, 2019) 389–407.

[92] Tullio Scovazzi, 'The "First Time Instance" as Regards Restitution of Removed Cultural Properties' (2012) 19 *Agenda Internacional* 9–19, 18.

[93] Judge Cançado Trindade argued in the *Temple of Preah Vihear* case that 'States, as promoters of the common good, are under the duty of co-operation between themselves to that end of the safeguard and preservation of the cultural and spiritual heritage'. See ICJ, *Request for Interpretation of the Judgment of 15 June 1962 in the Case Concerning the Temple of Preah Vihear (Cambodia v Thailand)* Provisional Measures, Order of 18 July 2011, Separate Opinion of Judge Cançado Trindade, para. 115.

[94] Ana Vrdoljak, *International Law, Museums and the Return of Cultural Objects* (Cambridge: Cambridge University Press, 2007) 301–302.

[95] Tullio Scovazzi and Laura Westra, 'The Safeguarding of the Intangible Cultural Heritage According to the 2003 UNESCO Convention: The Case of First Nations of Canada' (2017) 1 *Inter Gentes* 24–44, 39. It also protects economic aspects central to a community's culture.

[96] See Jochen von Bernstorff and Jakob Schuler, 'Wer spricht für die Kolonisierten? Eine völkerrechtliche Analyse der Passivlegitimation in Restitutionsverhandlungen' (2019) 79 ZaöRV 553–577, 576.

to Cameroon. It stated that return is not limited to looted objects, but can also be justified by the 'special — especially spiritual — significance of an object for the society of origin'.[97]

3.2 Relevance of justice considerations and the significance and value of objects

A benefit of the new consent approach is that it provides a means to reconsider the contemporary status of objects, without prejudging the outcome of solutions. It does not treat restitution or return as a zero sum game, but leaves flexibility for a plurality of approaches, based on the nature of objects and the underlying claims at stake.[98] The spectrum of options is guided by justice-related considerations and the value and significance of objects.[99]

Justice-related considerations, such wrongdoing or unjust enrichment, influence the choice of feasible remedies, based on where objects rightfully belong. For instance, the violent nature of takings may make it necessary to acknowledge and counter the force or coercion used in the original taking, express wrongdoing or discourage future violations.[100] This may limit the feasibility of permanent or temporary loans in certain instances and make physical return or a change in ownership the only viable option to recognize past wrong, make responsibility visible and tangible and/or provide relief to those affected by takings.

Heritage derives part of its value from the fact that 'it means something to the people who will ultimately live with it and care for it'.[101] Thus, it is important to consider the cultural value of objects and their significance to different stakeholders,[102] i.e. how objects are connected to, or dislocated from people or places.[103] Cultural objects carry different types of significance and value:[104]

---

[97] See Deutsche Welle, 'Germany to return looted artifacts to Africa' (29 June 2022).

[98] It reflects the practice of mutually beneficial return agreements (MBRAs) in heritage negotiations. See Losson, 'Opening Pandora's Box', 384.

[99] South African Cultural Observatory, *The Value of the Repatriation of South African Museum Artefacts: Debates, Case Studies and a Way Forward* (Port Elizabeth: Nelson Mandela University, 2021) 40.

[100] On expressivism, see Carsten Stahn, *Justice as Message* (Oxford: Oxford University Press, 2020).

[101] Lixinski, 'A Third Way of Thinking about Cultural Property', 588.

[102] See also Tolona Loulanski, 'Revising the Concept for Cultural Heritage: The Argument for a Functional Approach' (2006) 2 *International Journal of Cultural Property* 207–233, 215–216; Snowball, Collins, and Nwauche, 'Ethics, values and legality in the restoration of cultural artefacts', 5. Some inspiration may be drawn from the Burra Charter Process, adopted by Australian National Committee of the International Council on Monuments and Sites (ICOMOS) to provide guidance on the conservation and management of places of cultural significance. See International Council on Monuments and Sites, Burra Charter: The Australia ICOMOS Charter for Places of Cultural Significance (31 October 2013).

[103] Bénédicte Savoy, 'What Our Museums Don't Tell Us' (tr), *Le Monde Diplomatique* (2017) https://www.kuk.tu-berlin.de/fileadmin/fg309/dokumente/Translocations/Savoy_MDiplo_2017_EN.pdf.

[104] See South African Cultural Observatory, *The Value of the Repatriation of South African Museum Artefacts* 11–12.

(i) cultural significance, which is related to their artistic, aesthetic, spiritual, ritual or scientific functions;[105] (ii) social value, which is linked to cultural identity and includes the symbolic or historical significance of objects to people and communities, as well as access and education; and (iii) economic value, which includes not only market value, but also broader benefits derived from objects. These three different types of value and significance are helpful to determine the most appropriate form of reframing relations towards objects, such as return, exchange, loan-agreements, sharing-arrangements, digitalization, or circulation. They make it important to consider the place and use of objects for past, present, or future generations.[106]

For instance, the possibility of communities or individuals to use and have access to objects is an important feature of the cultural and social significance of objects. It may require return and/or new arrangements on the status of objects, such as shared or joint custody. The authenticity of objects, i.e. their originality and uniqueness, is an important part of their historical importance or role as 'witness to history'. This factor makes it critical to extend engagement beyond mere 'digital return'.

In other cases, the value of objects is closely linked to location. In some instances, the separation of objects over different places may be odds with their artistic value.[107] This may favour a return to the place of origin. Location also plays an important role in relation to spiritual value. Certain sacred or ceremonial objects can 'develop their aura only in their countries of origin'.[108] This makes it necessary to contemplate physical returns and/or new forms of ownership, access or circulation among public authorities and communities in societies of origin.

Human remains should be returned because of their relational bonds to ancestors and communities, the post-mortem rights of deceased (e.g. dignity) and/or need for a (re)burial in line with religious beliefs.[109] Co-ownership or physical return is an important means to secure a greater share in the economic value of objects, such as property rights, tourism, or reputational benefits, enhancing the value of collections or their ability to attract future support.

---

[105] See Art. 1.2 of the Burra Charter ('Cultural significance means aesthetic, historic, scientific, social or spiritual value for past, present or future generations').

[106] See Burra Charter, Preamble.

[107] A compelling example is the separation of the Parthenon marbles. It reduces not only the value of the site of origin, but also the value of marbles held in Britain. A return would enhance the 'value of both'. Thompson, 'Cultural Property, Restitution and Value', 261.

[108] They are placed in 'artificial coma', when they are closed off behind glass door in collections and inaccessible to communities. See Emery Patrick Effiboley, 'Reflections on the issue of repatriation of looted and illegally acquired African cultural objects in Western museums' (2020) 7 *Contemporary Journal of African Studies* 67–83, 78.

[109] See Chapter 5.

4 A spectrum of possibilities

Existing practices show that there are multiple pathways to reach new forms of consent in relation to 'entangled objects' in line with justice-related considerations and the value and significance of objects. New engagement with objects is not an antagonist choice between returning or not to return. There are various intermediate options. The spectrum comprises mutually beneficial return agreements, pluralistic ownership models, loans, object circulation, digital restitution, or epistemic restitution.

4.1 Mutually beneficial return agreements

One option is to negotiate returns based on mutually beneficial return agreements (MBRAs). This negotiated approach has a long tradition in repatriation practice.[110] It seeks to accommodate competing interests. It operates on the premise that return should benefit both sides. MBRAs may tie the commitment to return by the holding institution to certain promises or obligations by the source country or community, such as the possibility to host an exhibition before returning objects or a pledge to offer comparable objects in exchange for return.[111] For instance, return may be coupled with measures of cultural assistance, to support the establishment of new infrastructure in the claiming state, while enabling the holder country to retain the object for a specific period under a temporary loan back or cycle of loans.[112] This may enable a holding institution to organize an exhibition or complete ongoing provenance research to retrieve colonial histories. MBRAs may contain commitments by the claiming entity to allow international loans of similar works to the holding country, or stipulate modalities for the circulation of objects in order to take into account their importance to global, national, and local stakeholders.

An innovative approach is the two-step model towards return, applied by Germany[113] in relation to Benin objects, and by Belgium in relation to objects

---

[110] China has pursued negotiations for decades to recover cultural objects. Meng Yu, 'Approaches to the recovery of Chinese cultural objects lost overseas: a case study from 1949 to 2016' (2018) 24 *International Journal of Cultural Policy* 741–755; Ruida Chen, 'Healing the Past: Recovery of Chinese Cultural Objects Lost During the Colonial Era' (2022) 8 *Santander Art and Culture Law Review* 161–184, 172.

[111] Stacey Falkoff, 'Mutually-Beneficial Repatriation Agreements: Returning Cultural Patrimony, Perpetuating the Illicit Antiquities Market' (2008) 16 *Journal of Law and Policy* 265–304, 274.

[112] For instance, the Horniman museum cooperated with Nigeria's National Commission for Museums to enable a transfer of Benin objects, while maintaining the option to keep certain artefacts as a loan for purposes of display or education.

[113] Joint Declaration on the Return of Benin Bronzes and Bilateral Museum Cooperation Between the Federal Republic of Germany and the Federal Republic of Nigeria (1 July 2022), Agreement on the Return of Benin Bronzes between Stiftung Preußischer Kulturbesitz and the Federal Republic of Nigeria (25 August 2022).

acquired by force or as spoils of war in the Congo.[114] It provides a new methodology to realize the duty to seek new forms of consent. The separation of ownership
and return and the application of a phased-approach, starting with the unconditional return of ownership rights, and subsequent discussion on return, breaks the
traditional inequality in negotiations between holding countries and states and
communities requesting return. It provides a window of opportunity to find mutually agreed solutions. It has been branded as a 'pioneering model for the approach
to looted art from the colonial period' by Hermann Parzinger, the President of the
Prussian Cultural Heritage Foundation,[115] or as 'Copernican proposal' by Thomas
Dermine, Belgian State Secretary for Recovery and Strategic Investments.[116] Such
'immaterial returns' cannot and should not replace final consent,[117] but they open
room for a spectrum of possibilities. They may lead to agreement on the retention
of certain objects or commitments to broader circulation, based on the importance
or social value of objects and/or sharing of benefits with societies of origin (e.g. fee
for retention, profits from display or reproduction).[118]

New technological means, such as blockchain technology, can be used to
support diverse ownership relations. For instance, digitization, i.e. the creation
of a tokenized digital identity of objects, may facilitate the registration of objects, the tracing of their provenance or the development of 'shared ownership
structures',[119] based on division of specific rights (e.g. ownership, display, economic exploitation). For example, Western museums might be entitled to exhibit
objects, while 'ownership rights' and 'payment rights' are accorded to source
countries.[120]

---

[114] See Belgian Law of 3 July 2022 Recognizing the Alienability of Objects Linked to the Belgian
State's Colonial Past and Determining a Legal Framework for Their Restitution and Return, *Le Moniteur
Belge* (28 September 2022). Article 5 of the Law distinguishes material return from the object's legal
restitution. See Marie-Sophie de Clippele and Bert Demarsin, 'Retourner le patrimoine colonial: prop-
osition d'une lex specialis culturae' (2021) 19 *Journal des tribunaux* 345–353; Marie-Sophie de Clippele
and Bert Demarsin, 'Pioneering Belgium: Parliamentary Legislation on the Restitution of Colonial
Collections' (2022) 8 *Santander Art and Culture Law Review* 277–294.

[115] Federal Foreign Office, 'Federal Foreign Office on the signing of a Memorandum of Understanding
on museum cooperation with Nigeria' (14 October 2021) https://www.auswaertiges-amt.de/en/newsr
oom/news/museum-cooperation-nigeria/2489498.

[116] Thomas Dermine, 'Restitutie-het voorstel van Thomas Dermine' (6 July 2021) https://dermine.
belgium.be/nl/restitutie-het-voorstel-van-thomas-dermine; Bert Demarsin, 'Restitutie van koloniaal
erfgoed' (2022) 1 *Faro-Tijdschrift over cultureel erfgoed* 6–11 https://www.foliomagazines.be/artikels/
restitutie-van-koloniaal-erfgoed.

[117] They may be perceived as a 'symbolic act' which 'does not actually bring collections closer to the
people whose cultural heritage they ultimately embody'. See Basu, 'Re-mobilising colonial collections in
decolonial times', 66.

[118] Gracia Lwanzo Kasongo, 'Is Immaterial Restitution Enough?: A Belgian Approach to the
Human Right of Access to Cultural Heritage' *Völkerrechtsblog* (3 November 2021) doi: 10.17176/
20211103-110837-0.

[119] Amy Whitaker and others, 'Art, Antiquities, and Blockchain: New Approaches to the Restitution
of Cultural Heritage' (2020) 27 *International Journal of Cultural Policy* 1–18, 1.

[120] Ibid, 2.

4.2 Shared stewardship models

An alternative avenue is agreement on shared stewardship over objects. It enables plural ownership relations, which reflect the cultural importance of objects to multiple stakeholders. Shared stewardship agreements may be a powerful way to enable temporary preservation, care, or exhibition of objects, during ongoing conflict or humanitarian crisis in states or communities of origin.[121] In settler colonial contexts, it has been used to recognize different understandings regarding the nature of objects, enable joint responsibility, facilitate access to objects for spiritual or ceremonial purpose, or agree on display, narratives, and conservation practices. The practices of the Te Papa Tongarewa museum in New Zealand show that it is perfectly possible to represent indigenous and community perspectives meaningfully in a museum if the latter agrees to give up established curatorial privileges and include indigenous curators and agents. The Smithsonian Institution has openly recognized the 'shared stewardship' of collections as an important principle to show 'respect for a source community's fundamental and inalienable relationship to its intangible cultural heritage'[122] and provide 'opportunities for source communities to meaningfully engage with the collections'.[123] In circumstances, where objects are retained in Western collections, it is possible create special councils or commissions[124] in order to give source communities a voice in management and display, and/or grant them a share in the benefits.

4.3 Loans, reverse loans, or use of replica

A third option is the use of temporary or permanent loans. It enables return, even on a permanent basis, without altering the title to cultural property. This option provides a way for museums to bypass the principle of inalienability, which prohibits deaccessioning in several countries (e.g. France, UK). It has been convenient for holding states since it does not set a legal precedent. For instance, Germany used a permanent loan arrangement to return one of the famous Great Zimbabwe birds[125] to the Government of Zimbabwe in order to avoid a broader discussion on colonial restitution.[126] The British Museum has proposed to offer Benin Bronzes back

---

[121] Claire Voon, 'Smithsonian to display 77 looted artefacts from Yemen in shared stewardship agreement' *The Art Newspaper* (22 February 2023).
[122] Smithsonian Ethical Returns Working Group, Values and Principles Statement (3 May 2022) Principle 7.
[123] Ibid, Principle 8.
[124] Charity Gates, 'Who Owns African Art? Envisioning a Legal Framework for the Restitution of African Cultural Heritage' (2020) 3 *International Comparative, Policy & Ethics Law Review* 1131–1162, 1161.
[125] See Chapter 4.
[126] Shyllon, 'Repatriation of Antiquities to Sub-Saharan Africa', 143.

to Nigeria as permanent loans. The Victoria & Albert Museum (V&A) has applied a similar approach in relation to objects taken during the Maqdala looting. Such approaches enable access to objects in source countries. However, the concept or use of the term 'loan' carries political sensitivities. It may face critique in relation to entangled colonial objects from a justice and post-colonial perspective, since it may fail to recognize past wrongdoing or flaws in ownership relations and uphold traditional power inequalities. For example, the offer to 'loan' looted Asante artefacts back to Ghana was perceived as a humiliation, rather than as an act of good will.

The negotiations over the Parthenon Marbles are a paradigm example of such sensitivities. They have been ongoing for several decades. In secret negotiations over a deal, George Osborne, the chairman of the British museum has supported the idea of a loan in order to enable transfer to Greece under a mutually beneficial cultural exchange agreement within the framework of the British Museum Act, in exchange for rotating artefacts provided by Greece to the British museum. Greek Prime Minister Kyriakos Mitsotakis signalled openness towards a temporary transfer, with the hope that permanent return would be agreed on a later stage.[127] However, the language of a loan runs counter to Greek views on ownership.[128] There are several options to reconcile the divergent positions. A pragmatic way forward is to agree to disagree on the question of ownership, to use more neutral language, such as the word 'deposit' in order to describe the transfer,[129] or to treat return as a gradual process, combining an initial loan with longer prospects of permanent return. Another possible modality is collaboration under a joint curatorship or partnership agreement.

Return can be facilitated through reverse loans, namely loans from owners in the Global South to Western collections, for instance as part of MBRAs. This approach was negotiated by Western powers after the 1970s as part of an agreement over the return of stolen or illegally excavated objects. For example, in 2002, France negotiated the option to retain three Nok sculptures, which had been illegally exported from Nigeria. It obtained a loan for a period of 25 years in the permanent collection of the Quai Branly museum, 'in exchange' for France's recognition of Nigerian ownership.[130] The Nigerian NCCM agreed to offer occasional long-term loans of objects to the Smithsonian Institution with curatorial guidance from Nigeria. The circulation or temporary loan of objects from source countries

[127] Alex Marshall, 'After 220 Years, the Fate of the Parthenon Marbles Rests in Secret Talks' *NY Times* (17 January 2023).

[128] See Esther Addley and Helena Smith, 'British Museum in Talks with Greece over Return of Parthenon Marbles' *The Guardian* (4 January 2023).

[129] In March 2023, the Vatican agreed to return three sculpture fragments of the Parthenon marbles as a 'donation' to Ieronymos II, the head of the Orthodox Christian church, rather than as an interstate return. See James Imam, 'Vatican Returns Parthenon Sculptures to Greece in "Historic Event"' *The Art Newspaper* (8 March 2023).

[130] Folarin Shyllon, 'Negotiations for the Return of Nok Sculptures from France to Nigeria: An Unrighteous Conclusion' (2003) 8 *Art Antiquity and Law* 133–148, 147.

to former colonial powers reverses traditional power dynamics and enables source countries to present objects in Western collections, while maintaining ownership and benefits. It may be useful to create a connective memory culture and counter colonial amnesia.

A powerful example, in which return was successfully combined with the use of replica in Western collections, is the repatriation of the Ghost Dance Shirt[131] from the Kelvingrove Museum in Glasgow to the South Dakota Cultural Heritage Center. It is 'widely regarded as a model of good practice'.[132] The Glasgow City Council returned the original shirt to the current Lakota community in August 1999 at the site of the massacre because of its authenticity and historic importance. The Kelvingrove Museum received a faithful reproduction of the shirt from the Lakota community. It is shown in the museum, together with a story of the re-patriation process, which involved consultations with Glasgow city residents and Wounded Knee Survivors Association. The production of the replica, and its con-textualization in the Kelvingrove museum created a 'continuing relationship' with the source community and became 'an influential model for other museums oper-ating in a context without repatriation legislation'.[133] It might serve as an example for the return of other sacred objects.[134]

4.4 New forms of circulation and object mobility

Another possibility is the circulation of objects.[135] As the Dutch Expert guidance notes, 'cultural heritage objects have values that are not always tied to a particular physical place or owner' and 'are not always made to remain in a particular phys-ical location'.[136] Mobility and circulation can create 'new dynamics' for the objects and their perception.[137] For instance, in its mapping report of African artefacts and human remains, the African Foundation for Development (AFFORD), suggested a process of object 'restoration' in order to give 'context to objects that are currently denuded of a thorough object history'.[138] It includes 'moving of an object from a

---

[131] The shirt was removed from a Lakota body after the massacre at Wounded Knee. See Mark O'Neill, 'Repatriation and its discontents: the Glasgow experience' in Eleanor Robson, Luke Treadwell, and Chris Gosden (eds.), *Who Owns Objects? The Ethics and Legality of Collecting* (Oxford: Oxbow Books, 2006) 105–128.

[132] Neil Curtis, 'Repatriation from Scottish Museums: Learning from NAGPRA' (2010) 33 *Museum Anthropology* 234–248, 237.

[133] Ibid, 237.

[134] On the Hoa Hakananai'a, see Chapter 4.

[135] George Abungu, 'Museums: Geopolitics, Decolonisation, Globalisation and Migration' (2019) 71 *Museum International* 62–71.

[136] Dutch Report, 56.

[137] Ibid.

[138] African Foundation for Development, *Return of the Icons* (June 2020) 12 https://www.afford-uk.org/wp-content/uploads/2020/06/RoIMappingReportFinal.pdf.

restricted to public sphere, updating accompanying literature, translocation within a museum or between museums, a willingness to send an object on loan to other institutions, for a short period of time or indefinitely, or active engagement with diaspora communities who share a heritage with the objects.[139]

Circulation carries a negative connotation, if it is invoked as substitute to return or transfer of ownership.[140] However, it also offers new prospects to break the traditional geographical or cultural boundaries drawn through the colonial condition, enable new relationships and recognize the 'translocational' value of objects.[141] It is a way to acknowledge the diverse biographies of objects and the dynamics of connection and disconnection.[142] It enables a rethinking of museums and collections as mobile spaces, i.e. 'in terms of dispersion rather than accumulation, mobility rather than fixity, mutation rather than inertia.[143] It is a means to break existing biases. For instance, Emery Patrick Effiboley has argued that circulation should be extended beyond colonial objects and encompass sharing of 'artworks' of 'artists such as Pablo Picasso' in order to reflect 'entangled histories' and break cultural stereotypes.[144]

Mobility and sharing of objects may be important after return in order to resocialize objects and recreate affective bonds.[145] In international negotiations (e.g. the Benin Dialogue Group), debates often remain focused on return or preservation in state-sponsored national museums. However, returns may require new forms of collaboration between national, regional, and local museums or other forms of circulation.[146] Such types of collaborations may give returns a broader restorative dimension and enable new encounters with objects.[147] For example, community-run museums, heritage centres or 'living museums' with participatory models often provide a more direct and immediate access to objects. They may be better equipped than large national museums to change 'classificatory modes

---

[139] Ibid, 12–13.

[140] Felix Driver, Mark Nesbitt and Caroline Cornish, 'Introduction', 12. It may create distance from 'historical communities from which artefacts were sourced or plundered'. South African Cultural Observatory, *The Value of the Repatriation of South African museum artefacts* 27.

[141] Basu, 'Re-mobilising colonial collections in decolonial times', 66.

[142] It takes into account that source communities may have regrouped in new locations and that meanings of objects migrate with their cultural histories.

[143] Driver, Nesbitt, and Cornish, 'Introduction: mobilising and re-mobilising museum collections', 5–6.

[144] Effiboley, 'Reflections on the issue of repatriation of looted and illegally acquired African cultural objects in Western museums', 70.

[145] Joshua Bell, Kimberly Christen, and Mark Turin, 'After the Return: Digital Repatriation and the Circulation of Indigenous Knowledge' (2013) 1 *Museum Worlds: Advances in Research* 195–203.

[146] The strong focus on national structures creates critiques that returns simply replicate the 'colonial imprint' of Western museums or elitist structures of colonial contexts inside source countries. See Shahid Vawda, 'Museums and the Epistemology of Injustice: From Colonialism to Decoloniality' (2019) 71 *Museum International* 72–79.

[147] Njabulo Chipangura and Jesmael Mataga, *Museums as Agents for Social Change: Collaborative Programmes at the Mutare Museum* (New York: Routledge, 2021).

and forms of representation inherited from the colonial era' and render 'museums meaningful for the contemporary and local context'.[148]

This is recognized by cultural heritage instruments, which protect indigenous rights, heritage communities and intangible heritage.[149]

Mobility may be necessary to realize the different potentialities and meanings of objects.[150] For instance, ceremonial access and circulation of objects between museums and communities may be an important element to facilitate reconnection with objects in source communities after return. The Sarr and Savoy report mentioned the sharing of objects in Mali as a successful example:

> The National Museum of Mali regularly loans out specific ritual objects to communities. Once the ritual is finished, the Museum collects the object and brings it back to the National Museum to guarantee its preservation. The good preservation is also in the advantage of the community that performs the rituals.[151]

Another option is the creation of mobile museums.[152] For instance, Nana Oforiatta Ayim has established a mobile museum in Ghana in order to facilitate greater access to objects.

4.5 Digital restitution and use of non-fungible tokens (NFTs)

The development of technologies has increased the possibility to facilitate engagement with objects[153] through reproduction, visual restitution, and dissemination. Digital access to objects is an important means to provide transparency, increase awareness about the cultural significance of objects or stimulate provenance research. Projects like Digital Benin or the 'Transformative Heritage' project of Royal Museum for Central Africa in Tervuren have shown the virtues of digital reassembly in relation to colonial objects. For instance, cultural anthropologist Kokunre Eghafona has described the significance of Digital Benin to meaning-making through an analogy to the recomposition of a book. He noted: 'The looting was like a book being torn to pieces and then the pages were put in different

---

[148] Mataga, 'Museums in Africa', 18.
[149] See Chapter 7.
[150] Driver, Nesbitt, and Cornish, 'Introduction: mobilising and re-mobilising museum collections', 13.
[151] Sarr and Savoy, 'Restitution of African Cultural Heritage', 32.
[152] Driver, Nesbitt, and Cornish, 'Introduction: mobilising and re-mobilising museum collections', 4–5.
[153] Matholde Pavis and Andrea Wallace, 'Response to the 2018 Sarr-Savoy Report: Statement on Intellectual Property Rights and Open Access Relevant to the Digitization and Restitution of African Cultural Heritage and Associated Materials' (2019) 10 *Journal of Intellectual Property, Information Technology and Electronic Commerce Law* 240–271.

places.'[154] 'Gathering them together in one place' restores a fuller meaning that has been lost.

The process of digital restitution itself offers both prospects and risks. It is an important means to enhance transparency, visible access to objects or their educational value. However, it does not restore cultural value to the same extent as physical return. It may exclude societies or communities that lack digital access and can fail to be perceived as a 'respectful' or meaningful form of return or repatriation, if it is not complemented by an actual return of objects.[155] Its operationalization poses delicate challenges. Digitization is not a neutral process. It is more than mere copying. It may dematerialize objects[156] or preclude alternative conceptions towards objects, disregard community ownership, or fail to protect older or ancient works or traditional forms of knowledge.[157] It poses complex in relation to language or the application of Western intellectual property frames.

The Sarr and Savoy Report has recommended a 'radical practice of sharing', namely the digitization and 'open access' availability all of the African heritage objects which are envisaged for restitution.[158] This solution has been criticized for introducing a digital 'system of appropriation and alienation'.[159] Digitization can cause privacy or religious concerns (e.g. human remains, sacred objects) or re-enact erasure and violence.[160] It requires input of communities of origin in relation to the feasibility of digital reproduction, access and framing of intellectual property.[161] Experiences from settler colonial contexts suggest that '[m]any indigenous communities' seek to 'maintain control over the circulation of certain types of knowledge and cultural materials based on their own cultural systems' or 'add their expert voices and histories to the public record'.[162] As Lucas Lixinksi has cautioned, digitization may also 'backfire, and instead of bridging the divide, render all cultural heritage that has a digital surrogate a lesser form of heritage' and 'lower the value' of objects to the detriment of heritage communities.[163]

---

[154] C. Hickley, 'Digital Benin: a milestone on the long, slow journey to restitution' *The Art Newspaper* (8 June 2020) https://www.theartnewspaper.com/2020/06/08/digital-benin-a-milestone-on-the-long-slow-journey-to-restitution.

[155] Kimberly Christen, 'Opening Archives: Respectful Repatriation' (2011) 74 *The American Archivist* 185–210.

[156] Temi Odumosu, 'The Crying Child: On Colonial Archives, Digitization, and Ethics of Care in the Cultural Commons' (2020) 61 *Current Anthropology* 289–302.

[157] Christen, 'Opening Archives, 190.

[158] Sarr and Savoy, 'Restitution of African Cultural Heritage', 67–68.

[159] Pavis and Wallace, 'Response to the 2018 Sarr-Savoy Report'.

[160] Odumosu, 'The Crying Child', 294.

[161] Ibid, 295; Supriya Singh, Meredith Blake, and Jonathan O'Donnell, 'Digitizing Pacific Cultural Collections: The Australian Experience' (2013) 20 *International Journal of Cultural Property* 77–107.

[162] Christen, 'Opening Archives', 192.

[163] Lucas Lixinski, 'Digital Heritage Surrogates, Decolonization, and International Law: Restitution, Control, and the Creation of Value as Reparations and Emancipation' (2020) 6 *Santander Art and Culture Law Review* 65–86, 80.

One possibility to mitigate dilemmas is the creation of 'a third space' around digitized objects, i.e. the establishment of a novel environment[164] which presents the digital record in conjunction with contextualized narratives of histories and meanings and offers communities the possibility to add 'their own descriptions without approval from the museums that have the objects in custody' and to 'decide to whom they give access to see and use their digitally curated objects and collection'.[165]

A novel way of digital reproduction is the use of NFTs, i.e. the creation and sharing of digital codes of artworks.[166] It provides new opportunities for engagement and virtual restitution. In the field of cultural colonial objects, the turn to NFTs emerged as virtual counter-reaction to the looting of objects throughout the nineteenth and twentieth centuries. The Looty project, a group of 'artists, philosophers and future thinkers', named after the famous dog looted from the Chinese summer palace in 1860, has started to create digital files of looted art objects in Western collections, based on 3D scans of objects, such as Benin Bronzes.[167] It thereby creates a new form of virtual reality, which goes beyond classical means of reproduction (e.g. images, replica), and spreads the commercial benefits of objects held in public collections in a digital form. The project regards its activity not only as an 'art money heist' but as a form of digital repatriation and reparation. It sells the files as assets in order to support young artists in Africa.

Thus far, the creation of NFTs is only loosely regulated. NFTs do not provide legal ownership or copyrights relating to the objects,[168] but simply ownership over a digital transaction code, i.e. the hyperlink to the file with the piece of art. This method diversifies the forms and possibilities of virtual restitution. It is not 'a substitute for physical restitution' but a way to compensate physical absence through digital means.[169] It enables museums to restitute physical objects, while keeping NFTs of these works and distributing the proceeds of sale. It also provides a means to create new virtual collections, in which people may engage with objects through digital access to 3D reproduction of objects.

---

[164] An example is the 'Reciprocal Research Network' created by the Museum of Anthropology at the University of British Colombia in collaboration with Indigenous communities.

[165] Charles Jeurgens and Michael Karabinos, 'Paradoxes of Curating Colonial Memory' (2020) 20 *Archival Science* 199–220, 216.

[166] Manuel Charr, 'Looty NFT Project Challenges Museums that Refuse to Return Looted Works' *Museum Next* (5 May 2022) https://www.museumnext.com/article/looty-nft-project-challenges-museums-that-refuse-to-return-looted-works/.

[167] The Looty project defines itself as the 'world's first Digital repatriation of Art to the Metaverse'. See the self-description of Looty, 'Returning stolen loot' on the project website, https://www.looty.art/.

[168] Sunny J. Kumar and others, 'The NFT Collection: A Brave NFT World: A Regulatory Review of NFTs (Part 2)' (2022) 12 *National Law Review* https://www.natlawreview.com/article/nft-collection-brave-nft-world-regulatory-review-nfts-part-2.

[169] Chidirim Nwaubani, the founder of Looty, regards it as a platform to close a 'physical gap' in 'the digital realm'. See Min Chen, 'With Looty, The Case For Digital Repatriation Gains A New Ally: NFTs' *Jing Culture & Crypto* (25 May 2022) https://jingculturecrypto.com/looty-nfts/.

4.6 Facets of epistemic restitution

Another important modality that goes beyond physical return of objects is epistemic restitution, i.e. the sharing of knowledge. It has different facets. One element is return and/or sharing of archives. As Kenyan writer Patrick Gathara has argued, the return of colonial archives is an important 'path to colonial reckoning' since it may provide a 'better and more grounded understanding of what it is that Europe owes'.[170] Colonial archives are repositories of history' and were a 'form of violent control' and part of the 'ideology of white power'.[171] Article 27 of the Charter for African Cultural Renaissance expressly mandates African States to 'take the necessary measures to ensure that archives and other historical records which have been illicitly removed from Africa are returned to African Governments in order that they may have complete archives concerning the history of their country'.[172] From a heritage perspective, restitution of archives and cultural objects are closely interconnected. However, archival returns pose certain complex challenges.[173]

At present, the 'worlds of archives and objects are mostly separated'.[174] As Jos van Beurden has shown, the meaning of archives and approaches towards return differ. In many international contexts (e.g. Ethiopia–Italy, Indonesia–Netherlands), archives have been requested prior to the return of objects.[175] Archival returns have served as a prelude to return of objects, but also cause political sensitivities[176] and tensions or revive tensions or trauma. In practice, archival access has thus often been negotiated on a case-by-case basis, leading to the return of originals or digitized copies. In certain cases, 'stewardship' models may offer a way to address conflicting interests. For instance, historian Joel Wurl has argued that archival material should be 'viewed less as property and more as cultural asset, jointly held and invested in by the archive and the community of origin'.[177] In the U.S., specific protocols have been developed by professional organizations to guide archival returns to indigenous communities.[178]

---

[170] Patrick Gathara, 'The Path to Colonial Reckoning Is Through Archives, Not Museums' *Al Jazeera* (14 March 2019) https://www.aljazeera.com/opinions/2019/3/14/the-path-to-colonial-reckoning-is-through-archives-not-museums.

[171] Simon Gikandi, 'Rethinking the Archive of Enslavement' (2015) 50 *Early American Literature* 81–102, 92.

[172] Charter for African Cultural Renaissance, adopted by the 6th AU Assembly held in Khartoum, Sudan (26 January 2006) Art. 27.

[173] See with respect to the archives of British anthropologist Northcote W. Thomas, Basu, 'Re-mobilising colonial collections in decolonial times', 57.

[174] Jos van Beurden, 'Claims for Colonial Objects and for Colonial Archives Can the Two Meet?' in James Lowry (ed.), *Disputed Archival Heritage* (London: Routledge, 2022) 262–281, 277.

[175] Ibid, 275–276.

[176] See Jeurgens and Karabinos, 'Paradoxes of Curating Colonial Memory', 217.

[177] Joel Wurl, 'Ethnicity as Provenance: In Search of Values and Principles for Documenting the Immigrant Experience' (2005) 29 *Archival Issues* 65–76, 72.

[178] See First Archivist Circle, 'Protocols for Native American Archival Materials' https://www2.nau.edu/libnap-p/PrintProtocols.pdf.

A second facet is the return of knowledge regarding objects themselves. Colonial takings did not only dislocate objects from their cultural environment, but also destroyed traditions of knowledge associated with them. For instance, South African curator Bongani Mkhonza has argued that the 'looting of African art by imperial collectors "dismembered" the objects from their spirituality' and rituals,[179] turning them into 'symbolic objects without a spirit'[180] and led to a loss of knowledge.[181] The skills of how to create, or relate to objects, have often vanished. For example, the taking of the Benin bronzes affected the know-how and techniques of how to create brass figures in the kingdom.[182] The taking of the Luf canoe, hosted in the Humboldt Forum, contributed to the demise of the boat-making tradition of islanders. Epistemic restitution is thus critical for contemporary generations to preserve and continue traditions. Stanley Inum, one of the descendants of the builders of the Luf boat, made this clear in an interview:

> We want the old knowledge of how to make such a boat to come back to us. This knowledge must be brought back to us. You should help us and take us there so that we can see the boat. Then we can take photos and see exactly how the boat was built. This will help us to build a boat exactly like the one in the museum in Berlin.[183]

A third element is the return of racially biased visual documentation. Archives, film, and photography were often shaped by racial world views and colonial lenses. They misrepresented object histories or identities. The legal frameworks of intellectual property rights are often not adjusted to address the ongoing detrimental effects of past racial injustices. A good illustration is the dispute over the return of daguerreotype portraits of two enslaved people, Renty and Delia Taylor, in the case of *Tamara Lanier v Harvard University*.[184]

In this case, the two subjects, Renty and Delia, were photographed naked from various angles, without their consent or any form of compensation. The photographic material was commissioned by Harvard biologist Louis Agassiz

---

[179] Bongani Mkhonza, 'Towards Epistemic Repatriation: Re/Membering as the Moral Responsibility of Museums' (2021) 43 *South African Museums Association Bulletin* 10–17, 10.

[180] Ibid, 12.

[181] The notion was coined by Boaventura de Sousa Santos. See Boaventura de Sousa Santos, *Epistemologies of the South: Justice Against Epistemicide* (Boulder: Paradigm Publishers, 2014).

[182] Barnaby Phillips, 'The Benin Bronzes Aren't Just Ancient History: Meet the Contemporary Casters Who Are Still Making Them Today' *Artnet News* (13 May 2021) https://news.artnet.com/art-world/barnaby-philips-benin-1967703.

[183] See Interview, Stanley Inum by film-maker Martin Maden, Exhibition Humboldt Forum Berlin.

[184] For a discussion, see Jarrett Martin Drake, 'Blood at the Root' (2021) 8 *Journal of Contemporary Archival Studies* 1–24; Commonwealth of Massachusetts Supreme Judicial Court, No. SJC-13138, *Lanier v Harvard*, Amicus Brief, Dan Hicks and David Mirzoeff (11 October 2021).

to support research establishing polygenism and White biological superiority. Harvard University retained the daguerreotypes and charged fees for reproduction. Tamara Lanier, a descendant of Renty, claimed the return of the daguerreotypes and the profits, which Harvard derived from the photos. She argued that Harvard did not acquire ownership, based on the lack of consent, and that it should not be able to benefit from exploitative acts that violated the dignity and autonomy from the subjects.[185] Her lawyers argued that Lanier's ancestors could be deemed to enjoy a possessory title to the photographs, since property can be understood as relation, and that the daguerreotype carries synergies to a remain for Lanier, since it constitutes her only tangible link to her ancestors.

The Middlesex County Superior Court dismissed the claim based on a legal gap theory, which is reminiscent of initial objection to return human remains or cultural objects collected for purposes of racial science. The Court held that Renty and Delia Taylor 'did not possess a property interest in the photograph' since 'the negative and any photographs are the property of the photographer' even 'where an image is taken without the subject's consent'.[186] It refuted a contextual reading, and blended out the slavery context, arguing that 'the law, as it currently stands, does not confer a property interest to the subject of a photograph regardless of how objectionable the photograph's origins may be'.[187] It defended this position by the fact that the 'Court is constrained by current legal principles'.[188]

The ruling disregarded that transitional justice principles may also be applicable to identity-related objects.[189] The judgment failed to engage with the question of whether it would be suitable to make an exception to intellectual property rights for historical images which were taken without 'free and informed consent', which may constitute a link to ancestors and perpetuate ongoing racial stereotypes.[190]

---

[185] Harvard denied any obligation of return or compensation, arguing that Lanier lacked property rights to the daguerreotypes. It stated that the Peabody Museum would be best equipped to tell the story of the photographs.

[186] Middlesex County Superior Court, *Lanier v President and Fellows of Harvard College*, Civil Action No. 1981CV00784 (1 March 2021).

[187] Ibid.

[188] Ibid.

[189] As Dan Hicks and David Mirzoeff have stated '19th-century daguerreotypes of enslaved people were not simply historical documents evidencing racial violence' but 'enduring sites' of a 'transformational violence' that turned the human body into 'a scientific profile, a negroid type, an anthropological debate'. See Amicus Brief, Dan Hicks, Nicholas and David Mirzoeff, 10–11.

[190] The plaintiff invoked arguments of historical justice on appeal, arguing that Harvard should not be allowed to benefit from the 'fruits of their unlawful and outrageous conduct': 'Harvard's Agassiz and team were not journalists innocently chronicling an atrocity; rather, they were perpetrators' orchestrating the atrocity. Renty and Delia were not "subjects" of a "photograph" in any traditional sense that may apply in property law.' See Commonwealth of Massachusetts Appeals Court, *Lanier v President and Fellows of Harvard College*, Motion for Direct Appellate Review by Supreme Judicial Court, No. 2021-P-0350 (12 May 2021) 13–14.

5 Relational procedures

The functioning of a relational cultural justice model depends on process-related elements. Procedures may restore agency and equality in discourse and provide a means to transform museums from 'places of conquest to places of collaboration'.[191] They are necessary to connect objects and people, clarify the value and significance of objects in a dialogical way or build 'new and balanced relationships based on trust and dialogue'.[192]

There is a strong ethical case to extend processes beyond inter-state negotiation.[193] Colonial structures often suppressed local forms of authority. The interests of cultural communities, whose objects were removed in the colonial era, do not necessarily coincide with the interests of contemporary nation-states, which are deemed to represent them. The colonial past, and its dominant way of knowledge-production, can only be meaningfully reworked through joint initiatives and collaboration, including common engagement with histories and epistemologies, cooperative provenance research or initiatives beyond return.[194] It is thus important to include affected groups, communities, or stakeholders (e.g. descendants of former rulers) in return processes[195] in order to renew relations and enable them to gain authority over their past.

This importance of consultation and listening became evident in the context of the German/Namibian negotiations on colonial reparation. Bernadus Swartbooi, the Ovaherero Traditional Authority (OTA), and eleven Nama Traditional Authorities challenged the validity of the joint declaration adopted by Germany and Namibia, which is deemed to 'settle all financial aspects of the issues relating to the past'[196] before the High Court of Namibia due to the 'superficial level of participation' of affected communities.[197] They argued that it 'is impossible to remedy the violent past in a truly restorative manner when the affected communities are not included in the negotiation process, rendering them invisible'.[198] Legally, such an entitlement may be derived from the participatory rights relating to the protection

---

[191] Chip Colwell, *Plundered Skulls and Stolen Spirits: Inside the Fight to Reclaim Native America's Culture* (Chicago & London: University of Chicago Press, 2017) 265.

[192] Ibid, 388.

[193] Von Bernstorff and Schuler, 'Wer spricht für die Kolonisierten?', 576.

[194] This may require a departure from established 'scientific' or artistic interpretations or traditional concepts of management and conservation. For instance, NAGPRA seeks to balance interests of science against entitlements of native communities. See Chapter 6.

[195] Lixinski, 'A Third Way of Thinking about Cultural Property', 599.

[196] Joint Declaration by the Federal Republic of Germany and The Republic of Namibia, 'United in Remembrance of our Colonial Past, United in our Will to Reconcile, United in our Vision of the Future' (September 2021) para. 20 https://www.parliament.na/wp-content/uploads/2021/09/Joint-Declarat ion-Document-Genocide-rt.pdf.

[197] High Court of Namibia, *Bernadus Swartbooi vs The Speaker of the National Assembly*, Case No. HC-MD-CIV-MOT-REV-2023/00023, Founding Affidavit (20 January 2023) para. 336 https://ejustice. jud.na/ejustice/f/caseinfo/publicsearch.

[198] Ibid, para. 341.

of cultural rights under international human rights law[199] as well as specific cultural heritage instruments.[200] It may enable source communities to reclaim collective identities, and allow returning entities to take distance from the past or demonstrate how professional identities and knowledge structures have evolved.[201]

A major implication of a relational approach to procedures is that it challenges the traditional theory that objects should not be returned in case of doubts about the proper addressee. The issue 'to whom' objects should be returned is part of the relational process.[202] It should be addressed in a proactive way and through involvement of stakeholders, rather than serving as a pretext or excuse for inaction. This may render negotiations more complex. But it is necessary to build mutual trust, understand competing views and prevent that return processes are hijacked for one-sided political purposes.[203] In case of divisions between state representatives and heritage communities in source countries, joint stewardship or the creation of community museums provides an option to reconcile competing patrimony interests.

From a procedural perspective, return processes play an important role in cultural transmission, reaffirming agency or recreating or strengthening collective identity. Some lessons may be derived from the Expert Mechanism on the Rights of Indigenous Peoples, which has noted that successful examples of the repatriation of human remains involve demonstration of dignity and respect for subjects/objects, tracing origins, individual histories and biographies, engagement with local stakeholders and local histories, respectful ways of handover, ceremonies at appropriate places, which leave room for re-engagement or mourning, and/or the 'rehumanization' of objects or ancestral remains.[204] The Sarr and Savoy report

---

[199] See Art. 15(1)(a) ICESCR and Art. 27 ICCPR. Article 18 UNDRIP states that 'indigenous peoples have the right to participate in decision-making in matters which would affect their rights, through representatives chosen by themselves in accordance with their own procedures, as well as to maintain and develop their own indigenous decision-making institutions'. The German government argued that human rights instruments did not grant individual representatives of affected communities a right to participate in the joint settlement. This reading was criticized in a Joint Communication by Special Procedure mandate holders. See UN OHCHR, Joint Communication from Special Procedures, AL DEU 1/2023, 23 February 2023, 8, at https://spcommreports.ohchr.org/TMResultsBase/DownLoad PublicCommunicationFile?gId=27875.

[200] See the Preamble of the UNESCO Convention for the Safeguarding of the Intangible Cultural Heritage (17 October 2003) 2368 UNTS 3, Arts. 2(3) and 7(1) of the UNESCO Convention on the Protection and Promotion of the Diversity of Cultural Expressions (20 October 2005) 2440 UNTS 311, or Art. 3(8) of the UNIDROIT Convention on Stolen or Illegally Exported Cultural Objects (24 June 1995) 34 ILM 1322.

[201] Yann LeGall, 'If These Skulls Could Talk': Subjectification and Memory Practice in Repatriation and Reburial of Colonial Human Remains (MA Thesis, Berlin: 2016) 57–58.

[202] Van Beurden, *Incovenient Heritage*, 222–224.

[203] This is one of the lessons of the format of the Benin Dialogue Group.

[204] 2020 Report Mechanism Indigenous People, para. 65. The Belgian Advisory Committee on Bioethics mentioned three principles which are key for the successful return of human remains: A relationship of trust between the parties, their equal footing, and fairness, i.e. impartial treatment of the application. See Belgian Advisory Committee on Bioethics, Opinion No. 82 of 9 January 2023 on the Status of Human Remains in Museum, Scientific and Private Collections, 34.

stressed that additional measures, such as acknowledgement, dialogue, amends and cooperation, may be necessary to give meaning to returns and reflect engagement with past injustices. If returns are meant to have a broader social justice dimension, the traditional sequence of returns, i.e. the filing of claims, provenance research in holding institutions, and transfer of objects, needs to be revisited.[205] Ceremonial features play a key role. They may accommodate the emotional dimensions of return processes.[206] They are able to express that objects or human remains are more than 'things' and may contribute to a 'personification' of objects or remains, which have been collected or stored as 'anthropological material'.[207]

It is more difficult to determine under what conditions returns may contribute to reconciliation or healing of trauma.[208] Wayne Modest and Viv Golding have argued that 'contestation and controversy – if imaginatively, respectfully, and sensitively addressed in the museum with reference to wider concerns of equality, human rights, and social justice – may offer a potent means of building bridges and even overcoming divisions among disparate groups'.[209] Some studies suggest that repatriation may contribute to well-being, reduce trauma or address grief of individuals or groups.[210] For instance, ceremonies of renewal may contribute to better mental and physical health.[211] The return of ancestral remains has shown that repatriation may help survivors or descendants to satisfy their duties towards their ancestors[212] or restore 'broken relationships'.[213] Where subjects or objects are perceived as 'missing persons', their return can open pathways for mourning and facilitate processes to cope with trauma.[214]

However, people relate to objects and their cultural histories in complex ways. Dialogue and re-engagement cannot be enforced. Respect of alterity also involves the need to respect the voice of those who do not wish to engage with the wounds of the past, accept gestures of apology, or renew relations. The decision not to support

---

[205] LeGall, 'If These Skulls Could Talk', 62.

[206] Yann LeGall, Remembering the Dismembered: African Human Remains and Memory Cultures in and after Repatriation (PhD, University of Potsdam, 2020).

[207] Ibid, 44.

[208] Russell Thornton, 'Repatriation as Healing the Wounds of the Trauma of History: Cases of Native Americans in the United States of America' in Cressida Fforde, Jane Hubert, and Paul Turnbull (eds.), The Dead and Their Possessions: Repatriation in Principle, Policy, and Practice (New York: Routledge, 2002), 17–24.

[209] Viv Golding and Wayne Modest, 'Introduction' in Viv Golding and Wayne Modest (eds.), Museums and Communities: Curators, Collections and Collaboration (London: Bloomsbury, 2013) 1–9, 1.

[210] Amy Lonetree, Decolonizing Museums: Representing Native America in National and Tribal Museums (Chapel Hill: University of North Carolina Press, 2012); Moira G. Simpson, 'Museums and Restorative Justice: Heritage, Repatriation, and Cultural Education' (2009) 61 Museum International 121–129.

[211] Laura Peers, 'Ceremonies of Renewal: Visits, Relationships, and Healing in the Museum Space' (2013) 1 Museum Worlds 136–152, 141.

[212] See Chapter 6.

[213] Chip Colwell, 'Can Repatriation Heal the Wounds of History?' (2019) 41 The Public Historian 90–110, 96–97.

[214] Ibid, 96–97.

any act which would lead to 'guilt relief' or 'whitewashing' of colonial violence is also a demonstration of agency.

Returns may help ease 'open wounds', but do not necessarily remove the 'scars' inflicted through the colonial past.[215] In some cases, they may cause friction or retraumatization of specific individuals or groups.[216] For instance, the Cameroonian government initially remained opposed to the return of the Afo-A-Kom[217] sculpture, a symbol of the political and religious heritage of the Kom people (the 'heart of the Kom'),[218] which was stolen in 1966 from the village of Laikom in northern Cameroon[219] and rediscovered at an exhibition at the Furman Gallery in New York in 1973, because it feared that the object would enhance tribal identities in the country to the detriment of national unity.[220] In other cases, objects may face objection or resistance by communities. For example, the return of the throne of King Gezo, which was looted by French General Alfred-Amédée Dodds from the Kingdom of Dahomey, triggers conflicting memories in communities,[221] since it marks not only a gesture of repair by France, but also serves a painful reminder of the crimes committed by Gezo against enemies of the rulers of Dahomey.[222] In the Democratic Republic of the Congo, communities have remained divided over the return of certain objects collected by missionaries, since they 'no longer recognize themselves' in these objects[223] or consider them to be in conflict with their contemporary Christian beliefs.

In some cases, historical human rights violations by native rulers have been invoked as arguments against returns. For instance, in October 2022, the Restitution Study Group, a US-based NGO promoting slavery justice, filed a motion in the US District Court for Columbia to block the transfer of ownership of 29 Benin bronzes from the Smithsonian Institution to Nigeria.[224] It argued that the bronzes should stay in the U.S. for the benefit of descendants of enslaved peoples, since the Kingdom of Benin was complicit in slave trade and produced the bronzes from copper-based metal that it obtained in exchange for slaves, i.e.

---

[215] Ibid, 92.

[216] Andrew Gulliford, 'Curation and Repatriation of Sacred and Tribal Objects' (1992) 14 *The Public Historian* 23–38.

[217] Afo-A-Kom means 'the Kom thing'.

[218] Alessandro Chechi, Anne Laure Bandle, and Marc-André Renold, 'Case Afo-A-Kom: Furman Gallery and Kom People', Platform ArThemis, Art-Law Centre, University of Geneva https://plone.unige.ch/art-adr/cases-affaires/afo-a-kom-2013-furman-gallery-and-kom-people/#F5.

[219] Shyllon, 'Repatriation of Antiquities to Sub-Saharan Africa', 127.

[220] Patrick J. O'Keefe, 'Repatriation of Sacred Objects' (2008) 13 *Art, Antiquity, and Law* 225–241, 229.

[221] Ana Lucia Araujo, 'Afterlives of a Dahomean Throne' (2021) 19 *British Art Studies*.

[222] The king surrounded his palaces by the remains of conquered rulers of neighbouring kingdoms. A postcard shows one of his thrones placed on four human skulls.

[223] Effiboley, 'Reflections on the issue of repatriation of looted and illegally acquired African cultural objects in Western museums', 78.

[224] US District Court for Columbia, *Deadria Farmer-Paellmann and Restitution Study Group v Smithsonian Institution*, Emergency Motion for Temporary Restraining Order and Preliminary Injunction, Civil Case No. 1:22-cv-3048 (7 October 2022) https://rsgincorp.files.wordpress.com/2022/10/221007-complaint-final.pdf.

through 'abductions and sales of innocent people and the loss of their liberty and lives'.[225] It noted:

> The Benin Bronzes are not simply valuable objets d'art: they have a unique and special historical relationship to descendants of enslaved African-Americans whom Europeans forcibly brought to North America. Many, but not all, of these objects were crafted from metal ingots, melted down from a currency called manillas, that European slave traders paid to the oba (the Beni term for king) of the Kingdom of Benin, or to members of the Benin nobility, in exchange for abducted and enslaved neighboring non-Beni people.[226]

The Restitution Study Group claimed that the Smithsonian Institution has 'a moral and legal obligation to not enrich descendants of [human traffickers] with the assets they obtained through their brutality of kidnapping and trafficking human beings'.[227] This argument is flaws since it plays different types of coloniality against each other. It invokes one set of historical injustices, namely the slave trade history of Benin bronzes and victimizations by past local rulers, against remedies for another type of injustice, namely return of objects looted by former colonial powers from the same rulers. The motion of the Restitution Study Group did not explain fully why the rights of descendants of enslaved peoples to access to objects in the US should be privileged over the right of access to culture of source communities in Nigeria. It was denied on 14 October 2022.[228]

6 Beyond return: Relation-building and new object possibilities

A key element of relational cultural justice is relation-building and development of object possibilities, even after and beyond actual returns. The development of object possibilities is essential to accommodate the changing biographies of objects over time, and to create new pathways towards the future. Returns do not end with physical transfer or handover. They often require measures which extend beyond the act of restitution itself, namely strategies of reconnection, which enable new engagement with objects in countries or communities of origin,[229] and strategies

---

[225] Ibid, para. 10.
[226] Ibid, para. 3.
[227] Ibid, para. 95.
[228] Cultural Property News, 'Restitution Study Group Unable to Stop Smithsonian's Benin Returns' (10 October 2022) https://culturalpropertynews.org/restitution-study-group-files-suit-to-stop-smithsonians-benin-bronze-returns/.
[229] As Felwine Sarr has noted, the 'return of objects does not mean restoring them as they once were, but reinvesting them with social function'. It is 'not a question of return of the same, but of an "other same"'. See Felwine Sarr, 'Restitution of African Heritage: History, Memory, Traces, Re-Appropriation', Geneva (24 September 2021) 4.

of disconnection, which preserve memory in former colonial powers or holding institutions. Such measures should not be unilaterally imposed or turned into conditions for return, but must be addressed as part of return processes.

The ability of returns to mitigate old divides between colonizers and colonized and to avoid novel internal frictions in source countries (e.g. between state institutions and communities) depends on affective reconnection. Examples, such as the return of Dahomey treasures or Benin objects, show that it may be necessary to create new structures in societies of origin in order to recentre histories and ontologies, develop locally owned narratives, resocialize objects, or facilitate relations towards objects, which go beyond colonial/Western models of imagination (e.g. material object conceptions, artistic value). This includes not only infrastructure for the housing of objects, such as museums, but education, sharing and reappropriation of object meanings or histories, renewal of affective or spiritual bonds or reanimation through cultural rituals or traditions or contemporary works. Through these practices, objects became 'carriers of new meaning'.[230]

Returns or restitutions are successful if they create new possibilities for engagement with objects or to develop object identities. For instance, in the context of the Dahomey returns, historical objects were exhibited side-by-side with works of thirty-four contemporary artists from Benin and the Beninese diaspora in order to build a bridge between past and present.[231] In 2022, Germany returned a doll acquired by a missionary from a Namibian child in the middle of the nineteenth century in exchange for livestock ('doll from Otjimbingwe').[232] The design of the doll served as inspiration for modern textiles. It was placed in a local Namibian museum for fashion, where it was used by designers and fashion-makers for contemporary designs.

It is at the same time necessary to develop successful 'disconnection' strategies from objects to fill the void left by returns in holder countries. One detrimental side effect of returns is that they may erase memory of colonial history or injustice in former colonial powers. Return may then turn into a gesture of absolution, through Western countries extinguish their colonial debt towards former colonies. This type of 'whitewashing' of the past stands in conflict with the idea of cultural relational justice. It is important to build a connective memory culture beyond the return of objects, which facilitates continuing engagement and critical learning from the colonial past, in partnership with former colonized societies.

---

[230] Ibid, 8.

[231] On 19 February 2022, Benin's Palais de la Marina in Cotonou staged a major exhibition ('Benin Art from Yesterday to Today, from Restitution to Revelation') to welcome the objects. It was accompanied by the display of works of thirty-four contemporary artists from Benin and the Beninese diaspora.

[232] Zorena Jantze, 'Rare Namibian Artefacts Returned from German Museums' *Informante* (31 May 2022) https://informante.web.na/?p=320308.

Returns may involve changes in the status of objects, their modalities of display, or even their preservation. The relational approach demands respect of alterity. It requires openness to the multi-dimensional nature of objects and respect of a different object ontology, even if it conflicts with Western-liberal conceptions. For instance, it may be legitimate for source communities to withhold certain objects from public view, if their display is incompatible with their sacred nature. Other objects may represent the mutation of life and are meant to perish and to be renewed. As Felwine Sarr has observed:

> In some African societies, statues also die. They have a certain lifespan and are caught in a cycle of regeneration, based on a fluid materiality. Some masks are buried after several years of life and are then reproduced, in order to renew the energetic influxes that give them operative power.[233]

Such a world view should be respected in the aftermath of return, even if it goes against the museology of encyclopaedic preservation. Relational cultural justice may involve acceptance of uncomfortable choices, which conflict with a 'universalist' conception of objects or a logic of material culture focused on preservation.

7 Beyond the *status quo*: Rethinking normative structures

The realization of relational cultural justice requires not only changes in approaches return or restitution but deeper systemic transformations. The existing normative environment needs to be rethought. At the moment, change occurs predominantly on the micro-level (museum or university practices) or the meso-level (policy guidelines, national practices).[234] Sub-state entities, such as cities, museums or universities have started to play an important role in return processes. New guidelines and policies may contribute to the formation of a sense of legal obligation (*opinio juris*) and generate more differentiated legal principles, based on mutually-beneficial return practices.[235] However, they do not in and of themselves constitute a form of 'international custom'. There is still a lack of targeted instruments on the macro level (e.g. Conventions, resolutions, identification of common principles).

Shifts in ethics and decolonial practices have often opened the path for changes in law. They challenge the theory that takings operated in a legal void, based on the discriminatory nature of positivist law in relation to cultural colonial takings,

---

[233] Sarr, 'Restitution of African Heritage', 6.
[234] See Chapter 8.
[235] Losson, 'Opening Pandora's Box'; Marie Cornu and Marc-André Renold, 'New Developments in the Restitution of Cultural Property: Alternative Means of Dispute Resolution' (2010) 17 *International Journal of Cultural Property* 1–31, 23.

decolonial readings of the intertemporal rule or the recognition of a more plural-istic understanding of international law.[236] They promote changing perspectives on return or an emerging duty to seek new forms of consent for entangled objects in order to enable fair and just solutions. But there are striking gaps or uncertain-ties. For instance, transnational claims are only marginally regulated. Returns, res-titutions and repatriations often continue to face significant resistance in domestic law. Procedures are slow and cumbersome. Domestic inalienability laws create obstacles and barriers for return or deaccessioning of objects from public collec-tions.[237] Modalities of private acquisition deserve fresh attention.[238] For instance, artefacts, such as the Benin bronzes, have been offered for sale at public auctions, despite their violent acquisition.

7.1 Reviewing domestic barriers

National frameworks governing the treatment of colonial cultural objects require critical review. Returns are often barred by national laws which specify that cul-tural objects become the patrimony of the host nation after a certain period of time and inalienable public property.[239] Domestic legal frameworks contain ex-ceptions or different regimes in relation to human remains[240] or Nazi-looted art.[241] However, cultural colonial objects fall in legal grey zones. This makes returns slow and subject to political decision-making, such as parliamentary or governmental consent.[242]

The ICOM Guidelines reflect a permissive logic. They encourage national mu-seums to deaccession objects from their collections, but only in circumstances where domestic law 'does not prohibit a museum from de-accessioning'.[243] In Europe, approaches differ across jurisdictions. Countries like Germany, the Netherlands or Belgium have adopted regulatory instruments to enable the

---

[236] See Chapter 6.

[237] Clara Cassan, 'Should They Stay or Should They Go? African Cultural Goods in France's Public Domain, Between Inalienability s Public Domain, Between Inalienability, Transfers, and Circulations' (2021) 31 *Fordham Intellectual Property, Media & Entertainment Law Journal* 1248–1301.

[238] See Von Beurden, *Inconvenient Heritage*, 177–205.

[239] Snowball, Collins, and Nwauche, 'Ethics, values and legality in the restoration of cultural arte-facts', 3.

[240] For instance, in the UK, s 47 of the 2004 Human Tissue Act authorized nine national museums to deaccession human remains which are under 1,000 years old.

[241] Charity Gates, 'Who Owns African Art? Envisioning a Legal Framework for the Restitution of African Cultural Heritage' (2020) 3 *International Comparative, Policy & Ethics Law Review* 1131–1162, 1159–1160.

[242] For instance, the principle of inalienability of State property has formed part of French cultural heritage law since the 16th century. See Halina Niec, 'Legislative Models of Protection of Cultural Property' (1976) 27 *Hastings Law Journal* 1089–1122, 1093 ff.

[243] ICOM, Guidelines on Deaccessioning of the International Council of Museums, approved by the Executive Board in September 2019.

transfer of ownership of cultural heritage objects. Belgium has adopted a new framework law that creates an exception to the general rule, according to which public property is inalienable. It expressly recognizes the alienable character of cultural assets linked to the colonial past of Belgium.[244] It is innovative since it facilitates 'large-scale restitutions of colonial collections'.[245] However, it only applies to objects acquired in Belgian colonies in a context of occupation, fails to recognize participation of local communities in proceedings, and does not cover privately-owned objects, archives, or human remains. Austria, which has served as colonial power under the Habsburg Monarchy in the eighteenth century and later profited from colonial networks, is considering the introduction of a new restitution procedure to facilitate claims relating to objects acquired by violence, looting, theft, coercion or deception. Other former colonial powers are less proactive. For instance, Portugal has not adopted specific legislation favouring return. The issue of return did not rank high on the political agenda and caused division among political parties.[246] Based upon pressure by ICOM-Portugal, Minister of Culture, Pedro Adão e Silva, decided in 2022 to make an inventory of cultural heritage from former colonies.[247]

One of the critiques of existing inalienability laws is that they protect entangled objects based on the logic of a 'finders keepers' law.[248] Domestic frameworks in France and the UK illustrate the deadlocks and frictions that may arise if return of individual objects is made subject to parliamentary approval in each case.

France has only made limited changes to its legislation. It has pursued a case-by-case logic, despite the recommendation in the Sarr and Savoy report to amend the inalienability provisions in French law to accelerate returns through bilateral agreements.[249] It has adopted individual parliamentary laws in nearly all major cases involving return from national collections, such as the repatriation of remains of Sara Baartman in 2002,[250] the return of Māori heads to New-Zealand or the return of the Dahomey treasures to Benin.[251] These laws have either created

---

[244] See Belgian Law of 3 July 2022.

[245] De Clippele and Demarsin, 'Pioneering Belgium', 280.

[246] In 2020, Partido Livre suggested initiatives to return the 'heritage of the former Portuguese colonies'. However, it faced strong resistance. See Ana Temudo, 'Current challenges for African cultural heritage: a case study of Guinea-Bissau' (2021) 13 Midas 1–18, 7.

[247] See 'Portuguese government advances with heritage list originating from former colonies', *Tekdeeps* (25 November 2022) https://tekdeeps.com/portuguese-government-advances-with-herit age-list-originating-from-former-colonies/. The director of the National Museum of Ethnology, Paulo Costa, has proposed to distinguish between objects obtained by force or looting and objects acquired through 'improper alienation'. See 'Ana Temudo, 'Current challenges for African cultural heritage: a case study of Guinea-Bissau' (2021) 13 *Midas* 1–18, 7.

[248] See Tanner J. Wadsworth, 'Ancient Heritage and Contemporary Causes of Action: A Conversation with Geoffrey Robertson QC', Bulletin, *Columbia Journal of Transnational Law* (3 November 2020).

[249] Sarr and Savoy, 'Restitution of African Cultural Heritage', 75–80.

[250] Law No. 2002–323 of 6 March 2002 concerning the restitution of the remains of Saartjie Baartman to South Africa.

[251] See Law No. 2020–1673 of 24 December 2020 on the restitution of cultural property to the Republic of Benin and the Republic of Senegal.

exceptions from inalienability or operated on the premise that certain items, such as human remains, do not qualify as 'public property' of French institutions. In this way, Parliament and the Executive have kept a 'tight grip on every transfer of cultural property' from colonial contexts.[252] Such a methodology makes sense, in an environment where request for return are the exception, rather than the rule. However, it is ill-suited to confront the challenges of the new restitution movement and to respond to systematic claims, involving large numbers of objects captured in punitive or 'scientific' missions. It contrasts with models which allow the executive branch to decide on restitution of Nazi looted based on advice by expert bodies, such as French Commission for the Compensation of Victims of Spoliation Resulting from the Occupation (CIVS), the Spoliation Advisory Panel in the UK, or the Dutch Restitutions Committee.[253] Such an approach may make decisions on return less dependent on party-politics.

In the UK, progress has been hampered for years by a 'ping pong between government and museums', in which each side blamed the other for inaction.[254] In many controversial cases, such as the Parthenon marbles,[255] the Benin bronzes or the Ethiopian tabots,[256] the government avoided to take a clear-cut stance on return, based on the independence of the museum and the authority of the trustees. The purpose of laws, such as British Museum Act of 1963, was to make collections independent from daily politics and short-term decision-making. They turned into a justification to use lack of authority as an argument not to engage with return or restitution demands. The British museum itself put the blame on Act which emphasizes 'the duty of the Trustees of the British Museum to keep the objects comprised in the collections of the Museum'[257] and the need to respect any condition imposed by donors at the time of the acquisition.[258] It allows deaccession only in narrow circumstances, including where an object is considered to be 'unfit to be retained in the collections of the Museum' by 'the Trustees' and can 'be disposed of without detriment to the interests of students'.[259] This provision has been interpreted in a narrow sense in the museum policy on 'De-accession of objects', which reflects the ideology of the 'universal museum', rather than a decolonial agenda. An object is considered 'unfit' to be retained if it is

---

[252] Gates, 'Who Owns African Art?', 1283.

[253] Annemarie Marck and Eelke Mulle, 'National Panels advising on Nazi-looted Art in Austria, France, the United Kingdom, the Netherlands and Germany' in Evelien Campfens (ed.), *Fair and Just Solutions? Alternatives to litigation in Nazi-looted art disputes: Status quo and new developments* (The Hague: Eleven Publishers, 2014) 41–89.

[254] Robert Hewison, 'When it comes to restitution, UK museums should be careful what they wish for' *Apollo* (24 July 2022) https://www.apollo-magazine.com/tristram-hunt-restitution-uk-museums-law/.

[255] See Geoffrey Robertson, *Who Owns History?* (London: Biteback, 2019) 126.

[256] Ibid ('My Lords, the museum is independent of the Government; it is up to the trustees').

[257] British Museum Act 1963, § 3(1).

[258] Ibid, § 5(1).

[259] Ibid, § 5(1)(c).

[n]o longer useful or relevant to the Museum's purpose and if its retention would not be of benefit either to scholars or the general public, whether for display or research or any other purpose for which the Museum is established.[260]

This reading protects the retention of many colonial objects which are not displayed, but kept in storage.

One possibility to overcome this impasse is a flexible reading of the 'unfit' to be retained test. For instance, in the case of the Ethiopian altar tablets looted at Magdala, the Scheherazade Foundation has taken the view that the tabots may be deaccessioned under this exception, because they have never been exhibited, photographed, or been used for purposes of research.[261] Taking a contemporary perspective, one might argue that structural factors, such as colonial violence facilitating the taking of colonial objects, might render objects 'unfit to be retained' in ethical categories. The advantages of the digital era may limit damage to science or education. For instance, returns do not necessarily cause 'detriment to the interests of students' if replica or digital images are retained. The barrier to return is thus partly self-inflicted.

Another avenue is legislative reform. For example, Tristram Hunt, the director of the V&A, has proposed to review the National Heritage Act of 1983, which limits deaccessioning by museums, such as the V&A or the Science Museum. He has suggested to strengthen the power of trustees of the museum to decide on the deaccessioning of contested objects. Modest steps in this direction are reflected in changes to the UK Charities Act in 2022. As Alexander Herman has shown,[262] they provide trustees of national museums with greater flexibility to seek authorization for deaccessioning objects based on a 'moral obligation' to do so,[263] or to dispose of low value objects on moral grounds on their own motion.[264] This would for instance allow greater space for trustees to seek approval from the Charities Commission to deaccession objects on moral grounds. For instance, in 2022, the Charity Commission has approved the return of Benin 116 by the University of

---

[260] British Museum policy, 'Deaccession of objects from the collection', § 3(5).

[261] Tessa Gregory, a representative of the Foundation, stated: 'It is quite clear that the Trustees of the British Museum have the power under the British Museum Act 1963 (the Act) to give the Tabots back to the Ethiopian Orthodox Church. The Tabots have no particular use or purpose for the Museum as they cannot be viewed, displayed, photographed, copied, or made available for research or educational purposes. In these unique circumstances the Trustees can within the provisions of the Act deem the Tabots unfit to be retained and, without causing any detriment to students, return them to Ethiopia where they are of such sacred importance'. See Leigh Day, Press Office, 'British Museum religious treasures could be legally restored to Ethiopian Orthodox Church' (11 October 2021).

[262] Alexander Herman, 'Museums, restitution and the new Charities Act', Institute of Art & Law (25 September 2022) https://ial.uk.com/museums-restitution-and-the-new-charities-act/, id. 'Museums, Restitution and the New Charities Act 2022' *Art Antiquity & Law* (2022).

[263] Section 16 of the 2022 Charities of 24 February 2022 permits the disposal of objects with approval from the Charity Commission, the Attorney General, or the courts, in cases where there may be a 'moral obligation' to do so.

[264] See s 15 of the 2022 Charities Act.

Cambridge, accepting the argument that the University was under 'a moral obligation' to do so.[265] However, in October 2022 the government decided to defer the commencement of the relevant sections of the Act in order to 'fully understand the implications for national museums and other charities'.[266]

Ultimately, there are different ways to break domestic impasses. One is the broadening of the powers of the Trustees to deaccession colonial objects, based on domestic legislation, creating exemptions from inalienability through a framework law, such as in the context of Nazi-looted art. The other one is entrusting decision-making to the executive branch of power, based on expert advice. Both approaches would enable museums to consider a wider spectrum of legal and moral considerations, based on the nature of colonial injustice and the complex structure of nineteenth century international law, as suggested by contemporary guidelines.[267]

A flexible approach to return or object mobility requires not only change in countries holding objects, but also in those states, which are at the receiving end of returns. Returns may require both preparation and meaningful access to objects after transfer. One important measure is the strengthening of cultural heritage frameworks to prevent objects from contemporary looting or illicit trafficking.[268]

7.2 Filling normative gaps

Domestic reforms at the meso—and micro-levels need to be complemented by further action at the macro-level. Existing international frameworks contain gaps. The strong reliance on country-specific legislation individualizes possibilities of return or repair. It is at odds with the structure of colonial takings which occurred through networks of power. Colonial takings were a collective effort and may partly trigger a 'collective European Responsibility'.[269]

An international framework should not delay ongoing domestic reform efforts, but may usefully support them. It has multiple advantages. It creates greater clarity. It would make chances of return less dependent on negotiations with individual nations. It may harmonize approaches and would have an important expressive effect.[270] It would help claimants. They would not have to rely solely on

[265] 'Cambridge University to return Benin Bronzes to Nigeria' *BBC News* (15 December 2022) https://www.bbc.com/news/uk-england-cambridgeshire-63973271.

[266] Lord Kamall, Parliamentary Under-Secretary of State, Department for Digital, Culture, Media and Sport, in UK Parliament, Debate National Heritage Act 1983 (13 October 2022) Hansard, Vol. 824 (2022).

[267] See Chapter 7.

[268] Sarr and Savoy, 'Restitution of African Cultural Heritage', 83–85.

[269] Wazi Apoh and Andreas Mehler, 'Mainstreaming the Discourse on Restitution and Repatriation within African History, Heritage Studies and Political Science' (2020) 7 *Contemporary Journal of African Studies* 1–16, 7.

[270] Erik Jayme rightly speaks of 'narrative norms'. See Erik Jayme, 'Narrative Norms in Private International Law: The example of Art Law' (2015) 375 *Collective Courses of the Hague Academy* 9–52.

the law of a particular state or museum where the object has landed. The turn to an international framework would also have an important expressive effect. It would counter the perception that the movement toward return of specific categories of objects, such as the Benin bronzes, is mere symbolism or a ritual of guilt relief or 'self-purification'.[271]

Some authorities have suggested that it would be appropriate to establish a new convention on repatriation and return of looted art.[272] For instance, it has been proposed to complement the 1970 UNESCO Convention by a multilateral treaty, which should:

(1) specify the application of restitution in a peacetime setting to significant objects removed during the colonial era; (2) be made expressly applicable to publicly-owned cultural objects, regardless of how they were acquired; (3) incorporate a balanced regime of ethics and values to be weighed during negotiations over transfer of ownership, including the respective needs and interests of possessing Western nations and the dispossessed countries; and (4) appoint the International Conference of Museums, or another international organizations, to manage the repatriation program.[273]

However, given the complexities of the issues at stake, the interplay between justice, ethics, and human rights and the divergences of opinion among stakeholders, it may be more realistic in the immediate future to provide elaborate guidance for national frameworks through common principles or guidelines.

Due to the diversity of national practices, including those states which are 'specifically affected' by debates on restitution and return, it is still difficult to trace clear customary law standards on return, except in the area of indigenous rights or egregious cases of looting.[274] General principles offer a more promising means, since they are able to balance competing interests, may accommodate the interplay between law and ethics, and enable progressive realization.

The Belgium principles, emphasize the need to establish 'guidelines for policy-makers and governments in tune with the present social and ethical issues' which place 'the individual and human values at the heart of a broad and transversal

---

[271] See David Frum, 'Who Benefits When Western Museums Return Looted Art?' *The Atlantic* (October 2022) https://www.theatlantic.com/magazine/archive/2022/10/benin-bronzes-nigeria-return-stolen-art/671245/.

[272] See Robertson, *Who Owns History?*, 226 ff. See also Teresa McGuire, 'African Antiquities Removed during Colonialism: Restoring a Stolen Cultural Legacy' (1990) 1990 *Detroit College of Law Review* 31–70, 66.

[273] McGuire, 'African Antiquities Removed during Colonialism', 66.

[274] Robertson has argued in favour of a customary rule of international law requiring restitution of cultural treasures of great national significance. See Robertson, *Who Owns History?*, xxi. However, it remains doubtful in light of divides in the application of the law (see Chapter 6) and previous treaty practice regarding cultural colonial objects (see Chapter 7).

concept of cultural heritage'.[275] Existing guidelines on colonial contexts are country-specific.[276] A logical step would be the adoption of a general frame for colonial contexts, similar to the Washington Principles on Nazi looted art, which mediate between the 'is' and the 'ought'.[277] For instance, Jos van Beurden has suggested to adapt the 1998 Washington Principles to 'objects of cultural or historical importance', which were taken 'without just compensation' or 'involuntarily lost' during the 'European colonial era'.[278] It would inter alia entail the establishment of a central register for objects,[279] a need to consider 'unavoidable gaps or ambiguities in the provenance' of objects 'in light of the passage of time and the circumstances' of the 'colonial era',[280] or an international commitment to promote just and fair solutions. In his 'Shared Heritage' report, Jean-Luc Martinez has proposed a common declaration by African and European States on principles of restitution, modelled after the Washington Principles, and the establishment of an Africa-Europe public-private fund to showcase the work of contemporary African artists on the continent.[281]

The disadvantages of the Washington Principles is that they remain rather vague and general. Given the rapid development of the restitution movement over recent years, and the plurality of domestic guidelines, it is important to add clarity and specificity. A new international framework would be helpful to fill gaps in domestic laws and specify generally recognized criteria of return, procedures for handling of claims, modalities of provenance research or good practices relating to return or object mobility, in line with the relational approach. It should complement the existing UNESCO Intergovernmental Committee on Return and Restitution under the 1970 UNESCO Convention. Given its previous work on decolonization and restitution, and its adoption of the 2005 'Basic Principles and Guidelines on the Right to a Remedy and Reparation' for Victims under Resolution 60/147,[282] the UN General Assembly would be an appropriate forum to develop future principles.

Some initiatives have been taken at the European level. The European Parliament has encouraged 'the development of EU guidelines on restitution and calls for Member States to continue or to initiate processes for the restitution of cultural

---

[275] Restitution Belgium, Ethical Principles for the Management and Restitution of Colonial Collections in Belgium (June 2021), Conclusions and Final Recommendations (Belgian Ethical Principles).

[276] See Chapter 8.

[277] See James Nafziger, 'An Anthro-Apology for Managing the International Flow of Cultural Property' (1982) 4 *Houston Journal of International Law* 189, 191. Erik Jayme qualifies such frameworks as 'narrative norms'. See Erik Jayme, 'Narrative Norms in Private'.

[278] Jos van Beurden, *Treasures in Trusted Hands* (Leiden: Sidestone Press, 2017) 252–253.

[279] Ibid, 252.

[280] Ibid, 252–253.

[281] Martinez, 'Shared Heritage: Universality, restitutions and circulation of works of art', 71.

[282] Basic Principles and Guidelines on the Right to a Remedy and Reparation for Victims of Gross Violations of International Human Rights Law and Serious Violations of International Humanitarian Law, UN Doc. E/CN. 4/2005/L. 48 (13 April 2005).

works and artefacts in a more consistent and timely manner'.[283] Salima Yenbou, the Rapporteur of the Committee on Culture and Education, has supported the development of guidelines to ensure greater transparency of objects in Western collections. She has encouraged states not only to update and coordinate their restitution policies, but to confront the 'history and legacy of racism in Europe and its structural and systemic nature'.[284] Of course, such guidelines cannot be unilaterally established. They would need to be developed in close dialogue with source countries and affected communities. Otherwise, they may be perceived as replicating colonial mindsets in decolonial practices.

7.3 Scrutinizing private transactions

Public collections are only the tip of the iceberg. Modalities of private acquisition deserve fresh attention. The market for cultural colonial objects is considerable. Selling and auctioning objects is a gigantic business. The violent history of acquisition, the exotic nature of objects, their rarity or imagined social functions, may be important business factors. High-profile auction houses are generally careful to identify the provenance history of objects. However, many transactions occur in legal grey zones: They may be deemed immoral, but are not formally prohibited in light of the existing gaps in legal instruments. Many 'entangled objects', which would face strict ethical or legal scrutiny under contemporary guidelines governing public collections, have been traded freely through private transactions. For example, artefacts, such as the Benin bronzes, have been offered for sale at public auctions, despite their violent acquisition.

Until now, the main strategy to block such transactions is protest, public shaming, or the commercial acquisition of objects by source countries or communities, e.g. through crowd-funding, intermediaries, or public resources. For instance, in 2010, the Nigeria Liberty Forum prevented the Sotheby sale of a Benin ivory mask depicting Idia, the queen mother of the Edo peoples, through an online campaign. The object was put on sale by descendants of Sir Henry Lionel Galway, who had played an instrumental role in the 1897 raid.[285] The government of the Edo State intervened and called on Sotheby to stop the auction, planned in February 2011. Based on the emerging public pressure, the Galway family and Sotheby decided to drop the sale.[286]

---

[283] <European Parliament, Committee on Culture and Education, Salima Yenbou, Draft Report on the role of culture, education, media, and sport in the fight against racism (2021/2057(INI)), 2021/2057(INI) (11 November 2021) para. 11.

[284] Ibid, Explanatory statement, 10.

[285] Rob Sharp, 'Sotheby's Cancels Sale of 'Looted' Benin Mask' *The Independent* (29 December 2010).

[286] For a critical analysis, see Kwame Opoku, 'Reflections on the Abortive Queen-Mother Idia Mask Auction: Tactical Withdrawal or Decision of Principle?'. Modern Ghana (2 January 2011) https://www.modernghana.com/news/310582/reflections-on-the-abortive-queen-mother-idia-mask-auction.html.

China intervened several times in auction proceedings to prevent the sale of objects looted in 1860 from the Chinese Summer Palace,[287] because of their historical significance.[288] For instance, it requested that Christie's, in 2009, withdraw the sale of two Qing dynasty bronze heads looted in 1860, which formed part of the estate of Yves Saint Laurent.[289] In April 2018, it sought to stop the sale of an object looted from the Summer Palace in another an auction, based on the 'spirit of international agreements and code of professional ethics, as well as ... the cultural rights and national feelings of the Chinese people'.[290] It was forced to buy back the objects or negotiate their return from owners.

In 2021, the Ethiopia protested against the sale of five horn beakers and a leather Coptic bible taken at the loot of Maqdala in 1868. The artefacts were put on sale by the family of Major-General William Arbuthnot (1838–1893), the Military Secretary to Lord Napier, at the Busby auction house in Dorset. Two horns bore an inscription 'Magdala'.[291] The Ethiopian embassy in London noted that 'the auctioning of these items is, at best, unethical and, at worst, the continuation of a cycle of dispossession perpetrated by those who would seek to benefit from the spoils of war'.[292] This led to an online campaign against the auction, which prompted the auction house to remove the objects from sale. They were purchased by the Scheherazade Foundation, a private charity[293] and returned to Ethiopia. The return was celebrated as 'the single most significant heritage restitution in Ethiopia's history'.[294]

These examples show that public pressure and mobilization is a powerful tool to influence private transactions. They express a changing public conscience.[295] However, from an ethical point of view, it is highly unsatisfactory to require source countries or communities to buy back objects that were forcefully taken from. The commodification of many objects developed through European capitalism. The lack of constraints on sales perpetuates the market logic[296] and reproduces

[287] See Chapter 2.

[288] Afolasade Adewunmi, 'Possessing Possession: Who Owns Benin Artefacts' (2015) 20 *Art Antiquity and Law* 229–242, 240.

[289] David Barboza, 'China pressures Christie's to hand over sculptures', *New York Times* (17 February 2009.

[290] Evelien Campfens, 'The Bangwa Queen: Artifact or Heritage?' (2019) 26 *International Journal of Cultural Property* 75–110, 103, fn. 160.

[291] Cassie Packard, 'Looted Ethiopian Artifacts Withdrawn from Sale at British Auction House' *Hyperallergic* (24 June 2021) https://hyperallergic.com/658298/looted-ethiopian-artifacts-withdrawn-from-british-auction-house-sale/.

[292] Lanre Bakare, 'Looted artefacts withdrawn from UK auction after Ethiopia's appeal' *The Guardian* (16 June 2021).

[293] Cultural Restitution, 'Return of looted artefacts is single most important restitution in Ethiopia's history' (11 September 2021).

[294] Ethiopian Embassy in London, Press Release, 'Artefacts looted in Maqdala in 1868 to be returned to Ethiopia' (9 September 2021).

[295] Emile Durkheim, *The Division of Labour in Society* (W. D. Halls tr, Basingstoke: Palgrave, 2013), 79.

[296] Paul M. Bator, 'An Essay on the International Trade in Art' (1982) 34 *Stanford Law Review* 275–384.

inequalities. It is often a question of chance whether objects ended up in public or private collections. Exempting the professional art market from due diligence requirements that apply in relation to public museums creates a strong imbalance. It contrasts with the fact that non-state actors may face international legal obligations under human rights law. Private property rights may conflict with rights of access of culture.

There are several options to introduce a greater degree of scrutiny over private transactions. One possibility is to create a global public inventory of entangled objects in order to provide greater transparency and limit possibilities of trafficking, as in done in relation to Nazi-looted art or illegally removed objects. A second option is to increase due diligence obligations of auction houses in order to limit commodification. Existing provenance methods often conceal the histories of objects or even seek to profit from their exotic, rare or violent nature. It may be feasible for auction houses to carry out deeper inquiries into provenance history on their own motion and display greater caution in order to avoid complicity in perpetuating colonial injustice. A possible step forward would be the adoption of voluntary codes of conduct, through which auction houses and art dealers commit themselves to not put entangled objects on sale. Such practices of self-commitment are common in the area of business and human rights.[297] They can be transposed to taking of cultural objects. A third option is to place greater due diligence obligations in the buyer. Such an approach is inter alia reflected in the 1995 UNIDROIT Convention. It limits the option of good faith acquisition[298] and requires purchasers to demonstrate due diligence in transactions[299] in order to achieve compensation. This logic could be applied by analogy to certain categories of objects in order to limit their circulation.

The most radical step to prevent a further commodification of objects through commercial transactions would be to recognize that certain objects (e.g. looted objects, sacred objects, objects of special cultural significance) are *res extra commercium*, i.e. objects 'outside the commercial space' which cannot be legally acquired or sold in private transactions.[300] It would make bona fide acquisition on global markets impossible. This doctrine is recognized in common law and inquisitorial traditions.[301] It is partially reflected in the 1970 UNESCO Convention,

---

[297] See UN Guiding Principles on Business and Human Rights (New York and Geneva, United Nations 2011) 14.

[298] Art. 4(1) 1995 UNIDROIT Convention.

[299] Due diligence includes 'the circumstances of the acquisition, including the character of the parties, the price paid, whether the possessor consulted any reasonably accessible register of stolen cultural objects, and any other relevant information and documentation which it could reasonably have obtained, and whether the possessor consulted accessible agencies or took any other step that a reasonable person would have taken in the circumstances'. See Art. 4(4) 1995 UNIDROIT Convention.

[300] Sara Gwendolyn Ross, 'Res Extra Commercium and the Barriers Faced When Seeking the Repatriation and Return of Potent Cultural Objects' (2016) 4 *American Indian Law Journal* 297–389.

[301] Kurt Siehr, 'The Protection of Cultural Heritage and International Commerce' (1997) 6 *International Journal of Cultural Property* 304–325; Marc Weber, 'Private international law and cultural

which allows states to 'classify and declare certain cultural property as inalien-able',[302] and in exclusions of time bars for return claims under the UNIDROIT Convention.[303] It would reverse the market logic associated with objects through their takings and display.[304]

7.4 Relational cultural justice principles regarding entangled objects

Both the competing frames of cultural nationalism and internationalism and the narrow focus of the restitution debate on return have impeded constructive and forward-looking thinking for many decades.[305] The rise of new principles and ap-proaches in emerging guidelines, and the underlying legal models,[306] provide a new way to break impasses. They show that it is not enough to 'apply the Master's tools', i.e. to reverse takings in order to 'dismantle the master's house'. The process needs to venture beyond determination where objects rightfully belong and ad-dress broader structural conditions, i.e. the drivers of takings and the perpetuation of *status quo*. An important element is the need to move from a logic of restitution to a logic of social repair. This involves several departures from narrow restitution frames.

It is important to recognize that the discussion on return of objects is not a 'neu-tral' act (i.e. a pure ownership determination), but a process addressing the con-nection between objects and people. The virtue of negotiations and returns lies in their transformative potential, namely their ability to facilitate a move from unjust to more just relations. It involves backward-looking elements, such as acknow-ledging the past, as well as prospective steps towards 'righting the future'. It requires a holistic understanding of restitution, which does not treat return as a zero sum game, but takes into account a broader spectrum of object possibilities and rela-tions beyond return of restitution.

The development of such a relational cultural justice approach towards entangled objects goes beyond legal cultural heritage principles or the lenses of cultural na-tionalism and internationalism. It may benefit from transitional justice principles, such as (i) access to truth, (ii) accountability, (iii) repair, (iv) memorialization or

---

property and art disputes' in Irini Stamatoudi (ed.), *Research Handbook on Intellectual Property and Cultural Heritage* (Cheltenham: Edward Elgar Publishing, 2022) 517–543.

[302] See Art. 13(d) of the UNESCO Convention.
[303] See Art. 3(4) of the UNIDROIT Convention.
[304] Ross, 'Res Extra Commercium', 388.
[305] See Soirila, 'Indeterminacy in the Cultural Property Restitution Debate', 1, who argues that the two concepts serve as 'entry points that echo each other without a way to end the debate'.
[306] See Chapter 8.

(v) non-recurrence.[307] It is not a way to come to terms with the past, but a process of 'working through' it in new ways and shaping the future. Building on object lessons and insights developed throughout this study, one may identify a few guiding principles, which rely on these five macro ideas. They are grounded in the interplay between human rights law, transitional justice and heritage law, and soft law instruments (e.g. professional guidelines), and the need to take into account the systemic nature of colonial injustice.

7.4.1 Access to history and culture

Some relational principles are linked to truth-seeking in relation to the past[308] and access to culture.

7.4.1.1 Principle 1: Transparency of collections and object histories

A starting point is transparency of collections and object histories. This principle is reflected in many modern ethical guidelines. It applies to both 'processes and accessibility of information'.[309] It requires a proactive and engaging approach towards provenance research in existing collections.[310] States should encourage their public institutions holding cultural colonial objects to provide a clear and thorough explanation of the events that led to the acquisition of the object. It should not only encompass acquisition chains or the context of origin, but should include inquiry into the 'circumstances in which objects left their communities'.[311] It should ultimately facilitate a broader international public inventory of entangled objects[312] and greater transparency in relation to what is held in existing collections.[313] It requires evidence-based reconstruction of historical events, based on a broader information pool than archival material and engagement with oral histories and multiple perspectives. Institutions should commit to undertaking such new forms

---

[307] International Bar Association, *Contested Histories in Public Spaces: Principles, Processes, Best Practices* (London: IBA, 2021) 281–290.

[308] The idea of a right to the right to truth in relation to heritage objects is plausible, if one accepts the ontological premise that certain objects have subject-like qualities and can be equated to missing persons. See Ciraj Rassool, 'Re-storing the Skeletons of Empire: Return, Reburial and Rehumanisation in Southern Africa' (2015) 41 *Journal of Southern African Studies* 653–670.

[309] Belgian Ethical Principles, 1.

[310] In the context of human remains, it is increasingly recognized that provenance research should no longer simply be carried out to enable a decision whether or not to return, but rather to gather all the information that is available on origin and acquisition. See Hermann Parzinger, 'Die Rückgabe ist alternativlos', *Die Zeit* (11 February 2023).

[311] Belgian Ethical Principles, Executive Summary.

[312] See also Principle 6 of the ILA Principles for Cooperation in the Mutual Protection and Transfer of Cultural Material (ILA Principles), James A.R. Nafziger, 'The Principles for Cooperation in the Mutual Protection and Transfer of Cultural Material' (2007) 8 *Chicago Journal of International Law* 147–167, 164.

[313] Report of the Expert Mechanism on the Rights of Indigenous Peoples, 'Repatriation of ceremonial objects, human remains and intangible cultural heritage under the United Nations Declaration on the Rights of Indigenous Peoples', A/HRC/45/35 (21 July 2020) para. 90, which recognized the need to develop 'databases of indigenous peoples' ceremonial objects and human remains held by State museums, universities and other repositories that are accessible to the indigenous peoples concerned'.

of provenance research as part of a commitment to establish the truth in relation to colonial objects. It applies not only to cultural artefacts or human remains, but also to certain objects in natural history collections.

Transparency involves the need for a 'proactive approach to communication and data sharing around colonial collections'. It is necessary to facilitate return claims or the burden of proof.[314]

7.4.1.2 Principle 2: Object accessibility

Transparency of collections needs to be complemented by accessibility of objects. This prerequisite follows not only from ownership rights or the nature of objects as 'patrimony of humanity', but is grounded in various rights relating to the interplay between objects and persons, namely the right of people to cultural self-determination and development, community rights[315] or human rights of access to cultural heritage. States should encourage existing public institutions to work through invisible objects in collections and storages and provide greater physical or digital access to objects. Exceptions may apply in relation to certain categories of objects, such as sacred objects, or human remains, whose public display may constitute infringement of dignity or post-mortem rights.[316] Source countries and communities should retain the liberty to determine alternative ways of accessibility, rather than preservation in classical museum spaces.

7.4.2 Accountability

The concept of accountability is a building block for another set of principles, including new forms of consent in relation to objects, access to justice and acknowledgement of wrong.

7.4.2.1 Principle 3: Seeking new forms of consent

The need to establish new forms of consent in relation to entangled objects is a first key element of confronting the past in new ways.[317] It is an obligation of means. States should seek to establish a new basis of consent regarding the treatment of objects which were forcibly removed from source communities through violence or obtained through any other unjust ways in situations of colonial domination or exploitation.[318] This procedural duty arises not only from past wrongdoing,

---

[314] Ibid, 3.2.

[315] Council of Europe Framework Convention on the Value of Cultural Heritage for Society (CETS No. 199) (27 October 2005) (Faro Convention).

[316] Expert Mechanism on the Rights of Indigenous Peoples, 'Repatriation of ceremonial objects, human remains and intangible cultural heritage', para. 90, encouraging states to develop 'respectful protocols, such as not showing photographs of human remains and sacred items'.

[317] See section 3 above.

[318] Principle 4 of the ILA Principles for Cooperation in the Mutual Protection and Transfer of Cultural Material (ILA Principles) foresees 'an obligation to respond in good faith to a request for the transfer of cultural material originating with indigenous peoples and cultural minorities'. See Nafziger, 'The Principles for Cooperation in the Mutual Protection and Transfer of Cultural Material', 162.

but can be grounded contemporary relations to objects. It takes into account that 'international law itself played an important role in consolidating the structures of racial discrimination and subordination throughout the colonial period, including through customary international law'.[319] It has a basis in ethical principles, such as the trusteeship-based nature of guardianship over cultural heritage and just distribution and access to cultural resources, as well as legal foundations, such as the principle of 'free, prior and informed consent of the indigenous peoples' in relation to preservation of their cultural resources,[320] way of life and cultural expression, the cultural dimensions of right to self-determination and minority rights, and the right to participate in cultural life.

7.4.2.2 Principle 4: Pluralistic access to justice

Access to justice is necessary to enable accountability. Source countries and communities of entangled objects should be given the opportunity to make requests regarding the return of objects. This option should not be solely confined to states and mediated through diplomatic channels. Both individuals and groups[321] are holders of cultural rights. Their interests do not necessarily coincide with the interest of states. Existing practices show that governments have sometimes used claims to hijack object histories or promote cultural nationalist agendas, which conflict with the interests of communities or indigenous people. Societal structures have often evolved in the aftermath of removal or takings of objects. From a relational justice perspective, states and museums should recognize the plurality of stakeholders in a claims process, namely source countries, source communities or diaspora communities.[322]

7.4.2.3 Principle 5: Recognition of injustice

Recognition of past wrongs is a third element of accountability. Cultural colonial takings may entail moral, economic, political, or legal responsibilities. States should not only provide ethical, political, or economic pathways to remedy past wrong, but also acknowledge the legal underpinnings of wrongful takings or the contradictions of legal frames barring restitution or return. Reducing responsibility to moral duties or acts of comity may be perceived as half-hearted and or cause secondary victimization. As the Expert Mechanism on the Rights of Indigenous Peoples has stated, the determinations whether an object was 'illicitly' taken or 'stolen' should not only

---

[319] Report of the Special Rapporteur on contemporary forms of racism, racial discrimination, xenophobia, and racial intolerance, A/74/321 (21 August 2019) para. 50.

[320] UNDRIP, Art. 11(2).

[321] For instance, the Faro Convention recognizes both the concept of heritage community, as well as a right to cultural heritage. Article 4(1)(a) states: 'Everyone, alone or in community with others, has the right to take advantage of cultural heritage and to contribute to its enrichment'. UNDRIP recognizes rights to equality, non-discrimination, self-determination, participation, and consultation of indigenous people.

[322] See also Belgian Ethical Principles, Thematic Recommendations, Restitution Process.

be assessed based on colonial state laws, but take a broader perspective on legality.[323] In cases where takings were based on past wrongdoing, the 'possibility of rectifying an injustice' should be the 'guiding principle',[324] and not necessarily be tied to considerations of 'cultural significance', which are evidenced by return claims.

7.4.3 Social repair
The idea of repairing relations provides the foundation of a further group of principles covering process-related elements, agreement on future arrangements relating to objects, collaboration, and meaningful forms of redress.

7.4.3.1 Principle 6: Inclusivity, equality, and multi-perspectivity
Processes are as important as legal frameworks for restitution and return. The establishment of connections and dialogue with communities of origin, descendants, and source countries is an essential part of social repair. Entities holding cultural colonial objects should create news of ways of engaging with objects, which ensure meaningful stakeholder involvement, dialogical engagement, and openness to other worldviews. As the Belgian principles make clear, 'equality' should be 'the starting point for renewed collaboration and relations among heritage institutions and between heritage institutions and communities of origin'.[325] Colonial structures were dominated by racial bias and subordination. Recognition of equality is essential to restore agency and facilitate respectful dialogue. An open mindset towards competing histories or object ontologies is necessary to enable mutual engagement and avoid neo-colonial approaches in negotiations, display, or the formulation of conditions of return, such as modes of access or preservation based on Western-centric object views.

7.4.3.2 Principle 7: Plurality of pathways to achieve just and fair solutions
The recognition of equality and multi-perspectivity requires dialogue and engagement with multiple possible pathways. There is no-one-size fit all format for return or restitution. The proper method and approach depends on the nature of the object, and its cultural, social, and economic value.[326] As the Smithsonian Institution

---

[323] Expert Mechanism on the Rights of Indigenous Peoples, 'Repatriation of ceremonial objects, human remains and intangible cultural heritage', para. 88 ('a determination of whether an item is "illicit" or "stolen" property must include analysis not only of State laws, but the laws of indigenous peoples that set out standards of alienability, ownership, treatment and custody of ceremonial objects, human remains and spiritual, intellectual and other properties').

[324] See Council for Culture, Advisory Committee on the National Policy Framework for Colonial Collections, *Guidance on the way forward for colonial collections*, 6, Recommendations 4 and 5, and 7, Recommendation 7.

[325] Belgian Principles, Executive Summary.

[326] The ILA Principles name a number of criteria: 'the significance of the requested material for the requesting party, the reunification of dispersed cultural material, accessibility to the cultural material in the requesting state, and protection of the cultural material'. Nafziger, 'The Principles for Cooperation in the Mutual Protection and Transfer of Cultural Material', 166.

has acknowledged, museums should 'move beyond the idea that possession of physical objects is the only value of a museum's work'.[327] Return is not necessarily a loss. Practices, such as 'equitable knowledge-sharing', 'shared stewardship', collaboration, digitization, or new forms of object mobility may offer new opportunities.[328] Title to ownership and possession may diverge. If return of entangled objects is sought, the modalities and possible future arrangements should, in principle, be agreed between the provenance stakeholder and the institution holding the object. Conditions relating to return, or alternative pathways, such as immaterial return, shared stewardship models, loans, cross-national exhibitions, digital returns, or use of replicas should not be unilaterally but commonly determined.

7.4.3.3 Principle 8: Collaboration

Collaboration is an important building block of social repair. It cannot be forced on source countries or communities, but it should guide mutual encounters and processes of restitution and return. The success of returns depends on active community engagement. Partnerships between governments, holding institutions, and communities are key to support the return of cultural heritage. They build trust and mutual understanding, and 'should be built into the mission of cultural institutions'.[329] This is reflected in the ICOM Code[330] and expert principles. For instance, the Smithsonian principles state that museums should 'nurture relationships with communities, as well as inter-governmental and regional stakeholders, to enhance the free flow of information, engage in dialogue and consultation, and seek opportunities to share benefits'.[331] The Belgian principles encourage 'co-creative projects and open communication with communities of origin' in order to enable joint research and exchange of knowledge. An innovative practice, used in Scottish repatriations, is to allow entities who are making return claims to nominate an ad hoc expert member to the decision-making body deciding on return.[332]

Long-term partnerships are essential to promote shared stewardship models, facilitate alternatives to return or enable new forms of object mobility, between source countries and communities, following return. They may also promote reform of museum structures. For instance, in the context of Te Papa Museum in New Zealand, collaboration has not only forged a lasting relationship with communities, but has also contributed to new forms of partnership in museum governance.

---

[327] Smithsonian Ethical Returns Working Group, Values and Principles Statement (3 May 2022).

[328] See also Lord Vaizey of Didcot, Debate National Heritage Act 1983 (13 October 2022) Hansard, Vol. 824 (2022) ('The debate on the provenance of objects and their location has become much more sophisticated, technology has changed'). Principle 3 of the ILA Principles lists 'loans, production of copies, and shared management and control' as alternatives to transfer of objects. Nafziger, 'The Principles for Cooperation in the Mutual Protection and Transfer of Cultural Material', 161.

[329] Belgian Principles, 3(2).

[330] ICOM Code of Ethics for Museums (Paris: ICOM, 2017), Principle 6.

[331] Smithsonian Ethical Returns Working Group, Values and Principles Statement.

[332] Curtis, 'Repatriation from Scottish Museums', 240.

7.4.3.4 Principle 9: Meaningful redress for wrongful action

Redress should be understood in a broad sense. It should address both 'historical individual and group wrongs' and 'persisting structures of racial inequality, discrimination and subordination'.[333] It is not limited to return or restitution of objects, but should include consideration of measures of satisfaction, such as an acknowledgement of wrong or an apology,[334] acceptance of responsibility, or measures to commemorate or pay tribute to victims and survivors. This connection is inter alia reflected in the Dutch National Policy Framework, which acknowledges that 'recognition' of 'historical injustice' and the 'readiness to rectify' it are 'a key principle of the policy on dealing with colonial collections'.[335]

In cases of wrongdoing by the returning state, it may be necessary to complement return by an appropriate expression of remorse or apology, acknowledging the wrongfulness of takings and the forms of harm caused in order to build relationships. Such forms of satisfaction should be closely consulted and coordinated with stakeholders to avoid an unintended negative side or colonial *déjà vu*.[336] Critical elements are the agency of the speaker (e.g. who apologizes on behalf of whom), the addressee (e.g. the subject to whom the apology is addressed), the language and approach toward the historical narrative, the scope (i.e. abstract acknowledgement versus recognition of particular wrongs)[337] and whether recognition makes a tangible difference in the lives of those affected.[338] The example of the Joint Declaration regarding the historical genocide against the Nama and Herero shows that it is unhelpful to market practices of humanitarian aid or development cooperation as a form of redress for cultural takings, since it evades responsibilities.[339]

---

[333] Report of the Special Rapporteur on contemporary forms of racism, racial discrimination, xenophobia and racial intolerance, para. 57.

[334] Return of colonial objects and apologies mark 'two forms of atonement'. Franziska Boehme, 'Normative Expectations and the Colonial Past: Apologies and Art Restitution to Former Colonies in France and Germany' (2022) 2 *Global Studies Quarterly* 1–12, 9.

[335] Advisory Committee on the National Policy Framework for Colonial Collections, *Guidance on the way forward for colonial collections*, 6, Recommendations 1 and 2. See also Recommendation 5 ('the redress of an injustice is not achieved only through an actual return but also particularly by making the acknowledgement and redress of this injustice a fundamental principle of the policy').

[336] Many apologies have caused division through partial acknowledgement of facts, isolation of specific episodes, use of sanitized language, or the blending of atonement with justifications of past behavior. See Tom Bentley, *Empires of Remorse: Narrative, Postcolonialism and Apologies for Colonial Atrocity* (Abingdon: Routledge, 2015).

[337] As Michael Marrus has argued, a complete apology for historical wrong would include (i) an 'acknowledgement of a wrong committed, including the harm that it caused'; (ii) an 'acceptance of responsibility' for the wrong; (iii) an 'expression of regret or remorse' concerning the harm and the infliction of wrong; and (iv) a 'commitment, explicit or implicit, to reparation' and 'when appropriate, non-repetition'. See Michael R. Marrus, 'Official Apologies and the Quest for Historical Justice' (2007) 6 *Journal of Human Rights* 75–105, 79.

[338] See e.g. Tom Bentley, 'Colonial apologies and the problem of the transgressor Speaking' (2018) 39 *Third World Quarterly* 399–417.

[339] See Henning Melber, 'Germany and Namibia: Negotiating Genocide' (2020) 22 *Journal of Genocide Research* 502–514.

7.4.3.5 Principle 10: Addressing epistemic injustices

Social repair requires a structural approach to redress. States and holding institutions should not treat restitution or return 'as a singular event' but rather as 'part of a wider process of decolonisation' that includes a 'proactive communication about collection contents', a 'cultivation of long-term relationships with communities' and engagement with ongoing harms caused by epistemic injustices.[340] This may require changes in the method of display, rewriting of object histories and representation of historical events, review of object classifications or scientific theories, including acknowledgement of links between collection and racial science, revisiting semantics[341] or new educative approaches.

Same valuable lessons may be learned from practices relating to other objects with contested histories, such as public monuments.[342] There are multiple ways to confront the histories of entangled objects or recognize their dual nature as both colonial and counter-hegemonic objects. They include 'contextualization', i.e. recognizing colonial background,[343] 'resignification, i.e. transformation of public meaning,[344] 'repurposing', i.e. altering the use,[345] 'relocation', i.e. moving the object to another site,[346] or full 'removal'.[347] Measures to limit the commodification of objects are themselves a form of confronting continuing epistemic injustice. For instance, recognizing that some objects (e.g. human remains, certain sacred objects) should not be displayed in museums anymore, is a way of addressing epistemic injustice.[348] In some settler colonial contexts, new relational treaty frameworks have been negotiated to recognize native sovereignty and remedy dispossession.[349]

7.4.4 Memorialization

Memorialization is another key aspect of relational cultural justice.[350] It is a long-term process which complements truth, accountability and social repair.[351] It is

---

[340] Belgian Principles, 3.2.

[341] See Chapter 7.

[342] International Bar Association, *Contested Histories in Public Spaces: Principles, Processes, Best Practices* (London: IBA, 2021).

[343] Ibid, 285.

[344] Ibid, 286.

[345] Ibid, 287.

[346] Ibid, 288.

[347] Ibid, 288.

[348] See Neil Curtis, 'A Welcome and Important Part of Their Role: The Impact of Repatriation on Museums in Scotland' in Louise Tythacott and Kostas Arvanitis (eds.), *Museums and Restitution: New Practices, New Approaches* (Abingdon: Routledge, 2014) 85–104.

[349] Harry Hobbs and Stephen Young, 'Modern Treaty Making and the Limits of the Law' (2021) 71 *University of Toronto Law Journal* 234–273; Harry Hobbs and George Williams, 'Treaty-Making in the Australian Federation' (2019) 43 *Melbourne University Law Review* 178–232.

[350] It is one of the pillars of transitional justice. See Report of the Special Rapporteur on the promotion of truth, justice, reparation and guarantees of non-recurrence, 'Memorialization processes in the context of serious violations of human rights and international humanitarian law: the fifth pillar of transitional justice', A/HRC/45/45 (8 July 2020).

[351] Ibid, para. 100 ('without memory, the rights to truth, justice and full reparation cannot be fully realized and there can be no guarantees of non-recurrence').

'part of a broader cultural framework in which different visions, values and nar-ratives come together'.[352] It is essential to enable 'societies to learn the truth and regain ownership of their history'[353] and to establish a 'dialogic truth' in relation to contested histories, namely 'to create the conditions for a debate within' and across societies on 'the causes and consequences of past crimes and violence'.[354]

7.4.4.1 Principle 10: Multi-dimensional memorialization

Memorialization strategies, i.e. political and memorial work, should be part and parcel of efforts to enable new engagement with cultural colonial object. They pro-vide a means to foster historical and political consciousness, promote 'recogni-tion of otherness'[355] and confront distinct meanings of object histories.[356] As the Expert Mechanism on the Rights of Indigenous Peoples has stressed, memorial-ization 'involves revisiting painful intergenerational histories of colonialism, loss of dignity, forced relocation, military occupation and loss of lands, territories and resources'.[357] States and entities deaccessioning cultural colonial objects should adopt multi-dimensional memory measures to supplement restitution or return and prevent an erasure of memory in former colonial powers. Memorialization requires both disconnection strategies, i.e. measures to keep memories of the past and its trajectory to the present alive in returning institutions, and reconnection strategies, i.e. efforts to resocialize cultural objects in source countries or com-munities. It strengthens the claim by former colonized states 'to obtain access to archives'.[358]

7.4.4.2 Displaying absence

A successful example of multi-dimensional memorialization is the repatriation of Ghost Dance Shirt. It has contributed to long-term care of the shirt in the Lakota Sioux community, while permitting continuing critical engagement with object histories in the Kelvingrove museum in Glasgow through display of the reproduc-tion and the integration of local narratives. In other cases, preservation of critical memory can be achieved through innovative exhibition practices and/or new tech-nologies. As Neil Curtis has argued, there are a creative ways to use the absence of objects as a means of critical memory.[359] For instance, the space created through

---

[352] Ibid, para. 32.
[353] Ibid, para. 70.
[354] Ibid, para. 108.
[355] Ibid, para. 32.
[356] Ibid, para. 36.
[357] Expert Mechanism on the Rights of Indigenous Peoples, 'Repatriation of ceremonial objects, human remains and intangible cultural heritage', para. 90.
[358] Report of the Special Rapporteur on the promotion of truth, justice, reparation and guarantees of non-recurrence, 'Memorialization processes', para. 70.
[359] Curtis, 'Repatriation from Scottish Museums', 244.

return of objects opens new ways to explain histories and movements of objects or show their connection to contemporary art forms.

7.4.5 Non-recurrence

The need to prevent recurrence of harm is a final building block of relational culture justice principles. Measures of non-recurrence establish a bridge between the past and future.[360] They are necessary to promote social, political, and economic transformation and address the intergenerational legacies of cultural takings. For instance, legal and institutional frameworks should not 'reproduce stereotypes or discriminatory practices from the colonial period, or any other persistent form of racism or exclusion'.[361] This may require inter alia a commitment to institutional reforms and education in both former colonial powers and colonized societies.[362]

7.4.5.1 *Principle 11: Reviewing object ontologies and cultural national foundations of inalienability and deaccession laws*

One key element is a rethinking of object conceptions and foundations of inalienability laws or deaccession constraints under national laws. Domestic law has been complicit in facilitating past takings. It continues to protect the *status quo* or market powers. Many contemporary inalienability laws or deaccession provisions are ill-equipped to address the challenges of entangled objects. They are grounded in a logic of cultural nationalism, rather than relational approaches. They treat objects as national cultural property, rather than as heritage items or subject-objects, or rely on moral criteria to justify return. As part of a non-recurrence policy, and promotion of greater equality and distribution of objects, States should commit themselves to adjust their laws or policies and enable more flexible and pluralistic decision-making processes regarding restitution and return, which go beyond the UNESCO framework and ethical guidelines. This process has started in relation to human remains, which are often distinguished from property or qualified as *res extra commercium*. It requires greater attention in relation to entangled cultural objects.

7.4.5.2 *Principle 12: Object protection in source countries or communities of origin*

Another side of the coin is the strengthening of heritage frameworks in source countries communities of origin. Objects are often vulnerable to cultural nationalist reappropriation or commodification after return. This may make it necessary

---

[360] Alexander Mayer-Rieckh, 'Guarantees of Non-Recurrence: An Approximation' (2017) 39 *Human Rights Quarterly* 416–448.

[361] See Report of the Special Rapporteur on the promotion of truth, justice, reparation and guarantees of non-recurrence, Transitional justice measures and addressing the legacy of gross violations of human rights and international humanitarian law committed in colonial contexts, A/76/180 (19 July 2021) para. 112 (Special Rapporteur 2021 Report).

[362] Report of the Special Rapporteur on the promotion of truth, justice, reparation and guarantees of non-recurrence, A/HRC/30/42 (7 September 2015) (Special Rapporteur 2015 Report).

to introduce additional safeguards to avoid illicit transaction or trafficking. Source countries should be encouraged to ratify relevant regional and international instruments to protect returned objects against illegal acquisition or theft or to create new frameworks to that effect.[363]

7.4.5.3 Principle 13: Due diligence duties of auction houses and private collectors

Private forms of acquisition require further scrutiny. Many current legal frameworks favour ownership titles or good faith acquisitions of entangled objects by private purchasers over the heritage rights of source countries or communities. This limits the ability to prevent sales and transfers to awareness campaigns, naming and shaming or appeal to corporate social responsibility. It is necessary to develop due diligence structures and integrate protection of the right of access to culture more effectively into emerging practices on human rights duties of businesses. Another means is the reversal of the presumption of good faith, requiring purchasers to prove due diligence in market transactions to protect cultural property against trafficking,[364] or broader recognition of certain entangled cultural objects as *res extra commercium*.

7.4.5.4 Principle 14: Decolonial education

Education is a further key element to promote non-recurrence.[365] Colonial histories have often been marginalized in public education or public spaces. As Special Rapporteur on the promotion of truth, justice, reparation and guarantees of non-recurrence, Fabián Salvioli has stated, states should include 'information on the legacy of colonialism in curricula and educational material at all levels'[366] and foster 'critical thought, analytic learning and debate' in order to create greater awareness of 'contemporary challenges of exclusion and violence'.[367] Educational materials should draw attention to marginalized systems of knowledge and provide a 'fair, accurate and informative picture' of indigenous peoples.[368] Museums play an important role as drivers of change. As Joanna Tidy and Joe Turner have argued, they can be 'read' as a space 'in which visitors are invited to intimately encounter' a 'system of power structured by colonially-forged racial logics and classifications'.[369] As guardians of 'other people's cultures', they have a special educational

---

[363] The Sarr and Savoy report recommends the use of the 1995 UNIDROIT Convention as a 'springboard'. See Sarr and Savoy, 'Restitution of African Cultural Heritage', 81.

[364] This stricter emphasis on due diligence is inter alia recognized in the 1995 UNIDROIT Convention and European Directive 2014/60/EU on Return of cultural objects unlawfully removed from the territory of a Member State (15 May 2014).

[365] Special Rapporteur 2021 Report, para. 86.

[366] Ibid, para. 86.

[367] Ibid, para. 118.

[368] Ibid, para. 86.

[369] Joanna Tidy and Joe Turner, 'The Intimate International Relations of Museums: A Method' (2020) 48 *Millennium: Journal of International Studies* 117–142, 120.

responsibility to make ongoing discriminations visible. They are uniquely equipped to promote inclusive histories or articulate new understandings or experiences through artistic means.[370]

8 Not a conclusion

In 2010, historian Steven Conn, asked the radical question of whether museums still need objects.[371] The digital age offers new prospects for encounter with objects. It enables greater sharing of objects across locations or new experiences. Digitization or NFTs may make us believe that material objects themselves became less relevant. However, the current turn towards restitution and return shows they still matter a great deal. Authenticity and aura continue to play an important role for both holding institutions and source countries and communities. The main change is that the ways of engaging with objects have become more pluralist and diverse. This provides an opportunity to approach the debate on restitution and return with fresh perspectives and break the traditional impasses.

The struggle for greater access and more equitable distribution of objects reflects changing global power relations. For a long time, negotiation of return has been used as a soft power instrument by states in the Global North. However, it is more broadly recognized as a moral necessity grounded in law and ethics. It is no longer confined to inter-state politics, but driven by non-state actors (e.g. museums), protest movements, professional networks, or individuals.[372] There are new options to accommodate objects in source countries or communities and to create novel partnerships. Western museums do not have to hold on to every single item of their collections.

The growing recognition of the need to return illegitimately acquired artefacts is supported by changes on the conception of museums. The traditional roles of acquisition, classification and preservation have come under critical scrutiny in line with the interrogation of colonial histories. This is an opportunity to rethink governance models and self-conceptions. Museums are 'not simply treasure houses in an unequal world' but places for 'public ethical debate' and transformation.[373] The experiential dimensions of collection and display have become more important. This provides new prospects to overcome the classical dichotomies of cultural nationalism and cultural internationalism. Returning can have a liberating effect. It creates new opportunities for creative forms of governance and collaboration. Allowing objects to return may have positive effects. The story of the repatriation of objects, such as the Ghost Dance Shirt, shows that return processes themselves

---

[370] Special Rapporteur 2015 Report, para. 95.
[371] Steven Conn, *Do Museums Still Need Objects?* (Philadelphia: University of Pennsylvania Press, 2010).
[372] Boehme, 'Normative Expectations and the Colonial Past', 3.
[373] Curtis, 'Repatriation from Scottish Museums', 244.

may have value for a museum. Combined with loans, use of replica or forms of digital reproduction, stories of repatriation and their illustration may become part of the experiential dimensions of museums. As Neil Curtis has shown, 'exhibiting the absence of an object' may have a powerful impact, 'no less than that achieved by displaying it'.[374] Classical physical ownership of objects is thus only a small piece of the puzzle in 'the long and tangled story of people and things',[375] which continues to be written in new ways through practices of relational cultural justice.

On the broader scale, changing approaches towards restitution are only one small piece in the broader challenge of confronting cultural colonial injustices. It requires new methodologies and reforms which are not yet part of the toolbox of the 'Master's House'. It must be connected to broader structural measures addressing the multi-faceted consequences of cultural takings, such as correcting stereotypes about non-Eurocentric systems of governance and object traditions, revisiting contemporary historical and artistic frames, building bridges to modern and living art forms, addressing ongoing forms of social, economic, or cultural exclusion,[376] and imagining new ways of dealing with the past. As Matthias Goldmann has emphasized, it 'is difficult to imagine the enjoyment of cultural rights in the absence of fair global economic conditions'.[377] This makes it necessary to confront market dynamics, including intellectual property rights and digitization, promote more equitable socio-economic conditions in source countries and communities, and encourage more inclusive access to heritage. Returns may provide a modest step to challenge the political economy of global resource flows in an unequal world order or the capitalistic conception of ownership of objects.

Ultimately, colonial takings were 'about much more than artefacts', and the 'debt' is 'about far more than their return'.[378] This is not only a task of governments, experts, curators, or museums, but an ethical prerogative of citizens in everyday life. Through our daily actions, inactions, or choices, we all play an important role in inspiring change and recasting the ways in which we encounter objects and the stories and meanings they convey.[379]

---

[374] Ibid, 244.

[375] Ibid, 244.

[376] For instance, punitive expeditions destroyed histories and suppressed local forms of order and governance, which may have contributed to the destabilization of political structures on the continent. See Howard W. French, *Born in Blackness: Africa, Africans, and the Making of the Modern World, 1471 to the Second World War* (New York: Liveright, 2022).

[377] Matthias Goldmann, 'Review of Bénédicte Savoy, Afrikas Kampf um seine Kunst' (2023) 34 *EJIL* 1–5, 5, https://doi.org/10.1093/ejil/chad007.

[378] Howard W. French, 'What Europe Stole from Africa' *Foreign Affairs* (17 January 2023).

[379] For an alternative experience of objects in the British Museum, see 'The Unfiltered History Tour' *Vice Works News* (2021) https://theunfilteredhistorytour.com/.

Index

For the benefit of digital users, indexed terms that span two pages (e.g., 52–53) may, on occasion, appear on only one of those pages.